Exceptions in EU Copyright Law

Information Law Series (INFO)

VOLUME 45

Editor

Prof. P. Bernt Hugenholtz, Institute for Information Law, University of Amsterdam.

Objective & Readership

Publications in the Information Law Series focus on current legal issues of information law and are aimed at scholars, practitioners, and policy makers who are active in the rapidly expanding area of information law and policy.

Introduction & Contents

The advent of the information society has put the field of information law squarely on the map. Information law is the law relating to the production, marketing, distribution, and use of information goods and services. The field of information law therefore cuts across traditional legal boundaries, and encompasses a wide set of legal issues at the crossroads of intellectual property, media law, telecommunications law, freedom of expression, and right to privacy. Recent volumes in the Information Law Series deal with copyright enforcement on the Internet, interoperability among computer programs, harmonization of copyright at the European level, intellectual property and human rights, public broadcasting in Europe, the future of the public domain, conditional access in digital broadcasting, and the "three-step test" in copyright.

The titles published in this series are listed at the back of this volume.

Exceptions in EU Copyright Law

In Search of a Balance Between Flexibility and Legal Certainty

Tito Rendas

Wolters Kluwer

Published by:
Kluwer Law International B.V.
PO Box 316
2400 AH Alphen aan den Rijn
The Netherlands
E-mail: international-sales@wolterskluwer.com
Website: lrus.wolterskluwer.com

Sold and distributed by:
Wolters Kluwer Legal & Regulatory U.S.
7201 McKinney Circle
Frederick, MD 21704
United States of America
Email: customer.service@wolterskluwer.com

ISBN 978-94-035-2395-8

e-Book: ISBN 978-94-035-2400-9
web-PDF: ISBN 978-94-035-2401-6

À Lígia

Table of Contents

Preface and Acknowledgements

This book is a revised and updated version of the doctoral thesis I defended at Universidade Católica Portuguesa on 25 September 2020, which has been granted the annual award *Prémio Professor Doutor José de Oliveira Ascensão* by Associação Portuguesa de Direito Intelectual (APDI). The research for this book was concluded on 30 September 2020. Developments in legislation and case law that have occurred after that date were therefore not taken into account.

My first words of gratitude go to my supervisors – Henrique Sousa Antunes and Bernt Hugenholtz. Henrique Sousa Antunes was not only a tireless supervisor but also a true friend during this journey. Without his advice and categorical belief in my capacity to cross the finishing line, this project would never have seen the light of day. As to Bernt Hugenholtz, much of what I have to say about copyright law bears his fingerprints. Whether in Lisbon or in Amsterdam, his questions and comments – and often his disagreement with my opinions – challenged me and had me sharpen the arguments in the thesis.

I am grateful to Christophe Geiger and Dário Moura Vicente for having accepted the task of acting as discussants of the thesis, in the hope that I have not plagued their summer of 2020 with too monotonous a reading. Any researcher who is familiar with the topic of this book will recognise the influence they have played in it, and in this field of law more generally. The remaining members of the jury – Fernando Ferreira Pinto, António Cortês, António Frada de Sousa, Ana Taveira da Fonseca, and Rita Lynce de Faria – have all contributed to this project in diverse ways. It was a true privilege to have had them as members of my doctoral jury.

I am also indebted to all those who have been fertile interlocutors and co-workers throughout this process, especially Armando Rocha, Bernd Justin Jütte, Fernando Sá, Gonçalo Almeida Ribeiro, João Pedro Quintais, Kacper Szkalej, Nuno Sousa e Silva, Patrícia Fragoso Martins, and Pedro Garcia Marques. Sketches of the thesis have been presented in conferences and seminars in Brno, Florence, Glasgow, Helsinki, Luxembourg, Szeged, Tilburg, and Warsaw. Those who have generously shared their thoughts with me on such occasions are far too many to enumerate, but I am obliged to all of them.

I would also like to thank those who have played a key role in the early stages of my academic career. Were it not for Henrique Sousa Antunes, José Lobo Moutinho, Luís Barreto Xavier, Maria da Graça Trigo, and Rui Medeiros and I would have probably followed a different path – and I am glad that I did not. I owe a special debt of gratitude to Maria da Glória Garcia. To this day, it escapes my understanding how she, as Rector of Universidade Católica Portuguesa and after that, found the time to send doctoral students regular messages asking about their progress and to meet with them. Without such messages and meetings, insignificant as they may sound to outsiders, I doubt I would have ever come to submit my thesis.

Also, much of the thesis and of its defence was prepared while I was working under the coordination of three people: Elsa Vaz de Sequeira at the Católica Research Centre for the Future of Law, and Filipe Mayer and Martim Bouza Serrano at CCA Law Firm. I could not have wished for a fairer assignment of workload and a healthier working relationship with all of them.

I extend my appreciation to Fundação para a Ciência e a Tecnologia for the financial support I received between the years 2015 and 2018, and to the Max Planck Institute for Innovation and Competition for the exceptional conditions they provided me with during my research stays in Munich.

Some debts, of course, extend much farther beyond payment. That is the kind of debt I owe to my friends and family, among which my grandmother, my brother, but especially my parents. It takes unconditional love to never have questioned the decision of pursuing yet another cycle of studies – one that took longer than any of the preceding ones. And they have supported me without reservations throughout all of them and throughout this one in particular.

Finally, my debt towards Lígia and Nicolau is of a unique order. Whatever scientific contribution this book may represent, it is certainly undeserving of the sacrifices they underwent over the last years. They have endured far too many moments of absence and – perhaps the greatest sacrifice of all – they have indulged my enthusiasm in talking about this book. It would not stray far from the truth to say that they have been co-authors of this work. But the greatest share of this burden was undoubtedly carried by Lígia. I am sure Nicolau, when he is able to read this book (assuming he will ever have the patience to read such tedious lines, which I sincerely hope he does not), will understand my decision of dedicating this work to his mother – my ever-present partner in this emotional rollercoaster of doctoral studies and in life.

Tito Rendas
Lisbon, October 2020

List of Abbreviations

AA.VV.	Autori vari; Various Authors
AG	Advocate General
AI	Artificial Intelligence
ALAI	Association Littéraire et Artistique Internationale
BGB	Bürgerliches Gesetzbuch; German Civil Code
BGH	Bundesgerichtshof; German Federal Supreme Court
BIRPI	*Bureaux Internationaux Reunis pour la Protection de la Propriété Intellectuelle*; United International Bureaux for the Protection of Intellectual Property
BVerfG	Bundesverfassungsgericht; German Federal Constitutional Court
cf.	Confer
Charter	Charter of Fundamental Rights of the European Union
CJEU or Court	Court of Justice of the European Union
CMO	Collective Management Organisation
CUP	Cambridge University Press
DG	Directorate General
DRM	Digital Rights Management
DSM	Digital Single Market

DVD	Digital Versatile Disk
e.g.	Exempli gratia; For Example
EC	European Communities
ECHR	European Convention on Human Rights
ECJ	European Court of Justice
ECS	European Copyright Society
ECtHR	European Court of Human Rights
EIPR	European Intellectual Property Review
EPRS	European Parliamentary Research Service
et al.	Et alii; and others
et seq.	Et sequens; and those which follow
etc.	Etcetera
EU	European Union
fn.	Footnote
GIF	Graphic Interchange Format
GRUR	Gewerblicher Rechtsschutz und Urheberrecht
GRUR Int.	Gewerblicher Rechtsschutz und Urheberrecht, Internationaler Teil
i.e.	Id est; That Is
ICCPR	International Covenant on Civil and Political Rights
IIC	International Review of Intellectual Property and Competition Law
IP	Intellectual Property
IPQ	Intellectual Property Quarterly
ISP	Internet Service Provider
JIPITEC	Journal of Intellectual Property, Information Technology and Electronic Commerce Law
JIPLP	Journal of Intellectual Property Law & Practice
MEP	Member of the European Parliament
MMR	MultiMedia und Recht
NGO	Non-governmental Organisation
NJW	Neue Juristische Wochenschrift
OUP	Oxford University Press
p(p).	Page(s)

P2P	Peer-to-Peer
para.	Paragraph
QMJIP	Queen Mary Journal of Intellectual Property
RAM	Random Access Memory
RDI	Revista de Direito Intelectual
RIDA	Revue Internationale du Droit d'Auteur
SAIF	Société des Auteurs des arts visuels et de l'Image Fixe
SWD	Staff Working Document
TDM	Text and Data Mining
TEC	Treaty Establishing the European Community
TEU	Treaty on European Union
TFEU	Treaty on the Functioning of the European Union
TPMs	Technological Protection Measures
TRIPS	Agreement on Trade-Related Aspects of Intellectual Property Rights
TV	Television
UCE	Universidade Católica Editora
UDHR	Universal Declaration of Human Rights
UGC	User-Generated Content
UK	United Kingdom
UK CDPA	UK Copyright, Designs and Patents Act of 1988
USA or US	United States of America
UWG	Gesetz gegen den unlauteren Wettbewerb; German Act against Unfair Competition
VAT	Value Added Tax
VHS	Video Home System
WCT	WIPO Copyright Treaty
WIPO	World Intellectual Property Organization
WIPO Treaties	WCT and WPPT
WPPT	WIPO Performances and Phonograms Treaty

WTO	World Trade Organization
ZGE	Zeitschrift für Geistiges Eigentum
ZUM	Zeitschrift für Urheber- und Medienrecht

Introduction

Copyright law impacts the quotidian life of millions of people. Most of us routinely engage in acts that, even if below our awareness, are regulated by copyright – acts such as quoting another author's work in an academic assignment, sharing a hyperlink on our personal blog, streaming a video clip of our favourite band on YouTube, storing an audio file containing that band's greatest hit in a cloud storage locker, or using a third-party image on a PowerPoint slideshow. The lawfulness of these and other similar actions is determined by a legal framework composed of a set of exclusive rights and their exceptions. This book is primarily concerned with the side of exceptions.

The core of the EU law on copyright exceptions lies in the so-called InfoSoc Directive, which provides most of the carve-outs to the harmonised rights of reproduction and communication to the public. The InfoSoc framework of exceptions has been at the centre of discord among copyright stakeholders, scholars and policymakers for a number of years. While some argue it should be fundamentally changed, others claim minor periodic adjustments would suffice. Almost two decades into InfoSoc – and to the disappointment of many –, the recently adopted DSM Directive tacitly endorsed the latter view, building on the existing body of rules.

To reform or not to reform the InfoSoc framework of copyright exceptions – that is the question that we will be dealing with over the next few hundred pages.

1 BACKGROUND AND PROBLEM DEFINITION

In this starting section, I will present a synopsis of the problem addressed in this book and delimit its scope. I will then articulate the research questions that I will attempt to answer (section 2) and outline the structure of this book and the methodological guidelines I held on to in my quest for answers (section 3). This introductory chapter closes with a brief excursus, where I discuss whether it is warranted to approach this study's topic from the perspective of EU copyright law (section 4).

1.1 Copyright Exceptions and Their Rationales

Copyright is the field within IP law that regulates the protection of literary and artistic works like books, films, paintings, and even computer programs. For copyright protection to vest in a work,[1] some requirements must be fulfilled, chief among which the threshold of originality.[2] If the work is deemed to meet such requirements, a set of rights will attach to it. These rights, such as the right to reproduce the work in copies and the right to communicate it to the public, are usually of an exclusive nature.[3] The holder of an exclusive right enjoys an *ius excludendi omnes alios* – a right to exclude all others from the use and exploitation of the work in any of the restricted forms. Put differently, for a third-party use of the work to be lawful, the authorisation of the rightholder will be necessary.

In certain situations, however, the rightholder's consent is not needed for a third party to be able to use the work in a non-infringing manner. That is so when the use at issue, though falling within the prima facie scope of an exclusive right,[4] is covered by some exception.[5] In case the protected work is used without the rightholder's permission and an exception to the exclusive right applies, the unauthorised user will *not* have infringed the rightholder's copyright.[6]

Copyright exceptions come in different shapes and sizes and, throughout the world, countries vary widely in both the number and the type of exceptions they provide. Some countries provide broad and open-ended exceptions, requiring courts to engage in a case-by-case analysis, while others prefer to have a list of permitted uses with a precise formulation and

1. The term 'work' is used throughout the thesis to refer indistinctly to subject matter protected by copyright, like books and songs, and by related rights, like performances and phonograms. The distinction will be made where necessary. Similarly, the term 'copyright' and its variations are used as covering both copyright and related rights.
2. On the meaning of originality in EU copyright law, *see infra* Chapter 4, section 5.3.1.
3. In some cases, the right granted by copyright is not an exclusive right, but a right of remuneration. *See infra* Chapter 1, section 1.
4. A prima facie position differs from a definitive position, in that the former corresponds to the exclusive right before the application of the exception, while the latter refers to the exclusive right after the application of the exception (if it is applicable). *See* Alexy (2010a), p. 179. *See also infra* Chapter 2, section 6.
5. I consciously employ the term 'exceptions', instead of 'limitations'. I explain why in Chapter 2, section 2.1 *infra*.
6. When using the term 'rightholders', I will be making undistinguished reference to original and derivative rightholders, comprising authors and the content industries alike, as well as to holders of copyright and related rights. Also, the term 'users' covers a broad spectrum of persons, such as individual consumers, commercial users, libraries, museums, educational institutions and technological intermediaries.

a relatively narrow scope.[7] As Robert Burrell & Allison Coleman explain, 'no country can be said to adhere rigidly to either approach', but 'some countries lean towards one approach rather than the other'.[8] While the US and its fair use standard sit closer to the first approach, continental *droit d'auteur* countries regulate permitted uses by enumerating specific categories thereof. Other countries, such as the UK, adopt what may be deemed a middle ground solution.[9]

Copyright exceptions also differ in terms of the extent of the privilege they grant. On the one hand, they may be adopted as outright exemptions of liability, in the sense that they allow the privileged user to engage in certain acts without the authorisation of the rightholder *and* without giving rise to the payment of compensation for the use. On the other hand, exceptions may come in the form of statutory licences, permitting the unauthorised use of the work but subject to the payment of compensation to the rightholder, the amount of which is determined by the legislator or by another public body. In such cases, the exclusive right is replaced by a claim to monetary compensation. Exceptions may also be enacted as compulsory licences, which force the rightholder to negotiate with the user. The essential difference in relation to statutory licences is that, under a compulsory licence regime, the amount of the compensation is to be set through an agreement between the rightholder and the user, failing which a public body will intervene.[10]

Generally put, copyright exceptions have their rationale in the need to balance the interests of rightholders with the broader public interest in the access to works and their dissemination.[11] By fine-tuning the reach of copyright's exclusive rights, exceptions allow for a reconciliation of the private interests of rightholders with those of society as a whole.[12] To be sure, exceptions are not the sole mechanism within copyright law to ensure such reconciliation. Copyright's inherent limits, such as the term of protection, the idea/expression dichotomy and the above-mentioned originality requirement, serve a similar purpose. Yet, in a system characterised by

---

7. Proposing a similar divide, *see*, *e.g.*, Spoor (1998), p. 30; Ascensão (2003), p. 91; Dusollier (2003), p. 64; and Burrell & Coleman (2005), p. 4.
8. Burrell & Coleman (2005), p. 4.
9. Burrell & Coleman (2005), pp. 4-5, however, argue that the UK leans towards the second approach: though the UK CDPA contains a somewhat vague 'fair dealing' defence for limited purposes, it includes more than sixty sections setting forth detailed exceptions.
10. The expression 'non-voluntary licences' is sometimes used to encompass both statutory licences and compulsory licences. On this distinction, *see* Guibault (2002), pp. 20-26, and Lewinski (2008), p. 152.
11. Numa Droz, the Swiss politician who presided over the three preparatory diplomatic conferences of the Berne Convention, stated, in the closing speech to the first conference in 1884, that 'limits to absolute protection are set, rightly in my view, by the public interest' – Berne Convention Records 1884, p. 68. *See also*, *e.g.*, Dreier & Schulze (2018), p. 948.
12. *See* Schricker (1997), p. 139.

long-lasting and wide-ranging exclusive rights, covering almost every conceivable use of a work, exceptions may be rightfully considered the tools *par excellence* for attaining that balance of interests.[13] They are, as James Boyle tastefully put it, 'the holes [that] matter as much as the cheese'.[14]

Copyright exceptions are thus provided out of a belief that society at large derives greater benefit from having the covered uses take place without the authorisation of rightholders, rather than with it. Within this broad rationale, an array of more specific justifications underlies the different exceptions. These justifications may be divided into several categories.

One of the most widespread categorisations identifies three distinct justifications for exceptions.[15] Some exceptions are designed to safeguard the *fundamental rights* of users, namely their freedom of expression and information.[16] This is the case, for instance, of the exceptions that permit news reporting, quotations, parodies, and the use of political speeches. Other exceptions serve *public interests* of various kinds, such as the promotion of culture and the dissemination of knowledge within society. Exceptions adopted to protect these interests include those covering educational uses, those exempting certain uses by libraries, museums and archives, and those for the benefit of print-disabled people. Exceptions may also address situations of *market failure*, such as when the negotiation between individual rightholders and interested users is too costly or when the enforcement of exclusive rights is impractical or simply impossible. The paradigmatic examples of market failure exceptions are the ones that cover reprographic uses and private copies.

Alternative (even if partly overlapping) categorisations have been offered. Lucie Guibault adds a fourth category for exceptions adopted with the purpose of regulating industry practice and competition or to facilitate commerce, such as the exceptions for ephemeral recordings made by broadcasting organisations and for advertising public exhibitions or sales of

---

13. As observed by Ohly (2014), p. 62, the lower the threshold of originality and the wider the exclusive rights are, the more relevant the exceptions will be. *See also* Samuelson (2017), p. 16, pointing out that '[a]s legislatures expanded authorial rights to cover a broader array of activities, they discovered the need to create limits on the exclusive rights'.
14. Boyle (2008), pp. 65 and 69. In a much-cited statement on the importance of the US fair use standard, Leval (1990), p. 1110, wrote that fair use should not 'be considered a bizarre, occasionally tolerated departure from the grand conception of the copyright monopoly. To the contrary, it is a necessary part of the overall design'.
15. This tripartite categorisation was first proposed by Hugenholtz (1997), pp. 14-17, and later adopted by numerous scholars from different jurisdictions, in some cases with slight modifications – *see, e.g.*, Dreier (2001), pp. 307-308, and Trabuco (2006), p. 478.
16. Senftleben (2004), p. 24, claims that '[f]reedom of expression by far is the most powerful justification of copyright limitation'. *See also* AG Opinion, *Funke Medien*, para. 38: 'copyright is compatible with fundamental rights through the application of various exceptions. Those exceptions enable works to be used in different situations which may fall within the scope of different fundamental rights and freedoms'.

artistic works and the exceptions covering uses of computer programs intended to determine the underlying ideas and principles or to achieve interoperability with other programmes.[17] The Wittem Group, in its 2010 proposal for a European Copyright Code, categorised the proposed exceptions according to four different purposes: (1) uses with minimal economic significance; (2) uses for the purpose of freedom of expression and information; (3) uses to promote social, political and cultural objectives; and (4) uses for the purpose of enhancing competition.[18] More recently, Pamela Samuelson offered six clusters of policy justifications for the existence of copyright exceptions: (1) ongoing authorship; (2) user autonomy and personal property interests; (3) public benefits; (4) economic goals; (5) political expediency; and (6) flexibility and adaptability.[19,20]

Naturally, some exceptions may have more than one justification.[21] For instance, the private copying exception, besides responding to market failure concerns, protects the fundamental right to privacy, by avoiding undesirable intrusions into the users' private sphere with the purpose of exercising control over uses of works.[22] Similarly, the exception for the benefit of print-disabled people is based primarily on the interest in ensuring greater access to knowledge, but it also addresses a market failure problem, in that the market for accessible format copies is generally too narrow to be interesting for publishers.[23]

The regime defined by the legislator for each exception typically varies depending on the underlying justification. In the case of exceptions belonging to the first category, the privilege will normally cover the authorisation *and* the monetary compensation, meaning that the public can use the protected work with no need to seek the rightholder's permission or to pay for the use. Differently, in the case of market failure exceptions, while the user is free to use the work without authorisation, the use can only take place against the payment of appropriate compensation to the rightholder.[24]

---

17. *See* Guibault (2000), pp. 128-142, and Guibault (2002), pp. 54-66.
18. Similarly, the ongoing Project on Permitted Uses in Copyright Law, coordinated by the Max Planck Institute for Innovation and Competition, divides permitted uses into five groups: (i) freedom of expression and information; (ii) social, political and cultural objectives; (iii) use of software; (iv) uses with minimal significance; and (v) exhaustion/free circulation. *See* Hilty & Moscon (2018), p. 19.
19. *See* Samuelson (2017), pp. 24-45.
20. The diversity of justifications and categorisations is in line with James Boyle's sceptical view of the unity of exceptions. According to the author, '[t]hese limitations on intellectual property do not fit a single theory, unless that theory is "avoiding the multiple and evolving dangers of intellectual property itself"' – Boyle (2008), p. 68.
21. *See, e.g.*, Guibault (2002), p. 26; Stamatoudi & Torremans (2014a), p. 442; and Samuelson (2017), p. 25.
22. *See infra* Chapter 4, section 3.2.2.
23. *See* Samuelson (2017), p. 41.
24. *See* Dreier (2001), p. 308.

1.2 InfoSoc Directive: The Centrepiece of EU Copyright Law

Of all the EU legal instruments dealing with copyright exceptions – and of all the instruments in the copyright *acquis communautaire* more broadly –, the InfoSoc Directive is by far the most important one.

Although the European Commission acknowledged the irreversibility of the move towards an information society as early as in 1993,[25] the process that led to the adoption of the InfoSoc Directive only gained true momentum with the 1995 Green Paper on *Copyright and Related Rights in the Information Society*. Back then, the Commission recognised that if the information society was to develop successfully, the numerous new products and services that were emerging (and which made frequent use of existing works or led to the creation of new ones) had to be able to take full advantage of this renovated environment. In order to respond to this new set of circumstances, IP laws, in particular copyright law, had to be adapted.[26] The Commission identified a series of issues relating to copyright and related rights that should be addressed so as to ensure the proper functioning of the information society. Among those issues, the Commission included the adaptation of the rights of reproduction and communication to the public and the need to protect technical systems of identification and protection of works.[27]

Following a consultation process, the Commission published a Follow-Up to the 1995 Green Paper. Four priority issues for legislative action were outlined therein: the right of reproduction, the right of communication to the public, the legal protection of the integrity of technical identification and protection schemes, and the distribution right (including the exhaustion rule).[28]

Before the Commission had submitted a proposal for a Directive, however, two treaties were adopted under the auspices of WIPO, with the purpose of shaping new standards for the international protection of copyright in the online environment: the WCT and the WPPT, which, in turn, built upon the Berne Convention (incorporating Articles 1-21 thereof by reference),[29] the Rome Convention, and TRIPS. As a result, besides harmonising the four issues mentioned above, the upcoming proposal would also seek to bring the EU law on copyright in line with these treaties.

In December 1997, the Commission presented a proposal for a directive on the harmonisation of certain aspects of copyright and related rights in the information society (the InfoSoc Proposal). Apart from undertaking the implementation into the EU legal order of a number of the obligations arising

25. *See* 1993 White Paper, pp. 107 et seq.
26. *See* 1995 Green Paper, p. 3.
27. *See* 1995 Green Paper, p. 4.
28. *See* 1996 Follow-Up, pp. 9 et seq.
29. *See* Article 1(4) WCT.

from said treaties[30] and addressing the four issues identified in the Follow-Up, the InfoSoc Proposal dealt with a matter that, up until then, had only been cursorily touched upon by the Commission[31] – that of exceptions to copyright. This proved to be a controversial move by the Commission,[32] contributing to the delay in the adoption of the Directive and its implementation by Member States.[33]

The InfoSoc Directive was eventually adopted in May 2001, putting an end to long years of negotiation and 'unprecedented lobbying'.[34,35] In contrast with the fragmentary and largely technology-specific approach to copyright harmonisation that had been followed in previous directives,[36] the InfoSoc Directive harmonised various issues across the board, most importantly the economic rights of reproduction (Article 2), communication to the public (Article 3), and distribution (Article 4), the exceptions to those rights (Article 5), the legal protection of TPMs and DRM (Articles 6 and 7), and sanctions and remedies (Article 8). Other issues were left unaffected,[37] as were earlier directives in the *acquis*.[38]

Besides the objective of implementing the WIPO Treaties, the InfoSoc Directive sought to achieve a set of substantive policy goals.[39] These objectives may be distilled from the InfoSoc Directive's preamble[40] and from its legislative history. In conducting such exercise, help may be found in the case law of the CJEU, which often relies on the Directive's preamble for teleological support for the outcomes of preliminary rulings on the interpretation of its provisions.[41]

---

30. *See* Recital 11 InfoSoc Proposal, the content of which was replicated in Recital 15 InfoSoc Directive.
31. *See* 1995 Green Paper, pp. 49-52.
32. For poignant criticism, *see* Hugenholtz (2000b).
33. *See* Guibault et al. (2007), p. 18.
34. Hugenholtz (2000b), p. 499. Arguably, however, even more aggressive lobbying battles were waged during the discussions on the DSM Directive. *See also infra* Chapter 4, section 2.1.
35. For more detailed accounts on the events leading up to the InfoSoc Directive, *see*, *e.g.*, Dietz (1998); Lewinski (1998); and Hugenholtz (2000b).
36. *See infra* 4.1.
37. *See* Article 9 (on contracts) and Recital 19 (on moral rights) InfoSoc Directive.
38. *See* Article 1(2) InfoSoc Directive.
39. The InfoSoc Directive also provides reliable cues about the objectives of the copyright *acquis* in general, since it is based on principles and rules already laid down in previous IP directives, placing them in the context of the information society. *See* Recital 20 InfoSoc Directive; CJEU, *Infopaq I*, para. 36; and CJEU, *Premier League*, para. 187.
40. On the function of InfoSoc recitals as providers of 'a remarkably broad foundation of European copyright law', *see* Leistner (2009), p. 882.
41. Favale et al. (2016) have analysed the teleological arguments used by the CJEU to justify these rulings. The authors claim that these arguments, though sometimes of a merely rhetorical nature, may be good predictors of whether the outcome of the ruling is 'pro-rightholder' or 'pro-user'. *See also* Quintais (2017a), pp. 349-357, drawing on this research to identify the objectives of the copyright *acquis*.

The first and foremost among those objectives is the *harmonisation of copyright law*,[42] which is intended to ensure a functioning internal market where competition is not distorted.[43] As noted by the legislator, copyright and related rights are essential for the attainment of the internal market, 'as they protect and stimulate the development and marketing of new products and services and the creation and exploitation of their creative content'.[44] Existing differences in Member States' legislation on copyright adversely affect the cross-border exploitation of copyright goods and services and, in the absence of approximation, future national legislative responses to technological changes can lead to a re-fragmentation.[45] InfoSoc thus aimed primarily at addressing these concerns.

The Directive's preamble makes clear that another of its crucial goals is to promote *technological development* and to render the law on copyright adjustable to such development. Early on in the preamble, the legislator refers to the objective of fostering the advancement of the information society in Europe by creating 'a general and flexible legal framework'.[46] Though acknowledging that new IP concepts were not necessary, the legislator further stated 'that the current law on copyright and related rights should be adapted and supplemented to respond adequately to economic realities such as new forms of exploitation'.[47] It was predicted that this adaptation would foster investment not only in the creation of content but also in the development of technology-related services and products.[48] The purpose of safeguarding the development and operation of new technologies is also frequently cited by the CJEU.[49]

---

42. *See* Pila & Torremans (2016), p. 340, noting that '[a]s legislative measures introduced under the precursors to Article 114 TFEU to support the establishment and functioning of the internal market, the Information Society Directive and other copyright and related rights directives have the harmonization of EU Member States' laws among their primary aims'.
43. The very title of the Directive indicates that harmonisation is its fundamental goal. *See also* Recitals 1, 2, 3, 4, 6, 7, 9, 23, 25, 31, 32, 47 and 56 InfoSoc Directive. Referring to this same purpose, *see* CJEU, *Laserdisken*, paras 26 and 31-34; CJEU, *Padawan*, paras 35-36; CJEU, *DR & TV2 Danmark*, paras 35-36; and CJEU, *ACI Adam*, para. 49. The goal of ensuring the functioning of the internal market in the information society context has, in recent times, been framed by the Commission in terms of a 'DSM'. *See, e.g.*, Communication on a Digital Single Market; Communication on a Modern European Copyright Framework; and DSM Directive.
44. Recital 2 InfoSoc Directive. Also, Recital 32 refers to the catalogue of exceptions as 'aiming to ensure a functioning internal market'.
45. *See* Recitals 6 and 7 InfoSoc Directive.
46. Recital 2 InfoSoc Directive.
47. Recital 5 InfoSoc Directive.
48. *See* Recital 4 InfoSoc Directive.
49. *See, e.g.*, CJEU, *Premier League*, para. 164; CJEU, *PRCA*, para. 24; and CJEU, *Tom Kabinet*, para. 47. *See also* CJEU, *Circul Globus Bucuresti*, para. 38 (using the objective to justify the exclusion of traditional public performances from the scope of the InfoSoc right of communication to the public); AG Opinion, *GS Media*, para. 50 (regarding the

Third, the objective of ensuring increased *legal certainty* in EU copyright law appears as a 'constant leitmotiv' in the InfoSoc recitals.[50] In and of itself, the approximation of Member States' legislation through the removal of major national differences provides rightholders and users alike with a higher degree of certainty regarding the cross-border exploitation of protected works, at least when compared to a strictly national and unharmonised scenario.[51] The concern around legal certainty is also reflected on the scope given by the EU legislator to the rights of reproduction and communication to the public. The breadth of coverage of these rights – which must, in addition, be interpreted broadly[52] – entails that most uses involving copy-making and dissemination of protected works will be prima facie infringing.

Fourth, copyright harmonisation should seek to ensure a *high level of protection of copyright.*[53] The justification for this pro-rightholder goal lies in the idea that the protection of copyright helps foster creativity to the benefit of all stakeholders and the public in general. The need to achieve a high level of protection is reinforced by the fact that copyright, as a type of IP right, is protected under the fundamental right to property.[54] The CJEU has gone as far as to characterise this goal as 'the principal objective' of the InfoSoc Directive,[55] which has been invoked to justify not only broad readings of

---

interpretation of the concept of 'act of communication' within Article 3(1) InfoSoc Directive); and AG Opinion, *VOB*, paras 28-30 (proposing that Articles 1(1), 2(1)(b) and 6(1) Rental and Lending Directive be read as covering acts of e-lending).

50. Guibault et al. (2007), p. 4. *See also* Ohly (2009), p. 235. References to the need to ensure legal certainty – or, negatively put, to eliminate existing legal uncertainties – can be found in Recitals 4, 6, 7, 21, and 25 InfoSoc Directive.
51. *See* Recitals 4, 6, and 7 InfoSoc Directive. *See also infra* Chapter 3, section 3.2.
52. *See* Recitals 21 and 23 InfoSoc Directive. On the wide coverage of the rights in the EU *acquis* and the canon of broad interpretation, *see infra* Chapter 1, section 3 (reproduction), section 4 (communication to the public), and section 5 (broad interpretation).
53. *See* Recitals 4 and 9 InfoSoc Directive. This 'principle of *favor auctoris*' – as Ohly (2009), p. 238, calls it – underlies the broad understanding of reproduction and communication to the public in Recitals 21 and 23. *See also* Recital 10 Enforcement Directive; Recital 14 Orphan Works Directive; Recitals 1 and 27 Collective Management Directive; and Recitals 3 and 62 DSM Directive (all mentioning the need to achieve a high level of protection).
54. *See* Article 17(2) Charter. *See also* Recital 9 InfoSoc Directive; Recital 32 Enforcement Directive; and Recital 70 DSM Directive. The CJEU has been including copyright within the scope of the fundamental right to property since before the entry into force of the Lisbon Treaty. Pre-Lisbon, the right to property had been treated as a fundamental right in several copyright cases. *See* CJEU, *Metronome Musik*, para. 21; *Promusicae*, para. 62 (both recognising it as a 'general principle of Community Law'); and CJEU, *Laserdisken*, paras 62 and 65 (citing Article 1 of Protocol 1 to the ECHR). Naturally, after Lisbon, those references have only increased. *See also* ECtHR, *Ashby Donald*, para. 40 (also stating that Article 1 of Protocol 1 applies to IP).
55. *See, e.g.*, CJEU, *SGAE*, para. 36; CJEU, *Infopaq I*, para. 40; CJEU, *BSA*, para. 54; CJEU, *Premier League*, para. 186; CJEU, *Painer*, para. 107; CJEU, *Renckhoff*, para. 18; CJEU, *Bastei Lübbe*, para. 30; and CJEU, *Tom Kabinet*, para. 48.

exclusive rights, but also strict readings of exceptions.[56] The Court has clarified, however, that none of this means that exclusive rights merit absolute protection.[57] What is required for authors and performers to continue their creative and artistic work and safeguard their independence and dignity is that they be allowed to obtain an appropriate reward or adequate compensation for the use of that work.[58]

Finally, despite the need to ensure a high level of protection, a *fair balance* must be struck between the rights and interests of the different categories of rightholders, on the one hand, and those of users of protected works, on the other.[59] The CJEU has repeatedly stated that the copyright *acquis* must be interpreted in a way that allows a fair balance between conflicting fundamental rights to be achieved.[60] Objectives of general interest like the promotion of learning and the dissemination of knowledge and culture should also be balanced against the rights and interests of rightholders.[61]

1.3 The Debate on the InfoSoc Framework of Exceptions

The most important and contentious provision within the InfoSoc Directive is the one addressing the issue of exceptions – Article 5.[62] Article 5(1)-(4) lays down a closed catalogue of exceptions to the rights harmonised therein. Most of the enumerated exceptions are optional, meaning that Member States may choose whether to implement them in their national legal orders or not. Article 5(5) subjects the concrete application of these exceptions to the control of an indeterminate clause, commonly known as the three-step test.

The controversy around Article 5 and copyright exceptions spans very different issues, including the contractual overridability of exceptions[63] and

56. *See, e.g.*, CJEU, *Infopaq I*, para. 40.
57. *See, e.g.*, CJEU, *Scarlet*, para. 43. The term 'absolute' is used here as a synonym for 'limitless'. Of course, copyright's exclusive rights are absolute in the sense that they enjoy *erga omnes* opposability.
58. *See* Recitals 10, 11 and 35 InfoSoc Directive. *See also* AG Opinion, *Padawan*, para. 79; CJEU, *SGAE*, para. 36; CJEU, *Infopaq I*, para. 40; CJEU, *GS Media*, para. 30; CJEU, *Filmspeler*, para. 27; and CJEU, *ITV Broadcasting II*, para. 22.
59. *See* Recitals 3 and 31 InfoSoc Directive.
60. *See infra* Chapter 4, section 5.2.2.1 (with references).
61. *See* Recitals 14 and 22 InfoSoc Directive, and CJEU, *VOB*, paras 51 and 60. Favale et al. (2016) isolate the 'circulation of culture' as an autonomous teleological argument employed by the CJEU.
62. *See* Cohen Jehoram (2001b), p. 387 (considering Article 5 'the most important provision of the entire text'); Leistner (2011), p. 440 (qualifying the revitalisation of the EU system of exceptions as 'the most pressing issue'); Spindler (2014), p. 2552 (stating that the field of exceptions is one of the most controversial ones within copyright law in general); and Lewinski (2018), p. 127 (observing that this is one of the most debated issues).
63. Commentators have been generally critical of the absence of a provision in the InfoSoc Directive explicitly forbidding the overridability of exceptions through contractual

the relationship between exceptions and TPMs.[64] These are not the issues I will focus on, nor will I aim at resolving all the deficiencies of the exceptions' regime.

Instead, I will be concerned with the debate around whether Article 5 should be rethought in light of the demands of two (somewhat elusive) concepts: *flexibility* and *legal certainty*. The debate revolves not only around the content of Article 5 itself but also around the meta-rules that guide their implementation, interpretation, and application, which have often been clarified (or, in some cases, actually established) by the CJEU through the preliminary reference procedure. For convenience, I will refer to this broad set of rules throughout this book as the 'InfoSoc framework of exceptions'.

Critics of Article 5 came to the foreground even before the actual adoption of the InfoSoc Directive in 2001. Bernt Hugenholtz's early remarks on the proposed provision are an example in point: 'How can a legislature in its right mind even contemplate an exhaustive list of limitations, many of which are drafted in inflexible technology-specific language, when the internet produces new business models and novel uses almost each day?'[65] The scarce flexibility offered by exhaustive lists like that of Article 5 InfoSoc Directive is, in Lucie Guibault's view, the 'decisive argument' against their adoption.[66] These lists have illustratively been called

agreements. This contrasts with the option previously made by the legislator in the Software Directive (Articles 5(2) and 8 and Recitals 13 and 16) and in the Database Directive (Article 15) and, post-InfoSoc, in the Marrakesh Directive (Article 3(5)) and DSM Directive (Article 7(1)). Due to such absence, it is not entirely clear whether InfoSoc exceptions may be overridden by contractual provisions. Some commentators, however, argue that InfoSoc tolerates the contractual disposition of its exceptions, based on Article 9 (according to which the InfoSoc Directive is without prejudice to provisions of contract law) and Recital 45 (which states that exceptions 'should not … prevent the definition of contractual relations designed to ensure fair compensation for the rightholders insofar as permitted by national law') – *see* Janssens (2009), pp. 341-342, and Walter & Lewinski (2010), p. 1062. The leading work on the topic is Guibault (2002).

64. The issue relates to the way in which TPMs and their legal protection can restrict the legitimate exercise of the privileges conferred by exceptions and to the effectiveness of Article 6(4) as a solution to this problem. *See*, *e.g.*, Dusollier (2003) and Mazziotti (2008), pp. 179-229. In this regard, the CJEU has stated in *Nintendo I* that TPMs must not go beyond what is necessary to prevent or eliminate activities of third parties that require the authorisation of rightholders (paras 31-32).
65. Hugenholtz (2000b), p. 501, making two further related predictions: first, that 'thanks to the Directive, if some unforeseen use that everyone agrees should be exempted emerges, one will have to wait at least three years, if not much longer, for the Directive to be amended', and second, that '[i]t would be surprising if national lawmakers or courts were that patient, or E.C. law-abiding' (as we shall see, time proved him right on both counts).
66. Guibault (2010), p. 57.

'statutory straitjackets':[67] providing for a closed enumeration in a harmonisation instrument means that this solution will be 'cast in concrete for the years to come'.[68]

The language used to cast InfoSoc exceptions has led scholars to call them 'narrow pigeonholes'.[69] The exceptions in Article 5 contrast with the economic rights in the preceding provisions: there is, in the words of Ansgar Ohly, an 'asymmetry between the rather flexible provisions which grant the rights and the very specific wording of copyright exceptions'.[70] This asymmetry is, in Ohly's opinion, '[t]he main trouble with the Infosoc Directive and many national copyright acts'.[71]

Moreover, as argued by Tatiana-Eleni Synodinou, '[t]he rigidity of the regime governing copyright exceptions and limitations has been accentuated by the concurrent application of the three-step test'.[72] Instead of serving as 'the guarantor of an evolutionary legal system',[73] the test is said to further aggravate what InfoSoc sceptics deem a 'structural problem of inflexibility'.[74]

But the positions espoused by these scholars are not limited to stressing the need for greater flexibility. Critics further claim that the InfoSoc framework does not hold the advantage that supposedly offsets the relatively low degree of flexibility – legal certainty. This is so for a threefold reason. First, the fact that Member States are free to implement most of the exceptions generates uncertainty around the legal status of cross-border services that rely on unauthorised uses of copyright-protected works and constitutes an obstacle to the establishment of an internal market for copyright goods.[75] Second, the three-step test, against which the concrete application of InfoSoc exceptions must be tested, ends up giving a vague effect to these (otherwise relatively precise) provisions. And third, despite the

67. Patry (2011), p. 214. Similarly, in a piece on the principle of *numerus clausus* of real rights, Ascensão (1968), p. 76, has qualified any *numerus clausus* as 'a straitjacket apposed upon life'. Arguing for a rethinking of such principle *de lege ferenda*, *see* Antunes (2015), pp. 186-190, and (2017), pp. 147-153.
68. Hugenholtz (2000b), p. 501. *See also* Hoeren (2000), pp. 4-5, criticising the German framework of narrow and precise exceptions, which, in his view, captures a historic moment and fixes it by law for the rest of time.
69. Hilty et al. (2008), p. 9.
70. Ohly (2009), p. 236. *See also* Samuelson (1998), p. 77 (confessing, in relation to the InfoSoc Proposal, that it was 'distressing to see that the proposed European directive … is so broad in its grant of rights and so narrow in its willingness to grant exceptions to these broad rights'), and Senftleben (2012b), p. 412 ('flexible rights in the field of copyright law require flexible limitations as a counterbalance').
71. Ohly (2009), p. 236.
72. Synodinou (2014), p. 95.
73. Geiger (2007b), fn. 46.
74. Griffiths (2010), p. 89.
75. *See*, *e.g.*, Hugenholtz (2000), pp. 500-501, alerting to that risk before the Directive's adoption, and Guibault (2010), explaining 'why cherry-picking never leads to harmonisation'.

low level of judicial discretion granted by Article 5-type exceptions, courts have occasionally been deciding cases on unauthorised uses in defiance of the framework's constraints.

These scholars therefore argue that the InfoSoc framework should be profoundly reformed with a view to attaining a better equilibrium between flexibility and legal certainty. Whereas some of them have proposed redefining the core economic rights provided therein,[76] most have suggested tackling the issue through the side of exceptions, e.g. by reinterpreting or rewriting the three-step test enshrined in Article 5(5),[77] by enabling the analogical application of listed exceptions,[78] or by importing a fair use standard modeled after that of the US.[79] Support for this kind of reform proposals has also come from the camps of policymakers,[80] civil society organisations,[81] and consumers.[82]

A stronghold of scholars has reacted to this critique, along with rightholders and CMOs. They argue that the InfoSoc framework is structurally sound, forcefully stressing its (alleged) major virtue: the legal certainty it provides to users and rightholders alike regarding the situations in which copyright-protected works can be lawfully used without authorisation. Users, in particular, 'must be clearly warned about the limit between legal and illegal behaviour'[83] – and the existing framework is said to give them such a warning.

The scholars who broadly support the InfoSoc framework highlight the narrow and precise manner in which its exceptions are drafted, especially when contrasted with US fair use, which purportedly contains 'a maximum of insecurity for right owners as well as users'.[84] They thus welcomed the

---

76. *See, e.g.*, Pihlajarinne (2017); Westkamp (2017); and the different contributions in Hugenholtz (2018).
77. *See infra* Chapter 5, section 4.2.2.
78. *See infra* Chapter 5, section 4.2.1.
79. *See infra* Chapter 5, section 4.2.3.
80. *See*, in particular, Recital 13 Draft Reda Report, which recommends the adoption of 'an open norm introducing flexibility in the interpretation of exceptions and limitations' subject to the verification of the three-step test. During the compromise stage that led to the final version of the resolution, however, the tone of the suggestion was significantly weakened. Nevertheless, the version approved by the European Parliament calls for exceptions to be interpreted in a flexible manner in the face of new technology-enabled uses of works – *see* Recital 43 EP Resolution Implementation InfoSoc Directive 2015.
81. *See, e.g.*, Communia Association (2015).
82. According to the Report Public Consultation 2014, p. 33, '[m]ost consumers who responded [to the public consultation on the review of EU copyright rules] consider that more flexibility is needed in order to ensure that copyright exceptions can adjust to technological changes and are forward-looking'.
83. Lucas (2010), p. 282.
84. Cohen Jehoram (1998), p. 58. *See also* Spindler (2002), p. 115; Lucas (2010), p. 282; Nordemann & Conrad (2010), p. 969; and Pollaud-Dulian (2013), p. 171. On the US fair use standard, *see infra* Chapter 5, section 4.2.3.1.

fact that fair use never made its way into EU copyright law.[85] These scholars also tend to praise the EU legislator's choice of setting forth an exhaustive list. This solution, according to Jörg Reinbothe, is based on 'very good reasons': it provides greater harmonisation and transparency than a non-exhaustive list.[86] A closed catalogue can only be enlarged by the EU legislator, not by courts or individual Member States. Had the Directive set an open catalogue, 'there would hardly be any harmonization effect'.[87] Such a solution, it is claimed, 'would simply not achieve the level playing field for the scope of protection that is needed'.[88]

Legal certainty is not the only argument raised by this side in defence of the InfoSoc framework. They claim, in addition, that the Directive provides sufficient flexibility in two different senses. First, it ensures the respect for the legal traditions of Member States, by offering a diverse catalogue that allows national legislators to select the exceptions that they find necessary considering their cultures and local needs.[89] Second, it is capable of dealing effectively with the ongoing emergence of new technological uses, by undergoing periodic legislative revisions.[90] These scholars therefore tend to applaud the path followed by the EU institutions in the recent DSM Directive of cautiously updating the list of exceptions, by re-assessing it in light of today's technological realities.[91]

In sum, there is a sharp disagreement over whether the InfoSoc framework of exceptions should be reformed or not. A number of scholars call into question the flexibility and legal certainty provided by this body of rules, while the opposing faction engages in the converse exercise. What all participants in the debate seem to agree on, implicitly or explicitly, is that the prevailing solution should seek to strike a compromise between flexibility and legal certainty. This book aims at making sense of this debate and hopefully (though perhaps naïvely) at settling it.

---

85. Herman Cohen Jehoram, in commenting on the Dutch government's proposal to introduce a fair use-type exception in the European Commission's Working Group before the adoption of InfoSoc, claimed that, because of 'all the resulting uncertainty for copyright protection', '[t]his would have opened up a real lawyers' paradise of fair use' – Cohen Jehoram (2001a), p. 542. Elsewhere, in noting that this proposal 'found no support whatsoever', the author rejoiced: '[t]his, at least, is an invisible but glorious achievement of the whole Information Society Directive' – Cohen Jehoram (2001b), p. 388.
86. *See* Reinbothe (1998), p. 65.
87. Walter & Lewinski (2010), p. 1020.
88. Reinbothe (1998), p. 65.
89. *See* Reinbothe (1998), p. 65, and Walter & Lewinski (2010), p. 1021.
90. *See* Lucas (2012), p. 379 ('the legislative reforms of recent years have shown that the legislator has the capacity to react'), and Lewinski (2015), p. 4 (the EU system 'has shown that it has so far adapted successfully to new technical developments').
91. *See* Lewinski (2018), pp. 134-135, commending the EU for following a 'step-by-step approach' in the new DSM Directive.

2 RESEARCH QUESTIONS

Against the background set forth in the previous section, this book will endeavour to answer two interrelated research questions:

(1) To what extent does the current InfoSoc framework of exceptions promote flexibility and legal certainty?
(2) If the InfoSoc framework fails to attain an adequate balance between flexibility and legal certainty, how should it be reformed?

These questions will be answered in light of a normative frame of reference that breaks down the concepts of 'flexibility' and 'legal certainty' into a set of objectives and assessment criteria. As has already been anticipated, these terms encapsulate the prevailing policy arguments in the InfoSoc debate. With this in mind, this book advances a more sophisticated understanding of 'flexibility' and 'legal certainty', in order to enable us to methodically examine if, and the degree to which, the existing InfoSoc framework of exceptions achieves an appropriate equilibrium between the two values.

Before proceeding to outlining this book, it is important to emphasise and clarify some aspects related to the scope of the foregoing questions and of the study as a whole.

In examining the InfoSoc framework of exceptions, I will be concerned not so much with the particularities of specific exceptions (even though the wording and scope of selected exceptions will be discussed), as with a structural analysis of Article 5. As stated above, by 'InfoSoc framework of exceptions', I mean the fundamental options and general structure of Article 5, as positivised by the EU legislator and as interpreted by the CJEU, namely the exhaustiveness of the catalogue, the optional nature of most exceptions, and the function of the three-step test. These elements, more than the particulars of each exception, are the drivers of the policy debate I am interested in.

In addition, it ought to be made clear that, in theory, the questions that will guide this study could also focus on (or extend to) the side of exclusive rights. However, proposals for reforming the EU *acquis* on rights, e.g., by excluding certain acts from their scope, fall beyond the reach of this book. The justification for the exclusion is twofold.

First, the rights of reproduction and communication to the public, as briefly explained in the following chapter, have expanded throughout a long process. Although various borderline questions keep arising, the far-reaching scope of these rights in the EU copyright *acquis* is a consolidated matter. This may explain why the level of scholarly attention devoted to the scope of exclusive rights has been lower than that devoted to exceptions and why some scholars go as far as saying that 'what counts in modern copyright law are no longer the exclusive rights but rather the limitations and exceptions'.[92]

Second, the policy options for reforming the InfoSoc Directive are considered here in light of the constraints that emerge from the treaty obligations of the existing international copyright *acquis*. Introducing fairness-based or other types of normative considerations into the formulation of exclusive rights not only runs against copyright tradition but is also the result of a 'blue skies' approach that this book does not follow.[93]

3 OUTLINE AND METHODOLOGY

This book will approach the issue of exceptions from the perspective of EU copyright law and, more narrowly, of the InfoSoc Directive. Although differences in the national implementation of InfoSoc will be analysed where relevant, a detailed domestic or comparative approach falls outside the scope of this book. Non-harmonised issues, such as moral rights, are also excluded.

EU law has been said to be an 'autonomous body of law' that is generally independent of Member State law.[94] Yet, some scholars have disputed the idea that a *corpus* of legal norms coherent enough to deserve the label of 'EU copyright law' actually exists[95] – a question that I address below.[96] For the time being, suffice to point out that, throughout almost thirty years, multiple copyright doctrines have been harmonised in no less than a dozen directives specifically dedicated to copyright law[97] and in a voluminous body of CJEU case law, composed of more than fifty preliminary rulings.[98]

This book is composed of five chapters, each of which is dedicated to examining one or more sub-questions that contribute towards unveiling the answers to the broader research questions articulated above. The methodological approaches adopted in this book naturally track the purposes of the sub-questions under consideration.

92. Dreier (2010), p. 52.
93. As admitted in Hugenholtz & Kretschmer (2018), p. 3, the project of redesigning the economic rights of the EU copyright *acquis* led by these authors was 'primarily a theoretical, "utopian" exercise'. Arguing against the restriction of the scope of economic rights, on grounds that this solution would contravene the minimum rights provided in international treaties, *see* Lewinski (2018), pp. 129-130.
94. Rösler (2012), p. 979.
95. *See, e.g.*, Dietz (2004); Hilty (2004); and, more recently, Lucas-Schloetter (2014).
96. *See infra* 4.
97. For an overview, *see infra* 4.1.
98. On the CJEU's role as one of the protagonists in copyright law harmonisation, *see infra* 4.2.

Chapters 1, 2, and 3 set the stage for Chapters 4 and 5, both in terms of the legal framework that will be assessed and the normative criteria that will guide the analysis.

Chapters 1 and 2 place the InfoSoc framework of exceptions within its broader international and EU law context. Because the issue of whether exclusive rights are triggered by a certain use logically precedes the analysis of exceptions, I begin by depicting the scope of the rights of reproduction and communication to the public (Chapter 1). I then move on to a general description of the system of copyright exceptions in international and EU law (Chapter 2).

In outlining the copyright system of rights and exceptions, attention is devoted mainly to the relevant EU legislative sources. Primary law, including the EU fundamental rights framework, is considered where pertinent, but the analysis focuses on secondary law, particularly on the relevant provisions of copyright directives. Within secondary law, the content of other unilateral EU acts – such as opinions, communications, recommendations, and white and green papers – is also explored. The case law of the CJEU is another fundamental source of the *acquis communautaire*. Under the preliminary reference procedure, the CJEU gives authoritative interpretations of EU law provisions that are relevant in the main proceedings.[99] These interpretations are binding not only on the referring court but also on all Member State courts. The preliminary rulings that are relevant for this book contain answers to questions relating to the interpretation of directives in the copyright *acquis*, mainly the InfoSoc Directive.

It should nonetheless be kept in mind that the copyright harmonisation process has largely occurred in tandem with internationalisation and that extensive international copyright agreements have been in place since the late nineteenth century.[100] The EU approved both the TRIPS Agreement and the WCT,[101] making them binding upon its institutions and Member States.[102] These agreements, in turn, incorporated by reference the key substantive provisions of the Berne Convention,[103] meaning that the EU, which is not a party to the Convention, is nonetheless required to comply with its provisions.[104] Moreover, as already mentioned, the InfoSoc Directive implemented various obligations arising from the WIPO Treaties into the *acquis*.[105] EU law must, in general and in so far as possible, be interpreted

99. *See* Article 267 TFEU.
100. A complicated web of bilateral copyright treaties was woven during the nineteenth century, eventually leading to the conclusion of the Berne Convention in 1886. *See generally* Ricketson (1987).
101. TRIPS was approved by Council Decision 94/800/EC of 22 December 1994 and the WIPO Treaties by Council Decision 2000/278/EC of 16 March 2000.
102. *See* Article 216(2) TFEU.
103. *See* Articles 9(1) TRIPS and 1(4) WCT.
104. *See* CJEU, *Luksan*, para. 59, and CJEU, *DR & TV2 Danmark*, para. 29.
105. *See* Recital 15 InfoSoc Directive.

in a manner consistent with international law,[106] but that is all the more so where its provisions are intended to give effect to an international agreement concluded by the Union.[107] For these reasons, the rights of reproduction and communication to the public and the exceptions thereto will also be examined in light of their international context.

Chapter 3 follows a conceptual approach. The focus of its research is on how 'flexibility' and 'legal certainty' ought to be understood in the context of the debate on the InfoSoc framework of exceptions. If the merits of the current framework are to be assessed by reference to the extent to which they promote flexibility and legal certainty, rich and theoretically grounded conceptualisations of these values are needed. The chapter identifies the different meanings with which these terms are used by scholars and policymakers in the field, with a view to laying the normative groundwork against which the prescriptive parts of the book will unfold. Though making sense of these two concepts in EU copyright law is a valuable exercise in and of itself, its ultimate purpose is to establish more refined criteria against which to judge the merits of the existing framework, as well as the proposals for improvement that have been formulated in copyright literature in recent years.

Chapter 4 then revisits the InfoSoc framework of exceptions, in light of the normative apparatus established in the preceding chapter. It isolates the contentious structural features of the framework and examines them in a critical fashion. The analysis of the relevant features will be made against the background of the scholarly discussions taking place in leading academic circles from both sides of the Atlantic, but especially in Europe. Although the methodological approach in this chapter is essentially analytical, lurking in its shadows is a normative ambition: the chapter offers a *critical* portrait of the existing framework, so as to understand if reform is needed. As shall be seen, the analysis reveals the framework's incapacity to foster flexibility and legal certainty to a proper extent. This finding inevitably leads to the question of how these often-conflicting values should be balanced.

Chapter 5 thus addresses the crucial normative question of the book: how should the InfoSoc framework be reformed in order to adequately balance flexibility and legal certainty? Against the background of the intermediate conclusions gathered throughout the book, this chapter puts forward a set of reform proposals, articulating their advantages and responding to potential objections. In doing so, the chapter also identifies, systematises, and synthesises the various reform proposals that have been advanced

---

106. *See, e.g.*, CJEU, *Commission v. Germany*, and CJEU, *Bettati*, para. 20. In the field of copyright, *see* CJEU, *Dimensione Direct Sales*, para. 23, and CJEU, *Titus Donner*, para. 23.

107. Making reference to this obligation in relation to the InfoSoc Directive, *see, e.g.*, the CJEU judgments in *Peek & Cloppenburg*, para. 30; *SGAE*, para. 35; *Premier League*, para. 189; *Infopaq I*, para. 32; *Painer*, para. 126; and *Tom Kabinet*, paras 38-39. *See also* Recital 44 InfoSoc Directive.

in the literature, by describing their main characteristics and effects from the standpoint of EU copyright law.

Having chosen to dedicate a lengthy academic piece to investigating a series of questions from the perspective of EU copyright law, it is vital to begin by discussing if – and the extent to which – a common copyright framework can be said to exist beyond and above the copyright laws of Member States. Therefore, before I follow the sequence promised in the previous paragraphs, I will ask the reader to indulge me while I attempt at answering this key preliminary question.

4 EXCURSUS ON ONTOLOGY: IS THERE SUCH A THING AS AN EU COPYRIGHT LAW?

A thorough analysis of the question of whether such a thing as an EU copyright law actually exists would require a book-length effort. In fact, entire volumes have been dedicated to issues closely affiliated with this query.[108] Nonetheless, the jurisdictional focus chosen for this book implies that it is not much of an overstatement to say that there is something that can appropriately be called 'EU copyright law'.

It is, of course, hard (and a rather artificial exercise) to define the point beyond which there is sufficient coherence in the copyright law of Member States for it to merit that label. Some commentators dealing with this question seem to think that an EU copyright law would only really come into existence with unification.[109] Ironically, this view defeats the very purpose of the question. Attempting to answer the question of whether there is an EU copyright law presupposes the belief that there can exist such a thing *before* unification, for it is common knowledge among copyright enthusiasts that true unification is yet to occur. But, despite the lack of a comprehensive EU regulation taking precedence over national laws, a remarkable degree of harmonisation has been achieved over the course of three decades thanks to the work of both legislative and judicial institutions.

108. *See* Eechoud et al. (2009) and Synodinou (2012).
109. According to Farrand (2014), p. 31, 'it is technically incorrect to refer to the copyright law of the EU. … [T]here is no European Copyright Code' – Farrand (2014), p. 31. Though not focusing on the conceptual question, Leistner (2009), p. 884, makes a related point: 'in a long-term perspective only a genuine unification of European copyright by way of a Community copyright regulation, partially pre-empting national copyright laws, will allow the creation of a genuine internal market for copyright based goods and services (in particular on the internet)'.

4.1 The Legislative Copyright *Acquis*

European harmonisation in the field of copyright law has been argued for since at least 1974. Back then, the European Parliament unanimously approved a resolution in which it called for the harmonisation of 'the protection of the cultural heritage, royalties and other related intellectual property-rights'.[110] Three years later, in an extensive comparative study on copyright in the European Community elaborated at the request of the Commission, Adolf Dietz identified a set of pressing issues in need of Community intervention and proposed a 'harmonization timetable'.[111] At that time, through to the 1980s, the intervention of the CJEU (then ECJ) in the field of copyright was limited to assessing the compatibility of national copyright rules with the fundamental freedoms and EEC competition law.[112]

It was not until the Commission released the 1988 Green Paper on *Copyright and the Challenge of Technology*[113] that copyright harmonisation gained true momentum. The Commission identified a series of issues that merited urgent attention at Community level, such as piracy, audiovisual home copying, and the protection of computer programs and databases. Thereafter, and throughout almost three decades, the EU has harmonised various copyright doctrines in numerous directives specifically dedicated to copyright law:[114] software (1991);[115] rental, lending, and certain related rights (1992);[116] rights applicable to satellite broadcasting and cable retransmission (1993);[117] term of protection (1993);[118] databases (1996);[119]

110. EP Resolution Cultural Heritage 1974, p. 6.
111. *See* Dietz (1978). *See also* Dietz (1979).
112. Among the CJEU judgments handed down in the 1970s and early 1980s are *SABAM*; *SACEM*; *Coditel I*; *Coditel II*; *GEMA*; and *GVL*. For an early analysis on the role of the CJEU in promoting the harmonisation of IP law in general, *see* Loewenheim (1995). Derclaye (2009), p. 1, traces the origin of EU copyright law back to the 1971 judgment in *Deutsche Grammophon*, in which the CJEU established its competence over copyright law. The Court decided therein that the exercise of an exclusive right conferred by national copyright law could amount to a restriction of the free movement of goods and services (paras 11-13).
113. Analysing the Green Paper in detail, *see* Schricker (1989).
114. The list excludes the Enforcement Directive, which refers not only to copyright, but to all IP rights.
115. The 1991 Software Directive was repealed and replaced on codification in 2009. Unless otherwise noted, references to the Software Directive will concern the codified version.
116. The 1992 Rental and Lending Directive was repealed and replaced on codification in 2006. Unless otherwise noted, references to the Rental and Lending Directive will concern the codified version.
117. The Satellite and Cable Directive has been recently amended by the Online TV and Radio Directive.
118. The 1993 Term Directive was repealed and replaced on codification in 2006. This latter Directive was amended in 2011, with the purpose of extending the term of protection for performers and sound recordings to 70 years. Unless otherwise noted, references to the Term Directive will concern the 2006 version as amended in 2011.
119. The Database Directive was amended by the DSM Directive.

copyright in the information society (2001);[120] resale right (2001); orphan works (2012); collective management (2014); people with print disabilities (2017);[121] online services ancillary to TV and radio broadcasts (2019); and copyright in the digital single market (2019).[122] The decade between 1991 and 2001 witnessed the enactment of seven of these directives and, after a slowdown, the pace has accelerated again in more recent years. In 2017, two regulations that fall within the broad field of copyright were also adopted – one on cross-border portability of online content services and another on cross-border exchange of accessible format copies for the print-disabled. Thus, although before the 1990s the harmonisation of copyright law might have seemed 'retarded' when compared to other fields of IP,[123] it is now fair to say that '[c]opyright is a favourite child in Europe'.[124]

These harmonisation efforts notwithstanding, there is no specific Treaty provision granting the EU competence to approximate national copyright laws. Absent a copyright-specific legal basis, harmonisation measures on copyright law have been contingent upon their potential to contribute to the establishment and functioning of the internal market. Article 114 TFEU (former Article 95 EC Treaty), which grants the EU competence to adopt harmonisation measures with the aim of promoting the construction of the internal market, has therefore served as the main competence norm for copyright harmonisation.[125]

Since the Lisbon reform, however, Article 118 TFEU grants the EU an explicit legal basis for the creation of European IP rights,[126] bestowing on the

120. The DSM Directive amended the InfoSoc Directive too.
121. Along with the Marrakesh Regulation, this Directive implemented the Marrakesh Treaty into EU law.
122. At the time of writing, the Polish Government had brought an action for annulment of the DSM Directive before the CJEU under Article 263 TFEU, with an emphasis on the contentious Article 17. Poland claims that the CJEU should annul Article 17(4)(b) (best efforts to ensure the unavailability of unlicensed works on online content-sharing platforms) and Article 17(4)(c), *in fine* (best efforts to prevent future uploads of such works) of the DSM Directive, or, alternatively, the provision in its entirety. In Poland's view, the contested paragraphs infringe the freedom of expression and information guaranteed by Article 11 of the Charter. It argues, in particular, that the imposition on online content-sharing platforms of the obligations contained in those rules makes it necessary for the platforms to carry out prior automatic verification of content uploaded by users in order to avoid liability, thereby forcing platforms to introduce preventive control mechanisms (also known as 'filters'). Such mechanisms, Poland maintains, undermine the essence of the mentioned freedom and do not comply with the requirement that its limitations be proportional and necessary.
123. Schricker (1989), pp. 466-467.
124. Hilty (2004), p. 760.
125. For a thorough analysis of the EU's competence in the field of copyright, arguing that there is a normative gap in copyright law-making based on Article 114 TFEU, *see* Ramalho (2016a).
126. According to this provision, the European Parliament and the Council shall 'establish measures for the creation of European intellectual property rights to provide uniform

EU the competence to enact an autonomous copyright title valid in all Member States.[127] Nonetheless, the achievement of such a uniform protection is still predicated on 'the establishment and functioning of the internal market', meaning that although Article 118 enables the EU to proceed with copyright unification, only the copyright doctrines that bear the potential of imposing obstacles to the internal market fall within the EU's legislative competence.[128]

This internal market legal basis is a possible explanation for the fragmentary approach to copyright harmonisation that has been adopted by the EU. The harmonisation process has so far addressed only a limited set of copyright doctrines, while leaving a number of other important ones unharmonised – an approach deemed by William Cornish as 'the art of the possible'.[129]

On the other hand, whereas the so-called first generation of copyright directives carried out a vertical harmonisation, focusing on selected aspects of copyright law usually in a content- or technology-specific fashion (think of computer programs, databases, and satellite and cable TV), the InfoSoc Directive represented a fundamental change in paradigm.[130] InfoSoc adopted a horizontal and largely technology-neutral approach, tackling, among other issues, the most important economic rights and their exceptions.[131] More recently, the DSM Directive followed a similar kind of approach, in

protection of intellectual property rights throughout the Union'. Article 118 TFEU has already been used as a legal basis for the enactment of Regulations concerning the unitary patent protection and the revision of the Trademark Regulation.

127. The adoption of a unitary copyright title is distinct from the harmonisation or approximation of national laws. As Ramalho (2016a), p. 10, puts it, 'the creation of a new, pan-European copyright title adds a new form of right to the legal order (regardless of whether or not it replaces national copyright entitlements), whereas harmonization of national copyright laws arguably adjusts existing national laws by approximating them'. The adoption of an EU copyright title would present specific difficulties. As explained in EPRS (2015), p. II-236, 'copyright presents the particularity that it is acquired by the act of creation, as soon as a record of the work can prove the ownership. It does not require registration. As a result, a European copyright system could coexist with difficulty with national copyright systems because the author of the work cannot easily opt for a protection (national or European) as its work is automatically protected under the applicable national law where the work is published.'
128. The CJEU has confirmed the connection between the internal market rationale and the competences set by Article 118 TFEU in *Spain & Italy v. Council*, para. 17.
129. Cornish (1995), p. 811.
130. *See* Stamatoudi & Torremans (2014a), p. 397. In reality, the Term Directive, though dealing only with one particular aspect of copyright law, already followed a more horizontal approach, in that it harmonised the term of protection for all types of subject matter.
131. Despite its title suggesting an exclusively digital scope of application, the provisions of InfoSoc apply in the analogue context too – *see* Vicente (2005), pp. 161-162; Vicente (2008), p. 123; and Stamatoudi & Torremans (2014a), pp. 397 and 399. The former author observed that the InfoSoc Directive, with its vast reach, served as the legislative basis for a new EU copyright law.

addressing a variety of issues – such as exceptions, licensing practices, and certain uses by online services – in a horizontal manner.

Despite the change in legislative approach, by 2004, in Agnès Lucas-Schloetter's opinion, 'there was still no genuine European copyright law', since 'the convergence of national copyright law was … still limited'.[132] Also writing in 2004, two other distinguished scholars disagreed with the existence of something that could be properly called an 'EU copyright law'. According to Adolf Dietz, there was, back then, 'no such a thing as a "European copyright law"'.[133] The author further forecasted that copyright law 'will be for a long time … a national matter of legislation'.[134] Likewise, Reto Hilty then declared that 'today's harmonisation of copyright in Europe is still composed of fragments rather than being a cohesive regulation. In other words, the evolution of a European copyright is somewhere in mid-stream – there is no way back to mere national law, but it is also nowhere near complete.'[135] Hilty further criticised the fact that the patchwork of directives failed to address some of the most basic aspects of copyright law, fundamental among which are the requirements for copyright protection.

Since 2004, however, another EU institution has taken centre stage in the process of copyright harmonisation.

---

132. Lucas-Schloetter (2014), p. 11.
133. Dietz (2004), p. 820.
134. Dietz (2004), p. 820.
135. Hilty (2004), p. 761. Hilty specifically condemned the largely speculative and imbalanced character of the justifications for the enactment of the InfoSoc Directive laid down in its recitals. The Directive's priority, he suggested, was to protect the entertainment industry, rather than to ensure the promotion of 'cultural creativity' and to safeguard 'the independence and dignity of artistic creators and performers', as stated in Recital 11 – Hilty (2004), pp. 761-762. To my mind, however, these are not persuasive reasons to justify the idea of the non-existence of a truly European copyright law. One may or may not agree with the orientation of these policy statements and with the solutions adopted in the Directive, but it is beyond dispute that the InfoSoc preamble constitutes a unique step towards the construction of a harmonised copyright law. As Adolf Dietz put it, InfoSoc – unlike most modern national constitutions and international instruments, from which a reflection on the need to grant copyright protection is wholly absent – has the virtue of 'reformulat[ing] and restat[ing] what, under contemporary conditions, copyright ultimately is all about' – Dietz (2004), p. 813. Indeed, the legislative scale may be tipped too much in favour of rightholders. But that does not mean that there is no generalised understanding at the EU level about the essential rationales of this field of law.

4.2 The Era of CJEU-Made Harmonisation

Besides EU primary and secondary laws, the case law of the CJEU is widely regarded as being part of the *acquis communautaire*.[136] As the legislative body of EU copyright grew, so did the judicial *acquis*, due to the increasing number of preliminary reference requests by Member States.[137] Since the mid-2000s the Court has assumed a key role in shaping the meaning of fundamental copyright concepts, such as reproduction, private copying and fair compensation;[138] communication to the public;[139] and distribution to the public and exhaustion.[140]

Among the most important and hotly debated decisions arising from these requests is *Infopaq I*. In this seminal ruling, the CJEU harmonised the concept of originality for all protectable subject matter,[141] overlooking the fact that the referred questions did not prompt it to do so. *Infopaq I* and the rulings that followed had a decisive influence on the issue of subsistence of

136. *See* Ramalho (2016a), p. 13 (and references cited therein). On the role of the CJEU in interpreting and developing copyright law, in detail, *see* Rosati (2019).
137. Highlighting the substantial growth in CJEU copyright case law in the 2009-2014 period and referring to the InfoSoc Directive as 'the catalyst' for such development, *see* Leistner (2014), pp. 559-561, and Leistner (2015a), p. 626. *Contrast* these analyses with the earlier one made by the same author in Leistner (2009).
138. *See* the rulings in *Infopaq I*; *Premier League*; *Padawan*; *Stichting de Thuiskopie*; *Luksan*; *SAS Institute*; *VG Wort*; *Amazon*; *ACI Adam*; *Ulmer*; *Copydan Båndkopi*; *Reprobel*; *Austro-Mechana*; *EGEDA II*; *Microsoft*; *Soulier & Doke*; *VCAST*; *Pelham*; and *Cofemel*.
139. *See* the decisions in *SGAE*; *Organismos Sillogikis*; *BSA*; *Premier League*; *Circul Globus Bucuresti*; *Luksan*; *SCF*; *ITV Broadcasting I*; *OSA*; *Svensson*; *C More Entertainment*; *BestWater*; *SBS Belgium*; *Reha Training*; *GS Media*; *SPA*; *Soulier & Doke*; *ITV Broadcasting II*; *Filmspeler*; *Ziggo*; *AKM*; *VCAST*; *Renckhoff*; *Tom Kabinet*; and *Stim & SAMI*.
140. *See* the rulings in *Laserdisken*; *Peek & Cloppenburg*; *Titus Donner*; *UsedSoft*; *Art & Allposters*; *Dimensione Direct Sales*; *VOB*; *Syed*; and *Tom Kabinet*.
141. Due to the disparities in the level of originality required by different Member States for copyright protection to attach (most notably, the UK, which applied the 'skill and labour' test, and Germany, which has traditionally required a somewhat higher level of creativity), the most that EU legislators could achieve was the vague formula of originality as the 'author's own intellectual creation', which, until *Infopaq*, had applied only to computer programs (Article 1(3) Software Directive), databases (Article 3(1) Database Directive) and photographs (Article 6 Term Directive). Works falling under these categories of subject matter were protected if they were considered original in the sense that they were the author's own intellectual creation. InfoSoc, however, left open the question of the originality requirement for all other copyright-protectable works. In *Infopaq I*, paras 37 and 48, the CJEU boldly determined that the InfoSoc reproduction right applied only in relation to subject matter which is original in the sense that it is the author's own intellectual creation, thus extending this formula to all protectable works. The Court has confirmed this extension and given more precise hints on the meaning of the formula in subsequent judgments – *see BSA*, paras 44-46; *Premier League*, paras 96-98 and 155; *SAS Institute*, paras 45 and 65-70; *Painer*, paras 86-94; *Levola Hengelo*, paras 32-46; *Cofemel*, paras 26-56; and *Brompton Bicycle*, paras 20-38. For further detail on this line of case law, *see infra* Chapter 4, section 5.3.1.

copyright protection in the EU. This set of rulings spawned an unprecedented level of scholarly discussion on the Europeanisation of copyright law, leading commentators to acknowledge the CJEU's 'increased determination to interpret the copyright *acquis* in a manner that promotes the construction of as complete a body of EU copyright law as possible'.[142]

Moreover, when harmonising the meaning of important copyright doctrines, the CJEU has been narrowing down the margin of discretion of national legislators in implementing such doctrines, most notably exclusive rights and exceptions.[143] In a series of rulings, the CJEU clarified that Member States may not adjust the scope of the economic rights as harmonised in the EU *acquis*[144] and that, where they choose to implement an (optional) InfoSoc exception, they are not entirely free to define its coverage beyond what is permitted by Article 5.[145] Insofar as the lawfulness of uses of protected subject matter turns on the scope and meaning of rules on reproduction and communication to the public, including the exceptions to these rights, it seems that the Member States' room for manoeuvre in regulating such uses is now significantly diminished.

In late years, a new high in this 'age of judicial activism'[146] has arguably been reached, with judge-made harmonisation stretching for other areas that had previously been left untouched by EU law, such as secondary liability[147] and the notion of 'work'.[148] These daring judgments, much like the early ECJ decisions in the field of IP,[149] ended up providing impetus for legislative intervention in some of these areas. The resulting legal provisions – some of them composed of exceedingly vague language, as a consequence of difficult political compromises (Article 17 DSM Directive being the prime

---

142. Griffiths (2014a), p. 1099. For other accounts on the CJEU-led harmonisation of copyright law, with particular emphasis on the effects of the *Infopaq I* judgment, *see* Derclaye (2010); Vousden (2010); Griffiths (2011); Eechoud (2012); Rosati (2013a), pp. 97 et seq.; and Rosati (2013b).
143. *See infra* Chapter 4, section 5.1.1. *See also* Rosati (2014) and Xalabarder (2016).
144. *See* CJEU, *Luksan*, paras 64-68; CJEU, *Football Dataco*, paras 48-52; CJEU, *Svensson*, paras 34-41; CJEU, *Funke Medien*, paras 27-54; and CJEU, *Pelham*, paras 75-86.
145. *See* CJEU, *Padawan*, para. 36; CJEU, *DR & TV2 Danmark*, paras 35-36; CJEU, *ACI Adam*, para. 49; CJEU, *Deckmyn*, para. 16; CJEU, *Funke Medien*, paras 27-54; and CJEU, *Spiegel Online*, paras 16-39. *See also* Communication on a Modern European Copyright Framework, fn. 22. For further detail, *see infra* Chapter 4, section 5.1.1.
146. Hugenholtz (2013a), pp. 513-516. Bently (2012) has famously qualified this process as one of 'harmonisation by stealth'. *See also* Strowel (2012), pp. 75-76; Halpern & Johnson (2014), pp. 102-103; and Griffiths (2019), p. 15.
147. *See* the CJEU judgments in *GS Media*, *Filmspeler*, and *Ziggo*.
148. *See* CJEU, *Levola Hengelo*; *Cofemel*; and *Brompton Bicycle*.
149. In a line of decisions in the 1970s and 1980s, the Court assessed the compatibility of the exercise of IP rights with the fundamental freedoms of the internal market, namely the free movement of goods and services – *see* the judgments in *Deutsche Grammophon*; *Coditel I*; *Dansk Supermarked*; *Musik-Vertrieb Membran*; *Coditel II*; *Warner Brothers*; *EMI Electrola*; and *Tournier*.

example) –, in turn, are likely to prompt further references to the CJEU, in what amounts to a true cross-fertilisation process.

4.3 The Future of Copyright Harmonisation

Despite the foregoing developments, harmonisation – of the judge-made kind, as of the legislative one – has not reached all corners of copyright law. Some areas of copyright have been generally left out of the harmonisation process – namely authorship/ownership[150] and moral rights[151] – and, as a result, non-negligible differences between the copyright laws of EU Member States still remain.[152]

Besides, even though harmonisation has spread its tentacles far and wide, one 'last frontier' rests largely unconquered: that of territoriality.[153] The territorial nature of national copyright laws – the 'Achilles' heel of the

---

150. The Commission explained the reasons for this ommission in the 2004 Staff Working Paper, p. 14: 'One of the reasons for the scarcity of international and Community rules governing the initial ownership is the sensitivity of the issue and the fact that it is so closely associated with the foundations of copyright and the objectives of the copyright regime in a given country.' The exceptions, at the EU level, are the provisions in the Satellite and Cable Directive (Article 1(5)), the Rental and Lending Directive (Article 2(2)), and the Term Directive (Article 2(1)) that attribute the authorship of a cinematographic or audiovisual work to its principal director.
151. In the 1988 Green Paper, the Commission felt it was 'unnecessary to include provisions on moral rights in a Community framework directive at the present time' (p. 197). A few years later, in the 1995 Green Paper, which eventually led to the InfoSoc Proposal, the Commission called for 'an examination of the question whether the present lack of harmonization will continue to be acceptable in the new digital environment' (p. 67). Although the Commission admitted, in the 1996 Follow-Up that 'the Single Market dimension of moral rights gains more shape than it had before in the traditional environment', it ended up concluding that 'the time is not yet ripe for concrete harmonisation initiatives' (p. 28). Accordingly, Recital 19 InfoSoc Directive, as well as Article 9 and Recital 20 Term Directive make clear that these instruments do not apply to moral rights. It is important to note, however, that some aspects related to moral rights have found their way into the Directives. Article 4(b) Software Directive grants the right to do or to authorise the translation, adaptation, arrangement and any other alteration of a computer program, indirectly protecting the moral right of integrity over the program. In the InfoSoc Directive, Article 5(3)(a), (c), (d) and (f) require the privileged user to indicate the name of the author of the used work – a requirement that bears a connection with the moral right of attribution. Also, in the Marrakesh Directive, Article 3(2) obliges Member States to ensure that accessible format copies respect the integrity of the work. Moreover, the CJEU has been said to have initiated a *de facto* harmonisation of moral rights in the *Deckmyn* judgment – *see* Rosati (2015), pp. 527-528. Arguing for further harmonisation in the area of moral rights, *see*, *e.g.*, Metzger (2005), and Janssens (2017).
152. Some disparities are commonly attributed to the divide between the two main copyright traditions – the continental *droit d'auteur* tradition and the common law copyright tradition –, notably regarding the originality threshold, the rules on initial ownership and the rules on transferability of rights. On the relevance of this divide, *see infra* Chapter 3, section 2.2.1.
153. Eechoud et al. (2009), p. 307.

acquis'[154] – entails that the effects of the exclusive rights granted by one such law are produced only within the borders of that Member State.[155] This means, in turn, that the licences granted to use in-copyright works have an equally national scope and that rights must be cleared in each and every Member State before an EU-wide content service can be provided.[156] Nonetheless, important steps to overcome the problem of territoriality have been given by both the CJEU and the legislature.[157]

Scholarly proposals for a greater degree of 'Europeanisation' have been around for some time now. Prudence has been the watchword for some of these scholars. As early as in 2002, Michel Walter proposed the consolidation of the existing *acquis*, as well as the clarification of a number of inconsistencies and the closing of the gaps therein.[158] Yet, Walter – in borrowing Federico Fellini's famous quote, '[t]he true realist is the visionary'[159] – seems to suggest that something more could be done. But whereas

154. Eechoud et al. (2009), p. 307.
155. The territorial nature of copyright and related rights was affirmed by the CJEU in *Lagardère*, para. 46.
156. *See* Eechoud et al. (2009), p. 307.
157. In 1971, the CJEU created the rule of exhaustion of the distribution right in *Deutsche Grammophon*, paras 11-13, which was later codified in Article 4(2) InfoSoc Directive. Decades later, in the seminal *Premier League* decision, the Court used competition law to strike another blow against territoriality: it held that exclusive licensing agreements between copyright holders and broadcasters that had the effect of enforcing territorial exclusivity were incompatible with competition rules. In particular, these agreements would contravene Article 101 TFEU if they obliged the broadcaster not to supply decoding devices enabling access to that rightholder's copyright-protected works with a view to their use outside the territory covered by that agreement (para. 146).
At the legislative level, an early effort to overcome the problem of territoriality was Article 1(2)(b) Satellite and Cable Directive, according to which '[t]he act of communication to the public by satellite occurs solely in the Member State where … the programme-carrying signals are introduced into an uninterrupted chain of communication', meaning that an act of satellite broadcasting would only require a license from its country of origin. However, as Eechoud et al. (2009), p. 314, note, 'the [Satellite and Cable] Directive does not actually prohibit territorial licensing. Right holders and broadcasters have therefore remained free to persist in these age-old practices, and will undoubtedly continue to do so as long as broadcasting markets remain largely local and a pan-European audiovisual space a distant utopia.' More recently, the Online TV and Radio Directive extended the principle of 'country of origin' to ancillary online services of broadcasters (e.g., their simulcasting or catch-up services). The rules on multi-territorial licensing in the Collective Management Directive are another effort in the same direction, but a similarly modest one, for they apply only to authors' rights in musical works for online use – *see* Articles 23-32. Further steps were taken with the adoption of the Portability Regulation, with the goal of broadening access to online content services for travellers in the EU, and with the enactment of a 'country of origin' rule in the context of the exceptions for digital teaching uses (Article 5(3)) and for the making available of out-of-commerce works by cultural heritage institutions (Articles 8(2) and 9(2)) in the DSM Directive.
158. *See* Walter (2002).
159. Walter (2002), p. 8.

he does not dismiss the adoption of a European Copyright Code via EU regulation as the culmination of this process,[160] he believes that a consolidating directive would be 'more realistic and sufficiently visionary'.[161] A few years later, Frank Gotzen proposed the adoption of a mixed solution: a European Copyright Code composed of a directive that would regroup the harmonised doctrines in a coherent fashion and harmonise other aspects of copyright law that are likely to generate little controversy, and of a second part that would resort to soft law instruments, such as recommendations, to tackle contentious issues.[162] In justifying this prudent proposal, Gotzen too borrows Italian wisdom: *chi va piano, va sano, e chi va sano, va lontano.*[163]

Proposals for the adoption of more permanent legislative solutions have also been put forward. The most extensively debated of such proposals has come from the Wittem Group – a group of European copyright scholars that drafted a project for a European Copyright Code to 'serve as a model or reference tool for future harmonization or unification of copyright at the European level'.[164] Widely acclaimed as a pioneering and inspirational effort,[165] the project has nevertheless been criticised for its limited scope, as it failed to address a number of important issues, like related rights, collective management, and enforcement.[166] As to the choice between further harmonisation or unification, the Wittem Group deliberately refrained from taking a stance.[167] Although policymakers have occasionally entertained the possibility of codification and/or unification,[168] its political feasibility raises

160. Favouring the adoption of a copyright Regulation, *see* Strowel (2012), pp. 88-90, and Hilty (2012). *See also* Hilty & Moscon (2017), pp. 21-22, making the argument that, under Article 118 TFEU, it may be considered that the EU is obliged to adopt regulations in cases where they are necessary for the functioning of the internal market.
161. Writing in co-authorship with Silke von Lewinski, in this case – *see* Walter & Lewinski (2010), p. 1523.
162. *See* Gotzen (2007), pp. 55-61. The 2005 Online Music Recommendation is mentioned as an example – *see* Gotzen (2007), p. 56. Strowel (2014), p. 1128, also considers the idea of further Europeanisation of copyright law based on soft law.
163. Gotzen (2007), p. 61.
164. Wittem Group (2010).
165. *See* Lucas-Schloetter (2014), p. 17, and Stamatoudi & Torremans (2014b), p. 1156.
166. *See* Lucas (2012), p. 376, and Stamatoudi & Torremans (2014b), p. 1156.
167. Wittem Group (2010): 'the Group does not take a position on the desirability as such of introducing a unified European legal framework'. Nonetheless, the personal view of one of the project leaders is that the advantages of unification over directive-driven harmonisation are plentiful – *see* Hugenholtz (2012b), p. 352.
168. *See, e.g.*, the Communication on a Single Market for IP Rights, p. 11: 'Another approach for a more far-reaching overhaul of copyright at European level could be the creation of a European Copyright Code. This could encompass a comprehensive codification of the present body of EU copyright directives in order to harmonise and consolidate the entitlements provided by copyright and related rights at EU level. This would also provide an opportunity to examine whether the current exceptions and limitations to copyright granted under the 2001/29/EC Directive need to be updated or harmonised at EU level. A Code could therefore help to clarify the relationship between the various exclusive rights enjoyed by rights holders and the scope of the exceptions and limitations

serious doubts. For one thing, it is not clear whether Member States would be willing to forego their national approaches to copyright. For another, any hopes of a coherent and systematised code would probably drown in waves of stakeholder lobbying.[169]

In any case, regrettably, such initiatives do not seem to be among the European Commission's priorities.[170] If any indications can be extracted from the copyright legislative cycle that came to an end with the adoption of the controversial DSM Directive, they point towards a preference for piecemeal harmonisation aimed at addressing specific problems that have not yet been regulated at the EU level.[171]

Evidently, the formation of an EU copyright law is a gradual process, and there is still much more to be done. At present and for the purposes of this book, references to 'EU copyright law' must be understood as references to the existing *acquis*, formed by the directives and regulations that are in force and by the harmonising case law of the CJEU.[172] Whatever direction the Europeanisation of copyright law takes, one thing seems clear now, just as a quarter-century ago: 'within Europe ... the determination of future legal policy is likely to be dominated by developments at the Community level'.[173] This, I believe, is a sound justification for exploring this project's research questions from the perspective of EU copyright law.

---

to those rights.' The Commission went even further and stated that it would 'examine the feasibility of creating an optional "unitary" copyright title on the basis of Article 118 TFEU and its potential impact for the single market, right holders and consumers' (p. 11). The DG Information Society and the DG Market had already expressed similar views in the 2009 Reflection Document, p. 18.

169. Hilty (2012), p. 371, shows scepticism as to the success of a European codification endeavour, arguing that it 'would most probably end up as a patchwork'. *See also* EPRS (2015), p. 23, doubting that the creation of a single EU title would be feasible, on grounds that 'it would most likely encounter the resistance of Member States and stakeholders in addition to being subject to complex and protracted negotiations'.
170. Nevertheless, in its Communication on a Modern European Copyright Framework, the Commission, after highlighting the complexities a codification effort would entail, stated that '[t]hese complexities cannot be a reason to relinquish this vision as *a long-term target*' (p. 12).
171. *See*, with a critical look, ECS (2017), p. 3: 'Despite its ambitious overarching goal and key objectives, as stated (inter alia) in the preamble of the proposed DSM Directive, the Commission's reform package does not seem to reflect an overall vision of the future of EU copyright law, and fails to deliver on its promise of wholesale copyright reform. The copyright package proposes only piecemeal solutions, leaving the existing – already fragmented and partly outdated – copyright acquis intact.'
172. *See* Farrand (2014), p. 31.
173. Cornish (1995), p. 812. *See also* Pereira (2005), p. 507; Vicente (2011a), p. 274; Silva (2014), pp. 1333-1334; and Leistner (2015a), p. 636. Acknowledging that Brussels will play a 'fatal role' in relation to copyright exceptions in particular, *see* Hoeren (2007), p. 269.

Chapter 1

The Rights of Reproduction and Communication to the Public in International and EU Law

1 INTRODUCTION

The issue of whether a certain act is covered by a copyright exception is naturally dependent on the question of whether that act falls within the scope of a right in the first place.

The rights granted by copyright are typically divided into two categories: economic rights and moral rights. Whereas economic rights are concerned with the control over the exploitation of the work, moral rights, grounded on the idea that the work is an extension of its author's personality, serve to protect the intimate relationship that exists between the author and her work.[174] As mentioned above, the EU legislator opted not to harmonise moral rights and, as such, they fall outside the scope of this study.

Generally, the economic rights granted by copyright law are *exclusive* rights. The holder has the right to exclude – that is, to prohibit – third parties

---

174. The origins of moral rights lie in nineteenth-century French case law, having been later exported to most countries in Continental Europe and recognised by the Berne Convention (Article 6*bis*) in 1928. Two main rights are commonly conferred upon authors: the right of attribution, i.e. the author's right of having the authorship of her works attributed to herself, and the right of integrity, i.e. the right to prevent the distortion, mutilation or any other modification of the work that affects the author's honour or reputation. Modern digital technologies pose difficult practical problems to moral rights, for they enable users to easily intervene in copyright-protected works. These interventions can degenerate into manipulations of works that affect the author's rights of attribution (by suppressing the details about the author's identity) and integrity (by making unauthorised modifications that may be prejudicial to the author's honour or reputation). For a book-length account on the challenges that moral rights doctrine has faced in the digital era, *see* Rajan (2011). For an older and shorter piece, *see* Torremans (2000).

from using the works in any of the restricted forms.[175] Albeit of a temporary nature, an economic right over the work can be qualified, similar to a property right,[176] as a right to exclude all others (*ius excludendi omnes alios* or *ius prohibendi erga omnes*) from the use and exploitation thereof.[177] Put in a positive perspective, as in the Berne Convention, the rightholder has the

---

175. In some cases, however, the right granted is one of remuneration: the rightholder is not entitled to authorise or prohibit the use of the work, but holds a claim to remuneration for that use. EU copyright law provides for such rights in different situations, such as the broadcasting of phonograms (Article 8(2) Rental and Lending Directive). In other cases, the right at stake is an exclusive one (e.g., reproduction), but the application of an exception *qua* non-voluntary licence (e.g., private copying) renders it a right to compensation. For an overview of these rights in the *acquis*, *see* Quintais (2017a), pp. 128-129. It is also worth mentioning that the right of cable retransmission, though it is an exclusive right, is subject to mandatory collective management, meaning that it may not be exercised on an individual basis, but only through a CMO (Article 9(1) of the Satellite and Cable Directive). This condition to the exercise of the right renders it, in practical terms, a remuneration right. Under Article 4 Online TV and Radio Directive, this system shall be extended to other equivalent digital retransmissions (with the caveat of Article 5).

    Dusollier (2007), p. 423, claims that, in these cases, the exclusive right is 'amputated', because the use is not entirely free, although the rightholder cannot prohibit it. The expression raises some doubts. What exclusive rights do is to reserve the exploitation of their object to the rightholder. The defining element of the exclusive right is the prerogative that the rightholder has to *exclude* others from the use covered by that right. If third parties want to use the work, they must first ask for the rightholder's permission, which may be granted (typically against some form of remuneration) or refused. As Waldron (2006), p. 115, explains, '[i]t is … this element of exclusion that transforms the right to use into an essentially *private* right'. Hence, if such prerogative is subtracted from the rightholder's sphere, the exclusive right is no more. Where a right to remuneration is nonetheless preserved within the rightholder's sphere, the exclusive right is *replaced* by such a right, and not merely amputated.

176. In the EU, Article 17 Charter lays down the right to property and its para. 2 (laconically) provides that 'Intellectual property shall be protected'. There is some historical pedigree to this option. As an example, in the report to the 1791 French Copyright Law, Le Chapelier famously qualified copyright as 'The most sacred, the most personal of all properties'. The very expression 'intellectual property' (or 'literary and artistic property') denotes the widespread acceptance of the qualification of these rights as forms of property. This qualification is not without controversy and has generated lengthy scholarly debates. Several alternative theories about the legal nature of copyright have emerged throughout history, most notably in Germany, where Otto von Gierke's theory of personality rights and Josef Kohler's *Doppelrecht* theory enjoyed significant popularity – *see* Gierke (1889) and Kohler (1907). Other scholars, like Rognstad (2018), regard this debate as 'hardly meaningful' (p. 1) and prefer to explore the implications that flow from the use of the term 'property' in relation to IP.

177. The exclusive nature of these rights is expressly indicated in several statutes throughout the world. *See*, in particular, Article L111-1 French IP Code; Section 15 German Copyright Act; and Section 106 US Copyright Act. At the EU level, the CJEU has repeatedly stressed that the rights of reproduction are preventive in nature, in the sense that any use covered by those rights requires the prior consent of the rightholder – *see* CJEU, *Renckhoff*, para. 29 (and case law cited therein).

right to *authorise* third parties to use the work.[178] That is to say that the lawfulness of any restricted use by a third party is, in principle, dependent upon the prior consent of the rightholder.

The harmonisation of economic rights was a priority for the EU legislator. InfoSoc harmonised the rights of reproduction (Article 2), communication to the public (Article 3), and distribution (Article 4) for works of authorship and related subject matter.[179] Before InfoSoc, these rights had already been partially harmonised, in relation to specific subject matter, like computer programs[180] and databases,[181] and for specific rightholders.[182] Other rights, such as adaptation[183] and rental and lending,[184] had also been

---

178. The Berne Convention employs the formula 'the exclusive right of authorising' in several provisions – *see* Articles 8, 9, 11, 11*bis*, 11*ter*, and 12.
179. It is undisputed that the list of rights harmonised by InfoSoc is not exhaustive. Member States may therefore legislate on other rights, such as adaptation, provided they do so in respect of international copyright law. *See* Ohly (2009), p. 236.
180. *See* Articles 4(a) (granting the right to reproduce a computer program, as well as to display and transmit it, insofar as these acts necessitate reproduction) and 4(c) (granting the right to distribute the computer program to the public) Software Directive. The InfoSoc Directive leaves these provisions intact, pursuant to Article 1(2)(a).
181. *See* Articles 5(a) (reproduction), 5(c) (distribution), and 5(d) (communication to the public) Database Directive. As in the case of the Software Directive, these provisions are not affected by the InfoSoc Directive.
182. Article 8(1) and (3) Rental and Lending Directive grants the right of communication to the public (but not the right of making available) to performers and broadcasting organisations, and Article 9(1) grants the distribution right to performers, phonogram and film producers, and broadcasters, though with a different terminology ('the exclusive right *to make available* these objects, including copies thereof, to the public by sale or otherwise' (emphasis added)). Article 1(2) InfoSoc Directive, read together with Article 11 of the same Directive, makes clear that Articles 8 and 9 Rental and Lending Directive are left intact. Article 7 Rental and Lending Directive also granted the right of reproduction to these categories of rightholders, but was expressly replaced by Article 2 InfoSoc Directive (*see* Article 11(1)(a) InfoSoc Directive). The Satellite and Cable Directive harmonises the right of communication to the public by satellite in Article 2, which is left intact by the InfoSoc Directive, but is without prejudice to the Rental and Lending Directive (*see* Article 4 Satellite and Cable Directive).
183. As noted earlier, Article 4(b) Software Directive grants the right to do or to authorise the translation, adaptation, arrangement and any other alteration of a computer program. Aside from this provision, the EU legislature has refrained from harmonising the adaptation right. This, according to Eechoud et al. (2009), p. 84, may be due to the 'strong moral rights undertone' in the issue of adaptation. Articles 12 and 14 Berne Convention nonetheless refer to the right of adaptation.
184. It is debatable whether rental and lending should be conceptualised as autonomous rights or whether they are included in a broader distribution right. German copyright law leans towards the latter option (*see* Section 17 German Copyright Act). Recital 28 InfoSoc Directive and Article 4(1)(c) Software Directive, by granting the right to do or to authorise 'any form of distribution to the public, *including the rental*, of the original computer program or of copies thereof' (emphasis added), also suggest that rental and lending are species of the distribution right. In contrast, Article 4(1) InfoSoc Directive and Articles 1(1), 2(1) and 9(1) Rental and Lending Directive do not require Member States to grant the rental and lending rights as part of a broad distribution right. Read in

laid down in earlier directives. But it was the InfoSoc Directive that sought to harmonise those three core rights across the board.

InfoSoc is widely regarded as having been successful in that effort,[185] since all Member States afford those rights to the beneficiaries mentioned in the Directive.[186] Despite this high level of harmonisation, different techniques are still used in different Member States to regulate these rights. For instance, whereas some Member States formulate the economic rights in very abstract terms, others prefer more fine-grained approaches.[187] To an extent, the descriptions of the harmonised economic rights in the EU directives reflect a compromise between the formulations adopted in the different Member States, while simultaneously taking into account the formulations adopted in international instruments.[188]

This chapter starts by excluding the right of distribution and the rule of exhaustion from the scope of this book and by justifying the focus on reproduction and communication to the public (section 2). It then depicts the origins, meaning, and coverage of the rights of reproduction (section 3) and communication to the public (section 4), with a particular emphasis on the

---

light of Article 4(2), Article 4(1) InfoSoc Directive requires some form of ownership transfer – which does not occur in rental and lending – for distribution to come into play. The Explanatory Memorandum of the Commission's Proposal for the Rental and Lending Directive hinted that these rights were to be treated separately, by explicitly saying that rental and lending were distinct from 'sale or gift, for example, being forms of making available for use for an unlimited period of time' (p. 33). The CJEU confirmed this separate treatment in e.g. *Metronome Musik* (para. 18), *Commission v. Portugal* (para. 34), and *VOB* (para. 59), where it held that other forms of exploitation, such as rental and public lending, are different in nature from a sale or any other lawful form of distribution. Moreover, in *Peek & Cloppenburg*, para. 36, the Court stated that 'the concept of distribution to the public, otherwise than through sale, of the original of a work or a copy thereof, for the purpose of Article 4(1) of Directive 2001/29, covers acts which entail, *and only acts which entail*, a transfer of the ownership of that object' (emphasis added). If Article 4 InfoSoc Directive only applies in cases in which ownership is transferred – typically, by sale or donation –, then rental and lending, where such transfer does not take place, are necessarily excluded.

185. *See, e.g.*, Guibault et al. (2007), p. 22 ('the implementation of articles 2 to 4 of the Information Society Directive has led to a convincing degree of harmonisation'); Leistner (2009), p. 851 ('in the field of commercial rights, the Information Society Directive has achieved a substantial degree of harmonization'); and Ohly (2009), p. 232 ('a look at the provisions of Community legislation which grant economic rights, at their interpretation by the ECJ and at their implementation in national jurisdictions will reveal a significant degree of common ground').
186. *See, e.g.*, Guibault et al. (2007), p. 22.
187. *Contrast, e.g.*, Article 1er(1) Belgian Copyright Law (in force at the time the InfoSoc Directive was adopted, but meanwhile codified in Title 5 Belgian Economic Law Code, which came into force on 1 January 2015) with Section 17 UK CDPA.
188. *See* Eechoud et al. (2009), pp. 67-68. The Berne Convention lays down minimum standards for the economic rights of translation (Article 8), reproduction (Article 9), public performance (Article 11), broadcasting (Article 11*bis*), public recitation (Article 11*ter*), and adaptation (Article 12). The WCT provides for the rights of distribution (Article 6), rental (Article 7), and communication to the public (Article 8).

InfoSoc Directive. As mentioned above, the EU is a contracting party to the TRIPS Agreement and the WIPO Treaties, which incorporated by reference the substantive provisions of the Berne Convention, and the InfoSoc Directive implemented into EU copyright law a number of the international obligations flowing from the WIPO Treaties. In light of this connection, this chapter's analysis of the EU *acquis* on reproduction and communication to the public is preceded by an account of the relevant international background.

In elucidating the contours of these rights within the *acquis*, the CJEU has embraced a general canon of interpretation, according to which these rights are to be construed broadly. The meaning and implications of this rule of interpretation is discussed towards the end of this chapter (section 5).

2 THE RIGHT OF DISTRIBUTION (EXCLUSION)

The debate on the suitability of the InfoSoc framework of exceptions focuses on the exceptions to the rights of reproduction and communication to the public. The right of distribution, which covers the distribution of originals or copies of the work by sale or otherwise, is generally excluded – and so will it be in this book. It is warranted at this point to pause and take a brief look at the InfoSoc right of distribution in order to explain this option.

The right of distribution has traditionally been understood as being limited to the transfer of ownership over *tangible* copies of works, thus failing to extend to the digital environment.[189] Recital 28 InfoSoc Directive, by referring to 'the exclusive right to control distribution of the work incorporated in a tangible article', suggests that the *corpus mechanicum* of the work circumscribes the applicability of the distribution right.[190]

The CJEU ruling in *UsedSoft* slightly complicated matters, however. As is known, the right of distribution exhausts on its first sale by the rightholder or with his consent, meaning that the rightholder is not entitled to control subsequent sales of the copies of his work. This rule of exhaustion is provided both in the Software and InfoSoc Directives.[191] In *UsedSoft*, the Court clarified that the rule of exhaustion in the Software Directive extends to copies of software *downloaded from the Internet* with the rightholder's

189. Ohly (2009), p. 219, for instance, defines the right of distribution as 'the right to control the marketing and circulation of tangible embodiments of the work'.
190. This much was also implied by the CJEU in *Peek & Cloppenburg*, when it stated that the distribution right only applies when a transfer of ownership *of an object* occurs – *see* CJEU, *Peek & Cloppenburg*, para. 36. This is in consonance with the Agreed Statements concerning Articles 6 and 7 WCT, according to which 'the expressions "copies" and "original and copies" … refer exclusively to fixed copies that can be put into circulation as tangible objects'.
191. *See* Article 4(2) Software Directive and Article 4(2) InfoSoc Directive. On copyright exhaustion in detail, *see* Mezei (2018).

consent.[192] The Court considered that, for the purpose of applying the distribution right and the exhaustion doctrine, the online distribution is functionally equivalent to the distribution of physical copies, provided an actual transfer of ownership occurs.[193] To this effect, the CJEU interpreted the concept of 'sale' broadly, extending it to cases where the rightholder granted a licence to use a copy of a computer program for an unlimited period of time.[194] The judgment thus opened the door to the application of the right of distribution within the digital environment.

Nonetheless, it remained doubtful whether the reasoning in *UsedSoft* and the rule of digital exhaustion extended to subject matter, other than software, falling under the scope of the InfoSoc Directive as *lex generalis.*[195] For one thing, the EU legislator expressly stated in the preamble to the InfoSoc Directive that 'exhaustion does not arise in the case of services and on-line services in particular'.[196] For another, the indications the CJEU gave after *UsedSoft* (mostly through *obiter dicta*) suggested that the answer would be in the negative. In *Art & Allposters*, for instance, the Court repeatedly stressed the usage of the expressions 'tangible article' in Recital 28 and 'that object' in Article 4(2) InfoSoc Directive, concluding that 'exhaustion of the distribution right applies to *the tangible object* into which a protected work or its copy is incorporated if it has been placed onto the market with the copyright holder's consent'.[197] This statement implicitly foreclosed the application of digital exhaustion beyond the case of software copies and as suggesting that, in general, Article 4 InfoSoc Directive should not be taken to encompass the distribution of intangible copies of books, music, films, and other protected subject matter available for online transfer.[198]

---

192. *See* CJEU, *UsedSoft*, para. 88.
193. *See* CJEU, *UsedSoft*, para. 61. *See also* CJEU, *Ranks & Vasiļevičs*, paras 36-43, where the Court confirmed *UsedSoft*'s case law, but held that the lawful acquirer of a copy of a computer program cannot resell back-up copies of such programs without the rightholder's permission.
194. *See* CJEU, *UsedSoft*, para. 49.
195. The CJEU confirmed that the Software Directive constitutes a *lex specialis* in relation to InfoSoc in *UsedSoft*, para. 56, and *Nintendo I*, para. 23. On the relationship between these two Directives, *see* Rendas (2015).
196. Recital 29 InfoSoc Directive.
197. *See* CJEU, *Art & Allposters*, para. 40 (emphasis added).
198. Two other decisions – after *UsedSoft*, but before *Tom Kabinet* – lent further support to the idea that the distribution right does not extend to the digital realm. In *VOB*, the Court found that the public lending right harmonised in the Rental and Lending Directive applied to the lending of electronic copies of books by libraries, but made a point of stating that this right is distinct from the right of distribution and that the provisions applicable to the latter in no way affect the regulation of the former – *see* CJEU, *VOB*, para. 56. Despite the view held by AG Szpunar that the judgment in *Art & Allposters* does not call into question the conclusions reached in *UsedSoft* (AG Opinion, *VOB*, para. 54), the CJEU hinted yet again that the scope of Article 4 InfoSoc Directive is restricted by tangibility and that the application of its exhaustion rule is dependent on the sale of the physical medium of a work – *see* CJEU, *VOB*, para. 59. In addition, in *Ranks &*

Finally, in *Tom Kabinet* the Court confirmed that the right of distribution under Article 4 InfoSoc Directive covers only the distribution of works incorporated in tangible articles and that, accordingly, there is no digital exhaustion of this right. The provision of subject matter like e-books falls instead within the right of communication to the public – more specifically within the 'making available' prong –, which tolerates no exhaustion under Article 3(3).[199] Thus, the door opened in *UsedSoft* for copies of computer programs downloaded from the Internet was closed for other subject matter in digital format protected under the InfoSoc Directive, such as e-books and audiobooks.[200]

Whereas the distribution right is generally limited to the transfer of ownership over physical copies of works, the boundaries of reproduction and communication to the public were unambiguously stretched by the WIPO Treaties and the InfoSoc Directive to cover digital uses of intangible copies. Given that one of the book's main concerns is with the adaptability of copyright to technological changes, particularly changes in the digital environment, it will focus on those two rights (more rigorously: on their exceptions), as the rights that most pervasively apply in that environment. Indeed, digital uses, whether online or offline, usually involve one or multiple acts that implicate the rights of reproduction and communication to the public.[201]

3 THE RIGHT OF REPRODUCTION

The inception of copyright is intimately related to the act of making copies. The very name of the field of law – *copy*right – hints at it: the right to make copies which embody the work is the most fundamental of all exclusive

---

Vasilevics, the Court concluded that, *UsedSoft* notwithstanding, the exhaustion rule did not apply in cases of resale of back-up copies of computer programs – *see* CJEU, *Ranks & Vasiļevičs*, paras 34-43.

199. *See* CJEU, *Tom Kabinet*, paras 33 and 72.

200. *See*, in particular, CJEU, *Tom Kabinet*, para. 54: 'an e-book is not a computer program, and it is not appropriate therefore to apply the specific provisions of [the Software Directive]'. Arguing in favour of the introduction of a general rule of digital exhaustion in EU copyright law prior to the *Tom Kabinet* judgment, *see* Sganga (2018b).

201. Digital technologies allow text, sound and images that make up copyright-protected works to be recorded in numeric code, typically in binary combinations of 0s and 1s. This allows vast amounts of works to be easily copied and transmitted with no loss in quality. *See* Dreier (1993), p. 190 (arguing, in the early 1990s, that the economic rights in relation to which the impact of digital technologies would be mostly felt were the right of reproduction and the right of communication to the public); Guibault et al. (2007), p. 22, (focusing their assessment of the impact of exclusive rights on online business models 'on the two rights … that bear the most significance for the digital networked environment: the right of reproduction and the right of making available to the public'); and, though in relation to reproduction only, Lehmann (2003), fn. 18 ('it is apparent that the right of reproduction … is also the core of copyright in cyberspace').

rights, being granted by most, if not all, national copyright systems.[202] In the 1995 Green Paper, the Commission echoed this idea by describing the reproduction right as 'the core of copyright and related rights'.[203]

The invention by Gutenberg of the movable-type printing press in the fifteenth century made it significantly easier to engage in copy-making. Gutenberg's mechanical device, though performing the same function as the human copyists before it, enabled the reproduction of literary works in a much faster way than by hand.[204] This was an essential factor for the emergence of the predecessors of modern copyright, the printing privileges.[205]

The 1710 Statute of Anne – the first copyright statute in history – granted authors of books 'the sole liberty of printing and reprinting' them.[206] This was the first piece of legislation to confer directly upon authors an exclusive right to make copies of their works, thus marking the beginning of the worldwide transition from the privilege system to the modern idea of

202. *See* Spoor (1996), p. 67, and Walter & Lewinski (2010), p. 964.
203. 1995 Green Paper, p. 49. *See also*, from a US perspective, Cohen et al. (2015), p. 248.
204. This is not to downplay the influence that other factors had in the emergence of the first forms of regulation of the reproduction of literary works. Evidently, '[p]rinting by itself was not the mother of author's copyright' – Birrell (1899), p. 49. The desire of the established political and religious powers to contain the dissemination of dissenting ideas and the related protection of book trade monopolies were pivotal factors, according to most historical accounts of copyright. *See* Birrell (1899), p. 49, and Patterson (1968), p. 6 (focusing on the evolution of English and Anglo-American copyright, respectively).
205. Under the system of printing privileges, by and large, sovereign and local powers discretionarily granted the permission to print literary works or classes thereof and put them into circulation. In contrast, under modern copyright, as a matter of law authors enjoy rights over their original works as a consequence of having created them. The printing privileges were normally granted to publishers and only rarely to authors themselves. In England, initially, the system of personal printing privileges (or printing patents, as they were also known) granted by the sovereign operated in parallel with the so-called stationers' copyright. With its incorporation by the royal charter issued by Queen Mary I in 1557, the Stationers' Company secured a monopoly in the publication of books, meaning that only the printers, bookbinders and booksellers that were members of the company could be eligible to hold copyright. Queen Mary's fundamental purpose in issuing the charter was to establish an organisation that, in exercising the monopoly, would effectively perform censorial control for the Crown. In case of conflict, however, the privilege granted by the sovereign would prevail. For a detailed description of this dual system, claiming that some form of stationers' copyright was already in place before 1557, *see* Patterson (1968), pp. 28-113.
206. Section II Statute of Anne. There are noticeable inconsistencies in the terminology used in the Statute of Anne to refer to the prerogatives being granted. The authors of books that had already been printed were granted 'the sole right and liberty of printing such … books', whereas the authors of books yet to be printed were granted 'the sole liberty of printing and reprinting' them. Deazley (2004), p. 49, while noting these specific inconsistencies, claims that 'the most problematic aspect of the statute' is a more general one: 'the lack of any attempt to define those concepts central to the Act'.

copyright as a right of the author. Since then, legislatures in other countries have granted similar rights to authors of literary and artistic works.[207]

3.1 The Right of Reproduction in International Law

The Berne Convention, the first multilateral treaty on copyright, provides an exclusive right of reproduction with a broad formulation.[208] Article 9(1) states that '[a]uthors of literary and artistic works protected by this Convention shall have the exclusive right of authorizing the reproduction of these works, in any manner or form'. WIPO's Guide to the Berne Convention confirms the definition's broad and technology-neutral character:

> [t]he words 'in any manner or form' are wide enough to cover all methods of reproduction: design, engraving, lithography, offset and all other printing processes, typewriting, photocopying, xerox, mechanical or magnetic recording

207. For instance, the 1793 French Copyright Law, which granted authors the right to sell, cause to be sold, and distribute their works (Article 1), of which the reproduction in print was a necessary previous step in the case of literary works. Article 3 made this necessary connection between reproduction and distribution clear, by providing that all copies of editions printed or engraved without the formal authorisation in writing of the authors could be seized. Although the prerogative comprised two distinct actions – making copies and distributing them –, it was conceptualised as one synthetic right of edition (*droit d'édition*). Only with the 1957 French Copyright Law was the right of reproduction expressly established in France. Nowadays, the French right of reproduction is the object of arguably the broadest conceivable understanding, under the so-called theory of the right of destination (*droit de destination*). According to this theory, the right of reproduction covers not only the act of making copies, but also the control of all post-sale uses of each copy of the work. This right of destination thus encompasses the right of distribution, which was not expressly transposed into French law (though, oddly, the rule of exhaustion was). Other countries clearly separate the two forms of exploitation. On the theory of the right of destination, *see* Desurmont (1987); Françon (1987); and Pollaud-Dulian (1989). Criticising the theory, *see, e.g.*, Dusollier (2006), and Lucas et al. (2017), pp. 271 et seq.
208. The Berne Convention was signed in 1886. Strangely, it then failed to include a general right of reproduction. Only in 1967, with the Stockholm Revision, was such a right included in the Convention text. Scholars generally attribute this delay to the lack of agreement between Berne signatory countries on the exact scope of the right – *see* Spoor (1980), p. 49; Ricketson & Ginsburg (2006), p. 624; Ohly (2009), p. 214; and Goldstein & Hugenholtz (2012), p. 301. Sterling (2008), p. 783, and Lewinski (2008), p. 139, offer an alternative explanation, arguing that the fact that the national legislation of most Berne countries accorded some form of protection against unauthorised acts of (re)printing or, more inclusively, against the making of copies, was regarded as sufficient. The former explanation, however, is in line with WIPO's statement in WIPO (1978), p. 54: '[t]hough the right was recognised, in principle, by all member countries, the problem was to find a formula wide enough to cover all reasonable exceptions but not so wide as to make the right illusory'. Be that as it may, the consequences of this absence were practically immaterial, since all countries already granted some form of reproduction right. In 1967, after a failed attempt in the 1948 Brussels Revision, Berne signatories decided to put an end to the situation, adding a general reproduction right to the Convention text – *see* BIRPI (1966), p. 41.

(disks, cassettes, magnetic tape, films, microfilms, etc.), and all other processes known or yet to be discovered. It is simply a matter of fixing the work in some material form.[209]

While the right is sufficiently broad to encompass the storage of protected works in digital form,[210] the question of whether the chosen formula covered reproductions of a merely temporary nature was not as uncontroversial. Temporary reproductions already existed in the analogue era.[211] But the issue only became truly acute when digital technologies – whose operation heavily relies on this type of copies – emerged. Visualising a work via a computer depends on the making of such temporary copies at least in the computer's RAM and on the screen. The arrival of the Internet led to a sharp increase in the frequency of these copies. Indeed, ordinary online transmissions unavoidably involve making a number of fleeting copies of the transferred files.[212]

As admitted by most scholars, the answer to the question of whether the reproduction right encompassed copies of a temporary nature was not clear, even against Article 9's wide scope.[213] It is true that the phrase 'in any manner or form' clarifies that all *methods* of reproduction are to be considered as falling within the scope of the right. But the doubt around this type of copies does not relate to the method, process, technique, or 'manner'

---

209. WIPO (1978), p. 54.

210. As maintained by Ulmer (1972), p. 53, '[i]n storing a work in a computer, a material fixation constituting a reproduction already takes place when, as is the current practice, the work is encoded on the input medium such as punched cards, punched tape, magnetic tape and magnetic cards. But the storage itself is also to be regarded as a reproduction'. Efroni (2011), p. 207, claims that there was disagreement about this question, citing, in support of this claim, Ulmer's report and Nimmer (1968). But what seemed to exist was not so much disagreement, as a difference in the sources on which the two authors relied for their analysis. Ulmer himself concedes that, under US law (on which Nimmer focuses), the answer to the question of whether stored works amounted to reproductions was unclear. It ought to be added that, at the time of Ulmer's writing, the US were not yet a party to the Berne Convention, having only adhered in 1989.

211. *See* Ulmer (1972), p. 57 ('there is some relationship with the so-called "ephemeral recording" which takes place during the preparation of a broadcast and which is allowed in Contracting States under certain conditions by Article 11bis(3) of the Berne Convention').

212. Illustratively, Lemley (1996-1997), p. 555, citing software developer Glenn Tenney, estimates that downloading a picture from the Internet involves a minimum of seven copies: 'the modem at each end will buffer each byte, as will the router, the receiving computer, the Web browser, the video decompression chip, and the video display board. Those seven copies will be made on each such transaction.' *See also* Spoor (1996), p. 78, stating that '[o]n the net transmission may be the goal, but copies are the tool'.

213. *See, e.g.*, Ulmer (1972), p. 53; Samuelson (1997), p. 392; and Ricketson & Ginsburg (2006), p. 645. Differently, co-authors Reinbothe & Lewinski (2002), pp. 42-44, seem to refuse the existence of any margin for doubt as to the coverage of temporary reproductions within Article 9 Berne Convention. Writing on her own, however, Lewinski (2008), p. 140, recognises that, regarding 'transient digital reproductions that may occur on cache servers, ... the Berne Convention is not completely clear'.

through which the copy is effected (e.g., digitisation), nor to the 'form' that copies assume (e.g., two- or three-dimensional), but to their *duration.* Regarding that aspect, Article 9(1) Berne Convention is silent. Therefore, on a textual basis, persuasive arguments could be made in favour of both answers.[214]

Adopted in 1994, the TRIPS Agreement likewise failed to provide definitive guidance on the question of temporary copies.[215] The first attempt to shed light on this issue was made in the Basic Proposal leading to the adoption of the WCT.[216] Back then, a proposal for the inclusion of temporary copies within the scope of the reproduction right was put forward. Article 7(1) WCT Proposal was worded as follows: 'The exclusive right accorded to authors of literary and artistic works in Article 9(1) of the Berne Convention of authorizing the reproduction of their works shall include direct and indirect reproduction of their works, *whether permanent or temporary*, in any manner or form.'[217] However, the proposal was met with such controversy that it was eventually dropped.[218]

In the end, due to the lack of agreement among Contracting Parties, the definition of the right of reproduction was left out from the WCT. As a replacement of sorts, an Agreed Statement on the scope of the right was inserted. The statement evaded the question of temporary copies, by providing that '[t]he reproduction right, as set out in Article 9 of the Berne Convention, and the exceptions permitted thereunder, fully apply in the digital environment, in particular to the use of works in digital form. It is understood that the storage of a protected work in digital form in an electronic medium constitutes a reproduction within the meaning of Article 9 of the Berne Convention.'[219] In addition, the treaty provides a mandate to comply with the substantive provisions of the Berne Convention in Article 1(4).

---

214. Efroni (2011), pp. 217-224, acknowledges that the text of Article 9 Berne Convention supports both a 'minimalist' and a 'maximalist' reading, though arguing that the former is more appropriate.
215. In what regards the making of copies, Article 14 TRIPS grants (i) performers the right of fixation of their unfixed performances and reproduction of such fixation; (ii) producers of phonograms the right to authorise or prohibit the direct or indirect reproduction of their phonograms; and (iii) broadcasting organisations the right of fixation and reproduction of fixations.
216. For a comprehensive description of the period between Ulmer's study and the adoption of the WCT, *see* Ficsor (2002a), pp. 96-102.
217. Emphasis added. *See* WCT Proposal, p. 29.
218. The issue of temporary reproductions is regarded as the most controversial one in the negotiations that led to the adoption of WCT. At the root of the controversy seemed to be the ISPs' concern about their potential exposure to infringement claims. For detailed accounts of this controversy, *see* Ficsor (1996-1997), p. 203-207, and Ricketson & Ginsburg (2006), pp. 681-687.
219. *See* WCT Agreed Statements, p. 2.

The issue, as shall be seen shortly, was explicitly addressed in the InfoSoc Directive.

3.2 THE RIGHT OF REPRODUCTION IN THE EU *ACQUIS*

The right of reproduction was first harmonised at the EU level in the Software,[220] Database,[221] and Rental and Lending[222] Directives. Later, Article 2 InfoSoc Directive horizontally harmonised the right for all authors of works,[223] performers, phonogram producers, film producers, and broadcasting organisations,[224] and, more recently, Article 15 DSM Directive extended the InfoSoc right to EU-based press publishers in relation to the online use of press publications by information society service providers, such as news aggregators and media monitoring services.[225]

The right of reproduction in Article 2 InfoSoc Directive has a very broad coverage, being defined as 'the exclusive right to authorise or prohibit direct or indirect, temporary or permanent reproduction by any means and in any form, in whole or in part'. Because Article 2 makes no reference to national law for the purpose of determining its meaning and scope, the CJEU has deemed 'reproduction' to be an autonomous concept of EU law that, as such, must be interpreted in a uniform manner throughout the Union.[226] The Court has further held that Article 2 constitutes a measure of full harmonisation, as it defines the reproduction right in unequivocal terms and is not

220. *See* Article 4(a) Software Directive.
221. *See* Articles 5(a) and 7(2)(a) Database Directive
222. *See* Article 7 in the original 1992 version of the Rental and Lending Directive. The provision was repealed by the InfoSoc Directive, pursuant to Article 11 thereof.
223. Authors of computer programs and databases are covered by the Software and Database Directives, which are not affected by the InfoSoc Directive (Article 1(2)(a) and (e) InfoSoc Directive).
224. Note that under Article 7 Rental and Lending Directive, performers and broadcasting organisations are granted a right of first fixation. It is the right to prohibit or authorise reproductions of those fixations that is covered by Article 2 InfoSoc Directive. Criticising this fragmented solution, *see* Ohly (2009), pp. 214-215.
225. Article 15(3) DSM Directive makes clear that the InfoSoc exceptions apply *mutatis mutandis* to this new right of press publishers. *See also* Recital 57 DSM Directive. Moreover, the right has its own specific limitations: it does not apply to private or non-commercial uses of press publications by individual users, acts of hyperlinking, or the use of individual words or very short extracts of press publications (Article 15(1)). This means that such acts continue to be governed by the *acquis* that preceded the DSM Directive.
226. *See* CJEU, *Infopaq I*, paras 27-29, and CJEU, *Premier League*, para. 154. On autonomous concepts of EU law in the copyright *acquis* and their implications, *see infra* Chapter 4, section 5.1.2.

qualified by any condition nor subject, in its implementation or effects, to any measure being taken in any particular form.[227]

Article 2 InfoSoc Directive dispelled the existing uncertainty around the issue of temporary copies explained above, at least at the level of EU law. In 1991, the Software Directive had already included the temporary reproduction of computer programs in the list of restricted acts.[228] In the 1995 Green Paper and in the 1996 Follow-Up, the Commission recommended the adoption of a general reproduction right, moulded after the one provided in the Software Directive[229] – a suggestion adopted in the InfoSoc Directive. The EU legislator thus provided broader protection than what was required under the international framework. Acts of permanent reproduction, such as photocopying a book, as well as temporary copies that occur below the end-user's awareness, like RAM copies, fall within the coverage of the InfoSoc right of reproduction.[230]

Nonetheless, scholars and policymakers widely agreed that such acts of temporary reproduction, essential as they are for the operation of digital technologies, should not give rise to copyright liability. Accordingly, an exemption of liability for these acts of usage was provided in Article 5(1).[231]

Apart from clarifying that both permanent and temporary reproductions come within the coverage of the exclusive right, the definition in Article 2 also mentions: (i) 'direct or indirect' copies; (ii) 'by any means and in any form'; and (iii) 'in whole or in part'.

The expression 'direct or indirect' is intended to cover copies of protected subject matter regardless of whether they are made via an intermediate act (e.g., the recording of a broadcast made out of a phonogram) or without such an act (e.g., burning a CD from a CD).[232] Given the indistinct inclusion of both direct and indirect copies, it is 'irrelevant whether a wooden

227. *See* CJEU, *Funke Medien*, paras 36-38 (in relation to the reproduction right of authors), and CJEU, *Pelham*, paras 84-85 (in relation to the reproduction right of phonogram producers).
228. Article 4(a) Software Directive. A similarly comprehensive version of the right was granted in Articles 5(a) and 7(2)(a) Database Directive.
229. According to the Commission, 'the digitization of works or other protected matter should generally fall under the reproduction right, as should such things as loading on to the central memory of a computer' – 1995 Green Paper, p. 52. *See also* 1996 Follow-Up, pp. 9-11.
230. *See* Explanatory Memorandum to InfoSoc Proposal, pp. 24-25. *See also* Ohly (2009), pp. 216-217.
231. A detailed analysis of this exception can be found in Chapter 4, section 3.2.1.
232. *See* Explanatory Memorandum to InfoSoc Proposal, p. 24, and Walter & Lewinski (2010), p. 1475. The inclusion of the 'direct or indirect' element was an innovation in relation to the Berne Convention, the Software Directive, and the Database Directive. The element was mentioned in Article 7 Rental and Lending Directive and, in deleting this provision, the InfoSoc Directive took it over, extending it to authors and owners of related rights alike. Walter & Lewinski (2010), p. 964, claim that the 'direct or indirect' clarification applies to software and databases, irrespective of the fact that these earlier directives failed to expressly mention it.

sculpture is photographed, copied by hand from the photograph into a marble, then photographed again and loaded on a site on the Internet. All these acts are considered to be reproductions.'[233]

The second expression ('by any means and in any form') entails that all formats, methods, processes, and techniques of reproduction – be they analogue or digital, online or offline – fall within the scope of the reproduction right. The right thus applies to 'all methods of reproduction, whether known – drawing, lithography, offset and other printing processes, photocopying, recording etc. – or unknown'.[234]

Finally, the segment 'in whole or in part' means that the right encompasses not only full reproductions of works, but also merely partial ones. Although the wording of Article 2 gives no guidance as to how much of a work can be reproduced before infringement occurs, the CJEU clarified in *Infopaq I* that the requirement of originality serves as the standard for partial reproduction: the copying of a part of a protected work will count as a reproduction if it 'contains an element of the work which, as such, expresses the author's own intellectual creation'.[235]

This legislative formula, complemented with the rule of broad interpretation extracted by the CJEU from Recital 21 InfoSoc Directive,[236] produces a sweeping exclusive right of reproduction. Looking at the right's wide coverage, 'a cynical observer might be tempted to reduce the definition of "reproduction" in article 2 to the sentence "reproduction means any reproduction"'.[237]

The far-reaching scope of the right of reproduction in the EU *acquis* has important implications in the technological realm. The right covers, for example, acts of downloading copies of works onto a device, uploading copies onto cloud lockers, visualising works in the context of browsing or streaming processes, copying on Internet servers and routers, storing and indexing works for purposes like plagiarism-checking, among many other acts.[238] As scholars have noted, in the digital environment the right 'covers virtually any use of a work or other subject matter, even where similar acts of usage in the analogue realm (such as receiving a television signal or

233. Stamatoudi & Torremans (2014a), p. 402.
234. 1995 Green Paper, p. 50.
235. CJEU, *Infopaq I*, para. 48.
236. For a discussion on this interpretative rule, *see infra* 5.
237. Ohly (2009), p. 236. Similarly, *see* Walter & Lewinski (2010), p. 968 ('This concept results in the mere use of a work being considered subject to the author's consent, whenever such use necessitates reproduction'), and Triaille et al. (2013), p. 120 ('a reproduction in the technical sense, a "copy", is equated to a reproduction in the legal sense').
238. *See* Quintais (2017a), pp. 163-164.

reading a book) would have fallen well outside the scope of what intellectual property aims to protect'.[239]

This broad approach is confirmed by the Court's case law on Article 2 InfoSoc Directive. The Court has interpreted the right of reproduction as extending to some technology-based copies, provided that they express the author's own intellectual creation. These include the storage of extracts of works during a data capture process;[240] the creation of transient copies of works within the memory of a satellite decoder and on a TV screen;[241] the making of copies in a computer program (or in a user manual for that program) of certain elements described in the user manual for another computer program;[242] and using a very short sound sample of a phonogram in another phonogram, unless that sample is modified to such a degree that it becomes unrecognisable.[243]

In sum, in order to respond to technological change, the EU legislator substantially expanded the scope of the reproduction right compared to the (already quite broad) formula adopted in the Berne Convention.[244] The result of this expansion is that virtually *any* copy in a technical sense will be prima facie covered by the right of reproduction as harmonised by the InfoSoc Directive, regardless of its purpose or economic value.[245]

The implication of such broad coverage is that the solution to conflicts about the lawfulness of reproductions in the digital environment is, in practice, 'shifted to the defences',[246] that is, to the field of exceptions. As shall be seen, some of the acts falling within the prima facie reach of Article 2 InfoSoc Directive may be privileged by certain exceptions to the reproduction right.

---

239. *See* Hugenholtz et al. (2006), p. 54. *See also* Hugenholtz (1996), pp. 92-93; Spoor (1996), pp. 67-79; Hart (2002), pp. 58-62; Triaille (2002), p. 11; and Westkamp (2004), p. 1087.
240. *See* CJEU, *Infopaq I*, para. 51.
241. *See* CJEU, *Premier League*, para. 159.
242. *See* CJEU, *SAS*, para. 70.
243. *See* CJEU, *Pelham*, para. 39.
244. *See* Depreeuw (2014), p. 205.
245. This approach to the right of reproduction has been deemed 'technical', as opposed to 'normative'. *See* Hugenholtz et al. (2006); Ohly (2009), p. 217; Triaille et al. (2013), p. 111; Depreeuw & Hubin (2014), p. 41; and Pihlajarinne (2017). *See also* AG Opinion, *Infopaq I*, para. 56, defining reproduction as the 'fixation of the work in a given information medium'.
246. Ohly (2009), p. 216.

4 THE RIGHT OF COMMUNICATION TO THE PUBLIC

The general notion of communication to the public refers to acts of *immaterial* exploitation of protected works.[247] These acts can be distinguished into: (i) public performances and other types of rendition in the presence of the public; (ii) broadcasting, rebroadcasting, and cable retransmission; and (iii) on-demand transmissions that enable the access by members of the public at a time and place individually chosen by them.[248]

Therefore, apart from encompassing communications where the audience is physically present at the moment where the communication originates (*inter praesentes*), the concept of communication to the public is understood as also covering communications where the audience is remote and composed of disperse individuals (*inter absentes*). Whereas performance and recitation rights are implicated only when the persons are present at the time and place of the communication, being thus able to directly perceive the work, the emergence of radio, TV, satellite and cable technologies, and ultimately the Internet enabled distant communications.

In international and EU law, prerogatives like performance, recitation, broadcasting, and on-demand transmission are distinguished and treated separately, although they all involve acts of communication. As will be seen, the result of this distinction is an intricate web of rights that are subject to diverging degrees of harmonisation.[249]

4.1 The Right of Communication to the Public in International Law

There is no single broad right of communication to the public in the Berne Convention. Instead, Berne Convention splits the notion of communication to the public into a number of discrete rights, depending on the type of act of communication and the subject matter involved.

247. *See, e.g.*, Ricketson & Ginsburg (2006), p. 706; Lucas-Schloetter (2012), p. 125; and Depreeuw (2014), p. 245.
248. Like the right of reproduction, the right to publicly perform or recite the work is one of the oldest prerogatives granted by copyright law. In France, for instance, the exclusive right of authors of dramatic works to perform their works in public was provided in the late eighteenth century with the 1791 French Copyright Law. As observed by Ginsburg (1990), p. 1005, the main motivation behind that statute was to put an end to the monopoly held by the Comédie Française over the works of Corneille, Racine, and Molière. In Germany, Section 15(2) German Copyright Act expressly includes performance as a discrete prerogative within the exclusive right to communicate the work to the public in non-material form. Note, however, that the expressions 'public performance' and 'communication to the public' are consistently used in a separate way in the Berne Convention.
249. *See* Ohly (2009), p. 225.

As to public performance, Article 11 grants authors of dramatic, dramatico-musical, and musical works the exclusive right to publicly perform those works and to communicate those performances to the public. Similarly, Article 11*ter* grants authors of literary works an exclusive right of public recitation and communication to the public of such recitation, while Article 14 grants them the right to authorise the public performance of cinematographic adaptations of their works.

Article 11*bis*, in contrast, deals with distant audiences, establishing minimum standards of protection for the right of broadcasting,[250] retransmission of broadcast signals,[251] and public communication by loudspeaker or analogous instruments.[252] For any of these rights to be implicated, '[w]hat matters is the emission of signals; it is immaterial whether or not they are in fact received'.[253] In other words, there may be no *actual public*, as long as there is a *potential public*. Relatedly, Article 14 TRIPS grants different communication rights to performers[254] and broadcasting organisations.[255]

A crucial common element between all these acts of communication lies exactly in the fact that they must be made to the *public*. The appearance of transmission technologies like the Internet raised the question of whether the millions of users that can receive protected works at the time and place of their *individual* choice are part of the concept of 'public' for purposes of the communication rights.[256,257] Unlike in public renditions and broadcasts, in the case of digital transmissions the public does not necessarily receive the work in a simultaneous and passive way. The main difference between the older forms of communication, on the one hand, and digital technologies, on the other, is that the latter allow users to play an active role in the transmission process, by choosing the circumstances in which a specific work is received.[258] The emergence and proliferation of these technologies thus challenged the traditional understanding of communication to the

250. *See* Article 11*bis*(1)(i) Berne Convention.
251. *See* Article 11*bis*(1)(ii) Berne Convention.
252. *See* Article 11*bis*(1)(iii) Berne Convention.
253. WIPO (1978), p. 66.
254. *See* Article 14(1) TRIPS.
255. *See* Article 14(3) TRIPS.
256. For early accounts on the challenges posed by digital technologies to the concept of communication to the *public*, *see* Dreier (1993), pp. 192-194, and Dreier (1995), pp. 123-124.
257. The emergence of satellite broadcasting had raised a similar question decades earlier. The question was whether the communication of protected subject matter via point-to-point and distribution satellites was made to the public. Unlike direct-broadcasting satellites, point-to-point and distribution satellites do not transmit the signals directly to the individuals' receiving sets, but to intercepting terrestrial stations that then diffuse them to the public. For a description of the controversy, *see* Ulmer (1977), pp. 14-24. Lewinski (2008), p. 150, points out that the contemporary dominant opinion, which finds support in the wording of Article 11*bis*(1)(i) Berne Convention, is that even indirect communications fall within the scope of communication to the public.
258. *See* Efroni (2011), pp. 255-256.

public, by blurring the distinction between private and public.[259] Paul Goldstein and Bernt Hugenholtz summarise the point neatly in the following passage:

> Arguably, Articles 11, 11*bis*, and 11*ter* of the Berne Paris Text have provided an adequate structure for balancing author and consumer interests within the context of most twentieth-century technologies. But these provisions, and the national legislation of a great many countries, fall short of resolving the question of whether newer technologies enabling interactive, on-demand transmissions, most notably on the Internet, come within copyright control. The issue under Berne is not whether such uses constitute performance, but whether they are public. Although works offered over the Internet may be accessible to publics much larger than those reached by traditional broadcast radio and television, access to the Internet will often entail transmission of a selected work to an individual user on demand, so that it is received only by that single user, typically in the privacy of his or her home.[260]

But, although it was not entirely clear whether the Berne communication rights, as they were (and still are) formulated, applied to digital transmissions of protected works, extensive agreement seemed to exist among policymakers that this sort of transmissions should be considered to fall within the sphere of rightholders' control.[261] The solution agreed upon to address the issue was to provide clarification through the expansion of an existing right. Back in the mid-to-late 1990s, the main question on the table was *which right* should be extended in order to cover the new acts of digital transmission – the right of distribution or the right of communication to the public?[262]

The latter ended up being chosen. The expansion of the right of communication to the public was led by Article 8 WCT, which included the act of making available online within its scope. Article 8 provides that 'authors of literary and artistic works shall enjoy the exclusive right of authorising any communication to the public of their works, by wire or wireless means, including the making available to the public of their works in such a way that members of the public may access these works from a place and at a time individually chosen by them'.[263] Articles 10 and 14 WPPT grant performers and phonogram producers the making available right in relation to phonograms.[264] The broad formula reveals the intention of

259. *See* Efroni (2011), p. 249.
260. Goldstein & Hugenholtz (2012), p. 328.
261. *See* Ficsor (2002a), p. 208.
262. *See* Ficsor (2002a), pp. 146 et seq.
263. Article 8 WCT does not cover public performance and it is without prejudice to the provisions of Articles 11(1)(ii), 11*bis*(1)(i) and (ii), 11*ter*(1)(ii), 14(1)(ii) and 14*bis*(1) Berne Convention. Public performances thus remain subject to the rules of the Berne Convention.
264. On the WIPO right of making available in detail, *see* Dimita (2017).

enacting a right that would resist against technological obsolescence – a right that would apply to '*any present and future* communication technology'.[265]

The second part of the provision makes clear that the act of transmitting a protected work over digital networks, by making it available to users on individual demand, is comprised within the broad right of communication to the public laid down in its first part.[266] The extension of the right's scope came hand-in-hand with the extension of the notion of 'public': as noted by Lucas-Schloetter, '[a]fter departing from the criterion of unity of place by making broadcast subject to the author's exclusive right, it is now the criterion of unity of time that is being abandoned, in order to apprehend the exploitation of works over networks'.[267]

The technology-neutral formula in Article 8 WCT was devised to apply to all forms of communication to the public that the more technology-specific Berne articles failed to cover. Mihály Ficsor, Assistant Director General of WIPO at the time of the preparation of the WIPO Treaties, outlined the idea behind this so-called umbrella solution: 'the most basic element of the "umbrella solution" is the neutral, legal-characterization-free description of interactive transmissions (neutral in the sense that it should not be characterized either as distribution or communication to the public)'.[268] The purpose was thus to provide for a solution that would leave Contracting States with room to manoeuvre in choosing the rights within which they would include the various restricted acts. Unlike in the EU, the prevailing understanding in the US was that the right to authorise on-demand digital transmissions of works was covered by the right of distribution enshrined in Section 106(3) US Copyright Act, such that a legislative amendment in order to add the making available right was found unnecessary. Although the WIPO Treaties include the act of making available online within the scope of the exclusive right of communication to the public, the US solution does not contravene the Treaty, thanks to the discretion given to Contracting States under the umbrella solution.

4.2 The Right of Communication to the Public in the EU *Acquis*

In line with Article 8 WCT, the InfoSoc Directive provides a similar broad right of communication to the public for all works of authorship.[269] Article

265. Efroni (2011), p. 272. *See also* Reinbothe & Lewinski (2002), p. 109.
266. Criticising this solution, on grounds that the making available prong involves, as its designation suggests, an act of making the work available online, but not necessarily an actual *communication* to recipients of the work, *see* Ascensão (1999), pp. 24-27.
267. Lucas-Schloetter (2012), p. 129.
268. Ficsor (2002a), p. 496.
269. Before InfoSoc, Article 5(d) Database Directive granted the author of a database the exclusive right to carry out or authorise 'any communication, display or performance to the public' thereof, a right that was left untouched by the InfoSoc Directive (Article

3(1) harmonises the authors' exclusive right 'to authorise or prohibit any communication to the public of their works, by wire or wireless means, including the making available to the public of their works in such a way that members of the public may access them from a place and at a time individually chosen by them'. This right must, as far as possible, be interpreted in consistency with international law, namely with the Berne Convention and the WCT.[270] It should, in addition, be given an independent and uniform meaning in all Member States, since communication to the public, like reproduction, is an autonomous concept of EU law.[271]

As to the beneficiaries, Article 3(1) grants *authors* a broad right to authorise or prohibit communications to the public, comprising the right of making available. Article 3(2) grants *holders of related rights* the latter right only, extending it to two categories of rightholders that are excluded from the WPPT formulation: producers of first fixations of films and broadcasting organisations.[272] Article 8 Rental and Lending Directive and the Satellite and Cable Directive, which are left intact by InfoSoc,[273] already contained harmonised rules on the right of broadcasting, thus supplementing Article 3(2) InfoSoc Directive. The CJEU clarified that the concept of 'communication to the public' in both directives is to be understood as having the same scope and meaning.[274] Moreover, Article 15 DSM Directive extends the InfoSoc right of making available to press publishers, in relation to the online use of their press publications by information society service providers.[275]

For the InfoSoc right of communication to the public to be triggered, an act of (re)transmission or making available of some kind must occur, irrespective of the technical means or process used.[276] A wide variety of acts are encompassed by the right, such as TV and radio broadcasting, rebroadcasting, cable retransmission, near-video on demand, webcasting, simulcasting, streaming, and other forms of online on-demand communication.

Although the right covers any making available or (re)transmission of a work to the public by wire or wireless means, it 'should not cover any other acts'.[277] In particular, the right does not apply to the mere provision of

1(2)(e)). Nevertheless, as pointed out by Ohly (2009), p. 226, and Eechoud et al. (2009), p. 82, it is hard to understand how a database can be performed in public.

270. *See* CJEU, *Premier League*, para. 189, and CJEU, *Stim & SAMI*, para. 29.
271. *See* CJEU, *SGAE*, para. 31. On the implications of this qualification, *see infra* Chapter 4, section 5.1.2.
272. Articles 10 and 14 WPPT refer respectively to performers and phonogram producers.
273. *See* Article 1(2)(b) and (c) InfoSoc Directive.
274. *See* CJEU, *Reha Training*, para. 33; CJEU, *GS Media*, para. 33; and CJEU, *Stim & SAMI*, para. 28.
275. This new ancillary right does not apply to acts of hyperlinking, but only to the use of snippets of press publications. The Directive further states that the rights granted to press publishers are subject to the exceptions laid down in Article 5 InfoSoc Directive. *See* Recital 57 and Article 15(3) DSM Directive.
276. *See, e.g.*, CJEU, *Premier League*, para. 193, and CJEU, *Filmspeler*, para. 36.
277. Recital 23 InfoSoc Directive.

physical facilities for enabling or making a communication, like the operation of a telecommunications network by an ISP[278] or the supply of a radio receiver forming an integral part of a hired motor vehicle.[279] The CJEU has clarified, however, that acts such as the distribution of TV signals in hotel rooms,[280] the sale of a multimedia player with pre-installed add-ons (also known as a 'Kodi box'),[281] and the operation of an online sharing platform like the Pirate Bay[282] *do not* amount to the mere provision of physical facilities, but to actual acts of communication to the public.

The CJEU has also confirmed that Member States are not allowed to construe the concept of communication to the public as including a wider range of acts than those referred in the Directive, for that would potentially lead to national legislative differences in copyright protection and undermine the harmonisation and legal certainty objectives pursued by the EU legislator, the achievement of which depends on the elimination of those very differences.[283] As the Court recently explained, the right of communication to the public is a measure of full harmonisation.[284] Provided these constraints are respected, the right is to be understood in a broad sense.[285]

On the other hand, the right harmonised by InfoSoc is not as broad in reach as the general notion of communication to the public outlined above. Specifically, it does not include public renditions, such as live performances in theatres or concert halls. Even though the Explanatory Memorandum to the InfoSoc Proposal states that Article 3(1) is to cover 'all forms of public communication and all categories of works',[286] Recital 23 clarifies that its scope is restricted to 'all communication to the public *not present* at the place where the communication originates'.[287] Within the meaning of the InfoSoc

278. *See* Recital 27 InfoSoc Directive. A similar clarification can be found in the Agreed Statements concerning Article 8 WCT.
279. *See* CJEU, *Stim & SAMI*, para. 34.
280. *See* CJEU, *SGAE*, para. 46.
281. *See* CJEU, *Filmspeler*, para. 41.
282. *See* CJEU, *Ziggo*, para. 38.
283. *See* CJEU, *Svensson*, paras 34-41. *See also* CJEU, *C More Entertainment*, paras 22-37, where the Court held that Article 3(2) InfoSoc Directive does not allow Member States to protect acts of hyperlinking to live broadcasts (because the making available right only covers transmissions that may be accessed from a place and *at a time* individually chosen by members of the public, which is not the case with *live* broadcasts), but not without clarifying that Article 8(3) Rental and Lending Directive does.
284. *See* CJEU, *Funke Medien*, para. 38. Prior to *Funke Medien*, commentators had already been arguing that the harmonisation of communication to the public was 'full', in the sense that 'if an act does not constitute a communication at EU level, national law cannot designate it one' – Angelopoulos (2017b), p. 23.
285. *See* Recital 23 InfoSoc Directive. *See infra* section 5.
286. Explanatory Memorandum to InfoSoc Proposal, p. 25.
287. Recital 23 InfoSoc Directive (emphasis added). *See also* Common Position (EC) No. 48/2000. The distinct treatment given to remote communications and public performances is also hinted at by the juxtaposition of the terms 'communications' and 'performance' in Article 5(d) Database Directive. Arguing that it would have been a

Directive, therefore, communication to the public does not comprise communications made *inter praesentes*. That much has been confirmed by the CJEU,[288] which deemed the direct performance of musical works in circuses or cabarets, where the audience is in direct physical contact with the performer, to fall out with the scope of the InfoSoc communication right.[289] The exclusion of these conventional forms of communication is a corollary of InfoSoc's objective of adapting copyright law to technological developments that have created new ways of using protected works.[290] Article 8 WCT, on which Article 3 InfoSoc Directive is based, also leaves out public performances. Member States are thus allowed to legislate on this type of acts on their own terms, provided they respect the minimum standards established in the Berne Convention.[291]

As the second part of Article 3(1) makes clear, acts of making available online form part of the wider scope of communication to the public.[292] Whereas in the 1995 Green Paper the Commission entertained the possibility of introducing a specific right of 'digital dissemination or transmission', as well as a 'digital broadcasting right',[293] in the 1996 Follow-Up the Commission had decided to propose the protection of digital on-demand transmission as part of a broad, harmonised right of communication to the public.[294] As seen, the WCT, which was adopted less than a month after the 1996 Follow-Up was published, introduced the new making available right within the right of communication to the public.

The InfoSoc right of making available covers the situations where the user can choose the time and place in which the work is received.[295] In these cases, unlike in broadcasting, the transmission of the work and its reception do not occur simultaneously. Users need not actually access the work for the right to be triggered; the mere *possibility of access* as a result of the transmission suffices. Put differently, it is the person who makes the work accessible to the public that may violate the right, not the member of the

---

better solution to clarify the exclusion of public performances in the very letter of Article 3 InfoSoc Directive, instead of in the preamble, *see* Eechoud et al. (2009), p. 82. The inclusion of public performance would have allowed the CJEU to develop and further harmonise this concept, as noted by Ohly (2009), p. 226.

288. *See* CJEU, *Premier League*, para. 201, and CJEU, *Circul Globus Bucuresti*, para. 35.
289. *See* CJEU, *Circul Globus Bucuresti*, paras 37-40.
290. *See* CJEU, *Circul Globus Bucuresti*, para. 38.
291. *See* Walter & Lewinski (2010), p. 1480.
292. *See* CJEU, *C More Entertainment*, para. 24.
293. *See* 1995 Green Paper, pp. 56-64.
294. *See* 1996 Follow-Up, p. 14.
295. According to the Explanatory Memorandum to InfoSoc Proposal, p. 25, this solution 'ensures legal certainty by confirming that the communication to the public right is also pertinent when several unrelated persons (members of the public) may have individual access, from different places and at different times, to a work which is on a publicly accessible site'. Similarly, *see* Recital 25 InfoSoc Directive.

public that accesses it (who may, nonetheless, be exposed to liability for infringing on the right of reproduction).[296]

The requirement of individual choice entails that the making available right covers all interactive transmissions such as uploading protected works onto P2P file sharing networks or providing on-demand streaming,[297] but not linear uses such as webcasting or simulcasting of predetermined programmes.[298] The latter ones are covered by the general right of communication to the public. For practical purposes, however, it seems to be largely indifferent whether a concrete act falls within the general formula of communication to the public or within the specific making available prong, since the criteria used to assess the prima facie infringement of this right, as harmonised by the CJEU, do not distinguish between the two modalities. Moreover, neither of these is subject to exhaustion.[299]

The CJEU has been playing a decisive role in the construction of the InfoSoc right of communication to the public. The meaning and scope of the notion of 'communication to the public' has been uncovered throughout more than twenty rulings handed down by the judges in Luxembourg.[300] This voluminous and rather intricate *corpus* of case law – which shall be analysed more thoroughly under a different context[301] – provides a set of criteria or factors to determine the existence of a communication to the public. One of the most striking effects of CJEU case law (in particular of recent judgments

296. *See* Stamatoudi & Torremans (2014a), p. 412.

297. On-demand streaming is distinct from non-interactive or linear streaming, where transmission and reception are simultaneous, and which are, therefore, analogous to broadcasting. In CJEU, *ITV Broadcasting I*, for example, the acts at stake – live streams of free-to-air TV broadcasts – fell within the latter category and therefore outwith the making available prong. *See* Borghi (2011).

298. *See*, *e.g.*, Explanatory Memorandum to InfoSoc Proposal, p. 26, and Lewinski (2008), p. 457. Highlighting the difficulties in precisely defining 'on-demand', *see* Hugenholtz et al. (2006), p. 56, and Guibault et al. (2007), p. 28.

299. *See* Article 3(3) and Recital 29 InfoSoc Directive, which have codified the view held by the CJEU since the *Coditel I* and *Coditel II* judgments that the rule of exhaustion does not apply to services. As a result, *each* act of making the work available to the public depends on the rightholder's authorisation. This much has recently been confirmed by the Court in *Renckhoff*, paras 32-33, and *Tom Kabinet*, para. 33.

300. The majority of cases concern the interpretation of Article 3 InfoSoc Directive: *SGAE*; *Organismos Sillogikis*; *BSA*; *Premier League*; *Circul Globus Bucuresti*; *ITV Broadcasting I*; *Svensson*; *OSA*; *BestWater*; *C More Entertainment*; *SPA*; *SBS Belgium*; *Reha Training*; *GS Media*; *Soulier & Doke*; *ITV Broadcasting II*; *AKM*; *Filmspeler*; *Ziggo*; *Renckhoff*; *VCAST*; *Spedidam*; *Tom Kabinet*; and *Stim & SAMI*. The scope of the right as provided in the Rental and Lending Directive (*PPI*; *SCF*; and *Verwertungsgesellschaft Rundfunk*) and in the Satellite and Cable Directive (*EGEDA I*; *Lagardère*; and *Airfield*) has also been the object of preliminary references. As already mentioned, in view of the requirements of unity and coherence of EU law, the concept of 'communication to the public' employed in the different directives must be interpreted as having the same meaning – *see* CJEU, *Premier League*, paras 187-188 and 190, and CJEU, *Reha Training*, paras 27-34.

301. *See infra* Chapter 4, section 5.3.2.

like *GS Media*, *Filmspeler*, and *Ziggo*[302]) was the expansion of the right of communication to the public onto territory that had previously remained outside the scope of harmonisation – that of secondary liability.[303]

Primary liability typically did not cover the acts of people who provided the means that direct users employed to engage in infringing behaviour. That used to be the difference between primary copyright infringement and secondary copyright infringement: whereas those who copied or disseminated in-copyright works could be found primarily liable for violating the rights of reproduction or communication to the public, those who were somehow linked to the primary acts of infringement in a relevant manner – by enabling, assisting, promoting, or benefiting from them – could be found secondarily liable. Following the mentioned rulings, however, the liability regime under Article 3 InfoSoc Directive became broad enough to cover the *indirect* intervention of at least some of these latter persons, blurring the long-held distinction between primary infringement and secondary infringement.[304] While this move by the CJEU has been criticised by some as an over-expansion of the right of communication to the public,[305] it may bear

302. As of the time of manuscript submission, two other preliminary references on this issue were pending before the CJEU, both originating from the BGH. The referrals essentially ask the CJEU to rule on whether a video hosting platform and a filehoster perform acts of communication to the public – *see* C-682/18, *YouTube* and C-683/18, *Cyando*. AG Saugmandsgaard Øe advised the Court to rule that these operators are not directly liable for the infringement of the right of communication to the public, when users of the platforms run by such operators illegally upload protected works. That conclusion, however, does not mean that those operators cannot be found *secondarily* liable. *See* AG Opinion, *YouTube/Cyando*, para. 93.
303. In the EU, secondary liability has largely escaped legislative harmonisation, with the exception of the liability exemptions for various types of information society providers established in the E-Commerce Directive (the so-called safe harbours), the Enforcement Directive's requirements for injunctions against intermediaries and the DSM Directive's new obligations of online content-sharing platforms. Consequently, this type of liability has been subject to different doctrinal constructions in different Member States. In most Member States – as pointed out by Frosio (2017), p. 570 – these constructions are composed of 'highly demanding conditions that are derived from miscellaneous doctrines of tort law, such as the doctrines of joint tortfeasance, authorization, inducement, common design, contributory liability, vicarious liability, or extra-contractual liability'. On the national regimes of secondary liability for copyright infringement, *see*, *e.g.*, Koelman & Hugenholtz (1999); Spindler & Leistner (2006); Dixon (2009), pp. 15-19; Angelopoulos (2013) and (2016) (the latter with proposals for a harmonised intermediary liability regime); and Husovec (2017) (focusing on injunctions against intermediaries). *See also* Leistner (2012) and the various contributions in Strowel (2009). On the new obligations for online intermediaries emerging in different sectors of the Digital Single Market, *see* Montagnani & Trapova (2019).
304. *See* Leistner (2017b), p. 5; Quintais (2017a), p. 386; Rosati (2017a); and Savola (2017), p. 143.
305. *See* Angelopoulos (2017a), with a critical view of this line of case law.

the advantage of 'efficiently achieving full harmonization with regard to copyright infringements in the digital single market'.[306]

Article 17(1) DSM Directive blurred the distinction even further, by creating a special right of communication to the public applicable to online content-sharing platforms.[307] The provision determines that large-scale user upload websites like YouTube and Vimeo perform an act of communication/ making available to the public when they give the public access to copyright-protected works or other subject matter uploaded by their users. In other words, these websites are primarily liable for their users' uploads and shall therefore obtain the rightholders' authorisation in order to communicate this content lawfully.[308] The Directive further clarifies that when online content-sharing platforms are liable for such acts, the exemption in Article 14(1) E-Commerce Directive for hosting providers shall not apply (to the copyright-relevant acts only).[309] Nevertheless, Article 17(1) DSM Directive operates as a *lex specialis* in relation to Article 3 InfoSoc Directive, creating a new liability regime for certain online intermediaries, without affecting the possible application of Article 3 to other platforms using copyright-protected content.[310]

5 THE (BROAD) INTERPRETATION OF RIGHTS IN EU LAW

As mentioned, the harmonisation of the rights of reproduction and communication to the public by the InfoSoc Directive has allowed the CJEU to

---

306. Leistner (2017b), p. 5. *See also* AG Opinion, *Ziggo*, para. 3.
307. Article 2(6) DSM Directive defines 'online content-sharing service provider' as 'a provider of an information society service of which the main or one of the main purposes is to store and give the public access to a large amount of copyright-protected works or other protected subject matter uploaded by its users, which it organises and promotes for profit-making purposes'. Recital 62 seems to restrict the scope of the definition by stating that it 'should target only online services that play an important role on the online content market *by competing with other online content services*, such as online audio and video streaming services, for the same audiences' (emphasis added). Importantly, certain platforms are excluded from the coverage of Article 17, namely not-for-profit online encyclopedias (e.g., Wikipedia), not-for-profit educational and scientific repositories (e.g., SSRN), open source software-developing and sharing platforms (e.g., GitHub), certain providers of electronic communications services (e.g., WhatsApp), online marketplaces (e.g., eBay), as well as business-to-business cloud services and cloud services that allow users to upload content for their own use (e.g., Dropbox).
308. Nonetheless, Article 17(2) adds that 'where an online content-sharing service provider obtains an authorisation, for instance by concluding a licensing agreement, that authorisation shall also cover acts carried out by users of the services falling within the scope of Article 3 of Directive 2001/29/EC when they are not acting on a commercial basis or where their activity does not generate significant revenues'.
309. *See* Recital 65 DSM Directive.
310. *See* Recital 64 DSM Directive. *See also* AG Opinion, *YouTube/Cyando*, para. 252.

clarify their meaning in a series of rulings. In doing so, the Court has proceeded on the basis of a general interpretative rule: reproduction and communication to the public are to be construed in a *broad* manner.

Recital 21 InfoSoc Directive states that a 'broad definition' of the acts covered by the reproduction right is 'needed', and Recital 23 adds that the right of communication to the public 'should be understood in a broad sense'. The CJEU has consistently read both recitals as requiring the scope of protection conferred by Articles 2 and 3 to be *interpreted* broadly.[311] According to the Court, this requirement, which is now a staple of the case law on InfoSoc rights,[312] stems from one of the main objectives of InfoSoc – that of ensuring a high level of protection of copyright.[313]

A double significance can be ascribed to this canon of broad interpretation in the copyright *acquis*: a formal one and a substantive one.[314]

From the formal standpoint, the requirement to interpret rights broadly refers to the relationship between the meaning of the words in the provisions

---

311. These recitals do not make entirely clear whether the broad scope of protection reflected in the very wording of Articles 2 and 3 is enough to satisfy their requirements or whether, *beyond that*, the recitals require the judiciary to interpret the provisions' wording broadly. Recital 21, in particular, refers to the need for a broad *definition* – a need that is arguably satisfied by the textual scope of Article 2, which, as seen, applies to copies that are 'direct or indirect', 'temporary or permanent', 'by any means' and 'in any form'. It does not follow from the fact that the legislator opted to provide the right with a wide coverage that the interpreter, faced with multiple admissible readings of the right's scope, should necessarily go for a broad reading. Put differently, it is one thing to recognise that the right, *qua* linguistic proposition, comprises a vast array of acts; and it is another thing to require that the law-interpreter, in drawing the meaning and extent of that formulation so as to arrive at the rule that will guide her in deciding a concrete case, concludes that the right is to be given a broad reading. The CJEU, nonetheless, seems to be of a different opinion. *See* CJEU, *Infopaq I*, paras 41-43, where the Court, after recognising that the requirement of a broad definition is to be found in the wording of Article 2, adds that '[c]*onsequently*, the protection conferred by Article 2 of Directive 2001/29 must be given a broad *interpretation*' (emphasis added).

312. Invoking the canon of broad interpretation in relation to the right of reproduction, *see* CJEU, *Infopaq*, paras 41-47; CJEU, *Painer*, para. 96; CJEU, *Soulier & Doke*, para. 30; and CJEU, *Spedidam*, para. 36, and, regarding the right of communication to the public, *see* CJEU, *SGAE*, para. 36; CJEU, *Premier League*, para. 186; CJEU, *Circul Globus Bucuresti*, para. 33; CJEU, *ITV Broadcasting*, para. 20; CJEU, *Svensson*, para. 17; CJEU, *OSA*, para. 23; CJEU, *SBS Belgium*, para. 14; CJEU, *Reha Training*, para. 36; CJEU, *GS Media*, para. 30; CJEU, *Filmspeler*, para. 27; CJEU, *Ziggo*, para. 22; CJEU, *VCAST*, para. 40; CJEU, *Renckhoff*, para. 18; CJEU, *Spedidam*, para. 36; and CJEU, *Tom Kabinet*, para. 49;

313. *See, e.g.*, CJEU, *Infopaq I*, paras 40-41 (implying the connection between that objective and the need for a broad interpretation of reproduction), and CJEU, *SGAE*, para. 36 (expressly establishing such connection in respect to communication to the public). For an account on the general objectives of InfoSoc, *see supra* Introduction, section 1.2.

314. Identifying four possible senses in which a broad interpretation may be contrasted with a strict one, *see* Engisch (2014), pp. 188-197. *See also infra* Chapter 2, section 3.3, for a description of the rule of strict interpretation of exceptions.

that confer the rights and the scope of application of these provisions.[315] Canons of interpretation give guidance to courts in interpreting statutes. The canon of broad interpretation does not refer to the *process* that should be followed in investigating the meaning and scope of a provision (unlike, say, the canon of teleological interpretation), but to the *result* that the interpreter should achieve. The result of the interpretative activity will be a broad one if the interpreter, faced with two or more possible meanings for the provision under consideration or for the main concepts thereof, goes for the more inclusive one, thus widening the provision's scope of application. This meaning may comprehend, to a greater or lesser extent, phenomena that are at a legal provision's fringe, instead of at its nuclear core.[316]

Take as an illustration the interpretation of the concept of 'act of communication' in Article 3 InfoSoc Directive. A broad interpretation of such a concept would widen the scope of Article 3, while a narrow one would constrain it. In its case law on the transmission of broadcast signals to different establishments, the CJEU has construed the concept as requiring an intervention that is indispensable, in the sense that, in the absence of such intervention, the public would not be able to enjoy the work.[317] However, in its recent case law on the online right of communication to the public, the Court has relaxed the criterion, doing away with the requirement of 'indispensability'. In *Ziggo*, the Court stated that it is sufficient that, in the absence of the user's intervention, the public 'would not be able to enjoy the broadcast work, *or would be able to do so only with difficulty*'.[318] This reading has allowed the Court to expand the circle of cases that come within the coverage of Article 3. Activities that are not indispensable for the public to enjoy protected works, but that reduce the complexity in accessing those works – such as the sale of a multimedia player with pre-installed add-ons containing hyperlinks to freely accessible websites where unauthorised works have been made available (*Filmspeler*) and the offer and management of an online platform that indexes torrent files, making it easier for users to

315. *See* Larenz (2012), pp. 500-501. *See also* Engisch (2014), pp. 188-197, opting for a conceptualisation of narrow/broad interpretation that is connected with a subjectivist theory of interpretation. According to this author, a narrow/broad interpretation is needed when a relatively strict/ample meaning corresponds to the legislator's intention. However, as explained by Larenz (2012), p. 500, legislative intention is not binding upon the interpreter; it is but one among the various admissible criteria of interpretation.

316. *See* Larenz (2012), pp. 500-501. Distinguishing between the 'core' and the 'penumbra' of legal rules, *see* Hart (1958), p. 607.

317. *See* CJEU, *SGAE*, para. 42; CJEU, *Organismos Sillogikis*, para. 38; CJEU, *Premier League*, para. 195; CJEU, *SCF*, para. 82; and CJEU, *PPI*, para. 31.

318. CJEU, *Ziggo*, paras 26 and 36 (emphasis added). *See also* CJEU, *Filmspeler*, para. 41 (referring to the intervention as one 'without which the purchasers would find it difficult to benefit from those protected works'), and CJEU, *Stim & SAMI*, para. 32 (using the expression 'indispensable role', but defining it as a role in the absence of which 'customers would not be able to enjoy the broadcast work, or would be able to do so only with difficulty').

locate and share protected works via a P2P network (*Ziggo*) – are therefore covered by the concept of 'act of communication'.

The canon of broad interpretation has, in addition, a substantive significance, in that it instructs the interpreter to favour readings that promote certain interests or values.[319] Because economic rights are entitlements granted upon authors, broad interpretations thereof will necessarily favour their interests (or those of rightholders, if they are different from the work's authors). Indeed, saying that rights must be interpreted broadly entails, in symbolic terms, an inbuilt bias in favour of the interests of authors or rightholders. When determining the scope of the rights of reproduction and communication to the public, judges should, in case of doubt between different admissible interpretations, give precedence to the interests of these parties. This *in dubio pro auctoris* canon finds normative support in the 'high level of protection' objective that is repeatedly mentioned in the InfoSoc preamble.[320] Such an interpretative rule, more than following from the 'high level of protection' objective, is said to be 'essential' to achieve it.[321]

6 CONCLUSION

The InfoSoc Directive followed a systematic and technology-neutral approach to harmonisation, dealing with the rights of reproduction, communication to the public, and distribution in relation to all categories of protected subject matter. Although earlier directives had partially harmonised selected economic rights in respect of specific categories of subject matter and rightholders, only with the InfoSoc Directive were the three most important rights harmonised across the board. Among these, the right of distribution bears less relevance for the present study, for its reach is generally limited to the transfer of ownership over the *corpus mechanicum* of works. Consequently, it does not extend (or extends only to a very limited degree) to the digital domain.

319. Exploring the substantive dimension that the distinction between broad and strict interpretation may have, with examples from German law, *see* Engisch (2014), pp. 191-194.

320. Besides Recitals 4 and 9 InfoSoc Directive, Recital 11 refers to 'a rigorous, effective system for the protection of copyright' and Recital 22 to the 'strict protection of rights'. Criticising the principle of *favor auctoris* and its implications for the interpretation of economic rights, *see* Ohly (2009), pp. 238-240. *See* Vicente (2008), p. 59, grounding the general *favor auctoris* inclination of the continental copyright system in the natural rights justification that underpins it, as opposed to the utilitarian justification that prevails in common law copyright. Nonetheless, as the author acknowledges, EU copyright law cannot be said to adhere strictly to a single conception, for it mixes elements of both (pp. 125-126).

321. *See*, *e.g.*, CJEU, *SGAE*, para. 36. *But see* AG Opinion, *YouTube/Cyando*, para. 238, defending that the InfoSoc right of communication to the public 'does not necessarily have to be interpreted in a manner which ensures *maximum protection* for rightholders'.

The reproduction right – the primeval entitlement in copyright law – was given a broad definition in the Berne Convention, covering copies of works made 'in any manner or form'. The scope of the right was further stretched during the EU harmonisation process. The InfoSoc legislator made clear that the right covered a sheer number of different copies, be they temporary or permanent, direct or indirect, total or partial, made by any means and in any form. What this means, in practice, is that most, if not all, uses involving copy-making will fall within the scope of the right, including modern digital uses such as cloud storage and Internet browsing.

Another crucial right within the digital networked environment is that of communication to the public. Different types of activities may constitute communications to a large number of people, namely public performances, broadcasting, rebroadcasting, cable retransmissions, as well as online on-demand transmissions. These latter acts were brought within the scope of exclusivity through the umbrella solution of Article 8 WCT. In the wake of this provision, Article 3(1) InfoSoc Directive harmonised a broad right of communication to the public for all works of authorship. The right covers all communications made *inter absentes*, including acts of making available online.

The right of communication to the public has motivated an array of preliminary references to the CJEU, whose contribution for the determination of the scope of the right has been key (if sometimes puzzling). These references have allowed the Court to find that right applicable to a series of uses that would otherwise hardly come within its textual scope – uses such as the offering and management of online platforms for sharing protected works or the sale of Kodi boxes.

Adding up to the wide coverage of the rights of reproduction and communication to the public, the CJEU has developed and consistently followed a canon of broad interpretation. According to the Court, this interpretative methodology is fundamental to achieve a high level of protection of rightholders. The broad coverage of Articles 2 and 3 InfoSoc Directive, combined with this interpretative rule, entails that numerous uses, old and new, will fall within the scope of exclusivity. In other words, these uses will be considered prima facie infringing.

As the Latin expression '*prima facie*' conveys, however, these uses are infringing *on their face* only. The expression is used to refer to situations in which the conditions for a legal entitlement to hold are verified, even though that entitlement may end up not being conclusively applicable because the conditions for the application of a defence are also present. In copyright law, unauthorised uses of protected works may be considered non-infringing if, while constituting acts that are restricted by exclusive rights, they fall under the scope of a certain exception.

Chapter 2

Exceptions in International and EU Law

1 INTRODUCTION

Not all unauthorised uses that fall within the prima facie scope of an exclusive right will amount to *actual* infringements of that right. Such uses may be covered by an exception. Exceptions subtract a subset of uses from the definitive scope of exclusivity and treat that subset as non-infringing. They grant immunity from copyright liability for certain categories of uses, out of social, cultural, economic, and/or technological reasons.[322] Procedurally speaking, copyright exceptions work as defences to the rightholders' claims of infringement,[323] providing a vital counterweight to the broad scope of exclusive rights in the EU *acquis*.

This chapter sketches the framework of exceptions to the exclusive rights of reproduction and communication to the public in international and EU copyright law. Although essentially descriptive, this chapter also seeks to resolve some hitherto unsettled issues with important implications for the remainder of this book. Namely, it tries to dispel the uncertainty and expand our understanding on issues such as the legal nature of permitted uses of copyright-protected works and the addressees of the InfoSoc three-step test. Critical observations on the features of the InfoSoc framework will be reserved for other chapters.

Apart from this short introduction, this chapter is divided into four sections. It begins with a foray into terminology, with the purpose of clarifying the legal nature of the permitted uses laid down in provisions like Article 5 InfoSoc Directive and of the entitlements they confer (section 2). The (relatively scant) international rules on exceptions are then outlined

322. On the justifications for the recognition of copyright exceptions, *see supra* Introduction, section 1.1.
323. The qualification of copyright exceptions as 'defences' presupposes a certain understanding on their legal nature. This understanding is made explicit in the following section (2.1.).

(section 3.1), before proceeding to a more detailed exploration of the EU *acquis* (section 3.2). The so-called three-step test – which, throughout its evolution, has become the international and European foundation of exceptions' regimes – is examined separately (section 4). Section 5 summarises the conclusions reached in this chapter.

2 EXCURSUS ON TERMINOLOGY

Terminology matters. It matters not only because inaccurate terminology may be a threat to clear thought, but also because, in the particular case that is of interest to us, the words we use to refer to permitted uses of copyright-protected works have – or are commonly thought to have – important practical consequences.

What follows is an attempt at a clarification of which term – 'exceptions' *or* 'limitations' – should be used to refer to the content of provisions like Article 5 InfoSoc Directive, which lays down permitted (though unauthorised) uses of protected works (section 2.1). After concluding that these norms are better described as 'exceptions', I will briefly examine the question of whether they confer true rights upon users (section 2.2). I conclude that we should refer to the entitlements granted by copyright exceptions as 'privileges', in lieu of 'rights'.

2.1 Permitted Uses as 'Exceptions' (Not 'Limitations')

There is wide disagreement on how to refer to norms that describe permitted uses of protected subject matter, such as Article 5 InfoSoc Directive and the domestic provisions that rely on it. The terminological choice is typically framed in the literature as one between the terms 'exceptions' and 'limitations'.

The international treaties and EU directives on copyright provide little guidance on the matter. When employing either term individually or both simultaneously, the international and EU legislators seem to do it in an interchangeable manner. While the Berne Convention does not use the terms 'exceptions' and 'limitations',[324] Article 15 Rome Convention uses both terms. At the EU level, the word 'exceptions' is used in the Database[325] and

324. When it refers to uses of protected works for which the rightholder's authorisation is unnecessary, the Berne Convention resorts to the verb 'to permit' (e.g., Article 9(2)) or to the adjective 'permissible' (e.g., Article 10(1)). It ought to be noted, however, that the Convention, as amended on 28 September 1979, includes a table of contents, which does not appear in the original text, referring to Article 9(2) with the title 'possible exceptions'.

325. *See* Articles 6 and 9 Database Directive.

Software[326] Directives, and the word 'limitations' is found in the Rental and Lending Directive.[327] The combined expression 'exceptions and/or limitations' is used in the InfoSoc Directive,[328] the Orphan Works Directive,[329] the Marrakesh Directive,[330] and the DSM Directive,[331] as well as in the WIPO Treaties[332] and the TRIPS Agreement.[333]

Commentators speculate on the reason behind the use of this combined expression, particularly in the context of the InfoSoc Directive. It has been hypothesised that the term 'exceptions' refers to the situations where the use is entirely free, meaning that neither authorisation *nor* payment of compensation is necessary, whereas the term 'limitations' refers to non-voluntary licences, in which the exclusive right is replaced by a compensated exception (like in the case of private copying). Under this view, therefore, exceptions correspond to those permitted uses that are uncompensated and limitations to those that require payment.[334] Scholars subscribing to this view often find support in the title and coverage of Article 5 InfoSoc Directive itself. The provision encompasses cases in which the use requires neither authorisation nor payment of compensation – such as temporary reproduction, quotation, parody[335] – and three cases of non-voluntary licences, in which compensation is due to the rightholder – reprography, private copying, and reproduction of broadcasts made by social institutions.[336] Since the title of Article 5 reads 'exceptions and limitations', each of the terms can only refer to each of the foregoing types of situations, so the argument goes.

---

326. *See* Article 5 Software Directive. In a different field, the Trade Secrets Directive employs exclusively the term 'exceptions' in providing for defences against claims of illegal acquisition, use or disclosure of a trade secret (Article 5).
327. *See* Article 10 Rental and Lending Directive.
328. *See* Recitals 14, 31-45 and 51-52 and Articles 5 and 6 InfoSoc Directive.
329. *See* Recital 20 and Article 6 Orphan Works Directive.
330. The Marrakesh Directive employs the expression 'exceptions and limitations' in the preamble only (Recitals 1, 2, 4, 5, 6 and 20). Article 3, on the other hand, uses only the term 'exception'.
331. Recitals 3 and 5-43 (though occasionally using only 'exception') and Articles 4, 5, 8(2)-(5), 9(2), 10, 12(4), 16, 17(7)-(10), and 25 DSM Directive. *But see* Articles 3 and 6, employing the term 'exception'.
332. *See* Article 10 WCT and Article 16 WPPT.
333. *See* Article 13 TRIPS.
334. *See*, referring specifically to Article 5 InfoSoc Directive, Caron (2002), p. 25, and Lucas et al. (2017), p. 322. *See also* Gervais (2010), p. 507, referring to Article 5 Wittem Code; Ficsor (2012), p. 2, referring to Article 13 TRIPS Agreement; and Samuelson (2017), fn. 2, referring to 'limitations and exceptions' in general.
335. *See*, respectively, Articles 5(1), 5(3)(d), and 5(3)(k) InfoSoc Directive.
336. *See*, respectively, Articles 5(2)(a), 5(2)(b), and 5(2)(e) InfoSoc Directive. Note that Recital 36 allows Member States to provide for fair compensation also in the cases of exceptions that do not expressly require it.

In *VG Wort*, the Court seemed to have embraced this view, by expressly stating that Article 5 makes a distinction between exceptions and limitations in its title[337] and that such distinction 'should therefore be given effect'.[338] In the Court's own words, the exclusive right of reproduction 'may, depending on the circumstances, be either, as an exception, totally excluded, or merely limited. It is conceivable that such a limitation may include, depending on the particular situations that it governs, in part an exclusion, a restriction, or even the retention of that right.'[339] What this interpretation suggests is that a limitation is a weaker restriction to exclusive rights than an exception and that only the provisions that lay down uses that are completely free qualify as exceptions.[340]

But while *VG Wort* may be read as lending support to the distinction outlined in the previous paragraphs, other judgments suggest that the CJEU understands the terms 'exceptions' and 'limitations' interchangeably. In *ACI Adam*, for instance, the Court, in referring to the permitted-but-compensated use of private copying, expressly qualifies it first as an 'exception' and then as a 'limitation'.[341] In *VCAST*, on the other hand, it refers repeatedly to the private copying *exception.*[342]

Moreover, a thorough analysis of the InfoSoc Directive, in particular of its preamble, shows that the interpretation according to which the term 'exceptions' is used for free uses and 'limitations' for non-voluntary licences is misguided. Whereas Recitals 35-39 and 52 refer to cases of non-voluntary licences by putting them under the combined label of 'exceptions and limitations', Recitals 40-42 use this same label to refer to situations where the Directive does not impose the payment of compensation. Similarly, in the DSM Directive the expression 'exception or limitation' is used in Articles 4, 5, and 8(2), whereas the term 'exception' is used in Articles 3 and 6. None of them, however, establishes a non-voluntary licence.[343] In view of this, the only conclusion that can be drawn from the use of the combined expression 'exceptions and limitations' in the copyright *acquis* is that the legislator employed it indistinctly.

---

337. *See* CJEU, *VG Wort*, para. 33.
338. CJEU, *VG Wort*, para. 35.
339. CJEU, *VG Wort*, para. 34. *See also* AG Opinion, *VG Wort*, para. 37.
340. Drawing the same conclusion, though by reference to the AG Opinion, *see* Rosati (2014a), p. 590. *See also* Pila & Torremans (2016), p. 343.
341. *See* CJEU, *ACI Adam*, paras 28 and 31.
342. *See* CJEU, *VCAST*, paras 34 and 39.
343. Nevertheless, Article 5(4) and Recital 24 expressly state that Member States *are free* to establish a fair compensation scheme in relation to illustration for teaching. In contrast, they are prohibited from doing so in the case of the TDM exception for scientific research (Recital 17).

The most credible explanation for the use of both terms lies in the lack of terminological uniformity at the national level. Before InfoSoc, different Member States used different terms to refer to the situations grouped under the current Article 5. 'Exceptions' was used, e.g., in Belgian copyright law, but the German legislator preferred the word *Schranken* (limitations) and the Spanish the word *limites* (limits). Other Member States had alternative formulations, such as France, which avoided these terms by resorting to expressions like *l'auteur ne peut interdire* ('the author may not prohibit'), and Portugal, which preferred *utilizações livres* ('free uses'). Faced with this diversity of terms, as commentators plausibly conjecture, the EU legislator simply decided to try and accommodate the different national traditions by going for a combined version.[344]

Against this context, different positions have been sustained in scholarship as to the term that is *more suitable* to describe the unauthorised uses whose non-infringing character is determined by Article 5 InfoSoc Directive and equivalent national provisions. The question has been discussed from a legal-technical perspective and from a normative perspective.

From the legal-technical point of view, four different positions can be identified. Some scholars, as already mentioned, see exceptions as norms describing uses that are subject neither to authorisation nor to the payment of compensation and limitations as situations where the exemption from authorisation is offset by a claim to compensation granted to the right-holder.[345] Others define exceptions as immunities from liability for specific uses of protected works and limitations as the exclusion of protection for particular categories of subject matter (such as news of the day or official legislative texts)[346] or, more generally, as boundaries of copyright protection (such as the term of protection).[347] A third position understands the distinction as being related to the different copyright traditions and their underlying justifications: while 'exceptions' fits the natural rights-based *droit d'auteur* tradition better, the term 'limitations' is more appropriate in common law countries with a utilitarian approach.[348] And yet other

344. *See* Dusollier (2007), pp. 426-427, and Vivant (2002), pp. 72-73.
345. Among the scholars that subscribe to this account of the distinction between 'exceptions' and 'limitations' are Ricketson (1998), pp. 9-16; Ficsor (2002a), p. 257; Lewinski (2008), p. 152; and Samuelson (2017), p. 13, fn. 2. Note, however, that Sam Ricketson follows an alternative understanding in Ricketson (2003), pp. 3-4.
346. *See* Ricketson (2003), pp. 3-4.
347. *See* Christie (2011), pp. 123-125, and Lucas et al. (2017), p. 324.
348. *See* Senftleben (2004), p. 22, attempting to explain the use of the expression 'exceptions and limitations' in Article 13 TRIPS and Article 10 WCT. *See also* Lucas (1998), p. 170.

commentators think that the terminology used to refer to permitted uses is largely irrelevant[349] and that the choice is but 'a matter of working convenience'.[350]

I wish to argue that, from a legal-technical perspective, 'exceptions' is the most appropriate term to describe permitted uses. 'Exceptions' is a well-established notion in the literature on legal theory and methodology and has a meaning that goes beyond the copyright-specific debate. The acceptance or rejection of the qualification of permitted uses as exceptions should therefore have that concept as its reference.

Exceptions are traditionally understood as legal provisions that derogate from the content of another rule with a general character, working as defeating conditions of that general rule. In order to be properly classified as an exception, the provision must cut out a subset of situations from another rule and treat that subset differently, providing a solution that is contrary to the solution offered by the general rule.[351] To give an example from outside copyright law: in contract law, freedom of form and formalities is the general rule, meaning that a contract will be valid regardless of the form (e.g., oral or written) chosen by the parties to it. Due to special concerns about legal certainty, the validity of *some* contracts is subject to certain form requirements, like being in writing or being signed in the presence of witnesses. The rules laying down those form requirements are *exceptional*: they subtract certain situations from the larger set governed by the general rule and treat them in the opposite way.

Now consider an example from Article 5 InfoSoc Directive: the rule exempting unauthorised copies made for private use, also known as the private copying exception (Article 5(2)(b)). This rule cuts out a set of situations that the right of reproduction prima facie prohibits. Under one norm (the rule recognising right) the unauthorised use is infringing, while under the other (the private copying rule) it is not. If a given fact-situation is covered by Article 5(2)(b) (*rectius*, by a domestic provision introduced in reliance thereon), that norm will *defeat* the exclusive right and liability for infringement will be removed. Under the conceptualisation described above,

---

349. *See* Gautier (2001), p. 10; Dreier (2001), p. 307; Dusollier (2007), pp. 426-427; Förster (2008), p. 5; and Kur (2009), pp. 292-293. Séverine Dusollier opts to use the term 'exceptions', because this is the most common term in Belgian law. Similarly, Spoor (1998), pp. 29-30, although not finding the terminological choice irrelevant, goes for 'exceptions' on grounds that it is 'more widely accepted'. While I agree with the qualification, I find the justification unsatisfactory. A non-legal example might aid in explaining why. Many people call alligators 'crocodiles'. Alligators and crocodiles do belong to the same order of reptiles (*Crocodilia*). Yet, they have certain distinctive characteristics: alligators have a rounded, U-shaped front end, which contrasts with crocodiles' V-shaped nose. It is therefore possible to carefully examine a specific crocodilian and tell whether it is an alligator or not, regardless of what most people call it. I believe the same happens with exceptions, as I shall make clearer below.

350. Kur (2009), p. 292.

351. *See* Ascensão (2011), pp. 448-449, and Larenz (2012), pp. 502-503.

the permitted uses like the one described in Article 5(2)(b) InfoSoc Directive are properly qualified as exceptions.[352]

The natural rejoinder here is to criticise this understanding as positivistic, claiming that whether a defeating condition of the exclusive right is established as a separate rule or is incorporated as an inherent part of the right's definition is but a matter of legislative technique.[353] And indeed, at least in theory, the permission to make copies of protected works for private use could be built into the exclusive right of reproduction by including a requirement to that effect in its definition (for instance, through a formula like 'authors enjoy the exclusive right to authorise or prohibit reproductions for non-private use'). On this view, the fact that private copying and all the other permitted uses were formulated in separate provisions, instead of appearing in the right's definition, amounts to little more than a question of legislative style or convenience. Exceptions, it could be argued, are but 'superficial products of a linguistic or stylistic decision'.[354]

I submit that, aside from considerations related to practicality in drafting, there are at least two reasons to omit certain defeating conditions from the right's definition.

First, carving permitted uses separately underscores their distinct purposes and background justifications. Permitted uses are established out of the recognition that the protection of rightholders must be balanced with competing public policy objectives, such as freedom of expression and information.[355] The purpose that finds manifestation in the exclusive right conflicts with the autonomous purposes behind permitted uses. Providing for permitted uses in separate rules renders this tension visible.

Second, the separate formulation of permitted uses highlights their function as defences against the prima facie claims of rightholders.[356] The

---

352. Ubertazzi (2003), p. 94, adds that the systematic placement of rules on permitted uses *after* those on exclusive rights is also a suggestion that the former are 'exceptional'.
353. *See* Hugenholtz (1997), pp. 4-5.
354. The expression is by Finkelstein (1999), p. 149, but the author opposes this view.
355. *See* Ricketson (2003), p. 3, and Ricketson & Ginsburg (2006), p. 756. *See also* Introduction, section 1.1.
356. *See, e.g.*, Goutal (2002), p. 11 (stating that exceptions do not offer users any offensive means, but only means of defence); Kur & Ruse-Khan (2009), p. 5 (drawing a distinction between limitations and 'defence-type' exceptions); Walter & Lewinski (2010), p. 1022 (observing that exceptions and limitations give users 'a defence against any reproach of copyright infringement'); Caron (2012), p. 23 (pointing out that, traditionally, exceptions are used as defences); and Bently et al. (2018), p. 221 ('The exceptions come into play only once a claimant has established that copyright has been infringed. Where this occurs, the onus of proof falls on the defendant to prove that one of the exceptions applies'). The expression 'affirmative defence' is common in the US, where the character of fair use as a defence, though not mentioned in the statutory text, has been established in case law. *See, e.g.,* US Supreme Court, *Harper & Row*, p. 561; US Supreme Court, *Campbell*, p. 591; US Court of Appeals for the Second Circuit, *American Geophysical Union*, p. 918; and US Court of Appeals for the Ninth Circuit, *Perfect 10*, p. 1158. This entails that fair use 'comes into play only if and after the

applicable permitted use enables the defendant/user to raise facts and arguments that, if proven, will defeat the claim made by the plaintiff/rightholder. Although the systematic placement of a defeating condition may not always produce clear conclusions as to its status as a defence, it usually gives reliable cues in that regard.[357] Whereas the elements of the exclusive right's definition are part of the rightholder's claim, exceptions act as defences thereto. In general, the party invoking a specific provision favourable to its interest in the action bears the burden of establishing the facts on which that provision stands.[358] This means that the rightholder wishing to assert an exclusive right against an unauthorised user must prove the subjacent facts – say, that a user made a copy of the rightholder's protected work. Conversely, the user who objects to the claim by raising facts that challenge, modify, or extinguish the invoked right is burdened with the proof of those facts – say, that the copy was made for parodic purposes. Placing the defeating condition (parodic use) within the right's definition, as a negative element thereof (reproductions for non-parodic use), would have the effect of shifting the burden of pleading and substantiating the non-applicability of that condition to the rightholder. Given the long list of permitted uses in copyright law, it seems reasonable to accept that the burden of establishing the verification of the factual circumstances that characterise *a certain* permitted use should fall on the shoulders of the unauthorised user. Otherwise, the rightholder would have to show or at least plead the absence of *all* permitted uses in order to establish a prima facie case of infringement.[359] By placing the defeating conditions separately, the legislator is signalling that, once the rightholder makes a prima facie case of infringement, the burden shifts to the allegedly infringing user, who must refute the claim by showing the consistency of her acts with the requirements of a permitted use.

On the other hand, the term 'limitations' is better used to describe other situations. These situations may be divided into two categories.

The first category is that of limitations to copyright protection. These are limitations to the very subsistence of copyright in a given work.[360] According to André Lucas, these limitations arise from the very nature and

---

plaintiff has made out a prima facie case' and that 'the party asserting fair use bears the burden of proving its availability' – Patry (2017a), pp. 70 and 72.

357. *See* Kur (2009), p. 294.

358. The nature of the burden (preponderance of evidence, proof beyond a reasonable doubt, etc.) may vary from rule to rule, of course.

359. Whether we should have a different, more normative definition of economic rights instead of having as long a list of permitted uses is a different matter and one that falls beyond the scope of this book, as clarified in the Introduction (section 2).

360. As pointed out by Ricketson (2003), p. 4, the policy basis for limitations *and* exceptions is different: whereas the former category 'proceeds on the assumption that there are clear public policy grounds that copyright protection should not exist in the works in question', the latter 'represents a more limited concession that certain kinds of uses of works that are otherwise protected should be allowed'.

object of copyright law; they need not be expressly written down in law to be widely accepted.[361] The most prominent examples of such natural limitations are: (i) the idea/expression dichotomy, according to which ideas, as opposed to their expression, are excluded from the monopoly granted by copyright; (ii) originality as a requirement that a work must meet to qualify for copyright protection; and (iii) the limited duration of such protection, which expires after a certain period of time has lapsed (generally, seventy years *post mortem auctoris*).[362]

The second category is that of limitations to the scope of rights that result from their very definition. Limitations, understood in this sense, are integral parts of the rights.[363] Unlike exceptions, they do not subtract a portion of the right that is within its prima facie coverage; rather, they outline their perimeter aprioristically.[364] Limitations are therefore inherent requirements for the prima facie applicability of the right, while exceptions are external to and distinct from the applicable right.[365] A fitting example of such limitations in EU copyright law is the concept of 'public' within the right of communication to the public. The 'public' element of the definition helps to delimit the scope of the right: had it not been included and the right would cover acts of communication directed at the communicator's circle of family and friends, like communications made via personal e-mail messages. Because the 'public' is part of the definition of the right, a transmission that is not directed to a fairly large and indeterminate number of potential recipients will not fall within its coverage. The idea that rights have limits of this kind may seem, in the words of Robert Alexy, 'an obvious – almost trivial – point'.[366] Yet, this distinction highlights again the non-negligible practical consequences related to the burden of proof: as part of the right's definition, the fact that the communication was directed to a public is to be

---

361. *See* Lucas (1998), p. 165. In contrast, *see* Vide & Gómez (2008), p. 55 (calling exceptions 'natural limits' to copyright, which are 'ingredients' of exclusive rights themselves) and Schack (2016), p. 268 (claiming that copyright exceptions – or at least what this book calls 'exceptions' – are really integral parts of the definition of exclusive rights).
362. For an overview of these limitations, *see* Dreier (2001), pp. 303-306.
363. *See* Christie (2011), p. 124.
364. *See* Alexy (2010a), p. 179.
365. Drawing a similar distinction, *see* Gautier (2001), p. 10 ('the exception subtracts from the rule, the limitation restricts its scope'); Drassinower (2009), p. 237 ('scope limitations define the nature of the copyright entitlements to the work', whereas exceptions 'preclude liability in respect of acts falling within copyright scope'); and Dreier (2015), p. 139 ('[w]here an exception is a – usually confined – *divergence* from the scope of a generally worded provision, then a "limitation" concerns the *definition* of the substance of the provision as such'). Thomas Dreier nonetheless argues that the restrictions laid down in Article 5 InfoSoc Directive are really limitations on the scope of the exclusive rights (p. 140).
366. Alexy (2010a), p. 178.

demonstrated by the rightholder, along with the other definitional elements of the right.

But this is not the end of this terminological disagreement. Even if the description of permitted uses as 'exceptions' is descriptively preferable, some scholars argue that, from a normative point of view, the term is undesirable. This is due to the commonly held view that the term implies the existence of a hierarchy of norms in copyright law (according to which exclusive rights are *above* exceptions), where such hierarchy simply does not exist: copyright law's gist is about achieving a fair balance between, on the one hand, the interest in protecting and rewarding authors and, on the other, the users' freedom and their interest in the access to literary and artistic works.[367] Because restrictions such as the ones provided in Article 5 InfoSoc Directive are key tools for achieving this balance, these scholars argue, it is a mistake to consider them as hierarchically inferior to exclusive rights. According to Christophe Geiger's well-known metaphor, the term 'exceptions' suggests that permitted uses are islands of freedom in a sea of exclusivity, whereas it is the exclusive rights that should be described as islands of exclusivity in a sea of freedom.[368] These scholars fear, moreover, that the term 'exceptions' conjures up the idea that provisions laying down permitted uses ought to be strictly interpreted. The idea would be that exceptions, ranking lower in the hierarchy vis-à-vis exclusive rights, are to be narrowly construed and should not apply beyond the cases that they plainly describe.

While I agree that no such hierarchy should be considered to exist and that provisions describing permitted uses need not be strictly interpreted,[369] I do not find the use of 'limitations' (instead of 'exceptions') to be material in that regard. These are, in essence, separate inquiries. Choosing the word 'limitations' to classify permitted uses, in and of itself, will not do much to counter the perception that these provisions should be subject to a rule of strict interpretation. Borrowing Annette Kur's words, 'prevailing attitudes and legal traditions can hardly be influenced, and even less be changed, by choice of terminology only'.[370] Instead of arguing in favour of a terminological choice that is at odds with the cues provided by the structure of legal texts, it would perhaps be more effective to dispute the conventionally accepted methodological practice that exceptions – to copyright or otherwise

367. *See, e.g.*, Hugenholtz (1997), p. 5; Ascensão (1999), p. 32; Guibault (2002), p. 16; Geiger (2004b), pp. 887-888; Hoeren (2006), p. 26; Geiger (2010), p. 525; Vicente (2011a), p. 260; and Karapapa (2012), pp. 9-10.

368. *See* Geiger (2004b), p. 882; Geiger (2010), p. 521; and Geiger & Schönherr (2014), fn. 6.

369. This is different from thinking that relying on broad interpretations of exceptions is a sustainable solution to the problem of adaptability of copyright law – *see infra* Chapter 4, section 5.2.2.1. For a descriptive account of the canon of strict interpretation of exceptions in EU copyright law, *see infra* 3.3.

370. Kur (2009), p. 292.

– are to be interpreted in a strict manner.[371] This interpretative canon is indeed subject to substantial criticism by methodologists and copyright scholars alike, who note that there is no valid reason to take it for granted and *a priori* exclude extensive readings of exceptions based on their purpose.[372] As shall be seen, the CJEU itself has been moving away from this practice.

In sum, qualifying permitted uses as 'exceptions' should not be taken as carrying a preference for a narrow interpretation or as admitting the existence of any hierarchy.[373] Under this view, *nomen non est omen.*[374] The qualification arises simply from the recognition that exceptions *and* limitations are two structurally and technically different categories and that permitted uses of protected works, as they stand in EU copyright law, are best described as exceptions. Both exceptions and limitations are of fundamental importance in copyright's overall design. But they are distinct notions and the terminology we employ should reflect the differences between them.

2.2 PERMITTED USES AS 'PRIVILEGES' (NOT 'RIGHTS')

A second source of terminological disagreement lies in the question of whether the entitlements conferred by copyright exceptions are 'users' rights' or something else that is different from a right.[375]

Some scholars claim that these provisions do grant true rights to users of copyright-protected works.[376] The majoritarian view, however, holds that,

---

371. *See infra* Chapter 4, section 5.2.2.1.
372. *See, e.g.*, Müller (1996), p. 274; Förster (2008), p. 107; Kur (2009), pp. 294-295; Leistner (2011), pp. 426-427; and Larenz (2012), pp. 502-503.
373. *See* Spoor (1998), p. 30, and Pereira (2008a), p. 540.
374. The Latin expression used in Hugenholtz (2000b), p. 500 (*nomen est omen*) is deliberately used in the negative form.
375. According to Burrell & Coleman (2005), p. 10, the two terms in dispute are 'exceptions' and 'users' rights': 'On the one hand, proponents of increased copyright protection tend to prefer the language of copyright "exceptions". ... On the other hand, pro-user commentators tend to prefer to style the "exceptions" as "users' rights" or as "rights of the public". This suggests that such provisions are to be treated on an equal footing with the rights given to copyright owners.' This description, I believe, is not entirely accurate, for the categories of 'exceptions' and 'rights' are not mutually exclusive. That is, a rule may be exceptional in relation to some other general rule and, simultaneously, confer a right. While the language of 'exceptions' refers to a rule in relation to another (general) rule, the language of 'rights' refers to the classification of the entitlements conferred by the rules. Thus, the question that is of interest in this section is whether the entitlements conferred upon users by Article 5-type exceptions are rights-properly-so-called.
376. *See* Karapapa (2012), p. 14 (regarding private copying). Other scholars, though not explicitly discussing the issue, use expressions like 'right of quotation' – *see, e.g.*, Ricketson (1998), p. 7; Leistner (2011), pp. 424-425; and Senftleben (2013c), p. 90. *See also*, from an American standpoint, Patterson (1992), p. 249 (defining fair use as 'the right to make a limited use of another's copyright'). The CJEU itself has referred to the Article 5 exceptions as rights – *see*, in particular, CJEU, *Ulmer*, paras 43-47; CJEU, *Funke Medien*, para. 70; CJEU, *Spiegel Online*, para. 54; and AG Opinion, *Painer*, para.

properly speaking, there is no such thing as a quotation right or a private copying right.[377] Whatever entitlements users enjoy, they are not comparable in nature with the prerogatives – rights proper – of authors or derivative rightholders.[378] Users' entitlements lack most of the general characteristics that are normally attributed to subjective rights: for instance, users do not have the power of control over the protected work, nor is there any available legal action to ensure the enforcement of the (supposed) right.[379]

But if these entitlements are not true rights, what are they?

In seeking an answer for this question, the work of Wesley Hohfeld, which has enjoyed significant influence in American theory, is particularly helpful.[380] In a seminal article published in 1913, Hohfeld addressed the existing confusion around the concept of 'right' and other fundamental legal concepts. In his own words, '[o]ne of the greatest hindrances to the clear understanding … of legal problems frequently arises from the express or tacit assumption that all legal relations may be reduced to "rights" and "duties"'.[381] Hohfeld points out that even renowned jurists tend to use the word 'right' loosely, 'to cover what in a given case may be a privilege, a power, or an immunity, rather than a right in the strictest sense'.[382] This, I submit, is precisely what is happening when scholars and courts claim that exceptions to copyright grant rights to users.

Because the term 'right' does not lend itself to a neat definition, Hohfeld proposed to analyse it in terms of its correlative – the duty.[383] According to Hohfeld, the term 'right' is commonly used to refer to one of the four distinct active entitlements – right (*stricto sensu*), privilege, power, and immunity – and the term 'duty' to the four distinct passive entitlements – duty (*stricto*

---

196. Noting this tendency of the CJEU, *see* ECS (2014), p. 5, and Rosati (2015), pp. 522-523. *See also* Supreme Court of Canada, *CHH Canadian*, para. 48, affirming that '[t]he fair dealing exception, like other exceptions in the Copyright Act, is a user's right'. Critically examining the use of the expression 'users' rights', with a focus on Canada, *see* Craig (2017). A different question, which will not be addressed here, is whether these rules should, *de lege ferenda*, be articulated as rights of users. For arguments in that direction, *see*, *e.g.*, Burrell & Coleman (2005), pp. 279-280, and Elkin-Koren (2017).

377. *See*, *e.g.*, Ginsburg (1997-1998), p. 3; Lucas (1998), p. 171; Sirinelli (1998), p. 136; Guibault (2002), p. 93; Goutal (2002), p. 11; Geiger (2004b), p. 886; and Walter & Lewinski (2010), p. 1022. *See also* Brussels Court of Appeals, *Test-Achats* and Paris Court of Appeals, *Mulholland Drive* both stating that the private copying provision does not constitute a right of users.

378. *See* Ballin (1956), p. 26.

379. *See* Guibault (2002), p. 93.

380. Other copyright scholars have found valuable help in Hohfeld's model, most notably Guibault (2002), pp. 90-99.

381. Hohfeld (1913), p. 28.

382. Hohfeld (1913), p. 30.

383. This is probably the greatest virtue of the Hohfeldian scheme. In Jeremy Waldron's words, 'it compels us to concentrate on the other side of the coin … . To think that R2 is a good sort of right to recognize in our society is to think that D2 is a good sort of duty to impose' – *see* Waldron (2006), p. 115.

sensu), no-right, liability, and disability.[384] In order to clarify the meaning of these entitlements, Hohfeld divided them into two groups of four pairs each: the group of jural correlatives and the group of jural opposites (*see* Table 2.1).[385]

Table 2.1 Hohfeld's Jural Correlatives and Jural Opposites

Jural correlatives	*Right*	*Privilege*	*Power*	*Immunity*
	Duty	No-right	Liability	Disability

Jural opposites	*Right*	*Privilege*	*Power*	*Immunity*
	No-right	Duty	Disability	Liability

Each concept is paired with its correlative, which is its inverse, and with its opposite, which is its negation. Put differently: if person A holds one entitlement (a right that person B stays off her land), some other person B will necessarily be under its correlative (a duty to stay off person A's land); and if person A holds one entitlement (a privilege to enter B's land), that same person A cannot hold its opposite (a duty to stay off B's land). Hohfeld's concept of 'right' (*stricto sensu*) corresponds to the concept of 'claim-right', with the clue to grasping its meaning lying in its correlative – the 'duty' (*stricto sensu*).

Having this conceptualisation in mind, let us examine the legal relations within the field of copyright that are of interest to us.

The copyright owner's right to exclude third parties from the use of the work has as its correlative the public's duty not to use the work without the owner's consent. This much is undisputed: users are certainly under a duty in relation to the holder of exclusive rights – a duty *inter alia* not to reproduce, communicate, or distribute the protected work. In case the duty is violated, the rightholder can take legal action against the duty-bearer in order to enforce her right not to be prevented from authorising or prohibiting the use of the work.

If this conceptualisation is correct, a user will only hold a right to use the work if the author is under a correlative duty not to prevent the user from using the work. In the case of most copyright exceptions, rightholders are under no duty whatsoever regarding users. Instead, the entitlement the user holds in the majority of cases is a *privilege*.

As Table 2.1 illustrates, the privilege is the opposite of the duty, and the correlative of the no-right. Therefore, if user C has a privilege, she has no duty to refrain from using the work, and rightholder D has no right to prohibit

384. *See* Hohfeld (1913), p. 30.
385. *See* Hohfeld (1913), p. 30.

user C from doing so. Just like '[t]he privilege of entering [the land] is the negation of a duty to stay off',[386] the privilege of using the protected work is the negation of a duty not to use it. And just like A's right that B stays off her land is the correlative of B's duty to stay off A's land, C's privilege of using D's work is the correlative of D's no-right that C does not use it.

The general rule is that users have the duty not to engage in the restricted uses, which correlates with the exclusive right of rightholders. Exceptionally, however, they are statutorily permitted to engage in certain uses without the rightholders' consent. In Hohfeldian terms, they hold the *privilege* to engage in those acts, which correlates with the authors' no-right that they do not. According to this scheme, therefore, the term 'privilege' is the most appropriate one to qualify the entitlements conferred by Article 5 InfoSoc Directive and equivalent national provisions (or at least the majority thereof).[387,388] This holds also for the Anglo-American copyright system and its exceptions.[389]

---

386. Hohfeld (1913), p. 32.
387. The qualifications proposed by scholars vary. Dreier (2010), p. 51, states that the entitlements conferred by Article 5 InfoSoc Directive 'are – at best – legal privileges devoid of any higher-ranking legal protection'. Gautier (2017), p. 354, argues that they are not mere tolerances, but 'prerogatives in the form of exceptions'. There are no significant differences between the qualification of Article 5-type entitlements as 'privileges' and the qualification as '*droits objectifs*' ('objective rights'), which has been subscribed by other scholars – *see* Guibault (2002), p. 98 (noting that 'the *privilege* in Hohfeld's theory would … be the practical equivalent of continental European law's notion of objective right'); Geiger (2004b), pp. 886-887 (arguing, however, that this objective right might be an embryonic form of a true subjective right); and Dusollier (2007), p. 486 (who prefers the expression '*règle de droit objectif*'). It seems, nonetheless, that the Hohfeldian term 'privilege' is better suited to qualify the prerogatives at stake than the expression '*droit objectif*', which makes use of the very term that ought to be avoided – 'right' ('*droit*').
388. Karapapa (2012), p. 14, argues that the CJEU judgment in *Padawan* may be read as developing 'a line of reasoning under which private copying should be treated as a user right'. According to this scholar, '[w]hat the Court has affirmed is that if users pay fair compensation in the final price of media and equipment to compensate for the possible harm they cause to the rightholders due to private copying, they are *rightly presumed* to use the levitated media and equipment to make such copies'. I see no reason to extract the conclusion that a true right is being granted from the existence of fair compensation. As Karapapa herself says, the compensation exists to make good the possible harm that acts of private copying cause to rightholders, not to compensate for the grant of a right to private copying. The expression 'rightly presumed', which Karapapa highlights, in no way bears that meaning either. It merely means that, when implementing a fair compensation scheme, Member States are allowed to rely on a presumption that consumers use the acquired media and equipment to make private copies, even though that may not be true in the case of every consumer.
389. *But see* Lucas (1998), pp. 172-173, arguing that the fact that the Anglo-American system is characterised by a closed framework of rights and an open framework of exceptions allows us to qualify the entitlements of users as 'rights'. Making similar qualifications, *see* Patterson (1992), p. 265, and Elkin-Koren (1997), p. 101. However, under the

The term 'privilege' may be understood as a synonym of 'liberty', meaning one's freedom from another's claim-right. Unlike rights, however, liberties cannot be remedied by legal action. As stated above, the fact that there is no specific legal action to react against the disturbance of Article 5-type entitlements is yet another reason why these prerogatives should not be qualified as 'rights'. The entitlements conferred by copyright exceptions cannot be invoked against the author *a priori*, but only *a posteriori*, as a means of defence in the context of an infringement action.[390]

Having said this, it is crucial to note that there are certain cases in which the entitlement users hold can be described as a 'right'.

One set of such cases relates to the tension between the protection of TPMs under Article 6 InfoSoc Directive and the permissibility of certain uses under Article 5. The implementation of TPMs by rightholders enables them to prevent consumers from engaging in uses that are permissible under the exceptions to exclusive rights, threatening the balance of interests that these exceptions are meant to promote. Article 6(4) InfoSoc Directive was the solution found by the EU legislator to address this tension, reading as follows:

> 4. Notwithstanding the legal protection provided for in paragraph 1, in the absence of voluntary measures taken by rightholders, including agreements between rightholders and other parties concerned, Member States shall take appropriate measures to ensure that rightholders make available to the beneficiary of an exception or limitation provided for in national law in accordance with Article 5(2)(a), (2)(c), (2)(d), (2)(e), (3)(a), (3)(b) or (3)(e) the means of benefiting from that exception or limitation, to the extent necessary to benefit from that exception or limitation and where that beneficiary has legal access to the protected work or subject-matter concerned.
>
> A Member State may also take such measures in respect of a beneficiary of an exception or limitation provided for in accordance with Article 5(2)(b), unless reproduction for private use has already been made possible by rightholders to the extent necessary to benefit from the exception or limitation concerned and in accordance with the provisions of Article 5(2)(b) and (5), without preventing rightholders from adopting adequate measures regarding the number of reproductions in accordance with these provisions.
>
> The technological measures applied voluntarily by rightholders, including those applied in implementation of voluntary agreements, and technological

conceptualisation described above, the fact that the framework of exceptions is based on a fair use-style clause does not affect the absence of the essential element of a right – the correlative duty.

390. Hence, in the context of infringement proceedings, the privilege may also be conceived of as an exemption from liability or, in Hohfeldian terms, as an immunity. As Hohfeld (1913), p. 56, admits, a privilege may in some cases comprise liability exemptions. Similarly, Ricketson (2003), p. 3, defines copyright exceptions as '[p]rovisions that allow for the giving of immunity … from infringement proceedings for particular kinds of use'. *See again* Brussels Court of First Instance, *Test-Achats*, stating that private copying is not a users' right, but a legally granted immunity against copyright liability.

measures applied in implementation of the measures taken by Member States, shall enjoy the legal protection provided for in paragraph 1.

The provisions of the first and second sub-paragraphs shall not apply to works or other subject matter made available to the public on agreed contractual terms in such a way that members of the public may access them from a place and at a time individually chosen by them.

When this Article is applied in the context of Directives 92/100/EEC and 96/9/EC, this paragraph shall apply mutatis mutandis.[391]

In the (strictly delimited) situations falling within the coverage of Article 6(4), users have a true right against the holders of exclusive rights over the works.[392] A number of conditions must be met for that to be the case: (i) the act that the user wants to engage in must be covered by one of the selected exceptions listed in Article 6(4);[393] (ii) rightholders must have implemented TPMs, but must have failed to adopt voluntary measures enabling users to benefit from one or more of those exceptions, like the provision of a key for decryption; (iii) the user must have had legal access to the work or other subject matter concerned;[394] and (iv) the work could not have been made available to the public on agreed contractual terms in such a way that members of the public could access it from a place and at a time individually chosen by them.[395]

Another set of cases where users seem to enjoy true rights can be found in the newly enacted Article 17 DSM Directive. After determining that, under certain circumstances, online content-sharing service providers may be obliged to disable access to or remove from their websites infringing works (paragraph 4), Article 17 stipulates that Member States shall ensure that users are able to rely on the quotation and parody exceptions when making

391. Note that the first, third and fifth sub-paragraphs of Article 6(4) apply in relation to other exceptions in the *acquis*, specifically the DSM exceptions on TDM, cross-border teaching and preservation of cultural heritage (Recital 7 and Article 7(2) DSM Directive), and the Marrakesh exception for the print-disabled (Article 3(4) Marrakesh Directive).

392. *See* Geiger (2004), pp. 886-887; Dusollier (2007), p. 485; and Vicente (2011a), pp. 260 and 265-267.

393. These are the exceptions covering reprography, reproduction by libraries and similar establishments, ephemeral recordings by broadcasting organizations, reproductions of broadcasts by social institutions, uses for teaching or scientific research, uses for the benefit of people with a disability, and uses for the purpose of public security, or administrative, parliamentary and judicial proceedings. In relation to the private copying exception, Member States are allowed, though not obliged, to implement such measures. As to all other unenumerated exceptions, Member States do not have that choice; they *cannot* take any measures to enable users to benefit from those exceptions.

394. If the user obtains the copy of the work from an illegal source, those measures will not be available to her and she will not hold any right *stricto sensu* against the holder of exclusive rights.

395. *See* Article 6(4)(4) InfoSoc Directive. According to Recital 53 InfoSoc Directive, the purpose of this exception to Article 6(4)(1) and (2) is to 'ensure a secure environment for the provision of interactive on-demand services'.

available UGC on those websites (paragraph 7) and provide that such services put in place an effective and expeditious complaint and redress mechanism that is available to users in the event of disputes over the disabling of access to, or the removal of, works uploaded by them (paragraph 9). In addition, users must be given access to a court or another relevant judicial authority to assert the exercise of the prerogatives conferred by these exceptions.[396] It may be argued, therefore, that, under this regime, users of online content-sharing platforms enjoy a *right* to upload parodies and to criticise, comment on, and quote others' content on such platforms. These platforms, in turn, could become liable vis-à-vis their users for breaching the duty of not preventing the availability of works covered by the mentioned exceptions.

In the circumscribed situations of Article 6(4) InfoSoc Directive and Article 17(7) and (9) DSM Directive, Member States are obliged to take appropriate measures to ensure that rightholders (in the former case) and platforms (in the latter case) make available to the beneficiaries of the relevant exceptions the means of actually exercising the prerogatives flowing therefrom.[397] In other words, rightholders and platforms are under a *duty* not to prevent users from making the uses described in those exceptions. Depending on the measures implemented by Member States, users may be entitled to set in motion certain proceedings to enforce the prerogatives in the exceptions.[398] Where this is so, the affected users will have at their disposal a truly offensive means of reaction, instead of a mere means of defence.

396. *See* Recital 70 DSM Directive.
397. The mandatory nature of these measures derives from the use of the word 'shall' in Article 6(4)(1) InfoSoc Directive and Article 17(7) and (9) DSM Directive. Contrariwise, the use of the term 'may' in Article 6(4)(2) makes clear that the measures are optional in relation to the private copying exception.
398. Article 6(4) InfoSoc Directive gives wide discretion to Member States by not specifying the measures that must be taken. Nonetheless, despite the diversity of solutions that have been adopted at the national level, most of them enable users to initiate some form of legal proceedings – either in court or via alternative dispute resolution mechanisms – against the rightholder. *See*, *e.g.*, Article 95b(2) German Copyright Act and Article XI.336(1) Belgian Economic Law Code. For an overview of possible measures, *see* Bechtold (2016), pp. 478-481. As to Article 17 DSM Directive, the nature of the means of reaction adopted by Member States will become clearer as the national implementation phase unfolds. At the time of writing, Germany had presented a proposal requiring platforms to create an internal complaint procedure (an obligation which may be fulfilled by resorting to a recognised external complaint body), while leaving unaffected the right to appeal to the courts.

3 EXCEPTIONS

3.1 EXCEPTIONS IN INTERNATIONAL LAW

There have always been significant disparities between national regimes of copyright exceptions. Whereas countries belonging to the continental *droit d'auteur* tradition usually provide for catalogues of precisely worded exceptions, common law countries tend to stipulate solutions with relatively vague formulations, such as the 'fair use' and 'fair dealing' clauses.[399]

This divergence is admissible in light of the fact that international copyright treaties largely failed to harmonise exceptions to copyright. Commentators attribute the scarce international harmonisation to the close connection that exists between a country's social and cultural individuality and its regime of copyright exceptions, with the resulting difficulty in achieving consensus and compromise on the matter.[400]

For this reason, only a limited number of exceptions have been included in the governing international treaties. The Berne Convention sets forth minimum standards in respect of a few specific exceptions or sets of exceptions: quotation (Article 10(1));[401] uses for teaching purposes (Article 10(2)); uses by the press (Articles 2*bis*(2) and 10*bis*(1) and (2)); ephemeral recordings made by broadcasting organisations (Article 11*bis*(3)); conditions on the broadcasting and related rights (Article 11*bis*(2)); and reservations and conditions on mechanical reproduction rights (Article 13).[402] Most of these exceptions leave member countries with discretion regarding their implementation in national law. As pointed out by Marie-Christine Janssens, '[c]opyright exceptions, apparently, were not the main concern of the drafters of the Convention'.[403]

Apart from the exceptions that are expressly mentioned in the text of the Berne Convention, scholars, stakeholders, and the international community in general have come to accept that there are other permitted uses that are to be implied from the so-called minor exceptions or minor reservations doctrine. This doctrine, which has been explicitly invoked in the Brussels (1948) and Stockholm (1967) diplomatic conferences for the revision of the

399. For a characterisation of US fair use and UK fair dealing in contrast with *droit d'auteur* exceptions, *see infra* Chapter 5, section 4.2.3.1.
400. *See* Eechoud et al. (2009), pp. 94-95.
401. The quotation exception provided in Article 10(1) is mandatory for all the Berne Union members, as made clear by the use of the term 'shall'. This exception is analysed in detail *infra* at Chapter 4, section 3.2.5.
402. The two latter ones are commonly read as allowing the Berne Union members to impose non-voluntary licences. Although neither provision explicitly uses that terminology, the reference to 'conditions' and 'reservations' on exclusive rights and to the fact that those conditions and reservations shall not be prejudicial to the rightholders' claim to an equitable remuneration are understood as referring to compensated exceptions. *See* Ricketson (2003), pp. 28-32.
403. Janssens (2009), p. 319.

Convention, allows member countries to provide for exceptions covering certain *de minimis* uses related to public performance and translation, such as uses for religious ceremonies and uses by military bands.[404]

In the field of related rights, the Rome Convention also allows signatories to impose exceptions on the conventional minimum rights. To that effect, Article 15(1) lists, in a less detailed fashion than Berne, exceptions for private use, reporting of current events, ephemeral reproductions by broadcasting organisations, and teaching or scientific research. These exceptions apply to all three categories of beneficiaries, that is, performers, phonogram producers, and broadcasting organisations. The list is not exhaustive, however. As Article 15(2) makes clear, national laws may impose on related rights the same exceptions they provide in connection with the protection of copyright over literary and artistic works, preventing holders of related rights from being treated more favourably than authors.[405]

Besides these itemised exceptions, the Berne Convention introduced a general provision on exceptions to the reproduction right. Article 9(2), introduced in the Stockholm Revision, establishes a three-step test (more on which in section 4.1. *infra*) to determine the admissibility of exceptions to the reproduction right. Under this test, member countries may permit the unauthorised reproduction of protected works (i) in certain special cases; (ii) provided that the reproduction does not conflict with a normal exploitation of the work; and (iii) does not unreasonably prejudice the legitimate interests of the author.

The major change that the international law on copyright exceptions has faced since 1967 has been the extension of the three-step test's scope.[406] The TRIPS Agreement (Article 13) and the WIPO Treaties (Article 10 WCT and Article 16 WPPT) incorporated Berne's three-step formula, extending its reach to *all* exclusive rights provided therein. As a result, the test's conditions became the general international criteria under which the introduction of exceptions to copyright and related rights in national laws ought to be assessed.

Two other developments are worth mentioning.

First, in 2013, the Marrakesh Treaty was concluded under the auspices of WIPO, creating a set of mandatory exceptions for the benefit of the blind, visually impaired, and otherwise print-disabled.

Second, the project of adopting a treaty on copyright exceptions for libraries and archives has been under discussion at WIPO since 2008, but negotiations have been stalling for years. More recently, ahead of the 37th

404. *See* Ricketson (2003), pp. 33-39, and WTO, *US-Copyright*, paras 6.33 et seq. It should be added that the Berne Appendix contains a series of non-voluntary licences in relation to the translation and reproduction of protected works that may be invoked by developing countries.
405. *See* WIPO (1981), pp. 58-59.
406. *See* Eechoud et al. (2009), p. 97, contrasting the international stagnation in the field of exceptions with the drastic extension in the scope of exclusive rights.

session of WIPO's Standing Committee on Copyright and Related Rights in November 2018, civil society organisations have advanced a proposal for a Treaty on Copyright Exceptions and Limitations on Education and Research Activities.[407] The proponents' expectation is that the treaty will be regarded as a model for future text-based work by the Committee. Whether any action will be taken on the basis of this proposal remains to be seen.

3.2 EXCEPTIONS IN THE EU *ACQUIS*

In the EU *acquis communautaire*, exceptions to copyright and related rights are currently dealt with in seven different directives – Software, Database, Rental and Lending, InfoSoc, Orphan Works, Marrakesh, and DSM.

The lion's share of exceptions to the rights of reproduction and communication to the public and the central aspects of the general regime are provided in the InfoSoc Directive. Accordingly, this section is divided by reference to it: the EU landscape of exceptions prior to the adoption of InfoSoc – including the exceptions in the Software, Database and Rental and Lending Directives, as well as the preparatory works leading up to InfoSoc – is briefly described in 3.2.1; the catalogue of exceptions in Article 5 InfoSoc Directive is depicted in 3.2.2; and, finally, the developments that have taken place post-InfoSoc – specifically the exceptions in the Orphan Works, Marrakesh, and DSM Directives – are analysed in 3.2.3.

3.2.1 Exceptions Pre-InfoSoc

Before InfoSoc, exceptions had been harmonised only for specific categories of subject matter – software and databases – and for related rights.[408]

---

407. The text of the proposed treaty is available at http://infojustice.org/wp-content/uploads/2018/11/tera11152018.pdf. Also, the Max Planck Institute for Innovation and Competition is currently coordinating a group of copyright experts that is working on a legal instrument containing a set of permitted uses that States should be obliged to implement in their national laws, which is designed to become an international treaty. Describing the project and its purposes, *see* Hilty & Moscon (2018).

408. It is important to stress once again that the exceptions found in previous directives are left intact by InfoSoc (Article 1(2) InfoSoc Directive). Yet, there are some specificities in relation to the Rental and Lending Directive. First, as explained in the main text, Article 10(2) thereof entails that the exceptions provided in the InfoSoc Directive may be implemented with regard to related rights too. Be that as it may, it seems that the InfoSoc exceptions apply altogether to the reproduction right of holders of related rights, since the reproduction right originally granted upon these rightholders by the Rental and Lending Directive was later replaced by the one in Article 2 InfoSoc Directive (*see supra* Chapter 1, section 3.2). Naturally, therefore, the exceptions that apply to Article 2 extend to the reproduction right of related rightholders. In scholarship, it is commonly accepted that Article 5 InfoSoc Directive applies to related rights as well, despite the overlap with the list of the Rental and Lending Directive – *see*, *e.g.*, Eechoud et al. (2009), p. 100; Janssens (2009), fn. 40; and Bechtold (2016), p. 370.

The Software Directive provides exceptions for the lawful acquirer of the computer program (Article 5(1)), for the making of back-up copies (Article 5(2)), for the observation, study, or testing the functioning of the program (Article 5(3)), and for decompilation (Article 6).

The Database Directive lists both mandatory and optional exceptions in relation to uses of copyright-protected databases (Article 6) and optional exceptions for databases protected by the *sui generis* right (Article 9), for purposes like private copying, illustration for teaching or research, and public security.

As to the Rental and Lending Directive, Article 10(1) (which closely tracks Article 15 Rome Convention) contains a catalogue of optional exceptions to the related rights harmonised therein, in respect of, e.g., private use, reporting of current events, and teaching or research. Furthermore, Article 10(2) expressly allows Member States to provide for the same kind of exceptions in respect of related rights as they provide to authors.[409]

In the 1995 Green Paper, which eventually led to the adoption of the InfoSoc Directive, the issue of exceptions was not among the areas identified by the Commission as requiring future harmonisation. Instead, only an *en passant* reference to exceptions to the reproduction right was made. Recognising that Member States had enacted a sheer number of different exceptions under Article 9(2) Berne Convention, the Commission stated that '[c]areful consideration' was needed in deciding which of those exceptions could remain in place.[410]

It did not take long for the Commission to change its mind, however. In the 1996 Follow-Up, it openly admitted that '[t]he traditional reproduction right and the legitimate exceptions to it ... need to be reassessed and adapted to the new environment'.[411] That was so due to the significant divergences between the national regimes of copyright exceptions: 'some of the national legislative measures provide for many copyright privileges, others for only minimal exceptions, and still others for none'.[412] This fragmented scenario created substantial legal uncertainty and negatively affected the functioning of the internal market for copyright-protected works, rendering the need for harmonisation across the EU palpable.[413] The need for 'careful consideration' was thus replaced by a more assertive statement: '[h]armonising the limitations/exceptions to the reproduction right will be of utmost importance'.[414] Regarding the exceptions to the right of communication to the public, the Commission admitted that harmonisation was also necessary and

---

409. In addition, Article 6(1) Rental and Lending Directive stipulates that Member States may derogate from the exclusive right of public lending granted under Article 1 thereof, as long as authors obtain a remuneration for such lending.
410. 1995 Green Paper, p. 52.
411. 1996 Follow-Up, p. 9.
412. 1996 Follow-Up, pp. 9-10.
413. *See* 1996 Follow-Up, p. 10. *See also* Recital 31 InfoSoc Directive.
414. 1996 Follow-Up, p. 11.

'could follow the line taken for the harmonisation of the reproduction right'.[415]

Accordingly, the 1997 InfoSoc Proposal ended up including a provision on exceptions to the rights of reproduction and communication to the public. As previously mentioned, the controversial character of the issue of exceptions is said to be one of the main reasons behind the delay in the adoption of the InfoSoc Directive and in its national implementation.[416,417] The change in the number of exceptions from the Proposal to the final 2001 text echoes the controversy. Throughout the legislative process, the number of exceptions and the detail in their definition increased considerably.[418]

The Proposal provided for a list of nine harmonised exceptions: one mandatory exception (for temporary reproductions), three optional exceptions to the right of reproduction (for acts of reprography; reproductions on audio, visual or audiovisual recording media; and reproductions made by publicly accessible establishments), and five optional exceptions to the rights of reproduction and communication to the public (for teaching and scientific research; disabled persons; reporting of current events; quotation; and public security and administrative or judicial procedures).[419] The only exception that the distribution right admitted was that of exhaustion laid down in Article 4(2) InfoSoc Proposal.

3.2.2 Exceptions in InfoSoc

In contrast to the proposal, the text that was finally adopted contains a long, detailed list of no less than twenty-one exceptions to the rights harmonised therein and in relation to all categories of subject matter (with the exclusion of software and databases). These exceptions are based either on the exceptions of the Berne Convention or on the exceptions that pre-existed in national copyright laws.[420] In laying down these exceptions, the InfoSoc legislator aimed simultaneously at respecting the 'different legal traditions in Member States' and ensuring 'a functioning internal market'.[421]

Article 5(1) sets forth the only mandatory exception in the InfoSoc Directive, privileging temporary acts of reproduction, with the purpose of

415. 1996 Follow-Up, p. 14.
416. *See* Gaubiac (2002), p. 17; Lehmann (2003), p. 526; Guibault et al. (2007), p. 21; Eechoud et al. (2009), pp. 98-99; and Guibault (2010), p. 55.
417. Pursuant to Article 13 InfoSoc Directive, Member States had to enact the legislation necessary to comply with the Directive before 22 December 2002. France, the last Member State to finish the implementation, only did so on 1 August 2006.
418. Noting this change, *see* AG Opinion, *VG Wort*, fn. 34.
419. *See* Article 5 InfoSoc Proposal.
420. *See* Eechoud et al. (2009), p. 99.
421. Recital 32 InfoSoc Directive.

protecting ISPs and preserving the proper operation of information technologies in general.[422] Whereas in Article 7(2) WCT Proposal the exception was devised as optional for Contracting States (the provision on reproduction was eventually dropped), the InfoSoc legislator decided to make it mandatory.[423] Under this provision, temporary acts of reproduction, which are transient or incidental and an integral and essential part of a technological process and whose sole purpose is to enable: (a) a transmission in a network between third parties by an intermediary or (b) a lawful use of a work, and which have no independent economic significance, are treated as non-infringing.[424]

All the remaining InfoSoc exceptions are optional,[425] meaning that Member States are 'free to reflect in their legislation as many or as few of them as they wish'.[426] By making use of the option of implementing a certain

422. *See* Recital 33 InfoSoc Directive, clarifying that the exception should be understood as covering acts like browsing and caching.
423. The exemption for temporary reproductions could have been formulated as an exception or as a definitional limit to the exclusive right of reproduction. As Efroni (2011), p. 218, suggests, this latter option could have been followed in negative terms (e.g., 'the reproduction right shall not apply to acts of temporary reproduction') or via a positive formulation that excluded temporary copies (e.g., 'the reproduction right shall only apply to acts of permanent reproduction'). Instead of excluding these copies from the *prima facie* scope of the right in Article 2 InfoSoc Directive, the EU legislator opted to include them therein, while subtracting them from its definitive scope via an exception. What may seem, from a practical point of view, a largely indifferent choice, has relevant practical consequences related to the burden of proof, as seen *supra* (section 2.1). Ascensão (2006), p. 93, posits that the reason why temporary reproductions were excluded via an exception was that, this way, they could be subject to other narrowing conditions and to the discipline of the three-step test in Article 5(5).
424. The meaning of each condition has been elucidated in a series of decisions: CJEU, *Infopaq I*, paras 54-55; CJEU, *Infopaq II*, para. 25-26; CJEU, *Premier League*, para. 161; CJEU, *PRCA*, para. 22; and CJEU, *Filmspeler*, paras 60-61. For a more detailed examination of the exception's scope, *see infra* Chapter 4, section 3.2.1.
425. Optional exceptions are not exclusive of the InfoSoc Directive. As mentioned, the Database Directive sets forth optional exceptions both in relation to copyright (four exceptions in Article 6(2)) and the *sui generis* right (three exceptions in Article 9). Note that Article 6(2)(d) gives significant freedom to Member States, by allowing them to provide for exceptions that are traditionally authorised under national law. The question arises whether this provision should be read restrictively – as meaning that it only allows the provision of exceptions that already applied to *databases* – or less so – as meaning that it extends to uses generally permitted under copyright law. On that question, siding with the second reading, *see* Triaille et al. (2013), pp. 246-247. Also, the Rental and Lending Directive, besides allowing Member States to derogate from the exclusive right of public lending (Article 6), provides in Article 10 a list of optional exceptions to the copyright rights harmonised therein, permitting Member States to apply such exceptions to related rights.
426. Martin-Prat (2014), p. 41. In *Pelham*, however, AG Szpunar made a ground-breaking (if rather discreet) statement: since some of the Article 5 exceptions reflect the balance that the EU legislator sought to strike between copyright and various fundamental rights, '[f]ailing to provide for certain exceptions in domestic law could therefore be incompatible with the Charter' (para. 77). The AG did not identify the exceptions that merited such status. The judges, instead, adopted the ambiguous statement that Article

exception, Member States will ultimately afford the rights of reproduction and communication to the public less protection than if they had not.[427] Nonetheless, as shall be seen, this freedom of choosing whether to implement a certain exception does not necessarily entail a wide margin of freedom in determining its scope.[428] In addition, the Court has understood key concepts of Article 5 InfoSoc Directive to be autonomous concepts of EU law, which must be interpreted uniformly throughout the Union.[429] Be that as it may, the fact remains that all exceptions but one are optional for Member States to implement into their own legal orders. This policy option has deserved substantial scholarly criticism since the early stages of InfoSoc, for its end result was likely to be a fragmented scenario of copyright exceptions, where the number of implemented exceptions would vary significantly from country to country.[430]

Moving on, Article 5(2) provides five exceptions to the right of reproduction: the reprography exception;[431] the private copying exception;[432] the exception for specific acts of reproduction by cultural heritage institutions;[433] the exception for ephemeral recordings made by broadcasting organisations;[434] and the exception for reproductions of broadcasts made by social institutions.[435]

---

5 exceptions 'may, or even must, be transposed by the Member States' – CJEU, *Funke Medien*, para. 58; CJEU, *Pelham*, para. 60; and CJEU, *Spiegel Online*, para. 43. However, the segment 'or even must' could well refer to the mandatory temporary reproduction exception.

427. *See* CJEU, *Opinion 3/15 – Marrakesh Treaty*, para. 121.
428. *See infra* Chapter 4, section 5.1.1.
429. *See infra* Chapter 4, section 5.1.2.
430. *See infra* Chapter 4, section 2.3 (with extensive references).
431. Article 5(2)(a) exempts 'reproductions on paper or any similar medium, effected by the use of any kind of photographic technique or by some other process having similar effects, with the exception of sheet music, provided that the rightholders receive fair compensation'.
432. Article 5(2)(b) covers 'reproductions on any medium made by a natural person for private use and for ends that are neither directly nor indirectly commercial, on condition that the rightholders receive fair compensation which takes account of the application or non-application of technological measures referred to in Article 6 to the work or subject-matter concerned'. *See infra* Chapter 4, section 3.2.2.
433. Article 5(2)(c) privileges 'specific acts of reproduction made by publicly accessible libraries, educational establishments or museums, or by archives, which are not for direct or indirect economic or commercial advantage'. This is without prejudice to the exceptions provided in the DSM Directive (Article 24(2)(a) DSM Directive), namely those in Articles 3, 6 and 8(2) thereof.
434. Article 5(2)(d) refers to 'ephemeral recordings of works made by broadcasting organisations by means of their own facilities and for their own broadcasts' and adds that 'the preservation of these recordings in official archives may, on the grounds of their exceptional documentary character, be permitted'.
435. Article 5(2)(e) applies to 'reproductions of broadcasts made by social institutions pursuing non-commercial purposes, such as hospitals or prisons, on condition that the rightholders receive fair compensation'.

Article 5(3) lists fifteen other exceptions concerning both reproduction and communication to the public. These exceptions cover the following uses: teaching and scientific research;[436] use by people with disabilities;[437] news reporting;[438] quotation;[439] use for public security purposes and other public proceedings;[440] political speeches;[441] use during religious or official celebrations;[442] use of works made to be located in public places;[443] incidental inclusion of a work in other material;[444] advertising the public exhibition or sale of artistic works;[445] parody;[446] demonstration or repair of

436. Article 5(3)(a) exempts the 'use for the sole purpose of illustration for teaching or scientific research, as long as the source, including the author's name, is indicated, unless this turns out to be impossible and to the extent justified by the non-commercial purpose to be achieved'. This is without prejudice to the teaching exception provided in the DSM Directive (Article 24(2)(b) DSM Directive). *See infra* Chapter 4, section 3.2.3.
437. Originally, Article 5(3)(b) read as follows: 'uses, for the benefit of people with a disability, which are directly related to the disability and of a non-commercial nature, to the extent required by the specific disability'. Following the adoption of the Marrakesh Directive, the consolidated version of InfoSoc now clarifies that it does not affect the obligations of Member States under the said Directive.
438. Article 5(3)(c) comprises two types of uses: (i) 'reproduction by the press, communication to the public or making available of published articles on current economic, political or religious topics or of broadcast works or other subject-matter of the same character, in cases where such use is not expressly reserved, and as long as the source, including the author's name, is indicated' and (ii) 'use of works or other subject-matter in connection with the reporting of current events, to the extent justified by the informatory purpose and as long as the source, including the author's name, is indicated, unless this turns out to be impossible'.
439. The quotation exception in Article 5(3)(d) privileges 'quotations for purposes such as criticism or review, provided that they relate to a work or other subject-matter which has already been lawfully made available to the public, that, unless this turns out to be impossible, the source, including the author's name, is indicated, and that their use is in accordance with fair practice, and to the extent required by the specific purpose'. *See infra* Chapter 4, section 3.2.5.
440. Article 5(3)(e) refers to 'use for the purposes of public security or to ensure the proper performance or reporting of administrative, parliamentary or judicial proceedings'.
441. Article 5(3)(f) encompasses the 'use of political speeches as well as extracts of public lectures or similar works or subject-matter to the extent justified by the informatory purpose and provided that the source, including the author's name, is indicated, except where this turns out to be impossible'.
442. Article 5(3)(g) exempts the 'use during religious celebrations or official celebrations organised by a public authority'.
443. The so-called freedom of panorama exception within Article 5(3)(h) refers to the 'use of works, such as works of architecture or sculpture, made to be located permanently in public places'.
444. Article 5(3)(i) excludes the 'incidental inclusion of a work or other subject-matter in other material'.
445. Article 5(3)(j) covers the 'use for the purpose of advertising the public exhibition or sale of artistic works, to the extent necessary to promote the event, excluding any other commercial use'.
446. Article 5(3)(k) applies to the 'use for the purpose of caricature, parody or pastiche'. *See infra* Chapter 4, section 3.2.4.

equipment;[447] building reconstruction;[448] research or private study via dedicated terminals in libraries;[449] and existing analogue uses of minor importance.[450]

Article 5(4) enables Member States to extend the reproduction exceptions in the foregoing paragraphs to the right of distribution, to the extent justified by the purpose of the privileged reproduction. It is only natural that a Member State which allows users, for instance, to quote third-party works similarly permits the unauthorised distribution of the works containing those quotations. Besides quotation, other exceptions to the reproduction right may reasonably be extended to distribution, such as the ones for scientific research, news reporting, and parody.

The catalogue in Article 5(1)-(4) is an exhaustive one, despite the absence of an international obligation in that regard. The exhaustiveness of the catalogue means, in essence, that no other exceptions can be applied to the rights harmonised by the InfoSoc Directive.[451] This is confirmed by Recital 32, which states that the Directive 'provides for an exhaustive enumeration of exceptions and limitations to the reproduction right and the right of communication to the public',[452] and by the case law of the CJEU.[453] While all exceptions enumerated in Article 5 InfoSoc Directive, optional and mandatory alike, are subject to the control of the three-step test, this provision is not to be read as allowing the expansion of the catalogue. In fact,

---

447. Article 5(3)(l) exempts uses 'in connection with the demonstration or repair of equipment'.
448. Article 5(3)(m) allows the 'use of an artistic work in the form of a building or a drawing or plan of a building for the purposes of reconstructing the building'.
449. Article 5(3)(n) is connected to Article 5(2)(c), permitting the 'use by communication or making available, for the purpose of research or private study, to individual members of the public by dedicated terminals on the premises of establishments referred to in paragraph 2(c) of works and other subject-matter not subject to purchase or licensing terms which are contained in their collections'.
450. Article 5(3)(o) allows Member States to exempt the 'use in certain other cases of minor importance where exceptions or limitations already exist under national law, provided that they only concern analogue uses and do not affect the free circulation of goods and services within the Community, without prejudice to the other exceptions and limitations contained in this Article'. Commonly known as the 'grandfather clause', this provision is more aptly qualified as a permission to preserve other exceptions, rather than an exception *proprio sensu*. In fact, what sub-paragraph (o) does is to allow Member States to retain existing exceptions in their national catalogues, provided they meet certain requirements. It does not, as such, describe a specific type of behaviour that may be exempted. On the grandfather clause in more detail, *see infra* Chapter 4, section 2.2.
451. Some commentators argue that the exhaustive character of the list is not unequivocal due to the presence of the grandfather clause therein – *see* Eechoud et al. (2009), p. 103. Still, the scope of exceptions allowed under that clause is very limited and, at any rate, irrelevant in the digital environment. A thorougher exploration of the implications of exhaustiveness is provided in Chapter 4 (section 2.1).
452. *See also* Explanatory Memorandum to InfoSoc Proposal, p. 28, stating that 'Article 5 sets out a list of permitted exceptions, which is exhaustive. Member States will not be allowed to provide for any exceptions other than those enumerated.'

the CJEU has clarified that the three-step test in Article 5(5) cannot be relied on by Member States to establish exceptions beyond the listed ones.[454]

3.2.3 Exceptions Post-InfoSoc

Since InfoSoc, three other Directives have added exceptions to the copyright *acquis*: the Orphan Works Directive, the Marrakesh Directive, and the DSM Directive. All the post-InfoSoc exceptions cut out specific situations from, among others, the right of communication to the public and/or the right of reproduction laid down respectively in Articles 2 and 3 InfoSoc Directive. As such, they add up to the exceptions enumerated in Article 5, which had originally set forth the totality of admissible exceptions to these rights, increasing the complexity of the *acquis*.

In 2012, in light of advances in technologies for large-scale digitisation of print materials and for search and indexing,[455] the EU passed the Orphan Works Directive, which provides for a mandatory exception to the InfoSoc rights of reproduction and making available to the public. Article 6(1)-(2) allows publicly accessible libraries, educational establishments, museums, archives, film or audio heritage institutions, and public-service broadcasting organisations established in the EU Member States to make orphan works available to the public and reproduce them for purposes of digitisation, making available, indexing, cataloguing, preservation, or restoration, provided that such use fulfils their public interest missions.[456]

In 2017, the Marrakesh Directive, along with its homonymous Regulation, operated the implementation of the Marrakesh Treaty into EU law.[457] With a view to ensuring that the corresponding measures would be applied consistently throughout the internal market, the Directive introduced, for the benefit of the print-disabled, a mandatory exception to the harmonised rights that are relevant for the uses and works covered by the Treaty, among which

453. *See* CJEU, *Soulier & Doke*, paras 26 and 34; CJEU, *ITV Broadcasting II*, paras 24-27; CJEU, *Renckhoff*, para. 16; CJEU, *Funke Medien*, paras 56 and 62; CJEU, *Pelham*, paras 58 and 63; CJEU, *Spiegel Online*, paras 41 and 47; and CJEU, *Spedidam*, para. 38. *See also* CJEU, *OSA*, para. 38.

454. *See* CJEU, *OSA*, para. 40.

455. *See* Recital 1 Orphan Works Directive.

456. According to Article 2(1) Orphan Works Directive, '[a] work or a phonogram shall be considered an orphan work if none of the rightholders in that work or phonogram is identified or, even if one or more of them is identified, none is located despite a diligent search for the rightholders having been carried out and recorded in accordance with Article 3'.

457. Criticising the regulatory approach followed by the EU of providing for two different legislative instruments for the implementation of the Marrakesh Treaty, *see* Hilty et al. (2017), pp. 52-53.

the InfoSoc rights of reproduction and communication to the public.[458] Postulated in Article 3(1), the exception covers any act necessary for: (a) a beneficiary person, or a person acting on their behalf, to make an accessible format copy of a work or other subject matter to which the beneficiary person has lawful access for the exclusive use of the beneficiary person; and (b) an authorised entity to make an accessible format copy of a work or other subject matter to which it has lawful access, or to communicate, make available, distribute, or lend an accessible format copy to a beneficiary person or another authorised entity on a non-profit basis for the purpose of exclusive use by a beneficiary person.[459]

In 2019, the DSM Directive introduced a number of rules to adapt certain exceptions to digital and cross-border environments.[460] The final text of the Directive contains five mandatory exceptions within the fields of research, innovation, education, and preservation of cultural heritage.[461,462] The scope of some of these exceptions is partially overlapping with that of previous exceptions in the InfoSoc and Database Directives. Having this in mind, the DSM legislator expressly provided that, for the uses or fields covered by DSM exceptions, Member States may adopt or maintain in force

---

458. *See* Recital 6 Marrakesh Directive. The recital clarifies that 'as the scope of the exceptions or limitations required by the Marrakesh Treaty also includes works in audio form, like audiobooks, the mandatory exception provided for under this Directive should also apply to related rights'.

459. Article 4 of the Directive further obliges Member States to ensure that an authorised entity established in their territory may carry out the acts referred to in Article 3(1)(b) for a beneficiary person or another authorised entity established in any Member State. Member States shall also ensure that a beneficiary person or an authorised entity established in their territory may obtain or may have access to an accessible format copy from an authorised entity established in any Member State. These provisions are supplemented by Articles 3 and 4 Marrakesh Regulation, which permit the cross-border exchange of accessible format copies.

460. *See* Recital 3 DSM Directive.

461. Furthermore, Recital 70 DSM Directive states that the parody and quotation exceptions enshrined in the InfoSoc Directive should be made mandatory. However, this obligation does not seem to refer to *all* uses covered by such exceptions. Rather, as suggested by preceding segments in the recital and by Article 17(7) DSM Directive, it appears to require simply that Member States ensure that users are allowed to make uploads of content for purposes of quotation, criticism, review, caricature, parody and pastiche onto online content-sharing platforms. Opposing the grant of mandatory status to the DSM exceptions, *see* Lewinski (2018), pp. 136-139 (writing before the Directive's adoption).

462. The reform of other exceptions was contemplated during the legislative process. In 2016, the European Commission launched a public consultation on, *inter alia*, the possibility of making the freedom of panorama exception mandatory – *see* 2016 Public Consultation. Despite the fact that the majority of respondents said that the introduction of an exception covering both commercial and non-commercial uses of works made to be located permanently in public places would have a strong positive impact, the DSM package did not address the issue – *see* Report Public Consultation 2016, p. 22. The introduction of an exception for UGC was also discussed in legislative committees, but the proposal did not make it through to the Directive's text – *see* Geiger et al. (2018c), fn. 7.

broader provisions, as long as they are compatible with the existing exceptions in those two instruments (Article 25).

The Directive contains two TDM exceptions.[463] Article 3 sets forth an exception covering acts of TDM for purposes of scientific research carried out by research organisations and cultural heritage institutions,[464] regarding works or subject matter to which they have lawful access. Additionally, in order to foster legal certainty and to encourage innovation in other sectors, Article 4 contains a general TDM exception for reproductions and extractions of lawfully accessible works and other subject matter, insofar as rightholders have not reserved those rights in an appropriate manner, for instance through the use of machine-readable means, like metadata or terms and conditions of a website or service.[465]

---

463. TDM is a research technique that involves the automated processing of vast amounts of text and data (such as articles, websites and databases), with a view to uncovering useful relationships, connections, patterns and trends in that content – *see* Article 2(2) DSM Directive. TDM offers extraordinary possibilities to researchers, by allowing the extraction of valuable information from enormous amounts of content at a speed that only automated processes can cope with. In one or more of its multiple phases, the process requires the making of copies of the relevant subject matter, which may be copyright-protected, thus triggering the right of reproduction harmonised by Article 2 InfoSoc Directive.
464. The definitions of 'research organisations' and 'cultural heritage institutions' can be found in Article 2(1) and (3) and in Recitals 12 and 13 DSM Directive.
465. Before DSM, doubts existed as to whether TDM could be covered by pre-existing exceptions in the *acquis*, namely the exception for temporary reproductions in Article 5(1) InfoSoc Directive and the teaching and research exception in Article 5(3)(a) InfoSoc Directive. The uncertainty was due to the fact that neither of these provisions adequately covered TDM activities. For one thing, TDM may involve reproductions that are not transient and that may be considered to have an independent economic significance, thereby excluding the applicability of the former provision. For another, the teaching and research exception, besides being optional and not featuring in all national catalogues (creating uncertainty for cross-border TDM), is limited to scientific research for non-commercial purposes. Discussing whether TDM was covered by any exceptions in the EU *acquis* prior to the DSM reform, *see* Triaille (2014), p. 116 (proposing that a new specific data analysis exception be added); Stamatoudi (2016), p. 281 (concluding that 'they all present obstacles to TDM'); and Geiger et al. (2018a), pp. 8-12 (finding that 'existing exceptions and limitations might not offer a stable legal framework to safely engage in TDM research projects and invest considerable resources'). *See also* Montagnani & Aime (2017). Nonetheless, prior to DSM, Member States have introduced specific TDM exceptions in their national copyright laws, relying for that purpose on Article 5(3)(a) InfoSoc Directive – *see infra* Chapter 4, section 2.1. In the DSM Proposal, the European Commission put forward a single mandatory exception covering TDM activities carried out by research organisations for purposes of scientific research. The proposal was welcomed with mixed reactions: while the policy choice of exempting TDM deserved approval, the exception's narrow scope, which limited the set of beneficiaries to non-commercial research organisations (thus excluding individual researchers, start-ups, government services, journalists, and others), was severely criticised – *see, e.g.*, ECS (2017), p. 5; Hilty & Richter (2017), p. 28; and Geiger et al. (2018b) and (2018c), p. 8.

Article 5 provides an exception for uses of works and other subject matter in digital and cross-border teaching activities, with the goal of increasing legal certainty in relation to cases where teaching is provided online and at a distance.[466] Whereas this exception complements the teaching and research exception in the InfoSoc Directive, its coverage is limited to teaching.[467]

Article 6 allows cultural heritage institutions to make copies of any works or other subject matter that are permanently in their collections, in any format or medium, for purposes of and to the extent necessary for their preservation (e.g., to address technological obsolescence or the degradation of original media). Copies made for any other purposes besides preservation are not covered and therefore require the authorisation of rightholders, unless they are exempted by different exceptions in the *acquis*, specifically the exception for 'specific acts of reproduction' in Article 5(2)(c) InfoSoc Directive.[468]

Finally, Article 8(2)-(3) contains an exception enabling cultural heritage institutions to make available out-of-commerce works subject to certain conditions.[469] This, however, is a fallback exception, in the sense that it only applies insofar as the conditions for collective management of out-of-commerce works are not met, for instance, where there is no practice of collective management of rights for a certain type of work or where the relevant CMO is not sufficiently representative.[470]

Having come this far, it is now time to take a broader look at the landscape of exceptions to the InfoSoc rights of reproduction and communication to the public. Table 2.2 summarises the picture that has been sketched in the previous sections.

466. *See* Recital 19 DSM Directive.
467. Exploring these two exceptions in further detail, *see infra* Chapter 4, section 3.2.3.
468. *See* Recital 27 DSM Directive. On the relationship between these exceptions, *see* Geiger et al. (2018c), pp. 12-13.
469. According to Article 8(5) DSM Directive, 'a work or other subject matter shall be deemed to be out of commerce when it can be presumed in good faith that the whole work or other subject matter is not available to the public through customary channels of commerce, after a reasonable effort has been made to determine whether it is available to the public'.
470. *See* Recital 32 DSM Directive.

Table 2.2 Exceptions to the InfoSoc Rights of Reproduction and Communication to the Public in EU Copyright Law

InfoSoc Rights	*Exception*	*Character*	*Source*
Reproduction	Temporary reproduction	Mandatory	Article 5(1) InfoSoc
	Reprography	Optional	Article 5(2)(a) InfoSoc
	Private copying	Optional	Article 5(2)(b) InfoSoc
	Specific acts of reproduction by cultural heritage institutions	Optional	Article 5(2)(c) InfoSoc
	Ephemeral recordings by broadcasting organisations	Optional	Article 5(2)(d) InfoSoc
	Reproductions of broadcasts made by social institutions	Optional	Article 5(2)(e) InfoSoc
	TDM for scientific research	Mandatory	Article 3 DSM
	TDM	Mandatory	Article 4 DSM
	Preservation of cultural heritage	Mandatory	Article 6 DSM
Reproduction and Communication to the Public	Teaching and scientific research	Optional	Article 5(3)(a) InfoSoc
	Use by people with disabilities	Optional	Article 5(3)(b) InfoSoc
	News reporting	Optional	Article 5(3)(c) InfoSoc
	Quotation	Optional (but Berne mandatory)	Article 5(3)(d) InfoSoc
	Use for public security purposes and other public proceedings	Optional	Article 5(3)(e) InfoSoc
	Political speeches	Optional	Article 5(3)(f) InfoSoc
	Religious or official celebrations	Optional	Article 5(3)(g) InfoSoc

InfoSoc Rights	*Exception*	*Character*	*Source*
	Freedom of panorama	Optional	Article 5(3)(h) InfoSoc
	Incidental inclusion	Optional	Article 5(3)(i) InfoSoc
	Advertising public exhibition or sale of artistic works	Optional	Article 5(3)(j) InfoSoc
	Parody	Optional	Article 5(3)(k) InfoSoc
	Demonstration or repair of equipment	Optional	Article 5(3)(l) InfoSoc
	Building reconstruction	Optional	Article 5(3)(m) InfoSoc
	Research or private study via dedicated terminals in libraries	Optional	Article 5(3)(n) InfoSoc
	Existing analogue uses of minor importance	Optional	Article 5(3)(o) InfoSoc
	Orphan works	Mandatory	Article 6 Orphan Works
	Accessible format copies for print-disabled people	Mandatory	Article 3 Marrakesh
	Digital teaching	Mandatory	Article 5 DSM
	Out-of-commerce works	Mandatory (but fallback)	Article 8(2) DSM

3.3 The (Strict?) Interpretation of Exceptions in EU Law

Though the rule is unwritten in most national laws, it is frequently said that exceptions are to be interpreted in a strict manner.[471] The rule of strict interpretation is generally taken to entail that the provisions at stake ought to be read as covering *only* the fact-situations that they specify. From a negative perspective, the rule means that the interpreter is *not* allowed to read into the exception cases beyond those that are expressly envisaged therein.[472] An

471. *See* Larenz (2012), p. 502. In copyright literature, *see, e.g.*, Janssens (2009), p. 323.
472. *See* CJEU, *Zuid-Chemie*, para. 22 (and case law cited therein), and, in the copyright domain, CJEU, *Copydan Båndkopi*, para. 87. *See also* Metzger (2010), p. 110, for whom the rule of strict interpretation entails a subjective-historical interpretation of exceptions.

extensive construction of exceptions, based, e.g., on their underlying purpose, is therefore not allowed. Logically, the rule also means that the interpreter cannot apply an existing exception by analogy to situations that do not come within its set of possible meanings, nor can she create entirely new ones[473] (two consequences that also flow from the closed character of the catalogue[474]).

Where the rules that are to be strictly interpreted have more than one admissible reading according to their wording, the canon of strict interpretation requires that the interpreter go for the narrowest, less inclusive one. In Latin terms, *exceptio est strictissimae interpretationis.*[475] According to Karl Larenz, the strictest meaning is equivalent to the 'nuclear scope' that one first intends to refer to when a given term is used.[476] Larenz gives the example of the term 'children'. The nuclear scope of the term comprehends biological children, that being its strictest meaning. An interpretation that included stepchildren within the term's coverage would be a broad(er) interpretation.[477]

Let us take the exception laid down in Article 5(2)(d) InfoSoc Directive as an example. This provision exempts from liability unauthorised 'ephemeral recordings of works made by broadcasting organisations by means of their own facilities and for their own broadcasts'. In the *DR & TV2 Danmark* case, the CJEU was asked whether this exception covered ephemeral reproductions *commissioned* by broadcasting organisations, but *made* by legally independent external TV production companies. Were the canon of strict interpretation to be followed and the answer would have to be in the negative, for the exception could only cover recordings actually *made* by broadcasting organisations by means of their own facilities.[478] Thus, from a formal perspective, the canon of strict interpretation means that if the factual situation at hand does not fit strictly within the statutory wording of the exception, the interpreter must return to the general rule (in this case, the exclusive right of reproduction) and apply it.[479]

But like the rule of broad interpretation of exclusive rights, the rule of strict interpretation of exceptions has inevitable substantive implications.[480] Since copyright exceptions are for the users' benefit, serving *inter alia* the

---

473. *See* Lucas et al. (2017), p. 327.
474. *See infra* Chapter 4, section 2.1.
475. Lucas et al. (2017) dispute the idea that the canon of strict interpretation demands the *strictest* interpretation. They seem to consider that, as long as the use corresponds to one of the possible meanings of the exception's wording, it may be found non-infringing without contravening the canon of strict interpretation.
476. *See* Larenz (2012), pp. 500-501.
477. *See* Larenz (2012), pp. 500-501.
478. The Court, however, opted for a broad reading of Article 5(2)(d) InfoSoc Directive, answering the question in the affirmative, in light of Recital 41 – *see* CJEU, *DR & TV2 Danmark*, paras 46-58.
479. *See* Lucas (1998), p. 171, and Geiger (2004b), p. 887.
480. *See supra* Chapter 2, section 3.3.

promotion of their fundamental rights and freedoms, the broader the reading, the better for users. Conversely, narrower readings favour the interests of rightholders. Holding that derogations to the general rule of exclusivity are to be construed strictly therefore implies awarding *a priori* precedence to these interests, to the detriment of those of users; it implies solving any controversy in interpretation *in favorem auctoris*.

Outside the field of copyright, the CJEU has been following the canon of strict interpretation in its rulings for a long time. The canon has been repeatedly used in the Court's case law on VAT exemptions: the terms used to specify these exemptions are to be interpreted strictly, for they constitute derogations to the principle of VAT as a general tax on consumption.[481] Like exemptions, reduced rates too must be interpreted in a strict manner, since they deviate from the general rule that all supplies of goods and services are subject to the standard VAT rate.[482]

Ever since it became an established principle in VAT case law, the canon of strict interpretation has been used in relation to a diversity of issues, such as the recognition of professional qualifications[483] or the mutual recognition of driving licences.[484] The Court has gone as far as to say that '*any* derogation from or exception to a general rule must be interpreted strictly',[485] elevating the canon to a general interpretative maxim applicable in virtually every legal field.

In copyright law, early references to this rule can be found in a series of cases on the incorrect transposition of the Rental and Lending Directive. Article 6(1) (then Article 5(1)) of this Directive allows Member States to derogate from the exclusive right of public lending, as long as authors receive a remuneration for such lending. However, Article 6(3) provides that Member States may exempt *certain* categories of establishments from paying the remuneration. The Court held in a line of rulings that Member States which exempted all, or almost all, categories of establishments undertaking the public lending of copyright-protected works from such payment were interpreting the exemption in a manner that was not in conformity with the duty of strict interpretation required by that provision, which constitutes a derogation from the general obligation to remunerate authors.[486]

But it was only in the *Infopaq I* judgment, which dealt with the interpretation of the mandatory exception for acts of temporary reproduction, that the canon was brought into the horizontal InfoSoc domain. The CJEU

481. *See, e.g.*, CJEU, *Stichting Uitvoering Financiële Acties*, para. 13, and CJEU, *SDC v. Skatteministeriet*, para. 20.
482. *See, e.g.*, CJEU, *Commission v. Spain II*, para. 20; and CJEU, *Commission v. France*, para. 30.
483. *See* CJEU, *Beuttenmüller*, para. 64.
484. *See* CJEU, *Kapper*, para. 72.
485. CJEU, *Oude Luttikhuis*, para. 23 (emphasis added).
486. *See* CJEU, *Commission v. Portugal*, para. 22; CJEU, *Commission v. Spain I*, paras 31, 39, and 41; and CJEU, *Commission v. Ireland*, paras 26 and 30.

started by recalling that, according to its settled case law, the provisions of a directive which derogate from a general principle established by that Directive must be interpreted in a strict manner.[487] It then moved on to state that this canon applied to the exception under examination, because the provision worked as a derogation to the general principle according to which the authorisation of the rightholder was needed for any reproduction of a protected work.[488] Although the canon was derived from the case law on other fields,[489] the Court found a basis for its import in copyright-specific objectives and rules. According to the Court, the fact that the exception is to be interpreted in light of the three-step test laid down in Article 5(5) InfoSoc Directive and the need for legal certainty for authors and rightholders lend support to readings of exceptions *in favorem auctoris*.[490] The Court then proceeded to interpret one of the conditions of Article 5(1) InfoSoc Directive – the one related to the transient nature of the act of reproduction – in accordance with that canon, holding that the printing out of extracts of eleven words failed to satisfy that condition.

What emerges from the reasoning in *Infopaq I* is, in essence, that the Court understands the exclusive exploitation of protected works by rightholders to be the general rule within the InfoSoc Directive. Hence, and in coherence with the idea that all derogations to a general rule ought to be strictly interpreted, the canon is to be applied in relation to each and every single one of the exceptions contained in Article 5, as well as to other exceptions in the copyright *acquis*.

And, in fact, the Court has extended the reach of this interpretative rule to other InfoSoc exceptions. In *ACI Adam*, for instance, the Court held that a strict interpretation of the private copying exception in Article 5(2)(b) InfoSoc Directive precluded the provision from being understood as requiring rightholders 'to tolerate infringements of their rights which may accompany the making of private copies'.[491] Accordingly, the exception was construed as *not* covering copies made from unlawful sources.[492]

---

487. *See* CJEU, *Infopaq I*, para. 56.
488. *See* CJEU, *Infopaq I*, para. 57. *See also*, in the context of the same national proceedings, CJEU, *Infopaq II*, para. 27.
489. This much is confirmed by the judgments cited in *Infopaq I*, para. 56. *See also* Westkamp (2012), p. 65, criticising the 'apodictic' acceptance of the canon by the CJEU.
490. *See* CJEU, *Infopaq I*, paras 58-59. *See also* CJEU, *ACI Adam*, paras 22-24, and CJEU, *Filmspeler*, paras 62-63. It is debatable whether the three-step test has anything at all to say about how exceptions ought to be interpreted. As shall be explained shortly, the test is an autonomous substantive provision, which must be applied after concluding that a given unauthorised use is covered by an exception. It is not a rule of interpretation.
491. *See* CJEU, *ACI Adam*, paras 22-31. The Court connected this strict interpretation to Recital 44 InfoSoc Directive, which states that the scope of exceptions may be more limited when it comes to certain new uses of protected works.
492. *See* CJEU, *ACI Adam*, para. 41. *See also* CJEU, *Copydan Båndkopi*, paras 74-79; CJEU, *Reprobel*, paras 57-64; and CJEU, *VCAST*, paras 32 and 39 (all confirming this understanding).

Moreover, post-*Infopaq I*, the CJEU has read exceptions provided in other directives in a stringent fashion. In *Ranks & Vasiļevičs*, the Court determined that the exception for the making of back-up copies of computer programs could not be read as covering copies made with the purpose of being resold to third parties.[493] The General Court too has followed the canon in interpreting the exception provided in Article 5(1) Software Directive, pursuant to which no authorisation is needed for the reproduction and adaptation of a computer program if those acts are necessary for its use by the lawful acquirer in accordance with its intended purpose, including for error correction.[494]

In the aftermath of *Infopaq I*, scholars criticised the import into copyright law of the 'dogma' of strict interpretation.[495] Matthias Leistner qualified this approach as 'highly problematic' and hoped that 'future cases will allow the ECJ to limit the *ratio decidendi* of the *Infopaq* case'.[496] And it did not take long for judges in Luxembourg to answer scholarly prayers.[497] The Court has been consistently toning down the strict approach to InfoSoc exceptions, by admitting that exceptions may be construed beyond the words that compose them.

Premier League was the first case in which the CJEU departed from the canon of strict interpretation of InfoSoc exceptions,[498] reading Article 5(1) in light of its purpose. This purposive reading of InfoSoc exceptions has then been confirmed in a series of cases. In developing this approach – which will be analysed in greater depth later in the book[499] – the CJEU has relied to a large extent on fundamental-rights-based reasoning. These broad interpretations of exceptions have enabled the Court to declare a number of technological uses of protected works lawful, such as Internet browsing[500] and the e-lending of books.[501]

---

493. *See* CJEU, *Ranks & Vasiļevičs*, paras 41-43.
494. *See* CJEU, *Systran*, para. 225.
495. Senftleben (2013c), p. 93.
496. Leistner (2011), fn. 40.
497. As noted by Matthias Leistner himself in a later piece – *see* Leistner (2014a), p. 585,
498. This mitigated approach was, like the canon of strict interpretation itself, brought into copyright from case law on other fields. In its VAT case law, for example, the Court has recognised that, despite the need for a strict interpretation, the interpretation of exemptions must have regard to their context and underlying purpose. *See, e.g.*, CJEU, *Temco Europe*, paras 17-18; CJEU, *Horizon College*, para. 16; and CJEU, *Canterbury Hockey Club*, para. 17. The Court has also acknowledged that a truly strict interpretation of exceptions to the VAT as a general tax on consumption may conflict with the principle of fiscal neutrality. *See, e.g.*, CJEU, *Gregg*, para. 20; CJEU, *Dornier*, para. 42; and CJEU, *Kingscrest*, para. 29.
499. *See infra* Chapter 4, section 5.2.2.1.
500. *See* CJEU, *PRCA*, confirming the purposive reading of Article 5(1) InfoSoc Directive and holding that on-screen copies and cache copies made by end-users in the course of web browsing are covered by that exception.
501. *See* CJEU, *VOB*. In reasoning that the exception covered acts of public lending of digital copies of books, the Court emphasised the importance of this activity, as well as its

It is important to note that the adoption of a more nuanced approach to exceptions has not led to the vanishing of the canon of strict interpretation from copyright case law. After *Premier League*, the CJEU has occasionally engaged in narrow interpretations of exceptions.[502] Moreover, even in those cases where it construes the relevant exception in a relatively broad manner, the Court continues to pay lip service to the canon of strict interpretation.[503] More often than not, however, the Court concedes the departure from strict interpretation immediately after referring to it.[504] This has enabled the CJEU to grant, in certain cases, a wider scope to copyright exceptions than that which would have been reached through a truly strict construction.

4 THE THREE-STEP TEST

Another fundamental element in the framework of exceptions to copyright is the so-called three-step test. The test is essentially a standard[505] composed of three conditions against which the admissibility and (at least in some of its versions) the applicability of exceptions is assessed. The three conditions are typically framed as follows: (1) exceptions must be confined to certain special cases; (2) they must not conflict with a normal exploitation of the work; and (3) they must not unreasonably prejudice the legitimate interests of the author or rightholder.

Over time, this formula has become the 'centrepiece of the exceptions regimes'.[506] The test has known a plurality of incarnations at the international level: Article 9(2) Berne Convention; Articles 13, 17, 26(2) and 30 TRIPS; Article 10 WCT; Article 16(2) WPPT; Article 13(2) Beijing Treaty; and Article 11 Marrakesh Treaty. Moreover, the test has been included in a variety of regional instruments, bilateral and multilateral alike, such as the US-Australia Free Trade Agreement[507] and, most notably, in the EU

---

purpose of fostering cultural promotion (paras 50-51). The fact that the case concerned the interpretation of an exception from a directive other than InfoSoc – namely Article 6(1) Rental and Lending Directive – did not deter the Court from resorting to the teleological approach that then began to characterise its case law on InfoSoc exceptions.

502. *See* CJEU, *ACI Adam*, paras 22-32; CJEU, *Ranks & Vasiļevičs*, paras 41-43; CJEU, *AKM*, paras 37-42; and CJEU, *Filmspeler*, paras 62-72.

503. The expression is borrowed from Hugenholtz (2017), p. 286.

504. *See*, *e.g.*, CJEU, *PRCA*, paras 23 (referring to the canon) and 24 (recognising the need to ensure technological development and to achieve a fair balance), and CJEU, *Spiegel Online*, paras 53 (referring to the canon) and 54-55 (claiming that exceptions confer true rights upon users and that their effectiveness and purpose must be safeguarded).

505. On the distinction between rules and standards adopted in this book, *see infra* Chapter 3, section 2.1.2.

506. Ricketson & Ginsburg (2006), p. 759. For a detailed analysis of the historical evolution of the three-step test, *see* the leading monograph Senftleben (2004).

507. *See* Article 17.4(10)(a) Australia-US Free Trade Agreement.

directives addressing the topic of exceptions.[508] Apart from their threefold structure, the test's multiple versions share a high degree of vagueness in their formulation, which has given rise to voluminous scholarly debate.[509]

The test is generally understood as a limit on *exceptions.*[510] Although Article 13 TRIPS and Article 10 WCT refer to 'limitations and exceptions', the systematic insertion of the test in the different instruments shows that it is supposed to act as a constraint on what, for purposes of this book, is called 'exceptions' to copyright: provisions that remove a subset of uses from the scope of exclusive rights, treating those uses as non-infringing, despite the lack of rightholders' authorisation.[511] Therefore, the test should *not* be conceived as applying to: (i) limitations to copyright protection; (ii) definitional limitations to the exclusive rights; or (iii) defences to copyright infringement that are external to copyright law, such as abuse of rights. On the other hand, the test is applicable to *all* exceptions, including those that are subject to the payment of compensation. Whether the obligation to pay compensation affects the exception's compliance with the test – namely whether it increases its chances of passing the 'unreasonable prejudice' hurdle – is a debated issue.[512]

Much has been written about the role of the three-step test in copyright law.[513] The following sections offer a succinct description of the test's origins, evolution, and function in international law (section 4.1) and in the EU *acquis*, with an emphasis on the InfoSoc Directive (section 4.2).

4.1 The Three-Step Test in International Law

The three-step test was first codified in the Berne Convention. It was a late arrival to the Convention's text, having been introduced only in the 1967 Stockholm Revision, along with the general reproduction right.[514] Before Stockholm, Berne Union members could, in theory, refrain from granting upon authors a right to authorise or prohibit the making of copies of their

508. *See infra* 4.2.
509. Referring to the common structure and vague character of the different versions, *see*, *e.g.*, Senftleben (2004), p. 105, and Quintais (2017a), p. 248. Espousing the view that 'there is no such thing as *the* three-step test' and that each version is 'uniquely different', *see* Christie & Wright (2014), p. 410.
510. *See*, *inter alia*, Senftleben (2004), p. 283; Ascensão (2006); Hugenholtz & Okediji (2008), p. 18; Vide & Gómez (2008), p. 56; and Loewenheim (2010), p. 479.
511. *See supra* section 2.1.
512. *See* Hugenholtz & Okediji (2008), p. 19.
513. Apart from the general commentaries on international and European copyright law cited throughout this section, *see* Ginsburg (2001); Ficsor (2002b); Senftleben (2004); Koelman (2006); Geiger (2006b); Geiger (2007b); Westkamp (2008); Kur (2009); He (2009); Griffiths (2009); Lucas (2010); Senftleben (2010); Geiger et al. (2008); Christie & Wright (2014); Geiger et al. (2014). *See also infra* Chapter 5, section 4.2.2.
514. Senftleben (2004), pp. 45-47, sees the recognition of the 'minor reservations' doctrine in the 1948 Brussels Conference as a precursor to the three-step test.

protected works. If they recognised such protection, they could establish whatever exceptions thereto they wished. As a result, the number, form, and content of the exceptions differed sharply across Union members.[515]

The opportunity to systematically debate the exceptions to the reproduction right at the international level only arose when the decision to introduce that very right became part of the agenda.[516] While Union members found it necessary to subtract certain copying acts from the definitive scope of the right, an agreement on the specific acts that should be exempted proved difficult to achieve. A wide number of proposals and amendments were made during the preparation works for the Stockholm Revision. In the end, it was a proposal submitted by the UK delegation that won the day.[517] The proposal consisted of a generalised and standard-like residual permission granted upon Union members to enact exceptions.

Article 9(2) emerged from this proposal, reading as follows: 'It shall be a matter for legislation in the countries of the Union to permit the reproduction of such works in certain special cases, provided that such reproduction does not conflict with a normal exploitation of the work and does not unreasonably prejudice the legitimate interests of the author.'

As its wording denotes, the test sets out three conditions that Berne signatories must fulfil in designing national exceptions to the right of reproduction. Despite the cumulative character of these conditions,[518] their open-ended formulation leaves national legislators with a measure of discretion when introducing exceptions.[519] Therefore, in addition to the specific exceptions mentioned in section 3.1 *supra*,[520] the Berne Convention

515. *See* Ricketson & Ginsburg (2006), p. 759. Nonetheless, a few specific exceptions, privileging certain acts of reproduction, were already part of the Berne Convention, namely in Articles 2*bis*(2), 10 and 10*bis*.
516. *See supra* section 3.1. for further details on the introduction of the right of reproduction into the Berne Convention.
517. For accounts on the drafting, *see*, *e.g.*, Senftleben (2004), pp. 47-52; Ricketson & Ginsburg (2006), pp. 759-763; Geiger (2007b), fn. 13; and Lewinski (2008), p. 160.
518. Underscoring the cumulative character of the conditions, *see*, *e.g.*, Ricketson (1987), p. 482; Ficsor (2002b), pp. 125-127; Reinbothe & Lewinski (2002), p. 124; Senftleben (2004), p. 125; and Lucas (2010), p. 281. In WTO, *US-Copyright*, para. 6.97, it was expressly stated that '[t]he three conditions apply on a cumulative basis, each being a separate and independent requirement that must be satisfied'. *See also* the Report by Main Committee I of the 1967 Stockholm Conference in Berne Convention Records 1967, p. 1145. The very consensual use of the expression 'three-*step* test' gives the idea that the conditions are cumulative hurdles and not balancing factors.
519. *See* Ricketson & Ginsburg (2006), pp. 182-183, and Lewinski (2008), p. 160.
520. Commentators generally think that those exceptions are unaffected by the three-step test. *See* Ricketson & Ginsburg (2006), p. 763; Hugenholtz & Okediji (2008), p. 20; and Lewinski (2008), p. 159. *See also* Aplin & Bently (2018), pp. 11-12 (arguing that the three-step test in Article 9(2) Berne Convention is irrelevant e.g. for the mandatory quotation exception laid down in Article 10(1)).

includes in Article 9(2) a conditional permission to enact *further* exceptions (on which, it ought to be noted, there is no authoritative interpretation[521]).

The Berne test has been used as the template for the regimes of exceptions at the international level. In 1994, the TRIPS Agreement took over the test, with Article 13 thereof largely borrowing Berne's formula.[522] Given that TRIPS is intended to provide a uniform standard of copyright protection worldwide, in order to 'reduce distortions and impediments to international trade',[523] Article 13 may be conceived as a Berne-plus element.[524] The provision states that 'Members shall confine limitations or exceptions to exclusive rights to certain special cases which do not conflict with a normal exploitation of the work and do not unreasonably prejudice the legitimate interests of the right holder.'[525] As a close reading of the provision shows, the TRIPS version bears two important differences in relation to the Berne one. First, the test now extends to *all* minimum rights provided by TRIPS (not just to reproduction), including the Berne rights that have been incorporated by reference into TRIPS[526] and the new rights, such as the rental right over computer programs and cinematographic works provided in Article 11.[527] Second, Article 13 TRIPS, being an international trade law incarnation of the test, refers to the legitimate interests of 'rightholders' instead of 'authors'. This change in terminology, as noted by Bernt Hugenholtz and Ruth Okediji, 'brings to the foreground the commercial

521. *See* Hugenholtz & Okediji (2008), p. 21.
522. Other provisions in Part II of the Agreement, relating to other IP rights, are inspired in Berne's test, namely Article 17 (trademarks), Article 26(2) (industrial designs), and Article 30 (patents). It was during the TRIPS negotiations that the expression 'three-step test' was coined – *see* Lewinski (2008), p. 160.
523. Preamble TRIPS Agreement.
524. *See* Senftleben (2004), p. 90.
525. Considering its encompassing formula, it is sometimes assumed that the three-step test in Article 13 TRIPS applies to all exceptions provided in the Berne Convention – *see, e.g.*, Helfer (2000), p. 147, and Dinwoodie (2001), p. 769. *But see* Aplin & Bently (2018), pp. 12-16, making the case that the test in TRIPS (and in the WCT) does not apply to the quotation exception in Article 10(1) Berne Convention, not least because Article 10(1) is an obligation on Contracting Parties and '[i]t would be odd to require compliance with an obligation and yet at the same time constrain such compliance'.
526. Article 9(1) TRIPS obliges Member Countries to comply with Articles 1 to 21 Berne Convention, with the exclusion of Article 6*bis* on moral rights. This means that the three-step test in Article 9(2) Berne Convention is also incorporated into the TRIPS Agreement. Pointing out this 'double insertion', *see* Senftleben (2004), pp. 84-87. The WTO Panel in *US-Copyright*, para. 6.80, expressly rejected the argument that Article 13 TRIPS applies only to the additional rights granted under TRIPS.
527. Article 14 TRIPS – the provision on related rights – contains no similar formula, raising doubts as to the applicability of Article 13's test thereto. However, Article 16 WPPT does away with any practical difficulties, by clearly extending the test to exceptions to the related rights.

interests of intermediaries ("right holders"), while downplaying the interests of the authors'.[528]

The enlargement of the set of exclusive rights in relation to which the three-step test bears relevance was confirmed a couple of years later in the WIPO Treaties. The two 1996 instruments aimed at creating an international framework to tackle the then-emerging challenges raised by digital technologies, which TRIPS did not specifically deal with. In what concerns exceptions to copyright, the Berne three-step formula was incorporated with the purpose of addressing those challenges.

Article 10 WCT and Article 16(2) WPPT introduce the test in regards to the minimum rights provided therein. The Agreed Statement on Article 10 WCT, which is applicable *mutatis mutandis* to Article 16 WPPT,[529] makes clear that this provision allows Contracting States 'to carry forward and appropriately extend into the digital environment limitations and exceptions in their national laws which have been considered acceptable under the Berne Convention'. In addition, Article 10 'should be understood to permit Contracting Parties to devise new exceptions and limitations that are appropriate in the digital network environment'.[530] This statement notwithstanding, some scholars observe that the test 'remains closely linked to the spirit and confines of the Berne Convention and therefore cannot be understood as giving carte blanche to the introduction of novel and potentially far-reaching limitations'.[531] Article 10(1) WCT, in particular, allows Contracting Parties, subject to the three hurdles, to provide for exceptions to the rights granted under the Treaty – these being distribution (Article 6), rental (Article 7), and communication to the public (Article 8) –, while Article 10(2)[532] is intended to constrain countries when applying the Berne Convention, serving as an 'additional safeguard'.[533] Nonetheless, the Agreed Statement, in clarifying that 'Article 10(2) neither reduces nor extends the scope of applicability of the limitations and exceptions permitted by the Berne Convention',[534] practically neutralises the effect of this provision on the Berne Convention exceptions.[535]

As to the interpretation of each of the three conditions, guidance has been given at the international level by four WTO panel reports: one on

528. Hugenholtz & Okediji (2008), p. 17.
529. *See* Agreed Statement on Article 16 WPPT.
530. Agreed Statement on Article 10 WCT. The statement has been regularly cited as providing support for flexible readings of the test – *see infra* Chapter 5, section 4.2.2.1.
531. Kur (2009), p. 347.
532. Articles 10(2) WCT provides that 'Contracting Parties shall, when applying the Berne Convention, confine any limitations of or exceptions to rights provided for therein to certain special cases that do not conflict with a normal exploitation of the work and do not unreasonably prejudice the legitimate interests of the author'.
533. Senftleben (2004), pp. 121-124.
534. Agreed Statement on Article 10 WCT.
535. *See* Hugenholtz & Okediji (2008), p. 20.

patents,[536] two on trademarks and geographical indications,[537] and one on copyright.[538] Our attention will naturally be devoted to the latter one, for it focuses on Article 13 TRIPS and sheds light on the specific implications of the three-step test in copyright law.[539]

The case was brought before the WTO by the EC against the US, and it required the panel to examine the so-called homestyle and business exceptions provided in Section 110(5)(A) and (B) US Copyright Act.[540] The report is particularly relevant not so much for the outcome reached, but for the relatively detailed exploration of the meaning of each step.

It should be stressed that the interpretation given by the WTO Panel concerns the three-step test in TRIPS *only*, not the Berne Convention version or the WIPO counterparts. It is nevertheless undeniable that the interpretation of Article 13 TRIPS has a 'de facto influence'[541] over the other versions of the test. It has been said that 'this WTO decision … serves as the pragmatic authoritative interpretation of the provision'.[542] It would therefore be imprudent to disregard that interpretation when examining the three-step test in international law.[543] In addition, because EU copyright law must be interpreted, so far as possible, in light of international law, this interpretation is also relevant to determine the scope and meaning of Article 5(5) InfoSoc Directive – the version of the three-step test that is of greater interest to this book.

Regarding the first step, the Panel started off by clarifying the demands that flow from the use of the term 'certain': an exception provided in national legislation 'must be clearly defined'. 'However', it added, 'there is no need to identify explicitly each and every possible situation to which the exception could apply, provided that the scope of the exception is known and particularised.'[544] What is required under this term is 'a sufficient degree of legal certainty'.[545]

536. *See* WTO, *Canada-Patents*.
537. *See* WTO, *EC-Trademarks I* and WTO, *EC-Trademarks II*. These reports relate to parallel complaints submitted respectively by the US and Australia.
538. *See* WTO, *US-Copyright*.
539. But note that the WTO Panel Reports are only binding upon the parties to the specific dispute. *See* Shabalala (2010), p. 149; Geiger et al. (2014), pp. 600-601; and Quintais (2017a), p. 250.
540. The first exception passed the test as interpreted by the WTO Panel, but the second one did not. *See* WTO, *US-Copyright*, para. 7.1.
541. Lewinski (2008), p. 161.
542. Hughes (2017), p. 245.
543. *See* Senftleben (2004), p. 110.
544. WTO, *US-Copyright*, para. 6.108.
545. WTO, *US-Copyright*, para. 6.108. This interpretation has led scholars to question whether the textually vague fair use standard laid down in Section 107 US Copyright Act is compatible with the demands of the three-step test. This issue is approached in Chapter 5, section 5.6 *infra*.

But in order to comply with the first condition, something more is needed: the exception must be confined to 'special' cases. This term means that the exception must have 'a narrow scope as well as an exceptional or distinctive objective'.[546] What it *does not* mean, according to the Panel, is that the legitimacy of the policy objective underlying the exception has to be assessed.[547] Indeed, 'a limitation or exception may be compatible with the first condition even if it pursues a special purpose whose underlying legitimacy in a normative sense cannot be discerned'.[548] What this statement suggests is that the qualitative requirement related to the exception's purpose will be met as long as there is *some* public policy objective behind the exception at stake (which there will inevitably be).[549] Thus, the first step is, in practice, a requirement of precision and narrowness in scope.

Under the second step, the Panel had to determine the meaning of 'conflict with the normal exploitation of a work'. Such a conflict will exist if the uses covered by the exception 'enter into economic competition with the ways that right holders normally extract economic value from that right to the work (i.e., the copyright) and thereby deprive them of significant or tangible commercial gains'.[550] The normal exploitation is affected not only by the actual impact of the exception on the market at a given point in time but also by its potential effects.[551] In order to account for the emergence of new, unforeseen uses with likely economic consequences, the assessment of these effects should have as its reference 'the commercial and technological conditions that prevail in the market currently or in the near future'.[552] In the context of this step, consideration ought to be given not only to 'those forms of exploitation that currently generate significant or tangible revenue' but also to 'those forms of exploitation which, with a certain degree of likelihood and plausibility, could acquire considerable economic or practical importance'.[553] Importantly, however, the Panel stressed that not every commercial use of a work will necessarily fail to pass muster.[554]

Finally, under the third step, the Panel focused on the unreasonableness of the prejudice caused by the exception.[555] The Panel defines 'prejudice' as 'damage, harm or injury', while 'not unreasonable' is understood as a

---

546. WTO, *US-Copyright*, para. 6.109.
547. *See* WTO, *US-Copyright*, para. 6.111. Criticising this interpretation, *see* Ficsor (2002b), pp. 215-231.
548. WTO, *US-Copyright*, para. 6.112.
549. *See* Senftleben (2004), pp. 140-141, observing that '[t]he qualitative aspect of specialty was therefore de facto ignored'.
550. WTO, *US-Copyright*, para. 6.183.
551. *See* WTO, *US-Copyright*, paras 6.184-6.188.
552. WTO, *US-Copyright*, para. 6.187.
553. WTO, *US-Copyright*, para. 6.180.
554. *See* WTO, *US-Copyright*, para. 6.182.
555. As noted in WTO, *US-Copyright*, para. 6.226, the parties to the dispute did not question the legitimacy of the interests of rightholders.

'slightly stricter threshold than "reasonable"'.[556] In the panelists' view, 'a certain amount of "prejudice" has to be presumed justified as "not unreasonable"'.[557] The prejudice will reach an unreasonable level 'if an exception or limitation causes or has the potential to cause an unreasonable loss of income to the copyright owner'.[558] Hence, as in the previous step, the inquiry under the third step revolves largely around economic considerations.[559]

In sum, according to the Panel's interpretation, an exception will comply with the international three-step test if: (i) it is not excessively vague or broad; (ii) does not deprive rightholders of significant income, whether actual or potential; and (iii) does not harm rightholders in an unreasonable way. The exceptions within Article 5 InfoSoc Directive have been cited as examples of exceptions that are 'presumably compliant' with the test.[560]

The literature on the interpretation of the three conditions offered by the WTO Panel is vast and need not be rehearsed here.[561] Suffice to point out that the tone is overwhelmingly critical. The criticism focuses on the absence of policy considerations from the report.[562] A number of commentators have accordingly been arguing for more flexible approaches to the test – approaches that reflect an understanding of the test as an enabling standard, rather than as a restrictive one.[563]

4.2 The Three-Step Test in the EU *Acquis*

A cornerstone of international copyright law, the three-step test was also imported into the EU copyright *acquis*. Every EU directive that deals with exceptions to copyright and related rights includes some version – full or abbreviated – of the test.[564]

---

556. WTO, *US-Copyright*, para. 6.225.
557. WTO, *US-Copyright*, para. 6.229.
558. WTO, *US-Copyright*, para. 6.229.
559. *See* Kur (2009), p. 324. *See also* Hugenholtz & Okediji (2008), p. 25, noting that, in the analysis of the third step, the Panel repeats much of what it had stated in relation to the second step.
560. Hugenholtz & Okediji (2008), p. 26.
561. *See*, *inter alia*, Ginsburg (2001); Lucas (2001); Ficsor (2002b); Senftleben (2004); Senftleben (2006). *See also infra* Chapter 5, section 4.2.2.
562. *See*, *e.g.*, Hugenholtz & Okediji (2008), pp. 23-24; Kur (2009), pp. 326-327; Shabalala (2010); and Geiger et al. (2014), pp. 593-597.
563. For a systematisation and analysis of those proposals, *see infra* Chapter 5, section 4.2.2.
564. Article 6 Software Directive provides the decompilation exception for the purpose of interoperability. Article 6(3), in referring to the Berne Convention, states that the exception 'may not be interpreted in such a way as to allow its application to be used in a manner that unreasonably prejudices the rightholder's legitimate interests or conflicts with a normal exploitation of the computer program'. Oddly, the Software Directive formula omits the Berne first step ('certain special cases') and applies only to the decompilation exception and not to the other exceptions set forth in its Article 5. Article 6(3) Database Directive essentially replicates the wording of Article 6(3)

The chief incarnation of the three-step test in the *acquis* is the one in Article 5(5) InfoSoc Directive, due to the Directive's cross-cutting character and the number of exceptions it contains. It was through the WIPO Treaties that the three-step test found its way into InfoSoc, which, as mentioned, served to implement a number of the obligations arising from those international instruments. Importantly, the inclusion of the test in the EU copyright *acquis*, in general, and in the InfoSoc Directive, in particular, entails that the interpretation of its meaning and scope comes within the competence of the CJEU under the preliminary reference procedure.[565]

In the preparatory works that eventually led to the adoption of the InfoSoc Directive, the Commission expressed doubts about the Berne three-step formula, claiming, in the 1995 Green Paper, that Article 9(2) Berne Convention 'considerably limits the effectiveness of the reproduction right', while suffering from 'uncertainty as to its exact scope' and leading to 'divergent interpretation by the authorities in different countries'.[566] Despite these problems, in the 1996 Follow-Up the Commission announced that, in designing the catalogue of exceptions, 'the guidance offered by Article 9§2 Berne Convention shall be taken fully into account'.[567] Recognising the need to interpret the WIPO tests in light of the *acquis* (back then, the tests in the *acquis* were limited to the ones in the Software and Database Directives),[568] the Commission accordingly proposed the incorporation of the three-step test in the InfoSoc text, with a wording similar to that of previous directives.

Article 5(4) InfoSoc Proposal stated that the exceptions harmonised in previous paragraphs 'shall only be applied to certain specific cases and shall not be interpreted in such a way as to allow their application to be used in a

---

Software Directive. Differently, however, the Database test applies to all exceptions to the database right, being further extended to the acts of lawful users of databases protected by the *sui generis* right – *see* Articles 7(5) and 8(2) Database Directive. The current formulation of Article 10(3) Rental and Lending Directive, initially incorporated by virtue of Article 11(1)(b) InfoSoc Directive, contains the InfoSoc version of three-step test, making it applicable to the exceptions to related rights. Similarly, the Orphan Works Directive makes clear that the exception established therein is to be applied in respect of that formula – *see* Recital 20 Orphan Works Directive. More recently, two other directives imported the InfoSoc formula: the Marrakesh Directive in relation to the exception for the making and dissemination of copies in formats accessible to persons who are blind, visually impaired or otherwise print-disabled (Article 3(3) Marrakesh Directive) and the DSM Directive in relation to the exceptions for TDM, cross-border teaching activities, and preservation of cultural heritage (Article 7(2) and Recital 6 DSM Directive).

565. *See* Cohen Jehoram (2005a), p. 364, highlighting the fact that the CJEU 'is not bound by diplomatic reticence towards states, like a TRIPs Panel'.
566. 1995 Green Paper, pp. 50-51.
567. 1996 Follow-Up, p. 12. The statement echoes the contributions received during the consultation process that resulted from the Green Paper. According to the Commission, '[a] number of parties suggest the general 'economic prejudice' clause in Article 9§2 of the Berne Convention as a point of reference' – 1996 Follow-Up, p. 11.
568. *See* Explanatory Memorandum to InfoSoc Proposal, p. 28.

manner which unreasonably prejudices the rightholder's legitimate interests or conflicts with the normal exploitation of their works or other subject matter'. The order of the two final steps is inverted, and they seem to be alternative steps, given the use of the conjunction 'or'.[569]

The Proposal's language underwent some changes and, in the end, a formula closer to that of the international tests was adopted. Article 5(5) states that the InfoSoc exceptions harmonised in Article 5(1)-(4) 'shall only be applied in certain special cases which do not conflict with a normal exploitation of the work or other subject-matter and do not unreasonably prejudice the legitimate interests of the rightholder'.[570] In Article 5(5), in contrast with the InfoSoc Proposal's version, the term 'specific' was replaced with 'special'; the definite article 'the' (normal exploitation of the work) was replaced with the indefinite 'a'; and the point of reference for the last two conditions is no longer the interpretation, but the application of exceptions.

In relation to its international counterparts, however, the InfoSoc three-step test takes up a new role. Whereas the test in the international copyright framework has historically been directed at national legislators when designing exceptions to exclusive rights,[571] it now has the renewed function of controlling the *application* of copyright exceptions. The use of the term 'applied' suggests that, within EU law, even if a certain unauthorised use falls within the scope of one of the listed exceptions, that use must, in addition, cumulatively satisfy the three hurdles,[572]

The term raises the controversial issue of the addressees of the InfoSoc three-step test: is the test directed: (i) at national legislators when implementing exceptions;[573] (ii) at judges when deciding cases about unauthorised uses of protected works that are potentially covered by an exception;[574] or

569. Criticising the wording of the InfoSoc Proposal, *see* Heide (1999), pp. 107-109.

570. In the 2008 Green Paper, p. 5, the Commission observed that '[t]he formulation of Article 5(5) reflects the Community's international obligations in the area of copyright and related rights'. Regarding coverage, the InfoSoc test goes beyond Article 16 WPPT, in that it applies to the exceptions to all four related rights laid down in Articles 2 and 3 InfoSoc Directive – *see* Walter & Lewinski (2010), p. 1061.

571. *See* Koelman (2006), p. 407; Walter & Lewinski (2010), p. 1060; and Geiger et al. (2014), p. 586.

572. Similarly, Recital 44 InfoSoc Directive states that '[s]uch exceptions and limitations may not be applied in a way which prejudices the legitimate interests of the rightholder or which conflicts with the normal exploitation of his work or other subject-matter'. *See also* CJEU, *Laserdisken*, para. 79, recognising that Article 5(5) places 'strict boundaries' on the InfoSoc system of exceptions.

573. Sponsoring this view, *see* Hart (2002), p. 61; Burrell & Coleman (2005), p. 298; and Walter & Lewinski (2010), pp. 1060-1061.

574. *See* Mazziotti (2008), p. 85, arguing that Member States 'are already bound to comply with the three-step test under international obligations' and that, as such, the InfoSoc test serves 'as a common benchmark for judicial interpretation'. *See also* Dusollier & Buydens (2001), p. 12; Cordeiro (2002), p. 218; Cohen Jehoram (2005a), p. 364, (2005b), p. 258, and (2009), p. 408; Koelman (2006), p. 408; Pereira (2008a), p. 552, and (2008b), pp. 862-862; and Lucas (2010), p. 277.

(iii) at both[575]? As noted by scholars, Article 5(5) InfoSoc Directive is not entirely clear in this respect.[576] Yet, it does hint that the test is addressed at judges at least. After all, legislators do not *apply* exceptions; that is 'the business of private parties and the courts'.[577] A further argument in support of the idea that the InfoSoc three-step test is directed at judges, as duly noted by Richard Arnold and Eleonora Rosati, is that 'Article 5(5) expressly embraces Article 5(1), which … is a mandatory (and tightly drafted) exception'.[578] In addition, there is a difference in the wording of Article 5(2) and (3), pursuant to which Member States may 'provide' exceptions, and Article 5(5), which uses the verb 'apply'.[579]

The CJEU too has been pointing in that direction. The Court has dealt with Article 5(5) InfoSoc Directive in a series of decisions.[580] In some of them, the Court has suggested, though not unambiguously, that Article 5(5) is relevant only at the national implementation stage. In *Stichting de Thuiskopie*, the Court stated that Article 5(5) 'makes the introduction of the private copying exception subject to three conditions',[581] with the term 'introduction' implicitly referring to the job of legislators. In *Painer*, it added that, in implementing exceptions, 'the Member States' discretion is limited by Article 5(5)'.[582] In *ACI Adam* – in a slightly more confusing statement, due to the use of the word 'applied' – the Court seemed to reinforce the point, by holding that the provision 'takes effect only at the time when they [the exceptions] are applied by the Member States'.[583]

These statements are nevertheless hard to reconcile with a more recent string of decisions. What emerges clearly from the current case law of the CJEU is that courts should take the three conditions into account when interpreting and applying exceptions. That much has been openly said by

---

575. This is the view held, implicitly or explicitly, in Guibault (2003), p. 571; Senftleben (2004), p. 281; Geiger (2006b), p. 683; Geiger (2007c), pp. 13-15; Xalabarder (2008), p. 817; Vicente (2012), p. 744; Arnold & Rosati (2015); and Bechtold (2016), p. 469.
576. *See* Senftleben (2004), p. 279; Geiger (2007b), p. 488; Griffiths (2009), pp. 431-433; and Arnold & Rosati (2015), p. 743.
577. Cohen Jehoram (2009), p. 409. *See also* Cohen Jehoram (2005a), p. 364, and Geiger (2007b), p. 488.
578. Arnold & Rosati (2015), p. 744.
579. *See also* Explanatory Memorandum to InfoSoc Proposal, p. 29, stating that '[w]hen *applying* [the exception in Article 5(1)], or any other exception listed in this Article, the "three-step test" … has, of course, also to be met' (emphasis added).
580. *See* the rulings in *Infopaq I*; *Stichting de Thuiskopie*; *Premier League*; *Infopaq II*; *Painer*; *OSA*; *ACI Adam*; *PRCA*; *Ulmer*; *Copydan Båndkopi*; *Reprobel*; *Filmspeler*; *Funke Medien*; *Pelham*; and *Spiegel Online*. *See also* CJEU, *PPI* (on the three-step test provided in Article 10(3) Rental and Lending Directive).
581. CJEU, *Stichting de Thuiskopie*, para. 21.
582. CJEU, *Painer*, para. 110. *See also* CJEU, *Opinion 3/15 – Marrakesh Treaty*, para. 125.
583. CJEU, *ACI Adam*, para. 25.

AGs. In *Stichting de Thuiskopie*, AG Jääskinen stated that, 'though being primarily a norm addressed to the legislature, the three-step test must also be applied by the national courts in order to ensure that the practical application of the exception to Article 2 of Directive 2001/29 provided by national legislation remains within the limits allowed by Article 5'.[584] Similarly, in *ACI Adam*, AG Cruz Villalón concluded that 'the provisions of Article 5(5) are not addressed solely to national legislatures', but also to courts.[585] Although the Court has consistently stated that the test is not intended to affect the substantive content of the different exceptions in Article 5 InfoSoc Directive and cannot, consequently, be used to extend their scope,[586] it has equally consistently held, from *Infopaq I* up to the *Filmspeler* judgment, that these exceptions must be construed in light of the test.[587] Further to that position, the Court has clarified that, when examining whether the acts of the unauthorised user are privileged, courts must assess, first, whether those acts fall within the scope of a given exception and, second, whether they fulfil the three conditions in Article 5(5).[588] The Court has considered these conditions to be automatically satisfied in some cases, namely where the unauthorised use already satisfies the requirements of the temporary reproduction exception.[589] In other cases, the Court has itself undertaken that analysis, though always in a more or less concise manner.[590]

Furthermore, the Court implicitly walked back its initial position on the function of the test when it narrowed down the margin of discretion of Member States in implementing exceptions. This line of case law suggests

584. AG Opinion, *Stichting de Thuiskopie*, para. 42.
585. AG Opinion, *ACI Adam*, para. 48. It is worth quoting the statement in full: '[w]henever a national legislature implements the private copying exception it must, in all cases, do so in accordance with the requirements of Article 5(2)(b), but it must also, at the same time, satisfy the requirements laid down by Article 5(5) of Directive 2001/29, in accordance with international obligations. That applies equally to the application by national courts of the private copying exception. Contrary to what the Netherlands Government argues, the provisions of Article 5(5) are not addressed solely to national legislatures.'
586. *See* CJEU, *ACI Adam*, paras 25-26; CJEU, *Ulmer*, para. 47; CJEU, *Copydan Båndkopi*, para. 90.
587. *See* CJEU, *Infopaq I*, para. 58; CJEU, *OSA*, para. 40; and CJEU, *Ulmer*, para. 47; CJEU, *Filmspeler*, para. 63; and, in relation to Article 10(3) Rental and Lending Directive, CJEU, *PPI*, paras 75-76.
588. *See* CJEU, *Premier League*, para. 181; CJEU, *PRCA*, para. 53; CJEU, *Ulmer*, para. 56; and CJEU, *VCAST*, paras 52-53. *See also* Arnold & Rosati (2015), p. 747.
589. *See* CJEU, *Premier League*, para. 181, and CJEU, *Infopaq II*, paras 55-57. *See also* Chapter 4, section 5.2.2.3 *infra*.
590. *See*, *e.g.*, CJEU, *ACI Adam*, para. 38-41; CJEU, *Ulmer*, paras 47-48; CJEU, *Filmspeler*, paras 63-72; and CJEU, *Spiegel Online*, para. 79. *See also infra* Chapter 4, section 5.2.2.3.

that national legislators have one fundamental choice – to implement or not to implement a given exception (provided it is optional). Once they choose to implement it, they have highly circumscribed freedom in adjusting its wording.[591] Whereas the scope of such freedom is to be determined on a case-by-case basis, Member States may only transpose optional exceptions if they comply with all the conditions laid down in the respective provisions. Therefore, assuming the wording of the exceptions in InfoSoc respects the three-step test, Member State legislators have little to no freedom to breach the conditions of the test in formulating national exceptions. Nonetheless, in recent judgments the CJEU has been repeating the idea that the Member States' discretion in implementing exceptions is also limited by Article 5(5).[592]

Given the initial doubts around the function(s) of the InfoSoc test, not all Member States have transposed it into their national copyright legislation.[593] Germany, the UK, and the Netherlands were among the Member States that, when implementing the Directive into national law, have refrained from including the language of Article 5(5).[594] Other countries – such as France,[595] Italy,[596] and Portugal[597] – have done otherwise, albeit in a relatively inconsistent manner.[598] In these countries, there is no doubt that the three-step test 'constitutes a directly applicable rule in substantive law as regards the interpretation of limitations'.[599] In the former set of Member States, despite the absence of the language in national law, courts are obliged

591. On this point in greater detail, *see infra* Chapter 4, section 5.1.1.
592. *See* CJEU, *Funke Medien*, para. 52; and CJEU, *Spiegel Online*, para. 37.
593. Reporting on the implementation of the three-step test in a 2007 study commissioned by the European Commission's Internal Market DG, *see* Westkamp (2007), pp. 48-49, pp. 92-94. Building on that study, more recently, *see* EPRS (2015), p. I-203.
594. Hart & Holmes (2004), p. 255, in examining the implementation of the InfoSoc Directive in the UK, state that '[t]he Government took the not unreasonable view that, as all the exceptions in the CDPA were drafted to comply with this test, it did not want to have time spent in argument before the courts as to whether the three-step test has been complied with every time such an exception is considered'.
595. *See* Article L122-5(11) French IP Code. *See also* Articles L211-3 and L342-3, in relation, respectively, to related rights and to the right of database producers.
596. *See* Article 71-*nonies* and, in relation to the private copying exception, Article 71-*sexies*(4) Italian Copyright Law.
597. *See* Article 75(4) Portuguese Copyright Code.
598. For instance, Article 75(4) Portuguese Copyright Code omits the first step ('certain special cases') and refers only to the legitimate interests of the *author* (not of rightholders). *See* Ascensão (2002), p. 925 (supporting the solution) and Rebello (2005), p. 152 (criticising the latter option).
599. Westkamp (2007), p. 48.

to interpret national legislation in light of the Directive[600] and, in fact, they have sometimes applied the test in their decisions.[601]

Irrespective of whether Member States implemented the test, current CJEU case law, in stating that the acts of defendants must be subject to a two-tiered analysis formed by the eligibility for the exception at issue and the fulfilment of the test's conditions, has made it clear that, in disputes involving the applicability of a national exception resulting from the implementation of an InfoSoc exception, national courts will be required to go through the three-step test. Logically, and taking into account the harmonisation objective of InfoSoc, this should be so 'independently of whether the applicable national law contains express reference to the language of Article 5(5)'.[602] Therefore, the transposition of the test into national law, if not mandatory, is at least advisable, in order to safeguard the expectations of national litigants.[603]

In light of the above, it can be concluded that while the international tests are shaped as criteria for the admissibility of any exceptions that are enacted by the national (or regional) lawmaker, Article 5(5) InfoSoc Directive essentially limits the judicial application of the exceptions provided for in the previous paragraphs. It therefore allows rightholders to invoke the test directly in litigation against users.[604] Whether the former function of legislative control is still relevant at the EU level is debatable, following recent CJEU case law restricting the discretion of Member State

---

600. According to longstanding CJEU case law, national provisions must be interpreted in conformity with the wording and purpose of the directive they aim at implementing. This principle of consistent interpretation was first articulated in *Von Colson*. National courts, stated the CJEU then, 'are required to interpret their national law in the light of the wording and the purpose of the directive in order to achieve the result [referred therein]' (para. 26). In *Marleasing*, the Court made clear that this obligation applies to national provisions for the implementation of the directive at hand, irrespective of whether those provisions were adopted before or after the directive (paras 7-8). Moreover, this principle of consistent interpretation, as the Court later added in *Pfeiffer*, 'is inherent in the system of the Treaty, since it permits the national court, for the matters within its jurisdiction, to ensure the full effectiveness of Community law when it determines the dispute before it' (para. 114).
601. A well-known decision is the one in BGH, *Elektronischer Pressespiegel*. The case concerned the exception for (analogue) press reviews laid down in Article 49(1) German Copyright Act and its possible extension to electronic press reviews. Such an extension was deemed compatible with the test as long as the rightholder was duly remunerated for such practice (paras 43-45), despite the fact that Germany, as mentioned above, refrained from transposing the test. *See also* Court of Appeal of Amsterdam, *Uitgevers*.
602. Arnold & Rosati (2015), p. 747.
603. *See* Senftleben (2004), p. 280, arguing that implementation of the three-step test into national copyright laws, though recommendable, is *not* mandatory. *But see* Bayreuther (2001), p. 839 (opposing implementation by Member States); Walter & Lewinski (2010), pp. 1060-1061 (holding that Member States need only take account of the test when drafting national exceptions); and Bechtold (2016), p. 469 (stating that Member States need not transpose the test literally into national law).
604. *See* Gotzen (2007), p. 26.

legislators in implementing exceptions. What is beyond doubt is that the three-step test, in its InfoSoc incarnation, works as a further limit to the typified exceptions, preventing the judge from applying them to acts of defendants that do not cumulatively meet the three conditions.

5 CONCLUSION

The purpose of this chapter that now comes to an end has been to lay part of the foundations for the normative inquiries that will be conducted later in Chapters 4 and 5. It has aimed at portraying the InfoSoc framework of exceptions to the rights of reproduction and communication to the public – a framework that has been at the core of scholarly controversy for some years now.

The term 'exceptions', instead of 'limitations', is deliberately used in this book. It has been submitted that the norms setting forth permitted uses of protected works fit the legal-technical notion of 'exceptions'. One point deserves particular emphasis: the qualification of permitted uses as exceptions is normatively indifferent, in that it *does not* entail a belief that exceptions are somehow inferior to exclusive rights and should be subject to narrow constructions.

As to the type of entitlement granted by copyright exceptions, it has been argued that their beneficiaries in most cases enjoy the *privilege* (and not a true right) of making unauthorised usage of a protected work. In the context of infringement proceedings brought against a user, this privilege translates into an immunity from liability. However, in the strictly delimited cases laid down in Article 6(4) InfoSoc Directive and Article 17(7) and (9) DSM Directive, the entitlement conferred upon the user may be appropriately qualified as a right.

At the international level, minimum standards have been established in relation only to a few exceptions. In contrast, the list of exceptions that are dealt with in EU instruments is much longer, spanning seven different directives. Although initially exceptions were not on top of the harmonisation priorities, the InfoSoc Directive ended up providing a comprehensive and exhaustive list of exceptions to the rights of reproduction and communication to the public (which can be extended, under certain circumstances, to the right of distribution). Apart from the exception for acts of temporary reproduction in Article 5(1), all exceptions are optional. Contrariwise, in the more recent Orphan Works, Marrakesh and DSM Directives, the EU legislator has preferred to adopt mandatory exceptions.

Pursuant to a conventionally accepted methodological practice, exceptions should be interpreted strictly. The Court has brought this canon of interpretation to bear on its copyright case law, grounding it on the idea that exceptions are to be interpreted in light of the three-step test and on the need for legal certainty repeatedly emphasised in the preamble to the Directive.

Yet, this restrictive approach has been mitigated in a sequence of more recent judgments (more on this in Chapter 4).

In addition, under EU law, even if a certain unauthorised use is eligible for protection under an exception, it must still pass the so-called three-step test. The test originally emerged in the Berne Convention, and it has since been incorporated in a series of international instruments, namely the TRIPS Agreement and the WIPO Treaties. In all these versions, the test serves the purpose of limiting the discretion of national lawmakers. As interpreted by the WTO Panel in *US-Copyright*, the test requires States *not* to enact exceptions that are excessively vague or broad and that deprive rightholders of significant income. In the InfoSoc Directive, however, the test assumes a new function, working as a limit on the judicial application of the listed exceptions. This much has been confirmed by the CJEU in its case law. The question that still lingers is whether, in the EU, the test is *also* addressed at national legislators. Recent decisions by the CJEU restricting the freedom enjoyed by Member States in implementing exceptions suggest that the answer might be in the negative: if Member State lawmakers have little discretion when crafting national exceptions (beyond the choice of implementing those that are optional), then the test is necessarily divested of any meaningful role at that stage, despite the Court's statements to the contrary.

Chapter 3
Understanding Flexibility and Legal Certainty

1 INTRODUCTION

The aptness of the InfoSoc framework of exceptions has been the object of much debate in scholarly and policymaking circles. Participants in the debate are largely split into two sides.[605] One side – which nowadays gathers the majority of academics, information technology companies, and digital rights NGOs – vigorously opposes the InfoSoc framework on grounds that it lacks sufficient flexibility to deal with the emergence of new uses and business models and that it fails to deliver on the legal certainty promise. Participants adhering to this view forcefully call for the framework's reform. The other side – composed of CMOs, creative industries, publishers, as well as some academics – generally supports the *status quo*, arguing not only that it provides ample legal certainty but also that it has so far proven to be adaptable to changes in the technological landscape. These stakeholders argue that, at most, minor periodic updates of the catalogue of exceptions would be needed.

Although the two sides disagree on whether the InfoSoc framework should be reformed, one idea seems to gather consensus: that EU copyright law, in general, and the framework of exceptions, in particular, must achieve a balance between flexibility and legal certainty. Calls for compromise between both values are commonplace in copyright literature and policy-making. Indeed, 'many agree that a framework adapted to the digital age needs to be both predictable and responsive to a changing environment'.[606] As Bernt Hugenholtz puts it, 'copyright law must mediate between the maxims of legal certainty, which favours precisely defined legal provisions that provide optimal predictability *ex post*, and of fairness, which favours

605. *See* the references cited in the Introduction, section 1.3.
606. Geiger & Schönherr (2014), p. 111. *See also* Geiger & Schönherr (2012), pp. 157 et seq.

open and flexible legal concepts that allow a wide margin of judicial appreciation *ad hoc*'.[607]

More than mere buzzwords, flexibility and legal certainty have been ever-present concerns in the harmonisation process, as revealed by the InfoSoc Directive and its history,[608] as well as by subsequent developments in EU copyright policy.[609] The Holy Grail therefore lies in having a framework of exceptions that combines 'the best of the two worlds'.[610]

---

607. Hugenholtz (2017), pp. 278-279. *See also* Reinbothe (1998), p. 64 ('particularly with regard to exceptions, there has to be a balance between the highest possible degree of harmonisation and utmost flexibility for Member States, in respect of their cultural and legal traditions'); Hugenholtz & Senftleben (2011), p. 2 (recommending the introduction of flexibility alongside the existing framework of exceptions, in order to 'combine the advantages of enhanced flexibility with legal security and technological neutrality'); Caron (2012), p. 25 (claiming that the attachment to legal certainty and predictability should not disregard the pragmatism of copyright, which is 'a kind of reed that knows how to bend itself to ensure its durability'); Hilty (2012), p. 366 ('a step in the direction of the "fair use" approach might be made, without losing the advantage of legal certainty provided by the "civil law" approach'); Geiger (2013b) (referring to *effectivité et flexibilité* as two imperatives); ECS (2014), p. 3 ('Harmonization, or even unification, of E&L should, so far as possible, respect the imperative of legal certainty, while allowing a degree of flexibility to permit the adaptation of the copyright system to changing circumstances and social needs'); and Dreier (2015), p. 142 (mentioning the need to 'coordinat[e] the objectives of harmonisation, legal certainty and flexibility' in the 'upcoming political debate').
608. The need to ensure adaptability and to eliminate existing uncertainties is repeatedly emphasised in the 1995 Green Paper (pp. 3, 16, 36, 50-51), the 1996 Follow-Up (pp. 2, 4, 7, 9-11), and the Explanatory Memorandum to the InfoSoc Proposal (pp. 7, 8, 12, 17, 19, 23, 25, 27, 29, 30, 31, 32). In the InfoSoc preamble, *see* Recitals 2 and 5, highlighting the need 'to create a general and flexible legal framework at Community level in order to foster the development of the information society in Europe' and 'to respond adequately to economic realities such as new forms of exploitation'; Recitals 4, 6, 21 and 25, stressing the importance of eliminating uncertainty and legislative inconsistencies; and Recital 32 recognising that the list of exceptions tries to take into account 'the different legal traditions in Member States, while, at the same time, aiming to ensure a functioning internal market'.
609. In late 2013, in its consultation on the review of EU copyright rules, the Commission emphasised the need for balance, stating that '[t]he main question here is whether a greater degree of flexibility can be introduced in the EU and Member States regulatory framework while ensuring the required legal certainty, including for the functioning of the Single Market, and respecting the EU's international obligations' – 2013 Public Consultation, p. 17. Following this consultation, and reporting on the implementation of the InfoSoc Directive, the European Parliament underscored that 'any reform of the copyright framework should … provide a stable, clear and flexible legal base that fosters investment and growth in the creative and cultural sector, whilst removing legal uncertainties and inconsistencies that adversely affect the functioning of the internal market' (EP Resolution Implementation InfoSoc Directive 2015, para. 19) – a statement that highlights once more the importance of achieving an equilibrium between flexibility and legal certainty.
610. Leistner (2011), p. 438.

Flexibility and legal certainty operate as two-sided claims in the InfoSoc debate, being part of the argumentative toolbox of supporters and critics alike. Upon closer inspection, however, it becomes apparent that these terms are regularly employed in a loose and unspecified manner, masking conceptual distinctions that are vital for the debate. The same expressions are frequently used to refer to autonomous and importantly different ideas that correspond to often-conflicting policy preferences and arguments. Identifying these preferences is a crucial exercise not merely to clarify the terms of the debate, but to understand *if*, *why*, and *how* the InfoSoc framework of exceptions should be reformed. The present chapter attempts at dispelling this conceptual entanglement and at getting a more specific grip on the concepts of 'flexibility' and 'legal certainty'.

Against this background, the present chapter addresses the following research questions: What is the meaning of 'flexibility' and 'legal certainty'? How have these concepts been used in EU copyright law? How can they be translated into criteria against which to assess the existing framework of exceptions? Answering these questions will serve a twofold purpose.

First, and more generally, it will allow us to organise the copyright literature on flexibility and legal certainty into a holistic picture and to remedy the lacuna of reflection on these concepts. Insofar as these terms embody the two most commonly employed policy arguments in the InfoSoc controversy, a more refined and theoretically grounded understanding of how they have been used will allow us to appreciate the extent to which the current framework and proposals for reforming it (would) succeed in furthering these goals.

This, in turn, leads us to the second purpose of this chapter. As a by-product of the investigation on how flexibility and legal certainty should be conceptualised, the chapter will define the assessment criteria that will guide the evaluation of the InfoSoc framework in the following chapter. The answers to the foregoing questions will thus provide essential background to the prescriptive parts of this book.

This chapter is divided into three other sections. Sections 2 and 3 respectively explore the meaning of flexibility and legal certainty.[611] Each section divides its concept into two broad normative objectives and provides evidence of why each of them can legitimately be understood as a goal of the copyright harmonisation process and where to find such evidence in the *acquis*. While 'flexibility' is typically employed to refer to the law's adaptability to technology-related changes (section 2.1) and to different

611. The meaning of these concepts will be investigated by analysing the way in which they are *used* in the InfoSoc debate. This conception of 'meaning as use' is characteristic of the later stages of Ludwig Wittgenstein's thought. In his seminal (but posthumously published) book *Philosophical Investigations*, Wittgenstein famously stated that '[f]or a *large* class of cases – though not for all – in which we employ the word "meaning" it can be defined thus: the meaning of a word is its use in the language' – Wittgenstein (1958), para. 43.

national traditions and specificities (section 2.2), 'legal certainty' is used as a synonym for guidance in relation to the legal status of unauthorised uses of protected works (section 3.1) and for the harmonisation of copyright law (section 3.2). These four objectives form the normative apparatus that will underlie our critical analysis of the InfoSoc framework of exceptions in Chapter 4. Finally, Section 4 concludes.

2 FLEXIBILITY

The copyright-relevant meaning of the term 'flexibility' naturally draws from the meaning of the term in common parlance. The noun 'flexibility' is used to mean 'the quality of bending easily without breaking', 'the ability to be easily modified', and the 'willingness to change or compromise'.[612] The meaning and sub-meanings of the adjective 'flexible' add relevant elements to the previous definitions: that which is flexible is 'able to be easily modified *to respond to altered circumstances*' or 'ready and able to change *so as to adapt to different circumstances*'.[613] In law, indeed, the term 'flexibility' is generally employed to refer to the law's *adaptability* to different or changing social, cultural, economic, or political circumstances.

In EU copyright law and, specifically, in the context of the controversy that is of interest to us, the term 'flexibility' and its derivatives are employed to refer to the framework's capacity to adapt to ever-changing technological circumstances (section 2.1), as well as to different national cultures within the EU (section 2.2). I will explore each of these objectives in turn.

2.1 Adaptability to Technology-Related Changes

In copyright law, the term 'flexibility' is more often than not used as a synonym to the law's adaptability to the phenomenon of technological change and the ensuing behavioural and market changes.[614] In fact, the

612. Oxford English Dictionary (2010), p. 669.
613. Oxford English Dictionary (2010), p. 669 (emphasis added).
614. It is in this sense that most copyright scholars employ the term. *See*, *e.g.*, Spoor (1998), p. 29 ('Not all copyright laws are equally flexible when it comes to accommodating new developments'); Samuelson (1998), p. 76 ('Open-ended exceptions can provide a flexible mechanism with which to adapt copyright law to meet the challenges of new technologies that legislators did not and could not have anticipated'); Hilty et al. (2008), p. 8 ('European copyright legislation needs the flexibility to adapt to evolving and future methods of disseminating knowledge, instead of being fixed to specific forms of use based on a temporary snapshot of ongoing developments'); Hugenholtz & Okediji (2008), p. 42 (an international instrument on copyright limitations and exceptions 'must contain principles that are sufficiently flexible to accommodate technological change'); Pereira (2008b), p. 862 (connecting 'greater flexibility' with the 'resulting capacity of adaptation to the challenges of new technologies'); Ohly (2009), p. 235 ('Since

'altered circumstances' that copyright stakeholders are chiefly concerned with are, or are caused by, changes in the technological landscape.

It is, by now, a cliché to say that copyright law has always been profoundly influenced by technological change. The idea is often put metaphorically: copyright law has been called 'a creature of technology'[615] and, perhaps more affectionately, it is said to have been 'technology's child from the start'.[616] Whatever metaphor one chooses, the truth is that, since its early stages, copyright law has largely been shaped by changes in the

---

copyright law tends to follow technological development, the importance of flexible solutions rises as technological progress gathers pace'); Janssens (2009), p. 337 ('the choice of a closed list should be abandoned and such a list should be replaced by a more flexible system that will allow a more rapid response to new business models, novel uses or urgent situations that will continue to arise, undoubtedly, in the dynamic information society'); Dreier (2010), p. 52 ('there is an urgent need for … a flexible – albeit *de minimis* – exception in view of the rapid technological development of the information society infrastructure and the different new business models and use possibilities'); Lucas (2010), p. 282 ('Often, one invokes the flexibility of fair use, which allows the law to be adapted to keep pace with a fast-changing reality better than a "necessarily somewhat fixed" legislation would do'); Leistner (2011), p. 442 (an opening provision 'might provide for a more flexible legal framework, allowing for new forms of use by infrastructural internet services which provide a benefit to society'); Torremans (2012), p. 337 ('to be able to introduce flexibility in the application of copyright exceptions in a rapidly developing technological environment'); Hugenholtz (2013c), p. 26 ('the general lack of flexibility in the laws of copyright in the EU and its Member States … allow little leeway for new technological uses not foreseen by the legislature'); Rosati (2014a), p. 585 ('Over the past few years, consensus has grown around the idea that the current EU legislative framework for copyright lacks the flexibility needed to accommodate emerging interests, specifically those arising in connection with technological development'); Xalabarder (2016), p. 635 (new criteria, like the proportionality principle, 'have allowed the Court to introduce some much-needed flexibility at a time when copyright laws are not always prepared to meet the challenges posed by technologically changing contexts'); and Quintais (2018), p. 399 ('ensuring that the concept of "act of communication" retains sufficient flexibility to survive technological obsolescence').

615. Sherman & Wiseman (2012), p. 1.

616. Goldstein (2003), p. 21. Employing the same metaphor, *see* Goldberg & Feder (1993), p. 37, and Rose (2005), p. 63. In a similar vein, *see* Hugenholtz & Okediji (2008), p. 42 ('The clarity of copyright doctrine has always been hostage to the vagaries of technological change'); Depoorter (2009), p. 1838 ('Copyright law has a symbiotic relationship with technology'); Walter & Lewinski (2010), p. 937 ('The development of copyright was always closely connected to technical evolution'); Synodinou (2012), p. 618 ('Copyright law is strongly connected to technological changes'), and (2014), p. 81 ('rather than being external to copyright law, technology forms an integral part of the very fabric of law'); Halpern & Johnson (2014), fn. 40 ('The tensions between technology and copyright are as old as copyright itself'); Quintais (2017a), p. 18 (copyright law 'has evolved in a dialectic relationship with technology'); and Finck & Moscon (2019), p. 77 (copyright law's 'development and enforcement have always been closely inspired by the technological state of the art'). As acknowledged by the European Commission, '[t]he history of copyright and related rights consists of a succession of reactions in which the law was adapted to technical developments, sometimes in great bounds' – 1995 Green Paper, p. 24.

technological environment. The history and prehistory of copyright are intimately tied to the history of copying and communication technologies. As already mentioned, it was one major advance in technology – Gutenberg's movable-type printing press – that led to the creation and attribution of printing privileges, the ancestors of modern-day copyright.[617] Hence, to say that '[c]opyright came into existence because of a technological challenge'[618] is not much of an overstatement. From then through to the piano roll, the photocopying machine, radio broadcasting, computer programs, and so on, technological change has consistently moulded copyright law.[619] The dawn and development of the Internet, in particular, led to wide-ranging legislative changes at the international, European, and national levels.

Arguably every doctrine in copyright law has been impacted by the appearance of new technologies. Throughout copyright history, technological change has enabled new types of creative works, such as photographs, phonograms, film, and computer programs;[620] new forms of authorship, like computer- or AI-generated works[621] and the so-called *wiki* authorship;[622]

---

617. *See supra* Chapter 1, section 3. On the history of copyright law, *see* Patterson (1968), Rose (1993), Deazley (2004), Izzo (2010), and the different contributions in Deazley et al. (2010) and Alexander & Gómez-Arostegui (2016).
618. Goldberg & Feder (1993), p. 46. As noted by Justice Stevens of the US Supreme Court in the seminal *Sony* judgment, '[f]rom its beginning, the law of copyright has developed in response to significant changes in technology. Indeed, it was the invention of a new form of copying equipment – the printing press – that gave rise to the original need for copyright protection' – US Supreme Court, *Sony*, p. 430.
619. *See* Sherman & Wiseman (2012), p. 1.
620. For accounts on the extension of copyright protection so as to cover these forms of creative expression, *see* the pieces by Bowrey (2012) (photographs), Okpaluba (2012) (phonograms), Bracha (2012) (film) and Samuelson (2012) (computer programs). Technological change has also raised interesting issues about new types of works that arise out of the combination of previously existing works, such as multimedia works. For pioneering studies on multimedia works, *see* Davies (1994), Lucas (1995) and Rocha (1996). The topic became particularly *en vogue* in the early 2000s, deserving book-length studies – *see* Stamatoudi (2002) and Aplin (2005).
621. Computer-generated works ought to be distinguished from computer-assisted works. The latter raise no particular concern, in that it is common for the creator to make use of some tool to facilitate creation: using a computer is, in this regard, no different from using a pen or a camera. As stated in AG Opinion, *Painer*, para. 121, protected human creations 'can also include those for which the person employs a technical aid, such as a camera'. In the case of computer- or AI-generated works, there is more than a mere technical aid: the work is created *by* the machine with minimal or no human intervention, rather than by a human *using* a machine. On the challenges raised by these works, *see* the early study by Samuelson (1985) and, more recently, Perry & Margoni (2010), Ramalho (2017a), Margoni (2018) and Gervais (2019).
622. The phenomena of mass authorship that characterise the Web 2.0 were facilitated by the appearance of websites that allow users to collaborate on the elaboration of literary and artistic works. The paradigmatic example of such a website is Wikipedia. Wikipedia articles arise from the successive adding and editing of content by potentially multiple authors, whose individual contributions may be rather small and unnoticeable. As noted by Phillips (2009), p. 204, the content of these articles can be 'worked and reworked by

new enforcement methods, such as TPMs and filtering technologies;[623] and, most importantly for the present study, new ways of using existing works, including uses as diverse and chronologically dispersed as photocopying, radio broadcasting, and TDM.

Indeed, chief among the concerns of scholars and policymakers is the emergence of new uses or forms of access and exploitation. Changes in the technological environment regularly enable innovative ways for end-users to engage with protected content, as well as new services and business models that rely on the use of such content.[624] Compared to the other technological challenges recurrently faced by copyright, new ways of *using* works are arguably the ones that arise more often and that have a more profound impact on copyright law's effectiveness.[625] This is all the more so in the current online era. As access to storage mechanisms and high-speed Internet increases, more and more people upload, download, stream, rip, and hyperlink to protected content.[626] Likewise, online platforms and the very

---

several authors with the result that the individual contribution of each cannot be detected'. Wikipedia articles have thus been deemed as 'perpetual work[s] in progress' – Simone (2014), p. 103. The obvious question then arises: who should be considered the author(s) of the work? The issue is fraught with uncertainty, though the practical implications of this uncertainty are minimized by the fact that Wikipedia contributors agree to license the content they produce to the public under well-known all-purpose licences, such as the Creative Commons' Attribution/Share-Alike Licence. Anticipating the difficulties raised by the phenomenon of mass authorship and suggesting possible solutions, *see* Dreier (1993), pp. 191-192 and 196-197.

623. In the face of digital infringement, one of the first reactions by rightholders was to develop technology-based mechanisms to ensure the protection of their works. TPMs rely on technologies like stenography and encryption to accomplish one (or more) of three functions: to control the access to the work; to control particular uses of the work, such as copying; and to protect the integrity of the work, preventing it from being modified. *See generally* Koelman & Helberger (2000). On the other hand, the use of filtering technologies – technologies that screen content on online platforms, blocking downloads or uploads of protected subject matter – is a more recent trend. On the use of filtering technologies for purposes of copyright enforcement, *see generally* Angelopoulos (2009). The idea of requiring the implementation of filtering systems by online platforms of user-uploaded content that engage in acts of communication to the public inspired the controversial Article 17 DSM Directive. The provision has generated unprecedented amounts of critical scholarship even before its adoption – *see*, among many others, Angelopoulos (2017b); Rendas (2017b); Frosio (2018); and Senftleben et al. (2018).

624. *See*, in this regard, Explanatory Memorandum to DSM Proposal, p. 2 ('New uses have emerged as well as new actors and new business models. In the digital environment, cross-border uses have also intensified and new opportunities for consumers to access copyright-protected content have materialised').

625. *See* Hardy (1999), p. 672, deeming the emergence of new uses as 'the most vexing of all' problems raised by technological change. Relatedly, *see* Synodinou (2014), p. 93, stating that 'the main and most popular critiques in respect of adapting copyright law to technological challenges concern the field of copyright exceptions and limitations'.

626. *See, generally*, Vicente (2005), pp. 155-157; Lessig (2008), pp. 36-50; Murray (2016), pp. 275-276; and Quintais (2017a), pp. 1-3.

Internet rely on a variety of copyright-relevant acts in order to operate properly. All these acts have been generating considerable volumes of litigation, policymaking debates, and scholarly writing. It is thus fair to say, borrowing Ben Depoorter's words, that 'most pages in the history of copyright law involve drawing boundaries around new uses of content created by technology'.[627]

In a context where technological change is accelerating and largely unpredictable, it is undisputed among stakeholders, regardless of the side on which they stand in the InfoSoc debate, that adaptability is key, in order to prevent copyright law from becoming antediluvian. EU policymakers have also consistently highlighted the importance of copyright law's adaptability to technological change, in general, and to the emergence of new uses and business models, in particular.[628] In the early stages of the legislative process that resulted in the adoption of the InfoSoc Directive, the Commission stated that:

> If the information society is to develop successfully, the many new services and products being created must be able to benefit fully from the information superhighway. … There is no doubt that laws will have to be adapted in order to respond to the new and varied requirements which may appear, raising unprecedented issues.[629]

As seen above, the InfoSoc Directive aimed at adapting legislation on copyright and related rights to the information society paradigm, with an emphasis on new forms of exploitation.[630] Recital 5 InfoSoc Directive clarifies this much:

> Technological development has multiplied and diversified the vectors for creation, production and exploitation. While no new concepts for the protection of intellectual property are needed, the current law on copyright and related rights should be adapted and supplemented to respond adequately to economic realities such as new forms of exploitation.

Almost twenty years after InfoSoc's adoption, the concern around the adaptability to technology-related changes remains pressing, as is apparent from the legislative history of the recent DSM Directive. As observed in the Explanatory Memorandum to the DSM Proposal:

> The evolution of digital technologies has changed the way works and other protected subject-matter are created, produced, distributed and exploited. … Even though the objectives and principles laid down by the EU copyright framework remain sound, there is a need to adapt it to these new realities.[631]

---

627. Depoorter (2009), p. 1839.
628. As noted by Vicente (2008), p. 121, technological development is a *leitmotif* of IP harmonisation in general.
629. 1995 Green Paper, p. 3.
630. *See supra* Introduction, section 1.2.
631. Explanatory Memorandum DSM Proposal, p. 2.

In light of what has just been said, the InfoSoc framework of exceptions will be deemed *flexible* for the purposes of this research if, when put before a new use of protected works, it is capable of being easily modified to respond to that circumstance.[632] It is crucial to note that this adaptability is not limited to expanding the number and/or scope of permitted uses. Rather, flexibility should 'cut both ways':[633] it may serve to clarify either that a new use falls within the realm of exclusivity or that the rightholder's authorisation is not necessary.[634] Flexibility is, in this sense, a normatively indifferent and unbiased concept.

As already hinted at, despite the fact that it is generally agreed that copyright law should be adaptable to technology-related changes, opposite sides of the debate disagree on the question of *who* should be entrusted with the task of adjusting the InfoSoc framework to such changes – the legislative branch or the judicial branch. In this context, the term 'flexibility' is often used in an indistinct manner to refer to *legislative flexibility* or *judicial flexibility*. While supporters of the existing framework argue that the leading role in responding to the challenges posed by technological development should rest in the hands of legislators, critics submit that judges should be granted wider discretion.

The objective of adaptability to technological change will therefore be split into two different paths for attaining it: legislative responsiveness (section 2.1.1) and judicial discretion (section 2.1.2).

2.1.1 Legislative Responsiveness

Commentators untroubled by the features of the InfoSoc Directive favour maintaining a list of precisely defined exceptions, which can be periodically updated by the legislator, rather than transferring the bulk of decision-making to judges through the adoption of a standard-like exception. 'The national lists', André Lucas argues, 'could very well be regularly fine-tuned, not to mention the other occasions offered by frequent legislative amendments.'[635] Critics of the *status quo*, in contrast, raise doubts over the legislator's – especially the EU legislator's – capacity to keep pace with technological change. Legislative responses at the EU level have been accused of being 'slow',[636] 'complex',[637] 'cumbersome and lengthy'.[638]

---

632. *See* Guibault et al. (2007) (using the term 'sustainable' to refer to copyright law's capacity to adjust to technological developments and new market conditions) and Renda et al. (2015), p. 124 (analysing the EU copyright framework's adaptability to technological or scientific advances under the criterion of 'relevance').
633. Martin-Prat (2014), p. 42.
634. *See* 2013 Public Consultation, p. 17.
635. Lucas (2010), p. 282.
636. Senftleben (2009), p. 1. *See also* He (2009), p. 306.
637. Hugenholtz & Senftleben (2011), p. 7.
638. Geiger & Schönherr (2012), p. 143.

As these arguments make clear, the quarrel revolves around the degree of *legislative responsiveness*. 'Responsive' is defined in dictionaries as 'reacting quickly and positively'[639] and responsiveness as 'the ability ... to adjust quickly to suddenly altered external conditions'.[640] Drawing on this ordinary meaning of the term 'responsiveness', legislative responsiveness will depend on two conditions: first, on the ability or freedom of legislators to change the law, which, in an area of shared competence,[641] must be raised at both the EU level and the Member State level; and second, on the speed at which legislators go about that change. The paragraphs that follow outline each of these interrelated conditions.

At the EU level, the freedom to change the law depends, first and foremost, on the EU having competence to legislate and adopt legally binding acts in a specific area. The competence system in the EU is governed by three principles: the principle of conferral; the principle of subsidiarity; and the principle of proportionality.[642] Whenever the EU intends to update the catalogue of copyright exceptions in the wake of changes in the technological environment, the legislative measure at stake must comply with these three principles. A brief description of each is thus in order.

Under the *principle of conferral*, the EU enjoys no inherent law-making competence. Instead, it is allowed to act only within the limits of the competences conferred upon it by the Member States in the Treaties in order to achieve the objectives enshrined therein.[643] In light of this principle, the legal basis on which a given Union action is founded must be indicated.[644]

In general, efforts to harmonise copyright law serve the declared purpose of fostering the internal market. This is not only the 'pre-eminent objective' of copyright harmonisation[645] but also one of the Union's fundamental aims.[646] It is the competence clause contained in Article 114 TFEU (former Article 95 TEC) that empowers the EU legislator to adopt measures designed to approximate Member State laws that have as their goal the establishment and functioning of the internal market. This is the legal

639. Oxford English Dictionary (2010), p. 1514.
640. Dictionary.com, http://www.dictionary.com/browse/responsiveness.
641. The CJEU has deemed IP to be an area of shared competence in *Opinion 1/94*.
642. *See* Article 5(1) TEU.
643. *See* Article 5(2) TEU.
644. *See* CJEU, *Commission v. Council*, para. 46.
645. *See* Hugenholtz et al. (2006), p. 9. As early as in the 1988 Green Paper, p. 3, the Commission stated that '[t]o the maximum extent possible, creators and providers of copyright goods and services should be able to treat the Community as a single internal market. This requires the elimination of obstacles and legal differences that substantially disrupt the functioning of the market by obstructing or distorting cross-frontier trade in those goods and services as well as distorting competition.'
646. The objective of creating the internal market is announced in Article 3(3) TEU. The definition of 'internal market' is laid down in Article 26(2) TFEU: 'an area without internal frontiers in which the free movement of goods, persons, services and capital is ensured in accordance with the provisions of the Treaties'.

basis behind the InfoSoc Directive,[647] as well as of most directives in the field of copyright.[648] For Article 114 TFEU to be considered a proper legal basis for a certain measure, a mere finding of disparities between national rules is not sufficient; the existing differences must constitute obstacles to cross-border trade and the measure in question must be designed to prevent them.[649] Article 114 can also be used to prevent the emergence of future obstacles to trade resulting from the heterogeneous development of national laws, as long as the emergence of such obstacles is likely and, again, the measure in question is designed to prevent them.[650] In addition to trade-related obstacles, distortions of competition may also be used as a justification for recourse to this legal basis.[651]

Thus, in the absence of a specific Treaty provision conferring on the EU competence to *approximate* national copyright laws (notwithstanding Article 118 TFEU[652]), harmonisation measures have been justified on grounds of their potential to contribute to the establishment and functioning of the

---

647. *See* Recitals 1-4, 6, 7, 9, 23, 25, 31, 32, 47 and 56 InfoSoc Directive.
648. *See, e.g.*, Recitals 4-5 Software Directive; Recitals 2, 3, 5, 14, 21 and 33 Satellite and Cable Directive; Recitals 3 and 10 Term Directive; Recitals 2-4 Database Directive; Recitals 8-15 and 22-23 Resale Right Directive; Recitals 8-9 Orphan Works Directive; Recitals 5 and 18 Collective Management Directive; Recital 6 Marrakesh Directive; and Recitals 1 and 2 DSM Directive. Of course, directives may be adopted with a view to pursuing additional and more specific objectives. For instance, the Orphan Works Directive aimed at allowing the mutual recognition of the status of orphan works on a cross-border basis on the grounds of Article 53(1) TFEU.
649. *See* CJEU, *Tobacco Advertising I*, paras 84-86. Various directives in the copyright *acquis* refer to the negative impact that national differences have on the internal market – *see, e.g.*, Recitals 4-5 Software Directive; Recitals 2-3 Database Directive; and Recitals 6-7 InfoSoc Directive.
650. *See* CJEU, *Spain v. Council*, para. 35, where the Court held that the 1992 SPC Regulation, which created the supplementary protection certificate for medicinal products, had been validly adopted on the basis of the provision conferring upon the EU the competence to harmonise national laws with the aim of creating the internal market. *See also, e.g.*, CJEU, *Data Retention*, para. 64, and CJEU, *Vodafone*, para. 33.
651. *See* CJEU, *Titanium Dioxide*, para. 23, and CJEU, *Tobacco Advertising I*, para. 95. But note that remote and indirect distortions are not enough to justify the use of Article 114 TFEU. The distortions need to be 'appreciable' or 'significant' – *see* CJEU, *Tobacco Advertising I*, paras 106-109, and CJEU, *Vodafone*, para. 47.
652. As already noted, since the Lisbon reform, Article 118 TFEU empowers the EU to establish measures for the creation of European IP rights, including e.g. a unitary copyright title valid in all Member States. The development of this uniform protection of IP rights throughout the Union must nevertheless be based on 'the establishment and functioning of the internal market'. This means that, although the EU is now competent to unify copyright law, such unification efforts can only cover the copyright doctrines that may constitute obstacles to the internal market. Hence, whatever competence source is invoked to legislate in the IP field, the EU must demonstrate an internal market rationale. European IP rights – namely, the Community trademark (now EU trademark) and the Community designs – had been established before the Lisbon reform. These were based on the Union's residual competence under former Article 308 TEC (current Article 352 TFEU), the so-called flexibility clause.

internal market. The internal market is one of the areas in which competence is shared between the EU and its Member States, pursuant to Article 4(2)(a) TFEU. This means that both the EU and the Member States may legislate in this area, though Member States can only exercise their competence to the extent that the Union has not done so (Article 2(2) TFEU).

In such areas of shared competence, the EU competence to legislate is dependent on the *principle of subsidiarity*, which is set forth in Article 5(3) TEU. According to this provision, the EU is allowed to act only if and in so far as the objectives of the proposed action cannot be sufficiently achieved at the national level and can be better achieved at Union level. The test of subsidiarity is thus a two-pronged one: it must be asserted, first, that the objectives in question cannot be attained in a sufficient manner by Member States and, second, that these objectives are more aptly achieved at the EU level. Therefore, assuming the EU enjoys competence to approximate national copyright laws under the internal market clause, the legitimacy of the Union's action in the field of copyright further depends on the provision of evidence that the action's objective is realised more effectively at the EU level than at the Member State level.[653]

The *principle of proportionality* constitutes yet another constraint on the freedom of the EU to legislate, governing the form and intensity of EU action. According to Article 5(4) TEU, the action undertaken by the EU cannot exceed what is necessary to achieve the objectives of the Treaties. As is well known, the proportionality analysis consists of a threefold inquiry: (1) the measure must be adequate to attain the objective in question; (2) it must be necessary, in the sense that it is the least restrictive among all the equally effective measures; and (3) it must be proportional *stricto sensu*, in that there must be a balance between the benefits gained with the adoption of the measure and the costs it entails. Therefore, before a harmonisation measure in the field of copyright (or, for that matter, in any other field) can be considered legitimate, the EU should first conduct a proportionality assessment.

But when discussing the issue of 'legislative flexibility', scholars and policymakers sometimes focus not on whether the EU is allowed to act, but on the latitude of *Member States* to legislate autonomously.[654] Based on the argument that the process of law-making in the EU is too complex and lengthy to deal adequately with law's lag in relation to technology, influential

653. *See* Ramalho (2016a), p. 110.

654. *See*, most notably, Hugenholtz & Senftleben (2011). *See also* Vinje (2000), pp. 553-554 ('the best intellectual property is generally the most flexible legislation, in particular so it does not become obsolete as technology develops, and this is especially true in times of great technological change. … [C]ontrary to the approach taken in the WIPO Copyright Treaty, the [InfoSoc] Directive goes so far as to prohibit Member States from adopting new exceptions that take account of technological change'); 2013 Public Consultation, p. 21 (pointing out that 'the formulation of certain of the limitations and exceptions is general enough to give significant flexibility to the Member States as to

commentators have advised Member States to explore the policy space left for national initiatives both within and outside the EU *acquis*, instead of waiting for action at the EU level.[655] The advice presupposes, however, that Member States are free to legislate in the field of copyright. Other commentators have questioned this premise, claiming that, in light of developments in CJEU case law, the room that is available for national legislative initiatives is narrower than may seem at first sight.[656]

The breadth of national elbowroom depends on the reach of the EU *acquis* and on its harmonising effect. EU harmonisation has not extended to all corners of copyright law.[657] Also, policy space for Member State initiatives may be available *within* harmonised terrain. The strength of the pre-emptive effects of the harmonisation measures in place reveals the extent to which national law has been set aside by EU law.[658] The freedom to legislate at Member State level is therefore inversely related with the harmonisation objective: the stronger the harmonising effects of a measure, the narrower the freedom left for national action.[659]

Moving on to the second condition identified above, legislative responsiveness depends not only on the freedom to legislate on a given area but also on *the rate* at which the legislator is capable of updating the law to adjust to technological change.[660] Whereas the freedom to legislate (either at the EU

---

how, and to what extent, to implement them'); and Martin-Prat (2014), p. 37 (noting that a 'reduction of flexibility of member states has happened with regard to limitations of rights').

655. *See* Hugenholtz & Senftleben (2011).
656. *See* Rosati (2014a).
657. *See* Hugenholtz & Senftleben (2011), p. 26, arguing that 'considerable flexibility outside the EU *acquis* can be identified in the field of the right of adaptation', which falls outside the scope of the InfoSoc Directive.
658. As mentioned, under Article 2(2) TFEU, in areas of shared competence between the EU and its Member States, 'Member States shall exercise their competence to the extent that the Union has not exercised its competence'. The wording of the provision seems to suggest that Member States are automatically pre-empted from legislating in such an area as soon as the Union exercises its competence. This understanding, however, is in contradiction with the Sole Article of Protocol No. 25, which reads: 'With reference to Article 2(2) of the Treaty on the Functioning of the European Union on shared competence, when the Union has taken action in a certain area, the scope of this exercise of competence only covers those elements governed by the Union act in question and therefore does not cover the whole area.' What emerges from these provisions, when read together, is that Member States are not *necessarily* pre-empted from legislating in fields where the EU has already acted. The extent to which Member States are free to legislate must be assessed on a case-by-case basis, looking at the content of the specific harmonisation measure and at the interpretative case law of the CJEU. For further detail, *see* Arena (2010-2011), pp. 525-527. *See also infra* 3.2.
659. *See infra* 3.2.1. and Chapter 4, section 5.1.1.
660. Response time is generally not taken as a relevant indicator in relation to the judiciary. For one thing, courts, unlike legislators, are in a passive position, in that they need to wait for the dispute to be brought before them. For another, although judicial proceedings may be long-lasting, the state of polarisation that currently characterises

or Member State levels) is related with the first condition of responsiveness – the ability to react –, the second condition raises the question of how quickly the reaction occurs.

The issue of legislative pace has been brought up by critics of the InfoSoc framework. They predict that the legislator is condemned to playing catch-up with technology, due to the unpredictability of technological development and its speed vis-à-vis that of legislative change.[661] In the words of Bernt Hugenholtz:

> Whereas, legislatures of the nineteenth and early twentieth century could still anticipate and adequately respond to the main technological changes that required modification of the law, the accelerating pace of technological change in the early twenty-first century no longer allows such legislative foresight. Conversely, the length of the legislative cycle in copyright has become ever longer, as copyright law is no longer perceived as a mostly 'technical' legal matter but has become highly politicized.[662]

Critics like Hugenholtz are particularly concerned with the average time it takes to pass legislation at the EU level.[663] Under the ordinary legislative procedure, which covers the vast majority of the EU's areas of competence, the Commission submits a proposal to the European Parliament and the Council, who must agree on a joint text in one of up to three readings. The duration of this procedure varies significantly, depending on the level of controversy surrounding the proposal and on how lobby-ridden the field is. In the case of directives, one must add to the duration of the EU procedure the deadlines for national implementation and the delays that frequently occur at this stage.

---

copyright law-making, and that is partly responsible for legislative delay in this field, can hardly spill over to the judicial process.

661. This relative speed seems largely ineluctable, not least because attempting to predict technological change and its implications is fated to failure. Technology predictions more often than not prove to be mistaken some years down the line. Among the most quoted predictions are those of Ken Olson, founder of Digital Equipment Corp., who, in 1977, said that, '[t]here is no reason anyone would want a computer in their home', and of IBM executives who turned down a deal with the eventual founders of Xerox under the argument that '[t]he world potential market for copying machines is 5000 at most'. On the topic of (failed) predictions of technological change *see also* Toffler (1970), p. 191, and Volokh (1995), pp. 1375-1376.
662. Hugenholtz (2017), pp. 280-281.
663. In fact, the time it takes to pass legislation at the national level is generally much lower. Relatedly, *see* Hugenholtz et al. (2006), p. 217 ('A non-exhaustive list of limitations would allow Member States to respond more quickly than the EC legislature to urgent situations that will arise, undoubtedly, in the dynamic information market'), and Lewinski (2018), p. 139 (claiming that legislative changes according to national needs that may change over time would be much more easily enacted than amendments to EU legislation following the EU legislative procedure).

2.1.2 Judicial Discretion

Several commentators and policymakers understand 'flexibility' not as a legislative phenomenon, but as the adaptability to changing circumstances *without* the need for any legislative intervention.[664] These participants in the InfoSoc debate generally believe that it would be preferable to have judges dealing with the accommodation of technological uses of protected works, instead of legislators. Should judges have enough autonomy to decide on the lawfulness of new uses, there would be no need for recurring legislative updates.

The primary way for granting discretion of this kind to the judiciary is through the wording of statutory provisions. In the context of the InfoSoc debate, two properties of the wording of copyright exceptions may be particularly relevant: their vagueness and their breadth.

The issue of vagueness is related to a fundamental distinction in the jurisprudence of norms: that between *rules* and *standards*. There is abundant literature on the distinction, a detailed analysis of which exceeds the scope of the present section.[665] For purposes of this research, I will take the difference between rules and standards to be one of degree.[666] These two ways of casting norms vary along a precision-vagueness spectrum, with rules being on the precision end and standards on the vagueness end.

Philosophers generally agree that a word or expression is vague if it has 'borderline cases'. Borderline cases separate the cases in which the vague term clearly applies from those in which it clearly does not.[667] According to a widespread definition, borderline cases are cases 'in which one just does not know whether to apply the expression or withhold it, and one's not knowing is not due to ignorance of the facts'.[668] Vagueness varies inversely

---

664. *See* Spoor (1998), p. 29.

665. The debate is particularly pervasive in American scholarship. Any list of leading references would include Dworkin (1967), pp. 22-29; Kennedy (1976), pp. 1687-1713; Schlag (1985), pp. 383-420; Kaplow (1992), pp. 571-586; Sullivan (1992), pp. 56-95; Grodin (1994); Sunstein (1995); Posner (1997), pp. 107-116; and Schauer (2009), pp. 188 et seq.

666. The distinction that I advance in the lines that follow largely borrows from the one adopted by Schauer (2009), pp. 188 et seq., who understands the distinction between rules and standards as a continuum. The fundamental point is summarised in the following passage: 'rather than thinking of a distinction between rules and standards, it might be better to think of a location on the vagueness-precision continuum, and "How vague?" or "How precise?" may be far more useful questions to ask than whether some directive is more like a rule or more like a standard' (p. 190). *See also* Ehrlich & Posner (1974), p. 258, and Schauer (2004-2005), pp. 803-804.

667. *See* Soames (2011), p. 31.

668. Grice (1989), p. 177. *See also* Alexy & Dreier (1991), pp. 74-75, calling borderline cases 'neutral candidates'.

with precision and words may be more or less vague (or, conversely, precise[669]), depending on the range of borderline cases they have.[670]

Typical (non-legal) examples of vague words are gradable adjectives like 'bald'.[671] Everyone knows someone who is clearly bald and someone who is clearly not bald, but they also know people that are borderline bald (I would count myself as one such person). As Charles Sanders Peirce explained, it is 'intrinsically uncertain'[672] whether people in this last group are bald and this intrinsic uncertainty is not due to 'any ignorance of the interpreter':[673] we know the meaning of the term 'bald' and we know how the person's scalp looks like,[674] but we are still unsure whether to qualify the

669. Waldron (1994), p. 522, importantly points out that the term 'specificity' is often mistakenly used as the inverse of 'vagueness'. The inverse of 'specific' is, as Waldron explains, 'general'. Hart (1994), p. 128, seems to have equated generality with vagueness when he wrote that 'uncertainty at the borderline is the price to be paid for the use of general classifying terms'. But, in truth, generality is different from vagueness and not necessarily correlated with it. In Waldron's example '[t]he term "tree" is more specific than the term "living thing", but it may be much easier to say whether a given object is a living thing (as opposed to inanimate) than whether it is a tree (as opposed, for example, to a bush)' – Waldron (1994), p. 522. Although I agree that vagueness and generality are independent from each other, I find the concept of 'generality' potentially misleading when used to explain the difference between a tree and a living thing (or, for that matter, between any other two categories) in a legal piece. That is so because, in law, generality is typically seen as an on/off phenomenon. A legal rule is general if it is designed to apply not to an individually considered person engaging in a (specific) behaviour, but to all people who come to find themselves in the situation described in the rule's antecedent. In contrast, a command directed at an individual person at a given time is typically characterised as 'specific'. That is why rules are frequently characterised as 'generalisations' – *see* Schauer (1993), pp. 17-37. Unlike the distinction between general and specific, the distinction between vague and precise is one of degree. A rule forbidding all 'acts of transmission or retransmission of a work to the public by wire or wireless means and of making such works available online' is *more precise* than a rule forbidding 'acts of communication to the public'. Yet, they are both general, in that they are designed to apply to *all* such acts and not only to a specific act. It is, I believe, more appropriate to describe the relation between 'tree' and 'living thing' by reference to the concept of 'breadth': 'living thing' is a broader category than 'tree'.
670. This range is itself open-ended, meaning that there is no clear border between borderline and non-borderline cases (or between the core and the penumbra of a norm, as H.L.A. Hart would have put it). Since people may disagree on where to draw the border, the question of whether a certain case is clear or not may be subject to controversy. The expression 'second-order vagueness' is sometimes used to refer to the idea that the borderline status of cases has itself borderline cases, i.e. that it can be unclear if a borderline case is a borderline case or not – *see, e.g.*, Keefe (2000), pp. 33-34.
671. Using 'bald' as an example of a vague word has become popular since Bertrand Russell did so in his seminal article on vagueness – *see* Russell (1923).
672. Peirce (1902), p. 748.
673. Peirce (1902), p. 748.
674. We may not know *exactly* how many hairs that person has, but that is a surmountable cognitive limitation. The requirement that the cognitive limitation be insurmountable is sometimes used to distinguish between absolute borderline cases and relative borderline cases, the former ones being due to some insuperable limitation and giving rise to true

person as bald. The same holds, for example, for the word 'rich': we may know the exact value of a person's assets, yet we may not be sure whether to qualify her as rich or not.[675]

Figure 3.1 Borderline Cases in Vagueness

Non-borderline cases of clear applicability	Borderline cases	Non-borderline cases of clear non-applicability

For the law, vagueness is sometimes considered problematic and undesirable. Vague norms arguably give less guidance than their subjects might expect in a certain situation.[676] But although it may reduce clarity, vagueness is a valuable mechanism at the disposal of those in charge of enacting legislation. The precision-vagueness or rules-standards continuum is 'an important way of allocating discretion between the issuer of the directive and those who must apply it, enforce it, or interpret it'.[677] Vague language is often used in legal provisions with the intent of delegating a share of decision-making power to law-applying officials like judges. Often, where legislators resort to vague language, they do it not out of carelessness in drafting, but out of a deliberate wish to pass off to courts the task of developing the law.[678] Standard-like norms – such as norms prohibiting 'inhuman or degrading treatment or punishment', or imposing liability for 'unjust enrichment', or requiring adherence to a standard of 'reasonable care', or relying on vague multi-factor tests like proportionality – give no definite answer to most litigated cases, granting latitude to the law-applier to

---

vagueness – *see* Sorensen (2004), pp. 21-39. The following example given by Poscher (2012), p. 131, helps understand why relative borderline cases do not generate true vagueness: 'In comparison to 3, 5, 11 it might be difficult to tell at first glance whether 11.197 is a prime number. The concept of prime number, however, is not vague. 11.197 is only a "relative borderline case" of a prime number – relative to our ad hoc capacities to handle the mathematical complexities of large numbers'.

675. Vague terms, like 'bald' or 'rich' or 'heap', generate what became known among philosophers as the *sorites* paradox. The paradox may be illustrated with the following example: Imagine a person that you would consider as being clearly not bald. Removing one single hair from that person's scalp would certainly not turn her into a bald person. No one hair can be said to make the difference between being considered bald and not bald. Under this assumption, the paradox arises when one considers what to say about the person's status as bald (or not bald) when the hair removal process is repeated a series of times: at a certain point, the person would cease to be considered a non-bald person, but at what exact point?
676. Vagueness-based judicial discretion is thus inversely related with the 'legislative guidance' criterion – *see infra* 3.1.1.
677. Schauer (2009), p. 194. *See also* Endicott (2011a), p. 26, noting that vagueness in the law has a 'power-allocation function', and Endicott & Spence (2005), p. 664, praising the use of vague standards to delegate power on courts to decide on the scope of copyright. *But see* Sorensen (2001), disputing the functionality of vagueness.
678. *See* Schauer (2009), pp. 148-149, and Ribeiro (2019), p. 261.

make her own judgment.[679] These norms may be contrasted with rule-like norms – such as norms setting the maximum speed limit at '50 kilometers per hour' or making presidential eligibility dependent upon the candidate being 'at least 35 years of age' –, which encapsulate value judgments and factual triggers defined *ex ante* by the legislator, leaving a very narrow set of borderline cases and little *ex post* discretion to the official in charge of applying the law. Generally put, whereas bright-line rules keep the bulk of decision-making at the legislative level, standards shift decision-making to the judicial apparatus.

Precision in statutory wording constraints judges by limiting the set of choices they have when rendering their decisions. To give a simplified example in the copyright realm, a hypothetical provision exempting 'quotations of no more than 100 words' grants less discretion and lies closer to the rules end of the continuum than a provision exempting 'quotations in accordance with fair practice and to the extent required by the specific purpose'.[680]

Figure 3.2 The Rules-Standards Continuum

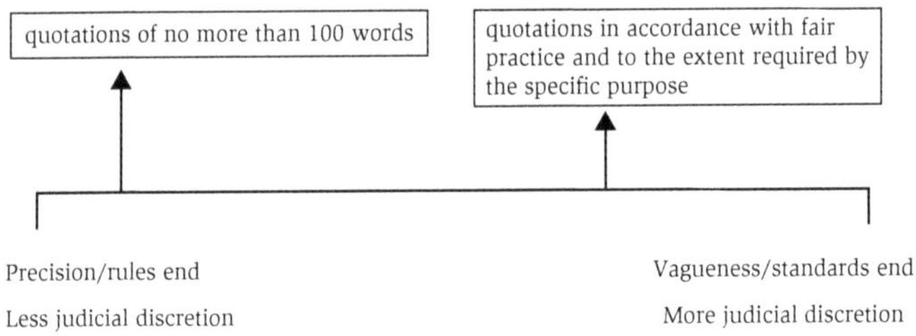

Standard-like provisions that come in the form of balancing tests commonly grant a considerable degree of discretion to those in charge of interpreting and applying them. Balancing tests involve comparing competing principles, values or interests on their own merits.[681] Such tests give ample freedom to courts, by asking them to weigh opposing considerations 'without being subject to rules of weight, presumptions, burdens of proof, or various other devices that influence the outcome in one way or another'.[682]

679. These cases where evaluative terms ('inhuman', 'unjust', 'reasonable', 'fair') are used in legal norms are called by Endicott (2011a) and (2011b) cases of 'extravagant vagueness'. These are distinct from the cases of 'trivial vagueness'. Lawmakers usually avoid trivially vague terms like 'rich'. If the legislature wants to tax rich people more heavily, it would normally do so by reference to a precise level of income, expressed in numerical currency terms – *see* Marmor (2014), p. 87. On the use of trivially vague terms in the DSM Proposal, *see* Rendas (2017b), pp. 42-43.
680. This formulation evidently draws on the wording of Article 5(3)(d) InfoSoc Directive.
681. *See*, in general, Alexy (2003b), pp. 436-439. *See also* Alexy (2003a).
682. Schauer (2012), p. 311.

Naturally, balancing tests vary in their constraining capacity: while some include a set of factors that the court must take into account, others are more open-ended. But even though these tests may award prevalence to some factors or preclude the decision-maker from considering others, they are less constraining than provisions whose application is a matter of subsumption, for they fail to provide textually conclusive reasons to decide either way.[683] A mandate to balance competing considerations constitutes a broad grant of discretion, authorising judges to render individualised decisions in each case and to reach what they think is the correct outcome on a case-by-case basis.

As stated in the beginning of this section, judicial discretion is also influenced by the breadth of scope of the provision that controls the dispute. Breadth is distinct from vagueness. Frederick Schauer uses the example of the word 'insect' to illustrate this distinction. While the category of insects covers more animals than all the other categories within the animal kingdom combined, the word 'insect' is a very precise one. Although it certainly has some borderline cases, these cases are fewer than, say, in the category of 'acts of heroism', which are very infrequent.[684] Schauer resorts to this example to extract the conclusion that broad categories can be very precise, whereas narrow categories can be vague. To illustrate this idea with a copyright example, contrast a hypothetical provision according to which 'reproductions of all kinds are infringing' with a provision stating that 'unfair reproductions are infringing'. The former provision is simultaneously broader and more precise than the latter.

This is also helpful to understand why the breadth of copyright exceptions is essential for judges to be able to adapt copyright law to technological change. An exception privileging 'fair quotations' is vague, but it only enables the judge to accommodate uses that fall within the category of 'quotations'.[685] In contrast, a similarly vague exception privileging 'fair uses' grants a much broader and discretionary mandate upon judges. Combining breadth *and* vagueness thus makes up for a particularly discretion-granting provision.

2.2 Adaptability to National Cultures

In the context of the InfoSoc debate, the term 'flexibility' is understood in a second sense (arguably less pervasive than the first one): EU copyright law

683. *See* Schauer (2012), pp. 313-314. *But see* Alexy (2003b), arguing that the formal structures behind balancing and subsumption exercises are roughly similar.
684. *See* Schauer (2009), pp. 200-201.
685. On the discretion provided by an exception modelled after the InfoSoc quotation exception laid down in Article 5(3)(d), *see infra* Chapter 4, section 3.2.5.

must be flexible enough to adapt to different Member States' cultures, by taking them into account in the harmonisation process.[686]

The respect for cultural diversity features prominently as one of the Union's aims in Article 3(3) TEU.[687] Although the EU lacks a specific competence to harmonise Member State laws in the area of culture,[688] it must take cultural aspects into consideration in its action under other clauses, in particular in order to respect and promote the cultural diversity within the Union.[689] Similarly, the preamble to the Charter of Fundamental Rights of the EU states that '[t]he Union contributes to the preservation and to the development of these common values while respecting the diversity of the cultures and traditions of the peoples of Europe as well as the national identities of the Member States'.[690]

In this context, it has been argued time and again that the harmonisation of copyright law should not unjustifiably eradicate national legal differences that aim at accommodating Member States' cultural needs and expectations. Harmonisation, in the words of Christophe Geiger and Franciska Schönherr, 'should not lead to uniformity – directives should thus leave some discretion to Member States to adapt to their domestic needs and local cultural traditions'.[691] This concern is expressed in the copyright *acquis* itself, the most notable piece of evidence being Recital 32 InfoSoc Directive, which conveys a concern regarding the compatibility of the list of exceptions laid down in Article 5 with the different Member States' legal traditions.[692]

---

686. Using the term with this meaning, *see*, *e.g.*, Reinbothe (1998), p. 64 ('particularly with regard to exceptions, there has to be a balance between the highest possible degree of harmonisation and utmost flexibility for Member States, in respect of their cultural and legal traditions'); ALAI (2010), p. 3 ('copyright exceptions and limitations are the primary means through which member States implement their national cultural policies under the fairly flexible Berne-TRIPs standards'); Ohly (2013b), pp. 258-259 ('EU law could give more flexibility to the Member States, especially with regard to copyright exceptions: copyright is linked to culture, and even in a unified Europe cultural diversity will and should remain'); and Ramalho (2016a), p. 179 ('The extension of the list [in Article 5 InfoSoc Directive], coupled with the broad wording of the exceptions contained therein, suggest that Member States have enough flexibility to accommodate most of their national specificities').
687. The last paragraph of the provision states that the Union 'shall respect its rich cultural and linguistic diversity, and shall ensure that Europe's cultural heritage is safeguarded and enhanced'.
688. *See* Article 167(5) TFEU.
689. *See* Article 167(4) TFEU.
690. *See also* Article 22 Charter, according to which 'the Union shall respect cultural, religious and linguistic diversity'.
691. Geiger & Schönherr (2012), pp. 137-138. *See also* Halpern & Johnson (2014), p. 23
692. *See also* Recitals 11, 12, 14, and 22 InfoSoc Directive, highlighting the objective of supporting and disseminating culture. More recently, Recital 33 DSM Directive, focusing on the legal framework for the digitisation and dissemination of out-of-commerce works, has stated that 'Member States should, within the framework provided for in this Directive, have flexibility in choosing the specific type of licensing

At first sight, the importance of respecting Member States' cultures may conflict with the project of copyright harmonisation and the establishment of an internal market.[693] The two objectives should nonetheless be regarded as reconcilable. Article 167(1) TFEU states that the Union shall bring 'the common cultural heritage to the fore', while simultaneously respecting the Member States' cultural diversity. The CJEU too has accepted that the objective of fostering culture may justify national legislation that negatively affects the internal market.[694] Moreover, the tension between harmonisation and the respect for Member States' cultural and legal diversity may be minimised by catering for national specificities in the harmonisation instruments themselves.

The goal of respecting national cultures may be understood as covering 'the culture and history of the European peoples',[695] but also, and more importantly for this research, the Member States' *legal* traditions. This understanding emerges from the recognition that 'cultural expressions are often intertwined with regulatory aspects, especially in fields that are strongly connected to cultural matters, as is the case with copyright law'.[696] In this sense, therefore, accommodating the legal traditions of Member States in the field of copyright, either by incorporating them in harmonisation instruments or by leaving Member States with the freedom to legislate autonomously, would be a way of abiding by this objective. Legal traditions in the domain of copyright include not only the broader system – Continental or Anglo-American – to which each Member State belongs (section 2.2.1) but also the specific (often quite 'traditional') exceptions listed in national catalogues (section 2.2.2).

2.2.1 Accommodation of Member States' Legal Traditions

As just mentioned, the harmonisation of copyright law must not iron out Member States' cultural differences with no reasonable justification. In particular, allowing for national *legal* differences, which often go hand in

mechanism … that they put in place for the use of out-of-commerce works or other subject matter by cultural heritage institutions, in accordance with their legal traditions, practices or circumstances.'

693. Reinbothe (1998), p. 64, notes this tension by calling for a 'balance' between both. *See also* Ramalho (2016a), p. 134.
694. *See, e.g.*, CJEU, *Cinéthèque*, holding that national legislation which prohibits the simultaneous exploitation of cinematographic works in cinemas and in video-cassette form for a limited period of time is justified by the objective of encouraging cinematographic production.
695. The expression is used in Article 167(2) TFEU.
696. Ramalho (2016a), p. 104. *See also* Ginsburg (2000), p. 267, observing that '[n]ational copyright laws are a component of local cultural and information policies. As such, they express each sovereign nation's aspirations for its citizens: exposure to works of authorship and participation in their country's cultural patrimony'.

hand with a Member State's cultural and historical background, may be desirable to accommodate local needs and expectations.

National copyright laws may generally be categorised as belonging to one of two traditions – the civil law or *droit d'auteur* tradition (comprised by Continental countries, most notably France and Germany) and the common law or copyright tradition (of which Cyprus, Malta, and Ireland are the current representatives in the EU, following the UK's exit).

A foundational difference between the two traditions lies in the theoretical justifications underpinning them. Copyright theories of justification draw from wider theories of IP, which, in turn, have deeper philosophical roots.

Two theories have had greater influence over the copyright laws of European countries: the natural rights theory and the utilitarian theory. Put briefly, the former – inspired by the works of Locke, Kant, and Hegel – understands copyright as a natural right of authors, either due to the existence of an intimate connection between the work and its author's personality or because the rights are regarded as the just reward for the author's labour. The latter – inspired by the works of Bentham, Mill, and Pigou – sees in copyright a State-granted incentive to the creation and dissemination of cultural goods for the benefit of society. While the *droit d'auteur* tradition rests primarily on natural rights justifications, the influence of the utilitarian theory is prevalent in the common law tradition. The predominance of one theory over the other is said to explain certain doctrinal dividing lines between the two systems, as, e.g., the diverging thresholds of originality and the different rules on initial ownership and on transferability of rights.[697]

To an extent, the distinct traits of each theory and tradition may be considered a product of cultural and identity differences between the respective countries.[698] Although no profound chasm exists between the two systems,[699] they differ in the way they approach copyright exceptions, with *droit d'auteur* countries tending to be more restrictive than countries

697. For further detail on such theories, *see* Hughes (1988); Fisher (2001); and Gompel (2011), pp. 215-284. It should nevertheless be emphasised that none of these theories, elusive as they are, is capable of justifying every characteristic feature of each tradition. Take moral rights as an example. Although a stronger protection of these rights is commonly regarded as a characteristic of *droit d'auteur* countries, in the UK, as in France, moral rights cannot be assigned to a third party. Moral rights can be waived in the UK (Section 87(1) and (2) UK CDPA), but so can they, though only partially, in some Continental European countries, like Belgium (Article XI.165(2) Belgian Economic Law Code, *a contrario*). In addition, the fact that every EU Member State has adhered to the Berne Convention entails that all of them share the minimum common ground set in Article 6*bis* thereof. Relatedly, it should be borne in mind that there is a body of literature that raises doubts on the accuracy of the accounts that divide copyright laws into distinct traditions – *see*, *e.g.*, Ginsburg (1990) and Davies (1995).

698. *See* Lewinski (2008), pp. 34 and 63.

699. *See* Strowel (1993), p. 655.

belonging to the common law tradition.[700] In this regard, it is undisputable that the EU law on copyright exceptions leans towards the continental tradition. Ideally, however, it should try to achieve a synthesis between these distinct approaches.[701]

2.2.2 Accommodation of Member States' Specificities

Important as the *droit d'auteur*/copyright divide may be, it is not capable of explaining all relevant differences between the national frameworks of exceptions. Some of these differences can hardly be credited to the distinguishing traits of both traditions. Rather, they are products of the Member States' own cultural environment or legislative evolution.

In approximating Member States' regimes of exceptions, these national legal peculiarities must not be disregarded. One way to go about this is to incorporate such particularities in the very harmonisation measure. Alternatively (or even cumulatively), the EU legislator may resort to techniques of partial harmonisation that leave Member States with freedom to autonomously accommodate local situations.[702]

In theory, this goal can also be satisfied by omission, that is, by not harmonising certain copyright doctrines.[703] However, refraining from intervening at the EU level in the field of exceptions does not seem to be an option. For one thing, the harmonisation of copyright exceptions is well established and backtracking is unlikely to be on the Commission's agenda. For another, exceptions, generally considered, have an important impact on the internal market,[704] unlike other areas where such impact is arguably not as clear.

700. Noting this difference, *see*, *e.g.*, Hugenholtz (2017), pp. 278-283. *But see* Burrell & Coleman (2005), pp. 201-208, casting doubt over the idea that a natural rights-based *droit d'auteur* tradition is characterised by weaker exceptions. The authors further argue that understanding the process of EU harmonisation in light of the two traditions entails the risk of hindering users' interests, by leading to the provision of narrower exceptions grounded on the fact that the majority of Member States belongs to the *droit d'auteur* tradition.
701. *See* Pereira (2001), pp. 106-107 (observing that harmonisation measures often achieve a compromise between both traditions); Pereira (2008a), pp. 252-253 (referring to the construction of EU copyright law as a *tertium genus* between the *Urheberrecht* and copyright traditions); and Ramalho (2016a), p. 175 (arguing that 'EU copyright legislation should take account of both systems … by formulating concepts or rules that comprise elements of both traditions, or that stand at middle ground between them').
702. *See* Ramalho (2016a), pp. 178-180.
703. *See* Ramalho (2016a), pp. 178-180.
704. As argued *infra* Chapter 5, section 3, however, not all exceptions can be considered to have such a decisive impact.

3 LEGAL CERTAINTY

Dictionary entries for the term 'certainty' define it as the '[f]irm conviction that something is the case'.[705] Relatedly, certainty may also be understood as an epistemic property of facts or beliefs. In this sense, a fact will be qualified as 'a certainty' if it is 'definitely true' or 'definitely going to take place'.[706] For the law, certainty is one among its most cherished values.[707] It is an *idée directrice*.[708]

But despite its importance, the concept of 'legal certainty' hardly lends itself to a tidy definition. Theorists understand legal certainty as comprising multiple related features. Franz Bydlinski divides it into five narrower categories: legal clarity (*Rechtsklarheit*), legal stability (*Rechtsstabilität*), legal accessibility (*Rechtszugänglichkeit*), legal peace (*Rechtsfrieden*), and legal enforcement (*Rechtsdurchsetzung*).[709] Similarly, Claus-Wilhelm Canaris understands the concept as encompassing determinacy and predictability, legislative and judicial stability and continuity, and practicability of the application of law.[710] Other scholars stress the connection between legal security/predictability and the rule of law.[711] It is also generally agreed among theorists of the rule of law that laws should abide by certain requirements, such as the requirement that they be validly enacted and adequately publicised, normally in an official journal, and that retroactive effects be subject to strict limitations.[712]

In EU law, legal certainty features as a general principle, alongside, e.g., proportionality, non-discrimination, and the protection of fundamental rights.[713] Although the Treaties make no explicit reference to the principle, Article 2 TEU includes the rule of law as one of the values on which the Union is founded.[714] In addition, the CJEU has invoked the principle of legal certainty on multiple occasions and in relation to diverse fields of law.[715] The

705. Oxford English Dictionary (2010), p. 284.
706. Oxford English Dictionary (2010), p. 284.
707. *See, e.g.*, Canaris (1996), p. 22, and Raz (2009), p. 211.
708. The expression is borrowed from Andreas von Arnauld's study on legal certainty in German law – *see* Arnauld (2006), p. 691.
709. *See* Bydlinski (1988), p. 293.
710. *See* Canaris (1996), p. 22.
711. *See* Arnauld (2006), p. 691; Maxeiner (2007), pp. 545-547; and Paunio (2013), p. 54.
712. *See, e.g.*, Fuller (1969), pp. 33-94; Summers (1999), pp. 1691-1695; and Raz (2009), pp. 214 et seq.
713. Including legal certainty among the general principles of EU law and exploring its role as an interpretative argument employed by the CJEU, *see, e.g.*, Arnull (1990), p. 3; Usher (1998), pp. 52 et seq.; and Tridimas (2006), pp. 242 et seq.
714. In the seminal *Les Verts* judgment, in 1986, the CJEU stated that the European Economic Community was 'a Community based on the rule of law' (para. 23).
715. The first reference to the principle by the CJEU dates back to 1961, in the *SNUPAT* case. For an overview of the Court's case law, *see* Raitio (2003), pp. 187 et seq., and Paunio (2013), pp. 64 et seq. The principle is also frequently alluded to by the ECtHR, through

principle requires that EU rules 'enable those concerned to know precisely the extent of the obligations which are imposed on them .... Individuals must be able to ascertain unequivocally what their rights and obligations are and take steps accordingly.'[716] Like legal theorists, the CJEU has drawn different corollaries from this general principle: legal acts must be publicised; they must be clear, precise, and predictable; judicial decisions are binding; the retroactive effects of legal acts must be limited; and legitimate expectations must be safeguarded.[717]

All the foregoing facets of legal certainty are interrelated and sometimes overlap with each other. Overall, they point towards one fundamental idea: law must be capable of guiding the behaviour of those who are subject to it. Guiding behaviour is, in the words of Jeremy Waldron, 'the mode of governance distinctive to law'.[718] Law, if it is to conform to the mandates of legal certainty, must give its subjects a *firm conviction* about the legal consequences that attach to their behaviour. The capacity to anticipate those consequences offers legal subjects the possibility to autonomously regulate their own conduct. In other words, legal subjects must be able to know what the law is so as to organise their affairs accordingly.[719]

With this theorisation in mind, I will divide the objective of legal certainty within the InfoSoc debate into two objectives: that of guiding

---

the definition of 'law' that is necessary to restrict fundamental rights in accordance with the Convention. In *Olsson*, para. 61, the ECtHR held that '[a] norm cannot be regarded as a "law" unless it is formulated with sufficient precision to enable the citizen – if need be, with appropriate advice – to foresee, to a degree that is reasonable in the circumstances, the consequences which a given action may entail'. However, in that same paragraph, the Court made clear that the importance of statutory precision should not be exaggerated: 'however, experience shows that absolute precision is unattainable and the need to avoid excessive rigidity and to keep pace with changing circumstances means that many laws are inevitably couched in terms which, to a greater or lesser extent, are vague'.

716. CJEU, *Stichting ROM-projecten*, para. 25 (and case law cited therein).
717. *See* Arnauld (2006), pp. 495 et seq. (with extensive references to CJEU case law).
718. Waldron (2011), p. 61.
719. *See* Raz (2009), pp. 214-220. In Friedrich von Hayek's formulation of the rule of law, rules should 'make it possible to foresee with fair certainty how the authority will use its coercive powers in given circumstances, and to plan one's individual affairs on the basis of this knowledge' – Hayek (1944), p. 72. It is important to note that the concept of 'legal certainty', as described herein, is wholly formal. As Raz (2009), p. 214, puts it, a conception of this kind 'says nothing about how the law is to be made: by tyrants, democratic majorities, or any other way. It says nothing about fundamental rights, about equality, or justice'. *See also* Maxeiner (2007), p. 547, and Alexy (2015), p. 444. This widely accepted conception of legal certainty differs from a twofold conception that has achieved significant popularity in Scandinavian literature, due to the influence of Aulis Aarnio and Aleksander Peczenik. According to these theorists, the concept of 'legal certainty' comprises two dimensions: formal legal certainty, which relates to the predictability behind rules and judicial decisions, and substantive legal certainty, which refers to the adequacy and rational acceptability of legal decisions. *See* Aarnio (1987), pp. 3-8, and Peczenik (2008), pp. 24-27.

rightholders and prospective users as to the legal status of unauthorised uses (section 3.1) and that of harmonisation in the field of exceptions (section 3.2).

3.1 Guidance on the Legal Status of Unauthorised Uses

Scholars and policymakers in the field of copyright often justify their proposals with the argument that they promote legal certainty (or legal security or predictability).[720] Likewise, the CJEU frequently invokes the need to foster legal certainty, or to overcome legal *un*certainty, as an argument for justifying its interpretative options in the field of copyright law.[721]

Not all facets of legal certainty enumerated above are relevant in the context of the InfoSoc debate. The 'firm conviction' that the InfoSoc framework of exceptions must be able to provide to copyright stakeholders relates to the legal consequences that arise from the use of protected works without the authorisation of rightholders. The guidance sought by rightholders and users is, in essence, guidance about the boundary between lawful and unlawful conduct, that is, about the infringing or non-infringing character of these uses.[722]

Guidance in relation to the legal status of unauthorised uses is, first and foremost, a function of the clarity of the legal materials that draw the line between infringing and non-infringing behaviour. Therefore, among the heterogeneous issues covered by legal certainty, the one about which stakeholders typically cross swords is the *clarity* of statutes and judicial decisions on the lawfulness of such uses. Unclear or incoherent rules and case law hinder the subjects' capacity to anticipate the legal consequences of their conduct. The InfoSoc framework and national laws relying on it will better conform to legal certainty if the content of their provisions is clear and

720. For instance, in the Communication on a Modern European Copyright Framework, p. 9, the Commission identified 'contentious grey areas and uncertainty' in relation to the definition of communication to the public in the online world. It then tried to tackle this uncertainty by clarifying that, in certain circumstances, information society service providers perform acts of communication to the public, for which the authorisation of rightholders is needed – *see* Article 17 DSM Directive (and accompanying Recitals 61-71).

721. *See* Favale et al. (2016), pp. 65-68. For example, in *Infopaq I*, para. 59, the Court stated that the requirements of Article 5(1) InfoSoc Directive, which contains the exception for acts of temporary reproduction, must be 'interpreted in the light of the need for legal certainty for authors with regard to the protection of their works'. Accordingly, the Court interpreted the 'transient' condition as requiring an automatic process that takes place without human intervention, on grounds that '[l]egal certainty for rightholders ... requires that the storage and deletion of the reproduction not be dependent on discretionary human intervention' (para. 62).

722. *See* Lucas (2010), p. 282.

if courts apply those provisions in a coherent and systematised fashion, to the effect that their decisions can be considered roughly predictable.

The InfoSoc framework's supporters maintain that preference should be given to legislative guidance, through a clear and precise set of statutory rules. In contrast, critics claim that statutory guidance is not the only way of ensuring legal certainty: guidance may be found in the courts' case law too.[723] Disagreement therefore exists on the ideal division of responsibility between legislators and judges in what regards the promotion of legal certainty. The use of a common label – 'legal certainty' – to refer to these two separate ideas blurs important distinctions that the following sections aim at clarifying.

3.1.1 Legislative Guidance

The concern with guiding conduct is reflected, first and foremost, in the very act of positing law. Translating norms of justice into positive law guides people by relieving them from the task of trying to understand what the demands of justice are in each and every concrete situation.[724] In a word, '[l]egal certainty demands positivity'.[725]

Nonetheless, in and of itself, the act of positing legal norms is not enough to adequately guide the behaviour of legal subjects. Legislative provisions, if they are to give their subjects any guidance, must be clear. 'The desideratum of clarity', as stated by Lon Fuller, 'represents one of the most essential ingredients of legality'.[726] Put differently, to borrow the words of another legal philosopher, '[a]n ambiguous, vague, obscure, or imprecise law is likely to mislead or confuse at least some of those who desire to be guided by it'.[727]

Indeed, the clarity of statutes may be impaired by the use of legal formulations that are *ambiguous* or *vague*. In colloquial language, the terms 'ambiguity' and 'vagueness' are often used indistinctly. In linguistics, however, ambiguity and vagueness are different phenomena, with diverging implications for the law.

Ambiguous terms are terms that have two or more different meanings. Whereas the meaning of a vague term is uncertain only at the borders, an ambiguous word may be ambiguous in abstract, simply by virtue of bearing multiple different meanings.[728] The paradigmatic example of an ambiguous word in English is 'bank', which may be used to refer to a financial institution or to the slope of land adjoining a river. In theory, this multiplicity

723. *See*, *e.g.*, Senftleben (2009-2010), p. 547, and (2010), p. 76; Griffiths (2010a), p. 91; Hugenholtz & Senftleben (2011), p. 8; and Halpern & Johnson (2014), pp. 155-156.
724. *See* Ribeiro (2015), p. 37.
725. Radbruch (1950), p. 109.
726. Fuller (1969), p. 63.
727. Raz (2009), p. 214.
728. *See* Poscher (2012), p. 129.

of meanings may make it hard to understand the mandates of a legal provision. Yet, only seldom will the use of an ambiguous term like bank be a problem in statutory construction, for '[i]f the law requires a deposit to be made in a bank, it is too far-fetched to assume this requires throwing the money into a river'.[729] The same holds, for example, for the term 'seizure' in a prohibition against 'unreasonable searches and seizures': the context makes clear that what the norm prohibits is the forcible taking of property by a law enforcer, not the abnormal electrical activity in someone's brain (a seizure in the sense of physical condition). The point is that, in law, the different meanings that a term may have are usually too distinct for context not to disambiguate.[730]

Ambiguity is a much less pervasive – and, for our purposes, much less remarkable – legal phenomenon than vagueness. In fact, copyright commentators who allude to the need for clarity in the definition of what counts as a lawful or unlawful use are not worried about ambiguity, as much as about vagueness. As explained earlier, vagueness varies inversely with precision along a continuum. The more precise the language used in a legislative framework – i.e., the closer its provisions lie to the rules end of the rules-standards spectrum –, the higher the degree of statutory clarity and the greater the subjects' capacity to anticipate the legal consequences that attach to their behaviour. To draw on examples that have been alluded to above, think of a hypothetical traffic norm that renders it punishable to drive at an 'unreasonably high speed' in residential areas. Whereas driving at 20 kilometres per hour in such an area is clearly not unreasonable and driving at 120 kilometres per hour is clearly unreasonable, we do not have that same certainty in relation to driving at 60 kilometres per hour. In some cases, thus, 'the person to whom [the norm] is addressed may not know exactly what is required of her'.[731] An alternative rule determining, without borderline cases, that driving at above 50 kilometres per hour is a punishable conduct provides drivers with much greater guidance. Under such a rule, drivers would know with *certainty* that driving at 60 kilometres per hour is punishable.[732] Similarly, a constitutional norm that makes presidential eligibility depend on the candidate's 'maturity' gives less guidance to potential candidates than a

729. Poscher (2012), p. 129.
730. *See* Solan (2005), p. 79, and Schauer (2009), fn. 30. Syntactic ambiguity – which is caused not by the multiple meanings of individual words, but by sentence structure – is relatively more prevalent. Ralf Poscher illustrates the phenomenon with a California statute on the discharge of teachers, which 'allowed the dismissal of permanent employees in case of a "conviction of a felony or of any crime *involving moral turpitude*"' – Poscher (2012), p. 129. The location of the words in the provision renders it 'syntactically ambiguous as to whether the moral turpitude requirement modifies only the last or both preceding expressions' – Poscher (2012), p. 129.
731. Waldron (1994), p. 534.
732. Whether the rule would actually be enforced is a different issue and one that falls beyond the scope of this book.

norm that determines that the President shall be at least thirty-five years of age. Under the latter norm, a twenty-year-old person, no matter how mature, will know that she is ineligible.

To be sure, standard-like norms do provide *some* guidance; they guide their subjects' 'practical reasoning through certain channels and in certain directions'.[733] The point here is merely that the level of guidance provided by precise norms is *higher* than that provided by norms on the vagueness end. Hence, the greater the degree of precision of its provisions, the better the InfoSoc framework of exceptions will score in terms of legislative guidance.

As should be clear by now, certainty *qua* statutory precision may evidently conflict with flexibility. Precision reduces flexibility in at least two ways: first, if harmonisation measures are cast in precise terms, Member States will have less freedom at the implementation stage;[734] second, if the provisions that govern a given dispute are closer to the precision end of the spectrum, courts will, at least in principle, be more constrained in their decision-making.[735]

3.1.2 Judicial Guidance

In rendering decisions on the lawfulness of unauthorised uses of protected works, courts may contribute towards either reinforcing or diminishing the guidance given by the wording of the relevant legal provisions.

Some InfoSoc critics claim that the rigid character of the framework of exceptions has led courts to circumvent some of its constraints, with prejudicial effects for legal certainty. The wording used in the statutory exceptions determines the range of choices granted by legislators upon courts. But this range of choices is merely a prima facie one, in that courts do not always stay within the set of choices given by legal provisions. The guidance given by the law is also, to an important extent, a function of judges' fidelity to statutory constraints.[736] Actually, narrowness and precision in statutory wording may not be sufficient conditions of judicial constraint, since strict judicial fidelity to the requirements of the governing provisions is in no way guaranteed.

Even though closed catalogues of rule-like exceptions are relatively constraining, judges may be unwilling to defer to their constraints. For instance, in a given case the deciding court may understand itself as not being bound by the closed nature of the catalogue and apply a listed exception to an unlisted (though comparable) use or simply create an *ad hoc* exception for

733. Waldron (2011), p. 67.
734. *See infra* 3.2.1. and Chapter 4, section 3.1.
735. *See supra* section 2.1.2 and Chapter 4, section 3.1.
736. As acknowledged by Schauer (2012), p. 315, '[t]he extent to which a given rule or a given legal text will in fact constrain legal decision-makers by narrowing the range of choice from what it would otherwise have been is … partly a question of the extent to which the decision makers will understand themselves as bound by that rule'.

that use. In such a case, the court will have disregarded the constraint on its discretion that arises from exhaustiveness. And indeed, as explored in detail below,[737] this type of attitude towards seemingly restricting provisions is not unheard of in European copyright law. Scholars have emphasised that European courts sometimes decide in disrespect for the mandates of the applicable provisions, in order to render what they think is the most reasonable decision in the circumstances at hand.

On the other hand, it has also been argued by InfoSoc critics that courts, if given vague provisions to work with, are capable of making them more predictable over time. Consider the US fair use doctrine. Due to its open-endedness, the fair use doctrine has a reputation for being 'the most troublesome in the whole law of copyright',[738] with several commentators ascribing it the disadvantage of unpredictability.[739] In fact, the standard-like formulation of fair use has led to epidermal accusations that it fails to provide legal certainty. In making such accusations, commentators rely, however implicitly, on the assumption that precision in statutory wording is a *necessary* condition of legal certainty. But even if the governing provisions lie closer to the vagueness end of the spectrum, the degree of guidance that legal subjects have at their disposal may be relatively high – or, at least, higher than one would expect by looking at the wording of the provisions alone. Put another way, statutory vagueness does not necessarily entail

---

737. *See supra* section 2.1.2 and *infra* Chapter 4, section 5.2.

738. The expression was first used by the US Court of Appeals for the Second Circuit in *Dellar*, and has since been used extensively in scholarship and case law.

739. In the words of Patry (2011), p. 217, a staunch fair use supporter, '[c]ritics of the U.S. fair use doctrine point to the alleged "open-ended" nature of fair use and argue that it lacks certainty. The term open-ended is used as a derogatory synonym to mean without boundaries or without any guidance; the term open-ended is used to conjure up fears that one simply never knows what a U.S. court might do'. In his influential piece, Leval (1990), p. 1106, wrote that '[j]udges do not share a consensus on the meaning of fair use. Earlier decisions provide little basis for predicting later ones'. The US scholar who has put the point most vividly is perhaps Nimmer (2003), p. 280: 'had Congress legislated a dartboard rather than the particular four fair use factors embodied in the Copyright Act, it appears that the upshot would be the same'. For similar observations on the lack of predictability in fair use case law in US scholarship, *see* Lessig (2004), p. 187 ('fair use in America simply means the right to hire a lawyer'); Madison (2004), p. 1666 ('Fair use is an *ex post* determination, a lottery argument offered by accused infringers forced to gamble, after the fact, that they did not need permission before'); Carroll (2007), p. 1106 ('leading courts and commentators generally acknowledge that the four-factor test as interpreted provides very little guidance for predicting whether a particular use will be deemed fair'); Lee (2008), p. 1468 ('Even though I am an expert of copyright law, my prediction of what is a fair use probably is no better than the person on the street – or it could be even worse, given that a jury will not typically be comprised of copyright experts and judges often are not well versed in copyright law'); and Netanel (2010), p. 66 ('Given the doctrine's open-ended, case-specific cast and inconsistent application, it is exceedingly difficult to predict whether a given use in a given case will qualify as the sort of transformative self-expression that enjoys the privilege'). But note that, in a later piece, Neil Netanel retracted this view – *see* Netanel (2011).

inexistent or insufficient guidance. This is so because, as some commentators have claimed in the context of the InfoSoc debate, 'legal certainty is not merely the role of the legislators' and 'need not be met purely at the stage of a law being drafted'.[740] The task of giving guidance to stakeholders as to the boundary between infringing and non-infringing conduct may be shared between the legislative and the judicial branch.[741] That is, even if legislators provide limited guidance by enacting a vague provision, courts may intervene to give *ex post* guidance through case law. As Bernt Hugenholtz & Martin Senftleben noted, 'vague norms may eventually become more predictable as sufficient precedents … are created by the courts'.[742] The point, in essence, is that vague doctrines may offer sufficient guidance to their subjects if a coherent and systematised body of interpretative case law develops over time.

US fair use is commonly offered as an example of an open-ended doctrine around which such a body of case law formed. InfoSoc critics point out that, when members of the opposite faction accuse fair use of giving little guidance to rightholders and users, they 'often do not go beyond the terms of the statutory provision itself'.[743] The truth is that recent scholarly studies show that, contrary to established wisdom, solid guidance can be found in fair use case law. As admitted by Neil Netanel – in citing empirical analyses on fair use case law by Barton Beebe,[744] Pamela Samuelson,[745] and Matthew

740. Halpern & Johnson (2014), p. 155. *See, in general*, Sunstein (1995), p. 965, on the capacity of standards to provide *ex post* certainty.
741. *See* Senftleben (2009-2010), p. 547, and Senftleben (2011), p. 149. *See also* Schauer (2009), p. 196, recognising that, in general, 'judicial opinions can also be sources of guidance'.
742. Hugenholtz & Senftleben (2011), p. 8.
743. Griffiths (2010a), p. 91.
744. *See* Beebe (2008), for an empirical study based on all reported federal opinions that significantly relied on the fair use standard between 1978 and 2005, showing which factors and sub-factors had a greater influence on case outcomes. Beebe ultimately concludes that '[t]o be sure, the data reveal many popular practices that impair the [fair use] doctrine: courts tend to apply the factors mechanically and they sometimes make opportunistic uses of the conflicting precedent available to them. These are systematic failures that require intervention. Nevertheless, as a whole, the mass of nonleading cases has shown itself to be altogether worthy of being followed' (p. 622).
745. *See* Samuelson (2009), building on Beebe's study and arguing that fair use cases tend to fall within a number of policy-relevant clusters. Within each cluster, Samuelson identifies a series of relevant and stable patterns that render the case law more predictable. Accordingly, her recommendation is that 'judges and commentators … stop wringing their hands about how troublesome fair use is and look instead for common patterns in the fair use caselaw upon which to build a more predictable body of fair use law. Analyzing fair uses in light of cases previously decided within the same policy cluster will make fair use more rule-like without a concomitant loss in its utility as a flexible standard for balancing a wide range of interests in a wide variety of situations' (p. 2621).

Sag[746] – 'leading scholars have found some order in fair use case law where others have seen only chaos'.[747] The accumulation of precedents allowed for consistent patterns and sub-factors in the case law to be fleshed out, enhancing predictability for concerned stakeholders. These elements amount almost to rule-like elaborations of the vague fair use standard.

Of course, these patterns are no guarantee of 100% predictability of outcome in fair use cases (which at any rate does not exist[748]). The emergence and identification of sub-factors and sub-rules does not change the fact that fair use is a balancing test that must be applied on a case-by-case basis. The upshot, however, is that the thickening of a *corpus* of case law that deals with a vague standard, combined with scholarly efforts to parse out the relevant trends and patterns and with searchable databases of court decisions intended to make them more accessible to the public,[749] promotes guidance even in the absence of statutory precision.

Given this book's focus on EU copyright law, the question of interest will be whether CJEU case law is capable of providing guidance when the governing norms are crafted as standards. Were a standard-like exception to be enacted at the EU level, the clarification of its meaning would end up falling on the shoulders of the CJEU, much like it has happened with other key doctrines and concepts within the copyright *acquis*. Some commentators have openly questioned the CJEU's capacity to develop a consistent line of case law on the basis of a standard modelled after fair use.[750] The question, therefore, is whether the CJEU can develop a coherent and systematised body of case law under a standard-like provision – a question that will be discussed in the following chapter, by examining the Court's jurisprudence on equivalently vague doctrines within EU copyright.

---

746. *See* Sag (2012), examining the outcome influence of unstated factual patterns – instead of the four stated factors – that are known to litigants before the judicial decision is rendered. The author concludes that 'fair use is not nearly so incoherent or unpredictable as is conventionally assumed' (p. 86).
747. Netanel (2011), p. 715. Note that in this 2011 paper, Netanel discusses Sag's manuscript, the final version of which was only published in 2012.
748. *See* Llewellyn (2015), p. 13, according to whom conceiving outcome predictability in terms of a dichotomy between 'absolute or 100 per cent certainty versus anything else at all as being "uncertainty"' is 'useless and misleading'. Instead, Llewellyn understood outcome predictability as a continuum, ranging from 'pure chance' to reckonability. Reckonability – the best any legal actor can hope for within this continuum – is the state of affairs in which making a prediction about the outcome of a particular case is, for a skilled lawyer, a 'good business risk'.
749. A good example of such a database is the Fair Use Index maintained by the US Copyright Office – *see* https://www.copyright.gov/fair-use/. Highlighting the benefits of this tool, *see* Jütte (2017), p. 321.
750. *See* Leistner (2011) and *infra* Chapter 4, section 5.3.

3.2 Harmonisation

Another meaning of 'legal certainty' that transpires in the InfoSoc debate is that of harmonisation.[751] Because the InfoSoc framework of exceptions covers numerous uses that may take place across national borders, including most copyright-dependent online services, the guidance given to copyright stakeholders will be better fostered by a harmonised framework of exceptions than by a combination of unharmonised national regimes. The co-existence of different national legal frameworks may naturally impair cross-border trade in copyright goods and services, not least because it increases the information and compliance costs of those interested in marketing such goods and services in multiple Member States.[752]

751. *See, e.g.*, Eechoud et al. (2009), p. 105 (in referring to the Member States' freedom under Article 5 InfoSoc Directive, points out that 'even where a specific limitation has been implemented in roughly similar terms in the different Member States, there is a risk that the national courts will give this limitation a diverging interpretation, thereby contributing to the legal uncertainty in respect of the use of copyright-protected works and other subject matter'); Guibault (2010), p. 55 (claiming that the InfoSoc Directive 'did not, and probably cannot, yield the expected level of harmonisation across the European Union and that, as a consequence, there still exists a significant degree of uncertainty for the stakeholders regarding the extent of permissible acts with respect to copyright protected works'); Geiger & Schönherr (2012), p. 139 (arguing that, as a consequence of the optional character of the exceptions contained in Article 5(2)-(4) InfoSoc Directive, 'legal certainty as to which unauthorised uses are permitted is reduced, in particular in relation to cross-border transactions'); Stamatoudi & Torremans (2014), p. 446 ('the fragmented landscape of limitations across Europe fails to offer legal certainty, even though, especially in the context of the online environment, certainty regarding allowed uses is crucial'); and Martin-Prat (2014), p. 37 (in commenting on the CJEU's holding, in the *Svensson* case, that Member States are not allowed to give wider protection to rightholders by including a wider range of activities within the concept of 'communication to the public' than those referred to in Article 3 InfoSoc Directive, recognised that 'the objective of the directives is to eliminate legislative differences and legal uncertainty, and reintroducing these differences would adversely affect the functioning of the internal market').
752. *See* Ohly (2013b), p. 260, and Halpern & Johnson (2014), pp. 12-13. The Commission recognised this much in relation e.g. to the reproduction right and the exceptions thereto: harmonising these issues was considered 'crucial' for the 'cross-border exploitation of information and entertainment products' – Explanatory Memorandum to InfoSoc Proposal, p. 16. Years later, the objective of furthering cross-border certainty became a hallmark of the Commission's Digital Single Market Strategy. In May 2015, the Commission announced that it would present legislative proposals 'to reduce the differences between national copyright regimes', including 'greater legal certainty for the cross-border use of content for specific purposes (e.g. research, education, text and data mining, etc.) through harmonised exceptions' – Communication on a Digital Single Market, p. 8. Observing that most copyright exceptions 'remain national and legal certainty around cross-border uses is not guaranteed', the Commission aimed at countering this state of affairs by enacting a number of *mandatory* exceptions in the DSM Directive – Explanatory Memorandum DSM Proposal, p. 2.

Harmonisation furthers legal certainty through the elimination of relevant national differences.[753] This relation between legal certainty and harmonisation is highlighted in the InfoSoc preamble. Recital 6 reads as follows:

> Without harmonisation at Community level, legislative activities at national level which have already been initiated in a number of Member States in order to respond to the technological challenges might result in significant differences in protection and thereby in restrictions on the free movement of services and products incorporating, or based on, intellectual property, leading to a re-fragmentation of the internal market and legislative inconsistency. The impact of such legislative differences and uncertainties will become more significant with the further development of the information society, which has already greatly increased transborder exploitation of intellectual property.[754]

As is known, harmonisation was not carried out for all copyright doctrines. But even in relation to the issues where harmonisation was found necessary, national differences may endure. The extent to which the InfoSoc framework precludes the discretion of national authorities – and, therefore, the tolerance for such national differences – is influenced both by the contents of legal provisions within harmonisation instruments (section 3.2.1) and by the interpretative case law of the CJEU (section 3.2.2).

3.2.1 Harmonising Effect of Legislation

The fact that the exceptions to the rights of reproduction and communication to the public have been the object of legislative harmonisation efforts does not fatally entail that national disparities no longer subsist. Harmonisation measures may leave Member States with a degree of freedom to legislate within the harmonised areas. The existence and extent of differences between Member State laws depends, first and foremost, on the amplitude of the freedom left by the EU legislator or, put differently, on the degree to which harmonisation measures supersede the powers of national authorities (legislative and judicial alike). In principle, the stronger the pre-emptive effects of harmonisation measures,[755] the lower the tendency of Member States to

753. *See* 2008 Green Paper, p. 17, acknowledging that the '[d]ifferent treatment of the same act in different Member States may lead to legal uncertainty with regard to what is permitted under the exception'.
754. *See also* Recitals 4 and 7 InfoSoc Directive and the EP Resolution Implementation InfoSoc Directive 2015, paras 37-38.
755. Commentators have sought to understand the harmonising effect of CJEU case law through the lens of the doctrine of EU pre-emption. *See*, in the copyright field, Rosati (2014a) and Rosati (2019), pp. 73 et seq. On the doctrine of EU pre-emption in general, *see*, *e.g.*, Cross (1992); Soares (1998); Weatherill (2002); Schütze (2006) and (2015), pp. 134-145; and Arena (2010-2011).

unilaterally deviate from the harmonised text and the lesser the level of fragmentation.[756]

Before proceeding any further, it should be pointed out that no clear correlation exists between the type of instrument used by the EU legislator and the strength of its pre-emptive effects. The issue revolves essentially around the effects of two different instruments: directives and regulations.[757,758] We learn from Article 288 TFEU that directives are binding as to the result to be achieved, but leave the choice of form and methods for achieving that result to national authorities.[759] Directives are thus indirect or two-stage legislation,[760] in the sense that implementation legislation must be adopted at the domestic level in order for them to have full effect. Differently, regulations are binding in their entirety and directly applicable in all Member States,[761] producing effects in national legal orders without the need for national implementation measures. The question is whether this difference implies a difference in the pre-emptive effects of regulations and directives. Although the CJEU seemed to adopt this view in its early case law, scholars currently agree that the answer is in the negative. As acknowledged by (nowadays CJEU judge) Sacha Prechal, the fact that a directive has been chosen as the instrument for EU intervention 'does not mean that Member States necessarily have a margin in terms of policy making'.[762] Conversely, '[w]hile regulations are clearly the most effective weapon in the E.U. legislature's arsenal for creating uniform rules, they are not invariably associated with exhaustive harmonisation'.[763]

---

756. *See* Arena (2010-2011), pp. 509-511, referring to the role of EU pre-emption as an 'anti-circumvention device'.
757. Article 114 TFEU provides that Member States shall adopt 'the measures for the approximation' of national laws that have as their object the establishment and functioning of the internal market, making no distinction as to the type of measures. According to the CJEU, the drafters of the provision intended to confer on the EU legislator discretion as to 'the method of approximation most appropriate for achieving the desired result' – CJEU, *Tobacco Advertising II*, para. 42 (and case law cited therein).
758. Besides directives and regulations, the EU legislator has also resorted to non-binding instruments in order to approximate national copyright laws. Nevertheless, the success of these instruments has been limited. The 2005 Online Music Recommendation is an example in point. The Recommendation attempted to promote a regulatory environment best suited to the management of copyright and related rights for the provision of legitimate online music services at the EU level. However, as recognised in the Collective Management Directive, 'the Recommendation has been unevenly followed' (Recital 6) and it 'has not been sufficient to encourage the widespread multi-territorial licensing of online rights in musical works or to address the specific demands of multi-territorial licensing' (Recital 39).
759. *See* Article 288 TFEU, third paragraph.
760. *See*, *e.g.*, Prechal (2005), p. 16.
761. *See* the second paragraph of Article 288 TFEU.
762. Prechal (2005), p. 73.
763. Arena (2010-2011), p. 529.

Therefore, the fact that exceptions to the rights of reproduction and communication to the public have been regulated through directives says little about Member State freedom. Rather, the harmonising effect of the InfoSoc legislative framework of exceptions is contingent on two elements.

The first element that directly affects the freedom of Member States is the harmonisation technique(s) followed by the EU legislator. The approximation of national laws can observe distinct models, which are classified according to the level of law-making freedom left to Member States.[764] Two major techniques may be distinguished: full harmonisation and partial harmonisation. Full harmonisation measures leave no leeway to the national legislator and, consequently, no room for disparities between the various national legal frameworks.[765] In contrast, partial harmonisation measures leave Member State legislators with a degree of freedom to make their own policy choices, thus allowing for divergence. Within partial harmonisation, one technique that is particularly relevant for our assessment of the InfoSoc framework of exceptions must be emphasised: that of optional harmonisation, which consists in the laying down of provisions that are not mandatory for Member States. Needless to say, full harmonisation measures have a higher harmonising effect than partial harmonisation measures and thus better further this objective. It must be noted, nonetheless, that multiple techniques may coexist within the same harmonisation measure.[766] This, as shall be seen, is the case of the InfoSoc Directive.[767]

The second element through which legislation may affect the Member States' autonomy is related to the provisions' wording. Naturally, 'the more precise and detailed the content of a directive, the less room for manoeuvre is left for the implementing authorities, with respect not only to the substance of the measures but also to the mode of implementation'.[768] Conversely, vague and conditional language provides national authorities with wider elbowroom and thus compromises the harmonising effect of a directive.[769] Vague concepts are therefore likely to be the object of a higher number of preliminary references by national courts seeking the CJEU's guidance on the unclear boundaries of such concepts.[770]

---

764. Commentators have offered different classifications for harmonisation models. *See*, *e.g.*, Slot (1996), pp. 382-388; Arena (2010-2011), pp. 537-544; Weatherill (2010), pp. 467-468; and Barnard (2016), pp. 580 et seq.
765. Total harmonisation is nonetheless different from unification: whereas the former is still a type of harmonisation, aiming at bringing national laws closer together, the latter aims to make national laws one and the same.
766. *See* Arena (2010-2011), pp. 537-538.
767. *See infra* Chapter 4, sections 2.1. and 2.3.
768. Prechal (2005), p. 74.
769. *See* Ramalho (2016a), p. 130.
770. It is arguably due to its imprecision that Article 3(1) InfoSoc Directive has been the object of more preliminary references than any other provision in the EU copyright *acquis*. *See infra* Chapter 4, section 5.3.2. The Court has nonetheless deemed it a measure of full harmonisation, as seen in Chapter 1, section 4.2.

3.2.2 Harmonising Effect of CJEU Case Law

The extent of the pre-emptive effects of harmonisation measures is sometimes left unclear by the EU legislator, who implicitly delegates the task on the EU judiciary.[771] In the field of copyright, the CJEU has been increasingly taking the issue into its own hands, dispelling the existing uncertainty around the scope of permissible national initiatives. In the absence of express legislative pronouncement, the Court frequently steps in to clarify the pre-emptive effects of EU legislation or to fill the harmonisation gap.[772] In fact, the preclusion of national law-making powers in the field of copyright has frequently resulted from a decision by the CJEU, which has been especially active in interpreting the residual space left for national policy choices in areas affected by the rules on exceptions.[773]

One of the mechanisms that is typically used by the Court to this effect is the identification and development of *autonomous concepts of EU law*. With a view to ensuring a coherent and uniform application of EU law and the respect for the principle of equality, the CJEU has held on numerous cases that certain legal concepts are to be considered autonomous concepts of EU law.[774] It is now a settled case law that, where a provision of EU law makes no express reference to national law for the purpose of determining its meaning and scope, the terms of such provision must be regarded as autonomous concepts and interpreted uniformly in all Member States, having regard to the wording of that provision, its context and the purpose of the legislation in question.[775] The Court has found concepts as diverse as 'teleshopping',[776] 'habitual residence of a child',[777] and 'human embryo'[778] to require an autonomous interpretation.

---

771. *See* Soares (1998), p. 133, arguing that EU pre-emption is more often than not implied, rather than express.
772. The judicial activism of the CJEU in the field of copyright has been summarised in the Introduction (section 4.2).
773. But also in the field of economic rights, as already mentioned. *See also infra* Chapter 4, section 5.1.1.
774. *See*, *e.g.*, CJEU, *Ekro*, para. 11; CJEU, *Linster*, para. 43; CJEU, *Yiadom*, para. 26; CJEU, *SENA*, para. 24; and CJEU, *Private Equity Insurance Group*, para. 39.
775. In what concerns the context of the provision, it must be taken into account whether the concept under interpretation is used in other instruments in the field of IP. If so, and given the requirements of unity and coherence of the EU legal order, the concept must be interpreted in light of the rules and principles of those instruments and given the same meaning, unless the EU legislator has expressed a different intention. *See* CJEU, *VEWA*, para. 27; CJEU, *Premier League*, para. 188; and CJEU, *Reha Training*, para. 28. On this conceptual unity that the CJEU attempts to develop, *see* Malenovský (2012). In *SCF*, paras 74-78, the different contexts and objectives of the right of communication to the public in Article 3 InfoSoc Directive (an exclusive right) and in Article 8(2) Rental and Lending Directive (a remuneration right) led the Court to engage in an 'individual interpretation' of the latter.
776. *See* CJEU, *Österreichischer Rundfunk*, paras 24-25.
777. *See* CJEU, *A*, paras 34-35.
778. *See* CJEU, *Brüstle*, para. 26, and CJEU, *International Stem Cell*, para. 23.

In sum, the stronger the harmonising effect of CJEU case law, namely through the identification of autonomous concepts within the InfoSoc framework, the greater the degree of legal certainty *qua* harmonisation.

4 CONCLUSION

In discussing the aptness of the InfoSoc framework of exceptions, both sides in the debate build their cases on flexibility- and certainty-related arguments, drawing on these notions to either praise or criticise various of its features. Nevertheless, a survey of the relevant sources in the debate shows that the terms 'flexibility' and 'legal certainty' are used with a plurality of meanings.

At a more general level, flexibility and legal certainty are understood as normative objectives that must be balanced within EU copyright law and, specifically, within the InfoSoc framework of exceptions.

With regard to flexibility, this framework should: (i) seek to prevent obsolescence, by remaining adaptable to technology-related changes; and (ii) respect the legal traditions and specificities of different Member States. Hence, the InfoSoc framework will be flexible if it is capable of adjusting to constantly changing technological circumstances and/or if it manages to accommodate diverse national cultural policies.

Likewise, the concept of 'legal certainty' is used to refer to two related policy goals: (i) the need to ensure that copyright law is able to guide the behaviour of users and rightholders regarding what amounts to infringing and non-infringing uses of protected works; and (ii) the importance of promoting the harmonisation of national laws. The framework of exceptions will thus foster legal certainty if it guides rightholders and prospective users on the legal status of unauthorised uses and/or if it holds a high harmonising effect.

Table 3.1 Flexibility and Legal Certainty as Normative Objectives of EU Copyright Law

Normative Objectives		
Flexibility	Adaptability to technology-related changes	The susceptibility of easy modification to respond to the emergence of new technological uses of protected works
	Adaptability to different national cultures	The capacity to accommodate the different Member States' legal traditions and specificities in the field of exceptions

Legal certainty	Guidance on the legal status of unauthorised uses	The existence of a clear legal framework that informs stakeholders about the boundary between infringing and non-infringing uses
	Harmonisation	The existence of a harmonised framework where the remaining national differences do not hinder cross-border uses of protected works

The four objectives may be organised into two pairs corresponding to two different tensions: one between technological adaptability and guidance (the first meanings of each pair) and one between Member State freedom and EU harmonisation (the second meanings of each pair). Where disagreement exists between participants in the debate is on how to manage these tensions. As to the first tension, the dispute focuses on the allocation of decision-making power between legislators and judges. Whereas some scholars understand adaptability and guidance to be tasks of the legislator, others would prefer the judiciary to have a greater share of the burden. The second tension refers to the division of competence between the EU and its Member States. In this regard, no consensus exists around the appropriateness of solutions like closed and open catalogues or optional and mandatory exceptions.

An itemisation of the different arguments advanced in the InfoSoc debate has allowed us to further translate the two pairs of objectives into eight criteria that will underlie a more refined assessment of the InfoSoc framework of exceptions.

Table 3.2 Flexibility and Legal Certainty as Criteria for Assessing the InfoSoc Framework of Exceptions

	Normative Objectives	*Assessment Criteria*
Flexibility	Adaptability to technology-related changes	Legislative responsiveness
		Judicial discretion
	Adaptability to national cultures	Accommodation of Member States' legal traditions
		Accommodation of Member States' specificities
Legal certainty	Guidance on the legal status of unauthorised uses	Legislative guidance
		Judicial guidance
	Harmonisation	Harmonising effect of legislation
		Harmonising effect of CJEU case law

As was highlighted throughout this chapter, these criteria sometimes overlap and stand in mutual tension. Generally, in case of conflict, the higher the framework scores on a certain criterion, the lower it will score on the competing one. For example, a rule that provides a high degree of judicial discretion due to its vague wording will, on the other hand, rank low in terms of legislative guidance. Similarly, a high degree of legislative freedom at the Member State level will likely entail a low level of harmonisation.

What is crucial is that the InfoSoc framework balances the conflicting objectives and achieves a compromise between them. As in all cases where an equilibrium between competing considerations is needed, however, this exercise 'might entail meeting all of them to a certain extent, rather than few of them to a large extent'.[779] What the next chapter does is to assess whether and to what extent such a balance has been reached within the InfoSoc framework of exceptions.

779. Ramalho (2016a), p. 147.

Chapter 4

Flexibility and Legal Certainty in the InfoSoc Framework of Exceptions

1 INTRODUCTION

The previous chapter served a twofold purpose. First, it aimed to systematise the main arguments used in the debate on the appropriateness of the InfoSoc framework of exceptions. Second, by examining the various senses in which the terms 'flexibility' and 'legal certainty' are used in copyright writings, it sought to introduce a measure of conceptual refinement in the debate and to lay down the criteria that will guide our critical assessment of said framework.

The task I take up in this chapter is to examine the InfoSoc framework of exceptions under the light of those criteria. This exercise will allow us, on the one hand, to highlight a number of the framework's shortcomings and, on the other, to recognise examples of features that meet the relevant benchmarks and that should be preserved or fostered in the future. The present chapter will therefore attempt to answer the following research questions: To what extent does the existing InfoSoc framework of exceptions promote flexibility and legal certainty? Does it achieve a balance between the different objectives and criteria described in Chapter 3? In a possible InfoSoc reform, which features should be maintained and which should be modified?

It is important to clarify at the outset what this chapter is not. This chapter will not offer a comprehensive analysis of each and every exception provided in InfoSoc and subsequent directives in the copyright *acquis*. That is a type of contribution which goes beyond the purpose of this book (and which, in any case, is more fittingly made by copyright law textbooks and commentaries).

This chapter will focus instead on the various *structural features* of the InfoSoc framework of exceptions – the features that lie at the core of the scholarly and policymaking controversy that this book aims to tackle. These features are grouped and critically explored under four main sections: the catalogue of exceptions and its fundamental attributes (section 2); exceptions themselves and their scope (section 3); the InfoSoc three-step test (section 4); and the role of the CJEU in interpreting and developing the framework (section 5).[780]

Section 6 concludes by revisiting the normative grid designed in the previous chapter and by setting out general recommendations on how the InfoSoc framework should be restructured so as to achieve a balance between the different objectives and criteria identified therein. These recommendations will pave the way for our last chapter, which puts forward a road map for reform.

2 THE CATALOGUE

The catalogue of exceptions to the InfoSoc rights of reproduction and communication to the public has a series of attributes that are above and beyond the exceptions themselves: it is an exhaustive, heterogeneous, and predominantly optional catalogue. Each of these features will be examined in turn in the subsections that follow. As shall be seen, they have a decisive influence on the extent to which the InfoSoc framework of exceptions achieves the policy objectives identified in the previous chapter and are therefore part and parcel of the controversy surrounding its appropriateness.

2.1 Exhaustiveness

In enacting an exhaustive catalogue, the EU legislator essentially prohibited any exceptions to the rights harmonised in InfoSoc beyond the ones provided in the *acquis*. Straightforward as it may seem, this implication deserves closer scrutiny. Three distinct effects emerge from the exhaustive character of the catalogue of exceptions.

The first two effects concern national legislative autonomy. First, exhaustiveness means that Member States are not allowed to *preserve* in their national laws any exceptions other than those provided in EU rules

780. Regarding the chapter's structure, two broad options were available. The chapter could be organised either around the criteria developed in the previous chapter or according to the InfoSoc framework's fundamental features. The second option was chosen in order to avoid unnecessary repetitions. Dividing the analysis according to the assessment criteria would force me to return to the same features of the framework at different points of the chapter. For example, the optional nature of the catalogue would have to be considered under at least the 'accommodation of Member States' specificities' and 'harmonising effect of legislation' criteria, whereas the three-step test would have to be assessed under the 'judicial discretion' criterion and again under the 'legislative guidance' one. Instead, each of the features – among which optionality and the three-step test – will be examined *in light of* the relevant criteria. The conclusions regarding each criterion are then summarised in the final section.

recognising exceptions to the InfoSoc rights. Second, it entails that Member States have no room to *enact* new exceptions beyond those ones, even if for the purpose of adapting their national laws to socio-economic, cultural, or technological changes that have occurred meanwhile. The fact that subsequent directives have provided for further exceptions to the rights of reproduction and communication to the public harmonised in InfoSoc, without explicitly mentioning that no other exceptions may be enacted at the national level does not undermine the exhaustive character of the catalogue. The exhaustiveness effect naturally extends beyond the InfoSoc Directive, which is *lex generalis*.

Some scholars prefer to describe the catalogue as 'quasi-exhaustive' due to the effects of the grandfather clause enshrined in Article 5(3)(o).[781] But the truth is that this provision does little to increase responsiveness to future changes. For one thing, the clause only authorises the maintenance of *pre-existing* exceptions (so, necessarily, not for unforeseen uses).[782] For another, the permission is limited to the maintenance of *analogue* exceptions, meaning that Member States cannot rely on it to pursue the objective of adaptation to technology-related changes, for most (if not all) emerging uses will be of a digital nature.[783]

The two foregoing effects have enabled the achievement of 'a certain degree of harmonisation', according to the Commission.[784] In fact, the exhaustive catalogue in the InfoSoc Directive is a type of full harmonisation requirement. By precluding most autonomous national measures falling within the field of exceptions to the harmonised rights, it practically pre-empts that entire field. Member States may change their own catalogues, but only within the tight boundaries set by the InfoSoc *acquis*. Exhaustiveness thus works as a prophylactic measure against the diverging expansion of lists of exceptions throughout the Union. Allowing for national legislative creativity beyond what is necessary to respect the cultural specificities of Member States would seriously prejudice the achievement of the harmonisation goal and is therefore unadvisable. That much has been recognised by the CJEU, in expressly negating the possibility of Member States laying down, in national law, exceptions other than those provided for in Article 5, such as the free use exception in Section 24(1) German Copyright Act or freedom-of-information-based exceptions. In that sense, the closed catalogue may be regarded as a positive measure.[785]

---

781. *See* Eechoud et al. (2009), p. 103, and Ramalho (2016a), p. 166.
782. This is made clear by the use of the expression 'where exceptions or limitations already exist under national law' in Article 5(3)(o).
783. On top of that, the CJEU has determined that the clause must be interpreted strictly – *see* CJEU, *AKM*, paras 36-38.
784. 2008 Green Paper, p. 5.
785. *See* 2008 Green Paper, p. 5, noting that '[t]he list of exceptions as contained in the Directive has achieved a certain degree of harmonisation: creating an exhaustive list of exceptions does not allow Member States to maintain or introduce exceptions which are

Its beneficial effects notwithstanding, the exhaustive nature of the catalogue may backfire against the EU. Reacting to changes in the technological environment, Member State legislators have tested the boundaries of the InfoSoc catalogue by introducing exceptions that were not *initially* provided therein.[786] The regulation of TDM provides a helpful example. Despite the fact that no specific provision existed then in EU copyright law, the UK Government introduced an exception privileging TDM for non-commercial research purposes in 2014 (Section 29A UK CDPA). The exception was adopted at a time when it was uncertain whether the exceptions in the *acquis* applied to TDM services and when solutions were already under discussion at the EU level. In this context, the legislative move by the UK may reasonably be understood as an expansion of the national catalogue contrary to EU law (though later confirmed by it).[787]

Like TDM, not all future emerging uses that may need to be accommodated will be covered by an exception within EU law. By precluding Member State legislators from updating national catalogues at their will, exhaustiveness leaves two options: either the EU legislator periodically updates the list or the task of adaptation will be carried out by the judiciary.

This, in turn, leads us to the third effect of the InfoSoc catalogue's exhaustive character. Exhaustiveness works as a limit not only on the freedom of national lawmakers but also on the freedom of law-appliers: in deciding disputes on unauthorised uses of protected works that are not expressly regulated by EU law, judges are not allowed to apply the existing exceptions by analogy.[788] The activity of analogical application entails going

---

not listed'. *See also* Reinbothe (2002), p. 46, commending the exhaustive nature of the catalogue for its harmonising effect.

786. *See* Renda et al. (2015), pp. 129-130.

787. *See*, in this regard, EPRS (2015), p. 18, observing that the UK added an exception 'not originally envisaged by the InfoSoc Directive'. Following the UK, a few other Member States have introduced exceptions specifically designed to cover TDM activities, namely France and Germany – *see*, respectively, Articles L.122-5(10) and L.342-3(5) French IP Code and Section 60d German Copyright Act. For commentary on these national exceptions, *see* Geiger et al. (2018a), pp. 17-18. Similarly, when negotiations on the DSM Proposal and its TDM exception were well underway, the Irish Government, relying on the InfoSoc research exception, proposed the introduction of its own TDM exception in a new Section 53A of the Irish Copyright Act, with a scope similar to the one in the UK. The proposal follows from a 2013 report published by the Irish Copyright Review Committee, where an exception for 'content-mining' cast in fair dealing terms had already been proposed. *See* Irish Copyright Review Committee Report 2013, pp. 85-88.

788. Of course, the prohibition against the application of listed exceptions by analogy may flow from the very qualification of these provisions as *exceptional*. *See*, *e.g.*, Lucas (1998), p. 175. The fact that the exceptions are part of a closed catalogue only reinforces such idea. Indeed, even where provisions are not properly qualified as exceptions, the fact that they are part of a *numerus clausus* entails a prohibition on their analogical extension. On the relationship between analogy and the principle of *numerus clausus* of real rights, *see* Antunes (2015), pp. 180 et seq., and Antunes (2017), pp. 142 et seq.

beyond the meaning of the relevant provision and extending it to fact-situations that do not come within its textual scope, but that may be considered 'similar'. The inquiry into whether an analogy is possible begins where the possible meaning of the relevant provision ends.[789] It is that meaning that marks the frontier – a well-established one in civilian methodology – between an extensive interpretation of the provision and the analogical extension thereof: the former, unlike the latter, implies that the judge stays within the linguistically possible meaning of the provision under interpretation. The application by analogy of statutory provisions is therefore commonly regarded as a form of judicial *development* of the law, rather than the regular interpretative activity of judges.[790] As such, the closed character of the catalogue necessarily precludes it.[791] Admitting the analogical application of exhaustively enumerated exceptions would mean, in practice, that Member States would be able to adopt additional exceptions through judicial decision-making.

If national judges and legislators are not allowed to update the catalogue of exceptions, the burden of adapting it to changes in technology-related circumstances will necessarily fall on the shoulders of the EU. The worthiness of this solution is predicated, first, on the competence of the EU to intervene to that effect and, second, on its capacity to keep pace with developments in technology. Let us consider each in turn.

As to competence, the Union has been legislating in the field of copyright by relying on the internal market legal basis.[792] As previously discussed, for a harmonisation measure to be sustained on the need to build the internal market, two requirements must be fulfilled: (1) an obstacle to cross-border trade *or* a significant distortion of competition must exist or must be likely to emerge and (2) the measure must be designed to prevent that obstacle or distortion.

The EU legislator understands these requirements in a very flexible way. As noted by commentators, the scope of the internal market competence 'is very wide indeed – at times almost unlimited'.[793] The breadth of the copyright *acquis*, in general, and the number and diversity of harmonised exceptions, in particular, lend support to the idea that 'where the EU legislators choose, with proper thought and drafting, they are able to legislate

789. *See, e.g.*, Engisch (2014), pp. 293-294.
790. *See, e.g.*, Posner (2006), p. 773, and Larenz (2012), pp. 519 et seq.
791. It nevertheless *does not* preclude the application by courts of extrinsic doctrines that may work, in specific disputes, as defences against claims of infringement. Despite exhaustiveness, courts may consider and apply defences based on doctrines from outside copyright law, the paradigmatic case being the abuse of rights doctrine. Concluding otherwise would imply that copyright law operates in isolation from other fields of law or that it is somehow hierarchically superior to them, which, quite obviously, is not the case. *See* Hugenholtz & Okediji, p. 19 (and references cited therein).
792. *See supra* Chapter 3, section 2.1.1.
793. Halpern & Johnson (2014), p. 122.

quite freely in relation to intellectual property'.[794] The narrow cross-border relevance of some of the exceptions laid down in EU law provides evidence of the lenient way in which the legislator interprets the internal market *vires*. The CJEU too has recognised that the EU enjoys broad discretion not only in what regards the nature and scope of the measures it adopts but also in relation to the finding of the basic facts that justify harmonisation.[795]

In addition, the internal market competence has a functional character, meaning that, although it defines the primary goal to be achieved by the EU legislator, it leaves the substantive content of the measures entirely to its discretion.[796] On the whole, this brings us to the conclusion that Article 114 TFEU is 'a rather flexible competence norm, in the sense that it enables the EU to harmonise a wide range of subjects, so long as there is a point of connection to the building of an internal market'.[797]

Establishing this connection seems to be a relatively easy task in cases of measures that amend or add copyright exceptions with the goal of responding to the emergence of new digital uses, by ensuring their legality across borders. Achieving legal certainty in the internal market regarding uses with a cross-border dimension is a goal that can hardly be pursued by Member States acting independently.[798,799] The justification for action by the EU will be all the more reasonable if the proposed exceptions are *mandatory*

794. Halpern & Johnson (2014), p. 125.
795. *See* CJEU, *Afton Chemical*, para. 33 (and case law cited therein).
796. *See*, *e.g.*, Weatherill (2004), pp. 6-7.
797. Ramalho (2014), p. 183. Halpern & Johnson (2014) take the argument further, stating that 'Article 114 … could be used to enact a Directive setting out an entire copyright code' (p. 125). The same may be said, *mutatis mutandis*, about Article 118 TFEU.
798. To be sure, the discretion to intervene on the basis of internal market-related competences is not boundless. Commentators have disputed the existence of an internal market rationale in the case of a legislative measure intended to create a related right for press publishers, such as the one enshrined in Article 15 DSM Directive – *see* Peukert (2016), pp. 5 et seq.; Bently et al. (2017), pp. 38-39; Ramalho (2017b); and Rosati (2017b), pp. 8-9. In fact, the existence of EU competence to create new rights appears harder to justify. This is so because the creation of a new right inevitably results in the introduction of an 'extra regulatory layer' that would need to be cleared for the uses that fall within its scope, with obvious negative consequences for the internal market – *see* Ramalho (2017b), p. 81. Contrary to rights, exceptions generally facilitate the building of the internal market, for they exempt interested users from clearance requirements.
799. The argument could be made, however, that the existing level of harmonisation in the field of exceptions forecloses the possibility of the EU to act on the basis of internal market-related considerations. Such argument would be based on the fact that the exhaustive nature of the catalogue already prevents the heterogeneous development of national catalogues, thus limiting the emergence of disparities between national copyright laws that may act as barriers to trade. However, it is the very fact that Member States are not allowed to unilaterally legislate on exceptions that justifies EU intervention in this field. As stated in the Impact Assessment accompanying the DSM Proposal, the impossibility of intervention at the national level combined with the need for exceptions that privilege certain new digital uses 'makes the amendment of EU legislation inevitable' – SWD DSM Directive, p. 81. Accepting the argument that the EU

for Member States to implement. Mandatory exceptions, as opposed to optional ones, undoubtedly improve the conditions for the establishment and functioning of the internal market in relation to the uses that fall within their scope, by forcing Member States to implement them and thus eliminating the fragmentation that could arise out of that discretion. And, indeed, since the InfoSoc Directive was adopted the exceptions' *acquis* has been updated with mandatory provisions accommodating uses connected to technological development.[800]

Assuming the EU enjoys the necessary powers to update the catalogue of exceptions to the rights of reproduction and communication to the public, the proposed measure would also need to satisfy the requirements of subsidiarity and proportionality. A firm conclusion on compliance would of course require testing the introduction of *concrete* exceptions against these principles. Nonetheless, some general considerations may be advanced independently of the content of would-be exceptions.

As to subsidiarity, if the exceptions to be added have a cross-border impact, the EU will in principle be in a better position to achieve the objectives underlying these exceptions. The cross-border nature of the uses covered by the exceptions would render national interventions insufficient.[801] It would certainly be harder for the EU to demonstrate that the goals of an amendment would be better achieved at the EU level where the new exceptions do not concern uses that take place across national frontiers and lack a noticeable impact on the internal market. However, and as mentioned above, the InfoSoc catalogue includes exceptions with limited cross-border impact, which suggests that the relevance of such impact is not a necessary condition for a measure to survive the subsidiarity test and that other public policy objectives may justify the added value of EU intervention in relation to Member State intervention.[802]

Regarding the principle of proportionality, the EU legislator has traditionally been given broad discretion in assessing its application.[803] In *Tobacco Advertising II*, the CJEU held that compliance with this principle by measures that involve political, economic, and social choices on the part of the EU legislator, and in which it is called upon to make complex

is precluded to legislate would be equivalent to proscribing any further EU action in the field of exceptions to the rights of reproduction and communication to the public – an evidently ludicrous idea.

800. *See supra* Chapter 2, section 3.2.3.

801. *See* Recital 83 DSM Directive. *See also* Explanatory Memorandum DSM Proposal, p. 5 (in relation to the exceptions proposed therein) and SWD DSM Directive, p. 81 (acknowledging that 'MS acting alone could not sufficiently address these problems and the objectives can be only achieved by EU action').

802. *See* Ramalho (2017b), p. 82.

803. *See* Hugenholtz et al. (2006), p. 16.

assessments, should only be negated if the measure is 'manifestly inappropriate' in relation to the objective that is being pursued.[804] The CJEU tends to adopt a deferential approach towards the legislator's policy choices, infrequently overturning them.[805] Furthermore, the Court has explicitly stated that the EU legislator's broad discretion 'implies limited judicial review of its exercise'.[806]

Thus far, the conclusion that emerges is that the EU would in principle enjoy competence to update the catalogue of exceptions. But beyond the EU legislator's competence to react, legislative responsiveness, as defined in the preceding chapter, is dependent on a second condition: the reaction must take place in a relatively swift manner.

Critics of the InfoSoc framework argue that having the EU legislator change the framework each and every time a new technology or service that needs to be assimilated emerges is not a viable solution.[807] The pace of technological change in relation to the EU legislative process entails that copyright law is fated to lagging behind technology and that new uses are to remain shrouded in uncertainty until legislative clarification is provided.

It is admittedly difficult to measure the legislative response time to technological change in a precise and reliable manner. One (undeniably rough) way to do it is to inquire into the average duration of the EU legislative procedure. The EU adopts legislation through different procedures, with the choice of procedure depending on the policy area of the instrument that will be proposed. The general procedure for adopting EU legislation is the ordinary legislative procedure (formerly known as the co-decision procedure).[808] The procedure, which applies to much of EU legislation, is essentially characterised by requiring a joint decision from the European Parliament and the Council, following a proposal prepared by the

---

804. CJEU, *Tobacco Advertising II*, para. 123 (and case law cited therein).
805. *See* Craig & Búrca (2015), p. 557. *But see, e.g.*, CJEU, *Buitoni*; CJEU, *Bela Mühle*; and CJEU, *ABNA*.
806. CJEU, *Afton Chemical*, para. 33 (and case law cited therein). It ought to be noted that in the case of an InfoSoc update the objectives pursued by any new or amended exceptions would have to be such as to justify the possible negative impact for rightholders – *see, mutatis mutandis*, CJEU, *Vodafone*, para. 53. As expressed in the Explanatory Memorandum DSM Proposal, exceptions should 'contain conditions that ensure the preservation of functioning markets and rightholders' interests and incentives to create and invest' (p. 5). Raising doubts as to whether the principle of proportionality has been observed in the DSM reform, on grounds that the Impact Assessment seemed 'to serve more as ex-post justification of a predetermined policy choice, rather than as ex-ante substantiation of the need for action', *see* Hilty & Moscon (2017), p. 20.
807. *See, e.g.*, Hugenholtz (2002), p. 69-1; Noll (2012), p. 25; Dnes (2013), p. 443; Hugenholtz (2013b), p. 65; Strowel (2014), p. 1135; Hugenholtz (2017), p. 281; Jütte (2017), p. 512; and Senftleben (2017), pp. 242-243. *See also* Förster (2008), p. 212, but citing as an example the enactment of the so-called second basket of German copyright reform, which was first announced in 2003 and only came into force in the beginning of 2008.
808. The procedure is described in Article 294 TFEU.

Commission. An agreement between the co-legislating institutions may be reached in any of up to three readings.

The duration of the procedure varies considerably depending on the stage at which the agreement is achieved.[809] Further delays are likely to occur if the file happens to be carried over from one parliamentary term to another. In addition, after the co-legislators have reached an agreement, the text must be translated into all official languages, verified by the lawyer-linguists, and finally published in the Official Journal, adding some extra months to the process.[810] As a result of these intricacies, 'even a relatively non-controversial directive takes several years to complete'.[811]

In the case of directives, as opposed to regulations, one must add the duration of national implementations. Each directive sets out a deadline for implementation, by which the Member States must send the text of the national implementing measures to the Commission. As is known, Member States often fail to meet the transposition deadlines.[812] The InfoSoc Directive itself is a case in point. Member States had until 22 December 2002 to transpose it into their national laws.[813] Yet, only Greece and Denmark complied with the deadline, with most Member States carrying out the transposition between 2003 and 2004.[814] The last Member State to complete the process was France, in August 2006.[815] This means that almost nine years elapsed from the date the Commission presented the InfoSoc Proposal to the end of the implementation stage.

To make things worse, copyright is nowadays a field of law where lobbying and political turmoil abound.[816] Not only is the legislative decision-making process lengthy and slow-moving, it is also permeable to the pressure exerted by interest groups.[817] During the process that led to the

809. *See* EP Report Ordinary Legislative Procedure, p. 12.
810. *See* EP Report Ordinary Legislative Procedure, p. 12 and fn. 25.
811. Hugenholtz (2013b), p. 65. *See also* Strowel (2014), p. 1135 ('the time between the first draft Directive by the European Commission and the last implementation by a Member State can take ten years or more'), and Hugenholtz (2017), p. 281 ('the total legislative response time to a new technological development may easily exceed ten years').
812. *See generally* König & Luetgert (2009), analysing patterns of transposition timeliness across Member States from 1986 to 2002.
813. *See* Article 13 InfoSoc Directive.
814. *See* Guibault et al. (2007), pp. vii-viii. *See also* Hugenholtz (2005), p. 117.
815. The Directive was implemented by the 2006 French Copyright Law. For the implementation acts and dates of the different Member States, *see* Westkamp (2007), pp. 79-81.
816. On copyright lobbying at the EU level, *see* Farrand (2015) (noting that '[c]opyright, at least academically, is a fiercely contested subject. Lobbyists, it has been suggested, dominate copyright policy' – p. 488); Vetulani-Cęgiel (2015) (focusing on the cases of the term of protection for sound recordings and of orphan works); Lewinski (2018), pp. 144-145 (pointing out that the activities of lobbyists have been intensifying in recent years); and, for a book-length account, Farrand (2014). On the role of lobby groups at the international level, *see* Lewinski (2005). *See also* Litman (1989) for an American perspective.
817. *See* Hugenholtz (2000), p. 500, and Hugenholtz (2013b), p. 67.

enactment of InfoSoc, stakeholder pressure had been considered 'unprecedented'.[818] However, the lobby battle fought over the DSM Directive has arguably been gorier. The process – which, from the presentation of the Commission's initial proposal to the publication of the Directive on the Official Journal of the EU, lasted almost three years – has been marked by successive voting delays and stalemates and by the pressure of rightholders' representatives (especially publishers, the recording industry, and music CMOs), on one side, and technology companies, Internet luminaries, and digital rights NGOs, on the opposite side. The outcome of this turbulent process was an extremely complex legislative text that is likely to lead to incompatible national implementations, posing a real threat to the creation of a true EU digital single market.

On top of all of this, technological uses that may justify an update in the field of exceptions often emerge far before the beginning of the legislative process. TDM may again serve as an illustration. While this technological use saw the light of day in the 1990s,[819] the Commission's intention to regulate it only came to the fore in the early 2013, when it set up a stakeholders dialogue called 'Licences for Europe' and, within it, a thematic working group dedicated to the issue of TDM. The stakeholders participating in that initiative failed to reach a consensus on the problems to be addressed and the results to be achieved.[820] Later, the Commission's public consultation on the review of the EU copyright rules asked a number of questions on copyright-related obstacles to the use and provision of TDM services.[821] Following the consultation and taking its results into account, the Commission published a Communication in 2015 where it acknowledged that '[t]he lack of a clear EU provision on TDM for scientific research purposes creates uncertainties in the research community', thus 'harm[ing] the EU's competitiveness and scientific leadership at a time when research and innovation (R&I) activities within the EU must increasingly take place through cross-border and cross-discipline collaboration'.[822]

A legislative proposal intended to clarify the legal status of TDM at the EU level was finally presented, as part of the DSM Proposal, on 14 September 2016. The time span that separated, on the one hand, the emergence and spread of TDM and, on the other, the realisation by EU institutions that such use needed to be expressly accommodated by the copyright *acquis* and the adoption of legislation to that effect strengthens the

818. Hugenholtz (2000b), p. 499.
819. Encyclopaedia Britannica reports that the first international conference on 'knowledge discovery' (the expression used by computer scientists to refer to the process) was held in 1995 and that the journal 'Data Mining and Knowledge Discovery' was launched in 1997, which coincided with the establishment of early data mining companies – *see* https://www.britannica.com/technology/data-mining.
820. *See* Memo Licences for Europe.
821. *See* 2013 Public Consultation, pp. 27-28.
822. Communication on a Modern European Copyright Framework, p. 7.

argument put forward by InfoSoc critics that the reliance on periodic amendments of the framework of exceptions in order to keep copyright law up-to-date is an impractical and unwise solution in light of the ever shorter intervals in which the legislator must act.[823] As new uses that do not fit the existing exceptions keep emerging, chances are that EU copyright law will require further updates, possibly with increasingly greater frequency.

In sum, as a by-product of exhaustiveness, the EU legislator will have to undertake recurring amendments to the framework of exceptions, either by reviewing the InfoSoc Directive itself or by enacting new instruments. A legislative failure to engage in these updates, due to inertia or political difficulties, will entail implicitly delegating the task of adapting copyright law to the judiciary.

2.2 Heterogeneity

The InfoSoc catalogue and the changes it suffered throughout the legislative process (even if such changes have been partly motivated by the need to achieve a political compromise[824]) are revealing of the EU legislator's interest in catering for Member States' distinct traditions. As seen, while the initial version of the catalogue in the Commission's proposal was composed of only nine exceptions, the final text of the Directive contains a total of twenty-one exceptions. This list, says the EU legislator, 'takes due account of the different legal traditions in Member States'.[825] And indeed, what the list seems to be, in the words of AG Sharpston, is 'a compilation of pre-existing exceptions and limitations under various national laws'.[826] This

---

823. This much has been recognised even by some policymakers, who feel no discomfort in admitting that legislative institutions cannot effectively handle the task of keeping copyright law up-to-date. Former MEP Julia Reda has openly acknowledged this – *see* Draft Reda Report, p. 12 ('In reality, it is most likely that legislation will lag behind such [technological] developments').

824. *See, e.g.*, Cohen Jehoram (2001b), p. 388 (claiming that '[t]he whole list represents the addition of all national restrictions which member states are unprepared to give up') and Janssens (2009), pp. 332-333 (pointing out that 'this situation was caused by the many heated discussions, resulting in political deals and concessions to lobbying pressure' and that 'the Community legislator was not strong enough to withstand the pressure of Member States, which all tried to consolidate existing provisions').

825. Recital 32 InfoSoc Directive. *See also* Hugenholtz & Senftleben (2011), p. 14, observing that the list in Article 5 'reflect[s] the diversity of national copyright traditions in EU Member States'.

826. AG Opinion, *VG Wort*, fn. 34. *See also* CJEU, *Laserdisken*, para. 80 (stating that, in general, 'the cultural aspects specific to the Member States ... have been fully taken into consideration by the Community institutions in the drafting and adoption of Directive 2001/29'); Hugenholtz et al. (2006), p. 63 ('The limitations listed in the Information Society Directive ... are modelled either on the provisions of the Berne Convention or on the provisions found in the legislation of many Member States'); Guibault et al. (2007), pp. 62-63 ('most limitations contained in the Directive are

compilation covers a wide spectrum of uses: it includes classic copyright exceptions, such as private copying and quotation, but also less common ones, such as the ones for use during religious celebrations or for use in connection with the demonstration or repair of equipment. This breadth and diversity allowed Member States to preserve most of their long-established national exceptions.[827] Moreover, some of the exceptions that were eventually included in the InfoSoc catalogue existed only in a few Member States prior to the Directive's adoption.[828] This, as pointed out by Ana Ramalho, 'speaks highly of the attempt to include national idiosyncrasies in the harmonization program'.[829]

Besides InfoSoc, other directives in the copyright *acquis* show a concern with respecting national specificities in the field of exceptions. For instance, Article 6(2)(d) Database Directive allows Member States to provide for exceptions to copyright protection in databases that are traditionally provided for in their national laws. More recently, Article 5 DSM Directive, along with Recital 23, also sought to safeguard the different national arrangements for implementation of the teaching exception.

Hence, from the perspective of the objective of adapting copyright law to national cultures and traditions, the diversified range of exceptions provided in the *acquis*, and in Article 5 InfoSoc Directive in particular, offsets the catalogue's exhaustive character and the limited freedom that Member States enjoy to adapt the wording of exceptions. While Member States are not allowed to add or maintain exceptions beyond the listed ones and have little discretion in designing exceptions at the implementation stage, they have a wide array of permitted uses to choose from.

The capacity to accommodate national particularities is further reinforced by the so-called grandfather clause set forth in Article 5(3)(o) InfoSoc Directive. This provision allows Member States to preserve exceptions beyond the ones described in the preceding paragraphs and sub-paragraphs (and in other instruments), as long as a number of conditions are met: (i) such exceptions cover only analogue (as opposed to digital) uses; (ii) those uses are of minor importance (presumably economic[830]); (iii) the exceptions already existed under national law; and (iv) they are not relevant for internal market purposes. While, as clarified in the preceding section, the clause does

inspired by the long internationally recognised limitations based on article 9(2) of the Berne Convention that already existed in the national legislation of the Member States'); and Hugenholtz & Senftleben (2011), p. 20 (mentioning that 'during the negotiations on the … Directive in the Council Working Group, EU Member States had insisted on the maintenance of the majority of limitations existing in their national laws').

827. *See* Hugenholtz (2000b), p. 500.
828. An example of such an exception is the one laid down in Article 5(3)(m), privileging the use of an artistic work in the form of a building or a drawing or plan of a building for the purposes of reconstructing the building. *See* Westkamp (2007), pp. 92-94.
829. Ramalho (2016a), p. 179.
830. *See* Walter & Lewinski (2010), p. 1058.

not give Member States sufficient discretion to enact exceptions for unforeseen uses, it promotes their capacity to accommodate national legal traditions by allowing the preservation of exceptions that already existed under national laws. The restriction to analogue uses does not significantly interfere with the goal of adaptability to national cultures, for most traditional uses prior to the adoption of the InfoSoc Directive were analogue.

A few exceptions in national copyright laws have been considered to be permitted under the grandfather clause.[831] These include, *inter alia*, pre-InfoSoc Belgian exceptions for the use of works by deceased authors in anthologies intended for teaching[832] and for the performance of a work during a public examination in the context of school activities,[833] as well as a German exception allowing the non-commercial reproduction and distribution of a portrait by its commissioner.[834] By contrast, the CJEU has held that an Austrian provision that permitted a multiplicity of economic operators to distribute, without authorisation, protected works in parallel by means of communal antenna installations with a limited capacity for connected subscribers was not covered by Article 5(3)(o). This use, the Court held, could not be considered as one of 'minor importance' due to its potential cumulative effects.[835]

2.3 Optionality

The harmonisation of copyright law 'has been a mixed process of partial and full harmonisation'.[836] The two types of harmonisation techniques have been employed even within the same instrument, as confirmed by the InfoSoc Directive.

In harmonising economic rights the EU legislator has typically opted for total harmonisation. As pointed out by the CJEU, the rights set out in

831. *See* Westkamp (2007), p. 48. *But see* Walter & Lewinski (2010), p. 1058, stating that 'it is unlikely that many exceptions and limitations will be covered by this provision'.
832. Prior to InfoSoc, the exception was laid down in Article 21 Belgian Copyright Law, being now provided in Article XI.191/1(5) Belgian Economic Law Code. *See* Westkamp (2007), p. 125, noting that the exception can also be justified under Article 5(3)(a) InfoSoc Directive, which allows exceptions for the sole purpose of illustration for teaching or scientific research.
833. Prior to InfoSoc, the exception was laid down in Article 22(1)(7) Belgian Copyright Law and can currently be found in Article XI.191/1(2) Belgian Economic Law Code. *See* Westkamp (2007), p. 130.
834. *See* Section 60(1) German Copyright Act. *See* Westkamp (2007), p. 230.
835. *See* CJEU, *AKM*, paras 39-42. *See also* AG Opinion, *Pelham*, para. 57, finding that the exception in Section 24(1) German Copyright Act, pursuant to which an independent work may be created in the free use of another work without the authorisation of the rightholder, does not meet the 'minor importance' requirement.
836. AG Opinion, *Titus Donner*, para. 25.

Articles 2 and 3 InfoSoc Directive are worded in unequivocal and unconditional terms.[837] The most notorious example is the reproduction right. Apart from being mandatory for Member States to implement, the provision defines the scope of the right in a remarkably broad and clear-cut way, leaving virtually no autonomy to the national legislator. As a result, a substantial degree of harmonisation across Member States has been achieved in regard to the reproduction right.[838]

In opposition to economic rights, copyright exceptions have been harmonised through what may be deemed a hybrid model – one that combines techniques of full harmonisation, such as the closed catalogue of exceptions (analysed above), and partial harmonisation.

The paradigmatic example of partial harmonisation within the copyright *acquis* is the optional nature of the twenty exceptions laid down in Article 5(2)-(3).[839] Member States are allowed to implement as many or as few of these twenty exceptions as they wish. This gives Member States some room for manoeuvre and, along with the grandfather clause, fosters the respect for the different national cultures within the EU. As noted in Chapter 3, the respect for national cultures is a normative objective pursued by the InfoSoc framework of exceptions. This is a goal that can be attained by not regulating certain culturally relevant aspects or by regulating them only partially, leaving important decisions to Member States. In the case of the exceptions in Article 5(2)-(3) InfoSoc Directive, the EU legislator has left in the hands of Member States the decision of whether to adopt them in their national laws or not. By allowing Member States to pick and choose the exceptions they wish to implement, this provision has the converse effect of *not imposing* exceptions upon Member States. Thus, to some extent, this regulatory technique furthers the achievement of the objective identified above. A given exception provided in Article 5 that, though being part of the copyright tradition in Member State A, has historically never been provided in Member State B, may be introduced or preserved by the former but is not obligatory for the latter. The optional character of exceptions leaves it to national legislators to assess the desirability of each such exception in their Member States, in full respect for the principles of subsidiarity and

837. *See* CJEU, *Funke Medien*, para. 36, and CJEU, *Pelham*, para. 84.

838. The first evaluation report of the InfoSoc Directive, commissioned by the European Commission's Internal Market DG, states that the reproduction right as harmonised by Article 2 InfoSoc Directive either already existed or was literally implemented by most Member States and that only minor differences existed regarding the requirement of fixation and the inclusion of temporary reproductions within or outside the *prima facie* scope of the exclusive right – *see* Westkamp (2007), pp. 1-4.

839. Other partial harmonisation measures have been adopted in the exceptions' *acquis*. In the InfoSoc Directive, Recital 36 establishes that Member States *may* provide for fair compensation for rightholders also when applying the optional exceptions that do not demand such compensation. Article 5(2) DSM Directive provides a further recent example, by determining that Member States may choose not to apply the exception for digital and cross-border teaching if suitable licensing mechanisms are available.

proportionality.[840] This seems to be the main advantage of a partial harmonisation measure like an optional catalogue of exceptions. In reforming the framework, this advantage should not be overlooked.

The greatest drawback of the facultative nature of the exceptions within Article 5(2)-(3) is, by far, the legal uncertainty it generates. Silke von Lewinski argues that 'the mandatory character of an exception or limitation does not increase legal certainty'.[841] I take this to mean that a mandatory exception, by virtue of the mere fact of its implementation being obligatory, is not necessarily more *precise* than an optional one. That much is, of course, true. But Lewinski herself implicitly concedes that mandatory exceptions increase legal certainty for *cross-border situations*: after claiming that 'legal certainty is the same whether a matter has been regulated at national or European level', she concedes that 'in the first case, it is however necessary to ascertain different national laws rather then one law if one wants to exploit or use a work beyond national borders'.[842]

EU law norms that are not mandatory attain at best a partial harmonising effect. Bernt Hugenholtz has pointedly labelled it 'fake harmonisation'.[843] The effects of partial harmonisation are aggravated by the fact that the principle of territoriality also applies to exceptions, meaning that an unauthorised act that is privileged in a certain Member State may still require the rightholder's permission in another Member State.[844] Making exceptions optional may have allowed the achievement of political consensus on the content of the catalogue. After all, exceptions are an aspect of copyright law that is closely linked to national cultural policy and that is therefore politically sensitive. But by making this concession, the InfoSoc legislator largely failed to achieve the goal of harmonisation.[845]

There is virtual agreement in the literature that, due to this feature, the InfoSoc legislative framework has been a fiasco in terms of harmonisation.[846]

---

840. *See* Hugenholtz et al. (2006), p. 59.
841. Lewinski (2015), p. 4.
842. Lewinski (2015), pp. 3-4.
843. Hugenholtz (2002), p. 69-1.
844. *See* EPRS (2015), p. III-288.
845. *See* Renda et al. (2015), pp. 27-28.
846. The opinion is almost unanimous, being shared by scholars from different nationalities and with diverging outlooks: Hart (1998), p. 169; Hugenholtz (2000), p. 501; Cordeiro (2002), p. 218; Hugenholtz (2002), p. 69-1; Gaubiac (2002), p. 17; Davies (2002), p. 316; Guibault (2003), p. 558; Gautier (2005), pp. 83-84; Rebello (2005), p. 150; Guibault et al. (2007), pp. 17-18; Favale (2008), p. 697; Hugenholtz & Okediji (2008), p. 27; Mazziotti (2008), pp. 78-79; Pereira (2008a), pp. 546-547; Eechoud et al. (2009), pp. 104-106; Janssens (2009), pp. 332-333; Guibault (2010), pp. 57-58; Rahmatian (2011), p. 141; Falce (2012), p. 206; Geiger & Schönherr (2012), p. 139; Lucas-Schloetter (2012), p. 116; Geiger & Schönherr (2014), pp. 111-114; ECS (2014), p. 2; Dreier (2015), p. 138; Bechtold (2016), pp. 453-454; Hilty & Köklü (2016), p. 291; Rocha (2016), pp. 87-89; Xalabarder (2016), p. 638; Angelopoulos (2017b), p. 23; Quintais (2017a), p. 205; and Bensamoun (2018), pp. 20-21.

Even some commentators who broadly support the InfoSoc framework as it is structured acknowledge that 'harmonization is absent on this point'.[847] EU institutions and policymakers have also been raising doubts about the soundness of the optional catalogue.[848] In fact, the possibility of Member States cherry-picking exceptions has led to a largely fragmented scenario throughout the EU.[849] To make things worse, most national legislators, instead of implementing exceptions *ipsis verbis*, have decided to do it in a way that reflects each Member State's traditions or to preserve old formulations.[850] Studies conducted after all Member States had finished implementing the Directive confirm this much.[851]

In this context, it is doubtful whether Article 5, as currently formulated, is capable of producing the much-needed level of harmonisation in a digital networked environment. A list of non-mandatory exceptions is especially problematic for cross-border services and activities that take place in such an environment and that rely on those exceptions. This includes, *inter alia*, social networks,[852] pan-European research projects,[853] and the offer of contents across borders by cultural heritage institutions such as online libraries.[854]

---

847. Lucas (2012), p. 374. *See also* Cohen Jehoram (2001b), p. 488, in the words of whom '[t]he purpose of harmonisation has largely been given up in order to accommodate the various "cultural" sentiments of the member states'.
848. Seven years after the Directive's adoption, the Commission acknowledged, more or less explicitly, that it had only partially succeeded in achieving the goal of harmonisation. In the 2008 Green Paper, the Commission recognised that '[d]ifferent treatment of the same act in different Member States may lead to legal uncertainty with regard to what is permitted under the exception' (p. 17) and asked whether certain categories of exceptions should be made mandatory in order to ensure greater harmonization (p. 6). *See also* 2009 Reflection Document, p. 15 (recognising that the uncertainty around exceptions to exclusive rights is 'neither beneficial for the internal market in knowledge products nor for the development in internet services'); 2013 Public consultation, pp. 16-17 (querying if some or all of the exceptions should be made mandatory and if a higher level of harmonisation of such exceptions was needed); EP Resolution Implementation InfoSoc Directive 2015, para. 37 (stating that 'some exceptions and limitations may … benefit from more common rules'); and EPRS (2015), p. 14 (observing that fragmentation at the level of exceptions 'continues to harm commercial users of copyright works, online intermediaries and end users').
849. Mapping the implementation status of copyright exceptions in all Member States, based on expert contributions from all over the EU, *see* http://copyrightexceptions.eu/. The table provided in the website is illustrative of this phenomenon of fragmentation. *See also* the early study by Favale (2008), pp. 697-705.
850. *See* Guibault (2010), p. 58, referring to a 'homing' tendency of Member State legislators. *See also* Hugenholtz et al. (2006), p. 38, and Hugenholtz & Okediji (2008), p. 27.
851. *See* Westkamp (2007), pp. 84-94; Gotzen (2007), pp. 14-16; and Renda et al. (2015), pp. 27-28.
852. *See* EPRS (2015), p. 16.
853. *See* Martin-Prat (2014), p. 42
854. *See* LIBER Europe (2016), *passim*.

The sudden move to online education caused by the Covid-19 lockdown is illustrative of the problem. The InfoSoc teaching exception is crucial to allow the use of third-party content in educational activities, particularly in periods of crisis. But this optional exception has been implemented in diverging manners throughout Member States. By way of example, Germany allows the reproduction and making available of 15% of a published work for the purpose of illustration for teaching in educational establishments in general.[855] In contrast, Spain allows the use of 'small fragments of works', but only by teachers in establishments integrated in the Spanish educational system or in public universities or research centres.[856] This kind of divergence palpably reduces legal certainty for providers of learning programmes with a cross-border character.[857]

The practical implications of a scenario characterised by multiple applicable exceptions across the EU are serious for services – particularly, those of enterprises with lower resources – operating in different Member States. As emphasised by Lucie Guibault and colleagues, '[t]he level of knowledge required for the conclusion of the necessary licensing agreements per territory is too high and costly to make the effort worthwhile. ... Moreover, finding proper legal counsel in the EU countries appears to be an onerous task, especially for innovative start-up companies.'[858] As a result, in what concerns the boundary between infringement and non-infringement at the cross-border level, 'there still exists a significant degree of uncertainty for the stakeholders'.[859]

Some commentators have tried to relativise the low harmonising effect of Article 5. Michel Walter and Silke von Lewinski have argued that the criticism is 'unjustified from the outset', since Article 5's goal has never been to achieve total harmonisation anyway,[860] but only a higher degree of approximation in relation to the pre-existing landscape in Member States.

---

855. *See* Article 60a German Copyright Act.
856. *See* Article 32(3) Spanish IP Code.
857. Granted, Article 5 DSM Directive mitigates the problem, by providing a 'country of origin' rule in relation to illustration for teaching in secure electronic environments. In any case, the exception has not yet been implemented in most Member States and its scope is rather narrow, not covering, e.g., the scanning and making available of entire textbook chapters by teachers (since that would not count as 'illustration') or the use of third-party content in open courses (since those courses are typically not offered in 'secure environments'). Moreover, Article 5(2) DSM Directive states that Member States may provide that the exception does not apply where suitable licences covering those acts are easily available on the market.
858. Guibault et al. (2007), p. 63. *See also* Janssens (2009), p. 338 ('Today, users across the EU have to acquaint themselves with the copyright laws of twenty-seven different jurisdictions. This is especially true with regard to uses in a digital environment').
859. Guibault (2010), p. 55. *See also* Hilty & Köklü, p. 291 ('It does not take a crystal ball to recognize that this hotchpotch of diverging national provisions, particularly on limitations and exceptions, leads to frustration in establishing new business models for the European market').
860. Walter & Lewinski (2010), p. 1021.

They rely, to this effect, on Recital 31, which says that 'exceptions and limitations should be defined *more harmoniously*'.[861] Even commentators with a critical stance concede that a *higher* degree of harmonisation has been achieved, because legislators in some Member States ended up implementing exceptions from the InfoSoc catalogue that they probably would not have implemented otherwise.[862] Article 5 therefore seems to have produced 'a sort of "spontaneous harmonization"'.[863] This, however, does not change the fact that, due to the optional character of exceptions, 'the harmonising effect is very modest at best'.[864] While the degree of harmonisation of copyright exceptions should be based on their impact on the proper functioning of the internal market,[865] the truth is that some exceptions with such a clear impact remain optional for Member States to implement.

Walter and Lewinski further note that 'the Directive conceived of the (partial) harmonization of exceptions and limitations as a process'.[866] Nonetheless, what EU institutions have been signalling since the implementation of InfoSoc is that partial harmonisation in the field of exceptions was an ill-advised choice from the beginning and that the process should shift to one of full harmonisation. The European Parliament has acknowledged that the smorgasbord approach followed in InfoSoc 'can be challenging for the functioning of the internal market in view of the development of cross-border activities and EU global competitiveness and innovation, and may also lead to legal uncertainty'.[867] It has accordingly called on the Commission to examine which of the optional exceptions laid down in the InfoSoc Directive could be rendered mandatory[868] and, as a result, the EU has clearly moved away from optional exceptions in the latest legislative initiative.[869]

---

861. Emphasis added. *See* Walter & Lewinski (2010), p. 1021.
862. *See* Eechoud et al. (2009), p. 104. *See also* Gotzen (2007), p. 16 (reporting that, following the adoption of the InfoSoc Directive, the vast majority of Member States introduced new exceptions into their national catalogues); Guibault (2010), p. 58; and Geiger & Schönherr (2014), p. 113.
863. Janssens (2009), p. 336, acknowledging that '[c]ountries have more limitations in common and share more notions and issues relating to exceptions than ever before'. *See also* Reinbothe (2002), p. 46.
864. Eechoud et al. (2009), p. 104. *See also* Janssens (2009), p. 336, noting that, despite the increase in harmonisation, 'the results are rather meagre'.
865. *See* Recital 31 InfoSoc Directive.
866. Walter & Lewinski (2010), p. 1022.
867. Report Public Consultation 2014, para. 37.
868. *See* EP Resolution Implementation InfoSoc Directive 2015, para. 40. *See also* 2009 Reflection Document, p. 15, stating that '[f]uture policy should make a clear distinction and proposals should clearly state which exceptions should be harmonised and made mandatory in scope as a matter of priority and the precise goals pursued in doing so'.
869. *See supra* Chapter 2, section 3.2.3. *See*, in particular, Recital 5 DSM Directive, admitting that 'the optional nature of exceptions and limitations provided for in Directives 96/9/EC, 2001/29/EC and 2009/24/EC in those fields could negatively impact the functioning of the internal market. This is particularly relevant as regards cross-border uses, which are becoming increasingly important in the digital environment'.

It is crucial to keep in mind that making certain exceptions mandatory should not entail the elimination of Member State freedom within the field of exceptions. Some room for national decision-making must be preserved so as to ensure the respect for 'the diverse traditions and *mentalités* of Member States'.[870] Despite recognising the challenges to the internal market posed by differences in national copyright regimes, the European Parliament remarked that 'differences may be justified to allow Member States to legislate according to their specific cultural and economic interests, and in line with the principles of proportionality and subsidiarity'.[871] Any reform of the InfoSoc framework of exceptions should therefore not lose sight of the need to balance between harmonisation and the respect for cultural diversity.

3 THE EXCEPTIONS

Besides the structural features of the catalogue of exceptions examined above, the very *wording* and *scope* of the provisions that are part of it have been reasons for discord among stakeholders. Whereas one faction in the debate praises the relatively narrow and precise formulae adopted by the EU legislator, the other would prefer a more standard-like approach inspired by the common law tradition. This policy choice naturally plays a crucial factor in determining, on the one hand, the level of legislative guidance on the legal status of unauthorised uses that the InfoSoc framework provides and, on the other, the level of discretion that judges enjoy in adapting copyright law to technology-related changes.

In the following sections, I will characterise the exceptions within the InfoSoc framework from the point of view of these two criteria. I shall start by making a general description of Article 5-type exceptions, before moving on to a more in-depth analysis of selected exceptions.

3.1 Article 5-Type Exceptions

Structural similarities in the field of exceptions have united Continental countries long before the beginning of copyright harmonisation. Most countries already granted users the privilege to engage in unauthorised uses for purposes such as private copying, quotation, administration of justice, and news reporting.

Besides this common core, however, the particular content of each country's list varied significantly. Individual countries had (and, in many cases, still have) their own very specific and narrowly tailored exceptions. For instance, the Belgian 1994 Copyright Act contained an exception

870. Pila (2013), p. 229.
871. EP Resolution Implementation InfoSoc Directive 2015, para. 37.

allowing the Cinémathèque Royale to make copies of films for purposes of preservation.[872] A similar peculiar exception can be found in the Italian Copyright Law, permitting the public performance of musical works by bands of the armed forces.[873] Yet another example comes from the Portuguese 1985 Copyright Code, which contains an exception allowing the author who reproduces, in a book or pamphlet, her articles, letters or other controversial texts that she had published in newspapers or magazines to also reproduce rival pieces without the permission of their author(s).[874] In a word, the scenario was fragmented.

In pursuing harmonisation, EU institutions gave preference to the legislative technique typical of the *droit d'auteur* tradition – that of rule-like exceptions.[875] Article 5 InfoSoc Directive (like the relevant provisions in subsequent directives) contains an enumeration of such exceptions.[876] Their antecedents generally contain triggering factual predicates that are formulated in fairly precise language. Striking examples include the exceptions for 'reproductions on paper or any similar medium, effected by the use of any kind of photographic technique or by some other process having similar effects' (Article 5(2)(a)), 'ephemeral recordings of works made by broadcasting organisations by means of their own facilities and for their own broadcasts' (Article 5(2)(d)), 'use in connection with the demonstration or repair of equipment' (Article 5(3)(l)), and 'use of an artistic work in the form of a building or a drawing or plan of a building for the purposes of reconstructing the building' (Article 5(3)(m)). If the exception's antecedent is satisfied, the consequent follows: the use under consideration is non-infringing, despite the absence of rightholders' authorisation.

The rule-like character of Article 5 exceptions has the benefit of giving more precise indications to those who rely on them. Most InfoSoc exceptions thus score well in terms of legislative guidance. This much seems to be uncontroversial: even commentators who are generally critical of the InfoSoc

---

872. *See* Article 22(1)(8) Belgian Copyright Law. With the transposition of the InfoSoc Directive, in 2005, the exception was absorbed by the one for specific acts of reproduction made, *inter alia*, by archives.
873. *See* Article 71 Italian Copyright Law.
874. *See* Article 77(2) Portuguese Copyright Code.
875. As opposed to exceptions that are positivised in the form of standards, rule-like exceptions lie closer to the precision end of the precision-vagueness continuum described above. *See supra* Chapter 3, section 2.1.2.
876. As shall be seen at a later stage, some of these exceptions may have moved closer to the standards pole as a result of the CJEU's construction of their meaning and scope. *See infra* 5.2.2.

framework concede that '[p]recisely defined exceptions in continental European countries may offer a high degree of legal certainty'.[877,878]

The degree of precision in the formulation of exceptions often comes hand in hand with their narrowness of coverage. When compared to a hypothetical exception that privileges 'uses that do not unreasonably prejudice the legitimate interests of the rightholder',[879] an exception covering the 'use during religious celebrations or official celebrations organised by a public authority' (Article 5(3)(g)) is both narrower – in that it covers a smaller range of unauthorised uses of protected works – and more precise – in that it bears less borderline cases. It is to this combination of properties that scholars allude to when they refer to the exceptions in the InfoSoc catalogue as being 'carefully defined'.[880]

It is important to note that this analysis holds not only for the formulation of exceptions at the EU level but also for their national implementations. When crafting national exceptions, Member States are

877. Senftleben (2010), pp. 68-69. *See also* Janssens (2009), p. 340 ('[w]hile this approach may lack flexibility, it does promote relative certainty'), and Guibault (2010), p. 64 ('While an exhaustive list obviously gives more legal security to established right holders and content providers, it also hinders the emergence of new services and business models'). But, to be sure, the mosaic of exceptions provided in the InfoSoc catalogue is not devoid of unclarities. Lack of clarity arises from the co-existence of the different exceptions' regimes in the multiple directives, such as the Software Directive and the Database Directive. Recall that Article 1(2) InfoSoc Directive establishes that the provisions of other directives remain unaffected by InfoSoc. The regimes in the various directives, besides having distinct requirements, apply to different rights and types of subject matter. As such, their 'concurrent application ... is bound to lead to incompatibilities and gaps between directives' – Hugenholtz et al. (2006), p. 64. A higher degree of uniformity between InfoSoc and the rest of the *acquis* would therefore be advisable – *see* 2004 Staff Working Paper, p. 7, and Hugenholtz et al. (2006), p. 69.

878. Their relative precision notwithstanding, most exceptions in the catalogue of Article 5 are drafted in technologically neutral terms. Technological neutrality implies that the formulation of legal provisions is 'independent of any particular technology, neither favouring nor discriminating against specific technologies as they emerge and evolve' – Craig (2013), p. 272. *See also* Bently (2004), pp. 175-176; Vicente (2005), p. 19; and Synodinou (2012), p. 618. Most exceptions in the catalogue regulate *the uses*, but not *the means* (i.e., the technologies) for the uses. They do not limit the applicability of exceptions to certain technologies that were known at the time they were enacted. A few of them, however, are drafted in technologically specific language, which makes them 'more vulnerable to changes in the technology and less suited for long-term application' – Guibault et al. (2007), p. 64. This is the case, for instance, of the reprography exception, which applies only to reproductions made on 'paper or any similar medium' through 'any kind of photographic technique' or a process with similar effects (Article 5(2)(a) InfoSoc Directive). Also, despite the European Parliament's call to ensure the technological neutrality in the design of exceptions, the new TDM exception is linked to the current state of technology – *see* EP Resolution Implementation InfoSoc Directive 2015, para. 44. Recent proposals to introduce exceptions for certain acts of hyperlinking – such as the one advanced by Sirinelli et al. (2016) – are also technology-specific.

879. The cited formula borrows from the three-step test, namely from its third step.

880. Senftleben (2009), p. 1.

generally expected to stay close to the formulae contained in Article 5.[881] But even where Member States have deviated from the EU wording, they have frequently opted for formulations that are narrower and more precise than their InfoSoc counterparts.[882] Consider the case of the quotation exception laid down in Article 5(3)(d), which privileges quotations for purposes such as criticism and review that, among other requirements, are made in accordance with fair practice and to the extent required by the specific purpose. Implementation divergences among Member States abound: some countries, like France, understand the exception as privileging only uses of 'small parts' of a work; others, such as Belgium, require that the 'intellectual legacy' of the quoted work be respected; and still others, like Italy, prohibit quotations for commercial purposes.[883] The exception for ephemeral recordings of works made by broadcasting organisations provides yet another example: while a similar provision existed in most Member States at the time of the adoption of InfoSoc, some of these national exceptions were only provided for specific purposes[884] or periods of time.[885]

---

881. On the implementation freedom of Member States, *see infra* 5.1.1.
882. An example of a relatively vague exception in national catalogues is the German free use (*Freie Benutzung*) doctrine in Section 24(1) German Copyright Act, according to which '[a]n independent work created in the free use of the work of another person may be published or exploited without the consent of the author of the work used'. The free use doctrine provides German courts with a measure of discretion in dealing with transformative uses of existing works. It has been used e.g. to address parodic uses, such as in BGH, *Alcolix*. More recently, the provision has been at the centre of the protracted *Metall auf Metall* saga. The case has known decisions by various German courts, including the BGH in 2008 and 2012 and the BVerfG in 2016. It was eventually referred to the CJEU, with the BGH questioning the Luxembourg Court about the compatibility of national free use provisions such as Section 24(1) German Copyright Act with EU copyright law. The Court answered in the negative, essentially on grounds that said provision is not included in the closed catalogue of Article 5 InfoSoc Directive – CJEU, *Pelham*, paras 56-65. *See also* AG Opinion, *Pelham*, paras 50-59. For commentary on the German decisions, *see* Duhanic (2016), Jütte & Maier (2017) and Mimler (2017), and, on the CJEU reference, ECS (2019), Jütte & Quintais (2019), Griffiths (2019), Jongsma (2019), Sganga (2019), Snijders & Deursen, and Geiger & Izyumenko (2020)
883. *See* the summary provided by Triaille et al. (2013), pp. 472-473. Hugenholtz & Senftleben (2011) draw a contrast between the Dutch implementation and the German one, focusing on the purpose element of the exception. Whereas the Dutch legislator allowed quotations for purposes of criticism or review as well as comparable ones – relying, for that matter, on the reference in Article 5(3)(d) to quotations for purposes 'such as' criticism or review –, the German one adopted a more restrictive enumeration of purposes. *Compare* Article 15a Dutch Copyright Act with Section 51 German Copyright Act. For a detailed analysis of the scope of the quotation exception in Dutch copyright law and its evolution, *see* Senftleben (2012b), pp. 365-374.
884. For example, in the UK, the exception is limited to the purpose of maintaining control and supervision over programs (Section 69 CDPA).
885. For example, in Germany, the copies must be deleted at the latest one month after the work is first broadcasted (Article 55 German Copyright Act).

3.2 Selected Exceptions

Having made a general description of the type of exceptions that make up the EU catalogue in general, and Article 5 InfoSoc Directive in particular, it is now time to individually scrutinise the scope of selected InfoSoc exceptions. Five prominent exceptions – the ones in relation to which there is a richer body of case law and literature – were selected: the temporary reproduction exception (section 3.2.1); the private copying exception (section 3.2.2); the teaching and research exception (section 3.2.3); the parody exception (section 3.2.4); and, last but certainly not least, the quotation exception (section 3.2.5).

Despite the general lack of judicial discretion that emerges from copyright exceptions of the Continental type due to their narrow and precise character, some InfoSoc exceptions are *relatively* broad and vague. The extent to which these specific exceptions, as formulated in InfoSoc, can be relied on to successfully accommodate emerging uses will be discussed in the sections that follow. As shall be seen, the analysis presents a grim picture, confirming that the catalogue is increasingly outdated and misaligned with prevailing socio-technological practices.

3.2.1 Temporary Reproduction

The controversy around the choice of exempting temporary reproductions from the scope of exclusivity through an exception, rather than through the negative delimitation of the reproduction right, has already been discussed.[886] As noted then, the EU legislator has opted to provide for a mandatory exception to that effect in Article 5(1) InfoSoc Directive.[887] This exception was implemented literally by almost all Member States.[888]

Article 5(1) is grounded on a twofold purpose: first, to enable the development and operation of new technologies and, second, to safeguard a fair balance between the rights and interests of rightholders and those of users who wish to avail themselves of those new technologies.[889] Without prejudice to a more nuanced analysis of certain CJEU rulings on Article 5(1)

886. *See supra* Chapter 1, section 3.
887. The special provisions in Article 5(1) Software Directive and Article 6(1) Database Directive govern the temporary reproduction of computer programs and databases, respectively. Article 5(1) InfoSoc Directive therefore does not apply to such subject matter.
888. *See* Westkamp (2007), p. 12; Renda et al. (2015), p. 150 (focusing only on six Member States); and Blásquez et al. (2017), p. 31. Compare, e.g., Article 44a German Copyright Act, Article 31(1) Spanish IP Code and Article 75(1) Portuguese Copyright Code, on the one hand, with Article 5(1) and Recital 33 InfoSoc Directive, on the other. The most notable exception is the Netherlands, which implemented the requirements of Article 5(1) as a limitation on the scope of the right of reproduction and not as an exception proper – *see* Article 13a Dutch Copyright Act.
889. *See* CJEU, *Premier League*, para. 164.

(which shall be conducted below[890]), let us now consider the relatively narrow textual scope of that exception.

Prima facie, the exception enshrined in Article 5(1) exempts all temporary (*i.e.*, limited in time or non-permanent) copies of protected works. However, the wording of the exception includes four other cumulative conditions that significantly restrict the range of exempted acts.[891] Unauthorised copies will only be deemed non-infringing under this provision if, besides being temporary: (i) they are transient *or* incidental; (ii) they form an integral *and* essential part of a technological process; (iii) their sole purpose is to enable a transmission in a network between third parties by an intermediary *or* a lawful use of a work or other subject matter to be made; and (iv) they have no independent economic significance. The meaning of each of these conditions will be considered in turn.

An act of reproduction will be *transient* if its duration is limited to the proper functioning of the technological process in the context of which it takes place. This amounts to a very short lifetime – shorter than what results from the leading requirement of temporariness. In addition, in order to be transient, the copy must be eliminated automatically with no need for human intervention. It should be noted that this requirement does not preclude the deletion from being preceded by human intervention directed at terminating the use of the technological process.[892] In the context of web browsing, for instance, the user may terminate the session (typically, by closing the browser) without the concerned copies losing their transient character.

To fulfil this first condition, the act need not be deemed transient. Copies that have a longer lifetime may alternatively be considered *incidental* (though they must still be temporary, which is longer than transient).[893] So as to be incidental, the copy must not exist independently from, nor have a purpose independent of, the technological process of which it is a part. The CJEU has considered, for instance, that the copies made in the Internet cache of a computer's hard disk – which may last for relatively long periods of time, depending on the user's navigation habits – count as incidental copies, even though they cannot be considered transient.[894]

The second of the conditions enumerated above states that the reproduction must be an *integral and essential part of a technological process*. Unlike the previous condition, this one is composed of two cumulative sub-conditions. The 'integral' requirement means that the copies must not be carried out, fully or partially, outside of the technological process, whereas 'essential' entails that the process could not function as correctly or

890. *See infra* 5.2.2.1.
891. Stressing the cumulative nature of the conditions, *see*, *e.g.*, CJEU, *Infopaq I*, para. 55; CJEU, *Infopaq II*, para. 26; and CJEU, *Filmspeler*, para. 61.
892. *See* CJEU, *PRCA*, paras 40-42.
893. *See* CJEU, *PRCA*, para. 39.
894. *See* CJEU, *PRCA*, paras 47-50.

efficiently without such copies. Regarding the latter, it is irrelevant whether an output produced outside of that process could be obtained *without* the acts of temporary reproduction.[895] As these requirements make clear, the exception in Article 5(1) only applies to copies that are technically necessary and automatically triggered by some other use.[896] Cached copies made in the course of Internet browsing are examples of temporary copies that are an integral and essential part of a technological process, since, according to the CJEU, 'without those copies, the internet would be unable to cope with current volumes of data transmitted online'.[897] Importantly, the CJEU has clarified that there is nothing in the provision indicating that the technological process must not involve any human intervention and, in particular, from being activated or completed manually.[898]

The third condition, too, is comprised of a pair of alternative criteria: the purpose of the reproduction must be either to *enable a transmission in a network between third parties by an intermediary* or *to allow the lawful use of a work*.[899] Recital 33 InfoSoc Directive develops the meaning of each sub-condition. As to the first, the intermediary should not modify the information nor interfere with the lawful use of technology. An example of an activity covered by the first criterion is that of an Internet router transmitting copies of works from sender to recipient. As to the second, a use should be considered lawful if it is authorised by the rightholder or not restricted by the applicable legislation (e.g., because it is permitted by any other exception in Article 5). Examples of uses not restricted by law include the reception of TV broadcasts in private circles[900] and the drafting of summaries of newspaper articles.[901] Differently, the reception of streaming content from third-party websites that offer the work without the rightholder's authorisation does not meet any of the alternative sub-criteria, with the temporary copies made in the context of such use thus being excluded from the scope of Article 5(1).[902]

---

895. *See* CJEU, *Infopaq II*, para. 38 (in relation to summaries of newspaper articles).
896. *See* Walter & Lewinski (2010), pp. 1024-1025, and Bechtold (2016), p. 457.
897. CJEU, *PRCA*, para. 35.
898. *See* CJEU, *Infopaq II*, para. 32, and CJEU, *PRCA*, para. 32.
899. Note that Articles 12, 13 and 14 E-Commerce Directive deal with the secondary liability of online intermediaries, exempting the routing, hosting and caching of information that may arise from unlawful activities, such as defamation, misleading advertising, trademark infringement, as well as copyright infringement. If certain copies are copyright-infringing under Articles 2 and 5(1) InfoSoc Directive, Articles 12-14 will determine if the online service provider that facilitates copy-making can be held liable for such copies. If, on the contrary, the copies are exempted under Article 5(1), the question of liability under the E-Commerce Directive does not even arise.
900. *See* CJEU, *Premier League*, paras 171-172.
901. *See* CJEU, *Infopaq II*, paras 44-45.
902. *See* CJEU, *Filmspeler*, paras 59-72. In *Filmspeler*, the CJEU pursued an integrated (and somewhat confusing) interpretation of the 'lawful use' criterion and the three-step test.

Finally, these reproductions must have *no independent economic significance*. This condition, as commentators have noted, 'is vague and does not refer to any known principle of international (or national) copyright law(s)' and therefore 'does not contribute to the increase of legal certainty'.[903] The CJEU has made clear that the technical copies may facilitate the use of subject matter, thus creating some economic value.[904] Nonetheless, such value must not be independent, in the sense that the economic advantage derived from the temporary copies must not be distinct or separable from the economic advantage derived from the work itself. According to the Court, distinctness and separability will exist: (i) if the author of the act at issue is likely to make an additional profit due to the economic exploitation of the temporary reproductions themselves; or (ii) if the act leads to a modification of the copied work.[905] In other words, the reproduction must be economically irrelevant *in itself*.

As the preceding analysis shows, the conditions for applying the exception are numerous and demanding, besides being cumulative. The scope of the exception therefore appears to be rather narrow, covering only a very limited range of acts of reproduction. These include on-screen copies made while watching TV broadcasts or browsing the web; copies made in Internet routers and proxy servers; and copies made in the computer's RAM and Internet cache.[906] While these copies are essential for the functioning of the technological systems of which they are part, the exception within Article 5(1) seems hardly capable of working as an escape valve to accommodate most unforeseen uses.

3.2.2 Private Copying

Article 5(2)(b) InfoSoc Directive lays down the well-known private copying exception.[907] The provision allows Member States to exempt copies made: (i) on any medium; (ii) by a natural person; (iii) for private use; (iv) for ends

903. Guibault et al. (2007), p. 35. *See also* Westkamp (2004), p. 1100 ('neither international conventions nor national legislation and judicature are capable of defining what can be economically significant'); Vicente (2005), pp. 162-163 (pointing out the risk of diverging judicial applications at the national level); and Lucas & Sirinelli (2006), p. 310 (observing that the expression is open to interpretation, raising concerns related to legal security).

904. *See* CJEU, *Premier League*, paras 174-175. *See also* CJEU, *Infopaq II*, paras 48-49, noting that acts of temporary reproduction are inherently intended to enable the achievement of efficiency gains and thus lead to an increase in profits or a reduction in production costs.

905. *See* CJEU, *Infopaq II*, paras 50-53.

906. *See* Recital 33 InfoSoc Directive. In Recital 9 DSM Directive, the legislator assumes that certain reproductions made in the context of TDM processes may fall under Article 5(1) InfoSoc Directive, provided they are temporary.

907. Less detailed versions can be found in Article 10(1)(a) Rental and Lending Directive and Articles 6(2)(a) and 9(a) Database Directive.

that are neither directly nor indirectly commercial; and (v) on condition that rightholders receive fair compensation in exchange for such unauthorised acts. The exception serves a plurality of purposes, namely the dissemination of knowledge and information, the technological development of recording media, and the acknowledgment that there is (largely unenforceable) mass copying of copyright-protected works taking place in the private sphere of consumers and the related desire to protect their privacy.[908]

The private copying exception is implemented in the majority of EU Member States – the most notable exception being Ireland (and, prior to Brexit, the UK)[909] –, though not without implementation discrepancies.[910]

As the first condition makes clear, the private copying exception, unlike the reprography exception in Article 5(2)(a),[911] is technologically neutral, in the sense that it covers reproductions made on *any medium*, whether analogue or digital, that is capable of carrying protected subject matter. This includes, for instance, copies made on magnetic tapes, CDs, computer hard drives, memory cards, and cloud storage lockers.

In order to be privileged by the private copying exception, the reproduction must be made by a *natural person*, as opposed to a legal person. A copy made by a natural person on behalf of a legal person, such as a company, would not fulfil this requirement.[912] On the other hand, according to the CJEU, the exception covers reproductions made by a third party providing copying services on behalf of a natural person. It is therefore not necessary that the natural persons concerned possess the reproduction equipment or media used to make the copies.[913] However, the CJEU has further held that a remote recording service which, besides organising the copy-making of its users, also provides access to the works that can be recorded is not protected by the private copying exception.[914]

---

908. On the rationales of the private copying exception in more detail, *see* Karapapa (2012), pp. 15-27.
909. Irish law provides for narrow exceptions covering the recording of a broadcast or cable programme for purposes of time-shifting and the making of photographs of TV broadcasts or cable programmes, unaccompanied by any compensation scheme – *see* Sections 101 and 102 Irish Copyright Act. The UK adopted the private copying exception in 2014, but it was later struck down due to the absence of a fair compensation scheme.
910. For an overview of such discrepancies, *see* EPRS (2015), p. I-137.
911. On the overlap between the reprography exception and the private copying exception, *see* Walter & Lewinski (2010), p. 1032.
912. *See* Walter & Lewinski (2010), p. 1033.
913. *See* CJEU, *VCAST*, para. 35. This statement in *VCAST* seems to stand in tension with paras 80-91 of *Copydan Båndkopi*, where the CJEU held that the question of whether the device used by the private individual to make the copies must belong to that individual or whether it may belong to a third party is not regulated by the Directive, meaning that it falls within the margin of discretion of Member States.
914. *See* CJEU, *VCAST*, paras 30-54. For a reflection on this case and its implications, *see* Quintais & Rendas (2018).

Crucially, the copy must be made for *private use*. The concept of 'private use' is narrower than the concepts of 'personal use' and 'own use', which may include certain professional or commercial uses.[915] The concept encompasses any use made by a natural person for personal (as opposed to professional) purposes within her private sphere. This includes copies made for consumption within a close circle of family and friends.[916] How many people may be granted access to the copy besides the user remains uncertain. João Pedro Quintais illustrates this uncertainty with the following example: 'is uploading a copy of a work to a cloud locker accessible only to a number of close friends and family a 'private' use? How big does that group have to be before the act loses its privileged nature?'[917]

Article 5(2)(b) further restricts the exception by stating that the *purposes of the act must be neither directly nor indirectly commercial*. The Directive does not define 'non-commercial purposes'.[918] In any case, the concept is certainly less demanding than the absence of economic significance required by the temporary reproduction exception, for otherwise the private copying exception would be without practical applicability.[919] It would therefore seem that the term 'commercial' refers only to copies that are made for profit.

Besides the textual requirements contained in Article 5(2)(b), the CJEU has added a condition of *lawfulness of source*. In *ACI Adam*, the CJEU held that the exception, read in conjunction with the three-step test in Article 5(5), must be interpreted as exempting only private copies made from lawful sources.[920] In practice, the ruling clarified, for instance, that acts of downloading content such as music and films with the aid of torrent aggregators and P2P networks are not covered by the private copying exception and are therefore infringing. Before *ACI Adam*, a few Member States explicitly excluded copies originating from unlawful sources from the scope of the exception,[921] whereas others made no specification regarding the source of the work.[922] Following *ACI Adam*, Member States who make no

915. *See* Walter & Lewinski (2010), pp. 1032-1033, and Poort & Quintais (2013), pp. 207-208.
916. *See* Walter & Lewinski (2010), p. 1032, and Poort & Quintais (2013), p. 207. A substantial degree of uncertainty exists, however, as to how narrow the private sphere needs to be for the act of reproduction to be privileged.
917. Quintais (2017a), p. 214.
918. For an attempt at defining 'commerciality' in a different context, *see infra* Chapter 5, section 4.3.2.
919. *See* Quintais (2017a), p. 214.
920. *See* CJEU, *ACI Adam*, paras 41 and 58. *See also* CJEU, *Copydan Båndkopi*, paras 74-79, and CJEU, *Reprobel*, paras 57-64 (the latter transposing the reasoning made in *ACI Adam* to the reprography exception).
921. *See* Article L311-1 French IP Code, which was amended in 2011 to include this requirement (the ruling having been delivered only in 2014).
922. This was the case of the Netherlands, from where the referral to the CJEU arose. *See* CJEU, *ACI Adam*, paras 9-10.

distinction between lawful and unlawful sources in their national copyright laws will not be in compliance with EU law.

A number of acts that users engage in on a daily basis – such as making back-up copies of works that have been lawfully acquired, format-shifting audio files from CDs to MP3 players, and making copies of TV broadcasts for time-shifting – would generally meet the foregoing substantive requirements. By contrast, acts of downloading or stream ripping will only be exempted by the private copying exception if they are made from lawful sources (e.g., from the rightholder's own website with unrestricted access).[923]

Apart from these requirements, which the acts of users must fulfil in order to be privileged, Article 5(2)(b) contains one other requirement directed primarily at national lawmakers. This requirement posits that the implementation of the exception by Member States is conditional upon the grant of *fair compensation* to rightholders. The idea underlying the requirement of fair compensation is that private copies are likely to cause harm to the concerned rightholders.[924] While the 'form, detailed arrangements and possible level of such fair compensation' depend on the 'circumstances of each case', the Directive acknowledges that the 'possible harm' caused to rightholders is a 'valuable criterion'.[925] In setting the level of the compensation, account must also be taken of the application of TPMs referred in Article 6 InfoSoc Directive. Nevertheless, where the harm is *de minimis* or where rightholders have already received payment in some other form (e.g., a licence fee), no obligation to pay the compensation may arise.[926] Beyond these general indications given by the text of the Directive, the concept of 'fair compensation' has been developed by the CJEU in numerous preliminary rulings (which fall largely outside the scope of this book).[927]

---

923. *See* Quintais (2017a), pp. 225-226.
924. *See, e.g.*, CJEU, *Padawan*, paras 44-46.
925. Recital 35 InfoSoc Directive. *See also* Recitals 17 and 24 DSM Directive, referring to the criterion of harm.
926. *See* Recital 35 InfoSoc Directive.
927. *See* the CJEU rulings in *Padawan*; *Stichting de Thuiskopie*; *Luksan*; *VG Wort*; *Amazon*; *ACI Adam*; *Copydan Båndkopi*; *Reprobel*; *Austro-Mechana*; *EGEDA II*; and *Microsoft*. For an overview of this line of case law, *see* Pereira (2017). It is important to mention that, in *Reprobel*, paras 44-49, the CJEU held that the fair compensation for private copying and reprography was only due to the rightholders mentioned in Article 2 InfoSoc Directive and that no part of such compensation could be allocated to publishers. As a direct legislative reaction against this ruling, Article 16 DSM Directive now explicitly *allows* Member States to authorise the sharing of the fair compensation between authors and publishers. *See also* Recital 60 DSM Directive, stating that the provision 'is particularly important for Member States that had such compensation-sharing mechanisms before 12 November 2015' (the date of the *Reprobel* judgment).

3.2.3 Teaching and Research

Article 10(2) Berne Convention contains an optional exception for purposes of teaching. The exception allows the 'utilization, to the extent justified by the purpose, of literary or artistic works by way of illustration in publications, broadcasts or sound or visual recordings for teaching, provided such utilization is compatible with fair practice'. As in the case of other exceptions, 'mention shall be made of the source, and of the name of the author if it appears thereon' (Article 10(3)). Article 15(1)(d) Rome Convention includes a similar, though less detailed version of the exception for related rights.

Inspired by these treaties, the InfoSoc Directive provides a similar exception. Article 5(3)(a) allows Member States to implement an exception privileging uses: (i) for the sole purpose of illustration for teaching or scientific research; (ii) as long as the source, including the author's name, is indicated, unless this turns out to be impossible; and (iii) to the extent justified by the non-commercial purpose to be achieved.[928] While the CJEU is yet to rule on this exception, some hints as to its scope and meaning can be derived from the very wording of the provision and from existing scholarly work.

In order to be exempted under Article 5(3)(a), the use must relate to *teaching* or *scientific research* activities. Since the exception makes no distinction, the reference to teaching should be read as covering teaching at all levels and in all types of educational institutions, including primary, secondary, vocational, and higher education.[929] Recital 42 makes clear that the exception is not limited to face-to-face teaching; uses made in the context of distance learning activities may also be covered. The exception also comprises acts made in the context of scientific research. The beneficiaries of this possibility will primarily be university professors and researchers.

The text of the exception adds an important restricting condition: the use must be made only for purposes of *illustrating* the ideas expressed by the teacher or researcher.[930] The term 'illustration' implies that only the use of extracts of works is allowed, in order to avoid the substitution effect in relation to the original works (e.g., the course textbook).[931] While this requirement should not be read as precluding the use of the entire work in all circumstances (think of the use of an image or a short poem), it makes it challenging to justify such a wide-ranging use in most cases.

---

928. Similar exceptions are set forth in Articles 6(2)(b) and 9(b) Database Directive (regarding, respectively, copyright and the *sui generis* right) and in Article 10(1)(d) Rental and Lending Directive. On the relationship between these provisions and Article 5(3)(a) InfoSoc Directive, *see* Walter & Lewinski (2010), pp. 1042-1043.
929. In the same direction, *see* Walter & Lewinski (2010), p. 1043.
930. It has been argued, however, that the illustration requirement applies only to teaching and not to scientific research – *see* EPRS (2015), p. I-132.
931. *See*, in this regard, Recital 21 DSM Directive.

The exception's scope is further restricted by the fact that illustration for teaching and scientific research must be the *sole purpose* of the use. Where the use serves an additional purpose besides those, it will not be exempted by Article 5(3)(a).[932]

The exception requires the user to indicate the source and the author of the original work, unless this is impossible. The indication of source (title, volume, year of publication, page/paragraph, publisher, website) is intended to facilitate the location of the full version of the work in question, while the indication of the author fosters the respect for the moral right of attribution. Interpreting Article 5(3)(a) in light of its Berne counterpart, it would seem that the latter obligation is limited to situations where the name of the author appears on the work in question.[933]

Furthermore, the purpose of the use must be *non-commercial* and the use must not go beyond what is necessary to satisfy such purpose. In this regard, Recital 42 InfoSoc Directive clarifies that 'the non-commercial nature of the activity in question should be determined by that activity as such' and that '[t]he organisational structure and the means of funding of the establishment concerned are not the decisive factors in this respect', meaning, for instance, that non-commercial uses by professors teaching in private universities are allowed under the exception. Purely for-profit teaching platforms and courses, which are not integrated in a recognised educational establishment, would however be excluded.

Article 5(3)(a) has been implemented by Member States heterogeneously,[934] raising serious obstacles to online and cross-border teaching activities.[935] In order to mitigate the harm to the internal market caused by

---

932. *See* Bechtold (2016), p. 464.

933. *But see* Walter & Lewinski (2010), p. 1044, arguing that even in such cases 'the user has the obligation to apply a certain minimal degree of care in searching for the author's name, be it on the internet or via a publishing house'. This, however, seems too burdensome a condition for users.

934. *See* SWD DSM Directive, pp. 87-89. For analyses of the different national implementations of Article 5(3)(a), *see* Xalabarder (2009); EPRS (2015), pp. I-132-I-133; and Communia Association (2017). Note, in this regard, that the InfoSoc Directive does not require the payment of fair compensation to rightholders, but some Member States provide for a compensation scheme nonetheless – *see, e.g.*, Section 60h German Copyright Act and Article 76(1)(c) Portuguese Copyright Code.

935. Janssens (2009), pp. 338-339, gives the following practical example: 'Let us consider the case of a professor who scans parts of a textbook, copies some digital articles, uploads them to the university's web server and refers his registered students – from home and abroad – to this material for further study by copying it or accessing it at the premises of a library. Before this occurs, the professor, the students and the relevant educational institutions themselves should carefully scrutinize the laws of each country in the EU to determine whether a specific use of the protected work is allowed without asking permission. Even a rough examination of the possibly applicable provisions, reveals that it would amount to a "mission impossible" to assess the permissibility of all these acts. National provisions do, indeed, not only differ in scope but also contain many variables relating to (analogue or digital) modes of copying, types of works and purpose

such discrepancies and to ensure that educational establishments benefit from full legal certainty, the DSM legislator complemented the InfoSoc exception with a mandatory exception intended to facilitate the digital use of copyright-protected content in the field of education.[936] Article 5(1) DSM Directive exempts uses of works or other subject matter made through digital means for the sole purpose of illustration for teaching[937] (research is excluded[938]), to the extent justified by the non-commercial purpose to be achieved.[939] Like in the InfoSoc exception, the use must be accompanied by the indication of the source and the author's name, unless this is infeasible.

The DSM exception applies to activities such as classroom use, digital whiteboards, and distance learning. However, the exception contains an important restricting condition. Any digital teaching uses made at a distance, such as in the context of online courses or access to teaching materials complementing a given course, must be made through a 'secure electronic environment'. As clarified in Recital 22, the expression 'secure electronic environment' should be understood as referring to a digital teaching and learning environment the access to which is limited to an educational establishment's teaching staff and to pupils or students enrolled in a study programme, in particular through appropriate authentication procedures including password-based authentication (e.g., a password-protected lecture via Zoom or WebEx). This means that certain modern digital teaching offers,

---

of use as well as limitations regarding quantity, numbers, premises, etc.' Analysing a similar case study under five different Member State regimes, *see* Ernst & Häusermann (2006). *See also* Xalabarder (2007), pp. 399-400, arguing that the exception in Article 5(3)(a) InfoSoc Directive should be made mandatory for Member States, on grounds that 'the different options taken by national legislators will likely result in a fragmentation of the internal market that may ultimately become an impediment to the development of on-line teaching within the EU'. Lewinski (2018), pp. 136-139, though claiming that mandatory exceptions should only be introduced in very limited circumstances, admits that cross-border teaching over the Internet is becoming increasingly popular, citing Harvard University's massive open online courses as an example. On the cross-border dimension of e-learning, *see* Triaille et al. (2013), pp. 381-382.

936. *See* Recital 19 DSM Directive. The existing InfoSoc exception should continue to apply, as long as it does not limit the scope of the mandatory exception provided for in the DSM Directive – *see* Recital 5 DSM Directive. The DSM exception extends not only to the InfoSoc rights of reproduction and communication to the public, but also to rights in the Database and Software Directives and to the new press publishers' right.

937. The DSM preamble clarifies that the underlying purpose is to 'support, enrich or complement the teaching, including learning activities' and that the use 'should be limited to what is necessary for the purpose of such activities' – Recitals 21-22 DSM Directive.

938. However, Article 25 DSM Directive safeguards the situation of those Member States that had previously implemented the InfoSoc teaching and research exception in broad terms.

939. In this case, too, the organisational structure and the means of funding of the educational establishment are not decisive factors in determining whether the activity is non-commercial in nature – *see* Recital 20 DSM Directive.

like Massive Open Online Courses, are excluded from the exception's scope.[940]

Moreover, pursuant to paragraph 2, Member States may override the applicability of the exception if licensing mechanisms for the acts privileged by the exception are easily available to educational establishments. Member States are therefore allowed to decide that Article 5(1) does not apply when suitable licences are available, covering the same uses as those allowed under the exception.[941] This is a surprising and rather criticisable option for a twofold reason. First, giving individual Member States this possibility of exclusion mitigates the harmonising effect produced by the mandatory character of the exception and threatens to preserve the existing fragmentation for digital educational activities in the EU, working against the stated goal of creating a digital single market.[942] Second, this implies that the EU legislator understands the digital teaching exception as being justified simply by a market failure rationale, disregarding the clear fundamental rights- and public interest-based justification for ensuring cross-border access to educational materials.[943]

3.2.4 Parody

Under Article 5(3)(k) InfoSoc Directive, Member States are allowed to provide for an exception to the rights of reproduction and communication to the public exempting uses for the purpose of caricature, parody and pastiche. The exception is naturally intended to foster the users' freedom of expression and should be interpreted in light of that purpose.[944]

The terms 'caricature', 'parody', and 'pastiche' – which are decisive to determine the meaning and scope of the exception – are left undefined in the Directive. The terms are partially overlapping, but each one has a meaning of its own. Caricature may be defined as a representation, typically of persons, in which their most striking features are exaggerated so as to produce a humorous or grotesque effect. The adaptation of someone's portrait by way of exaggerating certain characteristics would be covered by the concept of 'caricature'. Parody is commonly understood as a work that

---

940. *See* SWD DSM Directive, p. 91. Criticising this option, *see* Hilty & Lotte (2017), p. 37.
941. *See also* Recital 23 DSM Directive.
942. *See* Hilty & Lotte (2017), pp. 36-37, and Geiger et al. (2018c), pp. 11-12. Further contributing to fragmentation, Recital 21 DSM Directive provides that when implementing the exception, Member States should remain free to specify, for the different types of works, in a balanced manner, the proportion of the work that can be used for the sole purpose of illustration for teaching. Nonetheless, the exception mitigates the fragmentation effect by providing for a country-of-origin rule for secure electronic environments in Article 5(3).
943. *See* ECS (2017), p. 4. For the categorisation of justifications for copyright exceptions, *see supra* Introduction, section 1.1.
944. *See* CJEU, *Deckmyn*, paras 22-27. *See also supra* Chapter 2, section 3.3 and *infra* section 5.2.2.1.

imitates a pre-existing work with certain adaptations for comic effect. The popular mash-up novels *Pride and Prejudice and Zombies*, by Seth Grahame-Smith, and *Sense and Sensibility and Sea Monsters*, by Ben H. Winters (both crediting Jane Austen as co-author), may be cited as examples. Finally, pastiche may be defined as a work that imitates the style of another work or author. As Michel Walter and Silke von Lewinski rightfully point out, though, the reference to pastiche was not strictly needed, since copyright law's protection does not extend to mere styles.[945]

In *Deckmyn*, the Court was asked to clarify how the exception in Article 5(3)(k) should be interpreted and, in particular, whether the concept of 'parody' required certain conditions to be fulfilled.[946] The underlying national proceedings concerned a calendar that was handed out by the Flemish Nationalist Party in the New Year celebrations in the city of Ghent. The cover of the calendar was similar to the cover of a well-known comic book, but the altered version featured the mayor of Ghent throwing coins at coloured people and people wearing veils.

The CJEU began by holding that 'parody' is an autonomous concept of EU law that must be uniformly interpreted throughout the Member States. Since the Directive gives no definition of the term, its meaning must be determined by considering its usual meaning in everyday language, while taking into account the context in which it occurs and the purposes of the rules of which it is a part.[947] Such meaning, according to the Court, is composed of two essential characteristics: to count as a parody, the subsequent work must, first, 'evoke an existing work, while being noticeably different from it' and, second, it must 'constitute an expression of humour or mockery'.[948] The Court further clarified that a series of other conditions are not essential for a use to be exempted under the parody exception, namely (i) the parody need not display an original character of its own, other than that of displaying noticeable differences with respect to the original parodied work; (ii) it need not be reasonably attributed to a person other than the author of the original work itself; and, most importantly; (iii) it need not relate to the original work itself; nor (iv) mention the source of the parodied work.[949]

Having said this, the freedom of parody is not without limits. The exercise of such freedom must strike a fair balance between the interests and rights of rightholders and the freedom of expression of users.[950] Among the interests of rightholders is their legitimate interest in ensuring that their work

945. *See* Walter & Lewinski (2010), p. 1055.
946. For commentary on the judgment, *see* ECS (2014) and Rosati (2015).
947. CJEU, *Deckmyn*, para. 19.
948. *See* CJEU, *Deckmyn*, para. 20. *See also* AG Opinion, *Deckmyn*, para. 48.
949. *See* CJEU, *Deckmyn*, para. 33.
950. *See* CJEU, *Deckmyn*, para. 27.

is not associated with a discriminatory message.[951] In assessing whether such a fair balance has been preserved, the national court should take all circumstances into account.[952]

Being an optional exception, Article 5(3)(k) has not been implemented by some Member States and no equivalent exception is provided for in international treaties.[953] Where implementation has not occurred, the relevant uses may in some cases be covered by the quotation exception.[954] Be that as it may, the absence of a *mandatory* parody exception increases legal uncertainty, especially in the digital era where a variety of creative endeavours, like memes, GIFs, and other types of UGC are cheap and easy to produce.[955]

The DSM Directive may somehow mitigate this problem. In the recitals accompanying the controversial Article 17, namely in Recital 70, it is stated that the parody exception (as well as the quotation exception) provided in the InfoSoc Directive should be made mandatory. However, as suggested by preceding segments in that recital and by Article 17(7) DSM Directive, this obligation seems limited to the need to ensure that users are allowed to upload content for purposes of caricature, parody and pastiche onto online content-sharing platforms like YouTube. If this interpretation is correct, the DSM Directive makes the InfoSoc parody exception *de facto* mandatory, but only for situations falling within the coverage of Article 17.[956]

3.2.5 Quotation

Despite the generally narrow scope and precise wording of Article 5 exceptions, some of them lie closer to the standards end of the spectrum than others. The most notorious example of a *comparatively* broad and vague exception within the InfoSoc Directive is the quotation exception (Article 5(3)(d)).[957] Some commentators have argued that this exception provides a

---

951. *See* CJEU, *Deckmyn*, paras 29-31. Strikingly, though, the CJEU offers no criteria that may be used in identifying a discriminatory message.
952. *See* CJEU, *Deckmyn*, para. 28.
953. For a comprehensive investigation into the parody exception, analysing the situation in multiple jurisdictions, *see* Jacques (2019).
954. *See* EPRS (2015), p. I-135.
955. *See* EPRS (2015), p. I-136.
956. It may of course happen that the Member States which have not implemented the parody exception into their national laws will simply do so in relation to all uses, instead of limiting it to Article 17 situations.
957. As early as in 1988, the Commission admitted the possibility of adopting a vague provision on quotation, giving the judiciary the discretion to decide which acts are restricted on a case-by-case basis: 'the practical difficulties of resolving issues like the appropriate scope of the right to quote or borrow from existing works should not be underestimated. It may be that these issues can only be settled by legislation in a very general way, leaving it to case law to determine the precise parameters in specific circumstances' – 1988 Green Paper, p. 210.

template that is sufficiently flexible to compensate, at least in part, for the lack of a standard similar to US fair use.

Under Article 5(3)(d) InfoSoc Directive, Member States may implement an exception to the exclusive rights of reproduction and communication to the public that privileges quotations: (i) for purposes such as criticism or review; provided that (ii) they relate to a work that has already been lawfully made available to the public; (iii) the source, including the author's name, is indicated, unless this turns out to be impossible,[958] and (iv) their use is in accordance with fair practice and to the extent required by the specific purpose. The CJEU has clarified that there is no requirement that the quotation be used as part of a work protected by copyright[959] and that, under certain circumstances, the indication of the source, and not necessarily the name of the author, may be sufficient to satisfy the second requirement above.[960] It is relevant to note that, whereas the InfoSoc exception in Article 5(3)(d) is provided as an *optional* one for Member States,[961] as a matter of international law a quotation exception is *mandatory* for members of the Berne Union.[962]

Importantly, and notwithstanding the tradition of strict interpretation of exceptions, the CJEU held that the quotation exception must be interpreted in light of its purpose. That purpose, the Court added, is to strike a fair balance between the freedom of expression of users of protected content and the authors' right of preventing the use of their works.[963] In a similar vein, AG Trstenjak cited the 'interest in a free intellectual analysis', 'freedom of opinion' and 'freedom of the press' as the rationales behind Article 5(3)(d).[964]

---

958. On this requirement, essentially following the wording of Article 5(3)(d), *see* CJEU, *Painer*, paras 138-149. *See also* CJEU, *Nintendo II*, paras 83-85, interpreting the same requirement in the citation exception laid down in Article 20(1)(c) Community Design Regulation (which does not include the feasibility caveat).
959. *See* CJEU, *Painer*, paras 129-137.
960. *See* CJEU, *Painer*, paras 138-149. In his Opinion in *Pelham*, AG Szpunar expressed the view that the indication of source need not be made in the quoting work itself, but in its title or description – *see* AG Opinion, *Pelham*, para. 68.
961. *But see* Recital 70 DSM Directive, in relation to uses for purposes of quotation, criticism and review made through online content-sharing platforms. *See also supra* section 3.2.4 (in relation to parody).
962. This does not mean that the exception is imperative, in the sense that it cannot be contractually overridden or restricted through the application of TPMs. On the mandatory nature of Article 10(1) Berne Convention, *see*, *e.g.*, Xalabarder (2007), pp. 395-398, and Kur & Ruse-Khan (2009), pp. 38-39 (adding that, following the inclusion of the Berne *acquis* into TRIPS, 'in case a national copyright act were to prohibit quotations in any form, the conflict would lead to a Dispute Settlement, supposing that foreign publishers or other potential beneficiaries of the quotation right were strong enough to convince their government into action').
963. *See* CJEU, *Painer*, paras 132-135; CJEU, *Funke Medien*, para. 60; and CJEU, *Spiegel Online*, para. 45.
964. AG Opinion, *Painer*, para. 186.

The quotation exception in InfoSoc draws significantly from the quotation exception in Article 10(1) and (3) Berne Convention. Article 10(1) Berne Convention provides that '[i]t shall be permissible to make quotations from a work which has already been lawfully made available to the public, provided that their making is compatible with fair practice, and their extent does not exceed that justified by the purpose, including quotations from newspaper articles and periodicals in the form of press summaries'. Article 10(3) adds the requirement of attribution of source and authorship. Article 5(3)(d) InfoSoc Directive must be interpreted, insofar as possible, in light of these Berne provisions.[965]

Analysing the wording of Article 5(3)(d) InfoSoc Directive and the CJEU's interpretative case law, one can see that the quotation exception lies closer to what is conventionally called a standard than other *droit d'auteur*-type exceptions.[966] In relative terms, the exception is indeed broad and vague.

To begin with, the very notion of 'quotation' is, in itself, rather wide. First, quotations are not restricted to literary or textual works.[967] As the wording of Article 5(3)(d) makes clear, the exception applies to all types of subject matter, meaning that image or sound quotations are also possible.[968] Second, the exception extends beyond quotations of small parts of a work,

---

965. *See* CJEU, *Painer*, para. 126.

966. *See* Xalabarder (2007), p. 397 (pointing out that both Article 10(1) Berne Convention and Article 5(3)(d) InfoSoc Directive have an 'open, neutral and flexible scope'); Hugenholtz & Senftleben (2011), p. 7 ('[a]n example of a fairly open – but not general – exception commonly found in laws of the authors' right tradition is the quotation right'); and Bently & Aplin (2018) (dubbing the quotation exception in Article 10 Berne Convention a sort of 'global, mandatory fair use').

967. The view that quotations were in principle restricted to the literary domain prevailed in French scholarship for some time – *see, e.g.*, Desbois (1978), p. 317, and Françon (1999), p. 244 –, but has meanwhile been abandoned. *See* Geiger (2004a), pp. 345-349, for an account of this shift. Criticising the traditional approach in French law, *see* Bertrand (2010), pp. 337-338.

968. The wording of Article 5(3)(d) merely refers to 'a work or other subject-matter'. Similarly, Article 10(1) Berne Convention uses the expression 'quotations from a work' and its title is 'certain free uses of works'. In *Painer*, however, the CJEU refrained from ruling on the correctness of the assumption, made by the referring court, that a photographic work comes within the scope of the quotation exception (paras 122-123). *See also* AG Opinion, *Painer*, para. 212. Yet, AG Szpunar argued, in his opinion in *Pelham*, fn. 29, that the Court in *Painer* seems to have tacitly accepted quotation with regard to photographic works. He further claimed that 'there is nothing to indicate that, under EU copyright law, the quotation exception may not concern other categories of works [beyond literary works], in particular, musical works' (para. 62), an idea that was confirmed in the Court's judgment (para. 68). In relation to the Berne Convention version, *see* Dreier (2016), p. 48. Moreover, for what it is worth, the dictionary definition of 'quotation' comprises non-textual works: 'a group of words taken from a text or speech and repeated by someone other than the original author or speaker' and then as 'a short musical passage or visual image taken from one piece of music or work of art and used in another' – Oxford English Dictionary (2010), p. 1459.

encompassing lengthy quotations and, in some cases, even quotations of an entire work.[969] And third, the quoted work need not be inextricably integrated – through insertions or footnotes, for example – into the citing work. A quotation may therefore be made by way of a hyperlink to the quoted work.[970]

Furthermore, the enumeration of purposes that the quotations must respect is non-exhaustive. This results from the use of the expression 'for purposes *such as* criticism or review' in Article 5(3)(d). The term 'such as' clearly indicates that criticism and review are no more than *examples* of purposes that can justify quotations (but more on this shortly).[971]

Finally, the quotation must be made 'in accordance with fair practice and to the extent required by the specific purpose' – a vague requirement borrowed from the wording of Article 10(1) Berne Convention. Neither Berne nor InfoSoc provide any guidance as to the meaning of this requirement, and the indications given by the CJEU are also rather meagre.[972] While some commentators argue that Member States have significant autonomy in determining the meaning of 'fair practice' since '[n]ational norms of fairness may differ',[973] others claim that the requirement has a normative content of its own[974] and have posited that 'the practice must be fair, in and of itself, according to an objective appreciation'.[975]

This appreciation seems to require the law-interpreter to conduct a balancing exercise. In consonance with the purpose of the quotation exception as identified by the CJEU, the interests to be balanced include those of the rightholder in ensuring the respect for her work, on the one hand, and those of the user in exercising her freedom of expression, on the other. These interests may translate into different relevant factors within the 'fair practice' assessment resembling those of US fair use, namely the nature and purpose of the quotation, its size and substantiality, and the degree of market harm it causes.[976]

---

969. *See* Ricketson (2003), p. 12 (giving the example of the use, in historian's works, of representative pictures of schools of art for illustration purposes) and Aplin & Bently (2018), p. 6. *See also* AG Opinion, *Painer*, para. 212, and AG Opinion, *Spiegel Online*, para. 45, submitting that full quotations can also come within the scope of Article 5(3)(d). This will not be so in every case, since, as the Court clarified, the quotation cannot be 'so extensive as to conflict with a normal exploitation of the work or another subject matter or prejudices unreasonably the legitimate interests of the rightholder' – CJEU, *Spiegel Online*, para. 79.
970. *See* CJEU, *Spiegel Online*, para. 80.
971. *See* CJEU, *Spiegel Online*, para. 28, and CJEU, *Funke Medien*, para. 43.
972. *See* CJEU, *Pelham*, para. 69, and CJEU, *Spiegel Online*, para. 83.
973. *See* Ginsburg (2000), p. 288. *See also* Walter & Lewinski (2010), pp. 1049-1050.
974. *See* Aplin & Bently (2018), p. 10.
975. Dreier (2016), p. 48.
976. *See* Aplin & Bently (2018), p. 11. *See also* Dreier (2016), p. 48 (arguing that the practice will be fair 'if the quotation is made in support of the ideas expressed by the person

This broad and vague scope has led Lionel Bently and Tanya Aplin to claim that the exception for quotations 'comes very close to being a "fair use" exception'.[977] Similarly, Martin Senftleben has argued that the quotation exception, if implemented in a way that tolerates purposes comparable to criticism and review, comes close to a 'flexible standard capable of keeping pace with new technologies'.[978]

Pleasing as it may sound to the ears of a liberal-minded copyright enthusiast, this view seems overly optimistic, at least in what concerns the potential of the quotation exception to accommodate new technological uses of protected works. This exception, albeit broad and vague in comparison with other exceptions enumerated in Article 5 InfoSoc Directive and in the exceptions' *acquis* more generally, is subject to important limits.[979]

First, the concept of 'quotation', even if understood in the broadest possible sense, bears the limits that flow from the ordinary meaning of the term. Not every *use* of a copyright-protected work can fit the description of a *quotation*.[980] The CJEU has made this abundantly clear in the *Pelham* judgment. After clarifying that the usual meaning of the word requires the user who wishes to rely on the quotation exception to have the intention of entering into dialogue with the quoted work,[981] the Court said that if a musical sample is not identifiable, it cannot enter into such intellectual dialogue.[982] This is in line with AG Szpunar's view, according to which the act of musical sampling fell outside the scope of the exception because the quoted work, in order to qualify as a quotation, had to be incorporated into the new work without modification or at least in a way that makes the former distinguishable as a 'foreign element' within the latter – a requirement that sampling failed to fulfil.[983]

The sustainability of a solution that relies on the quotation exception is therefore limited, since we do not know if future technological uses will even

---

quoting, if it serves as an illustration of this person's views, if it encourages the seeking of more information, and if it does not merely substitute for the use of the work that has been quoted from').

977. Bently & Aplin (2018), p. 17. Making the same point, *see* Ricketson (2003), p. 13.

978. Senftleben (2013b), p. 27.

979. *See* Triaille et al. (2013), p. 464.

980. *See* Förster (2008), pp. 221-222, pointing out that even a broad formulation of the quotation exception in the German Copyright Act would continue to exclude completely new types of use, such as the Google Books digitisation project.

981. *See* CJEU, *Pelham*, para. 71. *See also* CJEU, *Spiegel Online*, paras 78-79: the user must 'necessarily establish a direct and close link between the quoted work and his own reflections', by using the quoted work for the purposes of 'illustrating an assertion', 'defending an opinion' or 'allowing an intellectual comparison' between the work and her assertions.

982. *See* CJEU, *Pelham*, para. 73.

983. *See* AG Opinion, *Pelham*, paras 62-67. Criticising this view for being based on a 'textual' or 'print-based' paradigm of quotation, *see* Jütte & Quintais (2019), p. 5. *See also* Jongsma (2019), pp. 8-11, opposing the introduction of restrictive requirements that do not clearly follow from the wording of the provision.

look like a quotation *proprio sensu*. Subsuming certain technological uses under the coverage of a quotation exception may thus be somewhat of a legal fiction. Evidently, a standard like fair use has the potential to cover a much wider spectrum of unanticipated uses than an exception that merely privileges 'acts of quotation', however broadly this category is understood. The very scholars arguing that quotation resembles fair use concede this much.[984]

Second, and relatedly, the non-exhaustive list of purposes in Article 5(3)(d) is not fully open-ended. The expression 'such as' has been said to entail a requirement that other possible purposes must be *comparable* to criticism and review (like teaching or other educational purposes). Under this understanding, the user, in making the quotation, would have to somehow refer back to the pre-existing work to make a statement on it.

There is ample support for this understanding in legal decisions.[985] In *Painer*, the CJEU stated that Article 5(3)(d) is intended 'to preclude the exclusive right of reproduction conferred on authors from preventing the publication, by means of quotation *accompanied by comments or criticism*, of extracts from a work already available to the public'.[986] AG Trstenjak argued in the same case that the general examples cited in Article 5(3)(d) point towards the requirement of 'a material reference back to the quoted work in the form of a description, commentary or analysis'.[987] Put briefly, '[t]he quotation must … be a basis for discussion'.[988] As seen above, in *Pelham* and *Spiegel Online*, the judges and the designated AG offered related arguments, adopting a definition of quotation based on the existence of an intellectual dialogue or comparison between works.[989]

---

984. *See* Bently & Aplin (2018), making such concession 'in relation to the technology-related uses, such as accessing interface information to ensure functional interoperability' (pp. 6-7) and admitting that the quotation exception in Article 10(1) Berne Convention 'is not as broad as "fair use" in US law'.
985. Not only in legal decisions, but also in the literature. *See* Walter & Lewinski (2010), p. 1050 ('The specific purpose may be criticism, review, or similar'); Senftleben (2012b), p. 372 (referring to statements made during the legislative process that led to the implementation of the InfoSoc Directive in the Netherlands, according to which there is 'a need to confine legitimate purposes in the sense of the quotation right to those comparable with criticism or review'); and Quintais (2017a), p. 231 ('the quoted work (whatever the extent of use necessary) should be ancillary to the subsequent work, and to the proposition the latter intends to illustrate or prove'). *Contra see* Bently & Aplin (2018), who dispute the consistency of purpose limitations with Article 10(1) Berne Convention. These authors note that Article 10(1) includes no examples of purposes that may justify the quotation, arguing that the objective behind the quotation is relevant merely for purposes of assessing the proportionality of the use (i.e., whether the extent of the quotation exceeds that justified by its objective).
986. CJEU, *Painer*, para. 120 (emphasis added).
987. AG Opinion, *Painer*, para. 210.
988. AG Opinion, *Painer*, para. 210.
989. *See* CJEU, *Pelham*, paras 71-73, and CJEU, *Spiegel Online*, paras 78-79. Similarly, in examining the meaning of 'citation' within the exception laid down in Article 20(1)(c) Community Design Regulation, the judges noted that the aim of this provision is 'to

Furthermore, the requirement of comparability with criticism or review had been adopted by a number of Member States in their national quotation exceptions, even before the *Pelham* and *Spiegel Online* decisions.[990]

Given this requirement, a series of technological uses that have purposes other than entering into some kind of dialogue with the quoted work will be excluded from the exception's coverage. In this context, it seems difficult to argue that automatically generated references, such as Internet search engine results, are covered by the quotation exception, since the purpose of such references can hardly be considered similar to criticism or review of the quoted work.[991]

Finally, there are other limiting conditions for the quotation to be lawful: the source and authorship must be indicated whenever possible,[992] and the quoted work must have been lawfully made available to the public.[993]

Granted, the InfoSoc quotation exception is broader and vaguer than most and, as such, confers a comparatively wide degree of discretion upon judges in charge of interpreting and applying it, especially when read in light of its purpose of ensuring a fair balance between competing interests. However, given the limiting conditions that have just been discussed, it is farfetched to argue that it gives courts the latitude they need to assimilate newly emerged and privilege-worthy acts of use without having to resort to recurring legislative updates. Although the quotation exception may provide relief in certain cases, it would hardly be a sustainable solution for the technological adaptability problem of the InfoSoc framework of exceptions

---

limit the rights conferred by the Community design so far as it concerns acts of reproduction that serve as *a basis for the explanations or commentary* of the person intending to rely on that limitation' – CJEU, *Nintendo II*, para. 76 (emphasis added).

990. *See, e.g.*, Article XI.189 Belgian Economic Law Code ('criticism, controversy or review'); Article L. 122-5(3)(a) French IP Code ('the critical, controversial, educational, scientific, or informative character of the work in which they are incorporated'); and Article 75(2)(g) Portuguese Copyright Code ('in support of its own theories or with the purpose of criticism, discussion or teaching').

991. *See* Senftleben (2012b) and Senftleben (2013b), finding support in the ruling by the Court of Appeal of Arnhem in *Zoekallehuizen.nl*, which concerned a search engine that collected information from online databases of housing agencies. The author claims that applying the quotation exception to the results provided by advanced search engines is a more consistent solution than, e.g., resorting to doubtful extensions of non-copyright doctrines, such as implied consent or abuse of rights. While the solution advanced by Senftleben has the advantage of keeping the resolution of the dispute within the realm of copyright law, it can hardly be argued that stretching the quotation exception to cover these types of uses is not an artificial solution or a 'legal fiction'. Only with a significant dose of interpretative generosity can it be considered that, for instance, the display of thumbnails in search engine results lists is made for the purposes of 'illustrating an assertion', 'defending an opinion' or allowing some form of 'intellectual comparison'.

992. As noted by commentators, many technological uses, such as digital adaptations and TDM activities, will fall short from attributing the source and authorship even where it is not impossible to do so – *see* Quintais (2017a), p. 232.

993. On the interpretation of this requirement, *see* CJEU, *Painer*, paras 124-128, and CJEU, *Spiegel Online*, paras 85-95.

as a whole. A more open-ended provision would be necessary for that purpose.

4 THE THREE-STEP TEST

Speaking of open-ended provisions, Article 5(5) is an unmistakable example of such within the InfoSoc framework of exceptions. It is useful at this stage to recall the wording of Article 5(5), according to which the exceptions provided for in the preceding paragraphs 'shall only be applied in certain special cases which do not conflict with a normal exploitation of the work or other subject-matter and do not unreasonably prejudice the legitimate interests of the rightholder'.

As explained in Chapter 2, the InfoSoc test (whose formula has been imported to other directives) primarily serves the function of controlling the *application* of exceptions. If a certain unauthorised use is considered to be privileged by one of the listed exceptions, that use must, in addition, cumulatively satisfy the test's three conditions.[994] In disputes involving the applicability of an exception arising from the InfoSoc Directive, national courts will be required to test the concrete use against the three-step test's conditions, irrespective of whether the test was expressly implemented into national law.[995] This, as I shall argue, raises a double problem for the InfoSoc framework of exceptions: not only does the test fail to foster the framework's adaptability to technological change (section 4.1), but it also creates significant unpredictability (section 4.2).

4.1 The One-Sided Character of the InfoSoc Three-Step Test

The three-step test is crafted in a standard-like manner. In particular, the second ('normal exploitation') and third ('unreasonable prejudice to the legitimate interests of the rightholder') conditions are arguably as vague as the US fair use factors. A parallel can even be established between such steps and the 'market harm' factor in Section 107 US Copyright Act, for they are all concerned with loss of licensing opportunities by the rightholder.

But the InfoSoc three-step test, though lying at the standards end of the continuum, does not grant courts the freedom they need to adapt copyright law to new technologies. This is so because Article 5(5) provides that exceptions *shall only be applied* in concrete cases if the three steps are met. If the deciding court understands that the steps are not met, it should refrain from applying the relevant exception and thus from considering the use at

---

994. *See* CJEU, *Premier League*, para. 181; CJEU, *PRCA*, para. 53; and CJEU, *Ulmer*, para. 56. *See also* Arnold & Rosati (2015), p. 747.
995. *See supra* Chapter 2, section 4.2.

stake lawful. In other words, the test cannot be applied to identify new use privileges, but only to strike down existing ones in specific disputes.

In addition, the conditions against which the 'excessive application'[996] of exceptions is to be analysed only mention the interests of rightholders. No reference is made in Article 5(5) to third-party interests, namely those of users of protected works and of the public at large. It could be argued that, if benevolently interpreted, the third step grants courts some leeway to consider countervailing interests, by implicitly admitting that the interests of rightholders may not be 'legitimate' and that the prejudice to those interests may be 'reasonable'.[997] Yet, this does not change the fact that these interests must be weighed as part of a second tier of scrutiny on exceptions. In these vests, the test functions, in practice, 'as a general presumption against the extension of exceptions'.[998] Thus, if there is some balancing to be conducted under the InfoSoc three-step test, it is a sort of one-sided, rightholder-centric balancing – which is not a true balancing exercise at all.

We therefore conclude that mere vagueness or standard-likeness may not be enough to deal adequately with the issue of adaptability to technological change. The three-step test *qua* judicial tool does grant discretion to law-appliers. The problem is that this discretion can only be used in favour of the rightholder, since the three steps work as hurdles that must be surmounted if an unauthorised use that already falls within a listed exception is to be conclusively deemed non-infringing. Hence, courts cannot employ the test as an enabling mechanism that allows the accommodation of new and unforeseen uses. As explicitly put by AG Maciej Szpunar in his opinion in *Pelham*:

> [The text] constitutes a restriction of the exceptions and limitations applicable to exclusive rights. By contrast, that provision cannot be understood as authorising the introduction of exceptions and limitations not provided for or as extending the scope of the existing exceptions on the grounds that they do not adversely affect the normal exploitation of the work or other subject-matter or the legitimate interests of the holders of exclusive rights.[999]

This one-sidedness of the three-step test has generated severe scholarly criticism. Jonathan Griffiths summarises the problem as follows: '[a]s communication technologies and potential methods for providing reward and incentive for creators are changing so rapidly, it seems unwise to pre-set policy balances in a manner that automatically favours copyright owners'.[1000] Some authors go as far as arguing that the biased nature of the test

996. Geiger et al. (2008), p. 708.
997. For a more detailed account of this alternative interpretation, *see infra* Chapter 5, section 4.2.2.1.
998. Griffiths (2009), p. 441. *See also* Westkamp (2008), p. 65, stating that 'the test reinforces notions of bias'.
999. AG Opinion, *Pelham*, para. 58.
1000. Griffiths (2009), p. 445.

undermines 'the social acceptance of copyright, which might intensify the crisis of legitimacy it is facing at the moment'.[1001]

This state of affairs should be reversed. Discretion with a view to adapting copyright law to the emergence of new technologies needs to 'cut both ways'[1002] – i.e., it must enable judges to render new uses infringing *or* non-infringing. When commentators suggest adjusting the three-step test in order to allow for a 'more flexible and balanced application',[1003] they are referring not merely to the idea of vagueness, but to the idea of having a true balancing and enabling test. In order for the test to be flexible in this sense, it would have to authorise the weighing of *competing* interests of rightholders and users in the determination of whether a certain use is lawful, regardless of whether it already falls within a rule-like exception. Even if no exception applies, the test could be used to identify new authorisation-free uses.

It should be noted here that some national courts have in the past applied the test in a flexible and enabling manner (the quintessential example being the Spanish Supreme Court's judgment in the *Megakini.com* case discussed below[1004]). These, however, remain exceptional cases.

Put briefly, insofar as the test is conceived of as a restrictive mechanism, it merely exacerbates the problem of inadaptability.[1005] As shall be seen, this predicament has led to a series of proposals to rethink the test, which will be analysed in detail in the following chapter.[1006]

4.2 The Uncertainty Created by a Judicial Three-Step Test

Understood as an extra layer of scrutiny in cases concerning the application of listed rule-like exceptions, the three-step test suffers from a fundamental certainty-related problem: it infuses imprecision in the analysis of exceptions that would otherwise be relatively precise. If potentially applicable exceptions must be controlled, on a case-by-case basis, by a standard composed of three open-ended criteria, users will not be able to confidently rely on their wording. As a result, the predictability that would prima facie arise from the

1001. Geiger (2007b), p. 490. *See also* Sganga & Scalzini (2017), pp. 429-430, claiming that the test has 'unidirectional, detrimental effects on the outcome of the copyright balance'.
1002. Martin-Prat (2014), p. 42.
1003. Senftleben (2009), p. 7.
1004. *See infra* 5.2.1.2. Writing before the Spanish Supreme Court had rendered judgment in *Megakini.com*, Griffiths (2009), pp. 436-440, cites as examples the cases BGH, *Kopienversanddienst* and Swiss Federal Supreme Court, *ProLitteris*. On the Swiss judgment in detail, *see also* Geiger (2008b).
1005. *See*, *inter alia*, Synodinou (2014), p. 95.
1006. *See infra* Chapter 5, section 4.2.2.

precise formulation of *droit d'auteur*-type exceptions ends up being eroded.[1007]

The French *Mulholland Drive* case is the most widely cited example of this effect.[1008] The plaintiff in this case had purchased a DVD copy of David Lynch's movie *Mulholland Drive*. He wanted to format-shift the copy into VHS format in order to watch it at his mother's house, but the TPMs installed in the DVD prevented him from doing so. The purchaser sued the producer and distributor of the movie, arguing that the private copying exception laid down in Articles L.122-5(2) and L.211-3(2) French IP Code entitled him to make copies of the content contained in the DVD.

The Paris Court of Appeals sided with the plaintiff, engaging in a literal interpretation of the provisions at stake, which provide that the author 'may not prohibit' acts of private copying. The exception, concluded the Court, 'can only be restricted subject to the conditions specified in the legislation'.[1009]

But the Court of Cassation overturned the decision.[1010] It explicitly stated that private copying is *not* an absolute right recognised to users.[1011] Moreover, in what matters for this section, it added that the private copying exception must be interpreted in light of the InfoSoc Directive (which, back then, was yet to be implemented into French law) and, consequently, in light of the three-step test enshrined in Article 5(5). The Court relied in particular on the second step, holding that the act at stake conflicted with the normal exploitation of the work 'in view of the risks inherent to the new digital environment as regards the protection of copyright and the economic importance that the exploitation of the work in DVD form represents for the amortisation of film production costs'. Hence, the unclear and largely hypothetical risk of income loss by the rightholder, in and of itself, was enough to render the private copying exception inapplicable to the dispute at hand.

1007. *See, e.g.*, Caron (2002), p. 26; Ernst & Häusermann (2006), pp. 18-19; Geiger (2007b), p. 489; Senftleben (2010), pp. 69-70; and Dreier (2015), p. 141. Also, as argued by Ascensão (2006), pp. 94-95, it is particularly bizarre to subject the concrete application of rule-like exceptions to a condition that they can only be applied in 'certain special cases'. The exceptions are already laid down for special cases. Should they then be applied only in special cases within the set of special cases that forms their factual predicate?

1008. For further national case law references, *see* Griffiths (2009); Senftleben (2009); and Rosati (2019), pp. 150-152.

1009. Paris Court of Appeals, *Mulholland Drive*.

1010. French Court of Cassation, *Mulholland Drive*. For discussion of the decision, *see* Maxwell & Massaloux (2006); Geiger (2006b); Ngombe (2007); Geiger (2008c), pp. 124-125; Griffiths (2009), pp. 433-436; and Hugenholtz & Senftleben (2011), pp. 19-20.

1011. *See supra* Chapter 2, section 2.2, on the legal nature of the entitlements conferred by copyright exceptions.

The application of the three-step test by the Court of Cassation resulted in the disapplication, in a concrete case, of an otherwise applicable exception, corroding the clarity of its strict wording.[1012] *Mulholland Drive* thus illustrates the idea put forward, among others, by Jonathan Griffiths: 'under art.5(5), a user of copyright works cannot ever be sure that his or her activities will fall within the terms of an exception in national law because the scope of the exception will always be subject to the uncertain conditions of the "three-step test"'.[1013] The criticism is almost consensual, for supporters of a restrictive InfoSoc framework like André Lucas concede that the test 'creates vagueness that is prejudicial to legal security'.[1014]

The first incarnation of the three-step test emerged as a flexible compromise solution in the 1967 Stockholm Conference for the Revision of the Berne Convention. In that capacity, the test has successfully enabled national legislators to preserve their own exceptions and to accommodate local needs and traditions.[1015] Nevertheless, when understood as an instrument intended to control the application of exceptions in concrete disputes, the test has proven to be hopelessly indeterminate, hindering the main advantage of the statutory exceptions in Article 5 InfoSoc Directive – the guidance that emerges from their reasonably precise wording. In its InfoSoc embodiment, thus, the test represents the worst of both worlds: it provides neither legal certainty nor the necessary flexibility in times of rampant technological change.[1016] A possible future reform of the EU copyright *acquis* will have to alter this sorry state of affairs.

5 THE ROLE OF THE CJEU

As briefly reported in the Introduction to this book, the CJEU has been playing a vital role in the copyright harmonisation process, particularly over the last decade. Irrespective of one's view regarding the appropriateness of such role, the fact of the matter is that, in developing this area of EU law, the CJEU has become as crucial a player as the legislative institutions.

When analysed through the lens of the criteria advanced in the previous chapter, the CJEU's activity may be divided into three related roles: the Court has been playing a harmonising role (section 5.1), a pragmatic role (section 5.2), and a guiding role (section 5.3).

1012. *See* Griffiths (2009), pp. 432 and 434, and Hugenholtz & Senftleben (2011), p. 20.
1013. Griffiths (2009), p. 446. *See also* Dreier (2015), p. 141, asserting that 'legal certainty is swept away where the CJEU also applies the vague criteria of the three-step test'.
1014. Lucas (2010), p. 277, adding that 'the three-step test could in practice rather result in paralysing these exceptions, or at least, in reducing their reach'.
1015. *See* Hugenholtz & Senftleben (2011), p. 21.
1016. *See* Senftleben (2010), p. 69, describing this as the 'worst case scenario'.

5.1 Harmonising Role

One of the natural consequences of the adoption of harmonisation measures is to have the CJEU interpret the concepts laid down in such measures, when prompted to do so by national courts under the preliminary reference procedure. In so doing, the CJEU has mitigated some of the 'harmonisation deficit'[1017] within the legislative copyright *acquis*.

In fact, legislation is not the sole vehicle for harmonisation. CJEU judgments have filled in important gaps in the harmonisation project, influencing both the freedom of national legislators in implementing copyright exceptions (section 5.1.1) and the freedom of Member State courts in interpreting the national versions of these exceptions (section 5.1.2).[1018]

5.1.1 Limiting the Implementation Freedom of Member States

As discussed earlier, the exceptions' *acquis* gives wide freedom to Member States by providing a number of *optional* exceptions in Article 5(2)-(3) InfoSoc Directive. However, other avenues of national legislative freedom exist beyond the 'to implement or not to implement' choice. If a Member State decides to transpose a certain exception into its national legal order, the question arises as to whether it needs to implement it literally or whether it is free to adjust its wording as it sees fit (e.g., in a way that maximises the level of discretion granted to national courts). Hence, in relation to optional exceptions, the question of national latitude emerges at two stages: *whether* to implement the exception and *how* to do it.

Commentators have claimed that the wording of some of the exceptions within Article 5 leaves Member States with significant leeway in the implementation phase.[1019] As seen, despite being generally cast in a rule-like manner, it is unquestionable that some exceptions employ open-ended expressions. When used in the provisions of an EU directive, these expressions may be understood as granting Member States a measure of implementation discretion.

Recognising this open-endedness, Bernt Hugenholtz & Martin Senftleben have argued that 'many exceptions listed in Article 5 ISD constitute *prototypes* for national law making rather than precisely circumscribed

1017. The expression is from Dreier (2015), p. 140. *See infra* Introduction, section 4.2 and Chapter 3, section 3.2.2.

1018. *See* Quintais (2017a), p. 199.

1019. *See, e.g.*, Benabou (2004), p. 35. The Commission also recognised this in the 2008 Green Paper, p. 5. *Contra, see* Zolynski (2007), pp. 145-148, arguing – even before the CJEU's copyright case law pointing in that direction – that national legislators had to transpose Article 5 exceptions verbatim.

exceptions with no inherent flexibility'.[1020] The authors point to eight examples of these so-called prototypes: Article 5(2)(b) (private copying), Article 5(2)(c) (libraries and similar institutions), Article 5(3)(a) (teaching and scientific research), Article 5(3)(c) and (f) (news reporting and political speeches), Article 5(3)(d) (quotations), Article 5(3)(i) (incidental inclusion), and Article 5(3)(k) (parody). These scholars argue that the freedom provided by the formulation of these exceptions is attested by the different ways in which Member States have implemented them into national law. Aside from the exception for acts of temporary reproduction, which was implemented in a literal manner in almost all Member States (arguably because of its mandatory nature and detailed wording), the national scope of InfoSoc exceptions varies considerably from Member State to Member State.[1021]

In addition, other exceptions contain wording that implies a grant of discretion upon national legislators to choose between different possibilities.

That is the case, for instance, of the exception in Article 5(3)(e), which covers uses 'for the purposes of public security or to ensure the proper performance or reporting of administrative, parliamentary or judicial proceedings'. Absent any indication in the text of the Directive about the circumstances in which the interests of public security can be raised, it is for the Member States to determine those circumstances in their own territory.[1022]

The same can be said about Article 5(2)(c), which allows Member States to provide for an exception for 'specific acts of reproduction made by publicly accessible libraries, educational establishments or museums, or by archives': the wording seems to leave Member States with some latitude to specify the acts of reproduction and the institutions covered by the exceptions.[1023] The result of this formula was that, as explained by Lucie Guibault and colleagues, '[i]n some Member States, the limitation applies to libraries and archives who may make reproductions of all types of works for purposes of preservation or restoration of their collection. In other Member States, this very limitation is restricted either to certain categories of works or to specific institutions.'[1024]

1020. Hugenholtz & Senftleben (2011), p. 14 (emphasis added). *See also* Hugenholtz (2017), pp. 284-285. The argument has since been picked up by other commentators – *see*, *inter alia*, Gotzen (2012), p. 46; Triaille et al. (2013), p. 248; and Quintais (2017a), pp. 204-205.

1021. *See* Westkamp (2007), pp. 11-48; EPRS (2015), pp. I-203-I-219; and Renda et al. (2015), pp. 27 and 30.

1022. *See*, in relation to the public security exception, CJEU, *Painer*, paras 101-102, and AG Opinion, *Painer*, para. 148. *See also* CJEU, *Stichting de Thuiskopie*, para. 23 (regarding the person who must be considered responsible for paying the fair compensation under the private copying exception), and CJEU, *Copydan Båndkopi*, paras 86-91 (on the use of third-party devices for private copying).

1023. Advancing this argument in relation to Article 5(2)(c), *see* Rosati (2014a), p. 592.

1024. Guibault et al. (2007), p. 64.

The CJEU has also clarified that, in relation to the transposition of the exceptions in Articles 5(3)(c), second part (reporting of current events) and 5(3)(d) (quotation), Member States enjoy significant discretion, even if they are subject to certain limits.[1025]

This (apparent) leeway has led Hugenholtz and Senftleben to claim that copyright harmonisation has left enough policy space for Member States to make their national copyright exceptions future-proof.[1026] This policy space could be used by national legislators to ensure the adaptability of copyright law to technology-related changes, while simultaneously sidestepping the complexity and lengthiness of the EU legislative process.

I, for one, do not entirely share such optimism regarding the breadth of national freedom to make copyright law fit for times of dynamic and unpredictable change. The scepticism is related to developments in CJEU case law that have taken place since Hugenholtz and Senftleben published their influential article. As of late, the Court has been narrowing down to a considerable extent the national flexibility that seemingly existed under the wording of some exceptions. Following a series of judgments, the pre-emptive effects of InfoSoc exceptions became stronger than could have seemed at first sight and the national elbowroom, which could legitimately be presumed to exist before those judgments had been delivered, was constrained.

In its early case law, the Court appeared to recognise broad discretion to Member States in the implementation of certain exceptions.[1027] Yet, recent judgments have shown a greater concern with ensuring a 'coherent application'[1028] (*rectius*: implementation) of exceptions throughout the Union, in the

1025. *See* CJEU, *Funke Medien*, paras 40-53, and CJEU, *Spiegel Online*, paras 25-38.

1026. Hugenholtz & Senftleben (2011), p. 2, have maintained that '[t]he EU copyright *acquis* leaves considerably more room for flexibilities than its closed list of permitted limitations and exceptions suggests'. Regarding the policy space that exists outside the copyright *acquis*, Hugenholtz & Senftleben (2011), pp. 26-27, put special emphasis on the possibility of Member States taking advantage of the unharmonised status of the right of adaptation in order to provide for exceptions privileging transformative uses of copyright-protected works. However, given the intersection between the (unharmonised) right of adaptation and the (harmonised) right of reproduction, the freedom left to Member States seems to be rather narrow. Were Member States to establish exceptions to the right of adaptation, they would be bound to do it in a way that respects the scope of reproduction. As pointed out by Eleonora Rosati, these exceptions would have to 'be designed in a manner that would not transform them into further – and, as such, forbidden – exceptions (in disguise) to other exclusive rights, notably the right of reproduction'; they would thus have to be 'limited to what can be considered pure adaptations, not transformative uses of a work that nonetheless also involve its simple reproduction' – Rosati (2014a), p. 597.

1027. *See* the already cited segment of the *Painer* judgment (paras 101-102).

1028. That is the expression used in Recital 32 InfoSoc Directive. *See also* CJEU, *ACI Adam*, para. 34 ('once [Member States] have made the choice of introducing a certain exception, it must be applied coherently').

interests of furthering the harmonisation project and the construction of the internal market.

The novel approach of the CJEU 'materialised in relation to classes of uses that Member States are not (or "no longer") entitled to modify or make more restrictive in scope, after having decided whether or not to maintain or implement a given exception or limitation'.[1029] In *ACI Adam*, the Court stated that Member States are not allowed to extend the scope of exceptions beyond the coverage provided in the InfoSoc Directive; rather, and in consonance with Recital 44, their margin of implementation is limited to the possibility of constraining the exceptions' scope.[1030]

This statement suggested that EU law only controls the *upper limits* of exceptions, meaning that Member States were allowed to restrict, but not extend, the scope of exceptions. However, the Court has also suggested that EU law also determines the *lower limits* of exceptions. In relation to the private copying exception,[1031] the exception for ephemeral recordings made by broadcasting organisations,[1032] the parody exception,[1033] and the exception for print-disabled people,[1034] the Court has explicitly stated that Member States are not free to determine their boundaries in an inconsistent and unharmonised manner.[1035] In such instances, the Member States' discretion must be exercised within the limits imposed by EU law, meaning that those exceptions must be implemented in a way that complies with all the conditions laid down in the respective paragraphs of Article 5.[1036]

Furthermore, in exercising their freedom to implement exceptions, Member States must comply with: (i) the general principles of EU law, including the principle of proportionality; (ii) the main objectives of the InfoSoc Directive, namely the establishment of a high level of protection of copyright and the smooth functioning of the internal market; (iii) the need for legal certainty for authors/rightholders with regard to the protection of their

---

1029. Renda et al. (2015), p. 30.
1030. *See* CJEU, *ACI Adam*, para. 27; CJEU, *Funke Medien*, para. 63; CJEU, *Pelham*, para. 64; and CJEU, *Spiegel Online*, para. 48.
1031. *See* CJEU, *Padawan*, paras 35-36, and CJEU, *ACI Adam*, paras 34 and 49.
1032. *See* CJEU, *DR & TV2 Danmark*, para. 36.
1033. *See* CJEU, *Deckmyn*, para. 16.
1034. *See* CJEU, *Opinion 3/15 – Marrakesh Treaty*, para. 122. *See also* CJEU, *OSA*, para. 39.
1035. This goes against what seemed to be the prevailing view among AGs. In *Padawan*, AG Trstenjak said that Article 5 'allows Member States considerable flexibility in the transposition of the directive' (para. 43) and, in *Painer*, that '[i]f the Member States are able to decide whether to provide for one of the constraints ..., they are also able, according to the principle of qui potest majus, potest et minus, to decide in principle how to organize such a constraint' (para. 148). Similarly, in *VG Wort*, AG Sharpston stated that '[t]he optional nature of the exceptions or limitations gives Member States a certain freedom of action in this area' (para. 35). *But see* AG Opinion, *Painer*, para. 190.
1036. *See* CJEU, *Opinion 3/15 – Marrakesh Treaty*, para. 123.

works; (iv) the three-step test in Article 5(5);[1037] and (v) the Charter of Fundamental Rights of the EU.[1038] Hence, as a result of this case law, the discretion granted upon Member States to implement the optional exceptions is 'highly circumscribed' by the requirements of EU law.[1039]

In this context, one of the proposals advanced by Bernt Hugenholtz and Martin Senftleben in their piece – that Member States can exercise discretion at the implementation stage in order to combine several InfoSoc exceptions into a semi-open provision[1040] – now seems to be inconsistent with the *acquis* and thus unavailable to national lawmakers. Instead, this line of cases may be interpreted as dictating the adoption of a more modest proposal made by these scholars: that of 'including literal copies of the prototypes in the Information Society Directive in national law',[1041] at least for those exceptions that are worded in more unconditional terms. Under this reading, where Member States choose to transpose one of those exceptions, they are not allowed to 'nationalise' it.[1042]

An obvious question then arises: what are the legal consequences that attach when Member States fail to implement exceptions in respect of the requirements imposed by EU law[1043]? It is a settled CJEU case law that EU directives cannot be applied in proceedings exclusively between private parties to the detriment of national provisions, even where they have not been correctly transposed by the Member State (they lack horizontal direct effect).[1044] Nonetheless, it is also an established case law that, when applying national legal provisions, a national court must make every effort to interpret them, so far as possible, in light of the wording and purpose of the relevant

1037. *But see supra* Chapter 2, section 4.2.
1038. *See* CJEU, *Painer*, paras 104-108, and CJEU, *Opinion 3/15 – Marrakesh Treaty*, para. 124.
1039. *See* CJEU, *Opinion 3/15 – Marrakesh Treaty*, para. 126.
1040. The semi-open norm envisioned by Hugenholtz & Senftleben (2011), pp. 17-18, is the result of the combination of various 'prototypes' with the criteria of the three-step test. For a description and critical analysis, *see infra* Chapter 5, section 4.2.2.2.
1041. Hugenholtz & Senftleben (2011), p. 17. Because the InfoSoc formulas often have a broader scope and a higher degree of vagueness than national implementations, an extra measure of judicial discretion would be guaranteed by transposing Article 5 exceptions verbatim. Therefore, the fact that Member States enjoy limited implementation freedom may end up ensuring *some* adaptability to emerging technologies, while simultaneously cultivating a level playing field. On the advantages of a literal implementation of InfoSoc exceptions, *see also* Senftleben (2004), pp. 265 and 281, and Rosati (2014a), p. 594.
1042. Zolynski (2007), p. 146. *See also* Rosati (2014a), p. 594, (2015), pp. 521-522, and (2019), p. 74, and Dreier (2015), pp. 138-139. This approach is in consonance with the case law of the CJEU in other fields – *see* CJEU, *Adidas-Salomon*, para. 18 (in relation to the implementation of optional provisions on the protection of trademarks with a reputation).
1043. *See* Rosati (2019), pp. 83-84.
1044. *See, e.g.*, CJEU, *Pfeiffer*, para. 109. *See also* CJEU, *OSA*, para. 48 (in relation to Article 3(1) InfoSoc Directive). *But see* AG Opinion, *OSA*, paras 44-47.

directive, in order to achieve an outcome consistent with the objective pursued by that directive.[1045] This principle of consistent interpretation allows courts to indirectly achieve, through judicial interpretation of national exceptions, the result that would be attainable by directly applying the InfoSoc formula. That said, this principle cannot be used as a basis for an interpretation of national law that is *contra legem*.[1046] In such cases – i.e., when a Member State court, in the context of a dispute between a rightholder and a user, concludes that it is unable to interpret the national exception in a manner that is compatible with the equivalent InfoSoc exception, because the national version is wholly inconsistent with EU law –, the party adversely affected by the incorrect transposition could nevertheless rely on the *Francovich* case law, with a view to obtaining from the Member State, if appropriate, compensation for any loss sustained.[1047]

With this growing *corpus* of case law limiting the implementation discretion of Member States, the Court looks determined to fill in the harmonisation gaps left by the legislator.[1048] An understanding according to which Member States enjoy ample freedom in transposing exceptions would undermine the goals of securing a harmonised copyright framework and ensuring that competition in the internal market for copyright-protected goods is not distorted as a consequence of national legal differences. Provided subsidiarity is respected and national legal traditions are not disregarded, this judicial harmonisation of copyright law is to be applauded, for it contributes towards the achievement of the overall goal of harmonisation – a goal that the InfoSoc legislator has been harshly criticised for not attaining.[1049]

5.1.2 Developing Autonomous Concepts of EU Law

Even where exceptions are implemented in broadly similar terms across Member States, fragmentation may occur at the level of interpretation by

1045. *See*, building on the *Marleasing* doctrine, CJEU, *Association de médiation sociale*, para. 38; CJEU, *Adeneler*, para. 111; CJEU, *Pfeiffer*, para. 119; and CJEU, *Dominguez*, para. 27. In the copyright context, *see* CJEU, *OSA*, para. 44.
1046. *See* CJEU, *Adeneler*, para. 110.
1047. *See* CJEU, *Dominguez*, para. 43, and CJEU, *Smith*, para. 56.
1048. Noting the CJEU's gap-filling role, *see*, *inter alia*, Geiger & Schönherr (2012), p. 136; Carre (2013) *passim*; Griffiths (2013), p. 65; Halpern & Johnson (2014), pp. 102-103; Rosati (2014a); Dreier (2015), p. 138; Renda et al. (2015), pp. 29-31; and Geiger (2016), pp. 436-440.
1049. *See supra* section 2.3. In future reforms, for reasons of legal certainty, the extent of the freedom that Member States have in implementing the wording of exceptions should be made clear in the legislative text. This would be consistent with the recommendations issued by the European Parliament, which has called on the Commission to ensure the 'proper implementation' of the InfoSoc exceptions and to 'improve legal certainty' – *see* EP Resolution Implementation InfoSoc Directive 2015, para. 38.

national courts.[1050] The CJEU's harmonising work on copyright law has also tried to alleviate this source of legal uncertainty by constraining the interpretative freedom of Member State courts. The development of autonomous concepts of EU law has been key in this regard.[1051]

EU law must recurrently borrow legal concepts from national law.[1052] In order to ensure the effectiveness of EU law, the CJEU often declares such concepts that pre-exist in domestic law to be autonomous concepts, reinterpreting them as having an independent meaning under EU law. In these cases, the Court super-imposes a separate meaning for concepts found in EU legal instruments, some of which already existed in national legal orders with their own specific meanings. With the development of autonomous concepts of EU law, the CJEU subtracts the determination of their meaning from the discretion of the authorities of each Member State on the basis of their national law, taking it into its own hands.

The CJEU has deemed a variety of concepts within EU copyright law to be autonomous concepts. This trend, which manifests itself especially in the interpretation of the InfoSoc Directive, extends to the entire copyright *acquis*, insofar as the Court makes a uniform interpretation of comparable terms across directives.[1053]

On the side of economic rights, as noted before, both 'reproduction' and 'communication to the public' have been given an autonomous meaning.[1054] In *Infopaq I*, the CJEU observed that Article 2 InfoSoc Directive makes no express reference to the laws of Member States. Accordingly, the Court has refused the Austrian Government's contention that it is for the Member States to provide the definition of the concept of 'reproduction in part'.[1055] As an autonomous concept of EU law, 'reproduction' must be interpreted in a uniform manner *under EU law*.[1056] The Austrian Government had previously advanced a similar argument in *SGAE*, a case on the interpretation of Article

1050. *See* Eechoud et al. (2009), p. 105; Janssens (2009), p. 333; and Guibault (2010), p. 58.
1051. *See* Eechoud (2012), p. 72. For a book-length account of the issue, *see* Roder (2016).
1052. *See* Azoulai (2012), p. 168.
1053. *See* Leistner (2015b), p. 252. In this respect, *see, e.g.*, CJEU, *Bastei Lübbe*, paras 26-28 (on the need for a complementary interpretation of the InfoSoc and Enforcement Directives).
1054. The concept of 'equitable remuneration' in the remuneration right granted by Article 8(2) Rental and Lending Directive and the concept of 'access to cable of broadcasting services' in Article 9 InfoSoc Directive have also been considered autonomous concepts of EU law – *see*, respectively, CJEU, *SENA*, para. 24, and CJEU, *ITV Broadcasting II*, para. 18. In the context of the distribution right over computer programs laid down in Article 4 Software Directive, the concept of 'sale', which triggers the exhaustion of said right, has likewise been given an autonomous meaning – *see* CJEU, *UsedSoft*, para. 40. More recently, in recalling that Articles 2 to 4 InfoSoc Directive oblige Member States to provide for a set of exclusive rights relating *inter alia* to 'works', the Court deemed the concept of 'work' to be an autonomous concept of EU law – *see* CJEU, *Levola Hengelo*, para. 33, and CJEU, *Cofemel*, para. 29.
1055. *See* CJEU, *Infopaq I*, paras 27-29.
1056. *See* CJEU, *Premier League*, para. 154, confirming the reasoning in *Infopaq I*.

3 InfoSoc Directive, where it claimed that the concept of 'public' in that provision was to be defined by the Member States. The Court rejected the argument and proceeded to interpret the concept of 'communication to the public' itself.[1057]

On the side of exceptions, the first concept to be given an autonomous meaning was that of 'fair compensation' in Article 5(2)(b) InfoSoc Directive. As previously explained, Member States that choose to introduce the private copying exception into their legal orders must provide for the payment of fair compensation to affected authors. In *Padawan*, the Court understood the Court of Appeal of Barcelona to be asking whether the concept of 'fair compensation' was an autonomous concept of EU law.[1058] The answer was in the affirmative: although Member States retain the power to determine, within the limits imposed by EU law, the form, detailed arrangements for financing and collection, and the level of fair compensation, this concept must be interpreted in a uniform manner in all Member States.[1059] The justification offered by the Court was twofold. First, Article 5(2)(b) does not refer to the national law of Member States in relation to the concept of 'fair compensation'.[1060] Second, the principle of equality and the harmonisation objective of the InfoSoc Directive 'requires the elaboration of autonomous concepts of European Union law'.[1061] Importantly, the Court further stated that the aim of achieving the most uniform interpretation possible of the InfoSoc Directive is especially palpable in the domain of exceptions, since Recital 32 calls on Member States to achieve a 'coherent application' thereof.[1062]

Grounded on the same reasoning, the Court has later deemed the concepts of 'by means of its own facilities' (in the context of the exception for ephemeral recordings by broadcasting organisations laid down in Article 5(2)(d) InfoSoc Directive)[1063] and 'parody' (Article 5(3)(k) InfoSoc Directive)[1064] to be autonomous concepts. Presumably, the qualification extends to the concepts in every other exception in Article 5, for none of them (except for the grandfather clause) refers to national law.[1065]

1057. *See* CJEU, *SGAE*, para. 31. On 'public' as an autonomous concept of EU law, *see* Lucas-Schloetter (2012), p. 129-131. *But see* Vousden (2010), claiming that there is a 'sleight of legal hand' in *SGAE*, because the doctrine of autonomous concepts was initially developed for areas of exclusive competence, which is not the case of IP.
1058. *See* CJEU, *Padawan* and compare the question's original formulation (para. 19) with the Court's rephrasal (para. 29).
1059. *See* CJEU, *Padawan*, para. 37. *See also* CJEU, *Reprobel*, para. 35, and CJEU, *EGEDA II*, para. 38.
1060. *See* CJEU, *Padawan*, para. 31.
1061. CJEU, *Padawan*, paras 32 and 35.
1062. *See* CJEU, *Padawan*, para. 35.
1063. *See* CJEU, *DR & TV2 Danmark*, paras 33-37.
1064. *See* CJEU, *Deckmyn*, paras 14-17.
1065. The Court has suggested that much through the use of the expression '*inter alia*' in passages like the following: 'an interpretation according to which Member States

The uniform understanding to be given to the concepts found in Article 5 exceptions is to be defined by the CJEU. In specifying the scope and conditions thereof, the Court obliges Member State courts to follow them in their own case law.[1066] What this means is that, where the CJEU has elaborated the autonomous interpretation of a certain concept, Member State courts are bound to adopt that interpretation, even if it conflicts with the specific conditions laid down in the national provisions and case law.

Where a ruling on the interpretation of an InfoSoc exception has not yet been handed down by the CJEU, national courts will, in theory, be free to adopt their own interpretations.[1067] Nevertheless, they should be mindful of their decisive role in the future and coordinated development of a genuinely European copyright law and make active use of requests for preliminary rulings,[1068] even where they are not obliged to do so under Article 267 TFEU and CJEU case law.[1069]

All in all, the harmonising agenda pursued by the Court in its recent case law must be welcomed. While the Court may be accused of being activist,[1070] expansionist, and undemocratic,[1071] the truth is that it has 'achieve[d] what the EU legislator failed to achieve'.[1072] The development of these uniform meanings, however piecemeal, is entirely consistent with the goal of harmonising copyright law. Autonomous concepts take legal certainty

---

which, exercising that option afforded to them by European Union law, have introduced an exception of that kind, are free to determine, in an unharmonised manner, the limits thereof, inter alia as regards the facilities used to make those ephemeral recordings, would be contrary to the objective of that directive' – CJEU, *DR & TV2 Danmark*, para. 36. *See* Stamatoudi & Torremans (2014a), p. 455. *See also* AG Opinion, *Pelham*, para. 76, proposing the extension of the qualification to the concept of 'quotation' within the meaning of Article 5(3)(d) InfoSoc Directive.

1066. To be clear, the application of the provision, as interpreted by the Court, is still within the province of national courts. Nonetheless, as recognised by Leistner (2014a), p. 595, 'the resulting margin of discretion is often rather limited – in some cases the Court even went so far as to practically decide on the facts which had been established by the referring national court'. *See also infra* 5.3.
1067. *See* Lewinski (2015), p. 4.
1068. *See* Leistner (2014b), pp. 868 and 872-873, also pointing out that Member State courts fulfil an important function as controllers of the correctness of EU case law, stressing the possibility to re-submit issues to the CJEU where they believe the existing case law is inaccurate or inadmissible.
1069. *See*, most notably, CJEU, *CILFIT*, articulating the *acte clair* doctrine, pursuant to which a national court of final resort is not obliged to refer where the answer 'is so obvious as to leave no scope for any reasonable doubt' (para. 21). The court is also not obliged to refer where the question raised has already been interpreted by the CJEU (*acte éclairé*) and where it is irrelevant.
1070. On the different possible meanings of the 'judicial activism' accusation, *see* Ribeiro (2015).
1071. *See*, *inter alia*, Bensamoun (2018), p. 21 (criticising CJEU-made harmonisation).
1072. Xalabarder (2016), p. 639. *See also* Lucas-Schloetter (2012), p. 132 (arguing that, although the CJEU's role may be 'a source of irritation to some', it is 'the *sine qua non* of effective harmonization').

from the national to the EU sphere and facilitate the establishment of a fully functional internal market for copyright goods and services where diverging national interpretations of common concepts are progressively reduced. If the definition of the InfoSoc concepts were a matter within the competence of national law, the meaning and scope of those concepts could vary from one Member State to another, giving rise to fragmentation and potential inconsistencies.[1073] Allowing Member State courts to interpret freely and in an unharmonised manner the concepts contained in the InfoSoc Directive would thus hinder the level playing field that the EU legislator intended to create.

This 'gradual diminution of Member States' legislative and interpretative freedoms'[1074] contributes towards the achievement of the InfoSoc Directive's main goal: that of furthering the project of copyright harmonisation. In the future, moreover, this approach may have the added benefit of pressing the EU legislator to claim back the lead in harmonising copyright law and make the extent of Member State freedom clearer in the harmonisation instruments themselves. Should it want to leave the meaning and scope of a certain EU copyright provision to be determined at the domestic level, it must make that intention explicit in the provision's text.[1075]

5.2 Pragmatic Role

As seen above, the general conclusion one reaches when examining the statutory wording of InfoSoc exceptions is that, in general, they are rule-like, discretion-constraining prescriptions.[1076] Even where, due to their vague wording, the provisions lie closer to the standards end of the spectrum, they fail to grant judges the freedom to adequately deal with the issue of technological adaptability – either because their scope is limited (as in the case of the quotation exception), or because they are one-sided (as in the case of the three-step test).

Having said this, in general, judges occasionally resist this kind of constraints by making use of techniques to evade the governing rules.[1077]

1073. *See* CJEU, *Padawan*, para. 35, and CJEU, *DR & TV2 Danmark*, para. 35, referring respectively to the private copying exception in Article 5(2)(b) and to the exception for ephemeral recordings made by broadcasting organisations in Article 5(2)(d) InfoSoc.
1074. Pila & Torremans (2016), p. 331.
1075. *See* Eechoud (2012), p. 72.
1076. *See supra* section 3.1.
1077. Whether and in what circumstances the avoidance of rules amounts to legitimate judicial behaviour are disputed questions. As Alexy & Dreier (1991) point out, '[t]here is no general formula by which to decide when the prima facie priority of the wording may be outweighed' (pp. 96-97). Drawing on the case law of the BVerfG, they cite a series of arguments that may be used to justify a decision against the statutory wording, e.g., 'the age of the norm', 'its contested character right from the beginning', 'changed ideas about the law among the population', and 'the unacceptability of having to wait for the legislator'.

These techniques are manifold and include, among others, the creation of *ad hoc* exceptions at the moment of application of the rule, based on values that mandate the opposite outcome from that of the governing rule;[1078] the appeal to considerations external to the rule in order to soften the rule's stringency; or the reliance on the purpose behind the rule to adjust its linguistically determinate scope.[1079]

In the field of copyright, European courts sometimes resort to this sort of judicial pragmatism in order to sidestep the constraints that arise from the restrictive system of exceptions.[1080] The effect of these techniques is to grant judges a degree of discretion that the controlling provisions fail to confer. As noted by some commentators, the constraints of the InfoSoc framework have not prevented courts from attaining flexible and technologically liberal solutions in some cases.[1081] While national courts have occasionally resorted to general civil law doctrines (such as abuse of rights) with that purpose, the CJEU has been searching for discretion within the copyright system itself.

I will begin by reviewing judgments rendered at the Member State level to show that national courts have been (sometimes rather ingeniously) finding alternative ways to accommodate certain uses of protected works (section 5.2.1). These judgments have been widely commented on in copyright literature and their analysis will serve as a segue to demonstrate that the CJEU too has been willing to avoid the constraints of the statutory framework, albeit in a stealthier style (section 5.2.2).

To be sure, this section is not intended to suggest that European courts have been deciding *all* cases in a flexible manner. There are notable examples of rulings adopting the opposite approach, both at the national[1082] and EU

1078. This technique roughly corresponds to what is known in Continental methodology as 'teleological reduction'. This doctrine has deserved significant attention from German methodologists – *see*, notably, Brandenburg (1983). For a shorter overview of the doctrine, *see* Larenz (2012), pp. 555 et seq.

1079. *See* Schauer (2003), pp. 312-315.

1080. Anticipating that Member States would work their way around the restrictive framework of exceptions, *see* Hugenholtz (2002), p. 69-1.

1081. *See* Kur (2009), p. 298; Hugenholtz & Senftleben (2011), p. 9; Leistner (2011); Westkamp (2012), p. 61; Xalabarder (2012b); and Dreier (2015), p. 141.

1082. In the Belgian case *Copiepresse v. Google*, the Brussels Court of First Instance and the Brussels Court of Appeals have both deemed the uses made in the context of Google News and Google Cache unlawful, reasoning in what can generally be called a formalist manner. Copiepresse SCRL, a CMO that represents the Belgian press publishers of French and German language, sought an injunction against Google with the purpose of removing from Google News and Google Cache any works of such publishers. The Brussels Court of First Instance ruled against Google, finding that the reproduction and making available of articles' headlines and excerpts on Google News and the storage and making available of the articles via the Google Cache service amounted to copyright-infringing acts, since none of the exceptions provided in the Belgian Copyright Act applied. Google was therefore ordered to remove the publishers' content from the aforementioned services. The Brussels Court of Appeals largely upheld the decision. It confirmed that the Google Cache uses were not covered by the

levels.[1083] But the rulings discussed in the following subsections illustrate a worrying trend in judicial behaviour – a trend that is both a symptom of the lack of statutorily granted discretion and a source of legal uncertainty.[1084]

5.2.1 Illustrative National Case Law

Some judgments delivered by national courts on the lawfulness of technological uses have deserved significant scholarly attention in recent years. These are cases in which the tango between (applicable) rights and (inapplicable) exceptions seemed to compel courts to render the use at stake infringing. In all of them, however, the deciding court reached the opposite result.[1085]

Yet, the main reason why commentators have lengthily discussed these decisions is not so much the outcome reached – an outcome that arguably most readers would find sensible –, but the pains the courts have taken to justify decisions that appear to run contrary to the statutory framework governing the dispute. Because the relevant copyright rules would produce an outcome that can plausibly be argued to be injudicious, courts found alternative doctrines to ground their decisions.[1086]

---

temporary reproduction exception, in that the acts were not technically necessary to ensure the efficient transmission of the work. Moreover, it noted that the act of reproduction in question could not be considered 'transient or incidental' (paras 24-26). As to the Google News service, the quotation exception was found inapplicable on grounds, *inter alia*, that the news excerpts were not used with the purpose of criticism or review (paras 31-35). Google could also not rely on the news bulletin exception, because this exception only covers situations in which the need to disseminate information urgently makes it impossible to request the rightholders' authorisation in a timely fashion (para. 37). This was not, as the court observed, the case of the excerpts featured in Google News, which remained listed for more than 30 days. The court stressed that, because the rights at stake are exclusive ones, the exceptions thereto are to be 'interpreted with reservation' (para. 45), and it employed the three-step test, in particular the normal exploitation prong, in a restrictive manner (para. 44). Furthermore, it also rejected the application of the E-Commerce safe harbours (paras 52-55) and of Google's abuse of rights and implied license arguments (paras 59-60). For a detailed analysis of the first instance decision, *see* Laurent (2007), Klein (2008), and Triaille (2008); and for the appellate decision, *see* Laurent (2011) and Xalabarder (2012a).

1083. *See* Rendas (2018), pp. 170-174, identifying judgments where the CJEU adopted a formalist approach.

1084. *See infra* 5.2.2.1 for an elaboration of this conclusion.

1085. This approach is contrary to the perception held by US copyright scholars according to which Continental European courts 'rarely, if ever, depart from these statutes to find limitations of their own for other types of conduct not envisioned ex ante by the legislature' – Cohen et al. (2015), p. 646.

1086. For an overview of the use of these doctrines in various countries, *see* Hilty & Nérisson (2012). *See also* Metzger (2010), p. 114 (calling these doctrines 'emergency valves') and Westkamp (2012) (deeming them 'escape clauses').

What follows is a discussion of two strings of cases – the *Vorschaubilder* saga in Germany (section 5.2.1.1) and the *Megakini.com* rulings in Spain (section 5.2.1.2) – where courts have resorted to such alternative doctrines.

*5.2.1.1 Implied Consent Constructions (*Vorschaubilder*)*

The *Vorschaubilder* cases decided by German courts concerned the display of reduced-size images, the so-called thumbnails, by Google through its image search engine (Google Images).[1087] Google's web crawlers automatically search the Internet, making small-size copies of the images they find and storing them in Google's servers. This allows users to search Google's index for images of interest, by using specific search terms or images as queries. The images that correspond to the user's request are then promptly displayed in the search results as thumbnails, with each thumbnail working as a hyperlink that redirects the user to the webpage where the full-size image can be found.[1088]

In the *Vorschaubilder I* case, an artist operated a website where she uploaded pictures of her own works. After realising that, following a Google query using her name, thumbnails of those pictures were displayed on the search engine results list, she sought injunctive relief against Google.

The Court of First Instance admitted that the display of the thumbnails in Google Images amounted to a prima facie infringement of the right of making available.[1089] The court held, nonetheless, that there was no actual infringement, because the artist, when publishing the pictures online, chose not to use any of the protection measures that are widely available, namely the robots exclusion standard (also known as robots.txt),[1090] and that would have prevented Google's crawlers from indexing her website. Since she elected not to implement any of such measures, the court reasoned, she essentially granted Google and other search engines an implied licence to

1087. For scholarly commentary on these judgments, *see*, *inter alia*, Ott (2009) (on the judgments of the lower courts); Clark (2010); Conrad (2010); Peguera (2012); Pihlajarinne (2012); Clark (2012); and Truyens & Eecke (2016). Citing them as illustrations of the EU framework's lack of flexibility, *see* Senftleben (2010), p. 72; Guibault (2010), p. 57; Spindler (2010), p. 792; Hugenholtz & Senftleben (2011); Leistner (2011); Westkamp (2012); Senftleben (2012b); and Senftleben (2013b).

1088. In the interests of textual economy, and on the assumption that readers are roughly familiar with how Google Images operates, I will refrain from describing this service in greater detail. For a thorougher description, *see* Peguera (2012), pp. 171-174.

1089. Articles 15(2)(2) and 19a German Copyright Act transpose the second part of Article 3(1) InfoSoc Directive, granting authors the right of making their works available to the public on demand.

1090. For a detailed description of the robots exclusion standard and other technical opt-out measures, *see* Peguera (2012), pp. 175-176.

crawl and index her website and to make the thumbnails available in the results list.[1091]

The application of the implied licence doctrine in these circumstances has raised some eyebrows. The use of implied consent, as noted by Orit Fischman Afori, 'is limited to the traditional framework of contractual, or at least quasi-contractual, relations. The implied licence doctrine functions as a gap filler, introducing a new term which the parties intended (subjectively or objectively) to include.'[1092] This function is drastically different from the function served by the implied licence doctrine in the first instance decision. In *Vorschaubilder I*, there was no contractual relation between the artist and Google. This is hardly the natural habitat of the implied licence doctrine.[1093]

On appeal, the existence of any implied licence was unambiguously denied.[1094] According to the Appellate Court, the fact that the rightholder had refrained from implementing protection measures when publishing her works online cannot be understood as a grant of an implied licence for search engines to crawl and index the website where the works could be found. The court nonetheless held that the use was non-infringing, relying on the doctrine of abuse of rights under Article 242 BGB.[1095] Because the plaintiff

---

1091. Regional Court of Erfurt, *Vorschaubilder I*. For a report of the decision in English, *see* Allgrove (2007).

1092. Afori (2008a), pp. 324-325. Relatedly, *see* CJEU, *Soulier & Doke*, para. 37 ('The objective of increased protection of authors ... implies that the circumstances in which implicit consent can be admitted must be strictly defined in order not to deprive of effect the very principle of the author's prior consent').

1093. Guibault (2010), p. 57, goes as far as to compare the application of the doctrine in these circumstances to the introduction of a copyright formality: 'The idea that by failing to technically prevent the reproduction and/or communication to the public of his work the rights owner gives implicit permission to others to do so puts the copyright rule on its head. It is the equivalent of making the application of technological protection measures mandatory for rights owners as a pre-requisite to copyright protection. This is a formality in disguise, which is contrary to Article 5(2) of the Berne Convention.'

1094. Higher Regional Court of Jena, *Vorschaubilder I*.

1095. The content of abuse of rights varies significantly among national legal systems. An exploration of these differences falls beyond the scope of this book, *but see*, *e.g.*, Bolgár (1975); Byers (2002); and Cordeiro (1984), pp. 661-901. In general terms, abuse of rights is a civil law doctrine intended to avoid the perversion of rights. This perversion may consist, for instance, in the exercise of the right in a manner that is contrary to its purpose or with the sole intent of causing harm to another. In the German Civil Code, the doctrine of abuse of rights was explicitly, though somewhat restrictively, codified in Article 226. Under the title 'prohibition of chicanery', this provision states that '[t]he exercise of a right is not permitted if its only possible purpose consists in causing damage to another'. The scope of this provision is limited to the exercise of rights with malicious intent. In the absence of malice, courts may still give relief if the exercise of the right at stake violates the requirements of good faith under Article 242 German Civil Code, which lays down the general principle of good faith (*Treu und Glauben*) in the performance of obligations. Moreover, Article 826 – which provides that a person who, *contra bonos mores*, 'intentionally inflicts damage on another person is liable to the other person to make compensation for the damage' – is also typically conceived

had engaged in 'search engine optimisation', by facilitating access to the content of her website and thereby attracting Google's web crawlers with the purpose of increasing website traffic, the court found that the exercise of the plaintiff's exclusive right – grounded on the fact that she had given no authorisation for the search engine to index her website and make available the thumbnails – amounted to *venire contra factum proprium*.

The artist finally appealed to the BGH. The BGH held that the use by Google Images fell prima facie within the scope of the making available right[1096] and that Google could not avail itself of any of the copyright exceptions, such as the exception for acts of temporary reproduction (Article 44a German Copyright Act)[1097] and the quotation exception (Article 51 German Copyright Act).[1098] Copyright exceptions, the court acknowledged,

---

as a manifestation of the abuse of rights doctrine in the German Civil Code. Scholars argue that copyright law cannot live in insulation from the general principles of law and that the exercise of authors' exclusive rights is subject to the control of the abuse of rights doctrine – *see* Caron (1998b), pp. 2-4, and, regarding moral rights only, Janssens (2013). Courts have also accepted the abuse of rights defence in cases on copyright infringement, especially in France – *see* Guibault (1998), p. 48, and Guibault (2002), p. 278. Accordingly, the topic has been explored with greater attention in French literature – *see, e.g.*, Carreau (1995), Caron (1998a) and Caron (1998b). But extending the abuse of rights doctrine to the improper exercise of authors' exclusive rights under copyright law is certainly not without controversy. Caron (1998b), p. 4 points out that 'it is a delicate matter to use this notion in literary and artistic property law'. 'Indeed', he continued, 'it may be difficult to accept the principle that authors may misuse their rights because it leads quite simply to the removal of the sacred aura surrounding those whom the gentlemen of the Enlightenment labelled "the most respectable citizens".' In the end, however, Caron argues that the abuse of rights doctrine *should* be used in copyright law, albeit in exceptional circumstances and in a moderate way. *See also* Sirinelli (1999), p. 36 (calling for moderation in the application of the abuse of rights doctrine in copyright law) and Geiger (2004a), pp. 390-391 (on the limits of the theory of abuse of authors' rights). In any case, abuse of rights constructions, like the implied license theory in the first instance judgment, are only necessary because the copyright system itself arguably fails to provide a *reasonable* outcome to the legal problem.

1096. Note that Google's use also implicates the right of reproduction, since it makes copies of the images and stores them in its servers. As to a potential violation of the reproduction right, however, the BGH, following the court of appeals, said that all acts of reproduction had taken place in the US and were thus not relevant for the purposes of these proceedings – BGH, *Vorschaubilder I*, para. 17. On the other hand, because the thumbnails are made available to German users in Germany, it had to be considered that the acts of making available were governed by Article 19a German Copyright Act.

1097. The exception provided in article 44a was found inapplicable because the case concerned a *prima facie* infringement of the making available right, whereas that exception's scope is circumscribed to acts of reproduction. The BGH clarified that even if it were to be extended to situations of making available, the condition that the act must not have independent economic significance would not be met, because the display of the thumbnails by Google is, in and of itself, a use with economic relevance – BGH, *Vorschaubilder I*, para. 24.

1098. According to the BGH, the quotation exception does not apply to the making available of thumbnails in the search engine results list because this use is not intended to foster the intellectual engagement with the work that is being used. The results list generated

are, in general, to be interpreted in a strict manner.[1099] Citing its previous case law,[1100] the BGH held that the existing framework of exceptions was not to be replaced by a general balancing of interests conducted outside the domain of copyright exceptions. (Ironically, however, that seems exactly what the BGH ended up doing in this judgment.[1101])

As to the existence of an implied licence, the BGH reached the same conclusion as the Court of Appeals: the fact that the artist had made the pictures freely available online, without blocking the automatic indexation by Google's web crawlers, did not mean that she had granted a true implied licence to use the pictures. This was all the more so given that the artist had inserted a copyright notice on the pictures.[1102]

---

by the user's query is but a tool for finding content on the Internet and that, in the Court's view, does not suffice for the quotation exception to be applicable – BGH, *Vorschaubilder I*, para. 27. On the need for some form of intellectual engagement for the application of the quotation exception, *see supra* section 3.2.5.

1099. BGH, *Vorschaubilder I*, para. 27. The BGH did not absolutely exclude broad readings of exceptions to copyright. Such readings may be necessary to adapt copyright law to new technologies or to fulfil the fundamental interests of the parties to the case. In this case, though, the BGH concluded that neither the users' freedom of information, nor Google's freedom of communication and freedom of trade required an extensive interpretation of the relevant exceptions. This conclusion is in contrast with the approach it followed some years earlier in the *Elektronischer Pressespiegel* case, which concerned the exception for (analogue) press reviews within Article 49(1) German Copyright Act. In that judgment, the BGH acknowledged that statutory exceptions might become obsolete as a result of technological change; the question was whether, considering the new technological possibilities and the exception's purpose, the exception could be construed in a broad manner – BGH, *Elektronischer Pressespiegel*, paras 27-28. The BGH further said that the interpretative rule according to which copyright exceptions must be interpreted strictly does not mean that only the technological paradigm under which the relevant exception was enacted is to be taken into account; if a privileged use, such as press reviews, is replaced by a new technology-enabled use, the exception may be interpreted in order to meet the needs of technological advancement (para. 30). In examining whether the exception should be extended beyond the technological possibilities of the time in which it was drafted, the interests of the author, notably the interest in being remunerated for the use of her work, must be taken into account (para. 31). Having this in mind, the BGH decided to extend the press review exception to electronic press reviews, on the condition that the author was duly remunerated. Although the case was decided before the InfoSoc Directive had been transposed into the German legal order, the BGH asserted that such an extensive interpretation of Article 49(1) German Copyright Act was compatible with the Directive, namely with Article 5(3)(c) and with the three-step test laid down in Article 5(5) (paras 43-45).

1100. Specifically, the decision in BGH, *Gies-Adler*.

1101. *See* Leistner (2011), p. 428.

1102. BGH, *Vorschaubilder I*, para. 30. As reported by Zimbehl (2010), p. 191: 'Since the licensing is a disposition of a right in rem, the strict requirements of such a disposition must be met. This means in particular that from an objective point of view it has to be clear that the copyright holder wants to license the use of the work. Such a disposition cannot be seen in the mere act of putting pictures on a website. And much less, if the applicant has used a copyright notice on the works.'

Nonetheless, the BGH judged Google's use non-infringing based on the argument that the plaintiff had given her 'simple consent' (*schlichte Einwilligung*).[1103] Simple consent, the BGH expounded, does not entail the actual licensing of any uses of the protected work; the user of the work is not authorised to exercise any right, nor does he benefit from any enforceable claim as a result of that consent. What simple consent does is merely to exclude the unlawfulness of the use, giving the third party a defence against copyright infringement claims. Consequently, no declaration of intent is necessary for simple consent to be established; it can be inferred from the rightholder's behaviour.[1104] The BGH concluded that the facts that the artist: (i) had made the works freely available on the Internet; (ii) without using any technical precautions; and (iii) engaging in 'search engine optimisation' were enough to infer that she has given her consent to Google's use of the works.[1105] In order to withdraw the consent, or to prevent it from being inferred in the first place, the rightholder would have to implement protection measures. Notifying the search engine operator would not suffice.[1106]

It is beyond doubt that Google's use serves 'a socially useful function, which is in the interest of internet users at large, the general public, and the majority of right holders'.[1107] The judges in Karlsruhe probably had this in mind when rendering their decision. It appeared unreasonable to declare such a valuable technology-enabled use infringing merely because the existing exceptions could not be construed to cover it. It seems that such an outcome would have left a bitter taste in the judges' mouth. Hence, so as to reach a sensible ruling[1108] and compensate for the restrictiveness of the system of exceptions, the BGH ended up assessing the permissibility of Google's use in light of a different dogmatic category. In practice, what the court did was to resort to a safety valve beyond the exceptions that are enumerated in the German Copyright Act in order to overcome 'the insurmountable fact that copyright had been violated'.[1109] The doctrine of simple consent allowed the court to strike a more appropriate balance between, on the one hand, the

---

1103. This was not the first time that the BGH resorted to this sort of construction. Before *Vorschaubilder I*, it had already held that an implied consent (*konkludente Einwilligung*) to reproduce protected works that were freely available on the Internet could be derived from the fact that those works were available online unshielded by any technical measures – BGH, *Drucker und Plotter*, paras 30-34. For an analysis of the role of implied consent in copyright law in light of the thumbnail decisions by the BGH, *see* Osken (2014). In the same vein, proposing the adoption of the implied license doctrine as a 'fine-tuning mechanism' within digital copyright law, *see* Afori (2008a).
1104. BGH, *Vorschaubilder I*, para. 34.
1105. BGH, *Vorschaubilder I*, para. 36.
1106. BGH, *Vorschaubilder I*, para. 37.
1107. Leistner (2011), p. 426.
1108. In Matthias Leistner's words, 'a fair and equitable *practical* solution' – Leistner (2011), p. 428.
1109. *See* Westkamp (2012), p. 61.

artist's exclusive right to prevent uses of her works and, on the other, the users' interest in searching for information on the Internet in an effective way.[1110] Commentators have qualified this move by the BGH as a 'substantially creative turn',[1111] a 'makeshift solution',[1112] a 'crutch',[1113] a 'legal fiction',[1114] and a 'lack of methodological honesty'.[1115,1116]

1110. The BGH had made similar considerations in a 2003 case on the lawfulness of deep linking – BGH, *Paperboy*. The case was decided on 17 July 2003, before the legislation that amended the German Copyright Act in order to bring it in line with the WIPO Treaties and the InfoSoc Directive came into force (the statute was adopted by the Bundestag on 11 April 2003, but came into force on 10 September 2003 only). The defendant operated a search engine called Paperboy, which was dedicated to freely accessible online newspaper articles. The results list of this news aggregator was composed of deep links. A deep link is a hyperlink that, instead of redirecting the user to a website's homepage, links directly to a specific page that can be found deeper in that website. The plaintiff – Verlagsgruppe, the publisher of the *Handelsblatt* newspaper and the *DM* magazine – sought injunctive relief based on copyright infringement and unfair competition. As to the alleged copyright-infringing uses, the BGH ruled that neither the right of reproduction nor the right of communication to the public were encroached upon. Regarding the reproduction right, the BGH said that a hyperlink was but an Internet address that directs the user to a protected work and, as such, it does not copy the work within the meaning of Article 16 German Copyright Act (para. 36). Therefore, because there was no *prima facie* infringement of the reproduction right, the applicability of exceptions to this right was immaterial (para. 41). It was this footnote-like nature of deep links that led the BGH to find no infringement of the right of communication to the public either, holding that it was the uploader of the (freely accessible) work that granted access to the work, not the provider of the hyperlink. The deep link merely facilitated access to a work that was already publicly accessible anyway; it would not be possible for the provider of the link to do so had the rightholder made use of TPMs (para. 56). It is crucial to note that, according to the BGH, the then-new InfoSoc Directive, in particular Article 3(1), did not affect this conclusion on the lawfulness of deep links (para. 46). Furthermore, the BGH rejected the claim that the setting of deep links, in allowing the users to bypass advertisements shown on the website's homepage, amounted to an act of unfair competition. More importantly, the BGH took the interest in the normal functioning of the Internet in due account: without search engines and the deep links they provide, navigating through the immense amount of information available on the web would be virtually impossible (para. 57).
1111. Truyens & Eecke (2016), p. 4.
1112. Leistner (2011), p. 430.
1113. Spindler (2010), p. 791.
1114. Senftleben (2013b), p. 65. The author argues that, had the German legislator implemented the quotation exception in a more flexible manner, 'this questionable expansion of the rules governing implicit consent could have been avoided' (p. 61). I have expressed doubts over this position *supra* section 3.2.5.
1115. Kleinemenke (2013b), p. 115, also calling it a 'detour' and a 'distortion'.
1116. Section 107 US Copyright Act, enshrining the fair use standard, has enabled US judges to accommodate similar uses internally, without having to resort to external doctrines. In *Perfect 10*, the US Court of Appeals for the Ninth Circuit considered Google's reproduction and making available of thumbnails of images of a men's magazine as 'highly transformative' – US Court of Appeals for the Ninth Circuit, *Perfect 10*, p. 1165. In analysing the first factor, the court argued that 'a search engine provides social benefit by incorporating an original work into a new work, namely, an electronic

In the second episode of the judicial tale of thumbnails in Germany – the *Vorschaubilder II* case –, the BGH confirmed this anti-formalist and technologically liberal approach.

The factual scenario differed from that of the first case in that it was not the author who had uploaded the copyright-protected works. Instead, the works – two photographs – were made available on third-party websites. While some website operators had been given permission to display the photographs online, the ones involved in the proceedings had not. Again, because these operators had implemented no protection measures, Google indexed the websites and displayed thumbnails of the photographs upon a user search.

The First Instance Court held in favour of the photographer,[1117] but the judgment was reversed on appeal.[1118] The dispute eventually reached the BGH, which not only reaffirmed the *Vorschaubilder I* precedent, holding that an act of making available that is prima facie infringing may be lawful where a simple consent by the rightholder may be inferred from the circumstances of the case, but also extended the scope of application of this doctrine: simple consent is available as a defence against copyright infringement where a work has been uploaded *by a third party* with the permission of the rightholder, but without taking any technical precautions against crawling and indexing by search engines. In those circumstances it may be assumed that, in licensing the use of the work, the rightholder agrees that the licensee consents on the indexing of the work by a search engine.

The rightholder claimed, however, that no authorisation had been given to the defendants in the proceedings to make the photographs available online. But the BGH went one step further: it held that simple consent might apply even where a third party has uploaded the work *without the rightholder's authorisation*. According to the BGH, the consent should be interpreted from the user's point of view. In this type of cases, the user – a search engine that crawls the Internet and indexes websites through a wholly automatic process – is unable to distinguish a work that has been made available with the necessary authorisation from one that has not. In other words, the BGH extended simple consent to cases where the work has been

---

reference tool' (p. 1165). The Ninth Circuit considered the search engine's public benefit as an information-gathering tool a decisive factor (p. 1166). The court added that it did not matter whether the indexed images were located on infringing websites, because Google was not 'intentionally misappropriat[ing] the copyright owners' works for the purpose of commercial exploitation', but 'operating a comprehensive search engine that only incidentally indexes infringing websites' (fn. 8). Hence, while in *Perfect 10* the Ninth Circuit, guided by the four statutory fair use factors, could openly balance all the relevant considerations, in *Vorschaubilder I* the BGH had to ingeniously come up with an alternative doctrine under which it could justify a balanced outcome. Using the case law on thumbnails as a starting point to highlight the relative benefits of the US fair use system, *see* Kleinemenke (2013b).

1117. Regional Court of Hamburg, *Vorschaubilder II*.

1118. Higher Regional Court of Hamburg, *Vorschaubilder II*.

illegally uploaded onto the Internet.[1119] Rightholders, the BGH clarified, would always have the possibility to act against the unauthorised uploader of the work.[1120]

The BGH's reasoning in this second instalment of the *Vorschaubilder* saga was even bolder than in the first one. Saying that the rightholder has consented to Google's use in this case is a far cry from saying that a rightholder who uploads a work online herself, without any technical precautions, has given consent. The link between the uses made by Google and the rightholder's will is significantly weaker in the former case. Unlike in *Vorschaubilder I*, it was not the rightholder who had made the images available online. However, according to the court, permission for Google's acts could be inferred from the authorisation to make the image available online given by the rightholder to a third party that was not the one who had uploaded the images from which the thumbnails at stake stemmed (and that was not the defendant in the proceedings). It would therefore seem that, under this reasoning, the rightholder's consent to search engine indexing and making available could be inferred as long as the rightholder had granted authorisation to upload the work to *any* third party.[1121]

*5.2.1.2 General Principles of Civil Law (*Megakini.com*)*

Search engine caching is yet another technological use that has prompted European national courts to look for discretion outside copyright law. The paradigmatic defendant in these cases is, again, Google. When crawling the web, Google's robots store on Google's own servers an archived version of

1119. Ohly (2014), p. 65, while deeming the decision in *Vorschaubilder I* 'dogmatically tenable', sees no justification for this extension of consent in *Vorschaubilder II*. In a commentary on the decision, Clark (2012), p. 789, argues that this question has not been fully addressed, because '[n]either *Vorschaubilder I* nor *Vorschaubilder II* concerned cases where images had been made publicly available via the internet without the copyright owner ever granting permission to anyone'. In those cases, where the rightholder has *never* authorised the making available of her works, can the search engine still rely on simple consent? Years later, in the *Vorschaubilder III* case, the BGH addressed a related situation. The plaintiff in that case had made available a series of photographs on a password-protected website. Some of these photographs were downloaded by users and illegally re-uploaded onto password-free websites. As a result, Google's system indexed the images and made thumbnails thereof available via Google Images. The question was whether this use by Google amounted to a violation of the plaintiff's right of communication to the public under Section 15(2) German Copyright Act. Relying on the CJEU's judgment in *GS Media*, the BGH decided in favour of Google, highlighting the particular importance of search services for the functioning of the Internet. For commentary on the decision, *see* Nordemann (2018).

1120. BGH, *Vorschaubilder II*, paras 31-32.

1121. *See* Geiger & Schönherr (2014), p. 124. As a side note, it may be added that this reasoning is hardly compatible with Article 3(3) InfoSoc Directive, pursuant to which the right of communication to the public is not subject to exhaustion. In that regard, *see* CJEU, *Renckhoff*, paras 32-33, and CJEU, *Tom Kabinet*, para. 33.

every website they index (the cached copy). This repository of websites' cached copies is called the Google Cache. These copies are also made available in the search engine's list of results, via a link placed next to the title of the website in question. This cache service allows users to visit websites that have been changed or taken down by their operators, who nonetheless have the option to block Google's caching.

Google Cache gave copyright aficionados what is arguably the definitive illustration of flexible judicial decision-making in this field – the *Megakini.com* case. In *Megakini*, Spanish courts, in particular the Spanish Supreme Court, have unabashedly ruled in contradiction with the statutory text, showing greater concern with the practical implications of the decision than with the consistency with the applicable legal materials.[1122]

In 2006, the operator of www.megakini.com, a gaming and betting website, brought a claim against Google Spain on grounds of infringement of exclusive rights over the contents of the website, seeking damages and an injunction to suspend the operation of Google's main search engine through the address www.google.es. The questions of law that courts had to answer related both to Google's main search engine and to its cache service: is there a copyright infringement: (i) in the reproduction and making available of snippets of Megakini's contents when the website appeared in the search engine results list and (ii) in the making available of a copy of the Megakini website in the Google Cache[1123]? All three courts – the First Instance, the Court of Appeals, and the Supreme Court – held in favour of Google, though relying on distinct arguments. I will examine each of the judgments in turn.

In dismissing Megakini's claims, the lower court stressed the fact that the operator could have made use of the possibility of blocking the indexation of his website and that it failed to do so with the implicit purpose of ensuring the widest possible dissemination of his website. Interestingly, the court added that the use of parts of website contents by search engines was a 'tolerated social use',[1124] which was, moreover, the only way to provide users with an effective search service. From the statutory standpoint, the lower court cited three rules: the rule privileging acts of temporary reproduction; the rule transposing the safe harbour for proxy caching provided in Article 13 E-Commerce Directive; and a specific Spanish rule containing a safe harbour for search engine/linking. An 'integrated interpretation' of these provisions led the court to conclude that Google's use of

1122. For a detailed analysis of the Spanish Supreme Court's decision, as well as of the lower courts', *see* Xalabarder (2012b). *See also* Fernández (2013).

1123. Google's web crawlers also copy the HTML code of the websites they visit. However, both parties agreed that this reproduction, inasmuch as it serves the purpose of indexing the websites to facilitate the requested searches, was privileged under Article 31(1) Spanish IP Code, which implemented the temporary reproduction exception provided in Article 5(1) InfoSoc Directive.

1124. Commercial Court No. 5 of Barcelona, *Megakini.com*, p. 4.

Megakini's contents did not infringe on the exclusive rights over such contents.[1125]

The Appellate Court upheld the conclusion reached by the Court of First Instance, but on substantially different grounds.[1126] As to the reproduction and making available of the snippets, the court considered them too ephemeral, incidental, and minimal to be held infringing. As to the main question – whether the making available of a copy of the website in the cache service was (un)lawful –, the court rejected the applicability of: (i) the temporary reproduction exception, because the act was neither necessary for the search engine to work, nor temporary, since the copy was often available even after the website had been modified by its operator; (ii) the safe harbour for proxy caching, because, given that Google is not an Internet access provider, the act was not performed in the context of a transmission service; and (iii) the safe harbour for search engines and linking, in that, although it evidently applied to search engine operators like Google, it served to exempt them from secondary liability for any infringement that occurred at the level of linked websites, while the question was whether the display of thumbnails amounted to primary (not secondary) infringement.

The court nonetheless declined to find infringement. To justify its decision, the court summoned a startling arsenal of doctrinal weaponry: the three-step test, the US fair use standard, and the *ius usus inocui* doctrine. According to the court, the three-step test ought to be read both in positive and negative terms, that is, as imposing limits not only on the scope of copyright exceptions but also on the scope of exclusive rights themselves. The court compared its construction with having the *ius usus inocui* doctrine – a property law doctrine that allows innocuous uses of movable and immovable property by third parties – translating into the IP domain, in order to avoid an abusive exercise of rights. As if the court had not been sufficiently inventive, it added that, in determining the harm caused by the use, judges should be guided by the fair use doctrine. The four factors were then expressly discussed.

The court thus brought a doctrine external to copyright law (*ius usus inocui*), as well as a foreign copyright doctrine (fair use), to bear on its reading of a provision enshrined in Spanish copyright law (the three-step test). The search for flexibility was conducted both *outside* and *inside* the copyright system of exceptions. Moreover, in a showing of judicial candor, the court admitted that its decision was ultimately guided by 'common sense'.[1127] Common sense, the court stated, should prevent courts from banning a use that not only does not harm the rightholder, but actually benefits her, by fostering her (implicit) goal of disseminating the contents as widely as possible.

1125. Commercial Court No. 5 of Barcelona, *Megakini.com*, p. 5.
1126. Court of Appeal of Barcelona, *Megakini.com*.
1127. Court of Appeal of Barcelona, *Megakini.com*, p. 5.

The tone of candor and realism marked the Spanish Supreme Court judgment as well. By way of introduction, the court stated that Megakini's operator presented his claim 'as if anything that is not written down in the statutory text is inexistent'.[1128] The court disagreed with the operator's view: general principles of law ought to be observed, particularly in cases that are not expressly regulated or that involve legal antinomies. The court added that the discrepancy between the reasoning of the First Instance and that of the Appellate Court illustrates the need for a special effort in interpreting written laws and asked whether such laws 'should be so precise, even in the case of a closed catalogue of exceptions, as to contemplate what is obvious and elementary'.[1129]

The court began the dispute's legal analysis by saying that it was clear that the exception for acts of temporary reproduction did not cover the making available of the cached copies by Google. This much seems obvious, although unmentioned by the Appellate Court: the exception covers acts of *reproduction*, not acts of making available such as that under consideration in the case.

What is less uncontroversial is the court's reading of the three-step test, which is similar to the one made by the Court of Appeals. According to the Supreme Court, Article 40bis Spanish IP Act, which lays down the test, has not only a 'negative interpretative value' but also a 'positive' one.[1130] The court construed the test as a special manifestation of the *ius usus inocui* doctrine, the principle of good faith, the abuse of rights doctrine, and the constitutional configuration of property as a right with limits. Megakini's claim, the court maintained, was not aimed at protecting the rightholder's exclusive rights; its fundamental purpose was to harm Google, by seeking suspension of the operation of its search engine, without any benefit for the claimant (beyond fame and monetary compensation). In fact, Megakini's initial petition not only omitted any allegation about the harm caused to the operator's exclusive rights, it also felt like a manifesto against Google as a 'corporate giant'.[1131]

Though acknowledging that copyright exceptions ought to be strictly interpreted, the court reasoned that none of the exceptions precluded the application of general doctrines. Resorting to these doctrines did not entail the judicial creation of a new exception. Rather, a closed list of exceptions should not go as far as acquiescing to 'absurd hypotheses', and the interpretation of the applicable provisions should not favour arbitrary claims that are aimed at harming others with no benefit for the claimant.[1132] For

1128. Spanish Supreme Court, *Megakini.com*, p. 9.
1129. Spanish Supreme Court, *Megakini.com*, p. 10.
1130. Spanish Supreme Court, *Megakini.com*, p. 10.
1131. Spanish Supreme Court, *Megakini.com*, pp. 10-11.
1132. Spanish Supreme Court, *Megakini.com*, p. 11.

these reasons, the Spanish Supreme Court found that Google's use was non-infringing.[1133]

There are diverging views among copyright scholars over the appropriateness of the court's approach. Raquel Xalabarder qualified the ruling as 'a major success in favour of a flexible interpretation and application of the copyright statutes, especially in the scenarios raised by new technologies and market agents'.[1134] The decision led her to wonder whether a fair-use-style standard was actually needed in European copyright law at all.[1135] Martin Senftleben, on the other hand, commented on the decision in less approving terms, accusing the court's reasoning of being opaque.[1136] They both agree on one point, however: that the appeal to general principles of civil law in *Megakini.com* was but a way of evading the stringent framework of copyright exceptions and producing a reasonable outcome through the backdoor.[1137]

The conclusion that emerges from the *Megakini.com* and *Vorschaubilder* cases is that the only reason why external doctrines need to be applied is the lack of adequately malleable solutions within the copyright system. The greatest advantage of external tools like the ones discussed above seems to be their 'pathological function'[1138] – they raise awareness around the fact that something is wrong with copyright law and that reform is needed.[1139]

1133. From the point of view of factual background, the American counterpart of *Megakini* is the case US District Court of Nevada, *Field*. Plaintiff Blake Field knew he could opt out of Google Cache but he deliberately refrained from doing so. Later, he sued Google, arguing that the company infringed on his copyright, because it copied and made available cached copies of websites where he published his own works. The District Court of Nevada found that Blake Field had granted Google an implied license to display the cached links. Interestingly, four years before the BGH decision in *Vorschaubilder I*, a US court similarly considered that the fact that the rightholder refrained from using meta-tags to prevent web crawlers from making cached copies of the pages was conclusive enough to amount to an implied license granted to the search engine operator. Google also successfully invoked the fair use doctrine. Apart from the four factors listed in Section 107 US Copyright Act, the Court took into account an additional factor: Google's good faith in operating its cache system, shown by its prompt removal of Field's cached pages when it learned that Field did not want them online.
1134. Xalabarder (2012b), p. 162.
1135. *See* Xalabarder (2012b), p. 166.
1136. *See* Senftleben (2013b), p. 79. *See also* Rodríguez-Cano (2017), p. 120, stating that the decision introduced some 'ambiguity' regarding the function of the three-step test.
1137. *See* Senftleben (2013b), p. 83, and Xalabarder (2012b), p. 162.
1138. Caron (1998), p. 66. *See also* Hugenholtz (1997), p. 8 ('If courts were to routinely resort to other bodies of the law to impose limits on the copyright monopoly, this would be a sign of crisis').
1139. In arguing in favour of the application of the UK public interest defence as a 'safety valve' allowing the unauthorised use of protected works when the use is not privileged by the listed exceptions, Jonathan Griffiths qualifies the idea according to which copyright disputes are to be solved only within the internal framework of copyright as

As cogently argued by renowned scholars, the instruments of balance should be included *within copyright law*.[1140] Copyright law has always included a series of provisions intended to accommodate interests that compete with those of rightholders, namely limitations to the scope of protection and exceptions to the exclusive rights.[1141] Moreover, there are benefits in copyright law being a self-contained field of law: in Thomas Dreier's words, it is made 'user-friendly (relevant legislation can be found easily)', 'more transparent (it is possible to understand what the legislature has done)', and 'more acceptable (the legislature is accountable for its actions)'.[1142] By contrast, reconciling competing interests of copyright stakeholders by relying on other bodies of law 'tends to fragmentise and obscure what should be a coherent body of law',[1143] with detrimental effects upon legal certainty.

In some cases, the application of external doctrines to copyright disputes requires somewhat artificial and controversial legal reasoning. Where courts have made use of these civil law doctrines, they have been accused of overextending them[1144] or of resorting to 'legal fictions'.[1145] For those concerned with the guidance value of the law, it seems preferable to have copyright disputes resolved internally rather than externally. Seeking flexibility within, instead of outside, copyright law is the most certainty-enhancing path. Even though these doctrines may provide some breathing space in specific contexts, they are not the natural *locus* for balancing the relevant interests in copyright law.

To be sure, in the absence of legislative reform, the helpfulness of non-copyright doctrines should not be neglected.[1146] But they should nevertheless be regarded as mechanisms of last resort that are only necessary because the copyright system *itself* fails to provide a balanced answer to

---

'unrealistically doctrinaire' – Griffiths (2014b), p. 298. However, the idea that the internal resolution of disputes is the best solution can only be considered unrealistically doctrinaire if the *status quo* is taken as a given, that is, if copyright law fails to incorporate a norm or set of norms that ensures the effective protection of competing and evolving interests. Griffiths himself seems to concede that an internal mechanism would be preferable, when he claims that the UK's public interest defence could serve as a model for a flexible norm in a possible EU regulation on copyright – *see* Griffiths (2014b), p. 308.

1140. *See* Dreier (2001) and Hugenholtz & Senftleben (2011), p. 12.
1141. *See* Dreier (2001), pp. 303-309.
1142. Dreier (2001), p. 311.
1143. Dreier (2001), p. 311.
1144. *See* Leistner (2011), p. 440.
1145. *See* Senftleben (2013), citing *Vorschaubilder I* and *Megakini.com* among the examples of judgments that rest on doubtful extensions of non-copyright doctrines. *See also* Geiger (2004a), pp. 390-391 (noting that, in most cases, it will be very challenging for the user to successfully demonstrate that the rightholder engaged in abusive conduct) and Westkamp (2012), p. 62 (in relation to the extension of the implied license doctrine).
1146. In this sense, *see* Metzger (2010), p. 122.

certain problems. They are, as commentators have deemed them, 'exceptional corrective measure[s]',[1147] '"emergency" solutions'[1148] or 'makeshift arrangement[s]'[1149] capable of delivering 'first aid'[1150] in some cases – cases that are 'symptomatic of a legal system that lacks an appropriate escape valve'.[1151] What is more, insofar as these external doctrines are not harmonised at the EU level and may therefore be accepted in some Member States but not in others, their independent application by national courts may negatively affect the goal of harmonisation.[1152]

None of this is to say that it is an easy task to determine how to best achieve the desideratum of technological adaptability, while at the same time preserving a measure of predictability. What is self-evident, however, is that the issue would be best addressed by copyright law itself.

5.2.2 Pragmatism at the CJEU Level

Like national courts, the CJEU has occasionally been bypassing the constraints imposed by the InfoSoc framework of exceptions in order to render somewhat pragmatic or flexible judgments. Unlike national courts in the rulings analysed above, however, the Court, in its typically minimalist and detached style of reasoning,[1153] tends to refrain from appealing to external doctrines (not least because some of them may not be harmonised).

The present section discusses selected judgments with the purpose of illustrating that trend in the CJEU's behaviour. The section is divided into three parts, according to the technique used by the Court to minimise or avoid the restrictive character of the InfoSoc framework of exceptions. The first part builds on section 3.3 of Chapter 2 (on strict interpretation) and examines cases in which the Court interpreted the relevant exceptions in a purposive way, often guided by the fundamental rights laid down in the Charter (section 5.2.2.1). The second part analyses the *Ulmer* judgment, where the Court read an 'ancillary right' into an exception that seemingly did not include it (section 5.2.2.2). Finally, the third part looks at cases where the Court either dispensed with the analysis of the three-step test or engaged in a summarised assessment thereof (section 5.2.2.3).

1147. Guibault (1998), p. 49. *See also* Caron (1998b), p. 8, and Geiger (2004a), p. 390, referring to the doctrine of abuse of rights. Caron (1998b), pp. 28-36, nonetheless, praises the doctrine's suppleness and flexibility.
1148. Leistner (2011), p. 440.
1149. Senftleben (2013), p. 77.
1150. Hugenholtz & Senftleben (2011), p. 2.
1151. Hugenholtz & Senftleben (2011), p. 12.
1152. *See* Westkamp (2012), pp. 61-64.
1153. *See*, *e.g.*, Weiler (2001), p. 224 (calling the CJEU's style 'cryptic' and 'Cartesian'); Perju (2009), p. 310 (noting that '[i]ts justificatory style has often been criticized as overly abstract, vague, and elliptical'); and Búrca (2013), p. 184 (describing the Court's discourse as 'self-referential and detached').

5.2.2.1 Purposive and Fundamental-Rights-Guided Interpretation of Exceptions

The CJEU has been mitigating the traditional canon of strict interpretation in recent years. The process began with the recognition, in successive rulings, that the task of interpretation must also take into account the exceptions' effectiveness and the observance of their purpose.[1154] This is consistent with the Court's settled case law according to which the interpretation of a provision of EU law should consider not only its wording, but also its context and *the objectives pursued.*[1155]

In the copyright domain, *Premier League* was the first case in which the CJEU engaged in an explicit departure of the canon of strict interpretation. The dispute in the main proceedings focused on the use, by a pub owner in the UK, of foreign satellite decoders in order to receive the broadcasts of Premier League football matches. The questions that were relevant for copyright purposes were those that concerned the use of the broadcasts containing the matches once they were received.[1156] The issue was whether the creation of transient sequential fragments of protected subject matter within the memory of a satellite decoder and on a TV screen, which are immediately effaced and replaced by the next fragments, was a restricted act under the InfoSoc Directive.[1157] Having determined that the right of reproduction in Article 2 could extend to such transient fragments (provided that they contain elements that meet the originality standard set forth in *Infopaq I*[1158]), the CJEU went on to analyse the applicability of the temporary reproduction exception.

The Court started by noting that the five conditions that must be fulfilled for a copy to be privileged under that exception 'must be interpreted strictly, because Article 5(1) of the Copyright Directive is a derogation from the general rule established by that directive that the copyright holder must authorise any reproduction of his protected work'.[1159] In the following paragraph, however, the Court conceded the departure from this traditional canon: 'None the less, the interpretation of those conditions must enable the effectiveness of the exception thereby established to be safeguarded and permit observance of the exception's purpose as resulting in particular from

---

1154. The European Parliament too has advocated that 'exceptions and limitations must be applied in such a way as to take account of the purpose for which they were designed' – EP Resolution Implementation InfoSoc Directive 2015, para. 35.
1155. *See* CJEU, *SGAE*, para. 34 (and case law cited therein). On the structure of teleological arguments in law, *see* Alexy (1989), pp. 240-244.
1156. *See* CJEU, *Premier League*, paras 57-146. The reception of encrypted broadcasts from other Member States raised a series of other questions on the interpretation of the Conditional Access Directive and the Treaty rules on the free movement of goods and services and competition law.
1157. *See* CJEU, *Premier League*, paras 147-152.
1158. *See* CJEU, *Premier League*, paras 153-159.
1159. CJEU, *Premier League*, para. 162.

recital 31 in the preamble to the Copyright Directive.'[1160] The purpose of the exception for acts of temporary reproduction, added the Court, is to 'allow and ensure the development and operation of new technologies' and to 'safeguard a fair balance between the rights and interests of right holders, on the one hand, and of users of protected works who wish to avail themselves of those new technologies, on the other'.[1161]

It was against these purposes that the Court interpreted the relevant conditions of Article 5(1). It was undisputed that the act was temporary, transient, or incidental, and formed an integral and essential part of a technological process. The Court's analysis was therefore focused on the remaining conditions.

The first such condition requires the copies to have as their sole purpose the enabling (a) of a transmission in a network between third parties by an intermediary *or* (b) a lawful use of protected subject matter. In this regard, the Court concluded that the ephemeral acts of reproduction at stake enabled the satellite decoder and the TV screen to function correctly. As the mere reception of the broadcasts containing the matches was not a restricted act under EU or UK law, the Court found that the condition was fulfilled.[1162]

Where the CJEU seemed to go beyond the plain meaning of the statutory language, reading it in light of the exception's purpose was in the analysis of the final condition, which requires that the acts of reproduction have no independent economic significance. The Court acknowledged that the copies in this case necessarily have economic significance, in that they make the access to the broadcasts and their visual display possible.[1163] But the Court placed special emphasis on the need for that economic significance to be *independent* for the condition not to be fulfilled. Independence means, in the Court's interpretation, that the economic advantage derived from the acts of temporary reproduction must go beyond the economic advantage derived from the reception of the broadcasts.[1164] In support of the finding that the economic significance of the copies in the satellite decoder and TV screen is *not* independent, the Court stated that such copies 'form an inseparable and non-autonomous part of the process of reception' and that they are performed 'without the influence or even awareness' of the persons receiving the broadcasts.[1165]

1160. CJEU, *Premier League*, para. 163.
1161. CJEU, *Premier League*, para. 164.
1162. *See* CJEU, *Premier League*, paras 169-173.
1163. *See* CJEU, *Premier League*, para. 174.
1164. *See* CJEU, *Premier League*, para. 175.
1165. CJEU, *Premier League*, paras 175-176. It ought to be noted that in paras 176-177 the CJEU seems to merge this requirement with the 'integral and essential part of a technological process' requirement. In the Court's own words, 'the temporary acts of reproduction, carried out within the memory of the satellite decoder and on the television screen, form an inseparable and non-autonomous part of the process of reception of the broadcasts transmitted containing the works in question. Furthermore,

This conclusion could plausibly be disputed. After all, the ephemeral reproductions carried out on the TV screen are the primary source of economic value in this technological process. It is because of such reproductions, and *only* because of them, that viewers are interested in the broadcasts. For this reason, these on-screen copies, unlike those that take place in the satellite decoder, arguably do not occur below the awareness of viewers. However, such a strict interpretation, as the Court implicitly admitted, would produce an absurd outcome: TV viewers using modern sets could be prevented from receiving broadcasts if they lacked the authorisation of rightholders.[1166] Concerned with this result, the Court opted for a purposive and consequentialist interpretation of Article 5(1).

After *Premier League*, the CJEU kept following the rhetorical strategy of citing the rule of strict interpretation, even where it ended up construing the relevant exceptions in a somewhat broad manner in light of their purpose.[1167]

The *PRCA* judgment is a case in point.[1168] The case was related with the applicability of the temporary reproduction exception to on-screen and cached copies of webpages made by an end-user in the course of browsing the Internet. The thorniest issue, which the Court deliberately left to the end, was whether the on-screen copies met the 'transient or incidental' condition. Somewhat surprisingly, the Court concluded that the on-screen copies qualified as 'transient'. The surprise arises from the fact that, in *Infopaq I*, the Court had stated that an act would be considered transient within the meaning of the second condition: (i) if its duration was limited to what was necessary for the proper completion of the technological process in question and (ii) if the copy was eliminated automatically without human intervention.[1169] In *PRCA*, the Court departed from this interpretation, by stating that 'the requirement of automatic deletion does not preclude such a deletion from being preceded by human intervention directed at terminating the use of the technological process'.[1170] This new reading allowed the Court to hold that the on-screen copies were not deleted by the end-user, but *by the*

they are performed without influence, or even awareness, on the part of the persons thereby having access to the protected works.' From this the Court seems to extract the conclusion that the copies have no independent economic significance: 'Consequently, those temporary acts of reproduction are not capable of generating an additional economic advantage going beyond the advantage derived from mere reception of the broadcasts at issue.'

1166. *See* CJEU, *Premier League*, para. 179.

1167. *But see, e.g.*, CJEU, *VCAST*, para. 32.

1168. The Court invoked the canon of strict interpretation, but cited *Premier League* in support of the need for a teleological interpretation right after – *see* CJEU, *PRCA*, para. 23. *See also* CJEU, *Spiegel Online*, paras 53-55 (in relation to Article 5 exceptions in general), and CJEU, *VOB*, para. 50 (in relation to the derogation provided in Article 6(1) Rental and Lending Directive).

1169. *See* CJEU, *Infopaq I*, para. 64.

1170. CJEU, *PRCA*, para. 41.

computer, though only at the moment when the end-user closed or moved away from the webpage.[1171] The Court added that 'it is irrelevant … that the on-screen copy remains in existence for as long as the internet users keeps his browser open and stays on the website concerned because, during that period, the technological process used for viewing that site remains active'.[1172] Given that it was the act of the end-user that determined, in and of itself, the deletion of the on-screen copies, this reasoning can only be qualified as a judicial sleight of hand. It nonetheless enabled the Court to 'save the Internet',[1173] by exempting on-screen copies from the need for rightholders' permission and furthering the purpose of ensuring technological operation and development.

In more recent rulings, the Court developed this teleological approach to InfoSoc exceptions in light of an added dimension – that of fundamental rights.[1174]

In *Painer*, the CJEU was asked, *inter alia*, whether the InfoSoc quotation exception was applicable where a press report that quotes protected

1171. *See* CJEU, *PRCA*, para. 44.
1172. CJEU, *PRCA*, para. 45.
1173. *See* Sherrell & Smith (2014).
1174. The approach evokes the doctrine of the indirect horizontal effect of fundamental rights. This doctrine entails that private parties in a dispute may invoke their fundamental rights against the court as law-interpreter, which ought to construe the relevant ordinary law in respect for the requirements of fundamental rights. Commonly regarded as having been founded by the BVerfG in the famous *Lüth* case, the doctrine of indirect horizontal effect has been recognized by most European countries. National courts have interpreted copyright exceptions in conformity with fundamental rights and freedoms. The BVerfG, in the *Germania 3* case, found support for a broad interpretation of the quotation exception in the constitutionally protected freedom of artistic expression, rendering non-infringing the unauthorised use of passages from two plays by Bertolt Brecht beyond the exception's limits – BVerfG, *Germania 3*. But the appeal to fundamental rights in a private dispute (i.e., between a rightholder and an unlicensed user) may come in a different shape. Fundamental rights may be invoked as having direct horizontal effects, meaning, e.g., that the unauthorised user raises her freedom of expression as a separate defence against the rightholder, in an attempt to escape liability. In the Dutch case *Scientology/Spaink*, journalist Karin Spaink successfully invoked her freedom of expression under Article 10 ECHR as a defence against copyright infringement for having posted documents of the Church of Scientology on her website – *see* Court of Appeal of The Hague, *Scientology/Spaink*, and, reporting on the decision, Daalen (2003) and Hugenholtz & Senftleben (2011), p. 11. This, however, seems to be a 'marginal trend', not least because the direct horizontal effect is generally rejected by national and supranational fundamental rights instruments – Guibault (1998), p. 44. For instance, Article 1(3) German Basic Law states that fundamental rights 'shall bind the legislature, the executive and the judiciary', and Article 51 Charter provides that its provisions are addressed at EU institutions and bodies, as well as at Member States when implementing EU law, thus excluding private actors. As observed by Deursen & Snijders (2018), p. 1088, so far the CJEU has never applied a fundamental right 'as an autonomous ground for the justification of a prima facie copyright infringement'.

content is not in itself a literary work protected by copyright.[1175] The underlying national case concerned the unauthorised publication by media outlets of a portrait photograph in the context of a search for a kidnapped girl. In answering the question, the Court, following *Premier League*, noted that the quotation exception must be interpreted in light of its purpose, which is to strike a fair balance between the freedom of expression of users and the protection of copyright.[1176] This was the first time that the CJEU acknowledged the role that fundamental rights should play in the interpretation of copyright exceptions. In the context of the referred question, the Court concluded that the users' freedom of expression should prevail over the interests of authors, provided that the author's name is indicated (if possible), and, therefore, that the quotation exception may apply where the press report quoting the content is not protected by copyright.[1177]

Since *Painer*, the CJEU has consistently been looking for guidance in the Charter[1178] in construing copyright exceptions and the copyright *acquis* in general,[1179] in a process that has been called one of 'constitutionalisation' of copyright law.[1180] In the field of exceptions, the Court has held, in *DR & TV2 Danmark*, that a broad interpretation of the ephemeral recordings exception found support the broadcasting organisations' freedom to conduct their business and, in *Deckmyn*, that the application of the parody exception must achieve a fair balance between, on the one hand, the interests and rights of copyright holders and, on the other, the freedom of expression of users. Of course, depending on the exception at stake, other fundamental rights may be relevant.[1181]

1175. *See* CJEU, *Painer*, paras 129-137.
1176. *See* CJEU, *Painer*, para. 134.
1177. *See* CJEU, *Painer*, paras 135-136. It is doubtful whether the Court needed to appeal to freedom of expression in order to reach this conclusion. As the judges themselves acknowledged, Article 5(3)(d) includes no requirement that a work must be quoted as part of a literary work protected by copyright (para. 130).
1178. With the adoption of the Lisbon Treaty, the Charter was granted the same legal status as the Treaties [Article 6(1) TEU] and has since become the main fundamental rights instrument in the case law of the CJEU.
1179. In the domain of exclusive rights, the Court has conceded in *GS Media* that qualifying all hyperlinks to works made freely available without the rightholder's permission would have highly restrictive consequences for freedom of expression and information – *see* CJEU, *GS Media*, paras 44-46. This and other fundamental rights and freedoms, like the right to the protection of private and family life (Article 7 Charter), the right to the protection of personal data (Article 8 Charter), and the freedom to conduct a business (Article 16 Charter), have also been raised by the CJEU to scrutinize remedies granted in cases of infringement – *see* the CJEU judgments in *Promusicae*, and, after the Lisbon Treaty came into force, *Scarlet*, *Netlog*, *UPC Telekabel*, *McFadden*, *Bastei Lübbe*, *Coty Germany* and *New Wave*.
1180. *See* Geiger (2006a); Griffiths (2013) and (2017); Mylly (2015); and Schovsbo (2015).
1181. For instance, in *Renckhoff*, AG Campos Sánchez-Bordona interpreted the exception in Article 5(3)(a) InfoSoc Directive in light of the right to education in Article 14 Charter – *see* AG Opinion, *Renckhoff*, paras 109-121.

In the 2019 triad of references made by the BGH, the CJEU confirmed that national courts, in applying copyright exceptions, must rely on an interpretation that, while consistent with their wording and safeguarding their effectiveness, fully adheres to the fundamental rights enshrined in the Charter.[1182] This need to interpret exceptions in light of fundamental rights standards seems to have influenced the Court's analysis of the scope of the relevant exceptions in each case.

In *Funke Medien*, the Court ruled that the publication of confidential reports by a media organisation – assuming that they amounted to protected works and that there had thus been a prima facie copyright infringement – was capable of falling within the exception for the reporting of current events. This was so because the reports had been presented on the newspaper's website in a structured form and in conjunction with an introductory note, further links, and a space for comments.[1183] The fact that the reports contained information on matters of public interest seemed to play a factor in the interpretation.[1184]

In *Pelham*, the Court considered sampling a form of artistic expression covered by the freedom of the arts guaranteed by Article 13 Charter.[1185] It then read the InfoSoc quotation exception in light of such provision to conclude that where the creator of a new musical work uses a sound sample taken from a phonogram which is *recognisable* to the ear in that new work, the use of that sample may amount to a quotation, provided that the remaining conditions in Article 5(3)(d) are met.[1186]

In *Spiegel Online*, which involved the making available of a politician's essays on morally controversial issues, the Court highlighted that the rationale of the exception for the reporting of current events is to contribute to the exercise of the freedom of information and the freedom of the media and that 'the purpose of the press, in a democratic society governed by the rule of law, justifies it in informing the public, without restrictions other than those that are strictly necessary'.[1187] Based on this, the Court rejected the idea that the exception for the reporting of current events includes a requirement that the user must seek the authorisation of the rightholder where reasonably possible.[1188]

1182. *See* CJEU, *Funke Medien*, para. 76, and CJEU, *Spiegel Online*, para. 59.
1183. *See* CJEU, *Funke Medien*, para. 75.
1184. *See* CJEU, *Funke Medien*, at [74].
1185. *See* CJEU, *Pelham*, at [35].
1186. *See* CJEU, *Pelham*, para. 72. As mentioned above, one such condition is that requiring the user to have the intention of establishing an intellectual dialogue with the work from which the sample was taken (paras 71 and 73).
1187. *See* CJEU, *Spiegel Online*, paras 45 and 72.
1188. *See* CJEU, *Spiegel Online*, para. 73.

Putting aside the question of its legitimacy,[1189] the practice of engaging in a purpose-bound and fundamental-rights-guided interpretation of copyright exceptions couched in relatively precise language gives judges leeway they would otherwise lack. Since the purposes of the law are generally open-ended, this teleological approach ends up compounding vagueness into statutory language. This has allowed the CJEU to grant a wider scope to some InfoSoc exceptions than that which would have been attained through a purely strict interpretation thereof and, as a consequence, to accommodate some uses that would otherwise arguably fall outside the scope of the relevant exceptions.[1190] But despite the 'pragmatic benefits' of purposive interpretations, they are but a next-to-best solution,[1191] for at least three reasons.

First, disagreement on the correct interpretation of copyright exceptions has historically been pervasive.[1192] Although it was generally accepted in the literature that exceptions, as restrictions to the rule of exclusivity, were to be interpreted in a strict fashion,[1193] some scholars started disputing this idea, arguing that the formal cloaking of a provision as an exception should not by

1189. The question is whether the principle of separation of powers is threatened by judicial behaviour of this kind. Zimmermann (1997), p. 321, sees no major issues, provided courts do not openly contradict the mandates of the law ('[t]he doctrine of separation of powers ... is not violated by the emergence of thick layers of case law in the interstices of codes and statutes: as long as judicial law-making *contra legem* is not (openly) tolerated, the prerogative of the democratically elected legislature remains substantially unaffected'). Peukert (2015), p. 147, however, referring specifically to IP cases, is of the view that deciding such cases 'directly on the basis of balancing fundamental rights runs afoul of the principle of separation of powers'.

1190. *See* Deursen & Snijders (2018), p. 1088 ('the CJEU has extended the scope of the limitations by interpreting their conditions in a more lenient way, especially in cases in which emerging technologies require so'). Commentators have praised the deflation of the influence of the rule of strict interpretation in CJEU's case law. According to Raquel Xalabarder, alternative methodological options, such as purpose-bound interpretations of listed exceptions, 'have allowed the Court to introduce some much-needed flexibility at a time when copyright laws are not always prepared to meet the challenges posed by technologically changing contexts' – Xalabarder (2016), p. 635.

1191. *See* Griffiths (2017), p. 25, according to whom the constitutionalisation of copyright law 'brings certain pragmatic benefits. Legislative reform of copyright law has become difficult because it takes place in such a hotly contested policy environment and the process of constitutionalisation provides courts with powerful tools to develop the law *in the absence of legislative instruction*' (emphasis added).

1192. *See* Spoor (1998), p. 31, reporting on the national diversity of approaches to the interpretation of exceptions.

1193. *See* Schricker (1997), p. 139 (*de lege lata*, provisions on exceptions must be interpreted narrowly and may not be analogically applied); Lucas (1998), p. 171 (new exceptions that have not been expressly laid down in statute cannot be admitted); and Cohen Jehoram (2005a), p. 360 (copyright exceptions are 'indeed exceptions to the main rules of the rights' and should, as such, be narrowly interpreted).

itself trigger the application of the rule of strict interpretation.[1194] Nowadays, most commentators see that interpretative mantra as misguided and acknowledge that exceptions can be interpreted holistically, taking into account *inter alia* their underlying purpose, which may be informed by fundamental rights.[1195]

1194. *See* Hugenholtz (1997), p. 5 ('the principle of narrow construction of copyright exemptions, so often found in copyright treatises and case law, is ill-conceived'); Spoor (1998), p. 30 ('it cannot be excluded off-hand that different interpretation rules may apply to foreseen and unforeseen situations'); Hoeren (2000), pp. 4-5 (criticising what he called 'the dogma of strict interpretation', but pointing out that German courts never really adhered to it); and Cornish (2004), p. 46 (calling the idea that exceptions should be construed narrowly a *non sequitur*). It is important to point out in this regard that legal methodologists had been expressing their scepticism regarding the strict interpretation of exceptions for some time – *see* Müller (1996), p. 274 (the rule is 'pseudo-normative' and based on circular reasoning); and Larenz (2012), pp. 502-503 (the rule has only a 'limited value' and does not entail that the provision must be interpreted as strictly as possible or that its analogical application is proscribed in all cases).

    This interpretative rule has also been rejected by courts in copyright disputes. The Supreme Court of The Netherlands in the famous 1995 judgment *Dior* held that, in the absence of an exception that could apply to the facts of the case, the conduct at stake could nonetheless be exempted using one or more of the existing exceptions as a point of reference (para. 3.6.2). The relatively precise exceptions could therefore be invoked as a model for the establishment of new privileges. In the UK, the Court of Appeal of England and Wales stated, in *Newspaper Licensing Agency* and in *Pro Sieben*, that the fair dealing exceptions for criticism or review and reporting of current events should be 'interpreted liberally'. In Germany, the BVerfG, *Kunstausstellung im Online-Archiv*, para. 18, held that exceptions – *in casu*, the exception for news reporting in Section 50 German Copyright Act – must be interpreted according to their wording, context and purpose.

1195. *See* Riis & Schovsbo (2007), p. 4. (making the argument that, in a copyright system where the interests of users and authors have equal weight, the rule of strict interpretation 'cannot be justified'); Geiger (2008a), pp. 192-193 ('In the search for a just balance between the different interests involved …, such rules of interpretation that *a priori* favour the right holders seem unjustified'); Ohly (2009), p. 239 ('When interpreting copyright law none of the interests involved should prima facie prevail'); Griffiths (2010a), p. 88 ('In the face of rapidly changing technological conditions, it seems foolhardy to set in place a firm predisposition in favour of one party to disputes in all circumstances'); Leistner (2011), p. 427 ('A priori, exceptions to a general principle have neither to be construed strictly, nor extensively – instead, according to most recent research into methodology, they have to be construed according to the general rules of interpretation'); Westkamp (2012), p. 65 (the rule of strict interpretation is 'based upon an alleged principle of European law, rather than on a principle of copyright law' and arguing that '[t]hat apodictic jurisprudence creates an imbalance and causes a division between European law and more lenient, and insightful, national approaches'); ECS (2014), pp. 4-5 (applauding the CJEU's move away from strict interpretation in cases like *Premier League*, *Ulmer* and *Deckmyn*); Geiger & Schonherr (2014), p. 116 (contending that 'in the context of the fast evolving digital environment, … rigorous application of the old adage [*exceptio est strictissimae interpretationis*] appears to be outdated'); Peukert (2015), p. 146 ('since exceptions and limitations form an integral part of IP laws, courts have to interpret these acts as a whole according to

Second, subjecting a copyright exception to such fundamental-rights-based scrutiny is comparable to converting it into a balancing test, for the interest the exception seeks to pursue will have to be weighed against the competing interest underlying the restricted exclusive right.[1196] Indeed, outcomes of cases on unlicensed uses presented as the result of purposive interpretations of exceptions often conceal a balancing judgment between the rights and interests of rightholders and those of users or society at large. This, in turn, begs the question: why insert a 'fair balance' component within a variety of exceptions, when we can simply have an open-ended norm that allows us to coherently and transparently engage in that balancing exercise? The latter solution would have the additional advantage of allowing a body of case law to form under the purview of one single provision. This would make the job of stakeholders seeking guidance on these matters significantly easier.[1197] Relying on purposive interpretations would add vagueness to multiple provisions, instead of using one provision as the repository of case law on unanticipated uses. The damage inflicted upon legal certainty by the recurrent use of purposive interpretations is greater than that of judgments based on patently vague norms around which guiding clusters and patterns may develop within case law over time.

Third, the technique of purposive interpretation is not without limits. As commonly recognised by legal methodologists, any interpretation of a statutory provision must remain within the boundaries of the linguistically possible meaning of that provision.[1198] It is not implausible to assume that, in the future, new technologies will enable uses that do not fall within the meaning of any listed exception, no matter how broadly we interpret them, despite being covered by their purpose.[1199] The adoption of a provision at the standards end of the continuum, with reference to the very values that

---

their wording, context, and purpose'); Quintais (2017a), p. 203 ('at least for limitations justified on the basis of fundamental rights, it does not seem consistent with EU and international law to impose a "horizontal" doctrine of strict interpretation'); and ECS (2019), pp. 4-7 (advising the CJEU, in the context of the *Pelham* reference, to interpret the quotation exception as covering the sampling of short extracts from phonograms, in light of the freedom of expression and freedom of the arts).

1196. On the nature of fundamental rights as principles that require balancing of opposing values, *see* Ribeiro (2017), pp. 226-232.

1197. *See* Geiger (2008a), p. 195, admitting that a fundamental rights-based interpretation of exceptions would be 'slightly detrimental to legal certainty'.

1198. *See* Larenz (2012), pp. 453-445. Of course, the extent of the 'linguistically possible meaning' is controversial in itself.

1199. *See* Förster (2008), pp. 211-212, rightfully pointing out that interpretation encounters its limit when there is simply no starting point for an extensive interpretation, because the use under consideration falls under no existing exception. The author cites the mass digitisation of books in the context of the Google Books project as an example. *See also* Jütte (2017), p. 278, illustrating the limits of interpretation with the following example: 'Article 5(2)(b) could not be interpreted widely to include reproductions made by a search engine as a search engine operator is very unlikely to qualify as a "natural person" making reproduction for "private use", neither is a search engine operator "the

exceptions typically instantiate, would avoid this problem of potential (and largely unpredictable) under-inclusiveness, in what would be a truly sustainable solution to the problem of adaptability.[1200]

Ideally, therefore, EU copyright law would contain doctrinal mechanisms of its own that would allow the fair balance between the competing interests to be struck internally and in a transparent and open manner. If the EU legislator is unwilling to engage in such ambitious reforms of the InfoSoc Directive, it could codify recent CJEU case law and clarify that the enumerated exceptions must be interpreted in light of the Charter rights, or in a way that enables their effectiveness to be safeguarded and that permits the observance of their purpose. This would amount to an explicit legislative authorisation for courts to engage in such exercise, dispelling any concerns that could be raised as to its legitimacy.[1201]

5.2.2.2 Combined Construction of Exceptions

In *Ulmer*, the CJEU took the trend of flexibly interpreting listed exceptions to a different level. The reference for a preliminary ruling was made by the BGH in the context of proceedings opposing the Technical University of Darmstadt and publisher Eugen Ulmer KG. The university had scanned a textbook published by Ulmer in order to make it available to patrons on the electronic terminals installed in its library. These terminals did not allow for a greater number of copies of the work to be consulted at any one time than the number owned by the library. Users of the terminals could print out the work on paper or store it on a USB stick, in full or in part, and take it out of the library in that form. The university did not accept Ulmer's offer of the possibility to purchase and use the e-book versions of its textbooks.

The dispute eventually reached the BGH, which referred questions on the interpretation of Article 5(3)(n) InfoSoc Directive. This provision allows Member States to provide for an exception privileging the use *by communication or making available*, for the purpose of research or private study, to individual members of the public by dedicated terminals on the premises of publicly accessible libraries (and similar establishments) of works not subject to purchase or licensing terms which are contained in their collections.[1202] The referred question that is of interest for purposes of this section is whether Article 5(3)(n) should be interpreted to mean that it allows Member States to confer on those establishments the possibility to *digitise*

---

press" in accordance with Article 5(3)(c) as this would require some editorial activity.' *See also* Chapter 5, section 4.2.1 (regarding analogy).

1200. *Contra, see* Poeppel (2005), pp. 507-511, making the argument that a broad interpretation or analogical extension of exceptions would be sufficient.

1201. *But see* Klimas & Vaiciukaite (2008), p. 27, claiming that purposive interpretations by reference to recitals diminish legal certainty.

1202. Criticising the narrow scope of this provision, *see* Guibault et al. (2007), pp. 56-57. *See also* LIBER Europe (2016), pp. 9-10, pointing out that the reference to 'dedicated

the works contained in their collections. Although the first sentence of Article 5(3) indicates that the exceptions provided in that paragraph concern the exclusive rights of reproduction and communication to the public, Article 5(3)(n), unlike other exceptions in that paragraph, makes no express reference to the former right – the one that is relevant when it comes to acts of digitisation. While the digitisation of works may be necessary for establishments like libraries to make the works available in electronic terminals, the wording of the exception refers solely to 'use by communication or making available'.[1203]

Aware of this limitation, the CJEU chose to read Article 5(3)(n) in conjunction with Article 5(2)(c), which exempts 'specific acts of reproductions' made by the same establishments. It held that the privilege – which the Court (misguidedly) called a 'right'[1204] – of making works available to the public via electronic terminals installed in libraries would be rendered meaningless or ineffective if the establishments in question did not have the 'ancillary right' to digitise those works.[1205] That 'ancillary right' flows from Article 5(2)(c). However, the requirement of 'specificity' as applied to acts of reproduction entails that the establishments are not allowed, as a general rule, to digitise their entire collections, but only *individual* works.[1206] On the other hand, the acts of printing out the copies on paper and storing them on USB sticks are not permitted under such provisions, since they are not necessary for making the works available to users via dedicated terminals.[1207]

Following this ruling, the question may be raised whether a national exception that corresponds to Article 5(3)(n) InfoSoc Directive includes the prerogative of digitisation even if the Member State has not implemented the exception for 'specific acts of reproduction'. Given the optional nature of these exceptions, a Member State may have implemented the former

---

terminals' is outdated, since library patrons now typically have their own devices, and proposing that they be allowed to access content on any device, as long as on the library premises.

1203. *See* CJEU, *Ulmer*, para. 40.
1204. The manifold references to 'rights' made in *Ulmer* are the apex of a tendency in CJEU's case law – *see* CJEU, *Padawan*, para. 43; CJEU, *Painer*, para. 132; and CJEU, *Deckmyn*, para. 26. *See also* ECS (2014), p. 5, and Geiger et al. (2015), p. 8. In Chapter 2, *supra* section 2.2, I explain why the use of the term 'rights' to refer to the entitlements conferred by InfoSoc exceptions should generally be avoided.
1205. CJEU, *Ulmer*, para. 43. This, *mutatis mutandis*, seems to contradict the statement in CJEU, *OSA*, para. 38, in relation to the exception for the reproduction of broadcasts made by social institutions: 'Article 5(2)(e) of Directive 2001/29, as can be seen from its wording, only forms the basis for an exception or limitation to the reproduction right, provided for in Article 2 of that directive. It cannot therefore form the basis for an exception or limitation to the exclusive right to authorise or prohibit any communication to the public of their works, provided for in Article 3(1) of that directive.'
1206. *See* CJEU, *Ulmer*, paras 44-45. *See also* AG Opinion, *Ulmer*, para. 38.
1207. *See* CJEU, *Ulmer*, para. 54.

(allowing the making available), but not the latter (allowing the reproduction). In such a case, would establishments like publicly accessible libraries be able to digitise the works? Although the ruling does not state so explicitly, it seems to follow from the circumstances of the case that when a Member State has transposed Article 5(3)(n), but not Article 5(2)(c), the establishments mentioned therein would nonetheless enjoy the privilege of digitisation. For one thing, Section 52b German Copyright Act, through which Germany had transposed Article 5(3)(n), referred only to the making available of works.[1208] For another, the CJEU's concern with the need to ensure the effectiveness of Article 5(3)(n) suggests that much, since otherwise – i.e., if both exceptions had been implemented – the question would not be raised and no effectiveness concerns would exist. It thus seems to be that, after *Ulmer*, the wording of Article 5(3)(n), *on its own*, also covers reproductions that are incidental to the acts of communication via dedicated terminals.[1209]

In practice, therefore, the effect of the CJEU's interpretation was to read an implied and ancillary privilege – the privilege of digitising books available in physical collections with the purpose of making them available via electronic terminals – into the one enshrined in the language of Article 5(3)(n), thus circumventing the problem caused by the optional nature of exceptions. Although the Court was cautious in delineating the scope of this privilege, clarifying that libraries are not entitled to digitise their entire collections, it openly extended the boundaries of Article 5(3)(n), by merging it with an exception to the right of reproduction. The Court's reasoning can either be read as a broad construction of Article 5(3)(n), guided by a contextual or systematic interpretation and by the desire to ensure the *effet utile* of the exception, or, more bluntly, as an outright creation of an autonomous and broader privilege arising from the combination of these two distinct exceptions,[1210] thus bypassing the exhaustive character of the list.

1208. The provision – whose title, it must be noted, is 'Reproduction of works at electronic reading points in public libraries, museums and archives' – is reproduced in CJEU, *Ulmer*, para. 9 and reads as follows: 'So far as there are no contractual provisions to the contrary, it shall be permissible *to make published works available* from the holdings of publicly accessible libraries, museums or archives, which neither directly nor indirectly serve economic or commercial purposes, exclusively on the premises of the relevant establishment at electronic reading points dedicated to the purpose of research and for private study. The number of copies of a work made available at electronic reading points shall not, in principle, be higher than the number held by the establishment. Equitable remuneration shall be paid in consideration of their being made available. The claim may be asserted only by a collecting society' (emphasis added).

1209. *See* AG Opinion, *Ulmer*, para. 34, clarifying that such acts of reproduction would not be covered by Article 5(1) InfoSoc Directive.

1210. On para. 54, the Court refers to the 'ancillary right stemming from the *combined provisions* of Articles 5(2)(c) and 5(3)(n)' (emphasis added).

While the Court's inventive and sensible approach in *Ulmer* deserves applause, it raises, yet again, doubts about the appropriateness of the InfoSoc framework of exceptions. As Eleonora Rosati puts it, '[w]hen there are exceptions and limitations that are so closely linked that they depend on each other to be effective, one may wonder indeed whether it makes sense to maintain a system of exceptions and limitations like that in Article 5 of the InfoSoc Directive'. The catalogue in Article 5, she rightfully notes, 'is so fragmented and über-specific as regards possible permitted uses to be misleading as to the actual importance of individual exceptions, if considered (and adopted) on their own'.[1211]

5.2.2.3 Avoiding the Three-Step Test

As previously explained, under the EU *acquis*, the inquiry into whether a certain unauthorised use that falls within the scope of an exclusive right is conclusively infringing is a two-tiered one: the deciding court must first assess whether the use is covered by one of the listed exceptions and, if so, it must examine whether the use cumulatively satisfies the hurdles of the three-step test.[1212]

However, in reading the CJEU's case law on InfoSoc exceptions, one cannot help but notice that the level of scrupulousness in the three-step analysis is not particularly high. In most cases where the Court engaged in such analysis[1213] – either on its own initiative or because the referred questions prompted it to do so –, it did so in a more or less concise manner.[1214] In some of these cases, like *Infopaq* and *Painer*, the requirements of the three-step test appeared to be met by merely reading the relevant exception(s) 'in light of' Article 5(5). In other cases, the Court did conduct an examination of the relevant use against each of the three steps, but only in a very superficial fashion.

In the *Ulmer* case discussed above, the Court was satisfied with noting: (i) that Section 52b German Copyright Act allowed the consultation of the digitised books on a one-copy/one-user basis and (ii) that, although the digitisation of the books did not give rise to an obligation to pay fair compensation, the subsequent making available of the copies did.[1215] This,

1211. Rosati (2014b).
1212. *See supra* Chapter 2, section 4.2.
1213. In some cases on exceptions, like *DR & TV2 Danmark* and *Deckmyn*, the Court simply does not mention the test.
1214. *See* Jütte (2017), p. 289, noting the lack of prominence of the test in the case law of the CJEU.
1215. *See* CJEU, *Ulmer*, paras 47-48. *See also* CJEU, *Ulmer*, paras 33-34 (on the compatibility with the three-step test of the requirement that the rightholder and the library have concluded a licensing agreement) and para. 56 (on the compatibility of the acts of printing out the works on paper and storing them on a USB stick).

according to the Court, was sufficient for the uses made by libraries to pass the three-step test.

More recently, in *Spiegel Online*, in discussing the admissibility of a reference made by means of a hyperlink to a file which can be downloaded independently and which included the protected work in its entirety, the Court simply stated, without further elaboration, that a quotation cannot be so extensive as to conflict with a normal exploitation of the work or prejudice unreasonably the legitimate interests of the rightholder.[1216]

ACI Adam is arguably the ruling in which the CJEU conducted the most detailed examination of the three-step test. The main question in that reference was whether the private copying exception in InfoSoc could be read as covering reproductions made for private use from unlawful sources. The Court answered in the negative, adding that such an interpretation of the exception would infringe the second and third steps of the test.[1217] Regarding the second step, the normal exploitation of the works would be affected since allowing reproductions made from unlawful sources would promote the circulation of pirated works, thus inevitably reducing the volume of sales or of other lawful transactions relating to the protected works.[1218] Still, as rightfully noted by João Pedro Quintais, '[t]hat assertion, which seems essential to the ruling and would rely at least partially on factual analysis, is not further explained'.[1219] As to the third step, the Court was similarly laconic. It merely stated that an interpretation according to which copies from unlawful sources would be privileged would unreasonably prejudice the legitimate interests of rightholders, for it would be equivalent to forcing them to tolerate infringements of their rights that may accompany the making of private copies.[1220]

In *Filmspeler*, the Court followed a similar reasoning, though analysing the second and third steps together. The Court held that streaming copies of unauthorised works made on a multimedia player could adversely affect the normal exploitation of the protected works *and* cause unreasonable prejudice to the legitimate interests of rightholders, because that practice would usually

1216. *See* CJEU, *Spiegel Online*, para. 79. *See also* AG Opinion, *Spiegel Online*, para. 50 ('A quotation which removes the need for the user to have recourse to the original work by substituting itself for the latter is necessarily prejudicial to its normal exploitation').

1217. *See* CJEU, *ACI Adam*, para. 38.

1218. *See* CJEU, *ACI Adam*, para. 39.

1219. Quintais (2015), p. 74. Later in the piece, Quintais adds that 'the Court's sporadic reasoning of substitution effects failed to argue or establish the existence of competing legal offers (which are scarce), of substitution between downloads from unlawful sources and legal channels (of which there is limited evidence), or the feasibility of enforcement of exclusive right of reproduction in these scenarios, which is unproven' (p. 88).

1220. *See* CJEU, *ACI Adam*, paras 31 and 40.

result in a diminution of lawful transactions relating to the protected works.[1221]

By contrast, in some cases concerning the temporary reproduction exception, the Court entirely and expressly dispensed with the analysis of the three conditions in Article 5(5). In *Premier League*, after concluding that the acts of reproduction that take place in the memory of a satellite decoder and on a television screen met the conditions of Article 5(1), the Court mentioned that those acts would still have to pass the three-step test. Yet, the Court did not go through each of the steps. It stated quite simply that if those acts of reproduction satisfy all the conditions of Article 5(1), it must be held that they also comply with the conditions in Article 5(5).[1222] In *Infopaq II*, the Court again assumed that the fulfilment of the requirements in Article 5(1) meant that the use at hand satisfied the hurdles of the three-step test.[1223] The Court provided no explanation in either case for why passing Article 5(1) necessarily entails passing Article 5(5). Although there may be some overlap between the analyses required under some of the conditions in both provisions – in particular, between the 'no independent economic significance' condition in Article 5(1) and the second and third steps of the test[1224] –, their wording and underlying purposes are fundamentally different.

Perhaps acknowledging this much, the Court refrained from adopting the same approach a few years later in *PRCA*. Having concluded that the uses under analysis fulfilled the relevant requirements of Article 5(1), the Court proceeded to examine whether the steps in Article 5(5) were satisfied. Nonetheless, the analysis was, again, rather brief and unclear. As to the first step, the Court merely stated that, given that the on-screen copies and cached copies were created only for the purpose of viewing websites, they constituted a special case.[1225] This seems to suggest that the Court interprets the first step as requiring the use at stake to have a limited purpose. Also, in analysing step two (which the Court did in the third place), the Court confusingly held that viewing websites constituted a normal exploitation and that, since the creation of on-screen and cached copies formed part of that viewing, it could not operate to the detriment of such exploitation.[1226] As regards the third step, the Court recognised that the copies could enable

1221. *See* CJEU, *Filmspeler*, para. 70.
1222. *See* CJEU, *Premier League*, paras 180-181.
1223. *See* CJEU, *Infopaq II*, paras 55-57.
1224. Both inquiries revolve essentially around economic considerations. The 'no independent economic significance' condition in Article 5(1) asks, *inter alia*, whether the temporary reproduction generates an additional profit, while the second and third conditions of the three-step test, in the Court's interpretation, seem to be largely focused on market harm. *See* Hugenholtz (2000a), p. 488; Guibault et al. (2007), p. 36; and Bechtold (2016), p. 458 (suggesting that the 'no independent economic significance' condition is derived from the three-step test).
1225. *See* CJEU, *PRCA*, para. 55.
1226. *See* CJEU, *PRCA*, paras 60-61.

Internet users to access works displayed on websites without the permission of rightholders, but it nevertheless found that the legitimate interests of rightholders were properly safeguarded because under Article 3(1) the website publishers already needed to obtain authorisation to make those works available online.[1227]

The point, in sum, is that although the three-step test is devised as yet another constraint on the freedom of courts to accommodate certain uses of protected works, the CJEU often deals with the test in a loose manner. More often than not, the analysis is concise and at times even simplistic. Occasionally, the analysis is dispensed with altogether. In CJEU case law, therefore, the three-step test, even in its restrictive vests, does not seem to be an autonomous and insurmountable obstacle to adapting copyright law to new technologies.

5.3 Guiding Role

As previously mentioned, commentators who support the existing framework of exceptions commonly argue that a standard-like exception would fail to provide any reasonable degree of legal certainty. The counter-argument put forward by the opposing camp is that the task of giving guidance to interested stakeholders need not be performed exclusively by legislators. These scholars point out that, as empirical research on fair use reveals, the judiciary may play an important role in that regard, by developing a coherent and systematised body of decisions that acts as a surrogate for statutory precision.[1228]

The argument for the introduction of a discretion-granting exception into EU copyright law is premised on the idea that the CJEU is capable of providing this type of guidance. Whereas some scholars suggest that the adoption of vague concepts could lead to the gradual formation of a body of case law that would render the law more predictable over time,[1229] others, like Matthias Leistner (who is nonetheless broadly supportive of a reform of the InfoSoc framework of exceptions), raise doubts about the CJEU's capacity to develop a consistent string of rulings on the basis of a fair use type of standard.[1230] Leistner's doubts are grounded on three fundamental reasons.

First, the emergence of clear and identifiable patterns in case law depends on the existence of a sizeable stock of decisions. Writing in 2011, Leistner claimed that the number of cases on the interpretation of EU

1227. *See* CJEU, *PRCA*, paras 56-59.
1228. *See supra* Chapter 3, section 3.1.2.
1229. *See*, *e.g.*, Ohly (2009), p. 240 ('While vague legal concepts in Community law may reduce legal certainty in the short term, common European concepts may well make life easier in the long run').
1230. *See* Leistner (2011), pp. 435-440.

copyright law that had reached the CJEU was 'rather limited'.[1231] However, the truth is that this number has been steadily increasing in recent years.[1232] Leistner himself conceded that, were such a standard to be enacted, the number of cases referred to the Court would certainly surge.[1233]

Second, he argues that, when interpreting EU secondary law, the Court acts as 'a rather "distant" appellate court ..., often leaving the application of certain rather abstract concepts or tests to the concrete facts of the case to the Member States' national courts'.[1234] Indeed, under the preliminary reference procedure, the CJEU is not supposed to apply the law to the facts of the case. The truth, though, is that the Court quite frequently does just the opposite,[1235] 'integrat[ing] the facts and national legal provisions into its interpretation of Community law so as to hand down a judgment that in reality determines the outcome of the main proceedings'.[1236]

1231. Leistner (2011), p. 437.
1232. This much has been recognised years later by Matthias Leistner himself, who, writing in 2014, noted that 'the body of relevant case law started to grow considerably' and that, since 2009, we have witnessed 'an explosive development of the ECJ's copyright case law' – Leistner (2014a), pp. 559-560. *See also* Eechoud (2012), pp. 75-76 (noting a sharp increase in the number of preliminary references in the 2003-2011 period in relation to the 1993-2002 period), and Favale et al. (2016), p. 31 (pointing to a 'dramatic recent increase in references to the Court').
1233. *See* Leistner (2011), p. 438.
1234. Leistner (2011), p. 437.
1235. Former AG Francis Jacobs wrote that the preliminary ruling resolves the dispute before the referring court 'in an extremely high proportion of cases' – Jacobs (1994), p. 29. *See also* EP Report Role of National Judge, according to which 89% of 123 judges that have made at least one reference for a preliminary ruling over the course of their career 'found the ECJ's ruling readily applicable to the facts of the case'.
1236. Broberg & Fenger (2010), p. 421. In the words of the late Federico Mancini, former AG and Judge at the CJEU, in these cases 'the national judge is ... led in hand as far as the door; crossing the threshold is his job, but now a job no harder than a child's play' – Mancini (1989), p. 606. EU copyright case law is fertile in rulings through which the CJEU effectively decided the main dispute. *VCAST* and *GS Media* are two recent examples.

    In *VCAST*, the referring court had asked whether, *in general*, the private copying exception covered the services of an online platform that allows users to store copies of free-to-air TV programmes in private cloud storage spaces. In answering the preliminary questions, the Court chose to focus exclusively on services like the one provided by VCAST, which did not merely organise the reproduction, but also provided customers with access to programmes of TV channels to which they did not have prior authorised access – *see* CJEU, *VCAST*, paras 37 and 46-49. The Court concluded that the making of unauthorised copies 'by means of a service such as that at issue in the main proceedings' was unlawful (para. 51), thus practically deciding the national dispute.

    The *GS Media* judgment provides another example, this time within the domain of exclusive rights. In that case, GS Media B.V. provided a hyperlink on a blog that it ran directing the user to photos that were to be published in a future issue of Playboy magazine. Not only did it not seek any authorisation for that purpose, but it also repeatedly ignored the removal requests sent by the rightholder. Against this background, the CJEU did not hesitate to apply its interpretation of the right of

Although these two arguments do not seem to hold up to scrutiny, Leistner's third argument requires closer examination. The author doubts that the Court could develop a reliable body of case law under a standard like fair use, due to the lack of 'a developed case law methodology' and, in particular, a consistent technique of distinguishing precedents.[1237] His idea is that the Court simply tends to accept existing precedents and to repeat them over the years in a somewhat superficial manner,[1238] preventing it from developing the sub-rules and factors that characterise US fair use case law and that make it more predictable than its wording actually suggests.

---

communication to the public to the facts of the main proceedings. Though cautioning that the concrete application of the law was 'subject to the checks' of the national court, the Court determined that GS Media had in fact made a communication to the public, essentially deciding the case on the facts: 'As regards the case in the main proceedings, it is undisputed that GS Media operates the GeenStijl website and that it provided the hyperlinks to the files containing the photos at issue … for profit. It is also undisputed that Sanoma had not authorised the publication of those photos on the internet. Moreover, it appears to follow from the presentation of the facts, as they result from the order for reference, that GS Media was aware of that latter fact and that it cannot therefore rebut the presumption that the posting of those links occurred in full knowledge of the illegal nature of that publication. In those circumstances, it appears that, subject to the checks to be made by the referring court, by posting those links, GS Media effected a "communication to the public", within the meaning of Article 3(1) of Directive 2001/29' (para. 54).

The upshot, as illustrated by these decisions, is that the CJEU's preliminary rulings often apply the law to the facts of the case and would be likely to do so under a vague standard as well.

1237. The doctrine of *stare decisis* requires courts to follow precedents, that is, to adhere to previous decisions on the same issue as the one dealt with in the case *sub judice*, regardless of their views about how that specific case should be decided. No such doctrine has been incorporated into the EU judicial system. Thus, unlike common law courts, the CJEU is *not* bound to follow its own prior decisions. In practice, however, the CJEU follows – in the words of former AG Maduro (2007), p. 146 – a 'precedent-oriented approach', treating its own decisions as binding *de facto*. Former AG Francis Jacobs recognised that 'in much the same way as other courts', the CJEU 'is reluctant to depart from them' – Jacobs (1994), pp. 29-30. The approach followed by the Court has been summarised by AG La Pergola in his Opinion in *Sema Sürül*, para. 36: 'The Court does not of course fail to ensure that its case-law displays continuity and that its judgments are logically compatible and not contradictory with each other. However, the Court is not technically bound by its earlier judgments, and may therefore … give a different answer to a preliminary question dealt with in an earlier decision, if such a result is justified by new matters brought to its attention in the later proceedings.' *See also* AG Opinion, *Cipolla*, para. 28. Discussing the precedential value of CJEU's rulings, *see, e.g.*, Toth (1984); Arnull (1993); Tridimas (2012); Barceló (2016); and Jacob (2016). In the field of copyright law, specifically on the long line of judgments about the concept of 'communication to the public', AG Sánchez-Bordona, in his opinion in the *Filmspeler* case, stated that '[t]he requirement of certainty in the application of the law obliges the court, if not to apply the *stare decisis* in absolute terms, then to take care to follow the decisions it has itself, after mature reflection, previously adopted in relation to a given legal problem' (para. 41).

1238. *See* Leistner (2011), p. 437.

The present section aims at investigating this very question: whether the CJEU is capable of giving adequate guidance when interpreting vague provisions.[1239] If an open-ended exception is to be adopted, a larger share of the burden of ensuring legal certainty will inevitably be transferred to the CJEU, which will be entrusted with the job of 'Europeanising' the doctrine on a case-by-case basis.[1240] Before a reform of this kind is undertaken, it must be examined whether the CJEU is up to the task of developing a sophisticated and harmonised body of case law.

Vague doctrines are part and parcel of EU copyright law.[1241] The paradigmatic example of a vague doctrine within the InfoSoc framework of exceptions – whose meaning *could* be further elaborated by the CJEU – is the three-step test. Yet, as previously discussed, the CJEU has not taken the opportunity provided by the referrals on the meaning of Article 5 exceptions to adequately densify the test.[1242] This fact lends some weight to Leistner's scepticism. But the case law the Court has been developing on the basis of other vague doctrines within the copyright *acquis*, namely originality and communication to the public, provides solid conflicting evidence.[1243]

Sections 5.3.1 and 5.3.2 thus attempt to show that the Court has managed to construe a fairly consistent *corpus* of case law in relation to these doctrines, with the sub-rules and factors that, over time, make standard-like doctrines more rule-like.[1244] While these sections do not examine the exceptions' *acquis* per se (and, for that reason, their systematic inclusion in this chapter may raise legitimate doubts), they lend important support to one of the key arguments in the InfoSoc debate.

1239. *See* Favale et al. (2016), researching the different and more general question of whether the CJEU has failed to develop a coherent, copyright-specific reasoning, due e.g. to the lack of pre-existing judicial expertise in the field.

1240. *See* Ohly (2009), p. 240.

1241. *See* Afori (2014), p. 891 ('The basic structure of copyright law features numerous "open standards", which are flexible, open-ended norms that facilitate broad judicial discretion, aimed at enabling the adjustment of the law to the intricate reality'). *See also* Hugenholtz & Senftleben (2011), p. 6 (citing originality and the idea/expression dichotomy as examples of doctrines with 'relative fluidity').

1242. *See supra* section 5.2.2.3.

1243. As noted by Rosati (2019), pp. 31-32, this may be due, in no small part, to a *de facto* specialisation that has occurred in the CJEU, through the appointment of repeated Judges-Rapporteur and Advocates General to copyright references.

1244. Making a similar argument in relation to the 'due cause' defence in EU trademark law, *see* Senftleben (2017), pp. 256-265.

5.3.1 The Case Law on Originality

Originality is the central requirement that must be satisfied in order for an authored work to be eligible for copyright protection.[1245] If the work is deemed original, it will be afforded copyright protection, meaning that its author will be granted a set of exclusive rights over that work.[1246]

'Originality' is an evidently vague concept that provides concerned stakeholders and decision-makers with limited guidance.[1247] In an attempt to concretise this (often unwritten) standard and to clarify what it means for a work to be original, different tests have been developed over time and in distinct jurisdictions, by courts and legislators alike.[1248]

Within the copyright *acquis*, three pre-InfoSoc Directives make reference to the originality standard, in relation to three distinct categories of works: computer programs (Software Directive), photographs (Term Directive), and databases (Database Directive). The standard's formulation is identical in all of them: works belonging to any one of these categories are to be deemed original if they are the 'author's own intellectual creation'.[1249]

1245. The leading monography on originality in EU copyright law is Rosati (2013a). *See also* Judge & Gervais (2010), pp. 378-389; Vousden (2010); Eechoud (2012); Margoni (2016); and Stamatoudi (2017).

1246. For copyright protection to attach, the subject matter in question must previously qualify as a 'work'. In this regard, the CJEU has stated that two cumulative conditions must be met: first, 'the subject matter concerned must be original in the sense that it is the author's own intellectual creation' and, second, 'only something which is the expression of the author's own intellectual creation may be classified as a "work"' – CJEU, *Levola Hengelo*, paras 36-37. The obvious tautology aside, with this statement the Court seems to conflate the concepts of 'work' and 'originality', by holding that only something that is original can qualify as a work. In this reference, the Court eventually decided that copyright protection could not subsist in the taste of a food product, specifically a spreadable dip containing cream cheese and fresh herbs.

1247. *See* Schricker (1995), p. 42 (speaking of the 'cryptic formula' of the 'personal intellectual creation' used in German Law); Bently et al. (2018), p. 93 ('it is very difficult to state with any precision what copyright law means when it demands that works be "original"'); and Margoni (2016), p. 87 ('generally speaking, originality lacks a precise statutory definition').

1248. In general, the threshold of originality may correspond to one of four different traditions: (i) the more demanding test of the 'author's own intellectual creation', which was the traditional test in Continental European countries, having later been adopted at the EU level; (ii) the US test requiring a 'minimal degree of creativity', which was developed by the US Supreme Court in the *Feist* case; (iii) the Supreme Court of Canada's test of 'non-mechanical and non-trivial exercise of skill and judgment' elaborated in *CCH Canadian*; and (iv) the less demanding 'skill and labour' test, prevalent in the UK and in other common law countries. Proposing this fourfold division, *see* Judge & Gervais (2009).

1249. *See* Article 1(3) Software Directive; Article 6 and Recital 16 Term Directive; and Article 3(1) of Database Directive. The formulation resembles the test that has traditionally been adopted in continental Member States, most notably in France, where originality is understood as *la marque d'un apport intellectuel* (*see*, *e.g.*, French Court of Cassation, *Babolat*), and in Germany, where works must be 'personal intellectual

The foregoing Directives carried out a vertical harmonisation only, focusing on selected aspects of copyright law in a content- or technology-specific fashion. As such, the originality test contained therein does not extend to other categories of subject matter besides the ones specifically mentioned in the Directives. Although the InfoSoc Directive works as a *lex generalis*, covering all categories of works, it makes no reference to the originality test that is to govern their protectability. The question of how to define the originality standard for all categories of subject matter besides computer programs, photographs, and databases was thus left open by the legislator.

The CJEU remedied this lacuna in a series of bold judgments.[1250] This process of judge-led harmonisation of the originality standard began in the landmark *Infopaq I* ruling. The relevant question was whether the concept of 'reproduction in part' in Article 2 InfoSoc Directive covered the storing and printing out of text excerpts. The Court reasoned that, in establishing a harmonised legal framework for copyright, the InfoSoc Directive draws on the same principle as the Software, Term, and Database Directives.[1251] Accordingly, the Court extended their originality formula to all protectable works, stating that the reproduction right in InfoSoc 'is liable to apply only in relation to a subject-matter which is original in the sense that it is its author's own intellectual creation'.[1252] Through a systematic and teleological interpretation of the InfoSoc Directive, the CJEU uncovered an autonomous EU originality standard for all categories of subject matter[1253] (which appears to have been recently codified in Article 14 DSM Directive[1254]). In what regards newspaper articles – the works that were at stake in the national proceedings –, the Court added that it is through the 'choice, sequence and

creations' in order for protection to attach (*see* Article 2(2) German Copyright Act). Note that Article 6 Term Directive allows Member States to provide for the protection of other (sub-original) photographs.

1250. Discussing some of these judgments, *see* Derclaye (2014) (with a consideration of their implications for UK copyright law).

1251. *See* CJEU, *Infopaq I*, para. 36.

1252. CJEU, *Infopaq I*, para. 37.

1253. It ought to be stressed that the question in *Infopaq I* concerned the reproduction of *parts* of protected works and not the works in their totality. Nevertheless, the Court said that this should not affect the conclusion on protectability: 'there is nothing in Directive 2001/29 or any other relevant directive indicating that those parts are to be treated any differently from the work as a whole. It follows that they are protected by copyright since, as such, they share the originality of the whole work' – CJEU, *Infopaq I*, para. 38.

1254. Article 14 DSM Directive states that 'Member States shall provide that, when the term of protection of a work of visual art has expired, any material resulting from an act of reproduction of that work is not subject to copyright or related rights, unless the material resulting from that act of reproduction is original in the sense that it is the author's own intellectual creation.' The provision essentially clarifies that simple reproductions of works of visual art belonging in the public domain do not give rise to new copyright rights. Unless the EU originality threshold is met, these reproductions

combination' of words that the author may achieve a result that is her intellectual creation.[1255]

In the *BSA* case, the CJEU confirmed that the originality standard was to be considered horizontally harmonised.[1256] In that preliminary reference, the Court was confronted with the question of whether a graphic user interface could be protected by copyright. After concluding that the interface did not constitute a form of expression of a computer program, thus falling outside the scope of the Software Directive,[1257] the Court considered whether the interface could be protected under the general InfoSoc Directive.[1258] Following its ruling in *Infopaq I*, the Court stated that the answer was in the affirmative provided the interface was *its author's own intellectual creation*.[1259] The Court added that, in making that assessment, the national court had to consider, among other elements, 'the specific arrangement or configuration of all the components which form part of the graphic user interface in order to determine which meet the criterion of originality'.[1260]

In subsequent case law, the CJEU elaborated upon the open-ended formula of the 'author's own intellectual creation', developing sub-criteria to facilitate its application and make it more predictable.

In the *Premier League* case, the Court denied protection to sporting events per se.[1261] In its reasoning, the Court added a specification that helps further illuminate the meaning of originality in EU copyright law. The exclusion from copyright protection, the Court said, 'applies in particular to football matches, which are subject to the rules of the game, leaving no *room for creative freedom* for the purposes of copyright'.[1262] As suggested in this passage, the freedom to make creative choices is a factor that must be taken into account in determining whether a given work meets the EU originality standard.

---

will also fall within the public domain. The reference to 'any material' suggests that a work, whatever its type, can only be protected by copyright if it is original in an *Infopaq I* sense.

1255. CJEU, *Infopaq I*, para. 45.

1256. Commentators have argued that the horizontal harmonisation of the originality standard hinders 'flexibility', in the sense that Member States will no longer be allowed to adopt different criteria for different types of subject matter. The German 'level of creativity' (*Schöpfungshöhe*) doctrine, pursuant to which works of applied art had to have a higher degree of originality in order to attract protection, is the paradigmatic example of such differentiation – *see* Schricker (1995) and Bently et al. (2018), p. 99. The question of whether the originality standard in InfoSoc extended to designs and applied art was the object of the *Cofemel* preliminary reference. In its judgment, the CJEU clarified that the only requirement for copyright protection to attach to these kinds of works is their originality. For a thorough opinion on the referred questions, *see* ECS (2018b).

1257. *See* CJEU, *BSA*, para. 42.

1258. *See* CJEU, *BSA*, para. 44.

1259. *See* CJEU, *BSA*, paras 45-46.

1260. CJEU, *BSA*, para. 48.

1261. CJEU, *Premier League*, para. 98.

1262. CJEU, *Premier League*, para. 98 (emphasis added).

In later cases, the 'room for creative freedom' factor was elevated to a *sine qua non* of originality in the EU. In *Painer*, in discussing whether portrait photographs deserved copyright protection, the Court emphasised the importance of creative freedom in the analysis of whether a work is original. A work's originality, the Court held, was dependent on whether 'the author was able to express his creative abilities in the production of the work by making *free and creative choices*'.[1263] Reasoning *a contrario* in relation to what it had held in the *Premier League* case, the Court said that a portrait photographer can exercise such creative freedom at various stages of the portrait's creation, for instance by choosing the background, the lighting, the angle of view, and the post-production techniques.[1264] The Court further suggested that the EU originality standard requires that the work carry the 'personal touch' of its author.[1265] Hence, a portrait photograph can be protected by copyright to the extent that: (i) the author can express her free and creative choices in the production of that photograph and (ii) those choices allow the author to stamp the photograph with her 'personal touch'.

More recently, in *Funke Medien*, *Cofemel*, and *Brompton Bicycle*, the Court confirmed that, for a work to be considered original, 'it is both necessary and sufficient that the subject matter reflects the personality of its author, as an expression of his free and creative choices'.[1266]

In *Football Dataco* – a case on whether football fixture lists could be considered 'intellectual creations' under the Database Directive –, the Court adopted the same criteria in elucidating the meaning of originality: 'As regards the setting up of a database, that criterion of originality is satisfied when, through the selection or arrangement of the data which it contains, its author expresses his creative ability in an original manner by *making free and creative choices* ... and thus *stamps his "personal touch"*.'[1267] 'By contrast', the judges added, 'that criterion is not satisfied when the setting up of the database is dictated by technical considerations, rules or constraints which leave no room for creative freedom'.[1268]

Besides clarifying the positive meaning of originality – what originality *is* –, the CJEU has also given guidance as to when originality *is not* present. In *BSA*, similarly to *Football Dataco*, the Court considered that when the expression of a work is *dictated by its technical function*, the originality threshold is not met, since the author is not allowed to express her creativity.[1269] The Court had also made a related point in *Premier League*, in

1263. CJEU, *Painer*, para. 89 (emphasis added). *See also* CJEU, *Renckhoff*, para. 14.
1264. *See* CJEU, *Painer*, paras 90-91.
1265. CJEU, *Painer*, para. 92.
1266. CJEU, *Funke Medien*, para. 19; CJEU, *Cofemel*, para. 30; and CJEU, *Brompton Bicycle*, paras 23 and 34.
1267. CJEU, *Football Dataco*, para. 38 (emphasis added).
1268. CJEU, *Football Dataco*, para. 39. *See also* CJEU, *Cofemel*, para. 31, and CJEU, *Brompton Bicycle*, paras 24 and 31.
1269. *See* CJEU, *BSA*, paras 48-50. *See also* CJEU, *SAS*, para. 39.

explaining why sporting events cannot be considered original: 'football matches, which are subject to rules of the game, leav[e] no room for creative freedom for the purposes of copyright'.[1270] The (negative) requirement that emerges from these judgments is that where the room for creative choices is severely limited due to the existence of certain rules or functional considerations, the originality standard will not be met.[1271]

In addition, the *Football Dataco* ruling helped clarify that the EU originality standard *is not* equivalent to (being more demanding than) the common law 'skill and labour' test. In that regard, the Court stated that 'the fact that the setting up of the database required ... significant labour and skill of its author ... cannot as such justify the protection of it by copyright under Directive 96/9, if that labour and that skill do not express any originality in the selection or arrangement of that data'.[1272]

In sum, throughout this line of cases the CJEU explored the meaning of the 'author's own intellectual creation' formula in relation to various types of subject matter. In that process, the Court developed a set of factors that provide more detailed guidance to stakeholders and litigators. Thanks to a series of landmark rulings by the Court, we now know that:

(i) The horizontal standard of originality in EU copyright law is the 'author's own intellectual creation'.
(ii) A work will be considered the author's own intellectual creation when its author had room for free and creative choices and when her personality is reflected on the work.
(iii) The work will not be original when the technical function or any underlying rules severely constrain the author's margin of creativity.

1270. CJEU, *Premier League*, para. 98. As Bently et al. (2018), p. 101, rightfully point out, 'to anyone who plays or watches football, the claim that there is no "creative freedom" because of the constraints provided by the "rules of the game" may seem misguided (so that the absence of copyright in football matches may need to be explained in some other way)'.
1271. *See* Bently et al. (2018), p. 100. In *Funke Medien*, AG Szpunar expressed doubts that a military report could be original in an EU copyright law sense, on grounds that the room for creative freedom enjoyed by its authors was limited: 'It seems to me to be rather unlikely that the author or authors of those documents, whose identity is unknown but who are probably civil servants or officers of the federal armed forces, were able to make free and creative choices in order to express their creative abilities when drafting those documents. The content of purely informative documents that are inevitably drafted in simple and neutral terms is entirely determined by the information they contain, so that such information and its expression become indissociable, thus precluding all originality' (para. 19). In its judgment, the CJEU left that determination to be made by the national court, answering the referred questions subject to that qualification (paras 16-26).
1272. CJEU, *Football Dataco*, para. 42.

(iv) The labour and skill invested by the author, even if significant, are not enough for the work to be considered original.[1273]

These factors or sub-rules have led the Court to exclude protection in relation to some subject matter (such as sporting events and lists of football fixtures) and to consider that protection would be possible – whether protection actually subsists is, in the end, for national courts to determine – in other cases (such as eleven-worded text extracts, portrait photographs, or graphic user interfaces).

To be sure, many questions of interpretation on the originality requirement still remain open.[1274] But while it cannot be argued that this case law provides full predictability, it does attest to the CJEU's capacity to draw clearer contours within vague doctrines on a case-by-case basis.

5.3.2 The Case Law on Communication to the Public

Notwithstanding the relevant evidence provided by the CJEU's case law on originality, the ideal set of judgments for investigation under the present section is the one on the right of communication to the public laid down in Article 3(1) InfoSoc Directive. This is so for a twofold reason.

First, this line of cases interprets a *statutory provision* within the InfoSoc Directive that lies on the vague end of the spectrum. The InfoSoc legislator, contrary to the intentions expressed by the Commission in the 1995 Green Paper,[1275] refrained from defining the notion of 'communication to the public'.[1276] In spite of its broad scope, which has been described in Chapter 1,[1277] the wording of Article 3(1), even when supplemented by the relevant recitals, leaves a series of open questions.[1278] The two components of the notion – 'communication' and 'public' – have been explored by the CJEU in order to provide guidance on such questions.

Second, the meaning of this provision has been the subject of numerous preliminary references. The emergence of relatively stable patterns in case law necessarily depends on the existence of a significant number of rulings. The notion of 'communication to the public' has been at the core of more than twenty references to the CJEU – more than any other doctrine in EU copyright law. The Court's growing and increasingly complex case law has

---

1273. *See* Margoni (2016), pp. 94-96, identifying similar 'principles'.
1274. *See* Bently et al. (2018), pp. 98-102, exploring some of these questions.
1275. *See* 1995 Green Paper, p. 54.
1276. *See* Angelopoulos (2017b), p. 19, noting, in this regard, that 'not much can be divined from the text of the Directive'.
1277. *See supra* Chapter 1, section 4.2.
1278. When CJEU-led harmonisation of the notion of 'communication to the public' was still at the onset, Ohly (2009), pp. 227-228, identified some borderline issues emerging from this notion, namely 'the line between public and private' and 'whether the posting of a hyperlink to a website where works are made available can amount to a communication to the public'.

been accompanied by scholarly studies that have identified relevant patterns and attempted to bring coherence where it was seemingly lacking,[1279] much like US scholars have been doing with fair use case law.

According to the Court's settled case law, the qualification of a given use as a communication to the public turns on the verification of two cumulative requirements flowing directly from the right's designation: (i) the existence of an *act of communication* of the work and (ii) the communication of the work *to the public*. This two-requirement approach has been consistently followed by the Court, forming the backbone of this case law. Over time, the Court has developed a series of sub-criteria to assess the fulfilment of these two requirements.

As to the first requirement ('act of communication'), the Court, pointing out that the Directive does not define the concept of 'communication' exhaustively,[1280] has clarified that a work must be made available to a public in such a way that the members of that public may access it, regardless of whether they avail themselves of that opportunity.[1281] In other words, for an act of communication to occur it is not decisive that members of the public actually enjoy the work. This criterion will be met when the user intervenes to provide access to the protected work, in full knowledge of the consequences of her actions.[1282] It is not sufficient, however, that the user provides a mere technical means to ensure or improve the communication.[1283] The user's intervention must be 'indispensable' – in the sense that the public would be unable to enjoy the work absent such intervention[1284] – or at least instrumental – in the sense that the public would be able to enjoy the work 'only with difficulty'.[1285] As previously discussed, the more recent judgments of the Court have interpreted this concept as covering acts of users who facilitate or enable infringing acts by third persons, broadening the primary liability under Article 3(1) to include behaviour that traditionally fell under the purview of (unharmonised) regimes of secondary or intermediary liability.[1286]

Regarding the second requirement ('to the public'), the text of the Directive provides no guidance on the meaning of the concept of 'public' either. Here too the CJEU took matters into its own hands, clarifying in a

1279. *See, e.g.*, Quintais (2018), offering a detailed conceptual framework for interpreting the right of communication to the public, with an emphasis on the hyperlinking case law.
1280. *See* CJEU, *ITV Broadcasting I*, para. 22.
1281. *See, e.g.*, CJEU, *SGAE*, para. 43; CJEU, *Svensson*, para. 19; and CJEU, *Renckhoff*, para. 20.
1282. *See* CJEU, *Reha Training*, para. 46; CJEU, *GS Media*, para. 35; CJEU, *Filmspeler*, para. 31; and CJEU, *Ziggo*, para. 26.
1283. *See, e.g.*, CJEU, *SGAE*, para. 42, and CJEU, *Premier League*, para. 194.
1284. *See* CJEU, *SCF*, para. 82; CJEU, *PPI*, para. 31; and CJEU, *GS Media*, para. 35.
1285. *See* CJEU, *Filmspeler*, para. 41, and CJEU, *Ziggo*, para. 26, which forwent the 'indispensability' element.
1286. *See supra* Chapter 1, section 4.2.

series of judgments that the term refers to an 'indeterminate' and 'fairly large number' of people.[1287] Whereas the 'indeterminate' nature of the public means that the work must be made perceptible to 'persons in general' instead of 'specific individuals belonging to a private group', the criterion of the 'fairly large number of people' denotes the existence of a '*de minimis* threshold', excluding groups of people that are too small or insignificant.[1288] Consequently, communications made via personal e-mail messages or within intranets whose participants are individuals with personal relationships fall outside the concept of 'public'.[1289]

Aside from being directed to a 'public', the use must meet one of two alternative sub-criteria in order to qualify as a communication to the public: the public targeted by the act of communication must be either (i) a 'new public', that is, a public that has not been taken into account by rightholders when they authorised the initial communication[1290] *or* (ii) a public targeted using 'specific technical means' that are different from those that have been previously used (i.e., through a technology that is different from the one used in the primary communication).[1291] Although both sub-criteria are now part of the Court's settled case law, they find no textual support in international or EU copyright instruments, having emerged both as judicial creations.[1292]

These two sub-criteria provide clear evidence of the CJEU's capacity to distinguish precedents (contrary to what Matthias Leistner has argued[1293]).

1287. *See, e.g.*, CJEU, *Mediakabel*, para. 30; CJEU, *Lagardère*, para. 31; CJEU, *SCF*, para. 84; CJEU, *PPI*, para. 33; CJEU, *ITV Broadcasting I*, para. 32; CJEU, *Reha Training*, para. 41; and CJEU, *GS Media*, para. 36.
1288. *See* CJEU, *SCF*, para. 86, and CJEU, *Reha Training*, paras 42-43. Prior to the CJEU's intervention, there was already a degree of common ground among Member States, most of which considered that the 'public' requirement was not fulfilled when the communication was made within the communicator's circle of family and friends – *see* Goldstein & Hugenholtz (2012), p. 318.
1289. In a pending reference before the CJEU, AG Hogan advised the Court to decide that the transmission by electronic means of a protected work to a court, as evidence in judicial proceedings between individuals, was not directed at an indeterminate number of people, since that communication would be aimed 'at a clearly defined and limited or closed group of people who exercise their functions in the public interest and who are, subject to verification by the referring court, bound by legal and ethical rules concerning, inter alia, the use and disclosure of information and evidence received in the course of court proceedings', even if it could very well surpass a *de minimis* threshold given the potentially high number of court officials – AG Opinion, *BY*, paras 42-44.
1290. The 'new public criterion' was introduced in CJEU, *SGAE*, paras 40-42.
1291. The 'specific technical means' criterion was introduced in CJEU, *ITV Broadcasting I*, para. 39.
1292. *See* Quintais (2017a), p. 171. Scholars have criticised the criteria for being at odds with international law – *see* ALAI (2014) (on both criteria) and Hugenholtz & Velze (2016) (focusing on the 'new public' criterion).
1293. *See supra* section 5.3.

As to the first sub-criterion ('new public'), the distinction established by the Court between the *Svensson* and *Renckhoff* cases is particularly illustrative. In *Renckhoff*, the Court addressed the question of whether the re-posting of a work, which was freely accessible to all Internet users on a third-party website with the rightholder's authorisation, on a person's own publicly accessible website amounted to an infringement of the right of communication to the public. The Court extensively cited its earlier decision in *Svensson*, where it had held that hyperlinking to freely accessible and authorised works should not be considered a communication to a new public. However, the *Svensson* ruling, as explicitly stated by the CJEU, 'was handed down in the specific context of hyperlinks'.[1294] The two cases were carefully distinguished on the facts: while *Renckhoff* concerned the communication of a work by *posting* it on a different website from that on which it was originally communicated, *Svensson* concerned the communication of such a work by *including a hyperlink* on a website that leads to the website on which the work was originally communicated. In the former case (re-posting), unlike in the latter (hyperlinking), the act of the user was deemed to constitute a communication to a new public. This was so, according to the Court, because: (i) hyperlinking, as opposed to re-posting, is essential to the sound operation of the Internet;[1295] (ii) re-posting the work, as opposed to hyperlinking thereto, makes it impossible or much more difficult for the rightholder to request the cessation of the communication;[1296] and (iii) holding otherwise would amount to extending the rule of exhaustion to the right of communication to the public, which is specifically prohibited by Article 3(3) InfoSoc Directive.[1297]

The development of the second sub-criterion ('specific technical means') provides further evidence. The sub-criterion was created in *ITV Broadcasting I*, a case that concerned a service, offered by a company called TV Catchup, which allowed users to receive online live streams of free-to-air TV broadcasts, including those transmitted by UK broadcaster ITV.[1298] The service was restricted to UK residents who held a UK TV licence and who could therefore already lawfully receive ITV's broadcasts in their catchment area. The Court was asked whether such a retransmission fell within the concept of 'communication to the public' within the meaning of Article 3(1) InfoSoc Directive. The retransmission in question was found to be a communication to a 'public'.[1299] TV Catchup contended, nonetheless, that its retransmission did not satisfy the 'new public' criterion (which had already been developed by the Court at the time, unlike the 'specific technical means'

1294. CJEU, *Renckhoff*, para. 39.
1295. *See* CJEU, *Renckhoff*, para. 40.
1296. *See* CJEU, *Renckhoff*, para. 30.
1297. *See* CJEU, *Renckhoff*, paras 32-33.
1298. *See* CJEU, *ITV Broadcasting I*, para. 9.
1299. *See* CJEU, *ITV Broadcasting I*, para. 36.

one), since the recipients were entitled to follow the broadcasts using their TV sets anyway.[1300] Crucially, the Court distinguished the proceedings under consideration from the *SGAE*, *Premier League*, and *Airfield* cases invoked by TV Catchup.[1301] Those cases related to 'situations in which an operator had made accessible, by its deliberate intervention, a broadcast containing protected works to a new public which was not considered by the authors concerned when they authorised the broadcast in question'.[1302] 'By contrast', the Court proceeded, 'the main proceedings in the present case concern the transmission of works included in a terrestrial broadcast and the making available of those works over the internet.' These two transmissions 'must be authorised individually and separately by the authors concerned given that each is made under *specific technical conditions*, using a different means of transmission for the protected works, and each is intended for a public. In those circumstances, it is no longer necessary to examine below the requirement that there must be a new public.'[1303]

Note that the Court did not overrule the legal reasoning in the applicable precedents, nor did it raise doubts on its soundness.[1304] What it did was to invoke a material difference in the facts of *ITV Broadcasting I* in order to apply those precedents only partially. In other words, the Court *distinguished* the cases.[1305]

Let us now return to outlining the criteria set forth by the Court in developing the notion of 'communication to the public'. Besides the two major requirements and their respective sub-criteria, the CJEU sometimes

---

1300. *See* CJEU, *ITV Broadcasting I*, para. 37.

1301. In the Court's words, 'it should be noted that the situations examined in the cases which gave rise to the abovementioned judgments *differ clearly* from the situation at issue in the case in the main proceedings' – CJEU, *ITV Broadcasting I*, para. 38 (emphasis added).

1302. CJEU, *ITV Broadcasting I*, para. 38.

1303. CJEU, *ITV Broadcasting I*, para. 39 (emphasis added).

1304. Only very seldom does the Court expressly overrule its own previous decisions. This much was recognised by AG Maduro in *Cipolla*, para. 28, where he stated that '[t]he Court has always shown itself to be circumspect with regard to reversing an interpretation of the law given in earlier judgments'. Similarly, AG La Pergola in *Sema Sürül*, fn. 35, admitted that cases of overruling are 'as few as they are celebrated', citing some examples. In the field of copyright, it is worth mentioning the proposal advanced by AG Wathelet in *GS Media*, paras 44-60, of departing from the *Svensson* precedent according to which posting hyperlinks on a website to protected works freely accessible on another website is an 'act of communication' within the meaning of Article 3(1) InfoSoc Directive (a proposal which was not followed in the Court's judgment). For commentary, *see* Ramalho (2016b) (suggesting that '[t]he aim of fostering the development of the information society is also probably what led the AG to depart from a path that had started to be carved out in previous decisions') and Rendas (2017a).

1305. The technique of distinguishing has been described by Jacob (2016), p. 127, as 'a process of reverse analogy whereby a putative precedent is declared not to bear on the present situation'. Jacob claims that '[t]he ECJ routinely makes use of distinguishing as an avoidance technique' (p. 130).

cites a third criterion: the profit-making nature of the communication.[1306] Taking the Court's reasoning at face value, it seems that this criterion has greater relevance in cases involving communications of subject matter protected by related rights than of copyright-protected works. While in *SCF*, a related rights case,[1307] the absence of a profit-making nature in the communication of phonograms broadcast by radio in a dentist's waiting room was found determinative,[1308] in copyright cases the Court has consistently deemed this factor to be neither 'necessary' nor 'essential' for the existence of a communication to the public, though simultaneously considering it 'not irrelevant'.[1309]

More recently, in the Court's case law on hyperlinking, the profit-making nature of the communication acquired a new role within the analysis of the existence of a new public. In *GS Media* – which concerned the question of whether hyperlinking to a freely accessible website where the work was available without the consent of the rightholder (unlike in *Svensson*) was a communication to the public – the CJEU attributed unusual importance to the pursuit of profit by the user.[1310] The relevance of this criterion manifested itself in a presumption of knowledge of illegality created by the Court, with the presumption's trigger lying in the profit-making nature of the act:[1311] when the posting of hyperlinks is carried out for profit, a *juris tantum* presumption that the linker knew of the illegal status of the works applies and, if the presumption is not rebutted, the linker is considered to have communicated the work to a new public.

The Court confirmed the significance of the for-profit criterion, as well as of the existence of knowledge of illegality, in *Filmspeler* and *Ziggo*. In the former judgment, the Court determined that the sale of multimedia players containing add-ons that linked to unauthorised audiovisual works, which was undeniably made 'with a view to making a profit', constituted a communication to the public.[1312] As held in the latter case, the same applied to the making available and management of a platform like The Pirate Bay, which 'generates considerable advertising revenues'.[1313]

1306. Arguing that there is no indication in international law that the concept of 'communication to the public', in any of its modalities, might be limited by the 'profit-making nature' element, *see* ALAI (2014), fn. 21.
1307. The case concerned the interpretation of the concept of 'communication to the public' within the remuneration right of performers and phonogram producers in Article 8(2) Rental and Lending Directive. The Court has stated that the profit-making nature of the communication is all the more relevant in cases concerning this right, given its essentially financial nature – *see* CJEU, *SCF*, paras 88-89, and CJEU, *PPI*, para. 36.
1308. *See* CJEU, *SCF*, paras 90, 97, and 99.
1309. *See, e.g.*, CJEU, *SGAE*, para. 44; CJEU, *Premier League*, para. 204; CJEU, *ITV Broadcasting I*, paras 42-43; CJEU, *Filmspeler*, para. 34; and CJEU, *Ziggo*, para. 29.
1310. *See* CJEU, *GS Media*, para. 38.
1311. *See* CJEU, *GS Media*, paras 47-54.
1312. *See* CJEU, *FIlmspeler*, paras 51-52.
1313. CJEU, *Ziggo*, para. 46.

Whether this role of the profit-making nature of the communication, as well as of knowledge of illegality, is relevant beyond the cases on hyperlinking is something that remains unclear.[1314] The subsequent ruling in *Renckhoff*, which involved re-posting of content (and not hyperlinking) and where the Court made no reference to these elements,[1315] suggests that the answer may be in the negative. Moreover, AG Szpunar and AG Saugmandsgaard Øe, in their opinions on two preliminary references which are pending at the time of writing, have called into question the subjective element of knowledge of the facts.[1316]

It is crucial to observe that neither the profit-making nature of the communication nor the sub-criteria that are relevant under each of the two cumulative requirements are treated by the Court as 'per se determinative of the qualification of the right'.[1317] In examining whether a communication to the public within the meaning of Article 3 InfoSoc Directive has been made, the Court understands these other criteria as being 'complementary', 'non-autonomous', and 'interdependent'. Depending on the situation under consideration, they may 'be present to widely varying degrees' and 'they must be applied individually and in the light of their interaction with one another'.[1318] These statements by the Court appear to indicate that the different sub-criteria work as *factors* that the Court balances on a case-by-case basis.[1319] When looking at the broader picture provided by this body of case law, one cannot help but have the impression that this is the type of exercise the CJEU is conducting. The Court hints at this much when it says that the concept of communication to the public 'requires an *individual*

1314. *See* Angelopoulos (2017b), p. 22.

1315. Unlike the designated AG – *see* AG Opinion, *Renckhoff*, paras 80-85, giving explicit relevance to the lack of profit motive of the users.

1316. *See* AG Opinion, *YouTube/Cyando*, para. 113 ('It is true that in *GS Media* the Court ruled that when the person who posts on a website hyperlinks to protected works published without the authorisation of their author on another website does so for the purpose of making a profit, it must be presumed (subject to rebuttal) that that person had knowledge of the protected nature of those works and of that lack of authorisation. However, aside from the fact that, in its subsequent case-law, the Court seems to have confined this approach to hyperlinks, I think that, in any event, this presumption cannot be applied in this present cases [*sic*]'), and AG Opinion, *VG Bild-Kunst*, para. 54 ('that solution is unorthodox from the point of view of general copyright rules, in particular in that it introduces a subjective criterion (knowledge of the facts) into the definition of an objective element, namely the scope of the acts subject to the exclusive right of the author').

1317. Quintais (2018), p. 388. *See also* Angelopoulos (2017b), p. 22, stating that 'all of these criteria are best seen as operating in a mutually supportive manner'.

1318. *See* CJEU, *SCF*, para. 79; CJEU, *PPI*, para. 30; CJEU, *Reha Training*, para. 35; CJEU, *GS Media*, para. 34; CJEU, *Filmspeler*, para. 30; and CJEU, *Ziggo*, para. 25.

1319. *See* Leistner (2014a), p. 570, and Quintais (2018), p. 388.

assessment'.[1320] This individual (or case-by-case) assessment is characteristic of standards, in the sense in which they are opposed to rules.[1321]

Nonetheless, in specifying the elements that must be taken into account under the vague formula of 'communication to the public', the Court provides guidance to stakeholders and helps litigators evaluate the merits of their cases. The consideration of the criteria described above has led the CJEU to hold that the right of communication to the public applies to a variety of uses of protected works. In the analogue environment, the right has been interpreted as covering the transmission of broadcast signals by means of TV or radio sets in hotels,[1322] pubs,[1323] restaurants,[1324] spas,[1325] and rehabilitation centres.[1326] The CJEU has also pondered over the meaning and scope of the right regarding an array of digital uses: retransmission by means of Internet streaming of terrestrial TV broadcasts (*ITV Broadcasting I* and *II*); hyperlinking to freely accessible and legally uploaded works (*Svensson*); embedded linking to freely accessible and legally uploaded works (*BestWater*); hyperlinking to live broadcasts in circumvention of a paywall (*C More Entertainment*); hyperlinking to freely accessible but illegally uploaded works (*GS Media*); digital exploitation of out-of-print books made by CMOs (*Soulier & Doke*); sale of a multimedia player with pre-installed add-ons containing hyperlinks to freely accessible websites where unauthorised works have been made available (*Filmspeler*); offering and management of an online platform that allows users to locate and share protected works via a P2P network (*Ziggo*); the services of an online platform allowing users to store copies of free-to-air TV programmes in private cloud storage spaces (*VCAST*); the posting on a website of a photograph previously posted, with no technical restrictions and with the rightholder's consent, on another website (*Renckhoff*); and the supply by downloading, for permanent use, of e-books (*Tom Kabinet*).[1327] While some of these uses have been held to come within the scope of exclusivity (e.g., *ITV Broadcasting I*, *GS Media*, *Ziggo*,

---

1320. CJEU, *GS Media*, para. 33 (emphasis added). *See also* CJEU, *SCF*, para. 76; CJEU, *PPI*, paras 29 and 38; CJEU, *Filmspeler*, para. 28; and CJEU, *Ziggo*, para. 23.
1321. On the difference between rules and standards, *see supra* Chapter 3, section 2.1.2. Noting that 'this flexible approach … almost turns Article 3 InfoSoc Directive into a "fair use" provision', *see* Ohly (2018), p. 103.
1322. *See* CJEU, *SGAE*, para. 47; CJEU, *Organismos Sillogikis*, para. 43; and CJEU, *PPI*, para. 47.
1323. *See* CJEU, *Premier League*, para. 207.
1324. *See* CJEU, *SPA*, para. 28.
1325. *See* CJEU, *OSA*, para. 41.
1326. *See* CJEU, *Reha Training*, para. 65.
1327. At the time of manuscript submission, a number of relevant references were pending before the CJEU, *inter alia* on whether online platforms of user-uploaded video content and cloud-based 'share-hosting' services could be considered to commit acts of communication to the public within the meaning of Article 3(1) InfoSoc Directive (C-682/18 and C-683/18, *YouTube/Cyando*) and on the lawfulness of frame linking and inline linking (C-392/19, *VG Bild-Kunst*).

and *Renckhoff*), liability for others has been ruled out (e.g., *Svensson* and *BestWater*).

None of the above should be read as suggesting that the CJEU's case law on communication to the public is problem-free or perfectly predictable. That, to be clear, is far from being the case. The interpretation of the right of communication to the public in relation to acts of hyperlinking is a particularly delicate and intricate matter,[1328] and the Court's approach in these cases has been characterised by scholars as a source of 'dogmatic difficulties'.[1329] Several problems and areas of uncertainty have been identified in that string of cases, namely the contours of the knowledge test introduced in *GS Media*, the meaning of 'for-profit' linking, and the line dividing primary and secondary liability under Article 3(1).[1330]

But the fact that the Court's interpretative case law has left (and will inevitably continue to leave) open issues *does not* entail that the Court is incapable of providing guidance on the basis of standard-like doctrines. The gradual, case-by-case judicial harmonisation and systematisation of a doctrine inescapably raises new questions, whose implications will have to be explored in upcoming references. Rome was not built in a day – and neither can we expect a coherent line of case law to be. We may disagree with certain aspects of the Court's case law on communication to the public (I, for one, disagree with some of them), but it is the very emergence of those aspects that shows the Court's capacity to construe a body of decisions with the sub-rules and factors that render a standard-like provision more predictable. What the foregoing analysis tells us, borrowing the words of Christina Angelopoulos, is that 'the CJEU is ponderously – and perhaps somewhat haphazardly – pulling together a harmonised European notion of a communication to the public for copyright. What the ultimate conclusion on what that notion looks like might be is still somewhat blurry. A picture is however emerging.'[1331]

6 CONCLUSION

This chapter attempted to conduct a critical assessment of the InfoSoc framework of exceptions. The underlying purpose was to examine whether the framework achieves a balance between the criteria and objectives identified in the previous chapter and, ultimately, to answer the question that

1328. Focusing on individual or multiple judgments within this line, *see* Arezzo (2014); Guibault & Quintais (2014); Headdon (2014); Savola (2014) and (2017); Leistner (2017); Rendas (2017a); Rosati (2017a); and Quintais (2018).
1329. Leistner (2017b), p. 28. *See also* Quintais (2017a), p. 187.
1330. Discussing these and other open issues left by the CJEU's recent hyperlinking case law, *see* Savola (2017), pp. 144-150, and Quintais (2018), pp. 398-414.
1331. Angelopoulos (2017b), p. 22.

has been dividing the copyright community for years: should the InfoSoc framework of exceptions be reformed?

The fundamental conclusion that emerges from this chapter is that most criteria are met to an insufficient extent. This unpalatable state of affairs undermines the attainment of the four normative objectives: (1) adaptability to technology-related changes, (2) adaptability to national cultures, (3) guidance on the legal status of unauthorised uses, and (4) harmonisation. Let us consider them in turn.

The framework is fundamentally flawed in what concerns the goal of ensuring *adaptability to technology-related changes*. Member States currently enjoy very limited freedom to legislate autonomously and, in any case, increasing such freedom would entail compromising the goal of harmonisation. The burden of updating the framework thus rests on the shoulders of the EU legislator, which are, in principle, authorised to update the catalogue of exceptions in order to adapt it to the emergence of new digital uses. Nonetheless, relying on periodic updates of the catalogue at the EU level is an impractical solution, given the pace of technological change. The EU ordinary legislative procedure is complex and lengthy and the level of lobbying that nowadays characterises copyright law-making, as illustrated by the recent DSM Directive, makes the adoption of new legislation or the revision of existing instruments even harder. This casts considerable doubt over the idea that the task of updating the framework of exceptions should be the job of legislators solely.

To make things worse, Article 5-type exceptions grant a limited degree of discretion on judges. The narrow and precise wording of the exceptions to the InfoSoc rights of reproduction and communication to the public contribute to EU copyright law's incapacity to adapt swiftly to technological change. The formulation of exceptions contrasts with the broad reach of economic rights. This imbalance might deter innovation in digital industries and the associated economic growth in the EU. In a rapidly evolving technological environment, the development and operation of new services depends on the existence of sufficient breathing space for unauthorised uses of protected works.[1332] The InfoSoc three-step test provides no relief either, since it works as a one-sided, rightholder-centric standard, adding to the restrictive character of the InfoSoc framework. The InfoSoc Directive thus lacks a doctrinal mechanism that allows courts to take account of the competing interests of rightholders and users in deciding whether to accommodate new uses. Judges, both at the national and CJEU levels, have tried to work around this lack of adaptability in creative ways, employing alternative constructions as a way to render certain uses non-infringing. Yet, judicial pragmatism can hardly be considered a sustainable solution to the problem.

1332. *See* Senftleben (2009), p. 6. For an overview of the main characteristics of online business models, *see* Guibault et al. (2007), pp. 7-16.

The framework would also benefit from an enhanced performance in terms of *guidance on the legal status of unauthorised uses*. Although the listed exceptions provide stakeholders with relatively precise indications, the need to apply the elusive three-step test as a second tier of scrutiny ends up blurring the line between lawful and unlawful behaviour and ultimately corrodes the certainty that emerges from the wording of exceptions.

In addition, the judges' search for adaptability has led them to soften the strictness of the framework of exceptions. Courts that find the solution dictated by the wording of the governing copyright provisions unsatisfactory will on occasion strip off the straitjacket and bypass those provisions (sometimes openly, other times less so), in order to deliver context-sensitive and case-specific decisions.[1333] These judgments also imply that the InfoSoc framework is producing less predictability than expected. Attempts to foresee the outcome of such cases based on the text of the applicable copyright exceptions alone would be largely deemed to fail, since judges either circumvented their literal application or summoned alternative legal doctrines.[1334] In these circumstances, the argument that users and rightholders are being 'clearly warned about the limit between legal and illegal behaviour'[1335] when relying on Article 5-type exceptions will no longer hold.[1336] Arguably, having judicial decisions sidestepping the governing rules – rules that concerned parties legitimately expect will guide the court – has a more adverse effect on legal certainty than having decisions guided by transparently open-ended provisions. If the most immediately applicable statutory provisions conferred greater discretion on judges, there would certainly be no need to resort to these 'interpretative gymnastics'.[1337] Courts would do significantly better if they could decide this type of cases in a methodologically transparent manner – that is, '*intra legem* rather than *praeter* or even *contra legem*'.[1338]

This trend in the behaviour of courts should not be read as confirming fears of transferring a greater share of the burden of guidance to the judicial branch. On the contrary, when interpreting vague doctrines and concepts of EU copyright law, the CJEU has proven capable of developing their meaning in a coherent and systematised manner. The Court's case law on 'originality'

1333. *See* Hugenholtz & Senftleben (2011), p. 9, and Dreier (2015), p. 141.
1334. Some of these doctrines were not obvious candidates to explain the decision. Of course, one may argue that the reasonably informed jurist would also look beyond copyright law, in search for other doctrines that might apply to the dispute at hand. But even if the answer to the legal question is clear under those alternative doctrines (which is not always the case), it is not copyright law *itself* that is providing such certainty. On the contrary: copyright law points towards an answer that is opposite to the answer provided by the application of those doctrines.
1335. Lucas (2010), p. 282.
1336. *See* Kleinemenke (2013b), pp. 115-116.
1337. The expression is borrowed from Aplin (2009), p. 71, who uses it in relation to the accommodation of new types of protectable subject matter.
1338. Ohly (2018), p. 119.

and 'communication to the public' shows that it is very much capable of sharpening the edges of open-ended concepts by introducing certain requirements, criteria, and factors that make judicial analysis more routinised and, over time, more predictable for stakeholders. This capacity further supports the introduction of a standard-like provision within the EU system of exceptions.

The goal of *adaptability to national cultures* is the goal that has been most successfully achieved. Although the InfoSoc framework of exceptions leans clearly towards the *droit d'auteur* tradition (to the detriment of the common law one), it takes national legal particularities into due consideration through three of its features. First, some of those particularities have been incorporated in the long and heterogeneous catalogue of exceptions itself. Second, the grandfather clause in Article 5(3)(o) grants Member States some latitude to accommodate local and long-established situations. Third, the optional nature of permitted uses has the effect of not forcing Member States to implement exceptions that they find unnecessary. It should not be forgotten, however, that the respect for national legal differences and for the cultural diversity within the Union must be balanced with the need to achieve a harmonised framework of exceptions.

And, in fact, in safeguarding national cultural autonomy the EU legislator has partly overlooked the objective of *harmonisation*. The InfoSoc legislative framework of exceptions has produced mixed effects. On the one hand, the catalogue in Article 5 has promoted a higher degree of harmonisation than before: it has led some Member States to implement exceptions that previously existed in other Member States and, due to its exhaustiveness, it has prevented them from increasing fragmentation by autonomously adding new exceptions. On the other hand, the fact that most exceptions in Article 5 are optional has contributed towards the preservation of an unharmonised mosaic of exceptions throughout the EU. This feature can be prejudicial for the functioning of the internal market, especially in the case of exceptions that are vital for activities and services that take place across borders. In future revisions of the *acquis*, these exceptions should be made compulsory for Member States to implement, in line with the approach that the EU has been following in recent legislative initiatives.

The CJEU has been filling some of the lacunae in copyright harmonisation, by reducing the freedom of national legislators and national courts in dealing with exceptions. Throughout a series of rulings, the Court has abandoned an approach of deference towards the implementation choices of Member State legislators. Additionally, it is steadily eliminating the interpretative freedom of Member State courts, by attributing the status of 'autonomous concepts of EU law' to fundamental notions in the exceptions' *acquis* and unilaterally defining their meaning and scope.

In light of the above, Table 4.1 summarises the conclusions and recommendations reached throughout this chapter according to the criteria developed in Chapter 3.

Table 4.1 Conclusions and Recommendations per Assessment Criterion

	Objectives	*Criteria*	*Conclusions/Recommendations*
Flexibility	Adaptability to technology-related changes	Legislative responsiveness	Tackling the issue of adaptability through the legislative side is ill-advised. Whereas increasing responsiveness at the EU level would be difficult, given the intricacy of the ordinary legislative procedure, promoting Member State autonomy would undermine the goal of harmonisation.
		Judicial discretion	In order to ensure adaptability and to avoid the uncertainty that flows from the use of makeshift judicial techniques, the level of judicial discretion and transparency should be increased through the introduction of an open-ended exception.
	Adaptability to national cultures	Accommodation of Member States' legal traditions	The InfoSoc framework follows the *droit d'auteur* tradition of rule-like exceptions, but could strive to reach a compromise with the contrasting common law technique of open-ended exceptions.
		Accommodation of Member States' specificities	The long list of exceptions and a grandfather-type clause should be maintained. Some exceptions should be made mandatory, while leaving optional those that are connected to national cultural policies.

	Objectives	*Criteria*	*Conclusions/Recommendations*
Legal certainty	Guidance on the legal status of unauthorised uses	Legislative guidance	The degree of guidance provided by narrow and precise exceptions should be preserved or furthered. The three-step test lacks sufficiently developed meaning and should thus be reviewed or simply eliminated.
		Judicial guidance	The CJEU's capacity to develop the meaning of vague doctrines in a coherent and systematised manner supports the introduction of an open-ended exception within EU copyright law.
	Harmonisation across Member States	Harmonising effect of legislation	The exhaustiveness of the catalogue should be maintained, preventing national legislators from autonomously adding exceptions. The exceptions with greater internal market relevance should be made mandatory, in line with the approach followed in recent directives. The extent of Member State freedom should be made clear in the text of the Directive.
		Harmonising effect of CJEU case law	The CJEU has abandoned an approach of deference towards the implementation choices of Member State legislators and has been steadily eliminating the interpretative freedom of Member State courts, which ought to resort to the preliminary reference mechanism to clarify the meaning of EU copyright doctrines.

The application of the conceptual apparatus developed in Chapter 3 has thus allowed us to identify the InfoSoc framework's shortcomings and to recognise examples of features that should be conserved or fostered in the future. In this regard, the main lessons that spill over to the next chapter are the following ones:

(i) a list of rule-like exceptions should be maintained, as well as a clause that allows for the accommodation of local diversities;
(ii) some of these exceptions should be made mandatory;
(iii) the role of the three-step test should be reconsidered; and
(iv) the issue of adaptability to technology-related changes should be tackled through the adoption of a provision that allows courts to exercise discretion in a transparent manner and whose meaning is to be developed by the CJEU.

All things considered, the analysis above lends support to the majoritarian position among copyright scholars according to which the InfoSoc framework of exceptions needs to be reformed. The following chapter builds on the conclusions that have just been outlined and advances concrete proposals in that regard.

Chapter 5
A Road Map for Reform

1 INTRODUCTION

The previous chapter established the need to reform the InfoSoc framework of exceptions in light of the purpose of achieving a balance between flexibility and legal certainty. It is now time to set forth a road map on how to go about such reform.[1339] Having concluded that the existing framework fails to attain a proper equilibrium between the goals uncovered in Chapter 3, we turn to our final research question: *how* should the InfoSoc framework of exceptions be reformed? How should it be redesigned so as to stand the test of time, while providing a high degree of guidance to interested parties and respecting European traditions?

The term 'reform' is used here in opposition to an alternative step-by-step approach characterised by sporadic amendments to the exceptions' *acquis*. The act of *reforming* EU copyright law, as it is understood in this book, does not refer to mere updates thereto, but only to changes with a view to improving it from a structural standpoint.[1340] The ambition of this chapter, however, is not to come up with a full-fledged set of statutory provisions that are ready to be adopted by the EU legislator. Given the quandaries of the legislative process, particularly at the EU level, that would most likely be a

1339. Given the scope of the book, the chapter will be concerned with proposals for reforming EU copyright law. Nonetheless, at specific points, it will discuss proposals for rewriting (or at least reinterpreting) international law, especially in relation to the three-step test, analysing them, *mutatis mutandis*, as potential EU-level solutions. Operating reform at the international level would, in any case, face much greater challenges, as generally recognised by commentators – *see, e.g.*, Koelman (2006), pp. 411-412; Mazziotti (2008), p. 305; Griffiths (2009), p. 442; and Janssens (2009), p. 320.

1340. *See* Lewinski (2018), p. 134, contrasting a step-by-step approach with a fundamental reform of exceptions (but supporting the former). The concept of 'reform' is, for some authors, more restrictive. Efroni (2011), pp. 415 et seq., generally refers to proposals for structural changes to the framework of exceptions as 'neoconservative approaches', in contrast to 'reformist approaches', the first being less radical than the second, in that they remain largely faithful to the principle of exclusivity that underlies the copyright system.

futile exercise. Rather, it aims at providing guidelines for a future (and direly needed) reform.

The chapter sketches a multi-tiered framework of exceptions that implements the lessons regarding the general direction of InfoSoc reform learned in the preceding chapter.[1341] By 'multi-tiered' (or 'hybrid') framework I mean a framework that combines an enumeration of rule-like exceptions for specific uses with an opening provision that grants courts the discretion to decide *ex post* whether certain uses should be considered infringing or non-infringing.[1342]

As already implied by this description, I oppose *entirely replacing* the catalogue of exceptions with an open-ended clause for deciding concrete cases of copyright infringement – what is sometimes called in German literature the 'grand solution' (*Große Lösung*).[1343] The benefits that this radical solution could entail in terms of flexibility would not make up for the severe lack of guidance that it would generate. This would, in another commentator's words, be akin to 'shooting sparrows with cannons'.[1344] Enumerating narrower privileges for recurring uses entails that these uses

---

1341. It should be clarified at the outset that, as this book is an exercise in legal analysis, considerations related to the proposal's political feasibility, important as they are, will play a secondary role only. On the political realism of amending the InfoSoc Directive, *see*, *e.g.*, Hilty (2010), p. 85.

1342. Other commentators before me have manifested their preference for such hybrid frameworks. *See* Senftleben (2004), pp. 304 et seq.; Geiger (2006b), p. 698; Guibault et al. (2007), pp. 65-67; Förster (2008), pp. 213-222; Lessig (2008), pp. 266-268; Janssens (2009), pp. 338-340; Wittem Group (2010); Christie (2011), pp. 134-135; Leistner (2011), pp. 438-439; Kleinemenke (2013a), pp. 557-558; Hugenholtz (2013c), p. 28; Ohly (2014), pp. 65-66; Westkamp (2014); and Samuelson (2017), p. 53. The model sketched in this chapter is elaborated on the assumption that a possible reform would focus only on *revising* the framework of exceptions within the InfoSoc Directive. The acts covered by the controversial Article 17 DSM Directive – which recognises a right that is *lex specialis* in relation to the InfoSoc right of communication to the public – would be excluded. On the qualification of Article 17 as *lex specialis*, *see* Husovec & Quintais (2020). Were such a reform to aim at consolidating the copyright *acquis* and the model could also refer to exceptions to rights harmonised by other directives, as proposed e.g. in the European Copyright Code drafted by the Wittem Group (*see infra* 4.2.1.1).

1343. *See*, *e.g.*, Förster (2008), pp. 213-222, and Schack (2016), p. 270.

1344. Förster (2008), p. 221, arguing that the frequency with which completely unforeseen uses emerge does not justify this 'grand solution'. Therefore – borrowing the similarly metaphorical words of Senftleben (2010), p. 77 –, 'it is unnecessary to sacrifice long-standing EC exceptions on the altar of a broad fair use provision'. Instead, Achim Förster advocates the partial and cautious opening of existing exceptions (a *kleine Lösung*), which would be combined with a supplementary standard for the cases that could not be accommodated by these listed exceptions. The author finds that this solution could be adopted in German law without the need for an amendment of the *acquis*. While I agree with the general direction of Förster's proposal, I disagree with the idea that no reform would be necessary. Given the closed character of the InfoSoc enumeration and the limitations meanwhile imposed by the CJEU on the leeway for

will not be exposed to the comparatively higher uncertainty of a case-by-case determination based on a standard-like exception.[1345]

This multi-tiered model of exceptions would allow us to achieve a better compromise between flexibility and legal certainty in the various dimensions identified in Chapter 3 – a compromise, first, between technological adaptability and guidance for stakeholders and, second, between the accommodation of different national cultures and harmonisation across Member States.

Section 2 describes the first tier of the proposed model and Section 3 the second one. Section 4 is dedicated to the third tier, arguably the most controversial part of the framework. Having identified, systematised and discussed different options for designing this tier, I ultimately recommend the adoption of a subsidiary 'CJEU-made' balancing test. I then address potential objections to the proposal and, after tackling each of them (section 5), I end by testing it against real-life cases (section 6).

2 THE FIRST TIER: AN EXHAUSTIVE CATALOGUE OF MANDATORY RULE-LIKE EXCEPTIONS

The fragmented landscape produced by the optional character of the vast majority of exceptions included in Article 5 InfoSoc Directive is harmful for legal certainty. Because national catalogues differ in terms of the listed exceptions as well as their wording, users that rely on the cross-border use of works may have difficulties in anticipating the legal consequences flowing from those uses. This approach, as observed by Christophe Geiger & Franciska Schönherr, 'is particularly problematic in the digital environment as the internet involves uses that, most of the time, affect several copyright legislations, leading to a major insecurity regarding what is allowed'.[1346] It also creates an imbalance vis-à-vis the most important economic rights, which have been fully harmonised and adapted to the digital era.[1347]

In view of this predicament, at least some InfoSoc exceptions (besides temporary reproduction) should be made mandatory for Member States to implement.[1348] As argued above, making exceptions mandatory is a path that

national implementation, it is highly doubtful that such a solution could be adopted at the national level without a legislative reform of EU law. In this sense, *see also* Hansen (2008), p. 407.

1345. *See* Kleinemenke (2014), p. 900.

1346. Geiger & Schönherr (2014), p. 111.

1347. *See* EPRS (2015), p. I-77, and Hilty & Köklü (2016), p. 291.

1348. *See*, *inter alia*, Guibault et al. (2007), pp. 65-66; Hilty et al. (2008), pp. 11-12; Janssens (2009), pp. 338-340; EPRS (2015), p. III-294; and Geiger et al. (2015), p. 19. On the introduction of mandatory exceptions at the international level, *see* Hugenholtz & Okediji (2008), pp. 43-44, and Kur & Ruse-Khan (2009). *But see* ALAI (2010), raising

the EU institutions seem willing to follow, judging by recent legislative initiatives in the field, namely the DSM Directive.

This enumeration of mandatory exceptions should remain exhaustive for Member State legislators. In other words, national lawmakers would not be allowed to introduce new exceptions without these being added to the EU catalogue beforehand. It would be incoherent to make some exceptions mandatory in the interests of harmonisation and then allow Member States to re-establish fragmentation by independently introducing new exceptions to their national catalogues.[1349] Were the catalogue to be an open one, the degree of legislative responsiveness to technological developments would likely increase, due to the higher national autonomy and the faster response time of Member State legislators when compared to that of the EU.[1350] Over time, however, this would result in only *some* Member States having exceptions for newly emerged uses, thus compromising the level playing field for rightholders and users that the copyright harmonisation process is intended to create.

I therefore disagree with the proposal, advanced by some scholars, of reinterpreting Recital 32 InfoSoc Directive, so as to clarify that it grants Member States some flexibility in this sense.[1351] While this solution would certainly allow room for creative experimentation by Member States,[1352] the negative effects for harmonisation across the EU would supersede that benefit.[1353] Instead, the exhaustive character of the enumeration – which could be established in a recital of the revised Directive, as is presently the case[1354] – would allow the preservation of the positive effects identified in section 2.1. of Chapter 4, whereas the negative ones would be mitigated by making some exceptions mandatory.

If *certain* exceptions are to become mandatory, the question then arises as to *which* of them should be granted that status.

---

doubts on the permissibility under the Berne Convention and TRIPS of a treaty providing mandatory exceptions.

1349. *See* Walter & Lewinski (2010), pp. 1020-1021.

1350. *See supra* Chapter 4, section 2.1.

1351. *See* Hugenholtz et al. (2006), p. 217.

1352. As noted by Hansen (2008), pp. 406-407.

1353. To make things worse, the interpretation of newly added exceptions at the national level would not fall within the realm of competence of the CJEU.

1354. *See* Recital 32 InfoSoc Directive. Ideally, the EU legislator would also clarify the specific meaning of exhaustiveness in the recital. As explained in Chapter 4, section 2.1, the exhaustive character of the catalogue produces a threefold effect. At the level of legislative law-making (i) it prohibits Member States from preserving in their national laws any exceptions other than the listed ones and (ii) it entails that Member States have no room to introduce new exceptions. Additionally, with regard to judicial law-making, (iii) it prevents judges from applying the listed exceptions by analogy to situations that are not expressly regulated by the catalogue. This latter effect, however, would be without prejudice to the proposed third tier.

Marie-Christine Janssens maintains that '[t]o achieve meaningful harmonisation, it is essential that as many exceptions as possible are uniformly applied in all Member States'.[1355] In the same vein, Christophe Geiger and colleagues, in analysing the DSM Proposal, argue that 'a true harmonisation of the DSM will only be achieved if *all* limitations and exceptions provided in the past EU copyright instruments are declared mandatory'.[1356]

This is a questionable proposition. Mandatory exceptions are a limitation of flexibility understood as the room for national cultural autonomy.[1357] As such, they should be carefully selected and justified, so as to balance flexibility (in this sense) with harmonisation. At the same time, it is no less true that if only the most widely implemented exceptions are made mandatory, not much would be done to improve the current situation. Later in the same piece, Janssens concedes that 'mandatory effect should particularly be conferred on exceptions that tend to have transnational or cross-border effects'.[1358] In principle, since the InfoSoc Directive is based on the internal market competence, it should not grant mandatory nature to exceptions beyond those that are necessary to guarantee the smooth functioning of the internal market.[1359] Also, there would be little point in imposing implementation in the case of uses that are unlikely to have any meaningful application across national borders.

Lucie Guibault and colleagues advance a list of exceptions that could be made mandatory based on their cross-border impact: the temporary reproduction exception (Article 5(1)), which is already mandatory; the reprography exception (Article 5(2)(a)); the private copying exception (Article 5(2)(b)); the exception for reproductions made by libraries and similar establishments (Article 5(2)(c)); the exception for research or private study via dedicated terminals in libraries and similar establishments (Article 5(3)(n)); and the exception for ephemeral recordings made by broadcasting organisations (Article 5(2)(d)). Besides these, the authors also propose that other exceptions be given mandatory status on grounds of their connection to the safeguard of fundamental rights and freedoms – specifically, the exceptions for quotation (Article 5(3)(d));[1360] news reporting (Article

1355. Janssens (2009), p. 338.
1356. Geiger et al. (2018c), p. 14.
1357. *See* Kur & Ruse-Khan (2009), p. 28.
1358. Janssens (2009), p. 339.
1359. This would be in consonance with Recital 31 InfoSoc Directive.
1360. The argument could also be made that the quotation exception should be granted mandatory nature so as to ensure consistency with Article 10(1) Berne Convention, under which it is already obligatory for Berne Union members. As stated by Xalabarder (2007), p. 398, 'since the [Berne Convention] obligation to exempt quotations remains effective among EU States, one can only regret that the [InfoSoc Directive] missed an opportunity to formally integrate such a prior common obligation into the EU *acquis*. Of course, this failure does not derogate the mandatory nature of the quotation exception within the Berne Union members, but may unnecessarily make things more complicated.' *See also* Xalabarder (2009), p. 110.

5(3)(c)); political speeches and public lectures (Article 5(3)(f)); parody (Article 5(3)(k)); teaching and scientific research (Article 5(3)(a));[1361] and use by disabled persons (Article 5(3)(b)).[1362,1363] Andrea Renda and colleagues offer a similar list, which includes the exception for the use of works made to be located in public places (Article 5(3)(h)).[1364]

Many of the foregoing exceptions have not been implemented in a number of Member States.[1365] Making them mandatory would therefore have tangible benefits. Moreover, the mandatory character of exceptions that are closely related to each other – such as the ones in Article 5(2)(c) and Article 5(3)(n) – would avoid the need for integrated or combined readings like the one carried out by the CJEU in the *Ulmer* case.[1366]

Some of these exceptions could be subject to the payment of fair compensation to rightholders, as is currently the case with reprography, private copying and reproduction of broadcasts made by social institutions – in relation to which the payment of fair compensation is made mandatory under the InfoSoc text itself (and not left to the discretion of Member States[1367]) – and as some scholars argue *should* be the case with other exceptions.[1368] In addition, the list could include other exceptions with an internal market impact, such as exceptions for UGC[1369] and for acts of non-deceptive hyperlinking.[1370]

1361. As seen, the DSM Directive has rendered (at least part of) this exception mandatory. *See supra* Chapter 4, section 3.2.3.
1362. The exception in Article 5(3)(b) has meanwhile been complemented by the Marrakesh exceptions with a view to stimulating the cross-border exchange of accessible format copies.
1363. *See* Guibault et al. (2007), p. 65. *See also* Hargreaves & Hugenholtz (2013), p. 8 (including in the list exceptions for information location, data mining, and UGC); Triaille et al. (2013), pp. 300-301 and 397 (adding that exceptions conveying a public interest of EU-wide importance could be made mandatory); and Voorhoof (2015), p. 351 (focusing on the exceptions that are based on the freedom of expression and information).
1364. On the cross-border importance of the so-called freedom of panorama exception, *see* EPRS (2015), p. I-136, stating that '[t]his exception is central in the modern digital age when both pictures and videos are posted on websites and platforms making these contents immediately available on a cross-border basis'.
1365. As evidenced in Westkamp (2007), pp. 84-94, and Renda et al. (2015), pp. 150-165. *See also* http://copyrightexceptions.eu/.
1366. *See supra* Chapter 4, section 5.2.2.2., describing the issue.
1367. *See* Recital 36 InfoSoc Directive.
1368. *See*, *e.g.*, Xalabarder (2007), p. 388 (suggesting the introduction of a compensation regime for some teaching uses under the exception for teaching and scientific research), and Hilty et al. (2008), p. 12 (proposing the introduction of fair compensation for revised exceptions for teaching and scientific research and for research and private study in libraries and similar establishments).
1369. *See*, *e.g.*, Ricolfi (2016), p. 464, and Quintais (2017b), pp. 204-205.
1370. *See*, *e.g.*, Schack (2016), p. 269 (focusing on German law), and Sirinelli et al. (2016), p. 5.

Furthermore, the statutory wording of these mandatory exceptions should provide as much guidance as possible.[1371] With that goal in mind, the EU legislator, in revising the catalogue, could codify the interpretative case law of the CJEU on the scope and meaning of specific exceptions. By way of example, it could clarify that:

- the private copying exception does not cover reproductions made from unlawful sources;[1372]
- under the exception for ephemeral recordings, a broadcasting organisation's own facilities include the facilities of any third party acting on behalf or under the responsibility of that organisation;[1373]
- the exception in Article 5(3)(n) does not cover the printing out of works on paper or their storage on devices like USB sticks;[1374]
- the quotation exception covers references made by means of hyperlinks to files which can be downloaded independently[1375]

These clarifications could be provided either in the text of the exceptions themselves or in the relevant recitals. Greater precision in the wording of exceptions would not only increase legislative guidance and lower the need for litigation and associated costs, but also signal the will of the EU legislator to ensure a uniform implementation,[1376] thereby reducing the space for diverging domestic implementations and judicial interpretations,[1377] as well as for creative constructions at the EU or national levels.[1378] Increased precision would furthermore reinforce the compatibility of the exceptions listed in the InfoSoc Directive with the international three-step test, namely with the first step ('certain special cases').

1371. Making similar suggestions, *see* Guibault et al. (2007), p. 66; Janssens (2009), p. 340; and Ohly (2014), pp. 65-66.
1372. *See* CJEU, *ACI Adam*, para. 58. The private copying exception proposed in the Wittem Code (Article 5.3(2)(a)), though formulated before *ACI Adam* was handed down, also takes the lawfulness of the source into account, privileging the 'reproduction by a natural person for private use, provided that the source from which the reproduction is made is not an obviously infringing copy'.
1373. *See* CJEU, *DR & TV2 Danmark*, para. 58. Recital 41 InfoSoc Directive currently says 'it is understood that a broadcaster's own facilities include those of a person acting on behalf of *and* under the responsibility of the broadcasting organisation' (emphasis added), while other language versions use the conjunction 'or'. Ideally, the clarification provided by the CJEU would be included in the exception's text.
1374. *See* CJEU, *Ulmer*, para. 57.
1375. *See* CJEU, *Spiegel Online*, para. 84.
1376. *See* Zolynski (2007), p. 43.
1377. *See* Janssens (2009), p. 340; Triaille et al. (2013), p. 397 (in relation to a possible revision of the exception for teaching and scientific research); and Lewinski (2018), p. 136 (in relation to the exceptions in the DSM Proposal).
1378. *See*, in general, Schauer (2003), p. 328 ('Recognising that sharp-edged rules will in practice be rounded, rule-makers may attempt to anticipate this effect by making the edges even sharper').

The risk of fragmentation caused by different implementations would also be alleviated by the mandatory nature of these exceptions. Judging by the way Member States have implemented the mandatory exception within Article 5(1), it would seem they are more prone to implementing exceptions in a literal or quasi-literal manner when these are of a compulsory character.[1379] In addition, the reduction in implementation freedom that the CJEU carried out over a series of rulings could be codified in a recital to a revised InfoSoc Directive, lending further strength to the harmonising effect of the catalogue.[1380] In parallel, the recitals could mention that the provisions recognising these exceptions are measures of full harmonisation,[1381] overturning, at least in part, the recent jurisprudence of the CJEU.[1382] The Court would most likely continue elaborating the autonomous interpretation to be given to the concepts within the various exceptions, provided that, as is currently the case, the exceptions make no reference to the national laws of Member States.[1383]

Of course, the selection of exceptions to be given mandatory status would be a highly controversial matter.[1384] Representatives of rightholders and users would cross swords in the Brussels battlefield, arguing, respectively, for shorter and longer lists.[1385] Although this section does not aim to provide a 'ready-to-use' catalogue of mandatory exceptions, it has no intention of belittling the difficulties linked with its fundamental proposal either. These difficulties notwithstanding, it is hoped that the suggestions in the preceding paragraphs could serve as a basis for further discussions, should the legislator decide to open the Pandora's box of InfoSoc exceptions in the future.

3 THE SECOND TIER: A QUASI-EXHAUSTIVE CATALOGUE OF OPTIONAL EXCEPTIONS

Despite the centrality of harmonisation, the regime of exceptions should also leave some room for diverse national solutions and independent cultural policies, in respect for the autonomy of Member States and for the principles

1379. As observed in Chapter 4, section 3.2.1, the temporary reproduction exception provided in Article 5(1) was implemented literally in almost every Member State, unlike most other exceptions.
1380. *See supra* Chapter 4, section 5.1.1.
1381. As was done, for instance, in the Unfair Commercial Practices Directive (recitals 14 and 15) and the Consumer Rights Directive (recitals 5-7).
1382. *See* CJEU, *Funke Medien*, para. 54, and CJEU, *Spiegel Online*, para. 39.
1383. *See supra* Chapter 4, section 5.1.2.
1384. *See* Eechoud et al. (2009), p. 94, noting that 'a broad, regional, consensus on the adoption of specific limitations is very difficult to achieve'. Hilty & Köklü (2016), p. 296, go further and call it a 'monumental task'.
1385. *See* Triaille et al. (2013), p. 302.

of subsidiarity and proportionality.[1386] Indeed, as pointed out by the ALAI, 'copyright exceptions are an area in which the warning that "one size does not fit all" is especially pertinent'.[1387]

In order to ensure the accommodation of Member States' particularities in the field of exceptions, two approaches can be followed.

The first option would be to include a single open-ended provision allowing Member States to provide exceptions for uses that have no (or merely negligible) impact on the internal market.[1388] This option should be considered second best for a twofold reason. For one thing, the expressions 'uses with no (or merely negligible) impact on the internal market' or, to borrow the wording of a condition in the grandfather clause, 'uses that do not affect the free circulation of goods and services within the Community', when unrestricted by any other conditions, could be interpreted by Member States in an excessively broad manner, thus undermining the goal of harmonisation. For another, the experience with the InfoSoc Directive shows that optional exceptions, when specifically enumerated, may nonetheless produce an unplanned harmonising outcome.[1389]

The second and better option is therefore to preserve a list of optional exceptions for those uses that: (i) are recurrent and can be described with some exactness; (ii) reflect the traditions within the different Member States; and (iii) lack a clear cross-border relevance. Because these exceptions would be optional and would not affect the internal market, they would need not be drafted in as precise a manner as the mandatory ones. This greater degree of imprecision would leave some leeway for Member States to adapt their wording to national specificities. At the same time, however, they could not be so broad or vague as to allow them to enter into territory that should be fully harmonised. A careful balancing in their wording would be required, if the enumeration were not to have unintended consequences.[1390]

Marie-Christine Janssens suggests that such a list of optional exceptions 'could include uses in relation to, for example, religious ceremonies, military

1386. Arguing that such a concern should be taken into consideration in a possible international instrument on copyright limitations and exceptions, *see* Hugenholtz & Okediji (2008), pp. 42-43. *But see* Janssens (2009), p. 339, contending that 'if one supports the ultimate goal of achieving a coherent European copyright system, it will be necessary to (gradually) abandon the long cherished belief that the notion of what constitutes a legitimate or public interest should always accommodate national particularities'.

1387. ALAI (2010), p. 3. *See also* Kur & Ruse-Khan (2009), pp. 28-30.

1388. *See* Janssens (2009), p. 344, discussing and opposing this solution.

1389. *See* Janssens (2009), p. 344. *See also supra* Chapter 4, section 2.3.

1390. It is important to point out that, given the narrow or non-existent cross-border relevance of these exceptions, concerns regarding the EU's competence to include such a list could legitimately be raised. Nonetheless, as previously noted, the internal market competence has typically been understood in a flexible (even lenient) way, as the very inclusion of a heterogeneous catalogue of optional exceptions in the InfoSoc Directive attests. The solution, thus, would not be unprecedented.

happenings and performances during public exams'.[1391] Lucie Guibault and colleagues, drawing on the list of exceptions in Article 5 InfoSoc Directive, argue that the following could remain optional: reproduction of broadcasts made by social institutions (Article 5(2)(e)); use for purposes of public security or to ensure the proper performance or reporting of administrative, parliamentary or judicial proceedings (Article 5(3)(e));[1392] use during religious celebrations or official celebrations organised by a public authority (Article 5(3)(g)); use of works, such as architecture or sculpture, made to be located permanently in public places (Article 5(3)(h));[1393] incidental inclusion of works in other material (Article 5(3)(i)); use for the purpose of advertising the public exhibition or sale of artistic works (Article 5(3)(j)); use in connection with the demonstration or repair of equipment (Article 5(3)(l)); and use of an artistic work in the form of a building or a drawing or plan of a building for the purposes of reconstructing the building (Article 5(3)(m)).[1394]

It is also recommended that the grandfather clause in Article 5(3)(o) be preserved.[1395] In order to avoid fragmentation that is prejudicial to the internal market, the clause should keep a narrow scope. The condition that the exceptions pre-exist in national law could possibly be eliminated, in order to allow Member States to respond to local cultural developments, provided that the remaining conditions (minor importance, analogue uses only, and lack of internal market relevance) are left intact.[1396]

The preservation of the grandfather clause, while not allowing for the accommodation by national legislators of new digital uses, would serve the double purpose of safeguarding the analogue specificities of the various Member States and ensuring that the enumeration of optional exceptions is not unduly long and detailed. The inclusion of such a clause means that this second catalogue is not strictly exhaustive, for it gives some – albeit very limited – discretion to Member State lawmakers.[1397]

1391. Janssens (2009), fn. 135.
1392. Within the context of this exception, and following the CJEU's case law in *Painer*, paras 102-112, it would be for each Member State to determine the requirements of public security in accordance with their national needs, provided they would do so within the limits imposed by EU law. On the other hand, as threats to public security have an increasingly transnational character, the 'public security' prong of the exception could be made mandatory.
1393. But note that the freedom of panorama has been considered a suitable candidate for the list of mandatory exceptions above – *see supra* section 2.
1394. *See* Guibault et al. (2007), p. 66.
1395. *See* Guibault et al. (2007), pp. 66-67.
1396. Making a similar suggestion, *see* Dreier (2015), p. 142.
1397. This quasi-exhaustiveness could be clarified in a recital to the revised Directive stating that the catalogue of optional exceptions is 'exhaustive, subject to the conditions of [the provision in which the grandfather clause is laid down]'.

4 THE THIRD TIER: A SUBSIDIARY STANDARD-LIKE EXCEPTION

In deciding whether to go for a rule-like or standard-like formulation of legal norms, there is no one-size-fits-all solution.[1398] In general, however, when the regulated phenomena are relatively simple and do not change unpredictably over time, categorical rules provide greater certainty.[1399] That is why I have proposed catalogues of rule-like provisions to deal with certain recurring uses.

By contrast, when the phenomena are particularly complex or variable, judicial discretion and context-specific decision-making may be essential.[1400] This is so for two interconnected reasons.

First, the legislator 'labours under one supreme handicap', as H.L.A. Hart once put it: 'the impossibility of foreseeing all possible combinations of circumstances that the future may bring'.[1401] This problem is especially palpable in fields, such as copyright law, that are permanently challenged by unpredictable changes in the digital environment. Judges, unlike legislators, do not work under such handicap: instead of having to determine the legal status of unanticipated uses *ex ante*, they make those determinations incrementally and after the uses emerge.

Second, giving wider discretion to the judiciary mitigates the problem of the lack of legislative responsiveness, by largely dispensing with the need

1398. *See* Grodin (1994), p. 572 ('[t]he overall lesson ... is that the tension between categorical and individualized decision making cannot equitably be resolved on the basis of a general preference for one over the other'). *See also* Schauer (2009), p. 194 ('there is no strategy that will be best in all contexts').

1399. *See* Braithwaite (2002), pp. 52-53.

1400. Endicott (2011b), p. 178, refers to this as '"the diversity principle": the principle that precise regulation cannot effectively be used to control a massively complex pattern of behaviour'. Of course, vagueness in statutory wording and the resulting judicial discretion are plainly inappropriate in some areas. Timothy Endicott gives the example of a hypothetical rule granting the right to vote upon 'adult' or 'mature' citizens. While adopting this vague formulation, as opposed to a precise voting age, would avoid problems of under- and over-inclusiveness, such discretion-granting norm in this area would increase the danger of corruption and promote a form of discrimination that is unacceptable in democracy – *see* Endicott (2011a), p. 22.

1401. Hart (1983), p. 270. In the words of Grant Gilmore, '[i]t is an unhappy fact of life that, while we can know the past only imperfectly, we know the future not at all. Our best informed guesses about what is going to happen next have an uncomfortable habit of missing the mark completely' – Gilmore (1967), p. 467 *See also*, referring specifically to the InfoSoc framework of exceptions, Hugenholtz (2002), p. 69-1 ('I think any lawmaker should realize that we do not understand that environment so well that we can predict what kind of exemptions are needed in the years to come'), and Patry (2011), p. 223 ('no legislature, no matter how careful or insightful, can think of all current uses, much less think of uses, technologies, or markets that are not yet existence [*sic*]').

for regular amendments to legislation.[1402] Since InfoSoc was adopted, many calls have been made by scholars and policymakers for the introduction of new exceptions for specific and relatively well-defined uses.[1403] The time it takes to pass these exceptions – coupled with the fact that the narrow and precise formulation they would predictably have would merely perpetuate the need for new exceptions whenever an unforeseen use emerges – makes relying on legislative intervention an ill-advised option. Besides being generally slow, legislative reforms may be further delayed 'because of politically strategic reasons or because of difficulties in reaching a consensus between various stakeholders'.[1404] Judges, unlike legislators, cannot take a *laissez-faire* approach and refrain from judging a claim submitted to them.[1405] Furthermore, they are less prone to the lobbying efforts by interest groups, while also able to hear the arguments made by both sides in a case. Provided they are shielded from external pressure, courts might thus be in a

1402. It may be argued that the same reason why it is impractical for the EU to keep updating the framework of exceptions – the lack of legislative responsiveness – should discourage us from advocating reform at all. In fact, a revision of the *acquis* with a view to introducing a solution as controversial as an opening provision could well take a decade (assuming it were ever to pass at all). The difference, however, is that the adoption of such a provision would aim precisely at eliminating the need for *multiple* amendments. As such, it would require only one amendment in order to provide the framework of exceptions with a sustainable source of adaptability.

1403. *See, inter alia*, Gowers Review (2006), p. 68 (recommending that the InfoSoc Directive be amended so as to include an exception for 'creative, transformative or derivative works'); 2008 Green Paper, pp. 19-20 (calling for the introduction of a specific exception for UGC); Geiger (2010a), pp. 532-533 (proposing the creation of a remunerated exception for creative reuses); Hargreaves Review (2011), p. 47 (recommending that the UK Government exert pressure at the EU level for the creation of 'an exception allowing uses of a work enabled by technology which do not directly trade on the underlying creative and expressive purpose of the work'); ALAI (2015), pp. 8-9 (reflecting on the possibility of introducing a carefully tailored exception for certain acts of hyperlinking, but within the WCT framework); Dreier (2015), p. 145 (claiming that there is a need for exceptions for 'the non-commercial sharing of images' and for 'the accidental and/or transformative, non-commercial use of copyright works on digital network platforms'); Sirinelli et al. (2016), p. 5 (proposing the introduction of a mandatory uncompensated copyright exception for acts of non-deceptive hyperlinking); Leistner & Metzger (2017), pp. 383-384 (suggesting the introduction of an exception allowing 'private users to share works with other private users on Internet platforms as long as such use is in accordance with fair practice and does not conflict with the exploitation of the work on the primary market'); and Quintais (2017b), pp. 204-205 (arguing in favour of a mandatory exception for UGC, in connection with an alternative reading of the 'normal exploitation' step in the three-step test).

1404. Depoorter (2009), p. 1859.

1405. To be sure, judicial proceedings may also be lengthy and cumbersome. Nonetheless, as noted by Depoorter (2009), 'legislative decision making, by the nature of its democratic processes, involves more deliberation and, ideally, the consultation of a wide range of stakeholders'. Legislators are therefore, in general, the 'slower rule-maker' (pp. 1858-1859).

better position to independently balance the competing interests of rightholders, users and the public at large.

Having this in mind, the third part of the proposed model is a subsidiary standard-like exception empowering courts to accommodate unlisted uses. The fundamental purpose of this tier is to account for the emergence of new uses, catering for the human inability to anticipate future changes in the technological landscape and minimising the need for legislative updates to the catalogue.[1406]

This standard would have the added advantage of promoting methodologically honest judicial decision-making, rendering unnecessary the use of doctrinal artifices by courts. With such a provision, judges would be given discretion to openly deal with changes in the technological environment against which copyright unfolds, instead of having to search for that discretion elsewhere. Simultaneously, it would help restore the catalogue of exceptions' original and frequently touted advantage of providing clear guidance on the permissibility of uses, in that the rule-like exceptions would no longer need to be twisted and expanded through makeshift interpretations to accommodate emerging uses.[1407]

4.1 Subsidiarity

Because a stand-alone exception with an open-ended nature would fail to attain an appropriate balance between flexibility and legal certainty, the third tier developed in this section is conceived to supplement an enumeration of rule-like exceptions.

It is submitted that a catalogue of such precisely defined exceptions coupled with a subsidiary standard is a superior solution to a standard combined with a list of typical examples of concretisations thereof. Apart from reducing the complexity of the framework, the former solution puts emphasis on the fact that the rule-like exceptions should be given prevalence over the opening clause, which exists primarily for those less frequent cases of unforeseen uses.[1408] Hence, the listed exceptions are *not* to be taken as specific examples of the broad and vague predicate of the standard-like exception, but as taking precedence over it.

Saying that the rule-like exceptions take precedence over the standard – or, differently put, that the standard has a subsidiary character – means that

1406. Of course, a residual standard-like exception would not preclude the introduction, in the future, of further rule-like exceptions, particularly of non-voluntary licences if they are deemed necessary. Adding new exceptions to the statutory catalogue would be advised if the legislators wanted to codify or clarify existing case law in statute as a way of increasing legal certainty – *see* Metzger (2010), p. 122. Naturally, the legislator could also use its prerogatives to correct the interpretative case law of the CJEU.
1407. *See* Ohly (2014), p. 65, and Kleinemenke (2014), p. 900.
1408. *See* Förster (2008), pp. 221-222.

the former should be deemed inapplicable before the deciding court in a given dispute can consider any claim under the latter.[1409] The court would therefore have to begin with an analysis of whether the disputed use is privileged by any exception listed in the paragraphs that precede the standard. Only where the conclusion is in the negative can the standard come into play.[1410]

Note that the price for this increase in the framework's adaptability to technology-related changes is the preservation of a measure of uncertainty regarding the legal status of unauthorised uses. After all, the subsidiary character of the standard means that prima facie infringing uses falling outside the scope of enumerated exceptions can still be considered in light of a vague norm and subject to a supplementary case-by-case examination. Under this residual opening standard, if a use were found not to be privileged by any of the exceptions, the infringement analysis could be reopened to examine if that use met the standard.

Nevertheless, such a norm would represent an improvement in relation to the current framework. Since the purpose of the secondary inquiry in each case would be different, the proposed subsidiary standard would *not* be the flip-side equivalent of having the three-step test working as a second tier of scrutiny in cases regarding the concrete application of exceptions, as it presently does.[1411] Whereas under the current three-step test the inquiry serves a restrictive function, simultaneously hindering flexibility and legal certainty, under the proposed model it would serve as an enabler of unlisted uses, thus fostering – not hindering – the framework's adaptability.[1412]

4.2 Design Proposals

Several commentators and policymakers have advanced proposals for a clause aimed at allocating greater decision-making power to courts, with the ultimate goal of increasing the adaptability of copyright law to variations in

1409. *See* Irish Copyright Review Committee Report 2013, p. 177.

1410. Users would naturally bear the burden of establishing the facts that underlie its application.

1411. *See supra* Chapter 4, section 4.2.

1412. Ohly (2014), pp. 65-66, in summarily proposing the adoption of a multi-tiered model, claims that experience both with the open catalogue of protected subject matter in Section 2(1) German Copyright Act and with unfair competition law indicates that courts would only resort to such a subsidiary clause in exceptional cases. Another way of minimising uncertainty would be to restrict the range of uses to which the subsidiary standard could apply. To this effect, the provision could be designed, for example, in a way that it would be triggered only in cases of digital uses. Uses permitted by digital technologies that are not clearly covered by the listed rule-like exceptions would thus have access to the case-by-case analysis enabled by the standard and would no longer need *ad hoc* and dogmatically questionable judicial constructions in order to be accommodated. This solution, however, would hardly solve the legal uncertainty issue, as it would then raise the difficult question of 'what counts as a digital use?'.

the technological landscape. Some proposals have common elements or overlap in specific parts.

For analytical purposes, I have systematised these proposals into three clusters, which will be described and critically discussed in turn: analogy-based proposals (section 4.2.1); proposals that focus on rethinking the three-step test (section 4.2.2); and proposals that favour introducing a fair use-style standard into EU copyright law (either verbatim or only partially) (section 4.2.3).[1413] As shall be seen, the proposals reflect the widespread disagreement on how to inject technological adaptability into the EU copyright system of exceptions.[1414] The insights gathered from the critical analysis of these proposals will help us outline the proposed third tier (section 4.3).

4.2.1 Enabling the Analogical Application of Listed Exceptions

As seen in Chapter 4, one of the effects of the exhaustive character of the catalogue of exceptions is a prohibition on courts to apply the listed exceptions by analogy. One way of widening the discretion enjoyed by courts in adapting the InfoSoc framework of exceptions to new socio-technological conditions is doing away with this effect, by explicitly providing for the admissibility of the analogical application of enumerated exceptions.

A group of European copyright scholars, who collaborated in drafting a proposal for a European Copyright Code, submitted a proposal to that effect. This proposal, which gathered expressive support from academics and policymakers, aims at allowing courts to extend rule-like exceptions to 'comparable uses'. The proposal is described (section 4.2.1.1) and critically assessed (section 4.2.1.2) in the following subsections.

4.2.1.1 The Wittem Group's Proposal

Established in 2002, the Wittem Project emerged as a joint effort of copyright academics from different Member States concerned with the future of EU copyright law.[1415] The output of the project, published in April 2010,

1413. In examining the proposals, I will consider only the criticisms that are specific to each of them. Those objections that may also be raised in relation to the solution I ultimately propose will be addressed towards the end of the chapter, after that solution has been outlined – *see infra* 5.
1414. Referring to this disagreement, *see* Kleinemenke (2013b), p. 105.
1415. For the background and method of the Wittem Project, *see* Hugenholtz (2012b), pp. 340-342. The Code was penned by a Drafting Committee of seven renowned scholars: Lionel Bently, Thomas Dreier, Reto Hilty, Bernt Hugenholtz, Antoon Quaedvlieg, Alain Strowel, and Dirk Visser. For a description and explanation of the Wittem Group's options, *see* Hugenholtz (2012b) and Dreier (2013). For commentary by external scholars, *see* Geller (2010), pp. 566-567; Gervais (2010); Griffiths (2010a), pp. 89-90; Rosati (2010); Belder et al. (2011); Derclaye & Cook (2011), pp. 267-268;

was a draft European Copyright Code (hereinafter, the Wittem Code) intended to serve as a model for the future EU harmonisation or unification of copyright law or for reforms at the national level.[1416] The proposed code is not a mere restatement or consolidation of the existing *acquis*. It does incorporate much of what had been achieved at the time and takes account of the obligations flowing from international treaties, but it also deviates from the existing solutions where the drafters considered necessary.[1417]

The group recognised that 'rapid technological development makes future modes of exploitation and use of copyright works unpredictable and therefore requires a system of rights and limitations with some flexibility'.[1418] While the chapter on rights has been accused of being cautious and timid,[1419] the same cannot be said about the one on exceptions, where deviation from the *acquis* is especially palpable.[1420] In order to remedy the existing lack of adaptability, the Wittem Group proposed the adoption of a 'half-open structure'[1421] of exceptions, reflecting both the civilian *droit d'auteur* tradition and the common law copyright tradition.[1422] The structure is twofold.

The first part – composed of Articles 5.1 through 5.4 – enumerates a series of exceptions to copyright's exclusive rights, either in the form of non-compensated exceptions[1423] or non-voluntary licences.[1424] These exceptions draw mostly, though not exclusively, from the InfoSoc *acquis*,[1425] reassembling them according to their primary purpose or *raison d'être*. The Code thus lays down exceptions for uses with minimal economic significance (Article 5.1),[1426] uses for the purpose of freedom of expression and

---

Ginsburg (2011); Kuhlen (2011); Geiger & Schönherr (2012), pp. 161-166; Lucas (2012); Gervais (2017), pp. 181-186; and Ficsor (2018).

1416. The Code is not comprehensive, however. Whereas it deals with the fundamental doctrines of any copyright law – subject matter (Chapter 1), authorship and ownership (Chapter 2), moral rights (Chapter 3), economic rights (Chapter 4), and exceptions (Chapter 5) –, it leaves out of its coverage issues like neighbouring rights, TPMs, and collective management.

1417. *See* Wittem Group (2010), pp. 10 and 12.

1418. Wittem Group (2010), p. 11.

1419. *See* Ginsburg (2011), p. 265.

1420. As recognised by some of its drafters – *see* Hugenholtz (2012b), p. 349, and Dreier (2013), p. 305. *See also* Ginsburg (2011), p. 265.

1421. Hugenholtz (2012b), p. 349.

1422. *See* Wittem Group (2010), fn. 48.

1423. *See* Articles 5.1, 5.2(1), 5.3(1), and 5.4(1) Wittem Code.

1424. *See* Articles 5.2(2), 5.3(2), and 5.4(2) Wittem Code.

1425. Exceptions provided in other directives, notably the Software Directive, are also included in the Code. *Compare, e.g.*, Articles 5(2) and 6(1) Software Directive with Articles 5.1(1) and 5.4(1)(b) Wittem Code.

1426. Article 5.1 exempts, without a remuneration requirement, the making of back-up copies; the incidental inclusion of a work in other materials; and the use in connection with the demonstration or repair of equipment.

information (Article 5.2),[1427] uses permitted to promote social, political and cultural objectives (Article 5.3),[1428] and uses for the purpose of enhancing competition (Article 5.4).[1429] While most of these exceptions may be said to be rule-like, some of them are drafted in relatively imprecise terms, bestowing on courts a significant degree of discretion.[1430]

The second and most innovative part of the Wittem framework of exceptions is Article 5.5. This provision allows courts to engage in analogical reasoning as a way to extend the catalogue of exceptions.[1431] Its wording goes as follows:

> Any other use that is comparable to the uses enumerated in art. 5.1 to 5.4(1) is permitted provided that the corresponding requirements of the relevant limitation are met and the use does not conflict with the normal exploitation of the

1427. Article 5.2 exempts uses of works for the reporting of contemporary events; uses of published articles on current economic, political or religious topics or of similar works broadcast by the media; use of works of architecture or sculpture made to be located permanently in public places; quotations; and parodies. It also exempts two categories of uses subject to the payment of remuneration: uses of single articles for the purposes of internal reporting within an organisation and uses for purposes of scientific research.
1428. Article 5.3 exempts uses for the benefit of disabled persons; uses to ensure the proper performance of administrative, parliamentary or judicial proceedings or public security; and uses for archiving by libraries and similar establishments. It also exempts two categories of uses subject to the payment of remuneration: private copying, provided that the source of the copy is not obviously infringing, and uses for educational purposes.
1429. Article 5.4(1) exempts uses for the purpose of advertising public exhibitions or sales of artistic works or goods and uses for the purpose of reverse engineering. Innovatively, Article 5.4(2) exempts uses of five types of informational or functional works (news articles, scientific works, industrial designs, computer programs and databases), against the payment of a remuneration negotiated by the parties in each individual case (i.e., without the intervention of CMOs), provided that (i) the use is indispensable to compete on a derivative market; (ii) the rightholder has refused to license the use on reasonable terms, leading to the elimination of competition in the relevant market; and (iii) the use does not unreasonably prejudice the legitimate interests of the rightholder.
1430. *See*, most notably, Article 5.4(2).
1431. The question has been raised whether the opening clause in Article 5.5 is directed at courts or legislators. Griffiths (2010a), pp. 89-90, assuming the addressees are legislators, finds the solution unsatisfactory: 'if it is directed solely at legislatures, either at national or at European, level, any flexibility will be significantly reduced because users would still depend upon the slow-moving and heavily lobbied legislative process'. This, however, seems to be a mistaken assumption. As noted by Thomas Dreier, one of the drafters of the Code's chapter on exceptions, Article 5(5) will only be addressed at the legislative power 'if the Code is regarded as the basis for further harmonization measures. But if the Code is regarded as a blueprint for national legislature or European regulation – as the Drafting Committee had hoped – then art. 5.5 is directed at the courts and gives them the opportunity to respond flexibly to rapidly changing circumstances and needs' – Dreier (2013), pp. 310-311. *See also* Kuhlen (2011), p. 21, assuming that the provision is directed at the judiciary. I, too, will proceed on that basis.

work and does not unreasonably prejudice the legitimate interests of the author or rightholder, taking account of the legitimate interests of third parties.

The provision amounts, in essence, to a special legal authorisation for the analogical application of listed exceptions. The exceptions in Articles 5.1 through 5.4(1) serve as anchors: as mentioned by the drafters, 'courts can only permit uses not expressly enumerated insofar as a certain analogy can be established with uses that are mentioned by the Code'.[1432] Flexibility is therefore restricted to the cases where a similarity between the litigated use and a previously enumerated exception is found. How such 'similarity' or 'comparability' is to be identified is an issue that is left unaddressed by the drafters (and one that will be analysed in the following section). The provision excludes the possibility of analogically applying the exception for purposes of enhancing competition laid down in Article 5.4(2) and a footnote to the provision clarifies that it does not allow new exceptions by blending the criteria of Articles 5.1 to 5.3.[1433]

In addition, the extension of listed exceptions *per analogiam* is subject to the verification of the criteria of the three-step test, considering, within the analysis of the third step, not only the interests of the author or rightholder[1434] but also those of third parties, like users and the public at large.

The drafters thus preferred reasoning by analogy to an open balancing of values, interests or factors similar to that required by US fair use. Bernt Hugenholtz, one of the project leaders, recognises that Article 5.5 Wittem Code 'goes considerably less far than section 107 of the US Copyright Act, by (1) requiring that uses are "comparable" to those enumerated; (2) applying the requirements (e.g., obligation to pay remuneration) of the corresponding exceptions; and (3) subjecting the exempted uses to the *three-step test*'.[1435]

This proposal has deserved widespread approval from the academic community, as well as from some policymakers. Naturally, the drafters of the Code highlight the merits of the proposal. Bernt Hugenholtz has argued that the Wittem framework of exceptions 'combines the advantage of legal security and predictability associated with the "closed list" approach of limitations and exceptions under the author's right tradition with the

1432. *See* Wittem Group (2010), fn. 48. *See also* Hilty (2010), p. 84 ('the application of the opening clause requires an analogy of sorts to existing statutory provisions'). The decision by the Supreme Court of The Netherlands in the *Dior* case – where it was held that the existing exceptions do not exclude the judicial establishment of further privileges 'in other cases on the basis of a comparable weighing of interests' – is commonly cited as a legitimising precursor to the Wittem solution. *See*, *inter alia*, Senftleben (2012b), pp. 388-395.

1433. *See* Wittem Group (2010), fn. 55.

1434. The focus on the interests of rightholders *only* in Article 13 TRIPS and in Article 5(5) InfoSoc Directive is therefore replaced by the consideration of the interests of rightholders *and* authors (which, of course, may be different persons).

1435. Hugenholtz (2012b), p. 351.

flexibility and adaptability to technological change of the American *fair use* doctrine'.[1436] Likewise, the scholars in charge of drafting the Code's chapter on exceptions – Reto Hilty and Thomas Dreier – emphasise the advantages of Articles 5.1-5.5: while Hilty sees the proposed framework as 'a step in the direction of the "fair use" approach …, without losing the advantage of legal certainty',[1437] Dreier claims that analogical reasoning, as proposed in the Code, 'would permit reservations about a lack of legal certainty to be dispelled as well as fears that the broadening of existing limitations on copyright that enhanced flexibility entails could dilute or even shift the borders of the scope of protection excessively at the expense of authors and right holders'.[1438]

Support for the Wittem model of exceptions has come from outside of the drafting committee as well. Martin Senftleben has advanced a proposal that is in line with Article 5.5 Wittem Code, by also incorporating the requirement of comparability.[1439] Matthias Leistner has expressed his preference for a Wittem-type solution over fair use, on grounds that purpose-based extension of listed exceptions is more akin to the CJEU's 'teleological method of reasoning' than a standard requiring the balancing of competing considerations.[1440] Others have made the argument that Wittem 'seems to better fit the European legal tradition than the US fair use doctrine'[1441] or that it is 'more likely to comply with the first step of the three-step test'[1442] (I shall dispute these claims below[1443]).

The influence of Wittem has spilled over to the policymaking field as well. Notably, the European Parliament has pronounced itself in favour of a

---

1436. Hugenholtz (2012b), pp. 349-350. Writing from a US perspective, Gideon Parchomovsky & Alex Stein have argued that legal frameworks composed of detailed enumerations of behaviours that share certain common characteristics and a clause explicitly empowering courts to accommodate unenumerated instances that have those same characteristics – a type of framework they call 'catalogs' – 'offer the legal system the certainty and predictability of rules and the flexibility of standards' – Parchomovsky & Stein (2015), p. 190.
1437. Hilty (2012), p. 366.
1438. Dreier (2015), p. 142.
1439. The proposal consists in rewording Article 5(5) InfoSoc Directive in the following terms: 'In certain special cases comparable to those reflected by the exceptions and limitations provided for in paragraphs 1, 2, 3 and 4, the use of works or other subject-matter may also be exempted from the rights provided for in Articles 2 and 3, provided that such use does not conflict with a normal exploitation of the work or other subject-matter and does not unreasonably prejudice the legitimate interests of the right holder.' Note that this proposal, contrary to Wittem, expressly uses the language of the first step of the three-step test. *See* Senftleben (2010), p. 76; Senftleben (2012b), pp. 393-394; and Senftleben (2017), p. 271.
1440. *See* Leistner (2011), pp. 438-439.
1441. Noll et al. (2012), p. 34. *See also* Spindler (2014), p. 2552.
1442. Triaille et al. (2013), p. 537, though ultimately opposing the injection of greater adaptability into the system of exceptions (pp. 538-539).
1443. *See infra* 4.2.1.2. and 5.6.

Wittem-style solution in its Resolution of 9 July 2015. Though not explicitly referring to the analogical application of exceptions, the Parliament stressed that

> where an exception or limitation already applies, new uses of content which are made possible by technological advances or new uses of technology should be, as far as possible, construed in line with the existing exception or limitation, provided that the new use is *similar* to the existing one, in order to improve legal certainty – this would be subject to the three-step test.[1444]

By contrast, other scholars have criticised Wittem's solution. In analysing Article 5.5, Jane Ginsburg adopts a disapproving tone, based on the fact that the provision is 'exceptionally open-ended'.[1445] André Lucas, faithful to his preference for having legislators accommodate new uses rather than courts, raises doubts as to the democratic legitimacy of the exercise authorised by Article 5.5[1446] (an argument that shall be rebutted at a later stage[1447]). He adds, moreover, that an analogy-based solution would be ill-advised because, from a methodological point of view, the extension of exceptions beyond their wording is not unanimously accepted by national legal orders.[1448]

These criticisms provide an appropriate segue for the next subsection, which critically engages with the Wittem proposal in greater depth.

4.2.1.2 Critical Analysis

As just described, the Wittem framework of exceptions is composed of two essential parts: (i) an enumeration of (mostly rule-like) exceptions spread through Articles 5.1-5.4 and (ii) a clause expressly allowing courts to analogically apply such exceptions to unenumerated uses. The assessment that follows is focused on the second part as an option for designing the third stage of a multi-tiered framework of exceptions.[1449] The objections I am

---

1444. EP Resolution Implementation InfoSoc Directive 2015, para. 43 (emphasis added). Furthermore, three months after the European Parliament adopted this non-legislative resolution, the Ex-Post Impact Assessment on the InfoSoc Directive conducted by the EPRS proposed to inject judicial discretion into the system of exceptions 'by relying on a mixed system where unauthorised uses of copyrighted materials could be permitted by analogy, *i.e.* when they are similar but not identical to the ones expressly intended by the law' – EPRS (2015), p. III-294.
1445. Ginsburg (2011), p. 296.
1446. *See* Lucas (2012), p. 379.
1447. *See infra* 5.3.
1448. *See* Lucas (2012), p. 379.
1449. I have reservations about the first part of the proposal too. It seems artificial to categorise exceptions according to their purpose, since many of them are grounded on a plurality of purposes or principles (or, more accurately, on a weighing of these purposes or principles, like freedom of expression, with the countervailing interests of rightholders). The drafters of the Code admit this much in fn. 48. For instance, the typical quotation is simultaneously a use with minimal economic significance, as well

about to express should not be read as meaning that I oppose a third tier modelled after Article 5.5 Wittem Code under *any* circumstances. To be clear, the opening clause put forward by the Wittem Group does represent an improvement in relation to the *status quo*, leading to an increase in the degree of adaptability of the framework of exceptions. My objections should rather be regarded as part of an effort to come up with a design that strikes the best possible balance between flexibility and legal certainty.

In applying Article 5.5 or an equivalent national provision, courts must depart from the enumerated uses in Articles 5.1-5.4(1), by discerning whether the (unenumerated) use *sub judice* is 'comparable' to any of the uses *sub legem*. But this is not the end of the analysis under Article 5.5. After finding comparability of uses, courts must inquire whether the use under consideration meets the corresponding requirements of the exception that covers the analogous use and passes the three-step test (crafted, in the Wittem Code, as an enabling clause). My doubts are related to each of these three moments of the analysis.

First, the nature of the legal reasoning required under the first moment (the finding of 'comparability', 'similarity' or 'analogy') raises issues related to *adaptability* and *transparency*. To understand why this is so, it is worth carefully dissecting how reasoning by analogy under Article 5.5 would operate.

For Article 5.5 to be relevant in a dispute, the court would have to be confronted with an unauthorised use that did not fit the wording of any of the listed exceptions, even if broadly interpreted.[1450] Facing such a use, the court would heuristically identify regulated uses that are prima facie similar, i.e. uses that dealt with the same kind of legal problem as the use *sub judice*.[1451] Suppose, for example, that the challenged use was the making available of book snippets by the Google Books service. While this use could be considered prima facie similar to a quotation (Article 5.2(1)(d) Wittem Code),[1452] we intuitively know that it bears no similarity whatsoever with uses in connection with the demonstration or repair of equipment (Article

as one that promotes freedom of expression and information and important cultural objectives. To make things messier, there are different and partially inconsistent categorisations of exceptions according to their rationales, as seen right at the beginning of the book (Introduction, section 1.1section .). *See* Lucas (2012), p. 378, and Ficsor (2018), with similar objections.

1450. Extensive interpretations may presumably be undertaken independently of the permission granted by Article 5.5. For instance, for those, like myself, who have trouble in qualifying, *per interpretationem*, automatic references generated by search engines as 'quotations' – grounded on the idea that the meaning of 'quotation' would not allow such a conclusion –, the analogical extension allowed by Article 5.5 could be a solution.

1451. *See* Brożek (2008), p. 191, defining *prima facie* similarity by reference to the kind of legal problem.

1452. *See* Ginsburg (2011), p. 296, considering the quotation exception the most obvious candidate to accommodate the Google book-scanning project under the Wittem Code.

5.1(3) Wittem Code) or with a use to ensure the proper performance of parliamentary proceedings (Article 5.3(1)(b) Wittem Code).

The need to depart from prima facie similar uses constrains the court's discretion – and this is exactly where the adaptability or sustainability problem arises. Granted, reasoning by analogy 'goes one step further than purposive interpretation'[1453] and, as such, confers greater discretion on the judiciary than the existing system. But it is not implausible to envisage that a new use may arise in the future that bears no prima facie resemblance to any of the listed uses.[1454] A new technological use may be so different from listed uses that an analogical application is not warranted at all.[1455] At the very least, we cannot know whether that will be the case, since unpredictability is at the essence of technological change. If such a use does emerge – and if it is a use that judges will feel compelled to accommodate –, courts will be confronted with the same choice they face under the current framework: they either refuse to accommodate it and await legislative intervention (which may take several years, if it is to occur at all) or they exercise questionably legitimate interpretative creativity.[1456]

Having identified a prima facie similar use that is regulated under Articles 5.1-5.4(1), the deciding court would proceed to reason (even if implicitly) in the following basic manner:

(i) Enumerated use *A* has a certain feature *x*.
(ii) Unenumerated use B – the disputed use – differs from use *A* in some respects, but shares feature *x*.
(iii) The Code treats use *A* as non-infringing.
(iv) It is inferred that use *B*, because it shares feature *x* with use *A*, should be treated in the same way.[1457]

1453. Langenbucher (1998), p. 482.

1454. I am assuming here that what Article 5.5 allows is what is commonly called *analogia legis* – which departs from a specific legal provision that regulates an analogous case – and not also *analogia juris* – which departs from a plurality of provisions, inferring therefrom a principle that is to be applied to the case *sub judice*. If it also allows the latter, then the deciding court will not need to go through the stage of identifying one or more *prima facie* similar exceptions. On the distinction between *analogia legis* and *analogia juris*, *see*, among others, Larenz (2012), pp. 544-552, and Engisch (2014), pp. 295-296.

1455. As stated by Depoorter (2009), p. 1848, 'technological breakthroughs, by their nature, make it more difficult to apply existing rules by analogy'. *See also* Kleinemenke (2013a), pp. 544-546, making a similar criticism to the Wittem proposal and arguing that, under such a solution, sooner or later legislative intervention would again be necessary.

1456. On the judicial use of makeshift reasoning to accommodate technology-enabled uses, *see supra* Chapter 4, section 5.2.

1457. This is an adapted version of the description of analogical reasoning provided in Sunstein (1993), p. 745. *See also* the formula in Alexy (2010b), p. 9: 'In every case *ci*, each case *cj* may be adduced with the argument that *ci* shares with *cj* the features $F^{j}l$,

The formula is meant to establish whether an unregulated use should be deemed non-infringing, given that an analogous use is also treated as non-infringing by a directly applicable exception.[1458] As such, the reasoning required under Article 5.5, like all instances of analogical reasoning, is grounded on the principle of equality, which requires us to treat like cases alike.[1459] Under the cited formula, sharing feature x is what makes the uses 'comparable' for the purpose of treating the use *sub judice* as non-infringing. However, neither this abstract formula nor Article 5.5 say anything about which features should be considered relevant for that purpose.[1460] In the words of Cass Sunstein, '[f]or analogical reasoning to operate properly, we have to know that *A* and *B* are "relevantly" similar',[1461] meaning that not every feature in common between the two uses will justify the extension of the exception that governs the regulated use. Hence, identifying and analysing the relevant features is the crucial step in any argument by analogy in law.

How, then, do we know if the uses are 'relevantly similar' for purposes of applying Article 5.5 Wittem Code (or of any analogical reasoning, for that matter)? In other words, what is to be used as the *tertium comparationis*? In order to know if two fact-situations – the regulated and the unregulated one – are relevantly similar, one ought to look at the purposes or principles that underlie the regulated situation. The features shared between the two situations, as opposed to their differences, must be closely related to the *ratio legis* of whatever provision serves as the source of the analogy. The process of extending such provision to situations that do not fall within its scope but are analogous is therefore done on the basis of the rationales that stand behind it.[1462] Having pinpointed a prima facie similar use, the court must

---

…, $F^j n$, and that ci, for that reason and because the rule $F^j l$, …, $F^j n \to Q$ is valid, ought to be treated, as cj, to the effect that Q.'

1458. Note that the conclusion that emerges from this type of reasoning is a conclusion from a particular case to another particular case, rather than from the general to the particular – *see* Engisch, pp. 288-289. Analogical reasoning is therefore not purely logical or deductive. As a consequence, the truth of the reasoning's premises does not necessarily entail that the conclusion reached is true; it only supports it as 'more likely to be true than false' – *see* Golding (2001), p. 45.

1459. *See* Langenbucher (1998), p. 482, and Larenz (2012), p. 541.

1460. Kleinemenke (2013a), pp. 544-546, also criticises the Wittem proposal for not providing any guidance on how to determine comparability between uses.

1461. Sunstein (1993), p. 745.

1462. As taught by Larenz (2012), p. 541, reasoning by analogy is a value-based type of reasoning and not merely a logico-formal mental operation. *See also* Langenbucher (1998), p. 488 ('Where an analogy to a statutory rule is drawn, its *ratio legis* provides this standard of comparison'); MacCormick (2005), p. 207 ('the relevance of analogy depends on the broader principle of which each of the cases can be shown to be an instantiation'), and Alexy (2010b), p. 14 ('the features in A1 and A2 acquire their relevance by virtue of the fact that they are related to reasons undergirding the rules that contain them as antecedents' and 'these reasons normally have the character of

identify those rationales and ask if they would be served by applying the provision to the unregulated situation.[1463]

Copyright exceptions are the result of a balancing of conflicting considerations undertaken by the legislator. To use quotation again as an example: the legislative decision to privilege quotations is the result of an exercise in which considerations such as 'cultural dissemination and intellectual criticism should be fostered' and 'authors/rightholders should control their works' are weighed against each other. In providing the exception, the legislator decided that the former should take precedence over the latter. The court must thus examine whether the use *sub judice* can be solved through the same precedence relation among principles as that of quotation (the prima facie similar use in our example), by balancing the conflicting considerations and judging if the prevailing one also applies to that use and is capable of providing justification for rendering it lawful. This exercise allows the court to determine if the prima facie comparable use is *relevantly* comparable to the unenumerated use.[1464] In sum, the existence of similarities in the mere external description of the situations does not suffice to establish an analogy; it is necessary that the justifying reasons of the regulated situation apply to the *casus omissus* as well.

Once we recognise this connection between analogy, exceptions and their underlying rationales, we understand that the key to establish 'comparability' is, in its second stage, not very different from a balancing exercise. Exceptions enumerated in Articles 5.1-5.4(1) cannot be extended by analogy without some sort of balancing of purposes, principles, values or interests. This is all the more so since Article 5.5 subjects the admissibility of analogy to the meeting of the second and third steps of the three-step test, with the latter one also incorporating the legitimate interests of third parties. Under this formula, the deciding court would have to weigh the interests of authors/rightholders against those of users in two stages. Article 5.5, much like true balancing tests, would suffer from the drawback of potential volatility.[1465] This, however, would only add to the disadvantage of its low(er) adaptability vis-à-vis a true balancing test. So the obvious question is: from a methodological point of view, would it not be more transparent to

principles'). *See also* Senftleben (2010), pp. 76-77, in relation to a solution modelled after that of the Wittem Group.

1463. Presumably, the purpose-based categorisation of exceptions in the Wittem Code was intended to facilitate such an exercise.

1464. *See*, by analogy, Brożek (2008), pp. 193-197, and Bustamante (2010), pp. 69-70.

1465. Ginsburg (2011), pp. 296-297, implies this much when discussing whether the Wittem quotation exception could be extended to cover Google Books: 'it is conceivable that Google's for-profit uses could be privileged. Depending on where one stands on the "balance" between creators and entrepreneurial users, this "flexibility" either is necessary to advance the public interest, particularly in light of evolving technology, or is a dangerous erosion of authors' rights, undermining their ability to profit from new markets created by new technologies'.

simply replace such a convoluted analogy-based exercise with a standard straightforwardly cast in the form of a balancing test that would reflect the interests of authors and rightholders, on the one hand, and those of users and society, on the other[1466]?

To make things worse, and as pointed out earlier, not all Member States would deal comfortably with having courts applying exceptions by analogy. In fact, the maxim *singularia non sunt extendenda*, though criticisable,[1467] is an entrenched constraint on judicial decision-making in some jurisdictions.

Moreover, apart from having to establish an analogy between uses, courts must ensure that the 'corresponding requirements' of the extended exception are met. It is not entirely clear what this formula means. If all the requirements of the relevant exception were fulfilled, then a mere exercise of subsumption would suffice and analogy would no longer be needed. After all, for analogical *extension* to be necessary, the use under consideration must *not* fall within the wording of the relevant exception. Instead, the most plausible reading of this second condition of Article 5.5 is that it imposes the fulfilment of the requirements laid down in the opening paragraph that precedes the description of individual exceptions. These requirements, where they exist, typically consist in the payment of compensation[1468] and in the use being made to the extent justified by its purpose.[1469] But, even if read in this benign way, the condition raises an important concern: it entails allowing courts to impose non-voluntary licences, by extending compensated exceptions to uses that are not originally covered by its wording – a problem that shall be analysed in section 5.5 *infra*.

A third condition for an unenumerated use to be rendered non-infringing under Article 5.5 is that it passes the second and third steps of the three-step test. Apart from the duplication of balancing exercises mentioned above, this option may be opposed for reasons related specifically to the meaning of the three-step test and which will be discussed in the section that follows.

1466. In a very sceptical tone, Judge Richard Posner claims that '[r]easoning by analogy tends to obscure the policy grounds that determine the outcome of a case, because it directs the reader's attention to the cases that are being compared with each other rather than to the policy considerations that connect or separate the cases' – Posner (2006), p. 765.

1467. Like the issue of broad interpretation of exceptions, the question of whether and in what circumstances exceptions may be applied by analogy is a contentious one in legal methodology – *see* Larenz (2012), pp. 502-503, and Engisch (2014), pp. 296-298.

1468. *See* Articles 5.2(2) and 5.3(2) Wittem Code. In the case of Article 5.1, for instance, the uses are permitted 'without authorisation, and without remuneration', so no extra requirements seem to apply.

1469. *See* Articles 5.2(1), 5.2(2), 5.3(1), 5.3(2), and 5.4(1) Wittem Code.

4.2.2 Rethinking the Three-Step Test

Among all the proposals for introducing adaptability to technology-related changes into the InfoSoc framework of exceptions, the proposal for having a discretion-granting provision modelled after the three-step test is the one with the widest currency in the literature. The idea, in a nutshell, is to convert the three-step test into a truly flexible, two-sided test,[1470] by reinterpreting or even rewriting it. Over the last two decades, a great many influential scholars have advanced proposals to that effect.[1471]

This trend in scholarship has first emerged as a reaction to the interpretation of the test adopted by the WTO Panel in *US-Copyright* (2000).[1472] This interpretation – which came to be known as the 'traditional' interpretation of the three-step test[1473] – has two fundamental characteristics. First, it understands the three conditions as separate steps that must be analysed successively (in the order they appear in the test) and met cumulatively. This means, for instance, that if a given exception (or a concrete use, under Article 5(5) InfoSoc Directive) fails the first condition, there will be no need to proceed to the second and third conditions. Second, it reads each step in a way that is commonly described as straitjacketing. The first step is understood as requiring that an exception be 'clearly defined'[1474] and 'narrow' in scope.[1475] The second step prohibits exceptions that enter into competition with the ways that rightholders ordinarily extract or could plausibly extract economic value from the work.[1476] The third step will not be met if the exception can cause an unreasonable loss of income to the rightholder.[1477] Overall, the test, to borrow the WTO Panel's own characterisation, is supposed to have a 'narrow sphere of operation'.[1478]

The three-step test was incorporated into the InfoSoc Directive via the WIPO Treaties. However, unlike its older international siblings, which constrain national *legislative* autonomy for the introduction of new exceptions, the InfoSoc test in Article 5(5) is crafted as a limit on the *judicial*

1470. On the one-sidedness of the test in the InfoSoc Directive, *see supra* Chapter 4, section 4.1.
1471. A non-exhaustive list includes Senftleben (2004); Senftleben (2006); Gervais (2005); Koelman (2006); Geiger (2007b); Hugenholtz & Okediji (2008); Mazziotti (2008); Westkamp (2008); He (2009); Kur (2009); Wright (2009); Geiger et al. (2008); Lucas (2010); Christie (2011); Hugenholtz & Senftleben (2011); Geiger *at al.* (2014); Geiger & Schönherr (2012) and (2014); and Quintais (2017b).
1472. For a description of the panel's interpretation of each step, *see supra* Chapter 2, section 4.1.
1473. *See* Goold (2017) (drawing a distinction between the 'traditional' and 'balanced' interpretations of the test) and Quintais (2017b), p. 201 (criticising the 'traditional view' of the concept of 'normal exploitation' within the second step);
1474. WTO, *US-Copyright*, para. 6.108.
1475. WTO, *US-Copyright*, para. 6.109.
1476. WTO, *US-Copyright*, paras 6.180 and 6.183.
1477. WTO, *US-Copyright*, para. 6.229.
1478. WTO, *US-Copyright*, para. 6.97.

application of exceptions. As seen in Chapter 2, the practical effect of this function shift is that, in deciding on concrete cases of liability for unauthorised use, courts must examine not only if the use is covered by an exception, but also if the use cumulatively meets the three conditions of the test. As discussed in Chapter 4, the CJEU often fails to develop the three-step analysis at any depth, but when it does engage with the test, it tends to accept the traditional interpretation.[1479]

The decision by the WTO Panel in *US-Copyright* has generated a vast body of (mostly critical) commentary. A number of scholars have argued against this traditional interpretation – criticising it for being 'strict',[1480] 'formalistic',[1481] 'problematic',[1482] and 'predominantly economic'[1483] – and in favour of 'rethinking' the test.[1484] These scholars' views are united under a common thread: the desire to have the three-step test reflect an appropriate balance of interests between rightholders and third parties. Guided by that purpose, they attempt to adjust the two main features of the traditional view identified above – the interpretation of the test's conditions and their separate and cumulative nature.

Accordingly, for ease of analysis, I will divide the proposals – which differ in some important respects, but overlap in others – into two categories: those that advocate reinterpreting one or more of the steps (section 4.2.2.1) and those that, at a more macro level, would prefer to restructure the test, by redefining the way in which the conditions interact with each other (section 4.2.2.2).[1485]

Before proceeding, a note of caution is in order. Not all of these proposals refer to Article 5(5) InfoSoc Directive as a judicial tool. Some of them are primarily concerned with international versions of the test and the restrictions they impose on national legislative autonomy. Nonetheless, and given the similarities in the wording and structure of the different tests, the different proposals will be discussed as possible candidates for a third tier of a hybrid InfoSoc framework of exceptions, intended to be applied by courts.

1479. *See supra* Chapter 4, sections 4.1 and 5.2.2.3. Note that the WTO Panel report is not mentioned in CJEU decisions, but only in AG Opinion, *VG Wort*, para. 9, and AG Opinion, *ACI Adam*, para. 55.
1480. Quintais (2017b), p. 200.
1481. Dinwoodie & Dreyfuss (2012), p. 80.
1482. Hilty (2010), p. 83, and Ruse-Khan (2016), p. 433.
1483. Geiger *at al.* (2014), p. 597.
1484. *See* Geiger (2007b), p. 486, speaking of an 'urgency over "rethinking"' the test. Sun (2007), pp. 330-331, adopts a more drastic tone, calling for 'a revolutionary earthquake to break down the very foundation on which the three-step test is founded'.
1485. *See* Christie (2011), pp. 128-129, making the distinction between the 'micro-level analysis' of the meaning of each step and the 'macro-level analysis' of the interrelation of steps.

4.2.2.1 Reinterpreting the Steps

Since the WTO Panel issued its report in *US-Copyright*, a number of scholars from different quadrants have questioned the soundness of its approach and proposed various alternative interpretations of the different steps. These proposals are premised on the idea that the reading endorsed by the WTO Panel need not be regarded as the last word on the three-step test.[1486]

The proposal for a reinterpretation of the three-step test with the greatest resonance in academic circles has been the 'Declaration on a Balanced Interpretation of the "Three-Step Test' in Copyright Law" – a joint project by the Max Planck Institute for Innovation and Competition Law and the Queen Mary University of London. Since its publication in 2008, the Declaration has occupied centre stage in the debate on recalibrating the three-step test. Whereas some have criticised it,[1487] others have proposed that it be taken one step further and adopted at the international level.[1488]

The Declaration is not the only proposal for reinterpreting the test's conditions. A pioneering effort towards reading the test in a more liberal light has been carried out by Martin Senftleben in his 2004 monograph on the three-step test. These two proposals, as largely representative of the spectrum of proposals for reading the test in a different way, will be discussed in the paragraphs that follow.

According to the Declaration, the first step ('certain special cases') does not prevent legislators from introducing standard-like exceptions, as long as the scope of those exceptions is 'reasonably foreseeable'.[1489] It also does not impede courts from developing existing (rule-like) exceptions by analogy, assuming this is possible within the legal system of which they form a part. It naturally follows that the test should be read as not requiring exceptions to be interpreted in a strict manner; they can be construed according to their underlying purposes.[1490] In Martin Senftleben's analysis, on the other hand, the terms 'certain' and 'special' are interpreted separately. The author claims that the term 'certain' means that exceptions 'must be delineated so as to become distinguishable from each other' and that such delineation need not be made by legislators, but may be trusted upon courts (as also suggested in the Declaration).[1491] The term 'special' should not be understood as imposing

1486. *See* Geiger et al. (2014), pp. 600-601, pointing out that WTO law is not governed by a formal doctrine of *stare decisis* and that '[a] report by the Appellate Body of course, due to its heighted position in the WTO hierarchy, could truly proceed *de novo* on the issue'.
1487. *See*, most notably, Lucas (2010) and Ficsor (2012), fn. 8. For a discussion of these critical views, *see infra* 4.2.2.3.
1488. *See* Geiger (2009b), proposing that a soft law instrument be adopted at the international level containing interpretation guidelines drawing from the Declaration.
1489. Geiger et al. (2008), p. 711.
1490. Geiger et al. (2008), p. 711.
1491. Senftleben (2004), p. 287.

any quantitative limits on exceptions, but as requiring that they be grounded on a 'clear reason of public policy'.[1492]

The second step ('normal exploitation') is the condition that most worries critical commentators. If the step is interpreted as precluding all exceptions that deprive rightholders of actual or plausible commercial gains, the risk is high that it will work in most cases as a 'showstopper'.[1493] Indeed, in the majority of disputes that courts are confronted with, the argument could be made that the challenged use could generate revenue in the future and should consequently be prohibited.[1494] To avoid this bleak outcome, scholars have tried to contain the broad definition of 'normal exploitation' proposed by the WTO Panel. Senftleben posits that this step should be interpreted not as encompassing all possible ways of extracting profit from protected works, but as prohibiting only the impairment of major sources of royalty revenue that belong to the 'economic core' of copyright.[1495] The Declaration, on the other hand, follows a more normative path, submitting that the definition of 'normal exploitation' should take into account any important competing considerations on which the exception is based,[1496] as well as its beneficial effects on competition, notably on secondary markets.[1497]

The fundamental purpose behind these alternative interpretations of the second step is to allow exceptions to progress more easily to the third step

1492. Senftleben (2004), p. 152.
1493. The expression is borrowed from Koelman (2006), p. 410.
1494. *See* Griffiths (2010b), p. 311. In theory, as noted by Ginsburg (2001), p. 14, 'there is a risk that even traditionally privileged uses, such as scholarship or parody, could be deemed "normal exploitations", assuming copyright owners could develop a low transaction cost method of charging for them'.
1495. Senftleben (2004), p. 226, and Senftleben (2006), p. 437. Attempts to read the second step in a more flexible manner are common in the literature, due to the fear that the WTO Panel's interpretation will prevent the accommodation of new and unforeseen uses whenever rightholders can find a way of exploiting them. Quintais (2017b), p. 202, argues that there should only be a conflict with the normal exploitation of the work when the exception at stake 'demonstrably deprives rights holders of substantive, reasonably expected and foreseeable sources of income under normal commercial circumstances'. Ginsburg (2001), pp. 51-53, proposes that an element of 'reasonableness of the exploitation' be taken into account under the second step. Koelman (2006), p. 410, suggests a similar softening of the second step, citing Article 30 TRIPS (under which exceptions may be created as long as they 'do not unreasonably conflict with a normal exploitation of the patent') and Ginsburg's proposal approvingly. Geiger et al. (2014), p. 600, follow the same approach, citing, in addition, Article 26.2 TRIPS (the twin of Article 30 for industrial designs). He (2009), pp. 294-300, submits that the second step should be re-understood as an 'adapted fair use test'.
1496. Lucas (2010), pp. 279-280, convincingly disputes this reading, on grounds, *inter alia*, that it would be based on a far-fetched reading of the word 'normal' and that it would deprive the third step of any meaningful role.
1497. *See* Geiger et al. (2008), p. 711. Also, the payment of adequate compensation is an element that should be taken into account under the second step, according to the authors of the Declaration.

('unreasonable prejudice to the legitimate interests of rightholders'), which would serve as a 'final adjustment tool', allowing a balancing between the interests of authors/rightholders and those of the users and the public in general.[1498] Overall, under Senftleben's model, the test can be understood as a 'refined proportionality test', where the first two steps serve as mechanisms to identify cases of 'evident disproportionality', while the last step, 'the kingpin of the three-step test', enables the decision-maker to strike a proper equilibrium between the competing interests involved.[1499] According to the Declaration, the interests of original and derivative rightholders, as well as those of third parties – including their fundamental rights, interests in competition and other public interests in social and scientific progress[1500] – must be duly considered.[1501] This reading of the third step brings to the fore the balancing of interests that its language seems to allow and that was largely overlooked in the Panel's economic interpretation of the step.

The scholars arguing for more flexible interpretations of some or all of the test's conditions often find support for their position in the drafting history, context and original purpose of the international three-step test.

They start by highlighting the fact that the test emerged in the Berne Convention as a compromise solution aimed at giving Member States sufficient discretion to accommodate different existing national exceptions. It was therefore intended to serve as an instrument of flexibility and tolerance for the choices of national lawmakers and not as a constraining mechanism. This original understanding should not be subverted by overly restrictive readings of each step and of the test as a whole.[1502]

In the context of TRIPS, these scholars observe that promoting technological innovation and ensuring a balance of rights and obligations was one of the objectives behind the agreement, as stated in Article 7.[1503]

1498. Senftleben (2004), pp. 289-290. *See also* Senftleben (2006), pp. 435-436.
1499. Senftleben (2004), pp. 287-290. Putting the spotlight on the third step is also the priority of Lucie Guibault and colleagues in the IViR study on the implementation of the InfoSoc Directive. According to the study, a flexible interpretation of the test 'could be achieved by not interpreting the first and second steps too narrowly, and thereby making the third step, which allows a certain balancing between the interests of right holders and the needs of society, the focal point of the three-step analysis' – Guibault et al. (2007), p. 67.
1500. *See also* Suthersanen (2005), p. 124, calling for a redrafting of Article 13 TRIPS that would include the following reference after the third step: 'taking note of the need to maintain a balance between the rights owners and the larger public interest'.
1501. *See* Geiger et al. (2008), p. 712. *See*, in agreement with the Declaration, Lucas (2010), pp. 277-278.
1502. *See, e.g.*, Hugenholtz & Senftleben (2011), p. 21, citing the Berne Convention Records 1967, p. 81, in support of their position.
1503. Article 7 TRIPS reads as follows: 'The protection and enforcement of intellectual property rights should contribute to the promotion of technological innovation and to the transfer and dissemination of technology, to the mutual advantage of producers and users of technological knowledge and in a manner conducive to social and economic welfare, and to a balance of rights and obligations.'

This reliance on the object and purpose of treaties as relevant elements for their interpretation is entirely consistent with the rules of interpretation of international law enshrined in the Vienna Convention (Article 31(1)).[1504]

Finally, these scholars argue that the nature of the three-step test as a flexible instrument emerges clearly from the text of the WCT. In support of that view, they cite the Treaty's preamble and the Agreed Statement concerning Article 10.[1505] Whereas the preamble expressly recognises 'the need to maintain a balance between the rights of authors and the larger public interest', the Agreed Statement provides that Article 10 allows Contracting Parties 'to carry forward and appropriately extend into the digital environment limitations and exceptions in their national laws' and 'to devise new exceptions and limitations that are appropriate in the digital network environment'. This forward-looking statement, they claim, is hard to square with a restrictive reading of the test.[1506] It is also submitted that this Agreed Statement is particularly relevant for the interpretation of the three-step test in the InfoSoc Directive. Drawing on the fact that one of the Directive's objectives was to implement the WIPO Treaties into EU copyright law, some commentators read Recital 44 – pursuant to which '[w]hen applying the exceptions and limitations provided for in this Directive, they should be exercised in accordance with international obligations' – as referring specifically to Article 10 WCT and its Agreed Statement and, therefore, as allowing a balanced reading of the three-step test under which new exceptions for technological uses can be introduced.[1507]

The differences between the so-called traditional interpretation and these alternative interpretations may thus be in Table 5.1.

1504. *See* Geiger et al. (2014), pp. 597-598.
1505. Article 31(1) and (2) Vienna Convention posits that Agreed Statements count as 'context' for purposes of treaty interpretation. The Agreed Statement concerning Article 10 WCT is also mentioned in the Explanatory Memorandum InfoSoc Proposal, p. 15.
1506. *See* Geiger et al. (2014), p. 610, and Quintais (2017b), p. 199.
1507. *See, e.g.*, Hugenholtz & Senftleben (2011), p. 23; Senftleben (2013b), p. 17; and Geiger & Schönherr (2014), p. 121. For this reason, it has been argued that the Agreed Statement holds greater weight for the interpretation of Article 5(5) InfoSoc Directive than the WTO Panel report – *see* Quintais (2017b), pp. 199-200. On the other hand, it must be noted that Recital 44 InfoSoc Directive also states that 'the scope of certain exceptions or limitations may have to be even more limited when it comes to certain new uses of copyright works and other subject-matter', pointing in the opposite direction of the Agreed Statement.

Table 5.1 Traditional and Alternative Interpretations of the Three-Step Test

	Traditional Interpretation	*Alternative Interpretations*
Step 1 ('certain special cases')	Exceptions must be clearly defined and have a narrow scope	Scope of exceptions must be reasonably foreseeable or distinguishable and it must be grounded on a rational justification
Step 2 ('normal exploitation')	Exceptions must not enter into economic competition with actual or potential (and plausible) forms of exploitation	Exceptions must not enter into unreasonable economic competition with actual or potential, plausible and major forms of exploitation
Step 3 ('unreasonable prejudice to legitimate interests')	Exceptions must not cause unreasonable loss of income to rightholders	Economic interests of authors and rightholders should be balanced against those of users and society at large

As applied to international instruments, where the three-step test works as a mechanism for controlling national autonomy, the proposed reinterpretations of the test's conditions would have the positive effect of increasing the legislators' freedom to adopt new exceptions, namely open-ended ones.[1508] However, the international three-step test cannot be used *by courts* to accommodate new uses in concrete disputes.

As explained in Chapter 2, the three-step test in InfoSoc and other directives is addressed primarily at judges as a restriction on the application of existing exceptions. What this means is that, in the context of the current Article 5(5) wording, the three conditions, even if reinterpreted, will always be part of a test that functions as a further constraint on listed use privileges. Absent an express change in the test's structure, '[o]nly an interpretation *contra legem* could use the test to open the closed list of exceptions and include uses that were not foreseen by the European legislature in 2001'.[1509] Of course, if the conditions are interpreted more liberally, the chances of a litigated use passing the test will increase. But even if a greater emphasis is placed on the public interest, the one-sided character of the test will remain largely unaltered. In addition, the test, as presently worded, would continue to undermine the legal certainty provided by enumerated and relatively

1508. Whether the test, in light of the traditional interpretation, already tolerates such open-ended exceptions is a question that will be discussed *infra* at 5.6.

1509. Jütte (2017), pp. 312-313. Such a (re)interpretation of Article 5(5), apart from its doubtful legitimacy, would also be harmful for legal certainty – *see* Mazziotti (2008), p. 306

precise exceptions, for their concrete application would still need to be examined against a set of vague conditions.

In order for these two problems to be addressed, a mere reinterpretation of the test's conditions would not be sufficient. Instead, as proposed by some commentators, a *structural revision* would be necessary. It is to those proposals that I now turn.

4.2.2.2 Restructuring the Test

Commentators have advanced proposals that are arguably more ambitious than simply re-reading the test's steps. Some of these proposals, when implemented in the EU *acquis*, could have the effect of conferring on judges the discretion they need to decide on the accommodation of new uses.

Some scholars question the established sequence of the steps, suggesting that the test be read in reverse. Christophe Geiger has proposed applying the test backwards,[1510] starting from the third step, which, unlike the two previous steps, opens the door for a balancing of competing interests. The second step would be analysed after the (nowadays) third step, serving as a 'corrective measure to eliminate the most abusive conflicts with the exploitation of the work',[1511] and the inquiry would end with the 'special cases' inquiry. Geiger's idea is to explore the 'psychological effect'[1512] of having courts consider the third step in the first place. He argues that 'after having balanced the different interests involved, they would certainly be less inclined to censor the use by adopting a purely economic approach and would therefore use the second step as a mere correcting tool'.[1513] While one can only speculate about its actual psychological impact, this reverse reading would certainly stress the normative assessment that is required by the terms 'unreasonable' (prejudice) and 'legitimate' interests in the third step. Such terms, by implying that there are *reasonable prejudices* and *illegitimate interests*, require the decision-maker to take into consideration possibly superior interests that conflict with those of the rightholder.[1514] Under the

1510. For a description of the proposal in detail, *see* Geiger (2005), (2006b), (2007c) and (2009b). A related proposal is the one submitted by Gervais (2005), who suggests a reverse reading of the test, but in a different (more radical) sense: what Daniel Gervais seems to propose is that the rightholder's entitlement be determined by the conduct that the three-step test *does not* allow, i.e. that the three-step test be understood as also defining *prima facie* infringements of copyright. As such, besides requiring a major reworking of the copyright system as a whole, this proposal does not strictly focus on exceptions and therefore falls outside the scope of this book.

1511. Geiger (2007c), p. 18.

1512. Geiger (2007c), p. 19.

1513. Geiger (2009b), p. 638.

1514. *See* Geiger (2007b), p. 490. *See also* Wright (2009), p. 610, maintaining that 'the ordinary meaning of the words [in the third step] appears to provide the greatest scope for the public policy intentions underlying an exception or limitation to form part of the interpretation'.

ordinary (non-reverse) reading of the test, this exercise could only be carried out *if* and *after* the second step was deemed to be met.

In the author's view, the reverse reading is not prohibited by any text.[1515] This seems disputable, however, at least at the international level. A look at the drafting history of the test in the Berne Convention sheds doubts on the permissibility of such a reading. In the initially proposed wording for Article 9(2) Berne Convention, what is now the second step ('normal exploitation') featured as the last step.[1516] But a proposal by the Drafting Committee suggesting that the 'normal exploitation' step be placed before the 'unreasonable prejudice' one was eventually accepted, on grounds that 'this would afford a more logical order for the interpretation of the rule'[1517] (presumably because it was understood that it was not possible for a use privilege to conflict with a normal exploitation of the work and not be unreasonably prejudicial to the interests of the author[1518]). The reverse reading is also questionable in light of the decisions by the WTO Panels. As Annette Kur notes, 'all three panels emphasise that the test actually does consist of three … clearly discernible stages, which must be passed through cumulatively and in a strict order'.[1519]

More importantly for our purposes, in what concerns the InfoSoc test, merely altering the order of the steps, as the CJEU occasionally does,[1520] would not change the nature of the test as a one-sided analysis. It could, in theory, increase the chances of a certain use meeting the test in a concrete dispute, by inclining the Court in a different direction. Nonetheless, it would not transform Article 5(5) into an enabling and fully discretion-granting standard.

Other proposals to rethink the test appear more promising as possible third levels of a multi-tiered model of exceptions. If implemented, these proposals could solve the problems of one-sidedness and certainty erosion described above.

A first set of such proposals attempts to redefine the function of the test, by proposing slight but crucial rewordings. Andrew Christie has proposed the introduction of a residual exception to the exclusive rights formulated with the very language of the three-step test. This would result in changing the role of the test: an autonomous exception would work not as a constraint on

1515. *See* Geiger (2006b), p. 697.
1516. *See* Berne Convention Records 1967, p. 1144.
1517. Berne Convention Records 1967, p. 1145. For a more detailed analysis, *see* Senftleben (2004), pp. 127-131.
1518. *See* Christie (2011), p. 127.
1519. Kur (2009), p. 314. *See also* Senftleben (2004), p. 125.
1520. *See* CJEU, *PRCA*, paras 54-63, switching the order of the second and third steps in its analysis of Article 5(5) InfoSoc Directive.

the application of other exceptions, but as a use privilege *proprio sensu*.[1521] Christie has suggested that the exception, which could be adopted in the EU and national legal orders, be worded as follows:

> In any particular case, it is not an infringement of copyright to do any act that does not conflict with a normal exploitation of the protected subject matter and that does not unreasonably prejudice the legitimate interests of the copyright owner.[1522]

Whereas step one is reformulated as the starting phrase of this residual exception, steps two and three remain cumulative conditions. In contrast to what happens in the current Article 5(5) InfoSoc Directive, these conditions must be met so as to autonomously determine that a given use is non-infringing and not to control the application of listed exceptions. The difference between Christie's proposal and the versions of the test that have been incorporated into EU directives is that the former, unlike the latter, 'permits all acts that are consistent with the three-step test'.[1523]

A related proposal has been made by Bernt Hugenholtz & Martin Senftleben. These scholars have recommended that EU Member State legislators adopt a 'semi-open' defence, by combining the language of some of the exceptions listed in Article 5 InfoSoc Directive with that of the three-step test:

> It does not constitute an infringement to use a work or other subject-matter for non-commercial scientific research or illustrations for teaching, for the reporting of current events, for criticism or review of material that has already been lawfully made available to the public, or quotations from such material serving comparable purposes, for caricature, parody or pastiche, or the incidental inclusion in other material, provided that such use does not conflict with a normal exploitation of the work or other subject-matter and does not unreasonably prejudice the legitimate interests of the rightholder.[1524]

Again, the difference between the starting formula of the current InfoSoc test ('The exceptions ... shall only be applied') and the proposed one ('It does not constitute an infringement'), though it may appear trivial to the unwary, is essential for assigning a new, opening function to the test.

A second set of proposals challenges the separate and cumulative nature of the test's conditions. Championing this challenge, Kamiel Koelman has

---

1521. Note that Article 5(5) Wittem Code, although employing the language of the test, is not a use privilege, but a permission to apply existing privileges by analogy, subject to the verification of the test's conditions. That is why I have analysed it above and not under the present heading.

1522. Christie (2011), p. 134. For an early proposal in the same direction, *see* Hoeren (2000), p. 5.

1523. Christie (2011), p. 134.

1524. Hugenholtz & Senftleben (2011), pp. 17-18. *See also* Hansen (2008), pp. 409-410, advancing a proposal along the same lines.

proposed redrafting the three-step test as a three-*factor* balancing test,[1525] inspired by the US fair use standard.[1526] Under Section 107 US Copyright Act, the four listed conditions are not decisive on their own; they work as factors to be weighed together, rather than as successive and separate hurdles. The idea is to use the vague language of the three conditions as models for the elaboration of fair use-type factors 'that courts or legislators have to weigh together when deciding on the scope of copyright'.[1527] Conceived in this way, the test would allow concrete uses to be accommodated even if they scored low on a certain factor. The proposal has garnered support not only from the academic community[1528] but also, quite remarkably, within the CJEU itself. The 'balancing of factors' approach has been followed by AG Campos Sánchez-Bordona in his opinion in *Renckhoff*. In analysing whether the unauthorised re-posting of a photograph on a school's website in the context of a class assignment constituted copyright infringement, the AG understood the three-step test as a standard requiring the weighing up of the different elements. The AG balanced the interests related to the exploitation of the work and those arising from the fundamental right to education to conclude that the use at stake passed the test.[1529]

In the context of a possible revision of the copyright *acquis* and of the InfoSoc Directive in particular, the two foregoing sets of proposals – which share the goal of explicitly restructuring the test, while essentially preserving

1525. The Declaration appears to formulate a similar proposal, in claiming that the test must be understood as an 'indivisible entirety' and, accordingly, that its conditions must be 'considered together and as a whole in a comprehensive overall assessment' – Geiger et al. (2008), p. 711. In its authors' view, no redrafting would be needed for the steps to be regarded as factors, as this could be achieved through a 'balanced interpretation' of the test. For the reasons offered above in relation to the reverse reading of the test, this does not seem to be an acceptable position in light of the test's history. A rephrasing of the test would be necessary for that purpose. *See* Lucas (2010), p. 281, and Ficsor (2012), fn. 8.

1526. *See* Koelman (2006), pp. 410-411. An alternative (and simpler) solution, in Koelman's opinion, would be to soften the interpretation of the second step.

1527. Koelman (2006), p. 410.

1528. *See* Mazziotti (2008), pp. 305-306 (supporting Koelman's proposal, but arguing that a redesign of the test would be easier to achieve at the EU level than at the international level). Other scholars have since made similar proposals – *see* Kur (2009), p. 340 (criticising the '"policy-blind" assessment' required under the traditional view of the test and proposing that the test be rethought as a 'comprehensive balancing exercise' based on the principle of proportionality); Geiger et al. (2008), p. 709 (claiming that a correct interpretation of the three-step test would understand it as requiring a 'comprehensive overall assessment rather than the step-by-step application'); Geiger & Schönherr (2012), pp. 145-146 (arguing for a reinterpretation of the conditions of the test as 'open-ended factors'); and Geiger et al. (2014), p. 585 (submitting that 'a sequential application does not mean that the third step should not be considered if the second step is not met').

1529. *See* AG Opinion, *Renckhoff*, paras 122-128, and, in particular, fn. 82 (expressly agreeing with the approach proposed in the Declaration).

the wording of its conditions – seem more auspicious than mere reinterpretations or reverse readings of the steps. The following section critically evaluates the fittingness of these proposals as candidates for a standard-like provision integrating a three-tiered framework of exceptions in InfoSoc.

4.2.2.3 Critical Analysis

As the previous analysis shows, much attention has been paid in recent years to the possibility of using a reworked three-step test as an instrument to inject adaptability into the copyright framework of exceptions. Two main arguments can be articulated in favour of that specific solution. The first one is that the three-step test has gone through various mutations throughout its history.[1530] Changing the test once again, by granting it a new function and structure, would not be without precedent. Second, and more importantly, rethinking the function of Article 5(5) InfoSoc Directive (and of equivalent provisions in other directives) would have undeniable political advantages vis-à-vis other solutions. The test's language is well established in international law and in the *acquis communautaire*, featuring in various directives. By using that same language and avoiding a major rewording of the legislative framework, a restructured three-step test would perhaps progress through legislative chambers more easily (although it would nonetheless be bound to be actively resisted by rightholders and their representatives). At the very least, it would escape the accusations of cultural specificity that US fair use often sustains.[1531]

It is presumably for these reasons that commentators regard the three-step test in Article 5(5) as the 'logical starting point'[1532] for the introduction of adaptability into the InfoSoc framework of exceptions. After all, by making simple changes to the wording of a provision that has some pedigree in the *acquis*, a standard-like exception could be created, allowing courts to transparently accommodate emerging and unforeseen uses.

However, before expanding the role of the three-step test as a judicial tool we should ruminate about how European courts, particularly the CJEU, have been dealing with the test and its conditions. Since it is the judiciary who will have the task of developing the test in its new vests, it is only to be expected that we look closely at the already existing case law. And this case law – as previously suggested and as other commentators have exposed[1533] – is disheartening.

On the one hand, national courts have been following radically divergent approaches when applying the test. Some of them, like the French

1530. Tracing those mutations, *see* Geiger (2007b). *See also supra* Chapter 2, section 4.
1531. This advantage is highlighted by Griffiths (2009), p. 447, and Griffiths (2010a), p. 90. On these objections in relation to the option of importing fair use, *see infra* 4.2.3.3.
1532. Senftleben (2010), p. 74.
1533. *See*, in particular, Griffiths (2009).

Court of Cassation in the *Mulholland Drive* case,[1534] have applied the test as a second tier of scrutiny in cases concerning the application of listed exceptions, as required by the wording of Article 5(5) InfoSoc Directive and relevant CJEU case law. Other courts – the definitive example being the Spanish Supreme Court in the *Megakini.com* judgment[1535] – have chosen to adopt a more flexible approach, weighing other factors besides the interests of rightholders in their analysis of the test. 'Viewed together', as argued by Jonathan Griffiths, these cases 'present a very strong impression of inconsistency', because '[t]he same formula is applied in remarkably different ways in different national courts'.[1536]

What unites these cases is that in none of them the adjudicatory body developed the three-step test reasoning in any satisfactory detail. Beyond the thorough interpretation provided by the WTO Panel in *US-Copyright* (however criticisable it may be), the meaning of each individual step in the eyes of courts is to a large extent a mystery. As a result, the test, despite being a staple of international copyright law, remains shrouded in haziness. As Geiger notes, '[i]t is the task of legal scholars to help the judges to find new readings of the test'[1537] – yet courts have so far failed to apply any such suggestions coherently. This lack of interest may be attributable to the fact that in academia too the interpretation of the steps is 'viciously contested'.[1538] There is very little consensus, among courts and academics alike, on what is required by the three-step test.

The scenario does not get any more promising when one examines the case law of the CJEU. As discussed before, the three-step test reasoning and the implications of each step are severely underdeveloped at the CJEU level.[1539] When the test is applied in its capacity as an instrument to restrict the application of exceptions, the reasoning is not elaborated to a sufficient extent.[1540] The clearer indications given by the Court relate to the second step, which is understood as a market harm inquiry focused on the reduction of lawful transactions concerning the protected works.[1541] The meaning of the first and third steps is, for the most part, up in the air. If the CJEU, who will be the main actor in charge of specifying the meaning of the terms within Article 5(5), has so far done such a wanting job at it, doubts should be raised as to whether it would perform any better even if the function of the test

---

1534. *See supra* Chapter 4, section 4.2.
1535. *See supra* Chapter 4, section 5.2.1.2.
1536. Griffiths (2009), p. 447.
1537. Geiger (2007b), p. 491.
1538. Goold (2017), p. 189.
1539. *See supra* Chapter 4, section 5.2.2.3.
1540. One can of course speculate and say that the CJEU has been avoiding the test precisely because it disagrees with the one-sided restrictive function of the test. But if that were the case, the Court could have simply interpreted the test in a more pro-user way, as proposed by scholars.
1541. *See* CJEU, *ACI Adam*, para. 39, and CJEU, *Filmspeler*, para. 70.

changed. Irrespective of whether the test serves a restrictive or enabling function, it seems presently incapable of performing as a useful doctrine for judicial application.

This uncertainty around the role and interpretation of the test is particularly problematic if the test is to decide concrete cases of liability.[1542] Given the scarcity of case law and the unsettled meaning of the steps at the EU level, the guidance offered by a new standard-like exception based on the language of the three-step test will be very little before further cases accumulate.[1543] Both rightholders and users will be at a loss. Under these circumstances the test may still be viewed as an international compromise that gives *legislators* some freedom to shape their exceptions' regimes, but it can hardly be argued that it is an appropriate analytical framework for *courts* to decide concrete disputes about unauthorised uses.[1544]

Jonathan Griffiths, the most prominent critic of the three-step test even in a restructured form, argues it is 'much too crude a tool'[1545] and a 'hopelessly blunt instrument unsuited for the making of policy distinctions on issues on which differing, but nevertheless legitimate, conclusions may be reached'.[1546] The courts' underdeveloped and confusing application of the test may well be related to its emergence as a 'capacious diplomatic compromise'[1547] and not as a doctrine directed at the judiciary (unlike US fair use, which emerged *from* the judiciary).[1548]

In light of the problems discussed in this and previous sections of the book, it would be pressing for the three-step test to be abandoned as a judicial tool. Instead of rethinking the test as a mechanism of judicial flexibility, the EU legislator would be well advised to simply remove it from InfoSoc and

1542. *See* Griffiths (2009), p. 448.
1543. *See* Griffiths (2010a), p. 90, pointing out that the test 'provides almost nothing in the way of normative guidance'. In this context of scant case law, it seems inconsistent to propose the adoption of a solution based on the three-step test and argue that '[a] sufficient degree of legal certainty can easily be secured by applying case law established under the old system as a basis of the new ... system' – Senftleben (2009-2010), p. 527.
1544. *See* Griffiths (2009), p. 430.
1545. Griffiths (2009), p. 451.
1546. Griffiths (2009), p. 453. Koelman (2006) makes similar criticisms to the test in the starting lines of his oft-cited piece, claiming that 'the three-step test is seriously flawed and not suited for application by the courts' (p. 407) and that 'the test is not fit to deal with the issue of which usage should exclusively be controlled by the right holder and which should not' (p. 408). Taking into account that he then advances suggestions for reform, he is presumably referring to the original version of the test – not to *any* version of the test, like Griffiths. *See also* Burrell & Coleman (2005), p. 298 (arguing, along the same lines, that the test is 'too vague and open to too many different interpretations to make it a useful guide for national courts').
1547. Griffiths (2009), p. 456.
1548. *See* Koelman (2006), p. 410, and He (2009), p. 294, observing that Section 107 US Copyright Act codified factors and language that were already in use by courts for a long time. More on US fair use history in 4.2.3.1. *infra*.

other directives, returning it to its original function in international law as a device for controlling legislative autonomy in devising domestic and regional exceptions. Eliminating the test would achieve the benefit of enhancing legal certainty, because, in its absence, courts would no longer be allowed to use it as a fuzzy constraining mechanism on the application of otherwise rule-like exceptions. At the same time, it would open the door for the exploration of alternative discretion-granting doctrines.

If this is not regarded as a viable solution, the three-step test could be redrafted to allow for a transparent balancing of interests. To be clear: this is far from being an ideal solution. But it would certainly represent an improvement in relation to the current predicament, especially if the EU legislator somehow densified the meaning of each factor (e.g., in the Directives' recitals).[1549] Some of the proposals described in the two previous sections could serve as guidelines for that purpose.

4.2.3 Importing Fair Use

Another solution for granting judges the discretion they need in times of rampant technological change is the introduction of an open-ended exception modelled after US fair use. This should not be equated with suggestions for drawing inspiration from fair use in order to rethink the three-step test, which have been addressed in the previous section. What is discussed under the present heading is whether a balancing standard *like* fair use – that is, containing language and reflecting considerations akin to those in Section 107 US Copyright Act – should be adopted in EU copyright law. One of the fundamental differences between the two sets of proposals therefore lies in the wording used in the suggested legal provisions: whereas some prefer to preserve the terms that have historically formed the three-step test, others advocate transplanting the wording of US fair use or at least part of it.[1550]

Proposals for the introduction of a fair use-type exception in Europe have been around since before the adoption of the InfoSoc Directive.[1551]

1549. Hence, while I agree with much of Jonathan Griffiths' criticism to the test, I do not side with him on the idea that 'any suggestions – no matter how well intentioned – that the role of the "three-step test" should be expanded must be resisted' – Griffiths (2009), p. 456.

1550. On legal transplants in general, *see* the seminal work Watson (1993). For a sceptical view of legal transplants – which he prefers to call 'legal irritants', using 'good faith' as imported into the UK through the Consumer Rights Directive as an example – *see* Teubner (1998).

1551. *See*, *e.g.*, Hoeren (1997), p. 871 (alluding to the possibility of widening the coverage of exceptions in German law through a solution based on US fair use); Samuelson (1998), p. 80 (arguing in favour of the adoption of fair use in Europe, accompanied by 'a set of guidelines or examples to demonstrate how various factors of a fair use defence would play out and apply to resolve various new technology issues'); and Bertrand (1999), p. 245 (defending the introduction of a fair use clause in French copyright law).

During the InfoSoc negotiations, the Dutch Copyright Committee, a body who advises the Ministry of Justice on copyright matters, made a plea for the introduction of fair use in the Dutch Copyright Act – a proposal that ultimately did not make it into the final text.[1552] After the adoption of the Directive, commentators kept endorsing the idea.[1553] Most of them have done it in somewhat unspecified terms,[1554] merely stating an abstract preference for the fair use paradigm. A few, however, have explored in greater detail the thought of importing fair use (or some version of it) into EU copyright law, having submitted concrete suggestions to that effect. But before we delve into such proposals, a thorougher understanding of the US fair use clause is useful.

4.2.3.1 The US Fair Use Doctrine

In general, continental copyright exceptions like the ones provided in Article 5 InfoSoc Directive stand in stark contrast to the broad and vague Anglo-American exceptions, the most prominent example being the US fair use standard.[1555]

The UK fair dealing clause is frequently equated with US fair use. It should be clarified, however, that they are not equally discretion-granting doctrines. Under UK fair dealing – which is provided in Sections 29, 30, 30A and 32 UK CDPA –, the prima facie infringing user must begin by showing that the use at stake (the 'dealing') fits within one of the specific categories of admissible uses: research and private study (Section 29(1) and (1C)); criticism or review (Section 30(1)); quotation (Section 30(1ZA)); reporting of current events (Section 30(2)); caricature, parody or pastiche (Section

1552. While Cohen Jehoram (2001b), p. 388, has regarded the rejection of this proposal as a 'glorious achievement', Mazziotti (2008), p. 79, qualified it as 'the most interesting and thoughtful proposal' submitted during the discussions between the European Commission and the Member States.
1553. *See* Patry (2011), pp. 223-225 (supporting the introduction of fair use or a functionally equivalent doctrine in EU copyright law, but approving lists of precisely defined exceptions for static, recurring and identifiable fact patterns); Westkamp (2014) (arguing in favour of a fair use clause coupled with a more detailed enumeration of exceptions); and Samuelson (2017), p. 53 (according to whom the 'optimal policy' in the field of exceptions is for nations to complement precise exceptions with a fair use-type clause).
1554. Noting the scarcity of wording proposals for such a standard, *see* Poeppel (2005), p. 496; Förster (2008), p. 214; and Kleinemenke (2013b), p. 104.
1555. It must be noted that the US Copyright Act also contains, along with the fair use standard, a set of precise exceptions e.g. for uses by instructors or pupils in the course of face-to-face teaching in physical classrooms or for the retransmission of broadcast signals by small establishments – *see* Sections 108-122 US Copyright Act. Most of these exceptions are narrower and far more detailed than InfoSoc exceptions. Also, unlike fair use, some of them apply only to certain categories of subject matter.

30A(1)); and illustration for instruction (Section 32).[1556] To be exempted under fair dealing, the use must necessarily fall within one of these purposes. Having made this preliminary demonstration, the user must then show that the dealing was 'fair'. Courts have been relying on a number of factors to reach a conclusion on fairness, such as the quantity of the work taken, whether the work has previously been made available to the public, the way in which the work was obtained, and the consequences of the use for the rightholder. Naturally, the weight of each factor varies according to the type of use and case.

Unlike fair use, the fair dealing doctrine exhaustively indicates the situations it applies to. For these reasons, commentators recognise that '[f]air dealing is by no means a broad open-ended exception'.[1557] As summarised by Robert Burrell & Allison Coleman, 'the key difference … is that US courts can, and do, find that a defendant's use is fair and hence non-infringing in cases where the use in question does not fall within the statutory list'.[1558]

In fact, Section 107 US Copyright Act allows for a more unconstrained exercise. The provision begins by stating that 'the fair use of a copyrighted work, including such use by reproduction in copies or phonorecords or by any other means …, for purposes *such as* criticism, comment, news reporting, teaching (including multiple copies for classroom use), scholarship, or research, is not an infringement of copyright'.[1559] As the italicised expression conveys, the list of purposes is an illustrative or open one (unlike in UK fair dealing).[1560] In any case, these purposes are intended only to give general guidance, playing a secondary role only.[1561] The crucial inquiry is whether the use in question is *fair*.

In assessing fairness, the court must take into account all the relevant considerations, including the four factors that are expressly laid down in Section 107. These are: (i) the purpose and character of the use, e.g. whether such use is of a commercial nature or is for non-profit educational purposes; (ii) the nature of the copyright-protected work; (iii) the amount and substantiality of the portion used in relation to the protected work as a whole;

1556. In determining whether the use was made for one of the listed purposes, the mental element of the alleged infringer (*e.g.*, whether the user had the belief that she was using the work for purposes of criticism) is irrelevant. Instead, a more objective analysis should be conducted. *See* Court of Appeal of England and Wales, *Pro Sieben*.

1557. Torremans (2012), p. 331.

1558. Burrell & Coleman (2005), p. 249.

1559. Emphasis added.

1560. The paradigmatic example of a purpose or category of use that is absent from the enumeration, but that may nonetheless be considered 'fair', is parody. Arguing for the expansion of fair use beyond the purposes listed in Section 107, *see* Samuelson (2010), pp. 1228-1229.

1561. *See* US Supreme Court, *Campbell*, p. 577. The Court also clarified that uses for enumerated purposes should not be considered presumptively fair (p. 584). *See also* US Supreme Court, *Harper & Row*, p. 561.

and (iv) the effect of the use upon the potential market for or value of the protected work.

The factors codified in the US Copyright Act have developed throughout more than a century of case law.[1562] They essentially correspond to the factors invoked by Judge Joseph Story in the 1841 case *Folsom v. Marsh*, which is generally considered the foundational decision of fair use in the US.[1563] In that case, the plaintiff had written a twenty-volume biography of US President George Washington and the defendant had copied 353 pages from the work to produce his own two-volume work. Justice Story refused to render the defendant's use non-infringing and explained how, in general, a fair abridgment claim should be assessed: 'In short, we must often, in deciding questions of this sort, look to the nature and objects of the selections made, the quantity and value of the materials used, and the degree in which the use may prejudice the sale, or diminish the profits, or supersede the objects, of the original work.'[1564] The factors Justice Story found relevant – the nature and objects of the use, the quantity and value of the materials used, and the prejudice to the market for the original work – bear striking similarities with the factors that were ultimately incorporated into Section 107. The judicially developed factors thus served as a source of guidance even prior to the doctrine's codification.

The four codified factors have no assigned weight and there is no predetermined hierarchical or sequential relation between them.[1565] The enumeration of factors is also non-exhaustive (as the expression 'shall

---

1562. A summary of the judicial origins of US fair use is provided in Litman (2001), pp. 68-69.
1563. *See* US Circuit Court for the District of Massachusetts, *Folsom v. Marsh*. The historical predecessor of US fair use is the English fair abridgment doctrine. One century before *Folsom v. Marsh*, the Court of Chancery of England, in the case *Gyles v. Wilcox*, ruled on the question of knowing whether summaries of a protected work amounted to copyright infringement or, on the contrary, whether they should be considered new and autonomous works. Lord Hardwicke, the reporting judge, distinguished between 'colourably shortened' books and true and legitimate summaries: 'Where books are colourably shortened only, they are undoubtedly within the meaning of the Act of Parliament and a mere evasion of the statute, and cannot be called an abridgement. … But this must not be carried so far as to restrain persons from making a real and fair abridgement, for abridgements may with great propriety be called a new book, because, not only the paper and print, but the invention, learning and judgment of the author is shown in them, and in many cases are extremely useful … .' For a detailed analysis of the early English cases on fair abridgment, *see* Patry (2017a), pp. 18-52. *See also* Deazley (2008).
1564. US Circuit Court for the District of Massachusetts, *Folsom v. Marsh*, p. 348. The expression 'fair use' only appeared in US case law years later, in US Circuit Court for the District of Massachusetts, *Lawrence v. Dana*, p. 60, and it was only recognised in statute by Congress with the 1976 US Copyright Act. On the legislative history of US fair use in detail, *see* Patry (2017a), pp. 759 et seq.
1565. *See* US House of Representatives 1976 Report ('The bill endorses the purpose and general scope of the judicial doctrine of fair use, but there is no disposition to freeze the doctrine in the statute, especially during a period of rapid technological change.

include' in Section 107 denotes) and courts sometimes give weight to alternative elements, such as the defendant's good faith.[1566]

The first factor is related to the way in which the protected work was used. Whereas the commercial or for-profit nature of the use weighs against a finding of fair use, its transformative character points the other way.

Within the analysis of the second factor, one must inquire into the degree of originality of the work and whether the work is publicly available or not. The more original and the less factual the work, the lower the probability of the use being found fair. Similarly, the fact that the work has not been published tips the scales against a finding of fair use.

The third factor asks how much of the work has been used in relation to the whole and how substantial that use was. Naturally, the wider the use, the less robust the user's defence will be.

With regards to the fourth factor, the negative effect of the use upon the market for or economic value of the work must be examined. According to the US courts' initial approach, the central question in fair use case law was whether the use at issue, if widespread, would adversely affect the potential market for the protected work and works derived therefrom.[1567] Later, this 'market-centered paradigm',[1568] in which the fourth factor had a decisive weight, lost its influence to an approach focused on the first factor, particularly on the transformative character of the defendant's use.[1569]

The analysis of whether a given unauthorised use is privileged under the fair use standard is to be conducted on a case-by-case basis, taking into account the various factors. In order to determine the (un)fairness of the unauthorised use, Section 107 requires the deciding court to balance competing interests, taking the specific facts of the dispute into account. As stated by the US House of Representatives, 'since the doctrine is an equitable

---

Beyond a very broad statutory explanation of what fair use is and some of the criteria applicable to it, the courts must be free to adapt the doctrine to particular situations on a case-by-case basis').

1566. *See, e.g.*, US Supreme Court, *Campbell*, p. 585; US Court of Appeals for the Eleventh Circuit, *Scientology*, p. 1312; and US Court of Appeals for the Second Circuit, *Rogers v. Koons*, p. 309.

1567. *See* US Supreme Court, *Harper & Row*, p. 568, citing also the 1984 decision in *Sony*, p. 451.

1568. Netanel (2011), p. 734.

1569. Since it was first formulated in Leval (1990), the transformative character of the use has gradually become the decisive criterion in fair use inquiries. In 1994, it was expressly adopted by the US Supreme Court in the *Campbell* case: 'The central purpose of this investigation is to see, in Justice Story's words, whether the new work merely 'supersede[s] the objects' of the original creation, or instead adds something new, with a further purpose or different character, altering the first with new expression, meaning or message; it asks, in other words, whether and to what extent the new work is "transformative"' (p. 579). On the relevance of transformativeness, *see, e.g.*, Netanel (2011), pp. 734 et seq.

rule of reason, no generally applicable definition is possible, and each case raising the question must be decided on its own facts'.[1570]

The decision on liability will come out of that balancing exercise. The factors are mere guidelines and do not work as 'a score card that promises victory to the winner of the majority'.[1571] Because the legislator did not establish the relative importance of the four factors, courts have ample freedom regarding how to take them into consideration.[1572] An aggregate assessment of those factors must be performed, meaning that no factor is determinative per se.[1573] In addition, US courts are not shackled by any canon of strict interpretation or by a restrictive three-step test, and fair use, unlike some exceptions in the Continental tradition, provides no compensation to rightholders for the exempted uses.

It is not hard to see that, from the formal point of view, the exceptions laid down in Article 5 InfoSoc Directive are fundamentally different from US fair use. The latter is not only evidently open-ended, but also very broad. Fair use can be invoked in relation to a wide variety of factual circumstances. The breadth of the doctrine results from the all-encompassing term '(fair) use', as well as from the non-exhaustive lists of uses ('the fair use of a copyrighted work, *including* such use by reproduction in copies or phonorecords *or by any other means* specified by [sections 106 and 106A]') and purposes ('for purposes *such as* … ') contained in the preamble to Section 107. In contrast to what happens with *droit d'auteur* exceptions and UK fair dealing, unenumerated uses and purposes may also be exempted under US fair use. This formula potentially covers all of the types of uses listed in Article 5 InfoSoc Directive and similar catalogues, as well as other unanticipated uses.

The upshot, however, is that the fair use standard delegates the balancing between competing considerations on the judiciary, while the Continental exceptions in Article 5 InfoSoc Directive and national equivalents are the result of balancing exercises that have been made *ex ante* by the legislator.[1574] It can thus be said that fair use functions logically as a rule, in that a court that finds a given unauthorised use unfair is bound do declare it copyright-infringing (and vice versa), but substantially as a principle, in that the court must weigh a variety of competing interests so as to determine whether the use is (un)fair.[1575]

1570. *See* US House of Representatives 1976 Report.
1571. Leval (1990), p. 1110.
1572. *See* Patry (2017a), pp. 62-63.
1573. *See* Patry (2017a), pp. 639-640, making the claim that '[n]o fair use analysis is complete until such an assessment occurs'.
1574. *See* Wandtke (2015), p. 223, noting the difference between the German system, where the balancing of competing interests is the task of the legislator, and the American model, where such task is trusted upon the judge.
1575. The statement draws on the teachings of Ronald Dworkin. As Dworkin (1977) puts it, the function of '[w]ords like "reasonable", "negligent", "unjust", and "significant"' is to make the application of the rule that contains them 'more like a principle' (p. 28).

The scope of fair use has allowed US courts to render a variety of uses non-infringing in an open and transparent manner. These uses include home videotaping of TV broadcasts;[1576] the borrowing of a song's opening musical tag and lyrics to create a parody;[1577] the use of brief quotations from texts posted on the Internet for purposes of news commentary;[1578] the display of thumbnails and cached websites in search engines' lists of results;[1579] the use of third-party photographs to create a collage;[1580] and the digitisation of library holdings in the context of the Google Books service.[1581] Of course, not all challenged uses have been deemed fair by US courts. Various digital uses have been considered unlawful due to the harm they caused to licensing markets, such as the display of a protected photograph on a website promoting a for-profit festival[1582] or certain uses of broadcast content by a subscription-based media monitoring service.[1583]

4.2.3.2 Fair-Use-Based Proposals

Two types of approaches may be followed in incorporating fair use into the *acquis* – either a verbatim one, performing a wholesale (and decontextualised) transplant of Section 107 US Copyright Act,[1584] or a customised one, adapting the language of the standard to the local circumstances. In submitting fair use-based proposals, commentators and policymakers in Europe have generally preferred the second approach.

Jonathan Griffiths is one of the leading supporters of the introduction of an EU-tailored fair use clause. Having dismissed the adapted three-step test as an ideal solution,[1585] he sets out to explore the possibility of adopting a

---

Dworkin gives the example of the US Supreme Court's reading of Section 1 US Sherman Antitrust Act. Although the rule determines that every contract in restraint of trade is void, the Supreme Court interpreted it as barring only 'unreasonable' restraints of trade. This, according to Dworkin, 'allowed the provision to function logically as a rule (whenever a court finds that the restraint is "unreasonable" it is bound to hold the contract invalid) and substantially as a principle (a court must take into account a variety of other principles and policies in determining whether a particular restraint in particular economic circumstances is "unreasonable")' (p. 28).

1576. *See* US Supreme Court, *Sony.*
1577. *See* US Supreme Court, *Campbell.*
1578. *See* US District Court for the Eastern District of Virginia, *Religious Technology Center.*
1579. *See*, respectively, the judgments in US Court of Appeals for the Ninth Circuit, *Kelly*, and US Court of Appeals for the Ninth Circuit, *Perfect 10*, and the judgment in US District Court of Nevada, *Field.*
1580. *See* US Court of Appeals for the Second Circuit, *Cariou.*
1581. *See* US Court of Appeals for the Second Circuit, *Authors Guild.*
1582. *See* US Court of Appeals for the Fourth Circuit, *Violent Hues.*
1583. *See* US Court of Appeals for the Second Circuit, *Fox News Network, LLC v. TVEyes, Inc.*
1584. This has been the approach adopted, by and large, in Liberia, the Philippines and Malaysia. For a description, *see* Yu (2018), pp. 4-6.
1585. *See supra* section 4.2.2.3 for his position.

standard based on US fair use within the EU – a possibility that, in his words, 'has not received the serious attention it deserves'.[1586] After reflecting on the merits and shortcomings of this solution, Griffiths submits that, in designing a fair use clause for EU copyright law, the factors provided in Section 107 US Copyright Act could be supplemented by European-specific considerations, such as EU fundamental rights.[1587]

Christophe Geiger & Elena Izyumenko have recently put forward a proposal along the same lines, though with some additional detail. Their underlying claim is that some form of 'fair use' is already a reality in Europe, given the increasing judicial application of fundamental rights, especially freedom of expression and information, in copyright disputes.[1588] Against this background, the authors rely on the ECtHR's case law on freedom of expression to shape a list of balancing factors analogous to those contained in Section 107. These factors grounded in freedom of expression would form the basis for a European 'fair use' exception.[1589]

In German academia, Jan Poeppel has advanced a possible design for a fair use standard in German law. Poeppel's version draws heavily from the language of the four factors, but is not a literal translation of Section 107. First, the expression 'fair use' is replaced with 'honest use' (*redliche Verwertung*), so as to ensure that the German standard is given an interpretation that is independent from that adopted in US case law. Second, the proposal deliberately foregoes the admissibility of fair use of unpublished works (which has been expressly admitted in the statutory language of Section 107 since its amendment in 1992), due to the higher ranking of authors' moral rights in German law. Finally, the legitimate purposes listed in the preamble of Section 107 are moved to paragraph 1 (the 'purpose and character of the use' factor) for systematic reasons. According to the author, the purposes enumerated within this hypothetical German standard would ultimately depend on which specific rule-like exceptions were to be replaced by the standard.[1590]

1586. Griffiths (2010a), p. 87.

1587. *See* Griffiths (2010a), p. 93.

1588. *See* Geiger & Izyumenko (2019b), pp. 9-13.

1589. Despite the fact that Geiger & Izyumenko (2019b) repeatedly state that the expression 'fair use' is employed throughout the article to refer to the need for an 'open-ended construction' of exceptions and that it is 'by no means identical to American fair use' (p. 9, fn. 75 and p. 58), the wording of the provision they propose (p. 59) appeals significantly to the wording of some of the fair use factors (strikingly, proposed factor 1 refers to 'the character of the use, including whether such use is commercial or transformative'). This is why their proposal was included under this Chapter's section on 'fair use-based proposals'. There are, however, important parallels between Geiger & Izyumenko's solution and the proposal advanced in this book – *see infra* 4.3.

1590. The exact wording proposed by the author can be found in Poeppel (2005), pp. 491-492. Nonetheless, the author ultimately stands against the solution of introducing a standard-like exception and claims that extensive readings or analogical applications of listed exceptions would be preferable.

Another German author who has entertained the possibility of importing fair use is Manuel Kleinemenke. His proposal is based on the premise that a transplant of US fair use *tout court* would be a 'suboptimal' solution for (German and) EU copyright law.[1591] In lieu of a transplant, Kleinemenke recommends the adoption of a residual clause blending the fair use factors with the conditions of a liberally understood three-step test.[1592,1593] The justification for this 'combined solution'[1594] is threefold. First, the author argues that the three-step test must be preserved, out of respect for the decision of the European legislator to explicitly include it in the InfoSoc Directive as a judicial tool.[1595] A second argument is that, by using the language of the test, this discretion-granting clause would not be seen as a 'foreign body' in EU copyright law.[1596] This, as shall be discussed below, is a commonly used argument against importing fair use. Third, considering

1591. Kleinemenke (2013b), p. 105.
1592. A summarised description of Kleinemenke's proposal would go as follows: Paragraph 1 provides that the use of a published copyright-protected work that does not fall within the scope of any of the listed rule-like exceptions is permitted without the authorisation of the rightholder, unless it unreasonably conflicts with the normal exploitation of the work and unreasonably prejudices the legitimate interests of the rightholder. Paragraphs 2 and 3 then elucidate how the two conditions borrowed from the three-step test are to be interpreted. In clarifying the meaning of the 'normal exploitation' factor, considerations that are relevant under the fourth fair use factor are used: it is said that, when assessing whether a given unauthorised use unreasonably conflicts with the normal exploitation of the work, the effects of the use on the actual and potential market for the work, the value of the work and the legitimate interests of third parties must be taken into account. Similarly, in the assessment of whether the use unreasonably prejudices the legitimate interests of the rightholder, consideration must be given to the legitimate interests of third parties. Moreover, under this condition, the judge must take into account the three other fair use factors – the purpose and character of the use, the nature of the copyright-protected work, and the amount and substantiality of the portion used in relation to the protected work as a whole –, as well as the possibility of paying fair compensation. Finally, paragraph 4 establishes that the author shall be fairly compensated for any use that is deemed permitted under this clause. The complete (and Byzantinely complex) formulation can be found in Kleinemenke (2013a), pp. 549-550; (2013b), pp. 122-123; and (2014), pp. 897-898. The sheer number of factors in Kleinemenke's proposed provision may increase the difficulty in predicting the outcomes of disputes governed by it. As stated by Liu (2008), p. 574, '[t]he more factors there are, the more difficult it is to determine which of these factors is dispositive'.
1593. The fair use clause in Article 35*ter* South Korean Copyright Act resorts to such a combination as well. Criticising the South Korean approach, arguing that the incorporation of the three-step test 'will burden those using the fair use provision with an additional layer of legal analysis', *see* Yu (2018), p. 6.
1594. Kleinemenke (2014), p. 897.
1595. *See* Kleinemenke (2013b), p. 121. The argument does not strike me as particularly convincing. If it is indeed concluded, as I think it should be, that transforming the three-step test into a judicial tool proved an ill-advised decision, the EU legislator may well want to backpedal. After all, in general, what the legislator giveth, the legislator may taketh way.
1596. *See* Kleinemenke (2013b), p. 128.

that it would hardly be appropriate to include the three-step test *and* fair use as separate clauses, the three-step test could be supplemented with the more developed assessment criteria contained in Section 107 US Copyright Act as a way to provide added certainty.[1597]

Proposals to introduce some form of fair use in Europe have also emerged from the camp of policymakers. In 2013, the Irish Copyright Review Committee[1598] recommended the inclusion of a 'specifically Irish' fair use clause.[1599] This clause borrows not only from Section 107, but also from the language of the three-step test and from the experience of other countries that have adopted a fair use standard in their copyright laws.[1600] Furthermore, the proposal admittedly tries to accommodate the concerns that critics of fair use have raised during the consultation process.[1601] The proposed clause is part of a multi-tiered model, comprising an enumeration of rule-like exceptions, and the Committee attempted to tie it as strictly as possible to such exceptions. To that effect, it proposed, first, that the enumerated exceptions be regarded as examples of fair use and, second, that, in any concrete case, those exceptions be exhausted before the deciding court can consider whether the use at stake amounts to a fair use.[1602] In order to aid the court in determining whether a given use is a fair use, a long and non-exhaustive list of factors is provided, which includes factors borrowed from US fair use, albeit in adapted form (e.g., 'the nature of the work, including in particular whether there is a public benefit or interest in its dissemination through the use in question'); factors inspired by the relevant literature (e.g., 'the extent to which the use in question is analogically similar or related to the other acts permitted by this Part'); factors drawn from the three-step test (e.g., 'whether the legitimate interests of the owner of the rights in the work are unreasonably prejudiced by the use in question'); and new factors (e.g., 'the possibility of obtaining the work, or sufficient rights therein, within a reasonable time at an ordinary commercial price, such that the use in question is not necessary in all the circumstances of the

---

1597. *See* Kleinemenke (2013b), pp. 121-122.
1598. The Committee was established on 9 May 2011 by the Minister for Jobs, Enterprise and Innovation. The Terms of Reference of the Committee expressly required it to '[e]xamine the US style "fair use" doctrine to see if it would be appropriate in an Irish/EU context' – *see* Irish Copyright Review Committee Consultation Paper 2012, p. 1.
1599. Irish Copyright Review Committee Report 2013, p. 90. In the UK, the Hargreaves Review (2011), though acknowledging that fair use could be 'the big once and for all fix of the UK' (p. 52), declined to recommend its introduction under the argument that 'importing Fair Use wholesale was unlikely to be legally feasible in Europe' (p. 5).
1600. *See* Irish Copyright Review Committee Consultation Paper 2012, p. 120.
1601. *See* Irish Copyright Review Committee Report 2013, p. 89.
1602. *See* Irish Copyright Review Committee Report 2013, p. 93, specifically the second paragraph of proposed Section 49A.

case'[1603]).[1604] Moreover, the Committee proposed the addition of ministerial powers over the definition of fair use, authorising the competent Minister to enact regulations prescribing what constitutes a fair use in specific cases.[1605]

4.2.3.3 Critical Analysis

Apart from its discretion-granting benefits, a fair use-based solution would have three specific advantages when compared with alternative designs for a third tier.

First, as a test that enables courts to openly balance opposing considerations without predetermined weights, fair use promotes transparent judicial decision-making. Instead of having to resort to intricate analogy-based exercises, courts, under a fair use standard, are allowed to take into account the interests of both rightholders and users and the way in which those interests play out in specific factual circumstances.

Second, unlike the three-step test, fair use originated as a judge-made doctrine. Section 107 codified factors and language that had already been in use by courts for decades. It may thus be assumed that judges generally feel comfortable in reasoning under its terms (but important qualifications to this argument shall be added shortly). Many scholars have noted this relative advantage of fair use. Writing from a US perspective, William Patry observes that fair use is a set of principles 'that have been tested in the forge of thousands of court cases and opinions'.[1606] European scholars have also praised fair use as a judicially created doctrine. Kamiel Koelman, contrasting the three-step test with fair use, points out that the latter 'was not conceived as a diplomatic compromise, but rather as a standard for the courts to actually apply' and concludes that '[n]ot surprisingly, therefore, it is better suited for that'.[1607]

Third, by adopting a fair use-inspired provision, the EU would be adhering to what seems to be a growing legislative trend spanning different jurisdictions around the world.[1608] Once a peculiarity of US copyright

1603. This factor is not exactly new, since it had already been expressly provided in the Singaporean fair use clause in Section 35 Copyright Act of Singapore and discussed in US case law, namely in US Supreme Court, *Harper & Row*, p. 562, and in US Court of Appeals for the Second Circuit, *American Geophysical Union*, pp. 930-931.

1604. In order to give guidance to courts as to whether the factors militate in favour or against a finding of fair use, the Committee ordered them accordingly – *see* Irish Copyright Review Committee Report 2013, p. 95.

1605. *See* Irish Copyright Review Committee Report 2013, p. 94, in particular the fifth paragraph of proposed Section 49A. The purpose of this solution, as Niva Elkin-Koren explains, 'was to reduce the uncertainty resulting from the open ended nature of the fair use doctrine' – Elkin-Koren (2016), pp. 21-22.

1606. Patry (2011), p. 224.

1607. Koelman (2006), p. 410.

1608. Tracing the global spread of fair use, *see* Decherney (2014) and Hughes (2017), pp. 256-262.

law,[1609] the doctrine has been introduced in several countries over the last few decades. Some form of fair use – either verbatim or adapted – has so far been adopted in Israel,[1610] Malaysia,[1611] the Philippines,[1612] Singapore,[1613] South Korea,[1614] Sri Lanka,[1615] and more.[1616] Policymakers in other jurisdictions have also entertained (or are currently entertaining) the idea of importing fair use, including Australia,[1617] Hong Kong,[1618] Ireland,[1619] the Netherlands,[1620] South Africa,[1621] and the UK.[1622] It can be argued that, by taking part in such a trend at a relatively early stage, the EU would be

1609. *See* Decherney (2014), p. 146 ('[f]or 150 years, fair use was a solely American doctrine').
1610. *See* Section 19 Israeli Copyright Act, adopted in 2007. For commentary, *see* Afori (2008b); Pessach (2010), pp. 189-193; and Zemer (2010).
1611. *See* Section 13 Malaysian Copyright Act, as amended in 2012.
1612. *See* Section 185.1 Intellectual Property Code of the Philippines, enacted in 1998, with amendments in 2012.
1613. *See* Sections 35 and 36 Copyright Act of Singapore, amended in 2004. It bears noting that Singapore introduced the fair use factors within its previously existing fair dealing provisions, expanding their reach, but preserving the *nomen iuris* 'fair dealing'. For commentary on the revised doctrine and its scope, *see* Loon (2009), pp. 173-179; Tan (2012); and Wei (2012), pp. 878-899.
1614. *See* Article 35*ter* South Korean Copyright Act, added in 2011. For discussion, *see* Hahn & Lee (2016).
1615. *See* Section 11 Sri Lankan Intellectual Property Act, enacted in 2003.
1616. For a compendium of fair use and fair dealing provisions in the IP/copyright laws of more than 40 countries, *see* Band & Gerafi (2015).
1617. In a report published in 2013, the Australian Law Reform Commission recommended the adoption of a fair use exception with non-exhaustive lists of fairness factors and illustrative purposes – *see* Australian Law Reform Commission Report 2013, pp. 90-98. More recently, on 19 March 2018, the Department of Communications and the Arts of the Australian Government released a consultation paper seeking stakeholder views, *inter alia*, on whether a fair use-style exception should be introduced in Australia – *see* Australian Government Consultation Paper 2018, p. 7.
1618. *See* Hong Kong Legislative Council Amendments 2015, p. 4. For a detailed discussion on the proposed amendment, *see* Yu (2016), pp. 319 et seq.
1619. *See* the proposal by the Irish Copyright Review Committee, discussed in the previous subsection.
1620. *See* Grosheide (2001), p. 325, on the proposal by the Dutch Copyright Committee to introduce fair use in the Dutch Copyright Act (deeming it 'an attractive alternative route compared to that now established in Brussels'). *See also* Hugenholtz (2017), p. 276, on the Dutch Government's commitment to start discussions at the EU level on the possibility of enacting a fair use clause.
1621. *See* South African Copyright Amendment Bill 2017, specifically draft Section 12A, converting the fair dealing provision into a fair use standard with non-exhaustive lists of purposes and factors. The bill was passed by the National Council of Provinces and sent to the President for assent. At the time of writing, the President had sent the bill back to the Parliament, raising concerns regarding its constitutionality.
1622. *See* Hargreaves Review (2011), pp. 44-52 (though ultimately rejecting the solution).

sending a relevant message about its attractiveness for technological innovation.[1623]

Be all this as it may, the idea of transplanting the language of US fair use into EU copyright law has not been met with universal acclaim. European commentators backing the reform of the InfoSoc framework of exceptions do commonly resort to fair use as an argumentative anchor,[1624] but the fact is that most of them end up rejecting the idea of adopting it, either implicitly, by supporting alternative solutions, or explicitly.[1625] Even those who advance such fair use-based proposals, as seen, tend to refuse an outright transplant of the US clause into EU copyright law.

Those who generally oppose the inclusion of *any* standard-like exception in EU copyright law deploy the 'legal uncertainty' bogeyman to justify their position.[1626] This, as discussed earlier, is an unfounded argument.[1627] But these scholars, as well as most of those who are in favour of reforming the framework, commonly invoke two other reasons for rejecting the import of a fair use-style standard.[1628]

1623. Making this argument in relation to Ireland, *see* Irish Copyright Review Committee Report 2013, p. 93. As acknowledged by the Australian Law Reform Commission Report 2013, p. 23, '[o]f course, innovation depends on much more than copyright law, but fair use would make Australia a more attractive market for technology investment and innovation'. *See also* Lohmann (2008), making the argument that the fair use doctrine encourages investment in socially desirable digital technologies.

1624. *See* Torremans (2012), p. 319 (observing that 'in recent years European copyright circles have been fascinated by the fair use doctrine and have wondered whether it would be worthwhile introducing the doctrine into European copyright law') and Birnhack (2015), p. 264 (generally noting that, in policy debates around copyright exceptions, '[t]he main reference point is the American fair use defence').

1625. It should furthermore be added that some US scholars suggest that fair use should be comprehensively rethought. *See*, *inter alia*, Gordon (1982) (understanding fair use in terms of market failure); Fisher (1988) (submitting that fair use should be recast according to a vision of what the 'good life' and the 'good society' is); and Madison (2004) (proposing a rethinking of fair use in light of socially accepted practices and patterns).

1626. *See supra* Introduction, section 1.3.

1627. *See*, in particular, *supra* Chapter 4, section 5.3.

1628. Others ground their opposition on doubts about the compatibility of fair use with the international three-step test. This is an important and frequently advanced argument, but I shall address it at a later point (section 5.6), since it is an argument that can also be raised against the solution I ultimately propose.

Another minor argument has been used: it is sometimes said that fair use does not fit well with the *pro auctoris* judicial attitude that (supposedly) prevails in Europe – *see* Burrell (2001), p. 388 (admitting, however, that the very adoption of such a provision 'could itself help to transform judicial attitudes'); Burrell & Coleman (2005), pp. 249 et seq.; and Brenncke (2007), p. 16. To the extent that a conservative pro-author/rightholder attitude was ever an established attitude at the CJEU level (an undemonstrated proposition), it seems to have dramatically changed, as has been made clear *supra* in Chapter 4, section 5.2.2.

It is contended, first, that fair use is not an appropriate solution for Europe because it is culturally alien to its tradition.[1629] At first sight, the claim appears shallow, for nothing in the wording of Section 107 US Copyright Act suggests any inherent connection to the culture of the US.[1630] But the argument is complemented by a further idea – the idea that standard-like provisions are foreign to the civil law tradition, in general, and/or to EU copyright law, in particular.

The argument is based upon the belief that judges from civilian traditions – the majority of Member States belonging to such tradition – lack the indispensable experience to apply and develop balancing tests. This idea, however, amounts to no more than 'mere rhetoric'[1631] or a 'red herring'.[1632] Although courts in the civil law tradition operate under no formal precedent system,[1633] it is not true that they are not used to or capable of applying such vague provisions consistently. In fact, important provisions in private law codifications within civil law countries are exceedingly open-ended (think of clauses on 'unjust enrichment' or 'abuse of rights') and courts have been applying them successfully for a long time.[1634]

It has also been maintained that CJEU judges, in particular, are unable or reluctant to work with balancing tests. According to Matthias Leistner, 'the very concept of a factor-based fair use test, essentially demanding a (more or less structured) balancing of interests, might be at odds with the limited methodology of the ECJ'.[1635] The Court's reasoning, says Leistner, is 'heavily based on the teleological method'[1636] and not so much on the

1629. *See, e.g.*, Report Public Consultation 2014, p. 34 (some stakeholders 'are particularly against the introduction of an open norm that is similar to the "fair use" principle in the US. They argue that this would not be in line with European legal traditions and that replacing statutory law by judge-made law would inevitably result in less legal certainty') and Jütte (2017), pp. 326-327 ('the doctrine, if implemented into EU copyright law without any further support or guidance, would constitute a foreign body that would hardly be expected to work smoothly'). Also, some raise doubts about the political feasibility of transplanting fair use or fear the strenuousness of the process leading to it – *see, e.g.*, Piotraut (2012), p. 157; Torremans (2012), p. 336; Triaille et al. (2013), p. 538; and Peifer (2014), p. 90.

1630. *See* Irish Copyright Review Committee Consultation Paper 2012, p. 116 ('there is nothing intrinsically or exclusively American about the fair use doctrine').

1631. Senftleben (2017), p. 265.

1632. Irish Copyright Review Committee Consultation Paper 2012, p. 117.

1633. *See* Griffiths (2010a), p. 93 ('[t]he fact-based and precedent-driven judicial enquiry mandated by s 107 sits uneasily within some European judicial traditions'). *See also* Leistner (2011), p. 437, specifically on the alleged lack of a true case law methodology at the CJEU level – an argument which has been disputed *supra* in Chapter 4, section 5.3.

1634. *See* Senftleben (2017), p. 250, giving the examples of the German *Treu und Glauben* and the Dutch *redelijkheid en billijkheid* doctrines. *See also* Hoeren (2000), p. 5, disputing the idea that the German judiciary is averse to case-by-case weighing.

1635. Leistner (2011), p. 438.

1636. Leistner (2011), p. 438.

balancing of competing values, interests or principles. Likewise, Paul Torremans claims that 'fair use in the US depends heavily on the judges. They have a lot of experience with fair use and they are used to the delicate balancing act it involves. … European judges, on the contrary, … lack the years of experience with fair use and its balancing act'.[1637]

This objection overlooks the fact that the CJEU is increasingly called upon to balance competing interests and values within the field of IP law and often does so at its own initiative.[1638] Although it is true that the CJEU regularly focuses on the purpose behind EU instruments or specific provisions contained therein, it is no less true that it has been engaging in balancing exercises rather frequently. On multiple occasions and in connection with different doctrines in the copyright *acquis*, the Court has tried to weigh IP as a fundamental right against the users' fundamental rights and freedoms.[1639]

The argument is occasionally narrowed down to mean that European IP law/copyright law is not familiar with such vague doctrines.[1640] But this, too, is far from being true. In areas of the law not distant from copyright, the use of standard-like norms is widespread and not fundamentally controversial. The defence of 'due cause' in EU trademark law and the prohibition against 'unfair commercial practices' come to mind.[1641] In EU copyright law, as seen, 'originality' and 'communication to the public' are everyday concepts, the latter one being increasingly applied as a balancing test of sorts. More generally, 'all of the foundational issues in copyright are equally fact-specific: did you contribute enough to be considered an author; did you imbue the work with enough originality for the work to be protected; is the material in question an idea or the expression of an idea?'.[1642]

A second argument against the introduction of a fair use clause in EU copyright law – and a more swaying one, in my view – is closely related to the argument that led me to reject a solution based on the three-step test. It has been repeatedly observed throughout the book that vague doctrines like fair use may be made more predictable by the accumulation of case law interpreting their terms and allowing consistent patterns to emerge. While the EU could indeed import all or part of the fair use wording into the copyright

---

1637. Torremans (2012), p. 333.

1638. *See*, *e.g.*, Strowel & Kim (2013).

1639. Relatedly, following the introduction of the notion of 'proportionality' in the InfoSoc (Article 8(1) and Recital 58) and Enforcement (Article 3(2)) Directives, the Court has been exploring the role of this principle in copyright law in a regular manner, particularly in cases concerning remedies for infringement. *See* the CJEU judgments in *Promusicae*, *Tele2*, *Scarlet*, *Netlog*, *Bonnier Audio*, *UPC Telekabel*, *Mc Fadden*, and *Bastei Lübbe*. For discussion, *see* Afori (2014).

1640. *See*, *e.g.*, Triaille et al. (2013), p. 536, making the claim that fair use 'would not fit easily in many Member States traditions and legal background regarding copyright law'.

1641. *See* Senftleben (2017), pp. 256-265.

1642. Patry (2017a), p. xiv.

acquis, such a newly created doctrine would nonetheless lack the vast body of case law on Section 107 that enabled the standard to become more precise over time.[1643] The argument, in essence, is that introducing only the statutory language would be equivalent to smuggling a lifeless doctrine into Europe, because '[f]air use lives from its case-law'.[1644] While it could be envisaged that European courts would occasionally cite US fair use case law,[1645] a massive borrowing should not be expected.[1646] The development of a comparable level of certainty in the EU, in the words of Thomas Dreier, 'would be delayed until sufficiently precise contours had evolved in Europe as well'[1647] – a process that would certainly take a number of years. This would also mean that an important advantage of fair use highlighted above – its judicial origins – would not hold on this side of the pond: fair use did originate from case law, but not from *EU* case law. Combining the language of US fair use with that of the three-step test, as proposed by some academics, would not solve this problem either. As discussed above, there is a dearth of developed case law on the three-step test. And if the three-step test offers limited guidance through case law in Europe, then, quite evidently, so does fair use, whose wording has no lineage in EU copyright law.

Having said all this, arguing that it is unadvisable to simply transplant the wording of Section 107 into the *acquis* is not the same as arguing that no lessons can be learned from the US experience with fair use. If it is agreed that the third tier of our framework should be designed as a balancing test, then the vast experience of the US in applying that type of test in the field of copyright exceptions can only be valuable. The example of fair use should indeed be looked at for purposes of crafting an EU-tailored standard – a standard with factors specific to EU copyright law, made up of concepts that

---

1643. *See* Jütte (2017), p. 327 ('[l]egal certainty is inextricably connected to the extensive body of fair use case-law, which gives guidance to the judiciary for an interpretation of the four factors. The lack of a comparable body of case-law would, at least in the short term, hinder its effectiveness in the EU') and Ficsor (2018), p. 32 (fair use 'may only work efficiently and adequately due to the long and rich legal traditions and the big body of case law which make it possible. It would be difficult to introduce such a system in countries where there is no such tradition and case law'). *See also* Geller (1994) (analysing methodological problems surrounding legal transplants in international copyright law) and Birnhack (2015) (warning against decontextualised legal transplants, using the Israeli fair use doctrine as a case study).

1644. Jütte (2017), p. 329.

1645. Interestingly, in its opinion on the liability of P2P file sharing platforms, AG Szpunar made reference to the related judgment of the US Court of Appeals for the Ninth Circuit in *Napster* – *see* AG Opinion, *Ziggo*, fn. 11. More recently, AG Saugmandsgaard Øe cited the judgments by the US Supreme Court in *Sony* and *Grokster* in his opinion on the *YouTube/Cyando* case – *see* AG Opinion, *YouTube/Cyando*, fns. 105 and 109.

1646. *See*, in general, Jacobs (2003) (though noting that, in certain specific fields like competition law, judicial dialogue and cross-fertilisation may be more likely). *See also* Rosas (2007), for a taxonomy of the various patterns of judicial dialogue, with a focus on the CJEU.

1647. Dreier (2015), p. 142.

are not foreign to it and that emerged from its own judicial practice. That is the task I take up in the next section.

4.3 Towards a CJEU-Made Standard

A standard-like exception in EU copyright law need not – or rather: *should not* – be a verbatim copy of Section 107 US Copyright Act. This does not mean, however, that it cannot draw inspiration from fair use. The proposal advanced in this section is similar to US fair use in a number of ways.

Like fair use, the proposed standard is a standard cast in the form of a balancing test. The term 'balancing' evokes the image of Lady Justice, the Ancient Roman anthropomorphisation of justice, conjuring up the idea of a set of scales on which two items are weighed. Balancing is a method of legal reasoning by which courts ponder conflicting considerations – rights, interests, purposes, principles, policies, values, factors – and decide which outweighs the other and should, for that reason, prevail in the case *sub judice*.

In addition, it is a balancing test that discriminates the factors that courts should consider in applying it, instead of leaving the choice of factors entirely to their discretion. Balancing tests vary in their ability to guide those who rely on them. The ones providing greater guidance usually do so by specifying weighing factors.[1648] Discriminating factors is a way not only of

1648. Discriminating balancing factors is not the only way that a fair use-style test can provide guidance. Other solutions – mostly of an institutional nature and therefore falling beyond the scope of this book – have been proposed in the literature. *See*, *e.g.*, Liu (2004) (granting authority to develop fair use guidelines to the US Copyright Office); Nimmer (2006) (creating arbitral panels charged with making fair use determinations); Carroll (2007) (giving the US Copyright Office the power to issue letters that would immunise petitioners from liability for the proposed uses); Mazzone (2009) (giving an administrative agency the authority to regulate fair use); Elkin-Koren & Afori (2015) (supplementing fair use with best practices); and Aufderheide & Jaszi (2018), pp. 119 et seq. (adopting codes of best practices and industry guidelines for different sectors and activities, such as documentary film-making, teaching, dance history, and online video-making). Some of these solutions have been adopted by legislators at different latitudes. The fair use transplant in Israel gave regulatory authority to the Minister of Justice to prescribe conditions under which a use shall be deemed privileged. Opposing this addition, on grounds that it has the potential to undermine the flexibility inherent in fair use, *see* Yu (2018), pp. 6-7. The Taiwanese fair use clause adds that industry-wide agreements should be taken as references in fair use determinations – *see* Yu (2018), p. 7. For a sceptical view over the beneficial effects of fair use guidelines and codes of conduct, *see* Crews (2001).

Alternatively, soft law instruments could be adopted, such as the documents or guidelines published by the Commission providing guidance on the implementation and application of directives in different fields of law. These instruments are nonetheless far from ideal. For one thing, as noted by Triaille et al. (2013), p. 288, they 'are not a habit of the European Union in the field of copyright'. For another, and most importantly, they are not legally binding (as recalled by AG Sharpston in her Opinion in *SGAE*, para. 45). In fact, only the CJEU has competence to authoritatively interpret

increasing guidance, but also of controlling the wide discretion given to courts.[1649] Although the US fair use provision is relatively non-constraining, it does not exempt 'fair uses' without more, nor does it require judges to reach the best outcome in each case or to do an all-things-considered review of circumstances. The enumeration of purposes and the list of factors set forth in Section 107 orientate the reasoning of judges and of those who rely on the standard through certain paths of inquiry.[1650] Moreover, as clarified above, the accumulation of judicial opinions has allowed the identification of sub-factors,[1651] policy-relevant clusters of cases,[1652] and unstated factual patterns[1653] that help predict the courts' decisions.[1654]

Finally, this is a standard composed of factors that have a track record in case law. In adopting a standard-like exception, the EU legislator could choose not to specify any balancing factors, leaving it to courts the working out of the relevant considerations in each concrete case. This, however, would be a failure to capitalise on the increasingly wealthy body of CJEU rulings in the field of copyright. To be sure, as noted by Bernd Justin Jütte, although CJEU case law 'is constantly growing, it does not relate remotely, quantitatively and substantively, to that of the fair use doctrine'.[1655] But relying on the lines of thought that arise from the EU copyright case law is the best first step at our disposal in order to increase the guidance value of a freshly enacted standard-like doctrine.[1656]

The purpose of this section is to provide useful guidelines for the content of a standard inspired in CJEU case law. The underlying idea is that this body of case law *can* and *should* be used as a source of EU-specific

---

EU law. *See*, in this regard, 2008 Green Paper, p. 6, opposing non-legally binding acts or non-legislative initiatives on grounds that they do not provide sufficient legal certainty.

1649. In the words of Endicott & Spence (2005), p. 680, 'vagueness allocates a power to the courts, and it is a power that calls for control. That control ought to be found in the development of principled criteria for the application of the doctrines.'

1650. *See* Jütte (2017), pp. 317-318, and Samuelson (2017), p. 49. *See also* Kleinemenke (2013b), p. 114.

1651. *See* Beebe (2008).

1652. *See* Samuelson (2009). For an early division of case law into clusters, even before the codification of fair use, *see* Schumann (1969).

1653. *See* Sag (2012).

1654. Whether such guidance is to be expected at the EU level is a question that has been addressed above (Chapter 4, section 5.3).

1655. Jütte (2017), p. 329.

1656. Besides, positivising normative considerations that originally emerged from CJEU judgments would not be unprecedented in EU copyright law. *See* Introduction, section 4.3 (referring to the creation, by the CJEU, of the rule of exhaustion in the *Deutsche Grammophon* case).

elements in designing a standard-like exception for InfoSoc and that codifying these elements is a more promising solution than restructuring the three-step test or transplanting US fair use.

The criteria suggested below are intended to serve as proxies to help judges reach a decision, while aiding stakeholders in anticipating the outcome of disputes. At the same time, they are sufficiently open-ended, so as to be able to react to changing circumstances and accommodate uses that are yet to be developed.

Of course, the contours of such criteria would need to be filled in gradually by the judiciary. If courts across Member States end up construing them in diverging ways, the recognition of this type of test within the *acquis* could arguably have a negative impact on copyright harmonisation.[1657] Notwithstanding this risk, some commentators believe that the job of developing the balancing factors 'could confidently be left to the courts in EU Member States – with the CJEU ensuring the evolution of consistent case law on the basis of prejudicial questions about the right interpretation'.[1658] Ultimately, the duty of elucidating and harmonising the meaning of each factor would lie on the shoulders of the judges in the Palais, provided that national courts practice a responsible culture of preliminary reference requests, as they have been doing with some copyright doctrines, most notably the right of communication to the public.[1659] Over time, the accumulation of preliminary rulings handed down by the CJEU could yield greater certainty concerning the factors' interpretation.

4.3.1 'Fair Balance'

In examining the lawfulness of uses that do not fall within the scope of any of the listed exceptions, courts should be guided by the very idea that informs the entire system of exceptions: the need to achieve a *fair balance* between the competing interests of authors/rightholders, on the one hand, and those of users, on the other.[1660]

The 'fair balance' concept finds pre-existing legal ground in the legislative *acquis*[1661] and has also been consistently cited by the CJEU in clarifying the meaning and scope of some exceptions, namely the ones for

---

1657. *See, e.g.*, Torremans (2012), pp. 333-334, and Triaille et al. (2013), p. 538. This much has been feared by AG Szpunar in *Spiegel Online*, para. 63.
1658. Senftleben (2017), p. 266. In a similarly optimistic tone, *see* Ohly (2009), p. 240.
1659. *See* Triaille et al. (2013), p. 538, though not without predicting that this will be a long process.
1660. *See* CJEU, *Funke Medien*, para. 70, and CJEU, *Spiegel Online*, para. 54.
1661. *See, e.g.*, Recital 31 InfoSoc Directive and Recital 6 DSM Directive.

private copying,[1662] temporary reproduction,[1663] quotation,[1664] parody,[1665] and library terminals.[1666,1667]

In the proposed standard, the need to establish a fair balance would work as an overarching principle, much like the preambular notion of 'fairness' in Section 107 US Copyright Act.[1668] This principle would expressly instruct courts to measure the intensity of both sets of interests and weigh them against each other. Essentially, courts would be required to balance the impact of the use on the interests of rightholders against the strength of the users' interests.

As attractive a metaphor as it may be, however, the need to strike a 'fair balance' in and of itself offers very limited guidance to courts, rightholders, and putative users. As a criterion for deciding concrete cases, it is too unspecified. In addition, it has been argued that the Court's application of the notion of 'fair balance' is underdeveloped and at times superficial.[1669] It is therefore essential to guide the judicial balancing exercise by spelling out which factors are to be balanced. These factors should bear a direct connection to the interests of rightholders and users and capture the types of considerations that typically influence the determination of fairness in cases on unauthorised uses. It is expected that the explicit codification of these considerations will lead the CJEU to engage in more meticulous reasoning under the 'fair balance' umbrella.

Before proceeding to the identification and description of possible balancing factors, a couple of clarifications are in order.

First, the following factors are not part of an exhaustive enumeration. Courts should be free to weigh other considerations in determining whether the use is privileged.[1670] Practical illustrations of the non-exhaustive character of the list of factors will be provided when testing the proposed standard against real-life cases (section 6).

1662. *See* CJEU, *Padawan*, paras 43-50.
1663. *See* CJEU, *Premier League*, para. 164, and CJEU, *PRCA*, para. 24.
1664. *See* CJEU, *Painer*, paras 132-135, and CJEU, *Spiegel Online*, para. 82.
1665. *See* CJEU, *Deckmyn*, paras 26-35.
1666. *See* CJEU, *Ulmer*, para. 31.
1667. *See supra* Chapter 4, section 5.2.2.1. Moreover, as noted by Griffiths (2013), p. 73, the concept 'has a well-established pedigree in European constitutional law', notably in the fundamental rights case law of both the CJEU and the ECtHR. *See also* Sganga (2019).
1668. In contrast, the preambular list of purposes in Section 107 would not be necessary in the proposed standard. The six illustrative purposes mentioned therein – criticism, comment, news reporting, teaching, scholarship, and research – would already be privileged by the mandatorily enumerated exceptions.
1669. *See* Griffiths (2013), p. 74.
1670. For instance, courts could consider whether the use of the copyright-protected work was in good or bad faith: if the user knew that access to the work was unauthorised or resulted from a violation of the law (e.g., the work had been leaked or stolen), this would weigh against her; differently, if the user obtained the work lawfully and properly credited the author, this would weigh in her favour. As mentioned before, the

Second, the factors are not to be applied in a mechanical and formulaic manner. It is not enough to merely count up the factors favouring one side versus the other. Rather, after the separate analysis of each individual factor, they would need to be weighed together in a holistic and fact-sensitive fashion.[1671] It is essential for the deciding court to consider the way in which the various factors are interconnected. In conducting such an exercise, no factor alone should be deemed dispositive (but, of course, they may individually be more or less decisive in a given case).[1672]

4.3.2 'Profit-making Nature of the Use'

The interests of authors and rightholders are primarily economic interests.[1673] These interests may be weighed under two related factors that emerge as

---

defendant's good faith (or lack thereof) has been taken into account by US courts in various cases – *see*, *e.g.*, US Supreme Court, *Harper & Row*, pp. 562-563; US Court of Appeals for the Second Circuit, *Rogers v. Koons*, p. 309; US Court of Appeals for the First Circuit, *Núñez*, p. 23; and US Court of Appeals for the Second Circuit, *NXVIM*, p. 478. Lately, knowledge of illegality has acquired a relevant status in EU copyright law as well – *see supra* Chapter 4, section 5.3.2.

1671. From a procedural perspective, the party asserting the standard in her defence would bear the burden of demonstrating its availability. Nonetheless, as with US fair use, the user would not need to meet the burden separately for each factor, precisely because the factors are to be weighed together. *See*, in this regard, US District Court for the Southern District of New York, *Video-Cinema Films* (stating that users 'need not establish that all of the factors favor them').

1672. A recital to the revised Directive could clarify this much, employing the language that the CJEU has consistently used to characterise the exercise that the right of communication to the public requires: the different factors are 'complementary', 'non-autonomous' and 'interdependent', and, depending on the case at hand, they may 'be present to widely varying degrees' and 'they must be applied individually and in the light of their interaction with one another' – CJEU, *SCF*, para. 79; CJEU, *PPI*, para. 30; CJEU, *Reha Training*, para. 35; CJEU, *GS Media*, para. 34; CJEU, *Filmspeler*, para. 30; CJEU, *Ziggo*, para. 25; and CJEU, *Stim & SAMI*, para. 31. In sum, the standard would require an 'individual assessment' – CJEU, *SCF*, para. 76; CJEU, *PPI*, paras 29 and 38; CJEU, *GS Media*, para. 33; CJEU, *Filmspeler*, para. 28; CJEU, *Ziggo*, para. 23; and CJEU, *Stim & SAMI*, para. 31.

1673. *See* Senftleben (2004), p. 289, and Quintais (2017a), p. 291. Despite the importance of economic interests, the analysis should not disregard the effect of the use upon other legitimate interests of authors and rightholders. As opposed to economic interests – which are at the core of copyright understood as a dimension of the fundamental right to property – these alternative interests will be interests of a more personal nature. The considerations that may be regarded as relevant here include, for instance, whether the use was accompanied by sufficient acknowledgment of authorship or source and whether the work had already been lawfully made available to the public. The privacy interests of the rightholder and/or her right to decide when to release the work to the public should also be taken into account. If the work used by the defendant was unpublished, this should weigh against her. Non-economic interests have also played a role in recent CJEU case law – *see*, *e.g.*, CJEU, *Deckmyn*, paras 29-31 (on the legitimate interest of rightholders in ensuring that their work is not associated with a

relevant considerations from a number of prior CJEU judgments on unauthorised uses.

The first such factor is the *profit-making nature of the use.*[1674] As explained above, in developing the notion of 'communication to the public', the CJEU makes frequent reference to this criterion. Although it does not see it as 'necessary' or 'essential' for the existence of a prima facie infringement of the right of communication to the public, the Court simultaneously deems it 'not irrelevant'.[1675] As also seen above, the profit-making nature factor acquired a renovated importance in the hyperlinking case law, with the CJEU establishing a connection between the existence of a profit-making intention and the knowledge of the hyperlinker regarding the protected nature of the work and the lack of rightholder's authorisation. The importance recognised to the commercial nature of the unauthorised use reflects the tacit idea that copyright law should protect authors and rightholders against the users' parasitic or otherwise unjust profits.[1676]

I posit that this trend of giving significance to commerciality should be taken one step further: in codifying a standard-like exception and listing the factors that ought to be weighed in the fair balance determination, this consideration should be expressly included.[1677] Under such a factor, any type of financial consideration that emerges in relation to the use of works – be it

discriminatory message), and AG Opinion, *Spiegel Online*, para. 79 (on the rightholder's freedom to change personal convictions).

1674. This factor would largely parallel the commercial/non-commercial distinction used by US courts under factor one of the fair use standard.

1675. *See supra* Chapter 4, section 5.3.2 (with references). The ECtHR too has given relevance to commerciality in determining whether the use *sub judice* is admissible as a restriction on copyright – *see* ECtHR, *Ashby Donald*, para. 39.

1676. *See* Ohly (2018), p. 110 (referring to the users' 'unjust enrichment').

1677. It could be objected that, by giving significance to the profit-making nature of the use, the proposed exception would stand in a tautological relationship with the right of communication to the public, for one of the factors that can be considered at the level of *prima facie* infringement is exactly the profit-making nature of the act of communication. Still, incorporating the commerciality of the use as a relevant factor at the level of exceptions would serve important functions. On the one hand, the element of commerciality is not part of the *prima facie* analysis under the (largely technical) right of reproduction. On the other, there is a non-negligible difference between, on the one hand, explicitly requiring that the commercial nature of the use be balanced against other factors and, on the other, qualifying that consideration as 'not irrelevant', as the CJEU has done in its communication to the public case law. If commerciality is not a mandatory requirement for a *prima facie* infringement of the right of communication to the public to be found (but only a possibly relevant consideration), the rightholder need not establish it in every case. In some preliminary references, the CJEU entirely disregards that element. In contrast, according to the proposed framework, at the stage of defences the commercial character of the use would *need* to be balanced against competing considerations, such as freedom of expression and information.

through sales, advertisement or any other paid channel[1678] – should be regarded as relevant.

The fact that a defendant's use of a protected work is commercial in nature would tend to weigh against a finding of non-infringement.[1679] Conversely, a finding that the use is in no way directed towards commercial advantage (e.g., a strictly personal or educational use) would influence the outcome in the opposite direction. The profit-making nature of the use should not be conceived of as an all-or-nothing inquiry; instead, it is more appropriately understood as a matter of degree.[1680] A user who directly derives 'conspicuous financial rewards'[1681] from the use has a weaker claim than a user who does not receive immediate payment, but hopes to benefit from the use remotely.[1682]

In determining the commerciality of the use, a combination of subjective considerations – related to the intention or purpose of the user – and objective ones – focused on whether the use actually generates revenue for the user, regardless of her intention – should be borne in mind. This would be in line with the existing case law of the Court.[1683]

1678. *See, e.g.*, CJEU, *Filmspeler*, para. 51 (regarding the sale of a Kodi box) and CJEU, *ITV Broadcasting I*, paras 41-44 (regarding a retransmission via online streaming that was funded by advertisement).

1679. The expression 'profit-making nature *of the use*' (be it a reproduction or a communication) instructs courts to analyse the character of the use being made, rather than the character of the person who is engaged in the use. A for-profit company may well make not-for-profit uses, and vice versa. This much is indicated in Recital 42 InfoSoc Directive, in relation to the teaching and research exception, as seen above (Chapter 4, section 3.2.3).

1680. *See*, in US case law, US Court of Appeals for the Second Circuit, *Maxtone-Graham*, p. 1262 ('The commercial nature of a use is a matter of degree, not an absolute').

1681. The expression is used by the US Court of Appeals for the Second Circuit in *American Geophysical Union*, p. 922.

1682. Contrast, for instance, CJEU, *Premier League*, para. 205 ('In a situation such as that in the main proceedings, it is indisputable that the proprietor transmits the broadcast works in his public house in order to benefit therefrom and that that transmission is liable to attract customers to whom the works transmitted are of interest. Consequently, the transmission in question has an effect upon the number of people going to that establishment and, ultimately, on its financial results') with AG Opinion, *Renckhoff*, para. 84 (noting that pupil and teacher lack a 'profit motive' and that '[i]n a school context … one cannot talk of "customers", in the commercial sense of the word, who obtain access to the photograph through the work posted on the school's website'). The former use would stand somewhere in the middle of the commerciality continuum – in that the use was not directly charged, but could indirectly benefit the commercial activity –, while the latter would be considered non-commercial. For an example of a use that would be deemed clearly commercial, *see* CJEU, *ITV Broadcasting I*, para. 11.

1683. In its analysis of the profit-making nature of communications, the CJEU has made reference to both types of considerations. *See, e.g.*, CJEU, *SGAE*, para. 44 ('the action by the hotel by which it gives access to the broadcast work to its customers must be considered an additional service performed *with the aim of obtaining some benefit*. It cannot be seriously disputed that *the provision of that service has an influence on the hotel's standing and, therefore, on the price of rooms*. Therefore, … it is in any event

Having said this, the profit-making nature should not determine conclusively whether a use is infringing or non-infringing (much like what happens in the communication to the public analysis under extant case law).

For one thing, most of the uses that will be assessed under this standard will involve some measure of economic benefit to the user, whether direct or indirect. Whether the economic value arising from uses that generate cost-savings to end-users – think of downloading or streaming audiovisual works from unlawful sources to avoid paying the price for lawful copies – should be considered under this factor is a debatable issue, since those uses are not exploitative per se. In any case, where these cost-savings are correlated with losses suffered by rightholders, they will be taken into account under the 'market harm' factor described below.

For another, the commerciality of a use is not necessarily connected to any actual or potential harm suffered by the rightholder. A for-profit use may be more likely to cause market harm than a not-for-profit one, but that will not always be so.[1684] Therefore, while the fact that the user derives an economic advantage from the use should weigh against her, it should not be a fatal blow to the defence.

4.3.3 'Effect Upon the Volume of Sales or of Other Lawful Transactions Relating to the Work'

As already hinted at, the economic interests of rightholders should be assessed in relation to a second factor: the level of market harm produced by the unauthorised use. This factor would command courts to consider the adverse impact of the use on the market for the rightholder's work, including the *effect of the use upon the volume of sales or of other lawful transactions relating to the work.*[1685] Courts would have to inquire into whether the use negatively impacted the commercial exploitation of the work, by impairing sales, advertising revenue, licensing opportunities and other business models, such as subscription, streaming or pay-per-download.

---

established that the communication is of a profit-making nature in circumstances such as those in the main proceedings' – emphasis added), and CJEU, *Ziggo*, para. 46 ('there can be no dispute that the making available and management of an online sharing platform, such as that at issue in the main proceedings, is carried out *with the purpose of obtaining profit* therefrom, it being clear from the observations submitted to the Court that that platform *generates considerable advertising revenues*' – emphasis added).

1684. For an example, *see infra* 6.2. (on the provision of a for-profit plagiarism detection service that relies on the unauthorised archival of student assignments).

1685. The effect upon 'the volume of sales or of other lawful transactions relating to the protected work' echoes the formula used by the CJEU in cases like *ACI Adam*, para. 39, and *Filmspeler*, para. 70, where market harm was explicitly weighed under the 'normal exploitation' requirement of the three-step test. Recognising the relevance of damage by market substitution, *see* AG Opinion, *Spiegel Online*, para. 50, and, though less explicitly, CJEU, *Spiegel Online*, para. 79.

Like the profit-making nature factor, market harm is a matter of degree,[1686] varying according to the amount and type of harm suffered (or likely to be suffered[1687]) by the rightholder. Rightholders should, in principle, have control over each distinct market where their works can be exploited. This is essential to ensure consistency with the goal of granting a 'high level of protection' to rightholders, which requires that they 'receive an appropriate reward for the use of their work'.[1688] If the use takes over such markets, conflicting with major sources of revenue of rightholders, it should not be tolerated. Naturally, the more significant the loss of income suffered by the rightholder, the more heavily this factor will weigh against the defendant.

But not all types of market harm would be material under this factor – only the harm that arises from the fact that the unauthorised use serves as a replacement for the original work in the marketplace. Relevant harm will exist where the use acts as a clear substitute to the original work, causing a negative impact on the rightholder's market position.[1689] If the work is used in its entirety and the third-party use stands in direct competition with the commercialisation by rightholders, market harm as contemplated by this factor is likely to occur. This will be the case, for instance, of the making available of digital copies of audiovisual subject matter (films, TV series, sporting broadcasts) for download or on-demand streaming by users. As noted by the CJEU, accepting uses like these would be equivalent to encouraging the circulation of pirated content, thus reducing the sales and the number of subscribers to lawful services and seriously prejudicing the level of protection of rightholders.[1690] In such cases, the balance between market displacement and increased public access to audiovisual works would tilt clearly in favour of rightholders, since the use is entirely superseding of the original work.

It is important to understand that the market harm factor bears the danger of circularity. As observed by Judge Pierre Leval in his seminal article on fair use, '[b]y definition every fair use involves some loss of royalty revenue because the secondary user has not paid royalties'.[1691] If taken

1686. *See*, relatedly, US Supreme Court, *Campbell*, p. 591.
1687. The harm need not be actual, otherwise the rightholder would be unprotected against predictable future harm. In this regard, *see* WTO, *US-Copyright*, paras 6.184-6.188, stating, in relation to the international three-step test, that the normal exploitation step should take into account not only the actual impact of the exception on the market at a given point in time, but also its potential impact.
1688. Recital 10 InfoSoc Directive. *See also supra* Introduction, section 1.2.
1689. As in the US, this factor should not be weighed against the user where the loss of market value of the original work arises not due to substitution, but due to criticism or unfavourable comment – *see* US Supreme Court, *Campbell*, p. 592.
1690. *See* CJEU, *ACI Adam*, para. 39, and AG Opinion, *Filmspeler*, paras 78-79.
1691. Leval (1990), pp. 1124-1125. Similarly, in relation to the concept of 'normal exploitation', *see* Kur (2009), pp. 317-318, and Quintais (2017a), p. 268.

literally, the market harm factor will necessarily be weighed against the user, because the rightholder can always offer to license the use. But the fact that all uses can *in theory* be licensed does not mean that all uses could or should *reasonably* be licensed. Hence, one way to break the circle, as suggested by US courts, is to say that market displacement should only be taken into account where the market is 'traditional, reasonable, or likely to be developed'.[1692] To give an example, a market for licensing website views could theoretically be developed, but that is neither a traditional nor reasonable licensing market. For harm to be relevant under this factor, the market must be one that the rightholder would have explored with reasonable likelihood. Market harm should thus be measured through the lens of the reasonably expected licensing fees and other profits.

Relatedly, if the rightholder's interest in the market is weak or if she does not intend to economically exploit the work at all, this factor should not lead courts to prohibit a beneficial secondary use. The fact that a system for collecting licensing fees is in place is relevant evidence of the rightholder's interest. Nevertheless, even if there is a licensing market that allows putative users to effortlessly seek the authorisation of rightholders, there may be cases where some overriding element of public interest justifies that the use goes unconsented and uncompensated.

It is crucial to stress that this factor, however important, should not be considered dispositive. Unlike 'normal exploitation' in the current three-step test, it does not function as a step, but as a *balancing factor*. Any negative economic consequences for rightholders should always be set off against the countervailing interests of users and society in general. The greater the market harm, the more compelling the users' interest will need to be in order for the use to be considered non-infringing. A use that causes substantial deprivation of reasonably expected revenue to the rightholder is not to be exempted unless there is some overwhelming interest that is capable of justifying such harm. Conversely, where the prejudice is minimal or inexistent, the users' interest need not be as weighty.

4.3.4 Users' Fundamental Rights

Under the proposed formula, the interests of authors and rightholders must be balanced against those of users. In instructing courts to consider users' interests, the standard should reflect the increasing reliance by the CJEU on

1692. *See* US Court of Appeals for the Sixth Circuit, *Princeton University Press*, p. 1387, and US Court of Appeals for the Second Circuit *American Geophysical Union*, p. 930.

users' fundamental rights as counterweights to copyright owners' proprietary interests.[1693,1694]

The recourse to fundamental rights-based argumentation in CJEU case law has sharply increased after the entering into force of the Treaty of Lisbon, which recognised fundamental rights among the core aims of the Union. Pursuant to Article 6(1) TEU, the Charter of Fundamental Rights of the EU – a modern human rights bill, codifying some fifty different rights – has 'the same legal value as the Treaties' and is now the text on which the CJEU primarily relies to ground its fundamental rights arguments.[1695]

Fundamental rights have served different functions in the copyright case law of the CJEU.

1693. To be clear, the copyright owners' exclusive rights also have fundamental rights status. The CJEU has been including IP, in general, and copyright, in particular, within the scope of the fundamental right to property – *see, e.g.*, CJEU, *Metronome Musik*, para. 21; CJEU, *Promusicae*, para. 62; CJEU, *Laserdisken*, paras 62 and 65; and CJEU, *Luksan*, paras 68-71. On the nature of copyright as a human right, *see* Torremans (2008) (with a focus on international human rights instruments) and Griffiths & McDonagh (2013) (on Article 17(2) Charter). Within the standard proposed in this chapter, however, the proprietary interests of copyright owners are given substantive content by the two preceding factors.

1694. It is submitted that analysing whether the use promotes the effectiveness of the users' fundamental rights makes up for a richer and more substantive inquiry than asking whether the use is 'transformative', as is done under factor one of the US fair use standard. As mentioned in section 4.2.3.1 *supra*, since the US Supreme Court's judgment in *Campbell*, which draws significantly from Leval (1990), the 'transformativeness' of the use has become highly influential in the fair use analysis (though some scholars claim that its influence has been exaggerated – *see* Beebe (2008), p. 604). The notion of 'transformative use' has been criticised for being overbroad, in that it covers not only uses that transform the pre-existing work itself, but also uses that simply give a new purpose to the work or change its original context, without actually altering it. *See*, *inter alia*, Madison (2004), p. 1670 ('As a beacon of fair use, the transformative use standard has become all things to all people'); Sag (2009) (proposing that non-expressive uses be regarded as a category outside that of 'transformative uses') and (2012), pp. 56-57 (arguing that the application of the notion to very different types of uses 'makes a precise definition of transformative difficult'); and Samuelson (2015), pp. 854-855 (recommending that 'different purpose' cases be removed from the inquiry on transformativeness). For example, while it is clear that the image search service of a search engine greatly improves access to information on the Internet, thus contributing to the practical realisation of users' freedom of information, it is not at all evident (despite US courts having stated it more than once) that the search engine's indexing and making available of protected images is a 'highly transformative' use. The transformativeness analysis in these cases – as the European courts' use of extrinsic doctrines in the cases discussed in the previous chapter – appears to be a makeshift technique for reaching a decision motivated by other considerations. I find it hard to deny that the actual reason why US courts have exempted such use by search engines was not so much the fact that it 'transforms' pre-existing works, but the social benefit of access to information that it provides.

1695. Mylly (2015), p. 105, noting a sharp increase in the CJEU's references to the Charter, goes as far as saying that '[d]uring the recent years, the CJEU has been transforming itself into a fundamental rights court'. *See also* Recitals 3 and 9 InfoSoc Directive.

Occasionally, the Court has assessed the compatibility of provisions in the copyright *acquis* with fundamental rights norms. This has been the case in *Metronome Musik*, regarding Article 1(1) Rental and Lending Directive, and *Laserdisken*, concerning the interpretation and validity of Article 4(2) InfoSoc Directive. In both cases, as scholars have pointed out, the validity of the provisions was upheld in a 'questionably cursory manner'.[1696] In addition, at the time of writing, a challenge filed by the Republic of Poland seeking the annulment of the controversial Article 17 DSM Directive was pending before the CJEU.[1697]

But fundamental rights have been playing another role in recent rulings. In its copyright case law the CJEU has repeatedly confirmed that fundamental rights have horizontal effects, asserting that the copyright *acquis* must be *interpreted* by courts in light of the Charter. The internalisation of fundamental rights in a copyright provision would not only echo the trend of analysing horizontal copyright disputes from the angle of these rights both at the national and European levels,[1698] but also stimulate the CJEU to elaborate its fundamental rights reasoning in a more coherent and systematised manner, allowing it to sidestep the critique that references to such rights are 'window-dressing',[1699] 'selective',[1700] 'inconsistent'[1701] and 'incoherent'.[1702]

Examining whether the defendant's conduct contributes towards the practical realisation of her fundamental rights (or of the fundamental rights of other potential users) is a way of determining whether that conduct serves a socially valuable end, such that it is preferable for the benefits arising therefrom to flow freely instead of subjecting them to the rightholder's veto.

1696. *See* Griffiths (2017), p. 3.
1697. Poland claims that the CJEU should annul Article 17(4)(b) (best efforts to ensure the unavailability of unlicensed works on online content-sharing platforms) and Article 17(4)(c), *in fine* (best efforts to prevent future uploads of such works) of the DSM Directive, or, alternatively, the provision in its entirety. In Poland's view, the contested paragraphs infringe the freedom of expression and information guaranteed by Article 11 Charter. It argues, in particular, that the imposition on online content-sharing platforms of the obligations contained in those rules makes it necessary for the platforms to carry out prior automatic verification of content uploaded by users in order to avoid liability, thereby forcing platforms to introduce preventive control mechanisms (also known as 'filters'). Such mechanisms, Poland maintains, undermine the essence of the mentioned freedom and do not comply with the requirement that its limitations be proportional and necessary.
1698. *See also* Geiger (2018), showing how national courts have been invoking fundamental rights as external limitations to copyright law.
1699. Griffiths (2013), p. 74. Griffiths' argument is that the CJEU resorts to fundamental rights talk in order to legitimize its harmonising agenda. On the other hand, it could also be argued that fundamental rights have 'the potential to aid intellectual property to overcome the serious crisis of legitimacy that it is facing at present in public opinion' – Geiger (2012), p. 238.
1700. Mylly (2015), p. 126.
1701. Griffiths (2019), p. 3.
1702. Jongsma (2019), p. 2.

It should be made clear that this factor should not be read as allowing courts to privilege every use that they see as socially beneficial. Whatever general benefit may arise from the use would always need to be balanced against the proprietary interests of rightholders. Naturally, the stronger the connection of the defendant's conduct with fundamental rights, the greater the impact on the rightholders' interests would have to be for the use not to pass muster.

Thus, in weighing this factor, courts should examine whether the concrete use of copyright-protected content can be considered as an exercise of one or more fundamental rights of users. The first step in this analysis lies necessarily in the identification of the relevant right(s).

The Charter rights that could provide weight to the users' side of the scale include e.g. the freedom of thought (Article 10), the freedom of the arts (Article 13), the right to education (Article 14), and the freedom to conduct a business (Article 16). Admittedly, however, in most cases the relevant right would be the freedom of expression and information (Article 11).[1703] Article 11(1) Charter provides that '[e]veryone has the right to freedom of expression. This right shall include freedom to hold opinions and to receive and impart information and ideas without interference by public authority and regardless of frontiers'.[1704] Article 11(2) adds that the 'freedom and pluralism of the media shall be respected'. The freedom encompasses the right to impart information and the public's right to seek and receive it. A wide variety of unauthorised uses may therefore be protected by the freedom of expression and information.[1705] In fact, a number of existing copyright exceptions find their core justification in this freedom.

1703. For early studies on the tension between copyright and freedom of expression in Europe, *see* Hugenholtz (2001) and Akester (2006). Arguing that the room for conflict between copyright and freedom of expression is limited, *see* Derclaye (2008), pp. 142-144. Examining the recent influence of freedom of expression and information on EU copyright law, *see* Izyumenko (2016); Jütte (2016); and, adopting a comparative EU-US perspective, Lucas & Ginsburg (2016). Opposing the use of this fundamental right as a way of injecting flexibility into copyright law, *see* Cohen Jehoram (2004).

1704. Article 11 finds its counterpart in Article 10(1) ECHR, which is worded in a similar manner. In spite of the pending EU accession to the ECHR, Article 10 thereof and the ECtHR case law are of relevance to EU copyright law, since, according to Article 52(3) Charter, the Charter rights that correspond to rights recognised by the ECHR shall have the same meaning and scope as the equivalent ECHR rights. *See also*, at the international level, Article 19 UDHR and Article 19 ICCPR. In the copyright *acquis*, Recital 3 InfoSoc Directive puts freedom of expression at the same level as IP: 'The proposed harmonisation will help to implement the four freedoms of the internal market and relates to compliance with the fundamental principles of law and especially of property, including intellectual property, and freedom of expression and the public interest.'

1705. In *Funke Medien*, AG Szpunar stated, in generalising terms, that 'the communication of a work covered by copyright, whether by the author himself, with his authorisation or without such authorisation, naturally falls within the scope of that freedom' – AG Opinion, *Funke Medien*, para. 35.

The importance of freedom of expression and information in the online environment is especially palpable. As scholars have noted, this freedom 'extends to the individuals' enjoyment of digital cultural goods, including activities like reading, listening, viewing, browsing, hyperlinking, and sharing works online'.[1706] In this regard, the ECtHR considered that this freedom covered the posting of photographs of fashion shows on the website of an online fashion magazine[1707] and the putting in place of a commercial P2P file sharing system.[1708]

Hence, whenever the unauthorised use at stake facilitates the reception or dissemination of cultural products and knowledge, the freedom of expression and information will be concerned. Of course, not every use of that type will have equal freedom-of-expression weight. This factor, as all the others, is a *gradual* factor. Different considerations can be taken into account in weighing the degree to which the use requires protection in the circumstances of the case, namely whether the work serves an informational or entertainment purpose, whether the use contributes to the public debate on an issue of general public interest,[1709] and whether alternative means of accessing the information are available. The value of the use must then be balanced against the opposing interest in protecting copyright owners.

5 POTENTIAL OBJECTIONS

Surely, the model proposed in this chapter, particularly its third tier, will not suit everyone's palate. Beyond the uncertainty-related arguments generally raised by critics of a standard-based solution (which have been addressed throughout the book), a number of other potential objections can be anticipated: the adoption of a standard-like exception will chill behaviour and favour affluent users (section 5.1); it will open the litigation floodgates (section 5.2); judges lack democratic accountability and should therefore not be in the business of deciding on the lawfulness of new uses (section 5.3); the model is inconsistent with the 'high level of protection' rationale (section 5.4); the uses exempted by the standard should take place against the payment of compensation to rightholders (section 5.5); and the proposed standard is incompatible with the international three-step test (section 5.6).

The present section examines these six objections, responding to each in turn. It ultimately concludes that none of them is capable of undermining the recommended model.

1706. Quintais (2017a), p. 299. *See also* Voorhoof (2015), pp. 337-338.

1707. *See* ECtHR, *Ashby Donald*, 36769/08, 10 January 2013.

1708. *See* ECtHR, *The Pirate Bay*. In both cases, though, the ECtHR concluded that the interference with freedom of expression did not amount to a violation of Article 10 ECHR. For a detailed analysis of these judgments, *see* Geiger & Izyumenko (2014) and, for an overview of the ECtHR case law on IP, *see* Geiger & Izyumenko (2018).

1709. This specific factor has played a decisive role in ECtHR, *Ashby Donald*, para. 39.

5.1 Chilling Effect and Defendant Inequality

In law, the expression 'chilling effect' is used to refer to the incidental and discouraging effect that laws or judicial rulings may have on legitimate behaviour. Vague laws, in particular, are thought to cause those who are subject to them to refrain from engaging in lawful conduct for fear of legal sanctions. This is so because legal subjects, when confronted with textually indeterminate provisions, cannot know with confidence whether their conduct crosses the line that separates infringement from non-infringement and thus prefer to steer far clear from the limits of those provisions.[1710]

According to this argument, a standard like fair use deters much behaviour that a court could eventually deem 'fair', since, due to the standard's vague character, copyright users act prudently to avoid the risk of infringement. Zohar Efroni puts the idea concisely: 'the unpredictability associated with the application of fair use exacerbates the chilling effect potential, as risk-averse (fair) users fear the consequences of having their defense ultimately dismissed by the court'.[1711] The likely consequence is that those who could benefit from the standard will play it safe, seeking a licence or simply not engaging in the use at all, even when proceeding without one would probably lead to no liability.[1712]

A related objection is that of defendant inequality. The argument is that a provision like fair use favours the interests of wealthier users only.[1713] Users with deep pockets, who can afford the costs of litigation and infringement, do not feel the chilling effects of vague provisions as harshly as the ordinary individual user. Ultimately, therefore, it is those users who do not have to financially shy away from disputes that benefit from a fair use-style standard.[1714]

1710. The 'chilling effects' concept is most commonly articulated in relation to freedom of expression or 'free speech'. *See, e.g.*, Schauer (1978) and Kendrick (2013). *See also*, for instance, Waldron (2011), pp. 75-76, regarding the case of a vague traffic rule ordering drivers to 'slow down'.

1711. Efroni (2011), p. 423.

1712. *See, e.g.*, Gibson (2007), p. 887 (noting that users tend to seek licences 'even when they have a good fair use claim'); Ohly (2014), p. 64 (claiming, in relation to an isolated fair use clause – i.e., a standard unaccompanied by rule-like exceptions –, that it generates the risk that investments in potentially permitted activities will not be made); and Elkin-Koren & Afori (2015), pp. 7-8 (submitting that the unpredictability of fair use leads users either to refrain from the use or to purchasing an unwarranted licence).

1713. Netanel (2010), p. 66, argues that fair use is but a merely theoretical defence for 'individuals and nonmarket speakers who can ill afford to risk being sued or fight a lawsuit if they are'. Relatedly, as previously quoted, Lessig (2004), p. 187, famously stated that 'fair use in America simply means the right to hire a lawyer'. *See also* Geiget et al. (2018b), p. 5 ('an open fair use or fair dealing norm alone would be unpredictable, increasing transaction costs and favouring economically stronger market players').

1714. *See* Hansen (2008), p. 413 (though also admitting that a vague exception could have positive effects for individual users if affluent defendants, such as Google, had services like Google Books exempted under the proposed provision); Torremans (2012), pp.

Whereas these objections are commonly encountered in the literature, they are not justified in the case of the proposal advanced in this chapter. It is crucial to emphasise, in this regard, that the solution advocated herein is *not* the replacement of rule-like exceptions with a single standard-like one. The proposed balancing standard would work as a subsidiary mechanism. Insofar as users, rich and poor alike, can continue to rely on a set of rule-like exceptions for categories of recurring uses, the arguments of chilling behaviour and defendant inequality lose much of their bite.[1715]

Under the current and rather restrictive regime, users are already engaging in some innovative and boundary-testing uses. This book's proposal can only improve the situation, by offering 'a zone for trial and error, for bolder risk taking',[1716] while simultaneously preserving the system's legal certainty in relation to run-of-the-mill uses.

5.2 Floodgates

Another frequently invoked argument against open-ended provisions (a largely non-substantive one, which seems to stand in contradiction to the previous one) is the risk of a 'litigation boom'. Critics essentially claim that the adoption of such provisions, by transferring discretion to the judiciary, might open the metaphorical floodgates to countless legal disputes. Courts would become overburdened with cases and this could, in turn, put the proper functioning of the judicial system at peril.

Concerns with caseload have been raised against the introduction of a fair use standard into EU copyright law too. Jean-Paul Triaille and colleagues fear the risk of 'increased litigation',[1717] conjecturing that 'the CJEU may be snowed under with a large number of cases concerning the application of open principles to very particular cases, which is arguably not its intended

---

332-333 (making the claim that fair use 'pushes particularly the smaller defendants with less deep pockets to settle, take a license or change their behaviour, even in those circumstances where ultimately they had copyright law on their side'); and Lewinski (2018), pp. 132-133 (submitting that standard-like exceptions favour 'big users', like Internet companies, who can 'impress judges with the best lawyers').

1715. In any event, the problem of the costs of legal aid and access to courts is not a copyright-specific problem. Patry (2017b), p. 21, makes the point in the following passage: 'Some studies have indicated that the average hourly income of a person needing legal services (of any type) is $25, while the average hourly rate for a new lawyer is about $350. Thus, for every hour of a lawyer's time, the person hiring the lawyer would have to work an extra 14 hours just to break even, or almost an extra week for just three hours of a lawyer's time. That doesn't happen, and therefore many middle-class people (in addition to the poor) cannot access the courts, regardless of the type of dispute. This is a national problem, not one of copyright law in general, much less fair use.'

1716. Hargreaves Review (2011), p. 44 (in relation to US fair use).

1717. Triaille et al. (2013), p. 536.

role'.[1718] Matthias Leistner deploys the same argument in similarly speculative terms: 'the pressing number of cases would arguably overextend the ECJ's capacities in its present state'.[1719]

The argument's fundamental flaw is that it overestimates the weight of copyright case law on the CJEU's workload. By way of example, of the 533 preliminary references brought before the CJEU in 2017 and of the 447 preliminary rulings delivered in that same year,[1720] only a minor proportion was related to copyright law.[1721,1722] While the CJEU is commonly said to be an overloaded court[1723] and while the adoption of an open-ended provision may certainly lead to an increase in the number of requests for preliminary rulings,[1724] it is unlikely that the Court will see itself drowned in requests on the interpretation of a copyright provision. There is indeed no indication that a possible increase arising from the enactment of a standard-like copyright exception would ever acquire relevant proportions within the context of the CJEU's overall workload.[1725] In the absence of such indication, the floodgates argument should not be given decisive weight.

5.3 Democratic Illegitimacy

Supporters of the existing InfoSoc framework assert that legislative amendments to the catalogue of exceptions are not only empirically *sufficient* to keep up with technological change, but also normatively *preferable* to

---

1718. Triaille et al. (2013), p. 538.
1719. Leistner (2011), p. 438.
1720. *See* CJEU 2017 Annual Report, pp. 36-37.
1721. The requests lodged before the CJEU in 2017 were *Bastei Lübbe*, *Renckhoff*, *Levola Hengelo*, *Funke Medien*, *Pelham*, *Spiegel Online*, *Syed*, and *Cofemel*, corresponding to 1,5% of the total. The preliminary rulings delivered were *VCAST*, *AKM*, *Verwertungsgesellschaft Rundfunk*, *Ziggo*, *Filmspeler*, *ITV Broadcasting II*, and *Biedrība*, corresponding to approximately 1,6% of the total.
1722. The data from the US points in the same direction, as reported by Patry (2017b), p. 21: 'In 2002, in our trial courts, the number of all copyright cases filed was finally separately broken out. In that year, there were 274,842 civil cases filed. Of those, 2,084 were copyright cases, or 0.75%. How many of those 2,084 resulted in fair use opinions in all of 2002? Only nine. As a percent of all civil cases filed, fair use rulings accounted for 0.004% of district courts' docket. Any doctrine that results in a defense being decided in only 0.004% of all cases decided at the trial level is hardly a "flood of litigation".'
1723. *See* Martins (2016), pp. 625-626 (with further references), listing the causes for such overload.
1724. Article 3 InfoSoc Directive is arguably one of the most indeterminate provisions in the *acquis* and the one on which more requests for preliminary rulings have been submitted.
1725. *See* Martins (2016), pp. 663-664, addressing the floodgates argument in relation to proposals favouring broader access by individuals to the CJEU and concluding that '[a]ll in all, one should not lose sight that issues of caseload should primarily be dealt with at the level of judicial reform'.

judicial updates. The argument, in a nutshell, is that the accommodation of new uses of copyright-protected works is a politically controversial issue that should be settled by legislators, who are electorally accountable and who (ideally, at least) consult with the various stakeholders. Courts, on the other hand, are unrepresentative institutions with no democratic credentials and do not allow the open participation of all parties interested in the decision-making process. As such, they should not be in charge of adapting copyright law to socio-technological developments. Arguing otherwise, according to these scholars, would be equivalent to accepting the usurpation of the legislator's role by the judiciary.[1726]

Focusing on the CJEU only – the highest authority on the interpretation of EU law, which will bear the greatest share of the burden of elaborating the third tier's meaning –, the foregoing argument seems to exaggerate this court's insulation from democratic processes. Not only are Luxembourg judges appointed by common accord of Member State governments,[1727] but national governments, under the preliminary reference procedure, also have the opportunity to submit written observations to the Court. Previous research has shown that these observations may have an important influence on the CJEU's copyright case law.[1728] On top of this, if EU legislative

1726. *See* Poeppel (2005), pp. 509-510 (claiming that legislators should not evade the decision-making task by transferring it to courts precisely because the issues underlying copyright exceptions are politically controversial); Lucas (2010), p. 282 (national lists of exceptions 'have been so adapted during democratic debates, which have allowed public opinion to coincide with the societal debates on authors' rights', and it is 'not reasonable to entrust a judge with the mission of searching by himself for the balance that is so important for the society – especially if he is equipped ... by very vague indications'); Lucas (2012), p. 379, ('in the legal tradition of civil law countries, it is not the role of the courts to conduct "political" arbitrations, because these are a matter for politics. It is up to the democratically elected legislator to make these choices'); Lewinski (2015), p. 4, ('too broad and flexible clauses may negatively affect the division of powers between the democratically elected legislature on the one hand and the judicial power on the other hand'); Peukert (2015), p. 148 ('an IP system is legitimate only if it is grounded on democratic decision making, if its boundaries are regulated in a foreseeable manner and if it is responsive to new technological and social circumstances. All these conditions can only be fulfilled by continuous legislative adjustments – if necessary, upon an exceptional wake-up call by the judiciary'); and Paulus (2016), p. 515 (questioning whether it would not be preferable, for reasons of democratic legitimacy, to have newly emerging situations addressed by the legislator). Intriguingly, the scholars raising this argument do not complain about democratic illegitimacy in relation to the InfoSoc three-step test, which, after all, is an open-ended provision that allows courts to trump the legislative decision of privileging certain uses.

1727. *See* Article 253 TFEU. Moreover, pursuant to Article 255, the candidates' suitability is assessed by a panel composed of seven persons chosen from among former members of the Court of Justice and the General Court, members of national supreme courts and lawyers of recognised competence, one of whom shall be proposed by the European Parliament.

1728. *See* Favale et al. (2018).

institutions disagree with the Court's interpretation, they have the power to amend the law accordingly.[1729]

The argument also overlooks the fact that a vital source of an institution's legitimacy lies in the degree of its acceptance by the relevant community. Eugene Rostow brought this point home in a passage on the legitimacy of the US Supreme Court: '[t]he weight of … history is evidence that the people do expect the courts to interpret, declare, adapt and apply these … provisions'.[1730] The same can be said about the CJEU, which has been filling in the gaps left by the legislative institutions and developing the meaning of indeterminate provisions in the *acquis communautaire* since the very beginning of EU integration. To paraphrase the famous words of Justice Benjamin Cardozo, judge-made law has always been one of the existing realities of the harmonisation project.[1731]

It may be further argued that the adoption of a standard-like provision would increase legitimacy vis-à-vis a state of affairs, as the existing one, in which courts recurrently circumvent the text of the law.[1732] A discretion-granting clause would reintroduce transparency, allowing courts to render their decisions as openly as possible, instead of underhandedly engaging in balancing exercises when the applicable statutory provisions do not seem to allow them to do so.[1733] Courts are already falling back on general principles and other vague overriding considerations when the outcome mandated by the controlling rules can plausibly be argued not to be a sensible one. The adoption of a standard would be no more than an *ex post* legislative acknowledgment of the CJEU's approach to these cases and its self-expanded power. Transparent reasoning under such an open-ended provision would also facilitate scrutiny of the rulings by interested stakeholders.[1734] Transparency and judicial legitimacy would therefore be important by-products of the proposed third tier.

1729. As they have done in the copyright field. *Contrast* the CJEU's judgment in *Reprobel* with Article 16 and Recital 60 DSM Directive.
1730. Rostow (1958), p. 590.
1731. The actual quote says 'I take judge-made law as one of the existing realities of life' – Cardozo (1921), p. 10. This much seems to be acknowledged by jurists from the civilian tradition as well – *see* Zimmermann (1997), p. 321, pointing out that '[j]udicial law-making *praeter legem* is not only a generally accepted phenomenon but an indispensable part of the *officium iudicis* in a legal system governed by statutes'.
1732. *See supra* section 4.
1733. *See* Bogdandy (2013), p. 376 ('a court can strengthen its democratic legitimacy, for example through transparent reasoning'). *See also* Fuller (1969), p. 64 ('[a] specious clarity can be more damaging than an honest open-ended vagueness'), and Grey (1983), p. 45 ('[i]n many situations decisions would be both more predictable and more acceptable if the ruling norm were a vague standard that allowed judges or juries to apply their intuitive sense of fairness case-by-case, rather than a clear rule that was sporadically and covertly evaded').
1734. In general, *see* Bogdandy (2013), p. 376.

Be all this as it may, the proposed discretion-granting clause, or any other provision with the same purpose, would inevitably be the result of a legislative enactment. Hence, the exercise conducted by courts under its terms would always hold democratic pedigree, albeit indirect.

5.4 Inconsistency with the 'High Level of Protection' Rationale

One of the dominant rationales behind the EU copyright harmonisation project, in general, and the InfoSoc Directive, in particular, is the need to secure a high level of protection for authors and rightholders.[1735] A further anticipated objection would posit that a standard-like exception would not be compatible with this rationale. Opponents of the introduction of a flexibilising clause are likely to object that it will lead to an over-expansion of use privileges and, as a consequence, to a weakening of the position of authors and rightholders in a manner that is inconsistent with the mentioned goal.[1736]

The argument is unconvincing for a twofold reason.

First, the 'high level of protection' is not the sole rationale underlying the EU copyright *acquis*. As discussed in the Introduction to this book, the preamble to the InfoSoc Directive and the interpretative CJEU case law allow us to identify four other fundamental objectives that the EU legislator sought to achieve with this instrument: (i) harmonisation of copyright law; (ii) technological development; (iii) legal certainty; and (iv) the need to strike a fair balance between the different rights and interests involved. All of these normative considerations play an important role in the shaping of the InfoSoc framework of exceptions and, as of late, the CJEU has been forcefully stressing that the protection of copyright, as a dimension of the fundamental right to property, must be balanced against the protection of other fundamental rights. The recommended reform would be a means of protecting these other fundamental rights, such as users' freedom of expression and information and their freedom of business. It would also foster the capacity of copyright law to accommodate new forms of exploitation of existing works, which ranks particularly high on the priorities of the *acquis*.

Second, in and of itself, the 'high level of protection' rationale says nothing about how many exceptions the InfoSoc Directive should recognise or how they should be drafted. Whereas the EU does indeed grant a high degree of protection to rightholders, there is nothing in this rationale to suggest that it bars the adoption of standard-like exceptions. Besides, rightholders/plaintiffs would remain in a privileged position under the proposed system. Despite the introduction of a vague exception, the prerogatives they enjoy would still be broad enough to effortlessly make out

1735. *See supra* Introduction, section 1.2.
1736. Anticipating this criticism in relation to a potential flexibilisation of the German catalogue of exceptions, *see* Förster (2008), p. 222.

a prima facie case of infringement and shift the burden of proof to users/defendants in most disputes. As any other copyright exception (in most cases, at least), the suggested clause could only be raised as a defence to a claim of infringement in the appropriate pleading, conferring no-right *proprio sensu* on users.

5.5 Lack of Fair Compensation

It can also be objected that while the analysis conducted so far may validate the recognition of a standard-like exception, it does not necessarily imply that the exception should be an uncompensated one. Indeed, under the standard recommended in this chapter, the user can proceed without obtaining authorisation *and* without paying compensation. Much like US fair use, it would work as 'an "all-or-nothing" system' in the sense that '[e]ither there is infringement or not, and there is no middle ground of compensation'.[1737]

The unpaid character of the proposed standard is justified by three arguments.

To begin with, a provision crafted in the form of a balancing test cannot suitably operate as a compensated exception. In practice, this would be tantamount to having the judiciary create statutory licences, which, in some jurisdictions, would be considered 'constitutionally improper'.[1738] Moreover, such licences are generally administered by collecting societies and, simply put, '[c]ollecting societies need clear rules. Levies could not be collected on an ad hoc basis'.[1739] Administering a statutory licence on the basis of a fair use clause would be virtually impossible.

Second, the framework outlined in this chapter is based on the co-existence of this unpaid standard-like exception with other exceptions, some of which give rise to the payment of compensation to rightholders, most notably the existing private copying exception. The statutory licence for cases of private copying is a tested system that should be preserved.[1740] In addition, under this framework, nothing prevents the legislator from enacting further compensated (rule-like) exceptions for particular uses, where appropriate.

1737. Triaille et al. (2013), p. 538. Deeming fair use an 'on/off switch' and arguing in favour of a 'permitted-but-paid' system in the US, *see* Ginsburg (2015).

1738. Griffiths (2009), p. 438. For instance, the Portuguese Constitutional Court has deemed private copying levies akin to taxes, with the implication that the 'tax rate' can only be determined by law. National provisions that allowed the rate to be decided by ministerial order or by agreement were therefore declared unconstitutional. *See* Portuguese Constitutional Court, Judgment No. 616/2003.

1739. Ohly (2018), p. 114. *See also* Triaille et al. (2013), p. 538: 'a system where courts may decide to allow or deny compensation and to set the amount thereof on a case by case basis would be highly impracticable'.

1740. *See* Ohly (2018), p. 118.

The third and final argument is related with the justifications for the adoption of statutory licences in copyright law. Statutory licensing typically concerns uses where there is a clear case for compensating rightholders due to the *harm* produced thereby. Some exceptions in the InfoSoc Directive are indeed subject to the payment of fair compensation, which must be linked to the harm caused to the rightholder by the permission-free uses,[1741] suggesting that these compensated exceptions are grounded on a market failure rationale.[1742] However, the standard proposed in this chapter is not directed at addressing market failures. It is intended at exempting unforeseen uses in relation to which the fundamental rights of users prevail, on balance, over the economic interests of rightholders. The standard's primary goal is not to accommodate cases of large-scale uses of works where transaction costs are too high for a licensing market to be viable. Furthermore, given that, as emphasised above, the standard would not cover uses that obviously act as substitutes for lawful transactions (e.g., downloading from unlawful sources), the case for fair compensation is weakened. Hence, if the use is considered fair, partly because it does not meaningfully affect the rightholders' market, then there is no need to license it (statutorily or otherwise).[1743]

5.6 Incompatibility with the International Three-Step Test

Notwithstanding the proposed elimination of the three-step test from the InfoSoc Directive, the EU copyright legislator would still have to comply with the *international* three-step test in enacting a new standard-like exception vaguely inspired in US fair use.[1744] The literature on the compatibility of Section 107 US Copyright Act with the three-step test is voluminous,[1745] with most commentators concluding that the claim that fair

1741. *See* Recital 35 InfoSoc Directive. *See also* CJEU, *Padawan*, para. 40, and CJEU, *Stichting de Thuiskopie*, para. 24, both stating that 'fair compensation must be regarded as recompense for the harm suffered by the author'.

1742. *See, e.g.*, Reinbothe (2016), p. 302, describing market failure as 'the main reasoning for the private copy levies'.

1743. It is worthy, in this regard, to quote Patry (2017a), p. xi: 'copyright law has become infested with a permission mentality in which all uses, no matter how trivial or remote from impacting on authors' wallets, are declared licensable and therefore must be licensed. Unlicensed uses are to be avoided at all costs, and tolerated, if at all, only when there is "market failure", a hypothetical economic construct antithetical to the actual reasons people create'.

1744. The Commission itself acknowledges this need to observe the test in the 2008 Green Paper, pp. 4-5 and 19-20.

1745. A (non-exhaustive) list of scholarship on the issue, with references from both European and US scholarship, includes Newby (1999); Okediji (2000), pp. 126 et seq.; Leaffer (2001); Ricketson (2003), pp. 68-69; Senftleben (2004), pp. 162 et seq.; Cohen Jehoram (2005), pp. 360-362; Förster (2008), pp. 191 et seq.; Lucas (2010), pp. 278-279; Geiger et al. (2014), pp. 612 et seq.; Halpern & Johnson (2014), pp. 147 et

use is compliant with international treaty obligations is strong.[1746] Given the structural similarities between US fair use and the test described above, the arguments that support such conclusion aid in explaining why the latter would be equally compliant.

It must be noted, first, that the proposed standard would explicitly command courts to consider the commerciality of the use and the risk of harm to the market for the original work. Moreover, since the factors are not exhaustively enumerated, other non-economic interests of rightholders may be taken into consideration in analysing the lawfulness of a given use, despite the absence of express reference in the provision. These elements should ensure that the test respects prongs two (no conflict with the normal exploitation of the work) and three (no unreasonable prejudice to the legitimate interests of rightholders) of the international three-step test.[1747]

As with US fair use, the most controversial issue would be whether the standard would comply with step one (the 'certain special cases' step).[1748] Is the proposed test sufficiently 'narrow in scope' and 'clearly defined' to pass this hurdle?

Scholars have pointed out that the WTO Panel in *U.S.-Copyright* was cautious enough *not* to state that fair use was per se incompatible with the first step.[1749] In the Panel's words, 'there is no need to identify explicitly each and every possible situation to which the exception could apply, provided that the scope of the exception is known and particularised. This guarantees a sufficient degree of legal certainty'.[1750] This formula has been read as a more or less implicit recognition that fair use and other open-ended exceptions are compliant with the test.[1751]

---

seq.; Samuelson (2015), pp. 850-853; Gervais (2017), pp. 64-66; Goold (2017), pp. 194-203; and Hughes (2017), pp. 236 et seq.

1746. However, some authors admit that the issue 'remains principally a theoretical question' (Hughes (2017), p. 247), while others go as far as calling this an 'imaginary conflict' (Sag (2013)).

1747. *See* Samuelson (2015), pp. 850-853, making the case that fair use satisfies the 'normal exploitation' step because market harm is a key consideration under Section 107.

1748. *See* Halpern & Johnson (2014), p. 148 ('The attacks on adopting (retaining) a flexible exceptions have been confined to the first step') and Hughes (2017), p. 242 ('The real issue is the first step'). Raising doubts on the compatibility of fair use with the first step, *see*, *inter alia*, Ricketson (2003), pp. 68-69.

1749. *See* Senftleben (2010), p. 76.

1750. WTO, *US-Copyright*, para. 6.108.

1751. *See* Senftleben (2010), p. 76 (arguing that this formula allows for the accommodation of both the civil law and common law traditions of exceptions, on grounds that otherwise 'an entire legal tradition of copyright law would be discredited and declared incompatible with international standards'); Geiger et al. (2014), p. 582 (noting that the history of the international three-step test 'demonstrate[s] that it was intended to serve as a flexible balancing tool offering national policy makers sufficient breathing space to satisfy economic, social, and cultural needs'); and Hughes (2017), p. 247 (calling it 'a clear attempt to give some breathing room to fair use and fair dealing doctrines').

Under the proposed test, similarly to Section 107, the CJEU-made factors would allow courts to identify 'certain special cases' on a case-by-case basis. Certainty would therefore follow from the accretion of a body of case law: as courts decide disputes and as preliminary rulings are handed down by the CJEU, more special cases of permitted uses would become 'known and particularised'.

The compatibility analysis must not disregard the standard's residual nature and its interaction with the preceding tiers enumerating rule-like exceptions. According to the framework outlined in this chapter, rule-like exceptions for specific uses take priority over the balancing test, thus guaranteeing a reasonable degree of legal certainty.[1752]

But however important the substantive discussion on compliance may be, the main reason why the international three-step test is not likely to pose an insurmountable obstacle to the recognition of an open-ended exception in EU copyright law is a political one. In the words of Justin Hughes, 'anyone who understands the international IP system knows that a frontal challenge to the fair use doctrine would be *politically* disastrous'.[1753] This arguably explains why, when the US joined the Berne Union in 1989, the compatibility of Section 107 with the Berne three-step test remained uncontested. Likewise, none of the several countries that have adopted fair use-style exceptions in their IP or copyright laws have been challenged in international *fora.*[1754] In any case, were the compliance issue to be raised, the fact that a significant number of States consider that open-ended exceptions of this kind comply with the three-step test is an element that would have to be weighed in the analysis.[1755]

In this context, it is not unreasonable to doubt whether, following the adoption of a residual standard-like exception within the InfoSoc framework, any country would ever bring a case against the EU for violation of the international three-step test.[1756]

1752. *See* Hughes (2017), p. 249, submitting that the retention of specific exceptions helps in ensuring compatibility. *See also* Hugenholtz & Okediji (2008), p. 26, claiming that '[t]he test most likely permits both discrete European-style limitations and broader fair-use-style exemptions, or possibly a combination of both'.

1753. Hughes (2017), p. 246. *See also* Griffiths (2010a), pp. 92-93 ('it is worth pausing for a moment to gain a little perspective on the question. Is it seriously to be suggested that the carefully evolved, minutely-scrutinised body of fair use doctrine under s 107 is to be invalidated by reference to a "test" which came into being as an intentionally vague political compromise formula and whose meaning and requirements remain almost entirely uncertain. It would certainly be ironic if this were the case').

1754. *See* Pessach (2010), pp. 192-193. On the global trend towards introducing some type of fair use, *see supra* section 4.2.3.3.

1755. *See* Hugenholtz & Okediji (2008), p. 25.

1756. *See* Ott (2009), p. 353, expressing such doubts.

6 TEST CASES

Having outlined the design of a multi-tiered framework of exceptions and addressed the main objections to it, I shall now explore the practical application of this framework against the background of cases inspired in real case law. The range of cases to which the framework could be applied is virtually infinite and exhausting them would be impossible. The purpose of this section is simply to provide the reader with some orientation on how the model and, in particular, the different balancing factors within the proposed standard would work out in concrete cases. Despite the usefulness of this exercise, it cannot be emphasised enough that every case must be decided *on its own facts*.

Three different situation-types will be analysed: (i) the online re-posting of a photograph in the context of a school assignment; (ii) the digital archiving of students' works by a plagiarism detection system; and (iii) the provision of downloadable files of a politician's essay on matters of general interest. These digital uses make up for interesting testing grounds for the solution advanced in this chapter. Each subsection starts by providing a description of the case, which is then examined in light of the proposed framework.

6.1 Online Re-posting of a Photograph in the Context of a School Assignment

Alice is a professional photographer based in Munich. She granted a licence to use one of her photographs – a panoramic shot of the city taken from the top of Frauenkirche – to the operators of an online travel magazine, who posted it on their website without any restrictive measures preventing it from being downloaded.

Bertolt is a student at a Munich secondary school who was tasked with preparing a presentation on the city's architecture, as part of a school assignment. He came across the photograph in the online portal, downloaded it and used it as an illustration in his slideshow. Bertolt was careful enough to identify the website where he had found the photograph, though he failed to mention Alice as the author because the magazine had omitted her name. Bertolt's presentation was selected as one of the best in his class and uploaded onto the school's website. Having found the pupil's presentation online, Alice decided to bring proceedings claiming that the posting of the photograph on the school's website infringed her copyright.[1757] How would the case be decided under the proposed model?

1757. The factual scenario is based on the dispute behind the *Renckhoff* preliminary reference. *See* CJEU, *Renckhoff*, paras 6-11.

A preliminary issue concerns the existence, or not, of a prima facie copyright infringement in this case. The inflated scope of the right of communication to the public (and a burden of proof that is relatively easy to satisfy) has tempted rightholders to litigate trivial cases such as this one. Deciding on a similar case, the CJEU held that the posting on one website of a photograph previously posted on another website, without any protection measures and with the consent of the rightholder, is covered by the exclusive right of communication to the public.[1758] In spite of the fact that the use was clearly non-commercial, it was found to fall within the scope of the right. The decision makes clear that a somewhat flexible economic right like the InfoSoc right of communication to the public (which, as explained above, requires an 'individual assessment') may not be enough to adequately reconcile the interests of rightholders and users. This broad prima facie allocation of exclusive rights makes the role of exceptions all the more important.[1759]

Given the subsidiary nature of the proposed balancing test, we are required to analyse first whether the use falls within a listed exception. The existing InfoSoc catalogue specifically provides for an exception that covers the use for the sole purpose of illustration for teaching or scientific research in Article 5(3)(a).[1760] This exception reflects a compromise between the right to education in Article 14 Charter and the protection of IP guaranteed by Article 17(2) Charter.[1761]

The posting of Bertolt's presentation containing Alice's photograph is certainly educational in nature. It may nonetheless be questioned whether it is covered by Article 5(3)(a).

In *Renckhoff*, AG Campos Sánchez-Bordona thought it was. In the AG's view, the exception would be reduced to a minimum if it were limited to allowing teachers to illustrate the content of their courses or lessons. Instead, he read Article 5(3)(a) in light of the Charter's right to education. In what regards the *teaching* dimension of the exception, the AG emphasised 'the active, rather than purely passive, role of the pupils, allowing them, too, to use images protected by copyright for the same teaching (or, in their case,

1758. *See* CJEU, *Renckhoff*, para. 47. Following the CJEU's judgment, the BGH confirmed that the posting amounted to copyright infringement – *see* BGH, *Cordoba II*.
1759. In its opinion on *Renckhoff*, the ECS has deemed the case 'symptomatic of the problems arising from the current copyright system's inability to adapt to the digital environment' – ECS (2018a), p. 1.
1760. On the scope and interpretation of the exception, *see supra* Chapter 4, section 3.2.3. The exception in Article 5 DSM Directive would not be a suitable candidate to resolve the dispute, due to its limited scope: to be exempted under this provision, the use must serve the sole purpose of illustration *for teaching* and it must be made through a secure electronic environment accessible only by the educational establishment's students and teaching staff.
1761. *See* CJEU, *Renckhoff*, para. 43.

learning) purpose'.[1762] As to the *research* dimension, the AG argued that the exception was not limited to scientific research, applying equally to students and teachers in the non-university sector, provided the other requirements were satisfied.[1763]

This rather extensive reading of the InfoSoc teaching and research exception was probably driven by the idea that this type of benign educational use should not be subject to the authorisation of rightholders. Under the existing framework, such a reading may be indispensable in order to exempt the use. However, under the model advanced in this chapter, the deciding court would not need to engage in such a questionable interpretation, since the subsidiary open-ended exception would allow for a more methodologically honest exercise.

It could also be argued that the InfoSoc quotation exception could privilege the digital use under consideration.[1764] But here, too, legitimate doubts around the exception's applicability would arise, mostly due to the 'criticism or review' requirement discussed above.[1765] A deciding court that favoured a strict reading of this requirement would be inclined to rule that the quotation exception failed to cover this type of situation. Yet again, the need to adopt a debatable interpretation of a rule-like exception in order to save the day illustrates why an opening clause is needed within the InfoSoc framework. A decision allowing this educational use would arguably stand on much firmer ground if based on a provision that explicitly required the consideration of the competing interests at stake, than if based on an elastic interpretation of exceptions tailored for specific uses.

Let us then examine the use described in the beginning of this section in light of the balancing factors outlined in 4.3.

The first factor (the profit-making nature of the use) would weigh in favour of fairness. The use was evidently made with no commercial intention and, in addition, any profit that the school might actually extract from posting the work online – through, say, increased website traffic and interest from students and parents – would be far too remote to be relevant under this factor. The non-profit educational purpose of the use may be outweighed by clear and significant harm to the rightholder's market position, but that does not seem to be the case either.

The question under that second factor (the effect of the use upon the volume of sales or of other lawful transactions) would be whether the posting of the photograph on the school's website was likely to have a substantially

1762. AG Opinion, *Renckhoff*, para. 115.
1763. *See* AG Opinion, *Renckhoff*, para. 116. The CJEU did not analyse whether the underlying situation could be privileged by any exception within Article 5 InfoSoc Directive, most probably due to the fact that the referring court had not submitted such a question. *But see* BGH, *Cordoba II*, paras 52-68, ultimately ruling against the applicability of the equivalent national exception.
1764. *See* ECS (2018a), p. 3.
1765. *See supra* Chapter 4, section 3.2.5.

negative impact on the work's market. The answer would appear to be in the negative.[1766] Licensing for school assignments is certainly not a plausibly exploitable market for professional photographers. Furthermore, the educational use in the case was unlikely to affect Alice's ability to license the photograph for other customary markets, such as travel magazines or news outlets. Of course, had the photograph not been used in an educational context, but in a commercial one, the reasoning would be different.[1767]

Moving to the users' side of the scales, the deciding court would have to ask whether the posting of the presentation on the school's website, including the photograph, contributed to the practical realisation of any of the Charter rights. On facts such as these, the most relevant right of users would be the fundamental right to education protected under Article 14 Charter.[1768] In weighing its relevance in a concrete case, the court would have to analyse whether the use of the protected work was related to the students' formal education and/or whether it was made in the context of some recognised educational establishment. This was clearly so in the hypothetical case under examination. The fact that the posting was made as recognition of the quality of Bertolt's work makes the connection with the fundamental right to education even stronger.

It could certainly be argued that displaying the student's work on the school's intranet would have been sufficient to achieve the desired purpose of giving publicity to his merit.[1769] Nonetheless, it is no less true, as noted by the AG in *Renckhoff*, that posting the work on the intranet or on the school's website would not make much of a difference, since the public that would access the work would most probably be the same in both cases, namely teachers, students and their families.[1770]

Finally, given that the list of proposed balancing factors is non-exhaustive, it should be asked whether any other considerations could influence the fair balance decision. In this regard, the fact that Bertolt was careful to acknowledge the source where the image was found could be seen as militating in favour of the use's lawfulness. Indeed, attribution may

---

1766. Reaching the same conclusion under the 'normal exploitation' inquiry, *see* AG Opinion, *Renckhoff*, para. 123. *See also* ECS (2018a), p. 3 ('There is arguably no economically significant market that the re-use of the photograph on the school website could negatively affect').

1767. *See, e.g.*, the decision by the US Court of Appeals for the Fourth Circuit in *Violent Hues*, which deemed infringing the unauthorised display of a photograph of the Adams Morgan neighbourhood in Washington, D.C. on a website promoting a for-profit festival, stating that '[i]f the ordinary commercial use of stock photography constituted fair use, professional photographers would have little financial incentive to produce their work'. In such a case, under the proposed standard, the negative impact on the market for the photograph would outweigh any arguments based on freedom of information and freedom of business.

1768. *See also* Article 2 Protocol No. 1 ECHR.

1769. *See* Hofmann (2018), p. 647.

1770. *See* AG Opinion, *Renckhoff*, fn. 81.

generally be considered a reliable indicator of the propriety of the user's conduct. Although Bertolt had failed to mention the name of the photographer, this would hardly tip against lawfulness since the magazine had also omitted it before.[1771]

6.2 Digital Archiving of Students' Works by a Plagiarism Detection System

The company iStudy owns and operates a technological system that assesses the academic originality of written works, namely student essays and exams, with the purpose of preventing plagiarism. Educational institutions may subscribe to iStudy's system and require their students to submit written assignments via the system. Upon submission, the iStudy software automatically performs a comparison of the student's assignments with content available online, assignments previously submitted by other students, and commercial databases of journal articles. After a given assignment is processed, the system produces a report indicating how likely the work is to have been plagiarised and sends it to the teacher. iStudy allows for the archival of student-submitted works in a non-public database for future plagiarism checks, a feature which must be specifically authorised by each subscribing school.

Charles and Dante attend the College of Letters & Science in their hometown. The college has contracted with iStudy and has activated the archival feature. Charles and Dante oppose this practice. They include a disclaimer on the cover of every assignment they submit indicating that they do not authorise the archiving. In spite of this, iStudy continues to archive their works. Charles and Dante claim that this feature constitutes copyright infringement.

The case concerns a digital use that the CJEU has not been confronted with, but that has been analysed in the US.[1772] Under the existing system of exceptions, a conservative reading of both the quotation exception (no critical dialogue is established with the archived essays) and the teaching and research exception (the essays are not being used to illustrate the contents of lessons[1773]) would preclude a finding of non-infringement. The private copying exception would also be unavailable, since the reproductions were

1771. Making the same argument, *mutatis mutandis*, in relation to the 'indication of source/author' requirement in Article 5(3)(a) InfoSoc Directive, *see* AG Opinion, *Renckhoff*, para. 119.

1772. The case is inspired in the factual background of the *iParadigms* decision rendered by the US Court of Appeals for the Fourth Circuit.

1773. In contrast, the expression 'non-profit educational purposes' in the US fair use clause seems to cover this use and arguably any use intended to promote an educational endeavour.

made by a legal person for commercial purposes. The deciding court would therefore progress to the subsidiary balancing test.

The first factor of the test would tip against fairness. There is a clear commercial purpose behind iStudy's archival of the student essays. In fact, the use is made in the context of a service that is provided to educational institutions with a view to making a profit.

However, the fact that the use is of a commercial nature does not mean that the market for the protected works will be affected. Archiving student essays for plagiarism check generates no loss of market opportunities, because there is no workable, reasonable or traditional market for that kind of use. Students would certainly fail to establish that any such market ever existed or was likely to exist.[1774]

The students could also invoke their legitimate interest in controlling the publication and dissemination of their essays, which had not been published yet. This is nonetheless an irrelevant fact in the context of this case. The system merely archived the essays, instead of disseminating them, making no use of those works beyond that necessary for purposes of comparison with other works. As such, it did not interfere with the students' right of first publication.[1775]

In weighing the interests of users in this case, it could be argued that, by protecting the students' written works from plagiarism, iStudy's activity furthered the fundamental right to education (Article 14 Charter). Even though the plaintiffs were the students themselves, this would not be an unreasonable line of argumentation. After all, the availability of a technological tool like iStudy promotes originality and independent student research in educational institutions. This can only be qualified as a substantial public benefit that results from the archival of the works.[1776]

The interests arising from the fundamental freedom to conduct a business would also militate in favour of privileging iStudy's use. The CJEU has defined this freedom as 'includ[ing], inter alia, the right for any business to be able to freely use, within the limits of its liability for its own acts, the economic, technical and financial resources available to it'.[1777] Several economic agents, in the course of conducting their affairs, make some kind

1774. The only available market would be to resell the essays to other students, but, in the *iParadigms* proceedings, the students themselves admitted that they were not willing to explore that market – *see* US Court of Appeals for the Fourth Circuit, *iParadigms*, p. 644. Be that as it may, this is not a reasonable market that copyright law should protect.

1775. *See* US Court of Appeals for the Fourth Circuit, *iParadigms*, p. 641. Although moral rights, including the right of first publication, lie largely beyond the reach of existing EU copyright law, they must be taken into account when interpreting the provisions of the *acquis*, according to AG Opinion, *Spiegel Online*, para. 77.

1776. In US Court of Appeals for the Fourth Circuit, *iParadigms*, p. 639, the use was considered 'transformative' because 'it had an entirely different function and purpose than the original works'.

1777. CJEU, *UPC Telekabel*, para. 49.

of use of protected works. Automatic plagiarism detection is an example of a business that necessarily relies on the use of such works to generate income.

In sum, while the profit-making nature of iStudy's use may favour Charles' and Dante's claim, the public benefit and the non-existent or immaterial market harm produced by the archival of the written assignments would likely lead a court to exempt this use under the standard-like exception outlined above.

6.3 Provision of Downloadable Files of a Politician's Essay on Matters of General Interest

Many years ago, Ernest penned an essay adopting a controversial position regarding an issue of public morality. The essay was published as a contribution to a collective volume. In compiling the contributions, the publisher changed the title and shortened one sentence of Ernest's essay without his consent. An influential affiliate of a political party, Ernest later became a Member of Parliament in his country. Having served for a few terms, he is now seeking reelection.

The original manuscript of his early essay was meanwhile rehashed and Ernest is facing unkind criticisms due to the views held therein. In that context, Ernest sent the manuscript version and the published version to newspapers, though he did not authorise their publication. Instead, he made the two versions available on his website and added a disclaimer on the pages of the latter distancing himself from its contents and asserting that the publisher had manipulated it by changing various parts of the original text.

Following this, an online news portal published an article claiming that Ernest had been misleading the public, since the essential content of the manuscript had remained unaltered in the published volume. As part of the article, the news portal provided full downloadable PDF files of both texts. The files did not contain Ernest's disclaimer, with the purpose of allowing readers to make their own unbiased judgment on the extent of the differences. The politician asked the news publisher to replace those files with hyperlinks to the versions that he had made available on his own website and that contained his disclaimer. The news portal refused to do so and Ernest brought proceedings intended to terminate the making available of the files, on grounds of copyright infringement.[1778]

Under our model, the first question would concern the applicability of the enumerated exceptions. Two exceptions appear to be relevant for this case: the exception for the reporting of current events and the quotation exception.

1778. This is an adapted version of the factual context underlying the *Spiegel Online* preliminary reference – *see* CJEU, *Spiegel Online*, paras 10-14.

The CJEU's interpretation of the former one in *Spiegel Online* suggests that it would apply to the case at hand. According to the Court, the exception may be found applicable even in cases where it is reasonably possible to make a prior request for authorisation with a view to using the work for purposes of reporting current events (thus implying, but never explicitly saying, that the exception could exempt the use made by Spiegel Online[1779]). Nonetheless, it seems that, as AG Szpunar argued in his opinion, this exceptions was not crafted for the type of situation described above. The exception's coverage is limited to cases in which it is unreasonable to expect the user to seek authorisation to use the work before reporting on a current event (e.g., background music in a newsworthy official ceremony). Interpreted in light of Article 10*bis*(2) Berne Convention – which requires the used works to have been 'seen or heard' in the course of the event –, the exception in Article 5(3)(c) does not seem to apply to the use of a literary work that must be read and carefully analysed by the reader.[1780] Again, the only reason why an expansive reading of the exception, as the one adopted by the CJEU, is necessary is the lack of a proper escape valve within the system.

It is also questionable whether the quotation exception could apply to the case at hand. AG Szpunar advised the CJEU to rule that it could not, arguing that, on the facts of the case, the making available of the work exceeded the limits of the exception, since a quotation is not supposed to compete with the quoted work by acting as a substitute thereto. In his view, the exception cannot cover situations in which a work is made available on the Internet as an autonomously accessible and downloadable file.[1781] Whereas the judges did not expressly exclude the applicability of the exception, they seem to have sided with the AG when they said that a quotation cannot be so extensive as to conflict with a normal exploitation of the work or prejudice unreasonably the legitimate interests of the rightholder.[1782]

Assuming that the two rule-like candidates would fail to exempt the use, the second step of the analysis would concern the residual open-ended exception.

The first factor would weigh slightly against fairness, for the use of the essay served a commercial purpose. Although the news portal does not directly charge its users for access to the politician's work, it shows advertisements in connection with the articles it publishes and/or charges subscriptions in order to allow readers to access those articles. Hence, the

1779. In the end, the BGH confirmed the lawfulness of Spiegel Online's conduct, finding that the exception for the reporting of current events – laid down, at the national level, in Section 50 UrhG – applied to the case. *See* BGH, *Spiegel Online*.

1780. *See* AG Opinion, *Spiegel Online*, paras 27-38.

1781. *See* AG Opinion, *Spiegel Online*, paras 44-48.

1782. *See* CJEU, *Spiegel Online*, para. 79.

news outlet commercially benefits, if indirectly, from readers opening the article that provides access to the copyright-protected essay. That said, the fact that the news publisher pursues a financial interest and tries to remain sustainable does not necessarily derogate from the fairness of the use. As shall be seen, the profit-making motivations of the publisher should not prevent it from relying on its freedom of information and freedom of the press.

In weighing market harm under the second factor, it would have to be acknowledged that the work has been made available in its entirety and as an autonomous file. As such, the use is likely to act as a competing substitute to the original work and have a negative impact on its market value.[1783] Nonetheless, the entire use of the original work should not automatically lead to the conclusion that the second factor favours a finding of infringement. In this case, the court could not ignore the fact that the rightholder had no intention whatsoever of economically exploiting the work.[1784] Market harm can only exist where the rightholder actually intends to profit from the work, which was clearly not the case here (as with most academic essays that are part of collective volumes). If the rightholder will never exploit the work, its marketability can hardly be impaired.

As to the third factor, the most obviously relevant Charter right is the freedom of expression and information.[1785] As seen, Article 11(1) Charter provides that such freedom includes the 'freedom to … receive and impart information and ideas', with paragraph 2 adding that the 'freedom and pluralism of the media shall be respected'. There is no doubt that the making available of the files falls within the scope of the outlet's freedom of information and freedom of the press. One of the most important functions of the fundamental freedom of the press, as a constituent element of freedom of expression and information, is to allow the electorate to know the politicians' position (actual or former) regarding issues of general interest, even where they would have liked that position to be concealed. This knowledge is vital for the normal functioning of any democratic society. A finding of infringement in this case would hinder the capacity of the press to participate in the analysis of those issues and to foster such knowledge.

In this regard, it is also crucial to note that the news portal's purpose could not be accomplished equally well without making the work available in its entirety. Given that its aim was to substantiate the allegation that there were no meaningful differences between the two versions of the essay, the

1783. As noted in AG Opinion, *Spiegel Online*, para. 49, any making available of a copy of a literary work in its entirety on the Internet and as an autonomous file effectively replaces the original work.

1784. In contrast, AG Szpunar, in relation to the 'normal exploitation' step, found the existence or absence of such intention irrelevant – *see* AG Opinion, *Spiegel Online*, para. 51.

1785. Secondarily, the news outlet could also conceivably rely on the freedom to conduct a business enshrined in Article 16 Charter.

full versions would necessarily have to be made available. If only mere excerpts had been posted, it would have been impossible to show the true extent of the modifications.

This case is a good example of why it is critical to consider the factors together instead of in isolation. In abstract, the making available of a work in its entirety would tip heavily in favour of infringement. Yet, if it is established that such a making available was key to satisfy the informational purpose of the use and that no significant market harm was caused, that abstract effect will no longer hold. The informational purpose associated with this specific use was far more significant than any incidental competitive effect or the indirect commercial benefit derived by the news publisher. In this case, the copyright-protected work is *the story itself*. The making available of the work is essential to illustrate the points made in the news report and has therefore a strong claim to non-infringement.[1786]

Other considerations beyond the listed factors may be of relevance in the case at hand.

The fact that Ernest seemed to be using his copyright to suppress unfavourable news and comment would have to be carefully balanced. In the US, courts have tended to exempt uses where rightholders were asserting their exclusive rights not for economic benefit, but to control the dissemination of information.[1787] In fact, Ernest had no intention of economically exploiting his work; rather, he was interested in having his own version of the story disseminated.

But a more benevolent perspective could be adopted. It could be argued, as did AG Szpunar, that politicians enjoy the right to freedom of thought, which comprises the freedom to change beliefs (Article 10 Charter), and that privileging the making available of the two versions without the added disclaimer would prevent the politician from exercising that right. Nevertheless, as reasonable as it may sound to enable a national politician to exercise his freedom to change beliefs, that exercise should not entail allowing him to control the circulation of an essay on issues of general interest. Such a solution would go far beyond what is necessary to achieve the intended aim. Alternative and more palatable ways of communicating a change of mind would always be available to politicians, who enjoy privileged access to the media.

Hence, in short, although one of the factors would perhaps weigh in favour of Ernest's claim, on balance it seems clear that the greater weight favoured the news publisher.

1786. For instance, if the news story relied on some other fact about Ernest that was wholly unrelated with the essay, the claim to non-infringement would be significantly weaker. As stated in US Supreme Court, *Campbell*, p. 589, 'in news reporting … context is everything'.

1787. *See* US Court of Appeals for the Seventh Circuit, *Ty*.

7 CONCLUSION

This chapter has tried to pave the way for a future reform of the InfoSoc framework of exceptions. The proposal that has been put forward is but a modest effort at striking a balance between flexibility and legal certainty – an effort that is mindful that 'the search for a doctrine that is both perfectly flexible and perfectly foreseeable is doomed to failure'.[1788] In order to achieve a compromise between the different policy goals outlined in Chapter 3, it has been submitted that the EU legislator should consider restructuring Article 5 InfoSoc Directive as a multi-tiered framework of exceptions.

The first tier is a closed catalogue of mandatory and precisely formulated exceptions for known uses with a relevant impact on the functioning of the single market. Recurring uses of protected works that have been anticipated by the legislator *can* and *should* be itemised. This tier would include time-tested exceptions that apply to specific kinds of uses, such as quotation and private copying, which, regardless of supervening changes in the technological environment, will predictably keep occurring along relatively stable fact patterns. These are socially common uses that, as such, lend themselves to *a priori* identification and settlement through a rule-like formulation.

Under this first tier, Member States would be obliged to introduce a number of exceptions, ensuring a certain balance with the (already mandatory) economic rights. By conserving a catalogue of exceptions that have a narrow scope and precise wording, the reform fosters one of the main advantages of the existing Article 5: the *ex ante* guidance it provides on the lawfulness of unconsented-to uses. The exhaustiveness of the catalogue, which prevents Member States from autonomously adding new exceptions, and the mandatory nature of the enumerated privileges aim at securing a high level of harmonisation and mitigating one of the principal handicaps of the framework currently in force. The closed character of the catalogue is without prejudice to the ability of courts to subsidiarily apply an opening, standard-like exception.

The second tier is a catalogue of optional exceptions that would reflect national specificities in this domain. These exceptions, although regarded as culturally important for certain Member States, do not impinge on the smooth functioning of the internal market as directly as the ones provided in the previous tier. For that reason, they need not be made mandatory and their conditions of application do not need as high a degree of uniformity as the ones in the first tier. This tier is therefore intended to uphold one of the main strengths of the extant InfoSoc framework – its capacity to accommodate different national cultures in the realm of copyright exceptions.

1788. Griffiths (2010a), p. 91.

This second catalogue would be quasi-closed, in that it would be combined with a grandfather clause, which would ensure that the enumeration is not excessively lengthy and detailed. In order to avoid fragmentation that is prejudicial to the internal market, the clause should have a narrow scope, much like that of current Article 5(3)(o).

The combination of the first two tiers attains a balance between internal market needs and the principle of subsidiarity. It also gives full realisation to Recital 31 InfoSoc Directive, according to which the degree of harmonisation of exceptions 'should be based on their impact on the smooth functioning of the internal market'.

Finally, the third tier is a mandatory standard-like exception, empowering courts to decide on the lawfulness of unenumerated uses on a case-by-case basis. This third tier reflects the acknowledgement that, as technology races forward, enumerated exceptions may be left in the dust. Because such exceptions are generally insensitive to unanticipated changes in the external environment they regulate and because, in the field of copyright, the expected rate of change is relatively high, with new uses emerging at a fast pace, exceptions of this type should be combined with a more responsive provision. The features of these new uses may vary significantly in important but unforeseeable respects. It is thus hopeless to have them regulated by narrow and precise provisions enacted in advance. The adoption of the third tier would do away with the need for incremental, time-consuming and costly updates to the catalogue at the EU level, while also eliminating the need for *ad hoc* constructions by courts willing to accommodate unlisted uses. At the same time, it would take advantage of the CJEU's capacity to elaborate the meaning of vague doctrines in a coherent and systematised manner.

The third tier is crafted as a subsidiary exception in the form of a balancing test, serving primarily as a safety net for unanticipated uses. The test would rely on pre-existing jurisprudential guidance, by incorporating criteria that have some lineage in CJEU copyright case law. It would require courts to examine whether a certain use achieves a fair balance between the interests of authors/rightholders and users, on the basis of a set of weighing factors: (i) the profit-making nature of the use; (ii) the effect of the use upon the volume of sales or of other lawful transactions relating to the work; and (iii) the capacity of the use to promote the effectiveness of users' fundamental rights. Over time, the level of predictability in the case law interpreting and applying these factors would expectedly grow. As decisions are rendered, the test would become increasingly refined and clusters of cases would emerge (the role of scholars in identifying and systematising such clusters would be essential). Additionally, the codification of normative arguments that already play a role in EU copyright law would arguably evade some of the cultural and ideological rancor that certain stakeholders feel towards fair use.

Towards its end, the chapter has argued against a number of expected objections and critiques to this framework. While they illustrate the difficulties involved in adopting the book's reform proposal, none of them truly undermines it.

Finally, the framework has been analysed against a series of test scenarios modelled after well-known cases on unauthorised digital uses, with a particular emphasis on the role played by the three balancing factors and on their interrelation. Alongside these cases, other uses related to the recent lockdown periods to fight the Covid-19 pandemic could be cited. These would include, for example, the scanning by teachers of entire textbooks for remote seminars and the making available to researchers of copies of books which could only be found in libraries that were shut to the public during such periods. Public interest organisations have called on the Commission to issue guidance on this kind of uses, proposing the adoption of exceptionally broad constructions of the relevant InfoSoc exceptions during government-imposed lockdowns.[1789] Under the model proposed in this Chapter, such inventive interpretations would not be necessary, as the residual balancing test would be openly capable of accommodating those uses, giving copyright law the capacity to adjust to emergency situations and to transparently weigh the interests of rightholders with those of users.

1789. *See* the statement by LIBER in https://libereurope.eu/wp-content/uploads/2020/04/LIBER-Statement-Copyright-Coronavirus-2020.pdf.

Conclusion

The debate over whether the system of copyright exceptions in the EU should be reformed is neither new nor settled. Stakeholders and scholars from different sides of the opinion spectrum have discussed the system's suitability ever since the European Commission tabled the proposal for the InfoSoc Directive. This book aimed at reopening the debate on the fittingness of the existing framework of exceptions, examining it against a normative background that combines the concepts of 'flexibility' and 'legal certainty', with an eye to future legislative reforms.

The new DSM Directive provided the ideal occasion to go about a structural review of the EU law on copyright exceptions that would tackle its most pressing problems. However, by introducing only a modest set of permitted uses, DSM was largely a missed opportunity in this regard. Some commendable choices have certainly been made, specifically that of providing for mandatory exceptions. But the broader course of action elected by the legislator – that of merely updating the *acquis* by adding further narrowly framed exceptions to the ones listed in previous directives – was unwise.

The chain of arguments articulated throughout this book has led us to the conclusion that this step-by-step approach is ill-conceived. While the predictability offered by rule-like exceptions is valuable, it should be supplemented with a higher degree of adaptability to technological change. Furthermore, the importance of achieving a balance between, on the one hand, harmonisation across Member States and, on the other, the capacity to adjust to national traditions and specificities should not be overlooked.

With these two pairs of goals in mind, it has been submitted that Article 5 InfoSoc Directive should be restructured as a multi-tiered framework, incorporating catalogues of relatively narrow and precise exceptions – some mandatory, some optional – along with a subsidiary balancing test enabling courts to accommodate unenumerated uses on a case-by-case basis.

The expected troubles in achieving a political agreement on the exceptions that should be made compulsory for implementation by Member States and on the wording of a European fair-use-style clause should not be discounted. Yet, such troubles should be weighed against the grim state of the current EU system of copyright exceptions – a system that promotes neither flexibility nor legal certainty to an adequate extent.

Besides striking a superior balance between these values, the proposed reform could have additional positive effects. Enhanced adaptability to emerging digital technologies would send important signals about the European openness to innovation, at the same time as it would reduce the existing chasm between EU copyright law and the socio-technological norms that govern the contemporary use of creative works. The reform could thus play an important role in promoting technological and market modernisation, while bringing the law closer to the reasonable expectations of the public. These benefits and, conversely, the risks associated with preserving the legislative *status quo* recommend giving serious consideration to avenues for rethinking the extant framework.

Given the present levels of polarisation in the copyright debate, some might see any proposal to comprehensively redesign Article 5 InfoSoc Directive as a non-starter. Admittedly, the hopes for adoption of the reform proposed in this book in the near future are dim. But the job of legal researchers is not limited to putting forward proposals that are likely to be adopted in the short run. Rather – and all the more so in as contested a field of policymaking as copyright –, academics are entrusted with the task of pursuing independent critical inquiry and delivering proposals for the benefit of society as a whole, however utopian they may be. And that is exactly what this book has sought to do.

Bibliography

Aarnio, Aulis (1987), *The Rational as Reasonable: A Treatise on Legal Justification* (Springer)

Afori, Orit Fischman (2008a), *Implied License: An Emerging New Standard in Copyright Law*, 25 Santa Clara High Technology Law Journal 275

Afori, Orit Fischman (2008b), *An Open Standard 'Fair Use' Doctrine: A Welcome Israeli Initiative*, 30(3) EIPR 85

Afori, Orit Fischman (2014), *Proportionality: A New Mega Standard in European Copyright Law*, 45(8) IIC 889

Akester, Patrícia (2006), *The Political Dimension of the Digital Challenge – Copyright and Free Speech Restrictions in the Digital Age*, 10(1) IPQ 16

ALAI (2010), *Report of the ALAI ad hoc committee on the proposals to introduce mandatory exceptions for the visually impaired*, http://www.alai.org/

ALAI (2015), *Report and Opinion on a Berne-compatible reconciliation of hyperlinking and the communication to the public right on the internet*, available at http://www.alai.org/

Alexander, Isabella & Gómez-Arostegui, H. Tomás (eds.) (2016), *Research Handbook on the History of Copyright Law*

Alexy, Robert & Dreier, Ralf (1991), *Statutory Interpretation in the Federal Republic of Germany*, *in* Neil MacCormick & Robert Summers (eds.), *Interpreting Statutes: A Comparative Study* 73 (Ashgate)

Alexy, Robert (1989), *A Theory of Legal Argumentation: The Theory of Rational Discourse as Theory of Legal Justification* (OUP)

Alexy, Robert (2003a), *Constitutional Rights, Balancing, and Rationality*, 16(2) Ratio Juris 131

Alexy, Robert (2003b), *On Balancing and Subsumption. A Structural Comparison*, 16(4) Ratio Juris 433

Alexy, Robert (2010a), *A Theory of Constitutional Rights* (trans. Julian Rivers) (OUP)

Alexy, Robert (2010b), *Two or three?*, *in* Martin Borowski (ed.), *On the Nature of Legal Principles* 9 (Nomos)

Alexy, Robert (2015), *Legal Certainty and Correctness* 28(4) Ratio Juris 441

Allgrove, Ben (2007), *The Search Engine's Dilemma: Implied License or Crawl and Cache?*, 2(7) JIPLP 437

Angelopoulos, Christina (2009), *Filtering the Internet for Copyrighted Content in Europe*, 4 IRIS-Plus 1

Angelopoulos, Christina (2013), *Beyond the Safe Harbours: Harmonising Substantive Intermediary Liability for Copyright Infringement in Europe*, 17(3) IPQ 253

Angelopoulos, Christina (2016), *European Intermediary Liability in Copyright. A Tort-Based Analysis* (Kluwer Law International)

Angelopoulos, Christina (2017a), *CJEU Decision on Ziggo: The Pirate Bay Communicates Works to the Public*, Kluwer Copyright Blog, http://copyrightblog.kluweriplaw.com/

Angelopoulos, Christina (2017b), *On Online Platforms and the Commission's New Proposal for a Directive on Copyright in the Digital Single Market*, https://papers.ssrn.com/

Antunes, Henrique Sousa (2015), *Revisitando o princípio da tipicidade dos direitos reais*, *in* AA.VV., *Estudos dedicados ao Professor Doutor Bernardo da Gama Lobo Xavier* 165, Vol. II (UCE)

Antunes, Henrique Sousa (2017), *Direitos Reais* (UCE)

Aplin, Tanya & Bently, Lionel (2018), *Displacing the dominance of the three-step test: the role of global, mandatory fair use*, University of Cambridge Faculty of Law Research Paper No. 33/2018, https://papers.ssrn.com/

Aplin, Tanya (2005), *Copyright Law in the Digital Society: The Challenges of Multimedia* (Hart)

Aplin, Tanya (2009), *Subject matter*, *in* Estelle Derclaye (ed.), *Research Handbook on the Future of EU Copyright* 49 (Edward Elgar)

Arena, Amedeo (2010-2011), *The Doctrine of Union Preemption in the E.U. Internal Market: Between Sein and Sollen*, 17 Columbia Journal of European Law 477

Arezzo, Emanuela (2014), *Hyperlinks and Making Available Right in the European Union – What Future for the Internet After* Svensson?, 45(5) IIC 524

Arnauld, Andreas von (2006), *Rechtssicherheit: Perspektivische Annäherungen an eine idée directrice des Rechts* (Mohr Siebeck)

Arnold, Richard & Rosati, Eleonora (2015), *Are national courts the addressees of the InfoSoc three-step test?*, 10(10) JIPLP 741

Arnull, Anthony (1990), *The General Principles of EEC Law and the Individual* (Palgrave Macmillan)

Arnull, Anthony (1993), *Owning up to fallibility: Precedent and the Court of Justice*, 30 Common Market Law Review 247

Ascensão, José de Oliveira (1968), *A Tipicidade dos Direitos Reais* (Minerva)

Ascensão, José de Oliveira (1992), *Direito Civil – Direito de Autor e Direitos Conexos* (Coimbra Editora)

Ascensão, José de Oliveira (1999), *O Direito de Autor no Ciberespaço*, 2(7) Revista da Escola da Magistratura do Estado do Rio de Janeiro 21

Ascensão, José de Oliveira (2002), *A transposição da Directriz N.º 01/29 sobre aspectos do direito de autor e direitos conexos na sociedade da informação*, XLIII(2) Revista da Faculdade de Direito da Universidade de Lisboa 915

Ascensão, José de Oliveira (2003), *O 'Fair Use' no Direito Autoral*, IV Direito da Sociedade de Informação 89

Ascensão, José de Oliveira (2006), *Os limites dos limites. A teoria dos três passos. A tensão entre os limites do direito e as medidas tecnológicas e outras relativas à informação e a gestão dos direitos*, *in* Carlos Rogel Vide (ed.), *Los Límites del Derecho de Autor* 83 (Reus)

Ascensão, José de Oliveira (2011), *O Direito – Introdução e Teoria Geral* (13th ed., Almedina)

Aufderheide, Patricia & Jaszi, Peter (2018), *Reclaiming Fair Use: How to Put Balance Back in Copyright* (2nd ed., University of Chicago Press)

Azoulai, Loïc (2012), *The Europeanisation of legal concepts*, in Ulla B. Neergaard & Ruth Nielsen (eds.), *European Legal Method in a Multi-Level Legal Order* 165 (Djøf Publishing)

Ballin, E.D. Hirsch (1956), *Author's rights compared with those of the community*, 20 RIDA 18

Band, Jonathan & Gerafi, Jonathan (2015), *The Fair Use/Fair Dealing Handbook*, http://infojustice.org/

Barceló, John J. (2016), *Precedent in European Community Law*, *in* Neil MacCormick & Robert Summers (eds.), *Interpreting Precedents: A Comparative Study* 407 (Routledge)

Barnard, Catherine (2016), *The Substantive Law of the EU: The Four Freedoms* (5th ed., OUP)

Bayreuther, Frank (2001), *Beschränkungen des Urheberrechts nach der neuen EU-Urheberrechtsrichtlinie*, 45(11) ZUM 828

Bechtold, Stefan (2016), *Directive 2001/29/EC*, *in* Thomas Dreier & Bernt Hugenholtz (eds.), *Concise European Copyright Law* 421 (2nd ed., Kluwer Law International)

Beebe, Barton (2008), *An Empirical Study of U.S. Copyright Fair Use Opinions, 1978-2005,* 156 University of Pennsylvania Law Review 549.

Belder, Lucky; Dijkman, Léon & Mombers, Arne (2011), *The age of copyright: Wittem's copyright reform proposal compared to Samuelson's Preliminary Thoughts*, 1(3) QMJIP 200

Benabou, Valérie-Laure (2004), *La transposition des directives en droit interne: l'exemple du droit d'auteur*, 30 Légicom 23

Bensamoun, Alexandra (2018), *La réforme du droit d'auteur dans la société de l'information: une histoire de norme(s)*, *in* Alexandra Bensamoun (ed.), *La Réforme du Droit d'Auteur dans la Société de l'Information* 15 (mare & martin)

Bently, Lionel & Aplin, Tanya (2018), *Whatever Became of Global, Mandatory Fair Use? A Case Study in Dysfunctional Pluralism*, https://papers.ssrn.com/

Bently, Lionel; Kretschmer, Martin; Dudenbostel, Tobias; Moreno, María del Carmen Calatrava & Radauer, Alfred (2017), *Strengthening the Position of Press Publishers and Authors and Performers in the Copyright Directive,* Study for the JURI Committee, http://www.europarl.europa.eu/

Bently, Lionel; Sherman, Brad; Gangjee, Dev & Johnson, Phillip (2018), *Intellectual Property Law* (5th ed., Oxford University Press)

Bently, Lionel (2004), *Copyright and the Victorian Internet: Telegraphic Property Laws in Colonial Australia*, 38 Loyola of Los Angeles Law Review 71

Bently, Lionel (2012), *Harmonization by Stealth: Copyright and the ECJ*, Address at the 20th Annual Fordham Intellectual Property Law and Policy Conference, http://fordhamipconference.com/

Bertrand, André R. (1999), Le Droit d'Auteur et les Droits Voisins (2nd ed., Dalloz)

Bertrand, André R. (2010), Droit d'Auteur (3rd ed., Dalloz)

Birnhack, Michael (2015), Judicial snapshots and fair use theory, 5(3) QMJIP 264

BIRPI (1966), *Intellectual Property Conference of Stockholm, 1967: Proposals for Revising the Substantive Copyright Provisions (Articles 1 to 20)*, Document S/1

Birrell, Augustine (1899), *Seven Lectures on the Law and History of Copyright in Books* (Cassell & Co.)

Blásquez, Francisco J.C.; Cappello, Maja; Fontaine, Gilles & Valais, Sophie (2017), *Exceptions and limitations to copyright*, IRIS-Plus – European Audiovisual Observatory

Bogdandy, Armin von (2013), *The Democratic Legitimacy of International Courts: A Conceptual Framework*, 14(2) Theoretical Inquiries in Law 361

Bolgár, Vera (1975), *Abuse of Rights in France, Germany, and Switzerland: A Survey of a Recent Chapter in Legal Doctrine*, 35 Louisiana Law Review 1015

Borghi, Maurizio (2011), *Chasing Copyright Infringement in the Streaming Landscape,* 42 IIC 316

Bowrey, Kathy (2012), *'The World Daguerreotyped: What a Spectacle!' Copyright Law, Photography and the Economic Mission of Empire*, *in* Brad Sherman & Leanne Wiseman (eds.), *Copyright and the Challenge of the New* 11 (Kluwer Law International)

Boyle, James (2008), *The Public Domain: Enclosing the Commons of the Mind* (Yale University Press)

Bracha, Oren (2010), *Early American Printing Privileges. The Ambivalent Origins of Authors' Copyright in America*, *in* Ronan Deazley, Martin Kretschmer & Lionel Bently, *Privilege and Property: Essays on the History of Copyright* 89 (Open Book Publishers)

Bracha, Oren (2012), *How Did Film Become Property? Copyright and the Early American Film Industry*, *in* Brad Sherman & Leanne Wiseman (eds.), *Copyright and the Challenge of the New* 141 (Kluwer Law International)

Bradley, Kieran (2011), *Powers and procedures in the EU Constitution: legal bases and the court*, in Paul Craig & Gráinne de Búrca (eds.), *The Evolution of EU Law* 85 (OUP)

Braithwaite, John (2002), *Rules and Principles: A Theory of Legal Certainty*, 27 Australian Journal of Legal Philosophy 47

Brandenburg, Hans-Friedrich (1983), *Die teleologische Reduktion: Grundlagen und Erscheinungsformen der auslegungsunterschreitenden Gesetzeseinschränkung im Privatrecht* (Schwartz)

Brenncke, Martin (2007), *Is 'fair use' an option for U.K. copyright legislation?*, *in* Christian Tietje, Gerhard Kraft & Rolf Sethe, *Beiträge zum Transnationalen Wirtschaftsrecht*, No. 71 (Martin-Luther-Universität Halle-Wittenberg)

Broberg, Morten & Fenger, Niels (2010), *Preliminary References to the European Court of Justice* (OUP)

Brożek, Bartosz (2008), *Analogy in Legal Discourse*, 94(2) Archiv für Rechts- und Sozialphilosophie 188

Brożek, Bartosz (2015), *Analogy and Balancing: A Reply to David Duarte*, 25 Revus 163

Búrca, Gráinne de (2013), *After the EU Charter of Fundamental Rights: The Court of Justice as a Human Rights Adjudicator?*, 20 Maastricht Journal of European and Comparative Law 168

Burrell, Robert & Coleman, Allison (2005), *Copyright Exceptions: The Digital Impact* (CUP)

Burrell, Robert (2001), *Reining in copyright law: Is fair use the answer?*, 5(4) IPQ 361

Bustamante, Thomas (2010), *Principles, Precedents and their Interplay in Legal Argumentation – How to Justify Analogies between Cases*, *in* Martin Borowski, *On the Nature of Legal Principles* 9 (Nomos)

Bydlinski, Franz (1988), *Fundamentale Rechtsgrundsätze: Zur rechtsethischen Verfassung der Sozietät* (Springer)

Byers, Michael (2002), *Abuse of Rights: An Old Principle, A New Age*, 47 McGill Law Journal 389

Canaris, Claus-Wilhelm (1996), *Pensamento Sistemático e Conceito de Sistema na Ciência do Direito* (trans. António Menezes Cordeiro) (2nd ed., Fundação Calouste Gulbenkian)

Canaris, Claus-Wilhelm (2003), *Direitos Fundamentais e Direito Privado* (trans. Ingo W. Sarlet & Paulo Mota Pinto) (Almedina)

Canotilho, José Joaquim Gomes (2003), *Direito Constitucional e Teoria da Constituição* (Almedina)

Canotilho, José Joaquim Gomes (2005), *Liberdade e Exclusivo na Constitutição*, *in* José Joaquim Gomes Canotilho, IV Direito Industrial 57

Cardozo, Benjamin N. (1921), *The Nature of the Judicial Process* (Yale University Press)

Carnelutti, Francesco (1955), *Teoría General del Derecho* (trans. Francisco Javier Osset) (Editorial Revista de Derecho Privado)

Caron, Christophe (1998a), *Abus de droit et droit d'auteur* (Litec)

Caron, Christophe (1998b), *Abuse of Rights and Authors' Rights: An illustration of the encounter between the special law and the ordinary law in French Civil Law*, 176 RIDA 2

Caron, Christophe (2002), *Les exceptions: L'impact sur le droit français*, 2 Propriétés Intellectuelles 25

Caron, Christophe (2012), *Les exceptions au regard du fondement du droit d'auteur en droit français*, *in* André Lucas, Pierre Sirinelli & Alexandra Bensamoun (eds.), *Les Exceptions au Droit d'Auteur: État des lieux et perspectives dans l'Union européene* 19 (Dalloz)

Carre, Stéphanie (2013), *Le rôle de la Cour de Justice dans la construction du droit d'auteur de l'Union*, *in* Christophe Geiger (ed.), *La contribution de la jurisprudence à la construction de la propriété intellectuelle en Europe* 1 (LexisNexis)

Carreau, Caroline (1995), *Propriété intellectuelle et abus de droit*, *in* AA.VV., *Propriétés Intellectuelles: Mélanges en l'honneur d'André Françon* 17 (Dalloz)

Carroll, Michael W. (2007), *Fixing Fair Use*, 85 North Carolina Law Review 1087

Carvalho, Catarina de Oliveira (2014), *Artigo 11.º*, *in* José Brandão Proença & Luís Carvalho Fernandes (eds.), *Comentário ao Código Civil – Parte Geral* 54 (UCE)

Casimiro, Sofia de Vasconcelos (2015), *A proteção da informação – História de uma evolução darwiniana e da ascendência da tecnologia*, *in* Dário Moura Vicente, José Alberto Coelho Vieira, Alexandre Dias Pereira, Sofia de Vasconcelos Casimiro & Ana Maria Pereira da Silva (eds.), *Estudos de direito intelectual em homenagem ao Prof. Doutor José de Oliveira Ascensão: 50 anos de vida universitária* 577 (Almedina)

Christie, Andrew & Wright, Robin (2014), *A Comparative Analysis of the Three-Step Tests in International Treaties*, 45(4) IIC 409

Christie, Andrew (2011), *Maximising Permissible Exceptions to Intellectual Property Rights*, *in* Annette Kur & Vytautas Mizaras, *The Structure of Intellectual Property Law: Can One Size Fit All?* 121 (Edward Elgar)

Clark, Birgit (2010), *Copyright: Google Image Search does not infringe copyright, says Bundesgerichtshof*, 5(8) JIPLP 553

Clark, Birgit (2012), *Google image search still does not infringe copyright, reaffirms Bundesgerichtshof*, 7(11) JIPLP 788

Cohen, Julie E.; Loren, Lydia Pallas; Okediji, Ruth L. & O'Rourke, Maureen A. (2015), *Copyright in a Global Information Economy* (4th ed., Aspen Publishers)

Cohen Jehoram, Herman (1998), *Exceptions and limitations to copyright: general review. Complete exemption, compulsory licensing, equitable remuneration – Interventions*, *in* Libby Baulch, Michael Green & Mary

Wyburn (eds.), *ALAI Study Days: The Boundaries of Copyright: Its Proper Limitations and Exceptions* 58 (Australian Copyright Council)

Cohen Jehoram, Herman (2001a), *European Copyright Law – Ever More Horizontal*, 32(5) IIC 532

Cohen Jehoram, Herman (2001b), *Some Principles of Exceptions to Copyright*, *in* Peter Ganea, Christopher Heath & Gerhard Schricker (eds.), *Urheberrecht – Heute – Morgen: Festschrift für Adolf Dietz zum 65. Gerburtstag* 381 (Beck)

Cohen Jehoram, Herman (2004), *Copyright and Freedom of Expression, Abuse of Rights and Standard Chicanery: American and Dutch Approaches*, 26 EIPR 275

Cohen Jehoram, Herman (2005a), *Restrictions on Copyright and their Abuse*, 27(10) EIPR 359

Cohen Jehoram, Herman (2005b), *The Evolution of Copyright Restrictions*, *in* Ansgar Ohly, Theo Bodewig, Thomas Dreier, Horst-Peter Götting, Maximilian Haedicke & Michael Lehmann (eds.), *Perspektiven des Geistigen Eigentums und Wettbewerbsrechts, Festschrift für Gerhard Schricker* 249 (Beck)

Cohen Jehoram, Herman (2009), *Is there a hidden agenda behind the general non-implementation of the EU three-step test?*, 31(8) EIPR 408

Communia Association (2015), *The importance of exceptions and limitations for a balanced copyright policy*, https://www.communia-association.org/

Communia Association (2017), *Copyright and Education in Europe: 15 everyday cases in 15 countries*, https://www.communia-association.org/

Conrad, Albrecht (2010), *Anmerkung zu BGH, Urteil vom 29. April 2010 – I ZR 69/08 – Vorschaubilder*, 54(7) ZUM 585

Cordeiro, António Menezes (1984), *Da Boa Fé no Direito Civil*, Vol. II (Almedina)

Cordeiro, Pedro (2002), *Limitações e excepções sob a 'regra dos três passos' e nas legislações nacionais – Diferenças entre o meio analógico e digital*, III Direito da Sociedade de Informação 211

Cornish, William R. (1995), *Copyright Across the Quarter-Century*, 26(6) IIC 801

Cornish, William R. (2004), *Intellectual Property: Omnipresent, Distracting, Irrelevant?* (OUP)

Craig, Carys J. (2013), *Technological Neutrality: (Pre)Serving the Purposes of Copyright Law*, *in* Michael Geist (ed.), *The Copyright Pentalogy: How the Supreme Court of Canada Shook the Foundations of Canadian Copyright* 271 (University of Ottawa Press)

Craig, Carys J. (2017), *Globalizing User Rights-Talk: On Copyright Limits and Rhetorical Risks*, 33(1) American University International Law Review 1

Craig, Paul & Búrca, Gráinne de (2015), *EU Law: Text, Cases, and Materials* (6th ed., OUP)

Crews, Kenneth (2001), *The Law of Fair Use and the Illusion of Fair-Use Guidelines*, 62 Ohio State Law Journal 599

Cross, Eugene Daniel (1992), *Pre-emption of Member State law in the European Economic Community: A framework for analysis*, 29 Common Market Law Review 447

Daalen, Ot van (2003), *NL – Court of Appeal Ruling in Scientology Case*, 9 IRIS-Plus 14

Davies, Gillian (1995), *The Convergence of Copyright and Authors' Rights – Reality or Chimera?*, 26(6) IIC 964

Davies, Gillian (2002), *Copyright and the Public Interest* (2nd ed., Sweet & Maxwell)

Davies, John (1994), *The Developing Law of Multimedia*, 10(1) Computer Law & Practice 6

Deazley, Ronan; Kretschmer, Martin & Bently, Lionel (2010), *Privilege and Property: Essays on the History of Copyright* (Open Book Publishers)

Deazley, Ronan (2004), *On the Origin of the Right to Copy: Charting the Movement of Copyright Law in Eighteenth-Century Britain (1695-1775)* (Hart)

Deazley, Ronan (2008), *Commentary on Gyles v. Wilcox (1741), in* Lionel Bently & Martin Kretschmer (eds.), *Primary Sources on Copyright (1450-1900)*, www.copyrighthistory.org/

Decherney, Peter (2014), *Fair Use Goes Global*, 31(2) Critical Studies in Media Communication 146

Depoorter, Ben (2009), *Technology and Uncertainty: The Shaping Effect on Copyright Law*, 157 University of Pennsylvania Law Review 1831

Depreeuw, Sari (2014), *The Variable Scope of the Exclusive Economic Rights in Copyright* (Kluwer Law International)

Depreeuw, Sari, & Hubin, Jean-Benoît (2014), *Study on the Making Available Right and Its Relationship with the Reproduction Right in Cross-Border Digital Transmissions*, Study for the European Commission, https://publications.europa.eu/

Derclaye, Estelle & Cook, Trevor (2011), *An EU Copyright Code: what and how, if ever?*, 15(3) IPQ 259

Derclaye, Estelle (2008), *Intellectual Property Rights and Human Rights: Coinciding and Cooperating*, *in* Paul Torremans (ed.), *Intellectual Property and Human Rights* 133 (Kluwer Law International)

Derclaye, Estelle (2009), *Introduction*, *in* Estelle Derclaye (ed.), *Research Handbook on the Future of EU Copyright* 1 (Edward Elgar)

Derclaye, Estelle (2010), *Infopaq International A/S v. Danske Dagblades Forening (C-5/08): wonderful or worrisome? The impact of the ECJ ruling in Infopaq on UK copyright law*, 32(5) EIPR 247

Derclaye, Estelle (2014), *Assessing the impact and reception of the Court of Justice of the European Union case law on UK copyright law: what does the future hold?*, 240 RIDA 5

Desbois, Henri (1978), *Le droit d'auteur en France* (3rd ed., Dalloz)

Desurmont, Thierry (1987), *Le droit de l'auteur de controller la destination des exemplaires sur lesquels son oeuvre se trouve reproduite*, 132 RIDA 2

Deursen, Stijn van & Snijders, Thom (2018), *The Court of Justice at the Crossroads: Clarifying the Role for Fundamental Rights in the EU Copyright Framework*, 49(9) IIC 1080

Dietz, Adolf (1978), *Copyright Law in the European Community: A comparative investigation of National copyright legislation with special reference to the provisions of the Treaty establishing the European Community* (Sijthoff & Noordhoff)

Dietz, Adolf (1979), *The Possible Harmonization of Copyright Within the European Community*, 10(4) IIC 395

Dietz, Adolf (1998), *The Protection of Intellectual Property in the Information Age – The Draft E.U. Copyright Directive of November 1997*, 2(4) IPQ 335

Dietz, Adolf (2004), *Marketing and Enforcing Intellectual Property in Europe – European Parliament Versus Commission: How to Deal with Collecting Societies?*, 35(7) IIC 809

Dimita, Gaetano (2017), *The WIPO right of making available*, *in* Paul Torremans (ed.), *Research Handbook on Copyright Law* 135 (2nd ed., Edward Elgar)

Dinwoodie, Graeme B. & Dreyfuss, Rochelle (2012), *A Neofederalist Vision of TRIPS: The Resilience of the International Intellectual Property Regime* (OUP)

Dinwoodie, Graeme B. (2001), *The Development and Incorporation of International Norms in the Formation of Copyright Law*, 62 Ohio State Law Journal 733

Dixon, Allen N. (2009), *Liability of users and third parties for copyright infringements on the Internet: overview of international developments*, *in* Alain Strowel (ed.), *Peer-to-Peer File Sharing and Secondary Liability in Copyright Law* (Edward Elgar)

Dnes, Antony W. (2013), *Should the UK move to a fair-use copyright exception?*, 44(4) IIC 418

Drassinower, Abraham (2009), *Exceptions Properly So-Called*, *in* Ysolde Gendreau & Abraham Drassinower (eds.), *Langues et droit d'auteur* 205 (Bruylant)

Dreier, Thomas & Schulze, Gernot (2018), *Urheberrechtsgesetz* (6th ed., Beck)

Dreier, Thomas (1993), *Copyright Digitized: Philosophical Impacts and Practical Implications for Information Exchange in Digital Networks*, *in* AA.VV., *WIPO Worldwide Symposium on the Impact of Digital Technology on Copyright and Neighboring Rights* 187 (WIPO)

Dreier, Thomas (1995), *L'Analogue, le Digital et le Droit d'Auteur*, *in* AA.VV., *Propriétés Intellectuelles: Mélanges en l'honneur de André Françon* 119 (Dalloz)

Dreier, Thomas (2001), *Balancing Proprietary and Public Domain Interests: Inside or Outside of Proprietary Rights?*, *in* Rochelle Dreyfuss; Diane Zimmerman & Harry First, *Expanding the Boundaries of Intellectual Property: Innovation Policy for the Knowledge Society* (OUP)

Dreier, Thomas (2010), *Limitations: The Centerpiece of Copyright in Distress – An Introduction*, 1 JIPITEC 50

Dreier, Thomas (2013), *The Wittem Project of a European Copyright Code*, *in* Christophe Geiger (ed.), *Constructing European Intellectual Property: Achievements and New Perspectives* 292 (Edward Elgar)

Dreier, Thomas (2015), *Thoughts on revising the limitations on copyright under Directive 2001/29*, 11(2) JIPLP 138

Dreier, Thomas (2016), *Berne Convention*, *in* Thomas Dreier & P. Bernt Hugenholtz (eds.), *Concise European Copyright Law* (2nd edition, Kluwer Law International)

Duarte, David (2015), *Analogy and Balancing: The Partial Reducibility Thesis and its Problems*, 25 Revus 141

Duhanic, Ines (2016), *Copy this sound! The cultural importance of sampling for hip hop music in copyright law – a copyright law analysis of the sampling decision of the German Federal Constitutional Court*, 65(11) GRUR Int. 1007

Dusollier, Séverine & Buydens, Mireille (2001), *Les exceptions au droit d'auteur dans l'environnement numérique: évolutions dangereuses*, 9 Communication Commerce Électronique 10

Dusollier, Séverine (2003), *Exceptions and Technological Measures in the European Copyright Directive of 2001 – An Empty Promise*, 34(1) IIC 66

Dusollier, Séverine (2006), *Le droit de destination: une espèce franco-belge vouée à la disparition*, 20 Propriétés Intellectuelles 281

Dusollier, Séverine (2007), *Droit d'auteur et protection des oeuvres dans l'univers numérique: Droits et exceptions à la lumière des dispositifs de verrouillage des oeuvres* (Larcier)

Dworkin, Ronald M. (1967), *The Model of Rules,* 35 University of Chicago Law Review 14

Dworkin, Ronald M. (1977), *Taking Rights Seriously* (Harvard University Press)

ECS (2014), *Limitations and Exceptions as Key Elements of the Legal Framework for Copyright in the European Union – Opinion on the Judgment of the CJEU in Case C-201/13 Deckmyn*, https://europeancopyrightsociety.org/

ECS (2017), *General Opinion on the EU Copyright Reform Package*, https://europeancopyrightsociety.org/

ECS (2018a), *Opinion of the European Copyright Society concerning the scope of the economic rights in light of case C-161/17, Land Nordrhein-Westfalen v. Dirk Renckhoff ('Córdoba case')*, https://europeancopyrightsociety.org/

ECS (2018b), *Opinion of the European Copyright Society in relation to the pending reference before the CJEU in Cofemel v. G-Star, C-683/17*, https://europeancopyrightsociety.org/

ECS (2019), *Opinion of the European Copyright Society in relation to the pending reference before the CJEU in Case C-476/17, Hutter v. Pelham*, https://europeancopyrightsociety.org/

Eechoud, Mireille van; Hugenholtz, P. Bernt; Gompel, Stef van; Guibault, Lucie & Helberger, Natali (2009), *Harmonizing European Copyright Law: The Challenges of Better Lawmaking* (Kluwer Law International)

Eechoud, Mireille van (2012), *Along the Road to Uniformity – Diverse Readings of the Court of Justice Judgments on Copyright Work*, 3(1) JIPITEC 60

Efroni, Zohar (2011), *Access-Right: The Future of Digital Copyright Law* (OUP)

Ehrlich, Isaac & Posner, Richard A. (1974), *An Economic Analysis of Legal Rulemaking*, 3(1) The Journal of Legal Studies 257

Elkin-Koren, Niva & Afori, Orit Fischman (2015), *Taking Users' Rights to the Next Level: A Pragmatist Approach to Fair Use*, 33(1) Cardozo Arts & Entertainment Law Journal 1

Elkin-Koren, Niva (1997), *Copyright Policy and the Limits of Freedom of Contract*, 12 Berkeley Technology Law Journal 93

Elkin-Koren, Niva (2016), *The New Frontiers of User Rights*, 32(1) American University International Law Review 1

Elkin-Koren, Niva (2017), *Copyright in a Digital Ecosystem: A User-Rights Approach*, *in* Ruth L. Okediji (ed.), *Copyright Law in an Age of Limitations and Exceptions* 132 (CUP)

Endicott, Timothy & Spence, Michael (2005), *Vagueness in the Scope of Copyright*, 121 Law Quarterly Review 657

Endicott, Timothy (2000), *Vagueness in Law* (OUP)

Endicott, Timothy (2001), *Law is Necessarily Vague*, 7 Legal Theory 379

Endicott, Timothy (2011a), *The Value of Vagueness*, *in* Andrei Marmor & Scott Soames (eds.), *Philosophical Foundations of Language in the Law* 14 (OUP)

Endicott, Timothy (2011b), *Vagueness and Law*, *in* Giuseppina Ronzitti (ed.), *Vagueness: A Guide* 171 (Springer)

Engisch, Karl (2014), *Introdução ao pensamento jurídico* (trans. J. Baptista Machado) (11th ed., Fundação Calouste Gulbenkian)

EPRS (2015), *Review of the EU copyright framework: European Implementation Assessment*, http://www.europarl.europa.eu/

Ernst, Silke & Häusermann, Daniel M. (2006), *Teaching Exceptions in European Copyright Law – Important Policy Questions Remain*, Berkman Center for Internet & Society Research Publication No. 2006-10, https://papers.ssrn.com/

Falce, Valeria (2012), *La Modernizzazione del Diritto d'Autore* (2nd ed., G. Giappichelli Editore)

Farrand, Benjamin (2014), *Networks of Power in Digital Copyright Law and Policy: Political salience, expertise and the legislative process* (Routledge)

Farrand, Benjamin (2015), *Lobbying and Lawmaking in the European Union: The Development of Copyright Law and the Rejection of the Anti-Counterfeiting Trade Agreement*, 35(3) Oxford Journal of Legal Studies 487

Favale, Marcella; Kretschmer, Martin & Torremans, Paul (2016), *Is there a EU copyright jurisprudence? An empirical analysis of the workings of the European Court of Justice*, 79(1) Modern Law Review 31

Favale, Marcella; Kretschmer, Martin & Torremans, Paul (2018), *Who is steering the jurisprudence of the European Court of Justice? The Influence of Member State submissions on copyright law*, https://papers.ssrn.com/

Favale, Marcella (2006), *Publication Review: Copyright Exceptions – The Digital Impact*, 28(9) EIPR 505

Favale, Marcella (2008), *Fine-tuning European copyright law to strike a balance between the rights of owners and users*, 33(5) European Law Review 687

Fernández, María Serrano (2013), *La doctrina del ius usus inocui y el principio de prohibición del abuso del derecho en el ámbito de la propiedad intelectual: comentario a la STS (Sala de lo Civil, Sección 1º) de 3 de abril de 2012 (RJ 2012, 5272)*, 32 Revista Aranzadi de derecho patrimonial 469

Ficsor, Mihály (1996-1997), *Copyright for the Digital Era: The WIPO 'Internet' Treaties,* 21 Columbia-VLA Journal of Law & the Arts 197

Ficsor, Mihály (2002a), *The Law of Copyright and the Internet: The 1996 WIPO Treaties, their Interpretation and Implementation* (OUP)

Ficsor, Mihály (2002b), *How Much of What? The 'Three-Step Test' and its Application in Two Recent Dispute Settlement Cases*, 192 RIDA 111

Ficsor, Mihály (2012), *Short paper on the three-step test for the application of exceptions and limitations in the field of copyright*, www.copyrightseesaw.net

Ficsor, Mihály (2018), *The hurried idea of a 'European Copyright Code' in the light of the EU's (desirable) cultural and copyright policy*, www.copyrightseesaw.net

Finck, Michèle & Moscon, Valentina (2019), *Copyright Law on Blockchains: Between New Forms of Rights Administration and Digital Rights Management 2.0*, 50(1) IIC 77

Finkelstein, Claire Oakes (1999), *When the Rule Swallows the Exception*, *in* Linda Meyer (ed.), *Rules and Reasoning: Essays in Honour of Fred Schauer* 145 (Hart)

Fisher, William W. (1988), *Reconstructing the Fair Use Doctrine*, 101 Harvard Law Review 1659

Fisher, William W. (2001), *Theories of Intellectual Property*, *in* Stephen R. Munzer (ed.), *New Essays in the Legal and Political Theory of Property* 168 (CUP)

Förster, Achim (2008), *Fair use: ein Systemvergleich der Schrankengeneralklausel des US-amerikanischen Copyright Act mit dem Schrankenkatalog des deutschen Urheberrechtsgesetzes* (Mohr Siebeck)

Françon, André (1987), *L'avenir du droit d'auteur*, 134 RIDA 2

Françon, André (1999), *Cours de propriété littéraire, artistique et industrielle* (Litec)

Frosio, Giancarlo (2017), *From horizontal to vertical: An intermediary liability earthquake in Europe*, 12(7) JIPLP 565

Frosio, Giancarlo (2018), *To Filter or Not to Filter? That Is the Question in EU Copyright Reform*, 36(2) Cardozo Arts & Entertainment Law Journal 331

Fuller, Lon (1969), *The Morality of Law* (Yale University Press)

Gaubiac, Yves (2002), *Les exceptions: La method suivie et les résultats obtenus*, 2 Propriétés Intellectuelles 17

Gautier, Pierre-Yves (2001), *De la transposition des exceptions: à propos de la directive 'droit d'auteur dans la société de l'information'*, 11 Communication Commerce Électronique 10

Gautier, Pierre-Yves (2005), *General Issue: The Diversity of Copyright Sources*, *in* ALAI Congress, *Exploring the Sources of Copyright* 79

Gautier, Pierre-Yves (2017), *Propriété littéraire et artistique* (Presses Universitaires de France)

Geiger, Christophe & Izyumenko, Elena (2014), *Copyright on the Human Rights' Trial: Redefining the Boundaries of Exclusivity Through Freedom of Expression*, 45 IIC 316

Geiger, Christophe & Izyumenko, Elena (2018), *Intellectual Property before the European Court of Human Rights*, *in* Christophe Geiger, Craig A. Nard & Xavier Seuba (eds.), *Intellectual Property and the Judiciary* 9 (Edward Elgar)

Geiger, Christophe & Izyumenko, Elena (2019a), *Freedom of expression as an external limitation to copyright law in the EU: The Advocate General of the CJEU shows the way*, 41(3) EIPR 131

Geiger, Christophe & Izyumenko, Elena (2019b), *Towards a European 'Fair Use' Grounded in Freedom of Expression*, 35(1) American University International Law Review 1

Geiger, Christophe & Izyumenko, Elena (2020), *The Constitutionalization of Intellectual Property Law in the EU and the Funke Medien, Pelham and Spiegel Online Decisions of the CJEU: Progress, But Still Some Way to Go!*, 51 IIC 282

Geiger, Christophe & Schönherr, Franciska (2012), *Defining the Scope of Protection of Copyright in the EU: The Need to Reconsider the Acquis regarding Limitations and Exceptions*, *in* Tatiana-Eleni Synodinou, *Codification of European Copyright Law: Challenges and Perspectives* 133 (Kluwer Law International)

Geiger, Christophe & Schönherr, Franciska (2014), *Limitations to copyright in the digital age*, *in* Andrej Savin & Jan Trzaskowski, *Research Handbook on EU Internet Law* 110 (Edward Elgar)

Geiger, Christophe; Bulayenko, Oleksandr; Hassler, Théo; Izyumenko, Elena; Schönherr, Franciska & Seuba, Xavier (2015), *Reaction of CEIPI to the Resolution on the Implementation of Directive 2001/29/EC on the Harmonisation of Copyright in the Information Society adopted by the European Parliament on the 9th July 2015*, Centre for International Intellectual Property Studies Research Paper No. 2015-01, https://papers.ssrn.com/

Geiger, Christophe; Frosio, Giancarlo & Bulayenko, Oleksandr (2018a), *The Exception for Text and Data Mining (TDM) in the Proposed Directive on Copyright in the Digital Single Market – Legal Aspects*, Study commissioned by the European Parliament's Policy Department for Citizens' Rights and Constitutional Affairs, http://www.europarl.europa.eu/

Geiger, Christophe; Frosio, Giancarlo & Bulayenko, Oleksandr (2018b), *Text and Data Mining in the Proposed Copyright Reform: Making the EU Ready for an Age of Big Data? Legal Analysis and Policy Recommendations*, 49 IIC 814

Geiger, Christophe; Frosio, Giancarlo & Bulayenko, Oleksandr (2018c), *The EU Commission's Proposal to Reform Copyright Limitations: A Good but Far Too Timid Step in the Right Direction*, 40(1) EIPR 4

Geiger, Christophe; Gervais, Daniel J. & Senftleben, Martin (2014), *The Three-Step Test Revisited: How to Use the Test's Flexibility in National Copyright Law*, 29(3) American University International Law Review 581

Geiger, Christophe; Griffiths, Jonathan & Hilty, Reto (2008), *Declaration on a Balanced Interpretation of the 'Three-Step Test' in Copyright Law*, 39(6) IIC 707

Geiger, Christophe (2004a), *Droit d'auteur et droit du public à l'information: Approche de droit compare* (LexisNexis)

Geiger, Christophe (2004b), *De la nature juridique des limites au droit d'auteur*, 13 Propriétés Intellectuelles 882

Geiger, Christophe (2005), *Right to Copy v. Three-Step Test: The Future of the Private Copy Exception in the Digital Environment*, 1(7) Computer Law Review International 7

Geiger, Christophe (2006a), *Constitutionalising Intellectual Property Law? The Influence of Fundamental Rights on Intellectual Property in Europe*, 37 IIC 371

Geiger, Christophe (2006b), *The Three-Step Test, a Threat to a Balanced Copyright Law?*, 37(6) IIC 683

Geiger, Christophe (2006c), *The Private Copy Exception, an Area of Freedom (Temporarily) Preserved in the Digital Environment*, 37(1) IIC 74

Geiger, Christophe (2007a), *Author's Right, Copyright and the Public's Right to Information: A Complex Relationship (Rethinking Copyright in the Light of Fundamental Rights)*, *in* Fiona Macmillan, *New Directions in Copyright Law* 24, Vol. V (Edward Elgar)

Geiger, Christophe (2007b), *From Berne to National Law, via the Copyright Directive: The Dangerous Mutations of the Three-Step Test*, 29(12) EIPR 486

Geiger, Christophe (2007c), *The Role of the Three-Step Test in the Adaptation of Copyright Law to the Information Society*, UNESCO e-Copyright Bulletin (January-March)

Geiger, Christophe (2008a), *Flexibilising Copyright – Remedies to the Privatisation of Information by Copyright Law*, 39(2) IIC 178

Geiger, Christophe (2008b), *Rethinking Copyright Limitations in the Information Society – The Swiss Supreme Court Leads the Way*, 39(8) IIC 943

Geiger, Christophe (2008c), *The Answer to the Machine Should not be the Machine: Safeguarding the Private Copy Exception in the Digital Environment*, 30(4) EIPR 121

Geiger, Christophe (2009a), *Copyright's fundamental rights dimension at EU level*, *in* Estelle Derclaye (ed.), *Research Handbook on the Future of EU Copyright* 27 (Edward Elgar)

Geiger, Christophe (2009b), *Implementing an International Instrument for Interpreting Copyright Limitations and Exceptions*, 40(6) IIC 627

Geiger, Christophe (2010a), *Promoting Creativity through Copyright Limitations: Reflections on the Concept of Exclusivity in Copyright Law*, 12(3) Vanderbilt Journal of Entertainment and Technology Law 515

Geiger, Christophe (2010b), *The Future of Copyright in Europe: Striking a Fair Balance between Protection and Access to Information*, 14(1) IPQ 1

Geiger, Christophe (2011), *Exploring the flexibilities of the TRIPS Agreement's provisions on limitations and exceptions*, *in* Annette Kur &

Vytautas Mizaras (eds.), *The Structure of Intellectual Property Law: Can One Size Fit All?* 287 (Edward Elgar)

Geiger, Christophe (2012), *Fundamental Rights as Common Principles of European (and International) Intellectual Property Law*, *in* Ansgar Ohly (ed.), *Common Principles of European Intellectual Property Law* 223 (Mohr Siebeck)

Geiger, Christophe (2013a), *The construction of intellectual property in the European Union: searching for coherence*, *in* Christophe Geiger (ed.), *Constructing European Intellectual Property: Achievements and New Perspectives* 5 (Edward Elgar)

Geiger, Christophe (2013b), *Effectivité et flexibilité: deux impératifs de l'adaptation du droit des 'exceptions'*, 94 Revue Lamy Droit de l'Immatériel 41

Geiger, Christophe (2016), *The Role of the Court of Justice of the European Union: Harmonizing, Creating and sometimes Disrupting Copyright Law in the European Union*, *in* Irini Stamatoudi (ed.), *New Developments in EU and International Copyright Law* 435 (Kluwer Law International)

Geiger, Christophe (2018), *'Fair Use' through Fundamental Rights: When Freedom of Artistic Expression Allows Creative Appropriations and Opens Up Statutory Copyright Limitations*, Centre for International Intellectual Property Studies Research Paper No. 2018-09, https://papers.ssrn.com/

Geller, Paul Edward (1994), *Legal Transplants in International Copyright: Some Problems of Method*, 13 UCLA Pacific Basin Law Journal 199

Geller, Paul Edward (2010), *A German Approach to Fair Use: Test Cases for TRIPS Criteria for Copyright Limitations?*, 57 Journal of the Copyright Society of the USA 553

Gendreau, Ysolde (2000), *A Technologically Neutral Solution for the Internet: Is It Wishful Thinking*, *in* Irini Stamatoudi & Paul Torremans (eds.), *Copyright in the New Digital Environment* 1 (Sweet & Maxwell)

Gervais, Daniel J. (2005), *Towards a New Core International Copyright Norm: The Reverse Three-Step Test*, 9 Marquette Intellectual Property Law Review 1

Gervais, Daniel J. (2010), *Fair Use, Fair Dealing, Fair Principles: Efforts to Conceptualize Exceptions and Limitations to Copyright,* 57 Journal of the Copyright Society of the USA 499

Gervais, Daniel J. (2017), *(Re)Structuring Copyright: A Comprehensive Path to International Copyright Reform* (Edward Elgar)

Gervais, Daniel J. (2019), *The Machine as Author*, https://papers.ssrn.com/

Gestel, Rob van; Micklitz, Hans-W. & Maduro, Miguel Poiares (2012), *Methodology in the New Legal World*, EUI Working Papers Law No. 2012/13, https://papers.ssrn.com/

Gibson, James (2007), *Risk Aversion and Rights Accretion in Intellectual Property Law*, 116 Yale Law Journal 882

Gierke, Otto von (1889), *Die soziale Aufgabe des Privatrechts* (Springer)

Gilmore, Grant (1967), *On Statutory Obsolescence*, 39 University of Colorado Law Review 461

Ginsburg, Jane C. (1990), *A Tale of Two Copyrights: Literary Property in Revolutionary France and America*, 64(5) Tulane Law Review 991

Ginsburg, Jane C. (1997-1998), *Authors and Users in Copyright*, 45 Journal of the Copyright Society of the USA 1

Ginsburg, Jane C. (2000), *International Copyright: From a 'Bundle' of National Copyright Law to a Supranational Code?*, 47 Journal of the Copyright Society of the USA 265

Ginsburg, Jane C. (2001), *Toward Supranational Copyright Law? The WTO Panel Decision and the 'Three-Step Test' for Copyright Exceptions*, 187 RIDA 2

Ginsburg, Jane C. (2011), *European Copyright Code – Back to First Principles (with Some Additional Detail)*, 58(2) Journal of the Copyright Society of the USA 265

Ginsburg, Jane C. (2015), *Fair Use for Free, or Permitted-but-Paid?*, 29 Berkeley Technology Law Journal 1383

Goldberg, Morton D. & Feder, Jesse M. (1993), *Copyright and Technology: The Analog, the Digital, and the Analogy*, *in* AA.VV., *WIPO Worldwide Symposium on the Impact of Digital Technology on Copyright and Neighboring Rights* 37 (WIPO)

Golding, Martin P. (2001), *Legal Reasoning* (Broadview Press)

Goldstein, Paul & Hugenholtz, P. Bernt (2012), *International Copyright: Principles, Law and Practice* (3rd ed., OUP)

Goldstein, Paul (2003), *Copyright's Highway: From Gutenberg to the Celestial Jukebox* (Stanford University Press)

Gompel, Stef van (2011), *Formalities in Copyright Law: An Analysis of their History, Rationales and Possible Future* (Kluwer Law International)

Gonçalves, Luís Manuel Couto (2019), *Manual de Direito Industrial* (8th ed., Almedina)

Gonçalves, Nuno (2015), *Notas sobre limitações e exceções no direito de autor*, *in* Dário Moura Vicente, José Alberto Coelho Vieira, Alexandre Dias Pereira, Sofia de Vasconcelos Casimiro & Ana Maria Pereira da Silva (eds.), *Estudos de direito intelectual em homenagem ao Prof. Doutor José de Oliveira Ascensão: 50 anos de vida universitária* 471 (Almedina)

Gonçalves, Nuno (2018), *A Função Social do Direito de Autor* (Princípia)

Goold, Patrick R. (2017), *The Interpretive Argument for a Balanced Three-Step Test*, 33(1) American University International Law Review 187

Gordon, Wendy J. (1982), *Fair Use as Market Failure: A Structural and Economic Analysis of the Betamax Case and Its Predecessors*, 82 Columbia Law Review 1600

Gotzen, Frank (2007), *Copyright in Europe: Quo Vadis? Some Conclusions after the Implementation of the Information Society Harmonisation Directive*, 211 RIDA 2

Gotzen, Frank (2012), *Une approche synthétique des exceptions au droit d'auteur dans le droit de l'Union européenne*, *in* André Lucas, Pierre Sirinelli & Alexandra Bensamoun (eds.), *Les Exceptions au Droit d'Auteur: État des lieux et perspectives dans l'Union européene* 43 (Dalloz)

Goutal, Jean-Louis (2002), *L'environnement de la directive 'droit d'auteur et droits voisins dans la société de l'information' en droit international et comparé*, 2002(2) Communication Commerce Électronique 4

Gowers Review (2006), *Gowers Review of Intellectual Property*, https://assets.publishing.service.gov.uk/government/uploads/system/uploads/attachment_data/file/228849/0118404830.pdf

Grey, Thomas C. (1983), *Langdell's Orthodoxy*, 45 University of Pittsburgh Law Review 1

Grice, Paul H. (1989), *Studies in the Way of Words* (Harvard University Press)

Griffiths, Jonathan & McDonagh, Luke (2013), *Fundamental rights and European IP law: the case of Art 17(2) of the EU Charter*, *in* Christophe Geiger (ed.), *Constructing European Intellectual Property: Achievements and New Perspectives* 75 (Edward Elgar)

Griffiths, Jonathan (2002), *Copyright Law and the Public's Right to Receive Information: Recent Developments in an Isolated Community*, *in* Eric M. Barendt & Alison Firth (eds.), *The Yearbook of Copyright and Media Law 2001/2* 29 (OUP)

Griffiths, Jonathan (2009), *The Three-Step Test in European Copyright Law – Problems and Solutions*, 13(4) IPQ 428

Griffiths, Jonathan (2010a), *Unsticking the centre-piece – the liberation of European copyright law?*, 1 JIPITEC 87

Griffiths, Jonathan (2010b), *Rhetoric & the 'Three-Step Test' – Copyright Reform in the United Kingdom*, 32(7) EIPR 309

Griffiths, Jonathan (2011), *Infopaq, BSA and the 'Europeanisation' of UK copyright law*, 16 Media & Arts Law Review 59

Griffiths, Jonathan (2013), *Constitutionalising or Harmonising? The Court of Justice, the Right to Property and European Copyright Law*, 38 European Law Review 65

Griffiths, Jonathan (2014a), *The Role of the Court of Justice in the Development of European Union Copyright Law*, *in* Irini Stamatoudi & Paul Torremans (eds.), *EU Copyright Law: A Commentary* 1098 (Edward Elgar)

Griffiths, Jonathan (2014b), *The United Kingdom's public interest 'defence' and European Union copyright law*, *in* Nari Lee, Guido Westkamp, Annette Kur & Ansgar Ohly (eds.), *Intellectual Property, Unfair Competition and Publicity: Convergences and Development* 289 (Edward Elgar)

Griffiths, Jonathan (2017), *Taking power tools to the acquis – The Court of Justice, the Charter of Fundamental Rights and European Union Copyright Law*, https://papers.ssrn.com/

Griffiths, Jonathan (2019), *European Union copyright law and the Charter of Fundamental Rights – Advocate General Szpunar's Opinions in (C-469/17) Funke Medien, (C-476/17) Pelham GmbH and (C-516/17) Spiegel Online*, ERA Forum 1

Grodin, Joseph R. (1994), *Are Rules Really Better than Standards?*, 45 Hastings Law Journal 569

Grosheide, F. Willem (2001), *Copyright Law from a User's Perspective: Access Rights for Users*, 23(7) EIPR 321

Guibault, Lucie & Quintais, João Pedro (2014), *Copyright, technology and the exploitation of audiovisual works in the EU*, 4 IRIS-Plus 7

Guibault, Lucie; Westkamp, Guido & Rieber-Mohn, Thomas (2007), *Study on the Implementation and Effect in Member States' Laws of Directive 2001/29/EC on the Harmonisation of Certain Aspects of Copyright and Related Rights in the Information Society*, Institute for Information Law Research Paper No. 2012-23, https://papers.ssrn.com/

Guibault, Lucie (1998), *Limitations Found Outside Copyright Law*, *in* Libby Baulch, Michael Green & Mary Wyburn (eds.), *ALAI Study Days: The Boundaries of Copyright: Its Proper Limitations and Exceptions* 42 (Australian Copyright Council)

Guibault, Lucie (2000), *Contracts and Copyright Exemptions*, *in* P. Bernt Hugenholtz (ed.), *Copyright and Electronic Commerce: Legal Aspects of Electronic Copyright Management* 125 (Kluwer Law International)

Guibault, Lucie (2002), *Copyright Limitations and Contracts: An Analysis of the Contractual Overridability of Limitations on Copyright* (Kluwer Law International)

Guibault, Lucie (2003), *Le tir manqué de la Directive européenne sur le droit d'auteur dans la société de l'information*, 15 Cahiers de Propriété Intellectuelle 537

Guibault, Lucie (2010), *Why Cherry-Picking Never Leads to Harmonisation: The Case of the Limitations on Copyright under Directive 2001/29/EC,* 1 JIPITEC 55

Hahn, Jee Young & Lee, Byoung Kyu (2016), *Brave New World: Issues and Implications of the New Fair Use Clause in the Korean Copyright Act*, 63 Journal of the Copyright Society of the USA 535

Halpern, Sheldon W. & Johnson, Phillip (2014), *Harmonising Copyright Law and Dealing with Dissonance: A Framework for Convergence of US and EU Law* (Edward Elgar)

Hansen, Gerd (2008), *Warum Urheberrecht? Die Rechtfertigung des Urheberrechts unter besonderer Berücksichtigung des Nutzerschutzes* (Nomos)

Hardy, I. Trotter (1999), *Copyright and 'New-Use' Technologies*, 23(2) Nova Law Review 659

Hargreaves, Ian & Hugenholtz, P. Bernt (2013), *Copyright Reform for Growth and Jobs: Modernising the European Copyright Framework*, 13 Lisbon Council Policy Brief 1

Hargreaves Review (2011), *Digital Opportunity: A Review of Intellectual Property and Growth*, https://assets.publishing.service.gov.uk/government/uploads/system/uploads/attachment_data/file/32563/ipreview-finalreport.pdf

Hart, H.L.A. (1958), *Positivism and the Separation of Law and Morals*, 71 Harvard Law Review 593

Hart, H.L.A. (1983), *Jhering's Heaven of Concepts and Modern Analytical Jurisprudence*, *in* H.L.A. Hart, *Essays in Jurisprudence and Philosophy* 265 (OUP)

Hart, H.L.A. (1994), *The Concept of Law* (2nd ed., OUP)

Hart, Michael & Holmes, Steve (2004), *Implementation of the Copyright Directive in the United Kingdom*, 26(6) EIPR 254

Hart, Michael (1998), *The Proposed Directive for Copyright in the Information Society: Nice Rights, Shame about the Exceptions*, 20(5) EIPR 169

Hart, Michael (2002), *The Copyright in the Information Society Directive: An Overview*, 24(2) EIPR 58

Hayek, Friedrich A. (1944), *The Road to Serfdom* (University of Chicago Press)

Hazucha, Branislav (2016), *Intellectual Property, Private Ordering and Legal Certainty*, *in* Mark Fenwick & Stefan Wrbka (eds.), *Legal Certainty in a Contemporary Context: Private and Criminal Law Perspectives* (Springer)

He, Huaiwen (2009), *Seeking a Balanced Interpretation of the Three-Step Test: An Adjusted Structure in View of Divergent Approaches*, 40(3) IIC 274

Headdon, Toby (2014), *An epilogue to Svensson: the same old new public and the worms that didn't turn*, 9(8) JIPLP 662

Heide, Thomas P., *The Berne Three-Step Test and the Proposed Copyright Directive*, 21(3) EIPR 105 (1999)

Helfer, Laurence R. (2000), *World Music on a U.S. Stage: A Berne/TRIPS and Economic Analysis of the Fairness in Music Licensing Act*, 80 Boston University Law Review 93

Hilty, Reto M. & Köklü, Kaya (2016), *Limitations and Exceptions to Copyright in the Digital Age. Four Cornerstones for a Future-Proof Legal Framework in the EU*, *in* Irini Stamatoudi (ed.), *New Developments in EU and International Copyright Law* 283 (Kluwer Law International)

Hilty, Reto M. & Lotte, Ricarda (2017), *Chapter 2: Digital and Cross-Border Teaching Activities*, *in* Reto M. Hilty & Valentina Moscon (eds.), *Modernisation of the EU Copyright Rules – Position Statement of the Max Planck Institute for Innovation and Competition* 35, Max Planck Institute for Innovation & Competition Research Paper No. 17-12, https://papers.ssrn.com/

Hilty, Reto M. & Moscon, Valentina (2017), *General Remarks*, *in* Reto M. Hilty & Valentina Moscon (eds.), *Modernisation of the EU Copyright Rules – Position Statement of the Max Planck Institute for Innovation and Competition* 13, Max Planck Institute for Innovation & Competition Research Paper No. 17-12, https://papers.ssrn.com/

Hilty, Reto M. & Moscon, Valentina (2018), *Permitted Uses in Copyright Law – Is There Need for an International Instrument?*, Max Planck Institute for Innovation and Competition Research Paper No. 18-14, https://papers.ssrn.com/

Hilty, Reto M. & Nérisson, Sylvie (2012), *Overview*, *in* Reto M. Hilty & Sylvie Nérisson (eds.), *Balancing Copyright – A Survey of National Approaches* 1 (Springer)

Hilty, Reto M. & Richter, Heiko (2017), *Chapter 1: Text and Data Mining*, *in* Reto M. Hilty & Valentina Moscon (eds.), *Modernisation of the EU Copyright Rules – Position Statement of the Max Planck Institute for Innovation and Competition* 25, Max Planck Institute for Innovation & Competition Research Paper No. 17-12, https://papers.ssrn.com/

Hilty, Reto M.; Krujatz, Sebastian; Bajon, Benjamin; Frueh, Alfred; Kur, Annette; Drexl, Josef; Geiger, Christophe & Klass, Nadine (2008), *European Commission – Green Paper: Copyright in the Knowledge Economy – Comments by the Max Planck Institute for Intellectual Property, Competition and Tax Law*, Max Planck Institute for Intellectual Property, Competition & Tax Law Research Paper Series No. 08-05, https://papers.ssrn.com/

Hilty, Reto M.; Lewinski, Silke von & Moscon, Valentina (2017), *Chapter 4: Implementation of the Marrakesh Treaty*, *in* Reto M. Hilty & Valentina Moscon (eds.), *Modernisation of the EU Copyright Rules – Position Statement of the Max Planck Institute for Innovation and Competition* 51, Max Planck Institute for Innovation & Competition Research Paper No. 17-12, https://papers.ssrn.com/

Hilty, Reto M. (2004), *Intellectual Property and the European Community's Internal Market Legislation – Copyright in the Internal Market – Harmonisation vs. Community Copyright Law*, 35(7) IIC 760

Hilty, Reto M. (2010), *Declaration on the 'Three-Step Test': Where do we go from here?*, 1(2) JIPITEC 83

Hilty, Reto M. (2012), *Reflections on a European Copyright Codification*, *in* Tatiana-Eleni Synodinou (ed.), *Codification of European Copyright Law: Challenges and Perspectives* 355 (Kluwer Law International)

Hoeren, Thomas (1997), *Urheberrecht in der Informationsgesellschaft – Überlegungen zu einem Rechtsgutachten von Gerhard Schricker et al.*, 99(12) GRUR 866

Hoeren, Thomas (2000), *Urheberrecht 2000 – Thesen für eine Reform des Urheberrechts*, 3(1) MMR 3

Hoeren, Thomas (2006), *Access Right as a Postmodern Symbol of Copyright Deconstruction?*, VI Direito da Sociedade de Informação 9

Hoeren, Thomas (2007), *Die Schranken des Urheberrechts in Deutschland*, *in* Reto M. Hilty & Christophe Geiger (eds.), *Impulse für eine europäische Harmonisierung des Urheberrechts – Urheberrecht im deutsch-französischen Dialog* 265 (Springer)

Hofmann, Franz (2018), *Die Systematisierung des Interessenausgleichs im Urheberrecht am Beispiel des Rechts der öffentlichen Wiedergabe*, 62(10) ZUM 641

Hohfeld, Wesley N. (1913), *Some Fundamental Legal Conceptions as Applied in Judicial Reasoning*, 23 Yale Law Journal 16

Hugenholtz, P. Bernt & Kretschmer, Martin (2018), *Reconstructing Rights: Project Synthesis and Recommendations*, *in* P. Bernt Hugenholtz (ed.), *Copyright Reconstructed: Rethinking Copyright's Economic Rights in a Time of Highly Dynamic Technological and Economic Change* 1 (Kluwer Law International)

Hugenholtz, P. Bernt & Okediji, Ruth L. (2008), *Conceiving an International Instrument on Limitations and Exceptions to Copyright*, Study supported by the Open Society Institute, https://papers.ssrn.com/

Hugenholtz, P. Bernt & Senftleben, Martin, *Fair Use in Europe: In Search of Flexibilities* (2011), Amsterdam Law School Research Paper n.º 2012-39 / Institute for Information Law Research Paper n.º 2012-33, https://papers.ssrn.com/

Hugenholtz, P. Bernt & Velze, Sam C. van, *Communication to a New Public? Three Reasons Why EU Copyright Law Can Do Without a 'New Public'*, 47(7) IIC 797 (2016)

Hugenholtz, P. Bernt; Eechoud, Mireille van; Gompel, Stef; Helberger, Natali (2006), *The Recasting of Copyright & Related Rights for the Knowledge Economy*, Study commissioned by the European Commission's Internal Market DG, https://papers.ssrn.com/

Hugenholtz, P. Bernt (1996), *Adapting Copyright to the Information Superhighway*, *in* P. Bernt Hugenholtz (ed.), *The Future of Copyright in a Digital Environment* 81 (Kluwer Law International)

Hugenholtz, P. Bernt (1997), *Fierce Creatures, Copyright Exemptions: Towards Extinction?*, IFLA/IMPRIMATUR Conference on Rights, Limitations and Expectations: Striking a Proper Balance, https://www.ivir.nl/

Hugenholtz, P. Bernt (2000a), *Caching and Copyright: The Right of Temporary Copying*, 11 EIPR 482

Hugenholtz, P. Bernt (2000b), *Why the Copyright Directive is Unimportant, and Possibly Invalid*, 11 EIPR 499

Hugenholtz, P. Bernt (2001), *Copyright and Freedom of Expression in Europe*, *in* Rochelle Dreyfuss, Diane Zimmerman & Harry First (eds.), *Expanding the Boundaries of Intellectual Property: Innovation Policy for the Knowledge Society* 343 (OUP)

Hugenholtz, P. Bernt (2002), *Commentary on the European Union Information Society Directive*, *in* Hugh Hansen (ed.), *International Intellectual Property Law & Policy – Volume 7* 69-1 (Juris Publishing)

Hugenholtz, P. Bernt (2005), *The Implementation of Directive 2001/29/EC in The Netherlands*, 206 RIDA 117

Hugenholtz, P. Bernt (2010), *Codes of Conduct and Copyright Enforcement in Cyberspace*, *in* Irini A. Stamatoudi (ed.), *Copyright Enforcement and the Internet* 303 (Kluwer Law International)

Hugenholtz, P. Bernt (2012a), *Harmonization or unification of EU copyright law, in* J. Axhamn (ed.), *Copyright in a borderless online environment* 189 (Kluwer Law International)

Hugenholtz, P. Bernt (2012b), *The Wittem Group's European Copyright Code*, *in* Tatiana-Eleni Synodinou (ed.), *Codification of European Copyright Law: Challenges and Perspectives* 339 (Kluwer Law International)

Hugenholtz, P. Bernt (2013a), *Copyright in Europe: Twenty Years Ago, Today and What the Future Holds*, 23(2) Fordham Intellectual Property, Media and Entertainment Law Journal 503

Hugenholtz, P. Bernt (2013b), *Is Harmonization a Good Thing? The Case of the Copyright* Acquis, *in* Ansgar Ohly & Justine Pila (eds.), *The Europeanization of Intellectual Property Law: Towards a European Legal Methodology* 57 (OUP)

Hugenholtz, P. Bernt (2013c), *Law and Technology: Fair Use in Europe*, 56(5) Communications of the ACM 26

Hugenholtz, P. Bernt (2017), *Flexible Copyright: Can the EU Author's Rights Accommodate Fair Use?*, *in* Ruth L. Okediji (ed.), *Copyright Law in an Age of Limitations and Exceptions* 275 (CUP)

Hugenholtz, P. Bernt (ed.) (2018), *Copyright Reconstructed: Rethinking Copyright's Economic Rights in a Time of Highly Dynamic Technological and Economic Change* (Kluwer Law International)

Hughes, Justin (1988), *The Philosophy of Intellectual Property*, 77 Georgetown Law Journal 287

Hughes, Justin (2017), *Fair Use and Its Politics – at Home and Abroad*, *in* Ruth L. Okediji (ed.), *Copyright Law in an Age of Limitations and Exceptions* 234 (CUP)

Husovec, Martin (2017), *Injunctions Against Intermediaries in the European Union: Accountable But Not Liable?* (CUP)

Husovec, Martin & Quintais, João Pedro (2020), *How to License Article 17? Exploring the Implementation Options for the New EU Rules on Content-Sharing Platforms*, https://papers.ssrn.com/

Izyumenko, Elena (2016), *The Freedom of Expression Contours of Copyright in the Digital Era: A European Perspective*, 19 The Journal of World Intellectual Property 115

Izzo, Umberto (2010), *Alle origini del copyright e del diritto d'autore: Tecnologia, interessi e cambiamento giuridico* (Carocci)

Jacob, Marc (2016), *Precedents and Case-Based Reasoning in the European Court of Justice: Unfinished Business* (CUP)

Jacobs, Francis G. (1994), *The Effect of Preliminary Rulings in the National Legal Order*, *in* Mads Andenas (ed.), *Article 177 References to the European Court – Policy and Practice* 29 (Butterworths)

Jacobs, Francis G. (2003), *Judicial Dialogue and the Cross-Fertilization of Legal Systems: The European Court of Justice*, 38(3) Texas International Law Journal 547

Jacques, Sabine (2019), *The Parody Exception in Copyright Law* (OUP)

Janssens, Marie-Christine (2009), *The Issue of Exceptions: Reshaping the Keys to the Gates in the Territory of Literary, Musical and Artistic Creation*, *in* Estelle Derclaye (ed.), *Research Handbook on the Future of EU Copyright* 317 (Edward Elgar)

Janssens, Marie-Christine, *Le droit moral en Belgique*, 25(1) Les Cahiers de Propriété Intellectuelle 91 (2013)

Janssens, Marie-Christine (2017), *Invitation for a 'Europeanification' of moral rights*, *in* Paul Torremans (ed.), *Research Handbook on Copyright Law* 200 (2nd ed., Edward Elgar)

Jongsma, Daniël (2019), *AG Szpunar on copyright's relation to fundamental rights: one step forward and two steps back?*, IPRinfo 1/2019, https://iprinfo.fi/

Judge, Elizabeth F. & Gervais, Daniel (2010), *Of Silos and Constellations: Comparing Notions of Originality in Copyright Law*, 27 Cardozo Arts & Entertainment Law Journal 375

Jütte, Bernd Justin & Maier, Henrike (2017), *A human right to sample – will the CJEU dance to the BGH-beat?*, 12(9) JIPLP 784

Jütte, Bernd Justin & Quintais, João Pedro (2019), *Advocate General turns down the music – sampling is not a fundamental right under EU copyright law*, https://papers.ssrn.com/

Jütte, Bernd Justin (2016), *The Beginning of a (Happy?) Relationship: Copyright and Freedom of Expression in Europe*, 38(1) EIPR 11

Jütte, Bernd Justin (2017), *Reconstructing European Copyright Law for the Digital Single Market: Between Old Paradigms and Digital Challenges* (Nomos)

Kaplow, Louis (1992), *Rules versus Standards: An Economic Analysis,* 42 Duke Law Journal 557

Karapapa, Stavroula (2012), *Private Copying* (Routledge)

Keefe, Rosanna (2000), *Theories of Vagueness* (CUP)

Kendrick, Leslie (2013), *Speech, Intent and the Chilling Effect*, 54 William & Mary Law Review 1633

Kennedy, Duncan (1976), *Form and Substance in Private Law Adjudication*, 89 Harvard Law Review 1685

Klein, Susanne (2008), *Search Engines and Copyright – An Analysis of the Belgian Copiepresse Decision in Consideration of British and German Copyright Law*, 39 IIC 480

Kleinemenke (2013a), Manuel, *Fair Use im deutschen und europäischen Urheberrecht?: eine rechtsvergleichende Untersuchung zur Flexibilisierung des urheberrechtlichen Schrankenkataloges nach dem Vorbild der US-amerikanischen Fair Use-Doktrin* (Nomos)

Kleinemenke, Manuel (2013b), *Fair Use, Dreistufentest und Schrankenkatalog: Plädoyer für ein „Kombinationsmodell' zur Flexibilisierung der urheberrechtlichen Schrankenbestimmungen*, 5(1) ZGE 103

Kleinemenke, Manuel (2014), *Google Books und Fair Use – Lehren für eine flexiblere Ausgestaltung und Anwendung urheberrechtlicher Schrankenbestimmungen (auch) im deutschen und europäischen Recht*, 63(10) GRUR Int. 892

Klimas, Tadas & Vaiciukaite, Jurate (2008), *The Law of Recitals in European Community Legislation*, 15 ILSA Journal of International and Comparative Law 1

Koelman, Kamiel J. & Helberger, Natali (2000), *Protection of Technological Measures, in* P. Bernt Hugenholtz (ed.), *Copyright and Electronic Commerce: Legal Aspects of Electronic Copyright Management* 165 (Kluwer Law International)

Koelman, Kamiel J. & Hugenholtz, P. Bernt (1999), *Online Service Provider Liability for Copyright Infringement*, WIPO Doc. OSP/LIA/1 Rev. 1, https://dare.uva.nl/

Koelman, Kamiel J. (2006), *Fixing the Three-Step Test*, 8 EIPR 407

Kohler, Josef (1907), *Urheberrecht an Schriftwerken und Verlagsrecht* (Enke)

König, Thomas & Luetgert, Brooke (2009), *Troubles with Transposition? Explaining Trends in Member-State Notification and the Delayed Transposition of EU Directives*, 39(1) British Journal of Political Science 163

Kuhlen, Rainer (2011), *Richtungsweisend oder eine nur begrenzt wahrgenommene Chance? Der Copyright-Code des Wittem-Projekts*, 2 JIPITEC 18

Kur, Annette & Ruse-Khan, Henning Grosse (2009), *Enough is Enough – The Notion of Binding Ceilings in International Intellectual Property Protection*, Max Planck Institute for Intellectual Property, Competition & Tax Law Research Paper Series No. 09-01, https://papers.ssrn.com/

Kur, Annette (2009), *Of Oceans, Islands, and Inland Water – How Much Room for Exceptions and Limitations under the Three-Step Test*, 8(3) Richmond Journal of Global Law & Business 287

Langenbucher, Katja (1998), *Argument by Analogy in European Law*, 57(3) The Cambridge Law Journal 481

Larenz, Karl (2012), *Metodologia da Ciência do Direito* (trans. José Lamego) (6th ed., Fundação Calouste Gulbenkian)

Laurent, Philippe (2007), *Brussels High Court confirms Google News' ban – Copiepresse SCRL v. Google Inc.*, 23 Computer Law & Security Review 290

Laurent, Philippe (2011), *Copiepresse SCRL & alii v. Google Inc. – In its decision of 5 May 2011, the Brussels Court of Appeal confirms the prohibitory injunction order banning Google News and Google's 'in cache' function*, 27 Computer Law & Security Review 542

Leaffer, Marshall (2001), *The Uncertain Future of Fair Use in a Global Information Marketplace*, 62(2) Ohio State Law Journal 849

Lee, Edward (2008), *Warming Up to User-Generated Content*, 5 University of Illinois Law Review 1459

Lee, Edward (2010), *Technological Fair Use,* 83 Southern California Law Review 797

Lehmann, Michael (2003), *The EC Directive on the Harmonisation of Certain Aspects of Copyright and Related Rights in the Information Society – A Short Comment*, 34(5) IIC 521Leistner, Matthias & Metzger, Axel (2017), *The EU Copyright Package: A Way Out of the Dilemma in Two Stages*, 48(4) IIC 381

Leistner, Matthias (2009), *Copyright Law in the EC: Status Quo, Recent Case Law and Policy Perspectives*, 46(3) Common Market Law Review 847

Leistner, Matthias (2011), *The German Federal Supreme Court's Judgment on Google's Image Search – A Topical Example of the 'Limitations' of the European Approach to Exceptions and Limitations*, 42 IIC 417

Leistner, Matthias (2012), *Common Principles of Secondary Liability?*, in Ansgar Ohly (ed.), *Common Principles of European Intellectual Property Law* 117 (Mohr Siebeck)

Leistner, Matthias (2014a), *Europe's Copyright Law Decade: Recent Case Law of the European Court of Justice and Policy Perspectives*, 51(2) Common Market Law Review 559

Leistner, Matthias (2014b), *Die Methodik des EuGH und die Garantenfunktion der nationalen Gerichte bei der Fortentwicklung des europäischen Urheberrechts*, *in* Wolfgang Büscher, Willi Erdmann, Maximilian Haedicke, Helmut Köhler & Michael Loschelder (eds.), *Festschrift für Joachim Bornkamm zum 65. Geburtstag* 859 (Beck)

Leistner, Matthias (2015a), *Copyright at the interface between EU law and national law: definition of 'work' and 'right of communication to the public'*, 10(8) JIPLP 626

Leistner, Matthias (2015b), *Nationales Recht unter dem Einfluss der EuGH Rechtsprechung*, *in* Thomas Dreier & Reto M. Hilty (eds.), *Vom Magnettonband zu Social Media – Festschrift 50 Jahre Urheberrechtsgezets (UrhG)* 251 (Beck)

Leistner, Matthias (2017a), *Closing the book on the hyperlinks: brief outline of the CJEU's case law and proposal for European legislative reform*, 39(6) EIPR 327

Leistner, Matthias (2017b), *Is the CJEU outperforming the Commission?*, https://papers.ssrn.com/

Leitão, Luís Menezes (2018), *Direito de Autor* (2nd ed., Almedina)

Lemley (1996-1997), Mark, *Dealing with Overlapping Copyrights on the Internet*, 22 University of Dayton Law Review 547

Lenaerts, Koen (1994), *Form and Substance of the Preliminary Ruling Procedure*, *in* Deirdre Curtin & Ton Heukels (eds.), *Institutional Dynamics of European Integration: Essays in Honour of Henry G. Schermers* 355, Vol. II (Martinus Nijhoff)

Lessig, Lawrence (2004), *Free Culture: How Big Media Uses Technology and the Law to Lock Down Culture and Control Creativity* (Penguin)

Lessig, Lawrence (2008), *Remix: Making Art and Commerce Thrive in the Hybrid Economy* (Bloomsbury)

Leval, Pierre (1990), *Toward a Fair Use Standard,* 103 Harvard Law Review 1105

Lewinski, Silke von (1998), *A Successful Step towards Copyright and Related Rights in the Information Age: The New E.C. Proposal for a Harmonisation Directive*, 20(4) EIPR 135

Lewinski, Silke von (2005), *Negotiation Methods and Role of Lobby Groups*, *in* ALAI, *Regards sur les sources du droit d'auteur – Congrès ALAI, 18-21 septembre 2005* 154

Lewinski, Silke von (2008), *International Copyright Law and Policy* (OUP)

Lewinski, Silke von (2015), *The Future of EU Copyright Legislation – Certain Issues*, Presentation to the European Parliament's Working Group on Intellectual Property Rights and Copyright Reform, 23 June 2015, http://www.europarl.europa.eu/

Lewinski, Silke von (2018), *Les exceptions au droit d'auteur*, *in* Alexandra Bensamoun (ed.), *La Réforme du Droit d'Auteur dans la Société de l'Information* 127 (mare & martin)

LIBER Europe (2016), *Limitations and Exceptions in EU Copyright Law for Libraries, Educational and Research Establishments: A Basic Guide*, https://libereurope.eu/

Lima, Fernando Andrade Pires de & Varela, João de Matos Antunes (1987), *Código Civil Anotado*, Vol. III (2nd ed., Coimbra Editora)

Litman, Jessica (1989), *Copyright Legislation and Technological Change*, 68 Oregon Law Review 275

Litman, Jessica (2001), *Digital Copyright* (Prometheus Books)

Liu, Joseph P. (2004), *Regulatory Copyright*, 83(1) North Carolina Law Review 87

Liu, Joseph P. (2008), *Two-Factor Fair Use?*, 31(4) Columbia Journal of Law & the Arts 571

Loewenheim, Ulrich (1995), *Intellectual Property Before the European Court of Justice*, 26(6) IIC 829

Loewenheim, Ulrich (2010), *Handbuch des Urheberrechts* (2nd ed., Beck)

Lohmann, Fred von (2008), *Fair Use as Innovation Policy*, 23(2) Berkeley Technology Law Journal 829

Loon, Ng-Loy Wee (2009), *Exploring Flexibilities within the Global IP Standards*, 13(2) IPQ 162

Lucas-Schloetter, Agnès (2012), *The Acquis Communautaire in the Area of Copyright and Related Rights: Economic Rights*, *in* Tatiana-Eleni Synodinou (ed.), *Codification of European Copyright Law: Challenges and Perspectives* 115 (Kluwer Law International)

Lucas-Schloetter, Agnès (2014), *Is There a Concept of European Copyright Law? History, Evolution, Policies and Politics and the Acquis Communautaire*, *in* Irini Stamatoudi & Paul Torremans (eds.), *EU Copyright Law: A Commentary* 7 (Edward Elgar)

Lucas, André & Ginsburg, Jane C. (2016), *Copyright, Freedom of Expression and Free Access to Information (Comparative Study of American and European Law*), 249 RIDA 5

Lucas, André & Sirinelli, Pierre (2006), *Chroniques – Droit d'auteur et droits voisins*, 20 Propriétés Intellectuelles 297

Lucas, André; Lucas, Henri-Jacques; Lucas-Schloetter, Agnès & Bernault, Carine (2017), *Traité de la propriété littéraire et artistique* (5th ed., LexisNexis)

Lucas, André (1995), *Droit d'auteur et multimédia*, *in* AA.VV., *Propriétés Intellectuelles: Mélanges en l'honneur de André Françon* 325 (Dalloz)

Lucas, André (1998), *Droit d'auteur et numérique* (Litec)

Lucas, André (2001), *Le 'triple test' de l'article 13 de l'Accord ADPIC à la lumière du rapport du Groupe spécial de l'OMC: Etats-Unis – Article 110 5) de la loi sur le droit d'auteur*, *in* Peter Ganea, Christopher Heath & Gerhard Schricker (eds.), *Urheberrecht – Heute – Morgen: Festschrift für Adolf Dietz zum 65. Gerburtstag* 381 (Beck)

Lucas, André (2010), *For a Reasonable Interpretation of the Three-Step Test*, 32(6) EIPR 277

Lucas, André (2012), *European Copyright Codification*, *in* Tatiana-Eleni Synodinou (ed.), *Codification of European Copyright Law: Challenges and Perspectives* 373 (Kluwer Law International)

Lucas, André (2018), *Le droit d'auteur, un droit fundamental comme un autre?*, *in* Alexandra Bensamoun (ed.), *La Réforme du Droit d'Auteur dans la Société de l'Information* 31 (mare & martin)

MacCormick, Neil (2005), *Rhetoric and the Rule of Law* (OUP)

Machado, J. Baptista (1989), *Introdução ao Direito e ao Discurso Legitimador* (Almedina)

Madison, Michael J. (2004), *A Pattern-Oriented Approach to Fair Use*, 45 William & Mary Law Review 1525

Maduro, Miguel Poiares (2007), *Interpreting European Law: Judicial Adjudication in a Context of Constitutional Pluralism*, 1(2) European Journal of Legal Studies 137

Malenovský, Jiří (2012), *La contribution de la Cour de justice à l'harmonisation du droit d'auteur dans l'Union européenne*, 13(3) ERA Forum 411

Mancini, Federico (1989), *The Making of a Constitution for Europe*, 26(4) Common Market Law Review 595
Margoni, Thomas (2016), *The Harmonisation of EU Copyright Law: The Originality Standard*, *in* Mark Perry (ed.), *Global Governance of Intellectual Property in the 21st Century* 85 (Springer)
Margoni, Thomas (2018), *Artificial Intelligence, Machine Learning and EU Copyright Law: Who Owns AI?*, CREATe Working Paper No. 2018/12, https://papers.ssrn.com/
Marmor, Andrei (2014), *The Language of Law* (OUP)
Martin-Prat, Maria (2014), *The Future of Copyright in Europe*, 38 Columbia Journal of Law & the Arts 29
Martins, Patrícia Fragoso (2016), *Rethinking Access by Private Parties to the Court of Justice of the European Union: Judicial Review of EU Acts before and after the Lisbon Treaty* (UCE)
Maxeiner, James R. (2007), *Legal Certainty: A European Alternative to American Legal Indeterminacy?*, 15(2) Tulane Journal of International & Comparative Law 541
Maxwell, Winston & Massaloux, Julie (2006), *French Copyright Law Reform: French Supreme Court Upholds Legality of DVD Anti-Copy Measures*, 5 Entertainment Law Review 145
Mazziotti, Giuseppe (2008), *EU Digital Copyright Law and the End-User* (Springer)
Mazzone, Jason (2009), *Administering Fair Use*, 51 William & Mary Law Review 395
Mello, Alberto de Sá e (2019), *Manual de Direito de Autor e Direitos Conexos* (3rd ed., Almedina)
Merges, Robert P. (1994), *Intellectual Property Rights and Bargaining Breakdown: The Case of Blocking Patents*, 62 Tennessee Law Review 75
Metzger, Axel (2005), *Europäisches Urheberrecht ohne Droit moral? – Status quo und Perspektiven einer Harmonisierung des Urheberpersönlichkeitsrechts*, *in* Ansgar Ohly, Theo Bodewig, Thomas Dreier, Horst-Peter Götting, Maximilian Haedicke & Michael Lehmann (eds.), *Perspektiven des Geistigen Eigentums und Wettbewerbsrechts, Festschrift für Gerhard Schricker* 455 (Beck)
Metzger, Axel (2010), *Urheberrechtsschranken in der Wissensgesellschaft: „Fair Use' oder enge Einzeltatbestände*, in Matthias Leistner (ed.), *Europäische Perspektiven des Geistigen Eigentums* 101 (Mohr Siebeck)
Mezei, Péter (2018), *Copyright Exhaustion: Law and Policy in the United States and the European Union* (CUP)

Mimler, Marc D. (2017), *'Metall auf Metall' – the German Federal Constitutional Court discusses the permissibility of sampling music tracks*, 7(1) QMJIP 119

Montagnani, Maria Lillà & Aime, Giorgio (2017), *Il text and data mining e il diritto d'autore*, 26 Annali italiani del diritto d'autore, della cultura e dello spettacolo 376

Montagnani, Maria Lillà & Trapova, Alina (2019), *New Obligations for Internet Intermediaries in the Digital Single Market – Safe Harbours in Turmoil?*, 22(7) Journal of Internet Law 3

Müller, Friedrich (1996), *Discours de la méthode juridique* (Presses Universitaires de France)

Murray, Andrew (2016), *Information Technology Law: The Law and Society* (OUP)

Mylly, Tuomas (2015), *The Constitutionalization of the European Legal Order: Impact of Human Rights on Intellectual Property In The EU*, in Christophe Geiger (ed.), *Research Handbook on Human Rights and Intellectual Property* 103 (Edward Elgar)

Netanel, Neil W. (2010), *Copyright's Paradox* (OUP)

Netanel, Neil W. (2011), *Making Sense of Fair Use*, 15 Lewis & Clark Law Review 715

Newby, Tyler G. (1999), *What's Fair Here is not Fair Everywhere: Does the American Fair Use Doctrine Violate International Copyright Law?*, 51(6) Stanford Law Review 1633

Ngombe, Laurier Yon (2007), *Technical measures of protection versus copy for private use: Is the French legal saga over?*, 29(2) EIPR 61

Nimmer, David (2003), *'Fairest of them All' and Other Fairy Tales of Fair Use*, 66 Law and Contemporary Problems 263

Nimmer, David (2006), *A Modest Proposal to Streamline Fair Use Determinations*, 24 Cardozo Arts & Entertainment Law Journal 11

Nimmer, Melville (1968), *Project: New Technology and the Law of Copyright: Reprography and Computers*, 15 UCLA Law Review 931

Noll, Rob van der; Gompel, Stef van; Guibault, Lucie; Weda, Jarst; Poort, Joost; Akker, Ilan & Breemen, Kelly (2012), *Flexible Copyright: The Law and Economics of Introducing an Open Norm in the Netherlands*, SEO-report nr. 2012-60, http://www.ivir.nl/

Nordemann, Jan Bernd & Conrad, Albrecht (2010), *Internationale Vereinigung für den Schutz des Geistigen Eigentums (AIPPI) – Berichte der Deutschen Landesgruppe für die Sitzung des Geschäftsführenden Ausschusses der AIPPI vom 3. bis 6. Oktober 2010 in Paris – Ausnahmen vom Urheberrechtsschutz und erlaubte Benutzungsformen urheberrechtlich geschützter Werke in den Branchen der Hochtechnologie und der Digitaltechnologie (Q216)*, 59(11) GRUR Int. 953

Nordemann, Jan Bernd (2018), *The German Bundesgerichtshof applies the latest CJEU case law on liability for linking to search engines*, Kluwer Copyright Blog, http://copyrightblog.kluweriplaw.com/

Ohly, Ansgar (2009), *Economic Rights, in* Estelle Derclaye (ed.), *Research Handbook on the Future of EU Copyright* 212 (Edward Elgar)

Ohly, Ansgar (2013a), *European Fundamental Rights and Intellectual Property, in* Ansgar Ohly & Justine Pila (eds.), *The Europeanization of Intellectual Property Law: Towards a European Legal Methodology* 145 (OUP)

Ohly, Ansgar (2013b), *Concluding Remarks: Postmodernism and Beyond, in* Ansgar Ohly & Justine Pila (eds.), *The Europeanisation of Intellectual Property Law: Towards a European Legal Methodology* 255 (OUP)

Ohly, Ansgar (2014), *Urheberrecht in der digitalen Welt – Brauchen wir neue Regelungen zum Urheberrecht und dessen Durchsetzung?* (Beck)

Ohly, Ansgar (2018), *A Fairness-Based Approach to Economic Rights, in* P. Bernt Hugenholtz (ed.), *Copyright Reconstructed: Rethinking Copyright's Economic Rights in a Time of Highly Dynamic Technological and Economic Change* 83 (Kluwer Law International)

Okediji, Ruth L. (2000), *Toward an International Fair Use Doctrine*, 39 Columbia Journal of Transnational Law 75

Okpaluba, Johnson (2012), *The Phonogram: A Tale of Vested Interests and Seized Opportunities, in* Brad Sherman & Leanne Wiseman (eds.), *Copyright and the Challenge of the New* 77 (Kluwer Law International)

Osken, Marc (2014), *Die schlichte Einwilligung im Urheberrecht: Eine Untersuchung unter Berücksichtigung der Vorschaubilder-Rechtsprechung des BGH* (Peter Lang)

Ott, Stephan (2009), *Bildersuchmaschinen und Urheberrecht: Sind Thumbnails unerlässlich, sozial nützlich, aber rechtswidrig?*, 25(5) ZUM 345

Oxford English Dictionary (2010) (3rd ed., OUP)

Parchomovsky, Gideon & Stein, Alex (2015), *Catalogs*, 115 Columbia Law Review 165

Pais, Sofia Oliveira (2011), *Entre Inovação e Concorrência – Em defesa de um modelo Europeu* (UCE)

Patry, William (2011), *How to Fix Copyright* (OUP)

Patry, William (2017a), *Patry on Fair Use* (Thomson Reuters)

Patry, William (2017b), *Fair Use is Good for Creativity and Innovation*, PIJIP Research Paper Series, Paper no. 2017-01

Patterson, Lyman Ray (1968), *Copyright in Historical Perspective* (Vanderbilt University Press)

Patterson, Lyman Ray (1992), *Understanding Fair Use*, 55 Law & Contemporary Problems 249

Paulus, Andreas (2016), *Europäischer Integrationsbedarf und nationale Regelungskompetenz: Referat auf der Konferenz »Die Zukunft des Urheberrechts – 50 Jahre Urheberrecht in Deutschland« am 2. Dezember 2015 in Berlin*, 60(6) ZUM 513

Paunio, Elina (2013), *Legal Certainty in Multilingual EU Law: Language, Discourse and Reasoning at the European Court of Justice* (Routledge)

Peczenik, Aleksander (2008), *On Law and Reason* (Springer)

Peguera, Miquel (2012), *Copyright Issues Regarding Google Images and Google Cache*, *in* Aurelio Lopez Tarruella (ed.), *Google and the Law: Empirical Approaches to Legal Aspects of Knowledge-Economy Business Models* 169 (Springer)

Peifer, Karl-Nikolaus (2014), *Selbstbestimmung im digitalen Netz – Privatkopie, Flatrate und Fair Use*, 58(2) ZUM 86

Peirce, Charles Sanders (1902), *Vague*, *in* James M. Baldwin (ed.), *Dictionary of Philosophy and Psychology* 748, Vol. II (Macmillan)

Pereira, Alexandre Dias (2001), *Informática, direito de autor e propriedade tecnodigital*, 55 Studia Iuridica (Coimbra Editora)

Pereira, Alexandre Dias (2005), *Direito de Autor, Liberdade Electrónica e Compensação Equitativa*, 81 Boletim da Faculdade de Direito – Universidade de Coimbra 441

Pereira, Alexandre Dias (2008a), *Direitos de Autor e Liberdade de Informação* (Almedina)

Pereira, Alexandre Dias (2008b), *Fair use e direitos de autor (entre a regra e a excepção)*, *in* António Menezes Cordeiro, Pedro Pais de Vasconcelos & Paula Costa e Silva (eds.), *Estudos em Honra do Professor Doutor José de Oliveira Ascensão* 853, Vol. I (Almedina)

Pereira, Alexandre Dias (2014), *Arquivos e bibliotecas digitais: os direitos autorais e a sentença Google*, 1 RDI 163

Pereira, Alexandre Dias (2015), *A digitalização de obras e sua colocação à disposição do público em terminais de bibliotecas universitárias: o acórdão Eugen Ulmer do Tribunal de Justiça da União Europeia*, 2 RDI 153

Pereira, Alexandre Dias (2017), *Levies in EU copyright law: An overview of the CJEU's judgments on the fair compensation of private copying and reprography*, 12(7) JIPLP 591

Perju, Vlad (2009), *Reason and Authority in the European Court of Justice*, 49 Virginia Journal of International Law 307

Perry, Mark & Margoni, Thomas (2010), *From Music Tracks to Google Maps: Who Owns Computer-generated Works*?, 26 Computer Law and Security Review 621

Pessach, Guy (2010), *The New Israeli Copyright Act – A Case-Study in Reverse Comparative Law*, 41(2) IIC 187

Peukert, Alexander (2015), *The Fundamental Right to (Intellectual) Property and the Discretion of the Legislature*, *in* Christophe Geiger (ed.), *Research Handbook on Human Rights and Intellectual Property* 132 (Edward Elgar)

Peukert, Alexander (2016), *An EU Related Right for Press Publishers Concerning Digital Uses. A Legal Analysis*, Research Paper of the Faculty of Law, Goethe University Frankfurt am Main No. 22/2016, https://papers.ssrn.com/

Phillips, Jeremy (2009), *Authorship, ownership, wikiship: copyright in the 21st century*, *in* Estelle Derclaye (ed.), *Research Handbook on the Future of EU Copyright* 193 (Edward Elgar)

Pihlajarinne, Taina (2012), *Setting the Limits for the Implied License in Copyright and Linking Discourse – The European Perspective*, 43(6) IIC 700

Pihlajarinne, Taina (2017), *Should We Bury the Concept of Reproduction – Towards Principle-Based Assessment in Copyright Law?*, 48(8) IIC 953

Pila, Justine & Torremans, Paul (2016), *European Intellectual Property Law* (OUP)

Pila, Justine (2013), *A Constitutionalized Doctrine of Precedent and the Marleasing Principle as Bases for a European Legal Methodology*, *in* Ansgar Ohly & Justine Pila (eds.), *The Europeanisation of Intellectual Property Law: Towards a European Legal Methodology* 227 (OUP)

Piotraut, Jean-Luc (2012), *Limitations and Exceptions: Towards a European 'Fair Use' Doctrine?*, *in* Ansgar Ohly (ed.), *Common Principles of European Intellectual Property Law* 147 (Mohr Siebeck)

Poeppel, Jan (2005), *Die Neuordnung der urheberrechtlichen Schranken im digitalen Umfeld* (V&R unipress)

Pollaud-Dulian, Frédéric (1989), *Le droit de destination. Le sort des exemplaires en droit d'auteur* (LGDJ)

Pollaud-Dulian, Frédéric (2013), *The dragon and the white whale: Three steps test and fair use*, *in* Toshiko Takenaka (ed.), *Intellectual Property in Common Law and Civil Law* 158 (Edward Elgar)

Poort, Joost & Quintais, João Pedro (2013), *The Levy Runs Dry: A Legal and Economic Analysis of EU Private Copying Levies*, 4(3) JIPITEC 205

Poscher, Ralf (2012), *Ambiguity and Vagueness in Legal Interpretation*, *in* Lawrence Solan & Peter Tiersma (eds.), *Oxford Handbook on Language and Law* 128 (OUP)

Posner, Eric A. (1997), *Standards, Rules, and Social Norms,* 21 Harvard Journal of Law and Public Policy 101

Posner, Richard (2006), *Reasoning by Analogy*, 91 Cornell Law Review 761

Prechal, Sacha (2005), *Directives in EC Law* (2nd ed., OUP)

Quintais, João Pedro & Rendas, Tito (2018), *EU copyright law and the cloud: VCAST and the intersection of private copying and communication to the public*, 13(9) JIPLP 711

Quintais, João Pedro (2015), *Private Copying and Downloading from Unlawful Sources*, 46(1) IIC 66

Quintais, João Pedro (2017a), *Copyright in the Age of Online Access: Alternative Compensation Systems in EU Law* (Kluwer Law International)

Quintais, João Pedro (2017b), *Rethinking Normal Exploitation: Enabling Online Limitations in EU Copyright Law*, 41(6) AMI – tijdschrift voor auteurs-, media- en informatierecht 197

Quintais, João Pedro (2018), *Untangling the Hyperlinking Web: In Search of the Online Right of Communication to the Public*, 21 The Journal of World Intellectual Property 385

Radbruch, Gustav (1950), *Legal Philosophy*, 4 Twentieth Century Legal Philosophy Series 43 (trans. Kurt Wilk)

Rahmatian, Andreas (2011), *Copyright and Creativity: The Making of Property Rights in Creative Works* (Edward Elgar)

Raitio, Juha (2003), *The Principle of Legal Certainty in EC Law* (Springer)

Rajan, Mira T. Sundara (2011), *Moral Rights: Principles, Practice and New Technology* (OUP)

Ramalho, Ana Bárbara (2014), *Conceptualising the European Union's Competence in Copyright – What Can the EU Do?*, 45(2) IIC 178

Ramalho, Ana Bárbara (2016a), *The Competence of the European Union in Copyright Lawmaking: A Normative Perspective of EU Powers for Copyright Harmonisation* (Springer)

Ramalho, Ana Bárbara (2016b), *The Opinion of AG Wathelet in GS Media: what's in a 'precedent'?*, Kluwer Copyright Blog, http://copyrightblog.kluweriplaw.com/

Ramalho, Ana Bárbara (2017a), *Will Robots Rule the (Artistic) World? A Proposed Model for the Legal Status of Creations by Artificial Intelligence Systems*, 21(1) Journal of Internet Law 12

Ramalho, Ana Bárbara (2017b), *Beyond the Cover Story – An Enquiry into the EU Competence to Introduce a Right for Publishers*, 48(1) IIC 71

Raz, Joseph (2009), *The Authority of Law: Essays on Law and Morality* (OUP)

Rebello, Luiz Francisco (1994), *Introdução ao Direito de Autor* (SPA/D. Quixote)

Rebello, Luiz Francisco (2005), *Implementation of Directive 2001/29/EC in Portuguese Law*, 206 RIDA 148

Reinbothe, Jörg, & Lewinski, Silke von (2002), *The WIPO Treaties 1996* (LexisNexis)

Reinbothe, Jörg (1998), *Provisions on exceptions in the European Community Proposed Directive on copyright and related rights in the information society*, *in* Libby Baulch, Michael Green & Mary Wyburn (eds.), *ALAI Study Days: The Boundaries of Copyright: Its Proper Limitations and Exceptions* 63 (Australian Copyright Council)

Reinbothe, Jörg, *Die Umsetzung der EU-Urheberrechtsrichtlinie in deutsches Recht*, 46(1) ZUM 43 (2002)

Reinbothe, Jörg (2016), *Private Copy Levies*, *in* Irini Stamatoudi (ed.), *New Developments in EU and International Copyright Law* 299 (Kluwer Law International)

Renda, Andrea; Simonelli, Felice; Mazziotti, Giuseppe; Bolognini, Alberto & Luchetta, Giacomo (2015), *The Implementation, Application and Effects of the EU Directive on Copyright in the Information Society*, CEPS Special Report, No. 120/November 2015, https://www.ceps.eu/

Rendas, Tito (2015), *Lex Specialis(sima): Videogames and Technological Protection Measures in EU Copyright Law*, 37(1) EIPR 39

Rendas, Tito (2017a), *How Playboy Photos Compromised EU Copyright Law: The GS Media Judgment*, 20(11) Journal of Internet Law 11

Rendas, Tito (2017b), *Form and Substance in the Value Gap Proposal*, *in* Julia Reda (ed.), *Better Regulation for Copyright: Academics Meet Policymakers* 39 (The Greens/EFA)

Rendas, Tito (2018), *Copyright, Technology and the CJEU: An empirical study*, 49(2) IIC 153

Ribeiro, Gonçalo de Almeida (2015), *Judicial Activism and Fidelity to Law*, *in* Luís Pereira Coutinho, Massimo La Torre & Steven D. Smith (eds.), *Judicial Activism: An Interdisciplinary Approach to the American and European Experiences* 31 (Springer)

Ribeiro, Gonçalo de Almeida (2017), *The Effects of Fundamental Rights in Private Disputes*, *in* Hugh Collins (ed.), *European Contract Law and the Charter of Fundamental Rights* 219 (Intersentia)

Ribeiro, Gonçalo de Almeida (2019), *The Decline of Private Law: A Philosophical History of Liberal Legalism* (Hart)

Ricketson, Sam & Ginsburg, Jane C. (2006), *International Copyright and Neighbouring Rights: The Berne Convention and Beyond* (OUP)

Ricketson, Sam (1987), *The Berne Convention for the Protection of Literary and Artistic Works: 1886-1986* (Centre for Commercial Law Studies – Queen Mary)

Ricketson, Sam (1992), *New Wine Into Old Bottles: Technological Change and Intellectual Property Rights*, 10(1) Prometheus: Critical Studies in Innovation 53

Ricketson, Sam (1998), *International Conventions and Treaties*, *in* Libby Baulch, Michael Green & Mary Wyburn (eds.), *ALAI Study Days: The Boundaries of Copyright: Its Proper Limitations and Exceptions* 3 (Australian Copyright Council)

Ricketson, Sam (2003), *WIPO Study on Limitations and Exceptions of Copyright and Related Rights in the Digital Environment*, SCCR/9/7, https://www.wipo.int/

Ricolfi, Marco (2016), *Towards an EU Copyright Code? A Conceptual Framework*, *in* Irini Stamatoudi (ed.), *New Developments in EU and International Copyright Law* 447 (Kluwer Law International)

Riis, Thomas & Schovsbo, Jens (2007), *Users' Rights: Reconstructing Copyright Policy on Utilitarian Grounds*, 29(1) EIPR 1

Rocha, Manuel Lopes; Carreiro, Henrique; Marques, Ana Margarida & Bernardo, André Lencastre (2005), *Guia da Lei do Direito de Autor na Sociedade de Informação (Lei 50/2004, de 24 de Agosto) Anotada e Comentada* (CentroAtlantico.pt)

Rocha, Maria Victória (1996), *Multimédia e Direito de Autor: alguns problemas*, Actas de Derecho Industrial y Derecho de Autor 175

Rocha, Maria Victória (2016), *Breves considerações sobre o future do Direito de Autor na Era Digital*, *in* AA.VV., *Direito de autor: Que futuro na era digital?* 79 (Guerra & Paz)

Roder, Verena (2016), *Die Methodik des EuGH im Urheberrecht: Die autonome Auslegung des Gerichtshofs der Europäischen Union im Spannungsverhältnis zum nationalen Recht* (Mohr Siebeck)

Rodríguez-Cano, Rodrigo Bercovitz (2017), *Manual de Propiedad Intelectual* (7th ed., Tirant Lo Blanch)

Rognstad, Ole-Andreas (2018), *Property Aspects of Intellectual Property* (CUP)

Rosas, Allan (2007), *The European Court of Justice in Context: Forms and Patterns of Judicial Dialogue*, 1(2) European Journal of Legal Studies 121

Rosati, Eleonora (2010), *The Wittem Group and the European Copyright Code*, 5(12) JIPLP 862

Rosati, Eleonora (2013a), *Originality in EU Copyright: Full Harmonisation through Case Law* (Edward Elgar)

Rosati, Eleonora (2013b), *Towards an EU-Wide Copyright? (Judicial) Pride and (Legislative) Prejudice*, 17(1) IPQ 47

Rosati, Eleonora (2014a), *Copyright in the EU: in search of (in)flexibilities*, 9(7) JIPLP 585

Rosati, Eleonora (2014b), *Copyright exceptions and user rights in Case C-117/13 Ulmer: A couple of observations*, IPKat Blog, http://ipkitten.blogspot.pt/

Rosati, Eleonora (2015), *Just a laughing matter? Why the decision in Deckmyn is broader than parody*, 52(2) Common Market Law Review 511

Rosati, Eleonora (2017a), *GS Media and its implications for the construction of the right of communication to the public within EU copyright architecture*, 54(4) Common Market Law Review 1221

Rosati, Eleonora (2017b), *The proposed press publishers' right: an actual solution?*, *in* Julia Reda (ed.), *Better Regulation for Copyright: Academics Meet Policymakers* 5 (The Greens/EFA)

Rosati, Eleonora (2019), *Copyright and the Court of Justice of the European Union* (OUP)

Rose, Mark (1993), *Authors and Owners: The Invention of Copyright* (Harvard University Press)

Rose, Mark (2005), *Technology and Copyright in 1735: The Engraver's Act*, 21(1) The Information Society 63

Rösler, Hannes (2012), *Interpretation of EU Law*, *in* J. Basedow, K. J. Hopt & R. Zimmermann (eds.), *The Max Planck Encyclopedia of European Private Law* 979 (OUP)

Rostow, Eugene (1958), *Supreme Court and the People's Will*, 33 Notre Dame Law Review 573

Ruse-Khan, Henning Grosse (2016), *The Protection of Intellectual Property in International Law* (OUP)

Russell, Bertrand (1923), *Vagueness*, 1(2) Australasian Journal of Psychology & Philosophy 84

Sag, Matthew (2005), *God in the Machine: A New Structural Analysis of Copyright's Fair Use Doctrine*, 11(2) Michigan Telecommunications and Technology Law Review 381

Sag, Matthew (2009), *Copyright and Copy-Reliant Technology,* 103 Northwestern University Law Review 1607

Sag, Matthew (2011), *The Pre-History of Fair Use,* 76 Brooklyn Law Review 1371

Sag, Matthew (2012), *Predicting Fair Use,* 73(1) Ohio State Law Journal 47

Sag, Matthew (2013), *The Imaginary Conflict Between Fair Use and International Copyright Law*, https://matthewsag.com/

Samuelson, Pamela (1985), *Allocating Ownership Rights in Computer-Generated Works*, 47 University of Pittsburgh Law Review 1185

Samuelson, Pamela (1997), *The U.S. Digital Agenda at WIPO*, 37 Virginia Journal of International Law 369

Samuelson, Pamela (1998), *Digitisation: Comments for Panel Session*, *in* Libby Baulch, Michael Green & Mary Wyburn (eds.), *ALAI Study Days: The Boundaries of Copyright: Its Proper Limitations and Exceptions* 76 (Australian Copyright Council)

Samuelson, Pamela (2009), *Unbundling Fair Uses,* 77 Fordham Law Review 2537

Samuelson, Pamela (2010), *The Copyright Principles Project: Directions for Reform*, 25 Berkeley Technology Law Journal 1175

Samuelson, Pamela (2012), *A Square Peg in a Round Hole? Copyright Protection for Computer Programs*, *in* Brad Sherman & Leanne Wiseman (eds.), *Copyright and the Challenge of the New* 251 (Kluwer Law International)

Samuelson, Pamela (2015), *Possible Futures of Fair Use*, 90 Washington Law Review 815

Samuelson, Pamela (2017), *Justifications for Copyright Limitations & Exceptions*, *in* Ruth L. Okediji (ed.), *Copyright Law in an Age of Limitations and Exceptions* 12 (CUP)

Sánchez, S. Iglesias (2012), *The Court and the Charter: The Impact of the Entry into Force of the Lisbon Treaty on the ECJ's Approach to Fundamental Rights*, 49(5) Common Market Law Review 1565

Sanctis, Vittorio M. de (2010), *Manuale del nuovo diritto d'autore* (Scientifica)

Savola, Pekka (2014), *Blocking Injunctions and Website Operators' Liability for Copyright Infringement for User-Generated Links*, 36(5) EIPR 279

Savola, Pekka (2017), *EU Copyright Liability for Internet Linking*, 8(2) JIPITEC 139

Schack, Haimo (2016), *Urheberrechtliche Schranken für Bildung und Wissenschaft*, 60(3) ZUM 266

Schauer, Frederick (1978), *Fear, Risk and the First Amendment: Unraveling the 'Chilling Effect'*, 58 Boston University Law Review 685

Schauer, Frederick (1993), *Playing by the Rules: A Philosophical Examination of Rule-Based Decision-Making in Law and in Life* (Clarendon Press)

Schauer, Frederick (2003), *The Convergence of Rules and Standards*, 2003 New Zealand Law Review 303

Schauer, Frederick (2004-2005), *The Tyranny of Choice and the Rulification of Standards*, 14 Journal of Contemporary Legal Issues 803

Schauer, Frederick (2009), *Thinking Like a Lawyer: A New Introduction to Legal Reasoning* (Harvard University Press)

Schauer, Frederick (2012), *Balancing, Subsumption, and the Constraining Role of Legal Text, in* Matthias Klatt (ed.), *Institutionalized Reason: The Jurisprudence of Robert Alexy* 307 (OUP)

Schlag, Pierre (1985), *Rules and Standards*, 33 UCLA Law Review 379

Schovsbo, Jens (2015), *Constitutional Foundations and Constitutionalisation of IP Law – A Tale of Different Stories?*, 7(4) ZGE 383

Schricker, Gerhard (1989), *Harmonisation of Copyright in the European Economic Community*, 20(4) IIC 466

Schricker, Gerhard (1995), *Farewell to the 'level of creativity' (Schöpfungshöhe) in German copyright law?*, 26(1) IIC 41

Schricker, Gerhard (1997), *Urheberrecht auf dem Weg zur Informationsgesellschaft* (Nomos)

Schumann, Heribert (1969), *Fair Use im amerikanischen Urheberrecht*, 18(4) GRUR Int. 125

Schütze, Robert (2006), *Supremacy without Pre-emption? The Very Slowly Emergent Doctrine of Community Pre-emption*, 43(4) Common Market Law Review 1023

Schütze, Robert (2015), *European Constitutional Law* (2nd ed., CUP)

Senftleben, Martin (2004), *Copyright, Limitations and the Three-Step Test: An Analysis of the Three-Step Test in International and EC Copyright Law* (Kluwer Law International)

Senftleben, Martin (2006), *Towards a Horizontal Standard for Limiting Intellectual Property Rights? WTO Panel Reports Shed Light on the Three-Step Test in Copyright Law and Related Tests in Patent and Trademark Law*, 37(4) IIC 407

Senftleben, Martin (2009), *Fair Use in The Netherlands – a Renaissance?*, 33(1) AMI – tijdschrift voor auteurs-, media- en informatierecht 1

Senftleben, Martin (2009-2010), *Bridging the Differences between Copyright's Legal Traditions – The Emerging EC Fair Use Doctrine*, 57 Journal of the Copyright Society of the USA 521

Senftleben, Martin (2010), *The International Three-Step Test: A Model Provision for EC Fair Use Legislation*, 1 JIPITEC 67

Senftleben, Martin (2011), *Overprotection and protection overlaps in intellectual property law – the need for horizontal fair use defences*, *in* Annette Kur & Vytautas Mizaras (eds.), *The Structure of Intellectual Property Law: Can One Size Fit All?* 136 (Edward Elgar)

Senftleben, Martin (2012a), *Ni flexibilité ni sécurité juridique: Les exceptions au regard du triple test*, *in* André Lucas, Pierre Sirinelli & Alexandra Bensamoun (eds.), *Les Exceptions au Droit d'Auteur: État des lieux et perspectives dans l'Union européene* 63 (Dalloz)

Senftleben, Martin (2012b), *Quotations, Parody and Fair Use*, *in* P. Bernt Hugenholtz, Antoon Quaedvlieg & Dirk Visser (eds.), *A Century of Dutch Copyright Law* 359 (deLex)

Senftleben, Martin (2013a), *Comparative approaches to fair use: An important impulse for reforms in EU copyright law*, *in* Graeme B. Dinwoodie (ed.), *Methods and Perspectives in Intellectual Property* 30 (Edward Elgar)

Senftleben, Martin (2013b), *Internet Search Results – A Permissible Quotation?*, 235 RIDA 3

Senftleben, Martin (2013c), *Breathing Space for Cloud-Based Business Models: Exploring the Matrix of Copyright Limitations, Safe Harbours and Injunctions*, 4(2) JIPITEC 87

Senftleben, Martin (2016), *Copyright Reform, GS Media and Innovation Climate in the EU – Euphonious Chord or Dissonant Cacophony?*, AMI – tijdschrift voor auteurs-, media- en informatierecht 130

Senftleben, Martin (2017), *The Perfect Match: Civil Law Judges and Open-Ended Fair Use Provisions*, 33(1) American University International Law Review 231

Senftleben, Martin; Angelopoulos, Christina; Frosio, Giancarlo; Moscon, Valentina; Peguera, Miquel & Rognstad, Ole-Andreas (2018), *The Recommendation on Measures to Safeguard Fundamental Rights and the Open Internet in the Framework of the EU Copyright Reform*, 40(3) EIPR 149

Sganga, Caterina & Scalzini, Silvia (2017), *From Abuse of Right to European Copyright Misuse: A New Doctrine for EU Copyright Law*, 48(4) IIC 405

Sganga, Caterina (2018a), *Propertizing European Copyright: History, Challenges and Opportunities* (Edward Elgar)

Sganga, Caterina (2018b), *A Plea for Digital Exhaustion in EU Copyright Law*, 9(3) JIPITEC 211

Sganga, Caterina (2019), *A Decade of Fair Balance Doctrine, and How to Fix It: Copyright versus Fundamental Rights before the CJEU from Promusicae to Funke Medien, Pelham and Spiegel Online*, 41(11) European Intellectual Property Review 683

Shabalala, Dalindyebo (2010), *United States – Section 110(5) of the US Copyright Act: Summary and Analysis*, *in* Carlos M. Correa (ed.), *Research Handbook on the Interpretation and Enforcement of Intellectual Property under WTO Rules – Intellectual Property in the WTO Volume II* 142 (Edward Elgar)

Sherman, Brad & Wiseman, Leanne (2012), *Copyright: When Old Technologies Were New*, *in* Brad Sherman & Leanne Wiseman (eds.), *Copyright and the Challenge of the New* (Kluwer Law International)

Sherrell, Phil & Smith, Will (2014), *CJEU decision in Meltwater – the internet is saved, browsing does not require a license*, Bird & Bird, https://www.twobirds.com/

Silva, Nuno Sousa e (2014), *Uma Introdução ao Direito de Autor Europeu*, Revista da Ordem dos Advogados 1331

Silva, Nuno Sousa e (2015), *A perspectiva do equilíbrio entre a propriedade intelectual e (outros) direitos fundamentais – A mais recente interpretação do artigo 8.º/3 da Directiva 2001/29 (UPC Telekabel Wien C-134/12),* 1 RDI 209

Simone, Daniela (2014), *Copyright or Copyleft? Wikipedia as a Turning Point for Authorship*, 25 King's Law Journal 102

Sirinelli, Pierre; Benazeraf, Josée-Anne & Bensamoun, Alexandra (2016), *Mission: Right of Communication to the Public – Report and Proposals*, High Council for Literary and Artistic Property, http://www.culture.gouv.fr/.

Sirinelli, Pierre (1998), *Rapport de synthèse*, *in* Libby Baulch, Michael Green & Mary Wyburn (eds.), *ALAI Study Days: The Boundaries of Copyright: Its Proper Limitations and Exceptions* (Australian Copyright Council)

Sirinelli, Pierre (1999), *Exceptions et limites aux droit d'auteur et droits voisins*, WCT-WPPT/IMP/1, http://www.wipo.int/

Slot, Piet Jan (1996), *Harmonisation*, 21(5) European Law Review 378

Snijders, Thom & Deursen, Stijn van (2019), *The Road Not Taken – the CJEU Sheds Light on the Role of Fundamental Rights in the European Copyright Framework – a Case Note on the Pelham, Spiegel Online and Funke Medien Decisions*, 50 IIC 1176

Soames, Scott (2011), *What Vagueness and Inconsistency Tell Us About Interpretation*, *in* Andrei Marmor & Scott Soames (eds.), *Philosophical Foundations of Language in the Law* 31 (OUP)

Soares, António Goucha (1998), *Pre-emption, Conflicts of Powers and Subsidiarity*, 23(2) European Law Review 132

Solan, Lawrence (2005), *Vagueness and Ambiguity in Legal Interpretation*, *in* Vijay K. Bhatia, Jan Engberg, Maurizio Gotti & Dorothee Heller (eds.), *Vagueness in Normative Texts* 73 (Peter Lang)

Sorensen, Roy (2001), *Vagueness has no function in law*, 7 Legal Theory 387

Sorensen, Roy (2004), *Vagueness and Contradiction* (OUP)

Spindler, Gerald & Leistner, Matthias (2006), *Secondary Copyright Infringement – New Perspectives in Germany and Europe*, 38(7) IIC 788

Spindler, Gerald (2002), *Europäisches Urheberrecht in der Informationsgesellschaft*, 104(2) GRUR 105

Spindler, Gerald (2010), *Bildersuchmaschinen, Schranken und konkludente Einwilligung im Urheberrecht – Besprechung der BGH-Entscheidung „Vorschaubilder'*, 112(9) GRUR 785

Spindler, Gerald (2014), *Die Reform des Urheberrechts*, 67(35) NJW 2550

Spoor, Jaap H. (1980), *Copies in Continental Copyright*, *in* Jaap H. Spoor, William R. Cornish & Peter F. Nolan (eds.), *Copies in Copyright* 1 (Sijthoff & Noordhoff)

Spoor, Jaap H. (1996), *The Copyright Approach to Copying on the Internet: (Over)Stretching the Reproduction Right?*, *in* P. Bernt Hugenholtz (ed.), *The Future of Copyright in a Digital Environment* 67 (Kluwer Law International)

Spoor, Jaap H. (1998), *General Aspects of Exceptions and Limitations to Copyright: General Report*, *in* Libby Baulch, Michael Green & Mary Wyburn (eds.), *ALAI Study Days: The Boundaries of Copyright: Its Proper Limitations and Exceptions* 27 (Australian Copyright Council)

Stamatoudi, Irini (2002), *Copyright and Multimedia Works: A Comparative Analysis* (CUP)

Stamatoudi, Irini & Torremans, Paul (2014a), *The Information Society Directive*, *in* Irini Stamatoudi & Paul Torremans (eds.), *EU Copyright Law: A Commentary* 395 (Edward Elgar)

Stamatoudi, Irini & Torremans, Paul (2014b), *Conclusion*, *in* Irini Stamatoudi & Paul Torremans (eds.), *EU Copyright Law: A Commentary* 1155 (Edward Elgar)

Stamatoudi, Irini (2016), *Text and Data Mining*, *in* Irini Stamatoudi (ed.), *New Developments in EU and International Copyright Law* 251 (Kluwer Law International)

Stamatoudi, Irini (2017), *Originality under EU copyright law*, *in* Paul Torremans (ed.), *Research Handbook on Copyright Law* 57 (2nd ed., Edward Elgar)

Sterling, J.A.L. (2008), *World Copyright Law* (Sweet & Maxwell)

Strowel, Alain & Kim, Hee-Eun (2013), *The Balancing Impact of General EU Law on European Intellectual Property Jurisprudence*, *in* Ansgar Ohly & Justine Pila (eds.), *The Europeanisation of Intellectual Property Law: Towards a European Legal Methodology* 121 (OUP)

Strowel, Alain (1993), *Droit d'auteur et copyright. Divergences et convergences. Étude de droit comparé* (Bruylant)

Strowel, Alain (ed.) (2009), *Peer-to-Peer File Sharing and Secondary Liability in Copyright Law* (Edward Elgar)

Strowel, Alain (2012), *European copyright: beyond the additions made by the European Court of Justice, some pieces are still missing, in* Marie-Christine Janssens & Geertrui van Overwalle (eds.), *Harmonisation of European IP Law: From European rules to Belgian law and practice. Contributions in honour of Frank Gotzen* 73 (KU Leuven/ HUB)

Strowel, Alain (2014), *Towards a European Copyright Law: Four Issues to Consider*, *in* Irini Stamatoudi & Paul Torremans (eds.), *EU Copyright Law: A Commentary* 1127 (Edward Elgar)

Sullivan, Kathleen M. (1992), *The Supreme Court 1991 Term – Foreword: The Justices of Rules and Standards,* 106 Harvard Law Review 22

Summers, Robert S. (1999), *The Principles of the Rule of Law*, 74 Notre Dame Law Review 1691

Sun, Haochen (2007), *Overcoming the Achilles Heel of Copyright Law*, 5(2) Northwestern Journal of Technology and Intellectual Property 265

Sunstein, Cass R. (1993), *On Analogical Reasoning*, 106(3) Harvard Law Review 741

Sunstein, Cass R. (1995), *Problems with Rules*, 83 California Law Review 953

Suthersanen, Uma (2005), *Towards an International Public Interest Rule? Human Rights and International Copyright Law*, *in* Jonathan Griffiths & Uma Suthersanen (eds.), *Copyright and Free Speech: Comparative and International Analyses* 97 (OUP)

Synodinou, Tatiana-Eleni (2012), *The principle of technological neutrality in European Copyright Law*, 34(9) EIPR 618

Synodinou, Tatiana-Eleni (2014), *Copyright law: an ancient history, a contemporary challenge*, *in* Andrej Savin & Jan Trzaskowski (eds.), *Research Handbook on EU Internet Law* 81 (Edward Elgar)

Tamanaha, Brian Z. (2004), *On the Rule of Law: History, Politics, Theory* (CUP)

Tan, David (2012), *The Transformative Use Doctrine and Fair Dealing in Singapore: Understanding the 'Purpose and Character' of Appropriation Art*, 24 Singapore Academy of Law Journal 832

Teubner, Gunther (1998), *Legal Irritants: Good Faith in British Law or How Unifying Law Ends Up in New Divergences*, 61 Modern Law Review 11

Toffler, Alvin (1970), *Future Shock* (Random House)

Torremans, Paul (2000), *Moral Rights in the Digital Age*, *in* Irini Stamatoudi & Paul Torremans (eds.), *Copyright in the New Digital Environment* 97 (Sweet & Maxwell)

Torremans, Paul (2008), *Copyright (and Other Intellectual Property Rights) as a Human Right*, *in* Paul Torremans (ed.), *Intellectual Property and Human Rights* 195 (Kluwer Law International)

Torremans, Paul (2012), *The Perspective of the Introduction of a European Fair Use Clause*, *in* Tatiana-Eleni Synodinou (ed.), *Codification of European Copyright Law: Challenges and Perspectives* 319 (Kluwer Law International)

Toth, A. G. (1984), *The Authority of Judgments of the European Court of Justice: Binding Force and Legal Effects*, 4(1) Yearbook of European Law 1

Trabuco, Cláudia (2006), *O Direito de Reprodução de Obras Literárias e Artísticas no Ambiente Digital* (Coimbra Editora)

Triaille, Jean-Paul; Dusollier, Séverine; Depreeuw, Sari; Hubin, Jean-Benoit; Coppens, François & Francquen, Amélie de (2013), *Study on the Application of Directive 2001/29/EC on copyright and related rights in the information society,* Study for the European Commission, https://publications.europa.eu/

Triaille, Jean-Paul (2002), *La directive sur le droit d'auteur du 22 mai 2001 et l'acquis communautaire*, 1 Auteurs & Media 8

Triaille, Jean-Paul (2008), *La question des copies 'cache' et la responsabilité des intermédiaires. Copiepresse c. Google, Field v. Google*, *in* Alain Strowel & Jean-Paul Triaille (eds.), *Google et les nouveaus services en ligne: Impact sur l'économie du contenu et questions de propriété intellectuelle* 251 (Larcier)

Triaille, Jean-Paul (2014), *Study on the legal framework of text and data mining (TDM)*, Study for the European Commission, https://publications.europa.eu/

Tridimas, Takis (2006), *The General Principles of EU Law* (2nd ed., OUP)

Tridimas, Takis (2012), *Precedent and the Court of Justice: A Jurisprudence of Doubt?*, *in* Julie Dickson & Pavlos Eleftheriadis (eds.), *Philosophical Foundations of European Union Law* 307 (OUP)

Truyens, Maarten & Eecke, Patrick van (2016), *Surprised by Embedded Assumptions: The Online Sector's Troubled Relationship with EU Case Law: The difficult relation of the online sector with EU copyright, data protection and ecommerce legislation*, 1 CRi – Computer Law Review International 1

Tsoutsanis, Alexander (2014), *Wby copyright and linking can tango*, 9(6) JIPLP 495

Ubertazzi, Luigi Carlo (2003), *I diritti d'autore e connessi: Scritti* (2nd ed., Giuffrè Editore)

Ulmer, Eugen (1972), *Copyright Problems Arising from the Computer Storage and Retrieval of Protected Works*, 8(2) Copyright 37

Usher, John (1998), *General Principles of EC Law* (Longman)

Vetulani-Cęgiel, Agnieszka (2015), *EU Copyright Law, Lobbying and Transparency of Policy-Making: The cases of sound recordings term extension and orphan works provisions*, 6(2) JIPITEC 146

Vicente, Dário Moura (2005), *Direito Internacional Privado: Problemática Internacional da Sociedade da Informação* (Almedina)

Vicente, Dário Moura (2008), *A Tutela Internacional da Propriedade Intelectual* (Almedina)

Vicente, Dário Moura (2011a), *O equilíbrio de interesses no direito de autor*, IX Direito da Sociedade de Informação 249

Vicente, Dário Moura (2011b), *Unkörperliche Güter im romanischen Rechtskreis*, *in* Stefan Leible, Matthias Lehmann & Herbert Zech (eds.), *Unkörperliche Güter im Zivilrecht* 75 (Mohr Siebeck)

Vicente, Dário Moura (2012), *Portugal*, *in* Reto M. Hilty & Sylvie Nérisson (eds.), *Balancing Copyright – A Survey of National Approaches* 737 (Springer)

Vide, Carlos Rogel & Gómez, Eduardo Serrano (2008), *Manual de Derecho de Autor* (Reus)

Vieira, José Alberto (2009), *Download de obra protegida pelo Direito de Autor e uso privado*, VIII Direito da Sociedade de Informação 421

Vieira, José Alberto (2016), *A cópia privada e o seu regime de compensação*, 1 RDI 51

Vinje, Thomas C. (2000), *Should we begin digging copyright's grave*, 22(12) EIPR 551

Vivant, Michel (2002), *Rapport de synthèse – La directive sur le droit d'auteur et les droits voisins dans la société de l'information. Bilans et perspectives*, 2 Propriétés Intellectuelles 71

Volokh, Eugene (1995), *Review: Technology and the Future of Law*, 47(6) Stanford Law Review 1375

Voorhoof, Dirk (2015), *Freedom of expression and the right to information: Implications for copyright*, *in* Christophe Geiger (ed.), *Research Handbook on Human Rights and Intellectual Property* 331 (Edward Elgar)

Vousden, Stephen (2010), *Infopaq and the Europeanisation of Copyright Law*, 1(2) The WIPO Journal 197

Waldron, Jeremy (1994), *Vagueness in Law and Language: Some Philosophical Issues*, 82 California Law Review 509

Waldron, Jeremy (2006), *From Authors to Copiers: Individual rights and social values in intellectual property*, *in* David Vaver (ed.), *Intellectual Property Rights: Critical Concepts in Law* 114, Vol. I (Routledge)

Waldron, Jeremy (2011), *Vagueness and the Guidance of Action*, *in* Andrei Marmor & Scott Soames (eds.), *Philosophical Foundations of Language in the Law* 58 (OUP)

Walter, Michel M. & Lewinski, Silke von (2010), *European Copyright Law: A Commentary* (OUP)

Walter, Michel M., *Updating and Consolidation of the Acquis: The Future of European Copyright* (2002), http://ec.europa.eu/

Wandtke, Artur-Axel (2015), *Schrankenlose Bildung und Wissenschaft im Lichte des Urheberrechts*, 117(3) GRUR 221

Watson, Alan (1993), *Legal Transplants: An Approach to Comparative Law* (2nd ed., University of Georgia Press)

Weatherill, Stephen (2002), *Pre-emption, Harmonisation and the Distribution of Competence to Regulate the Internal Market*, *in* Catherine Barnard & Joanne Scott (eds.), *The Law of the Single European Market: Unpacking the Premises* 41 (Hart)

Weatherill, Stephen (2004), *Competence Creep and Competence Control*, 23(1) Yearbook of European Law 1

Weatherill, Stephen (2010), *Union legislation relating to the free movement of goods*, *in* Peter Oliver (ed.), *Oliver on Free Movement of Goods in the European Union* 427 (5th ed., Hart)

Wei, George (2012), *A Look Back at Public Policy, the Legislature, the Courts and the Development of Copyright Law in Singapore: Twenty-Five Years On*, 24 Singapore Academy of Law Journal 867

Weiler, Joseph H. H. (2001), *The Judicial Après Nice*, *in* Gráinne de Búrca & Joseph H. H. Weiler (eds.), *The European Court of Justice* 215 (OUP)

Weinreb, Lloyd L. (1990), *Fair's Fair: A Comment on the Fair Use Doctrine*, 103(5) Harvard Law Review 1137

Westkamp, Guido (2004), *Transient Copying and Public Communications: The Creeping Evolution of Use and Access Rights in European Copyright Law*, 36(5) The George Washington International Law Review 1057

Westkamp, Guido (2007), *Part II – The Implementation of Directive 2001/29/EC in the Member States*, Queen Mary Intellectual Property Research Institute – Centre for Commercial Law Studies, http://ec.europa.eu/

Westkamp, Guido (2008), *The Three-Step Test and Copyright Limitations in Europe: European copyright law between approximation and national decision making*, 56 Journal of the Copyright Society of the USA 1

Westkamp, Guido (2012), *Emerging escape clauses? Online exhaustion, consent and European copyright law*, *in* Jan Rosén (ed.), *Intellectual Property at the Crossroads of Trade* 38 (Edward Elgar)

Westkamp, Guido (2014), *Copyright Reform and Necessary Flexibilities*, 45(5) IIC 497

Westkamp, Guido (2017), *One or Several Super-Rights? The (Subtle) Impact of the Digital Single Market on a Future EU Copyright Architecture*, *in* Kung-Chung Liu & Reto M. Hilty (eds.), *Remuneration of Copyright Owners: Regulatory Challenges of New Business Models* 21 (Springer)

WIPO (1978), *Guide to the Berne Convention for the Protection of Literary and Artistic Works (Paris Act, 1971)*

WIPO (1981), *Guide to the Rome Convention*

Wittem Group (2010), *European Copyright Code*, www.copyrightcode.eu

Wittgenstein, Ludwig (1958), *Philosophical Investigations* (trans. G.E.M. Anscombe) (Basil Blackwell)

Wright, Robin (2009), *The 'Three-Step Test' and the Wider Public Interest: Towards a More Inclusive Interpretation*, 12(6) The Journal of World Intellectual Property 600

Xalabarder, Raquel (2007), *On-line teaching and copyright: any hopes for an EU harmonized playground?*, *in* Paul Torremans (ed.), *Copyright Law: A Handbook of Contemporary Research* 373 (Edward Elgar)

Xalabarder, Raquel (2008), *Fair Use in Spain. The EUCD Aftermath*, *in* Gustavo Ghidini & Luis Mariano Genovesi (eds.), *Intellectual Property and Market Power: ATRIP Papers 2006-2007* 811 (Eudeba)

Xalabarder, Raquel (2009), *WIPO Study on Copyright Limitations and Exceptions for Educational Activities in North America, Europe, Caucasus, Central Asia and Israel*, WIPO Doc SCCR/19/8, http://www.wipo.int/

Xalabarder, Raquel (2012a), *Google News and Copyright*, *in* Aurelio Lopez Tarruella (ed.), *Google and the Law: Empirical Approaches to Legal Aspects of Knowledge-Economy Business Models* 113 (Springer)

Xalabarder, Raquel (2012b), *Spanish Supreme Court Rules in Favour of Google Search Engine... and a Flexible Reading of Copyright Statutes?*, 3 JIPITEC 162

Xalabarder, Raquel (2016), *The Role of the CJEU in Harmonizing EU Copyright Law*, 47 IIC 635

Yu, Peter K. (2016), *The Quest for a User-Friendly Copyright Regime in Hong Kong*, 32(1) American University International Law Review 283

Yu, Peter K. (2018), *Customizing Fair Use Transplants*, 7(1) Laws 1

Zemer, Lior (2010), *The Emancipation of Fair Use in Israel*, *in* Catherine Ng, Lionel Bently & Giuseppina D'Agostino (eds.), *The Common Law of Intellectual Property: Essays in Honour of Professor David Vaver* 281 (Hart)

Zimbehl, Philipp (2010), *Google Images, BGH Entscheidungung vom 29.04.2010, I ZR 69/08 (Vorschaubilder), English Introduction*, 1 JIPITEC 190

Zimmermann, Reinhard (1997), *Statuta Sunt Stricte Interpretanda? Statutes and the Common Law: A Continental Perspective*, 2 Cambridge Law Journal 315

Zolynski, Célia (2007), *Méthode de transposition des directives communautaires: Étude à partir de l'exemple du droit d'auteur et des droits voisins* (Dalloz)

Table of Cases

National decisions were cited using the respective national case law identifier. European decisions and opinions refer to the European Case Law Identifier (ECLI).

Court of Justice of the European Union (CJEU)

Judgments, Orders, and Opinions

AG Opinions

Renckhoff: Opinion of AG Sánchez-Bordona in Case C-161/17, *Land Nordrhein-Westfalen v. Dirk Renckhoff*, 25.04.2018, ECLI:EU:C:2018:279, 229, 255, 300, 326, 345–348

Sema Sürül: Opinion of AG La Pergola in Case C-262/96, Sema Sürül *v.* Bundesanstalt für Arbeit, 17.12.1998, ECLI:EU:C:1999:228, 242, 253

SGAE: Opinion of AG Sharpston in Case C-306/05, *Sociedad General de Autores y Editores de España (SGAE) v. Rafael Hoteles SA*, 13.07.2006, ECLI:EU:C:2006:479, 320

Spiegel Online: Opinion of AG Szpunar in Case C-516/17, *Spiegel Online GmbH v. Volker Beck*, 10.01.2019, ECLI:EU:C:2019:16, 190, 238, 322, 325, 327, 349, 351, 352

Stichting de Thuiskopie: Opinion of AG Jääskinen in Case C-462/09, *Stichting de Thuiskopie v. Opus Supplies Deutschland GmbH and Others*, 10.03.2011, ECLI:EU:C:2011:133, 108

Titus Donner: Opinion of AG Jääskinen in Case C-5/11, *Criminal proceedings against Titus Alexander Jochen Donner*, 29.03.2012, ECLI:EU:C:2012:195, 165

Ulmer: Opinion of AG Jääskinen in Case C-117/13, *Technische Universität Darmstadt v. Eugen Ulmer KG*, 05.06.2014, ECLI:EU:C:2014:1795, 236

VG Bild-Kunst: Opinion of AG Szpunar in Case C-392/19, *VG Bild-Kunst v. Stiftung Preußischer Kulturbesitz*, 10.09.2020, ECLI:EU:C:2020:696, 255

VG Wort: Opinion of AG Sharpston in Case C-457/11, *Verwertungsgesellschaft Wort (VG Wort) v. Kyocera and Others (C-457/11) and Canon Deutschland GmbH (C-458/11), and Fujitsu Technology Solutions GmbH (C-459/11) and Hewlett-Packard GmbH (C-460/11) v. Verwertungsgesellschaft Wort (VG Wort)*, 24.01.2013, ECLI:EU:C:2013:34, 64, 82, 163, 202, 291

VOB: Opinion of AG Szpunar in Case C-174/15, *Vereniging Openbare Bibliotheken v. Stichting Leenrecht*, 16.06.2016, ECLI:EU:C:2016:459, 9

YouTube/Cyando: Opinion of AG Saugmandsgaard Øe in Joined Cases C-682/18 and C-683/18, *Frank Peterson v. Google LLC, YouTube LLC, YouTube Inc., Google Germany GmbH (C-682/18) and Elsevier Inc. v. Cyando AG (C-683/18)*, 16.07.2020, ECLI:EU:C:2020:586, 54, 55, 58, 255, 319

Ziggo: Opinion of AG Szpunar in Case C-610/15, *Stichting Brein v. Ziggo BV and XS4ALL Internet BV*, 08.02.2017, ECLI:EU:C:2017:99, 55, 319

European Court of Human Rights (ECtHR)

World Trade Organisation (WTO) Panel Reports

National Case Law

Belgium

Canada

France

Germany

United States

Table of Legislation

The table lists not only binding legal instruments (e.g., treaties, laws, directives and regulations), but also non-binding ones (e.g., recommendations, resolutions and opinions) and preparatory documents (e.g., green papers, white papers and public consultations).

International Legal Texts

Treaties, Conventions and Proposals

Records of Treaties and Conventions

European Union Legal Texts

Treaties, Treaty Protocols and Charter

Directives

Regulations

Proposals and Explanatory Memoranda

European Commission Recommendations

European Commission Communications

European Parliament Resolutions and Reports

Common Positions

Public Consultations and Reports

Green Papers, White Papers, Working Documents, Reflection Documents and Memos

CJEU Reports

Council of Europe

National Legal Texts

Australia

Belgium

France

Germany

South Africa

South African Copyright Amendment Bill 2017: South African Parliament's Portfolio Committee of Trade and Industry, *Copyright Amendment Bill [B 13B-2017] final version 15/11/2018*, 315

South Korea

South Korean Copyright Act: Korean Copyright Act 2011, 312, 315

Spain

Spanish IP Code: *Código de Propiedad Intelectual, BOE núm. 97*, 22.04.1996, 169, 175, 219

Sri Lanka

Sri Lankan Intellectual Property Act: Intellectual Property Act, No. 36 of 2003, 315

The Netherlands

Dutch Copyright Act: *Wet van 23 september 1912, houdende nieuwe regeling van het auteursrecht (Auteurswet 1912)*, 23.09.1912, 174, 175, 305, 315

The Philippines

Intellectual Property Code of the Philippines: Intellectual Property Code of the Philippines, Republic Act No. 8293, 315

United Kingdom

Statute of Anne: An Act for the Encouragement of Learning, by Vesting the Copies of Printed Books in the Authors or Purchasers of such Copies, During the Times therein mentioned (1710), 8 Anne c. 19, 38

UK CDPA: Copyright, Designs and Patents Act 1988, c. 48, 3, 34, 134, 156, 305

United States

US Copyright Act: 17 United States Code §§101-810, 32, 49, 102, 194, 216, 222, 282, 300, 303–307, 310, 311, 313, 317, 320, 323, 341

US House of Representatives 1976 Report: US House of Representatives, *Copyright Law Revision*, Report No. 94-1476, 94th Congress – 2nd Session, 03.09.1976, 307, 309

US Sherman Antitrust Act: 15 United States Code §§1-7, 310

INFORMATION LAW SERIES

1. Egbert J. Dommering & P. Bernt Hugenholtz, *Protecting Works of Fact: Copyright, Freedom of Expression and Information Law,* 1991 (ISBN 90-654-4567-6).
2. Willem F. Korthals Altes, Egbert J. Dommering, P. Bernt Hugenholtz & Jan J.C. Kabel, *Information Law Towards the 21st Century,* 1992 (ISBN 90-654-4627-3).
3. Jacqueline M.B. Seignette, *Challenges to the Creator Doctrine: Authorship, Copyright Ownership and the Exploitation of Creative Works in the Netherlands, Germany and The United States,* 1994 (ISBN 90-654-4876-4).
4. P. Bernt Hugenholtz, *The Future of Copyright in a Digital Environment, Proceedings of the Royal Academy Colloquium,* 1996 (ISBN 90-411-0267-1).
5. Julius C.S. Pinckaers, *From Privacy Toward a New Intellectual Property Right in Persona,* 1996 (ISBN 90-411-0355-4).
6. Jan J.C. Kabel & Gerard J.H.M. Mom, *Intellectual Property and Information Law: Essays in Honour of Herman Cohen Jehoram,* 1998 (ISBN 90-411-9702-8).
7. Ysolde Gendreau, Axel Nordemann & Rainer Oesch, *Copyright and Photographs: An International Survey,* 1999 (ISBN 90-411-9722-2).
8. P. Bernt Hugenholtz, *Copyright and Electronic Commerce: Legal Aspects of Electronic Copyright Management,* 2000 (ISBN 90-411-9785-0).
9. Lucie M.C.R. Guibault, *Copyright Limitations and Contracts: An Analysis of the Contractual Overridability of Limitations on Copyright,* 2002 (ISBN 90-411-9867-9).
10. Lee A. Bygrave, *Data Protection Law: Approaching its Rationale, Logic and Limits,* 2002 (ISBN 90-411-9870-9).
11. Niva Elkin-Koren & Neil Weinstock Netanel, *The Commodification of Information,* 2002 (ISBN 90-411-9876-8).
12. Mireille M.M. van Eechoud, *Choice of Law in Copyright and Related Rights: Alternatives to the Lex Protectionis,* 2003 (ISBN 90-411-2071-8).
13. Martin Senftleben, *Copyright, Limitations and the Three-Step Test: An Analysis of the Three-Step Test in International and EC Copyright Law,* 2004 (ISBN 90-411-2267-2).
14. Paul L.C. Torremans, *Copyright and Human Rights: Freedom of Expression – Intellectual Property – Privacy,* 2004 (ISBN 90-411-2278-8).
15. Natali Helberger, *Controlling Access to Content: Regulating Conditional Access in Digital Broadcasting,* 2005 (ISBN 90-411-2345-8).
16. Lucie M.C.R. Guibault & P. Bernt Hugenholtz, *The Future of the Public Domain: Identifying the Commons in Information Law,* 2006 (ISBN 978-90-411-2435-7).

17. Irini Katsirea, *Public Broadcasting and European Law: A Comparative Examination of Public Service Obligations in Six Member States,* 2008 (ISBN 978-90-411-2500-2).
18. Paul L.C. Torremans, *Intellectual Property and Human Rights: Enhanced Edition of Copyright and Human Rights,* 2008 (ISBN 978-90-411-2653-5).
19. Mireille van Eechoud, P. Bernt Hugenholtz, Stef van Gompel, Lucie Guibault & Natali Helberger, *Harmonizing European Copyright Law: The Challenges of Better Lawmaking,* 2009 (ISBN 978-90-411-3130-0).
20. Ashwin van Rooijen, *The Software Interface between Copyright and Competition Law: A Legal Analysis of Interoperability in Computer Programs,* 2010 (ISBN 978-90-411-3193-5).
21. Irini A. Stamatoudi, *Copyright Enforcement and the Internet,* 2010 (ISBN 978-90-411-3346-5).
22. Wolfgang Sakulin, *Trademark Protection and Freedom of Expression: An Inquiry into the Conflict between Trademark Rights and Freedom of Expression under European Law,* 2011 (ISBN 978-90-411-3415-8).
23. Stef van Gompel, *Formalities in Copyright Law: An Analysis of their History, Rationales and Possible Future,* 2011 (ISBN 978-90-411-3418-9).
24. Nadezhda Purtova, *Property Rights in Personal Data: A European Perspective,* 2012 (ISBN 978-90-411-3802-6).
25. Brad Sherman & Leanne Wiseman, *Copyright and the Challenge of the New,* 2012 (ISBN 978-90-411-3669-5).
26. Ewa Komorek, *Media Pluralism and European Law*, 2012 (ISBN 978-90-411-3894-1).
27. Joris van Hoboken, *Search Engine Freedom: On the Implications of the Right to Freedom of Expression for the Legal Governance of Web Search Engines,* 2012 (ISBN 978-90-411-4128-6).
28. Natali Helberger, Lucie Guibault, Marco Loos, Chantal Mak, Lodewijk Pessers & Bart van der Sloot, *Digital Consumers and the Law: Towards a Cohesive European Framework*, 2012 (ISBN 978-90-411-4049-4).
29. Tatiana-Eleni Synodinou, *Codification of European Copyright Law: Challenges and Perspectives,* 2012 (ISBN 978-90-411-4145-3).
30. Heather Ann Forrest, *Protection of Geographic Names in International Law and Domain Name System Policy*, Second Edition, 2017 (ISBN 978-90-411-8839-7).
31. Sari Depreeuw, *The Variable Scope of the Exclusive Economic Rights in Copyright*, 2014 (ISBN 978-90-411-4915-2).
32. Vikrant Narayan Vasudeva, *Open Source Software and Intellectual Property Rights*, 2014 (ISBN 978-90-411-5228-2).
33. Frederik J. Zuiderveen Borgesius, *Improving Privacy Protection in the Area of Behavioural Targeting*, 2015 (ISBN 978-90-411-5990-8).
34. Paul L.C. Torremans, *Intellectual Property Law and Human Rights*, Fourth Edition, 2020 (ISBN 978-94-035-1304-1).

35. Irini A. Stamatoudi, *New Developments in EU and International Copyright Law*, 2016 (ISBN 978-90-411-5991-5).
36. Lodewijk W.P. Pessers, *The Inventiveness Requirement in Patent Law: An Exploration of Its Foundations and Functioning*, 2016 (ISBN 978-90-411-6731-6).
37. Susy Frankel & Daniel Gervais, *The Internet and the Emerging Importance of New Forms of Intellectual Property*, 2016 (ISBN 978-90-411-6789-7).
38. Axel M. Arnbak, *Securing Private Communications: Protecting Private Communications Security in EU Law – Fundamental Rights, Functional Value Chains, and Market Incentives*, 2016 (ISBN 978-90-411-6737-8).
39. Christina Angelopoulos, *European Intermediary Liability in Copyright: A Tort-Based Analysis*, 2017 (ISBN 978-90-411-6835-1).
40. João Pedro Quintais, *Copyright in the Age of Online Access: Alternative Compensation Systems in EU Law*, 2017 (ISBN 978-90-411-8667-6).
41. P. Bernt Hugenholtz, *Copyright Reconstructed: Rethinking Copyright's Economic Rights in a Time of Highly Dynamic Technological and Economic Change*, 2018 (ISBN 978-90-411-9103-8).
42. Manon Oostveen, *Protecting Individuals Against the Negative Impact of Big Data: Potential and Limitations of the Privacy and Data Protection Law Approach*, 2018 (ISBN 978-94-035-0131-4).
43. Tatiana Eleni Synodinou (ed.), *Pluralism or Universalism in International Copyright Law*, 2019 (ISBN 978-94-035-0355-4).
44. Martin Senftleben, *The Copyright/Trademark Interface: How the Expansion of Trademark Protection Is Stifling Cultural Creativity*, 2021 (ISBN 978-94-035-2370-5).
45. Tito Rendas, *Exceptions in EU Copyright Law: In Search of a Balance Between Flexibility and Legal Certainty*, 2021 (ISBN 978-94-035-2395-8).

www.ingramcontent.com/pod-product-compliance
Ingram Content Group UK Ltd.
Pitfield, Milton Keynes, MK11 3LW, UK
UKHW020228290926
15470UKWH00001B/412

9 789403 523958